The Fabrics of Culture

World Anthropology

General Editor

SOL TAX

Patrons

CLAUDE LÉVI-STRAUSS
MARGARET MEAD†
LAILA SHUKRY EL HAMAMSY
M. N. SRINIVAS

MOUTON PUBLISHERS · THE HAGUE · PARIS · NEW YORK

The Fabrics of Culture

The Anthropology of
Clothing and Adornment

Editors

JUSTINE M. CORDWELL
RONALD A. SCHWARZ

MOUTON PUBLISHERS · THE HAGUE · PARIS · NEW YORK

General Editor's Preface

Food and sex are direct biological necessities for the survival of *Homo sapiens*. In this sense, adornment of our bodies seems unessential; yet it is ubiquitous. Anthropologists have argued the necessity for clothing, both for warmth and to provide carrying devices which free the hands for other necessities. But body adornment and jewelry, and the decoration of clothing — not to mention changes in fashion — serve more subtle aesthetic and expressive needs. The present book, remarkably, provides the first full-scale treatment of these long-recognized phenomena. It had to await development of the theory of cultures as systems of symbols. It also awaited a spirit in which all cultures — one's own included — could be treated as fully comparable; and this spirit required the end of colonialism. It is not surprising then, that this book is a product of a world Congress.

Like most contemporary sciences, anthropology is a product of the European tradition. Some argue that it is a product of colonialism, with one small and self-interested part of the species dominating the study of the whole. If we are to understand the species, our science needs substantial input from scholars who represent a variety of the world's cultures. It was a deliberate purpose of the IXth International Congress of Anthropological and Ethnological Sciences to provide impetus in this direction. The *World Anthropology* volumes, therefore, offer a first glimpse of a human science in which members from all societies have played an active role. Each of the books is designed to be self-contained; each is an attempt to update its particular sector of scientific knowledge and is written by specialists from all parts of the world. Each volume should be read and reviewed individually as a separate volume on its own given subject. The set as a whole will indicate what changes are in store for anthropology as scholars from the developing countries join in studying the species of which we are all a part.

The IXth Congress was planned from the beginning not only to include as many of the scholars from every part of the world as possible, but also with a view toward the eventual publication of the papers in high-quality volumes. At previous Congresses scholars were invited to bring papers which were then read out aloud. They were necessarily limited in length; many were only summarized; there was little time for discussion; and the sparse discussion could only be in one language. The IXth Congress was an experiment aimed at changing this. Papers were written with the intention of exchanging them before the Congress, particularly in extensive pre-Congress sessions; they were not intended to be read aloud at the Congress, that time being devoted to discussions — discussions which were simultaneously and professionally translated into five languages. The method for eliciting the papers was structured to make as representative a sample as was allowable when scholarly creativity — hence self-selection — was critically important. Scholars were asked both to propose papers of their own and to suggest topics for sessions of the Congress which they might edit into volumes. All were then informed of the suggestions and encouraged to re-think their own papers and the topics. The process, therefore, was a continuous one of feedback and exchange and it has continued to be so even after the Congress. The some two thousand papers comprising *World Anthropology* certainly then offer a substantial sample of world anthropology. It has been said that anthropology is at a turning point; if this is so, these volumes will be the historical direction-markers.

As might have been foreseen in the first post-colonial generation, the large majority of the Congress papers (82 percent) are the work of scholars identified with the industrialized world which fathered our traditional discipline and the institution of the Congress itself: Eastern Europe (15 percent); Western Europe (16 percent); North America (47 percent); Japan, South Africa, Australia, and New Zealand (4 percent). Only 18 percent of the papers are from developing areas: Africa (4 percent); Asia-Oceania (9 percent); Latin America (5 percent). Aside from the substantial representation from the U.S.S.R. and the nations of Eastern Europe, a significant difference between this corpus of written material and that of other Congresses is the addition of the large proportion of contributions from Africa, Asia, and Latin America. "Only 18 percent" is two to four times as great a proportion as that of other Congresses; moreover, 18 percent of 2,000 papers is 360 papers, 10 times the number of "Third World" papers presented at previous Congresses. In fact, these 360 papers are more than the total of *all* papers published after the last International Congress of Anthropological and Ethnological Sciences which was held in the United States (Philadelphia, 1956).

The significance of the increase is not simply quantitative. The input of scholars from areas which have until recently been no more than subject matter for anthropology represents both feedback and also long-awaited theoretical contributions from the perspectives of very different cultural, social, and historical traditions. Many who attended the IXth Congress were convinced that anthropology would not be the same in the future. The fact that the Xth Congress (India, 1978) was our first in the "Third World" may be symbolic of the change. Meanwhile, sober consideration of the present set of books will show how much, and just where and how, our discipline is being revolutionized.

In this series on *World Anthropology* readers of the present volume will find others of interest: books on the theory of culture; on particular culture areas exemplified in the present volume; on other universal aspects of human culture, including the food and shelter which are so often mentioned together with "clothing"; and on other expressive aspects of culture, including music, dance, and the visual arts as well as all religious and ritual phenomena — surely a large world to explore!

Chicago, Illinois   SOL TAX
August 17, 1979

Preface

Most papers contained in this volume were presented in sessions of the IXth International Congress of Anthropological and Ethnological Sciences. Several Congress symposia dealt with aspects of art and aesthetics but none was organized specifically around the theme of clothing and adornment. A reading of the program, however, revealed there were a significant number of scholars interested in the topic and we felt it would be useful to bring the relevant papers together in a single volume. We discussed this with Dr. Sol Tax, President of the Congress, and Karen Tkach, an editor with Mouton Publishers. With their permission and encouragement we reviewed the papers on clothing and adornment and contacted several persons who we believed could make valuable contributions to the proposed project. Response to the idea of a special volume and to requests for additional articles was favorable and provided us with the papers needed to produce *The Fabrics of Culture*.

We wish to express our appreciation to Sol and Karen for their encouragement, support, and patience. We hope this effort makes the results of the Congress more accessible to students and professionals in many disciplines who share an interest in the technical, social, and symbolic aspects of "getting dressed."

JUSTINE M. CORDWELL
RONALD A. SCHWARZ

Table of Contents

General Editor's Preface   V

Preface   IX

Introduction   1

SECTION ONE: CLOTHING, CULTURE, AND COMMUNICATION

The Language of Personal Adornment   7
    by *Mary Ellen Roach* and *Joanne Bubolz Eicher*

Uncovering the Secret Vice: Toward an Anthropology of Clothing
    and Adornment   23
    by *Ronald A. Schwarz*

The Very Human Arts of Transformation   47
    by *Justine M. Cordwell*

You Dance What You Wear, and You Wear Your Cultural Values   77
    by *Joann W. Keali'inohomoku*

SECTION TWO: SIGNS, SYMBOLS, AND THE SOCIAL ORDER

Living Art Among the Samburu   87
    by *Herbert M. Cole*

Beads and Personal Adornment   103
  by *Ila Pokornowski*

Symbol and Identification in North American Indian Clothing   119
  by *Evan M. Maurer*

Badaga Apparel: Protection and Symbol   143
  by *Paul Hockings*

SECTION THREE: MAN, MASKS, AND MORALS

Analysis of an African Masked Parade   177
  by *Simon Ottenberg*

Pageantry and Power in Yoruba Costuming   189
  by *Henry John Drewal*

Mende Secret Societies and their Costumed Spirits   231
  by *Loretta R. Reinhardt*

Hortelanos: An Investigation into a Masking Tradition in a
  Changing Society   267
  by *Janet Brody Esser*

SECTION FOUR: THE CLOTH OF CULTURE CHANGE

Siona Clothing and Adornment, or, You Are What You Wear   297
  by *E. Jean Langdon*

Sexual Differentiation and Acculturation in Potawatomi Costume 313
  by *Margaret Thompson Miller*

Yoruba Dress in Five Generations of a Lagos Family   331
  by *Betty M. Wass*

Social Hair: Tradition and Change in Yoruba Hairstyles in Southwestern Nigeria   349
  by *Marilyn Hammersley Houlberg*

Clothing and Power Abuse   399
  by *U. R. von Ehrenfels*

The Garments of the Present-Day Azerbaidzhan Population: Traditional and Modern Elements 405
by *A. G. Trofimova*

The Social Symbolism of Women's Dress 415
by *Mary Ellen Roach*

SECTION FIVE: TECHNOLOGY AND TEXTILES

Tablet Weaving by the Jews of San'a (Yemen) 425
by *A. Klein*

Sierra Leone Resist-Dyed Textiles
by *Maude Wahlman* and *Enyinna Chuta* 447

The History and Development of Wax-Printed Textiles Intended for West Africa and Zaire 467
by *Ruth Nielsen*

Biographical Notes 499

Index of Names 505

Index of Subjects 511

Introduction

All visible things are emblems; what thou seest is not there on its own account; strictly taken, is not there at all: Matter exists only spiritually, and to represent some Idea, and *body* it forth. Hence Clothes, as despicable as we think them, are so unspeakably significant. Clothes, from the King's mantle downwards, are emblematic, . . . On the other hand, all Emblematic things are properly Clothes, thought-woven or hand-woven: must not the Imagination weave Garments, visible Bodies, wherein the else invisible creations and inspirations of our Reason are, like Spirits, revealed, . . .

THOMAS CARLYLE, *Sartor resartus*, p. 70.

In order to grasp the social functions of costumes we must learn to read them as signs in the same way we learn to read and understand languages.

PETR BOGATYREV, *The function of folk costume in Moravian Slovakia*, p. 83.

Compared to other dimensions of human behavior, we anthropologists are relatively silent about the meaning and function of dress and adornment. While we rigorously analyze kinship, language, and movement, clothes are usually ignored and rarely given systematic consideration. In contrast, the natives who are the subject of our queries are generally very cognizant of how they and others are dressed. Clothing and adornment are universal features of human behavior and an examination of what they reveal, and attempt to conceal, contributes to our knowledge about the fabric of cultures and to our understanding of the threads of human nature.

The articles in this volume are a sample of recent research by social scientists and reflect a diversity of theoretical, comparative, and ethnographic approaches to the study of dress and bodily decoration.

Section One, "Clothing, Culture, and Communication," deals primarily with theoretical and cross-cultural issues. Two papers examine the function and meaning of clothes (Roach and Eicher, Schwarz) while a third focuses on specific items of adornment and bodily modification (Cordwell). These papers also include valuable surveys of related literature. Roach and Eicher summarize the major problem areas and examine the role of clothing in relation to various aspects of social organization. Schwarz reviews what others have said about the origin and functions of clothing and outlines an approach based on biological and ecological models. He suggests we consider clothing as part of a total system of communication within cultures and illustrates his position through a symbolic analysis of the dress worn by an Indian society in the Colombian Andes. Cordwell documents the role of cosmetics in a cross-cultural and historical survey of many societies. She examines how and why the "arts of transformation" are a significant part of social life, citing numerous examples of body painting, tattooing, and scarification. She also details some of the technical procedures used in decorating the body. Keali'inohomoku discusses the influence of clothing on dance movements in several cultures. Although her paper focuses on dance, the problem she considers and her treatment of the subject has broad implications for the study of clothing in relation to behavior.

Section Two, "Signs, Symbols, and the Social Order," covers some of the aesthetic and symbolic aspects of clothing and adornment within limited cultural boundaries. Cole deals with the full range of items and procedures used by the Samburu in northern Kenya. He examines the role of adornment in expressing differences between and within age and sex categories, and explains variations linked to wealth and social status. Pokornowski reviews the history, utility, and problems of conducting research on beads. She provides a detailed description of Yoruba beads and examines their relationship to social, political, and religious life. Maurer describes a variety of clothing styles used by North American Indian societies. He discusses ways in which clothing is used to express status differences within and between cultures. Hockings analyzes the expressive and protective functions of clothing worn by the Badagas of India. He considers the role of dress in communicating social and moral traditions.

Section Three, "Man, Masks, and Morals," deals with the role of ceremonial costume and masks in the definition and maintenance of the social and moral order. Ottenberg, Drewal, Reinhardt, and Esser focus on societies and situations in which costumes and masks are used to identify the statuses of persons and spirits. They consider the function of clothing and masks in mediating relations between supernatural beings and society and analyze their symbolic role in ceremonies. There is also emphasis on their significance in role reversal as social sanctions are brought to bear on individuals whose wrongdoing may have otherwise escaped punishment through customary channels of civil law courts.

Ottenburg, Drewal, and Reinhardt present analyses of data from West
African societies, while Esser's analysis of data from Mexico reveals
common patterns with that of the preceding scholars. An examination
of her photographic illustration shows why this is so. The fishermen,
whose masking traditions she describes, are an ethically mixed population of Indians, mestizos and Afro-Americans, descendants of the
African fishermen slaves brought to the New World by the Spanish.

Section Four, "The Cloth of Culture Change," explores the effects of
imperialism, colonialism, and modernization on modes of dress and
adornment. Langdon describes a changing pattern of relationships
among authority, power, and adornment within a small tropical forest
society in southern Colombia. She examines traditional styles of body
decoration and clothing, and interprets the meaning of changes in dress
adopted by and imposed on the population during several historical
periods. Miller presents a longitudinal comparison of similarities and
differences in items worn by Potawatomi men and women. She considers
the influence of other cultural styles in the evolution of these changes.
The papers by Wass and Houlberg both deal with the Yoruba of southwestern Nigeria. Wass describes modifications in clothing worn by a
Lagos family through five generations. Houlberg considers the "multivocal" function of hair styles among the Yoruba as well as their role in the
evolution of Yoruba fashion. She views their activity as part of their
rich tradition in the sculptural arts. Von Ehrenfels describes changes
in attitudes toward traditional clothing among representatives of
colonial governments and the adoption of Western-style garments
by the native inhabitants of tropical countries. He discusses some
of the physiological, social, and psychological effects of extending
the use of European fashions to these regions. Trofimova details the
clothing worn by the Azerbaidzhan people of the Soviet Union before
the revolution and examines stylistic changes during this century. Roach
focuses on symbolic and social aspects of American women's dress
in the nineteenth and twentieth centuries. She examines the history of
women's groups that addressed the issue of dress reform and traces
events which influenced the evolution of more practical and comfortable
apparel.

Section Five, "Technology and Textiles," considers different methods
of textile production, distribution, and consumption. Klein presents a
brief historical account of the ancient and widely diffused art of tablet
weaving and a detailed description of the techniques used by a Jewish
population in Yemen. Wahlman and Chuta analyze the technological,
economic, and ideological aspects of resist-dyed textiles in Sierra Leone.
They describe technical procedures involved in producing different types
of fabrics including the preparation of dyes from commercial and local
sources. Nielsen's long article is a comprehensive account of the

development of designs and manufacturing techniques for wax-printed textiles which are widely distributed throughout Africa and other parts of the world. Her approach is historical but some attention is given to the use of these fabrics in West Africa.

REFERENCES

BOGATYREV, PETR G.
  1971 *The function of folk costume in Moravian Slovakia.* Translated by Richard G. Crum. Approaches to Semiotics 5. The Hague: Mouton. (Originally published 1937.)
CARLYLE, THOMAS
  1869 *Sartor resartus: the life and opinions of Herr Teufelsdröckh.* London: Chapman and Hall. (Originally published 1831.)

SECTION ONE

Clothing, Culture, and Communication

The Language of Personal Adornment

MARY ELLEN ROACH and JOANNE BUBOLZ EICHER

Personal adornment is characteristic of all societies, whereas coverings that protect are not. For many people, dressing oneself can be an aesthetic act, and all aesthetic acts are acts of speaking, through which an individual may speak as an individual, what is said having meaning only because of relationships with other people. Aesthetic acts do not grow out of a vacuum, but from what is learned from others. For example, no one individual invents fine dress, instead, the language of personal adornment is acquired from others. Personally unique inventions embellish or modify the "tongue" learned from human associates, but do not represent a new language of dress.

The form of a society's language of personal adornment depends upon environmental resources, technical developments, and cultural standards for judging what is fine or beautiful; and an individual may speak the dialect of a specific sub-group within a society. Beautiful dress or finery in one group may be represented by clean and neat dress, in another by a jewel-studded crown, in still another by an array of body scars. The form of what is *most* or *least* "fine" also depends upon the social group from which the standards for judging "fineness" emerge. Clean and neat dress may be a maximum standard for beauty in dress among those in American lower economic levels for example, but only a minimum standard for middle levels.

ADORNMENT AS AESTHETIC EXPERIENCE

The individual can derive aesthetic pleasure from both the act of creating personal display and from the contemplation of his own display and that of others. In either the creative or contemplative act a person is concerned with the characteristics of body and dress that prompt aesthetic responses. The body itself has its aesthetically describable qualities — color, texture, shape, and dimension — and the added materials of adornment modify the total arrangement displayed by an individual.

Reactions to the three-dimensional, and mobile, presentation of body and dress on the basis of its aesthetic qualities alone are almost impossible; for as human beings receive stimuli they continually process and respond to these stimuli attributing meaning to them. Thus, what is seen may stimulate an aesthetic response, but it also carries a number of other messages, frequently of social and psychological significance.

Individualistic Expressions Through Personal Adornment

MOOD. Personal adornment may reflect inner emotional states called mood. It may also reinforce, disguise, or create mood. An individual caught up in a certain mood may wish to externalize it so it can be conveyed to and shared with others. Perhaps an individual feels light-hearted and energetic. In America, a culturally recognized way to create this effect is to choose costume with colors and linear arrangements that show contrast rather than sameness. Typically, color contrast can be attained by using a number of different colors together, by using bright colors that contrast with a somber background, and by using sharp differences in lightness and darkness of color. Linear contrast occurs if lines suddenly change direction or intersect when proceeding in different directions. The culturally encouraged interpretation is that the redirection of eye movements required by line contrasts is symbolic of a dynamic inner state within the wearer. Thus, at least for Americans, contrasting line and color in costume can express exuberant mood to others and also reinforce the same mood in the wearer.

Dressing in a certain way, however, may contradict rather than support mood. To banish depression and melancholy, an individual may deliberately wear dress of color and design which is thought to express opposite feelings, the joyful and buoyant, for example. Success in changing mood may depend also on other environmental changes, such as change in activity or human company. A more complex kind of mood change can come with the putting on of new clothes. Part of the reorientation of mood that some people receive from new clothes results from response to crisp new textures and the unblemished quality of the color and design that has not been altered by wear. A new item may affect mood by reinforcing an individual's feeling of uniqueness and providing a break from the sameness of appearance that an individual had been presenting for a period of time. However, the reaction of an individual is also likely to be highly social in reference. New clothes may be a way of acquiring the confidence that comes with "good" timing within the fashion cycle. The anticipation is that new clothing places one more surely within the range of the most admired appearances of the moment and, therefore, in a position of social approval. Thus mood change may grow out of adjustments to social environment as well as aesthetic responses.

Dress may be used to hide feelings from others with no expectation of transforming one's mood. If the disguise of mood is to be convincing, gesture, body stance, and voice tones must complement dress, otherwise associates will not be deceived.

An individual who consciously decides to "dress up" or "dress down" perceives the possibility of creating mood through dress, particularly if the act of "dressing up" or "dressing down" is isolated from any particular social event or occasion. In the theater and in dance performances, such conscious use of dress is the rule, for performers are expected to use dress to create a mood that can be communicated to and participated in by their audience. The dress is a cue that communicates mood from performers to audience, a mood which may in turn be conveyed back to performers.

Dress used in ceremonial rites contributes to the creation of mood. For example, because of sentiments attached to traditional bridal attire, it can add to the solemnity or joy inspired by the traditional music, precise movements, and recitations of a wedding ceremony. The lively spirit of festivals may be promoted by clothing clearly designated to be festival dress and not everyday attire. Festive dress ordinarily presents colors, materials, accessories, and designs that are different from dress worn every day.

DIFFERENTIATION FROM OTHERS. Complementing, yet opposing, forces that influence people's lives are those that provide feelings of individual worth and those that assure social value. Preservation of some kind of balance between these forces contributes to emotional survival. Although one learns the language of personal adornment from peers, and thus may be expected to conform somewhat to their patterns of dress, one can also show determination to be an individual and declare uniqueness through dress. Differentiation of one's self from others on the basis of dress relates to rarity. Acquiring the most expensive clothing is often a way of achieving differentiation through rarity, which usually commands social admiration. Rarity, however, sometimes has quite an opposite social effect. The least expensive clothing may be comparatively rare within a society with widely dispersed economic resources, and may be owned by the poor. The type of clothing may be their possession exclusively, but its quality of rarity does not automatically bring social value; instead, it is more likely just the opposite. For those who reject the expensive, or wish to identify with the poor, the inexpensive (like bib overalls) may express individual philosophy and ethical stance.

The new and fashionable also has the quality of rarity for a time and may set one apart. The position of a form of dress within the fashion cycle, from introduction to obsolescence, has interesting effects on rarity. An item just out of fashion may be relatively rare but, because of its recent descent into the realm of the unfashionable, socially unpopular. However, given sufficient age, an out-of-date fashion takes on the aura of the antique and it may become a device used to show uniqueness. English and American youth discovered this route to individual expression in the 1960's and early 1970's. The display of attic discoveries or secondhand store finds were sources of unique expressions of dress by youth, regardless of their economic level.

Individual differentiation also depends on reference group. Thus individual differentiation from general societal norms for dress is different from subgroup differentiation in that the individual who is differentiated in appearance from general society may still be conforming to group code, that of the subgroup. The individualist looks for differentiation no matter what group he is in. Thus "hippies" of the 1960's sought individuality within the accepted code of dress of their peers, whereas Liberace or Tiny Tim in their early careers were truly individuals.

Contrary to popular belief, widespread mass production of clothing does not eliminate possibilities of dressing uniquely. It places its own peculiar limitations on forms produced, but the high volume of goods produced, in America at least, allows room for greatly varied combinations of clothing, especially in color and texture, and in type of combinable items. For some observers this can be a confusing variety, since the communicative efficiency of dress is reduced as the possible types of expected appearance multiply in number.

ADORNMENT AS DEFINITION OF SOCIAL ROLE

Adornment is communicative of many subtleties in social relations. It suggests the behaviors (roles) expected of people on the basis of their various and sometimes multiple connections with each other and can, therefore, distinguish the powerful from the weak, the rich from the poor, the hero from the outcast, the conformer from the nonconformer, the religious from the irreligious, the leader from the follower. It *can* make these distinctions, but not necessarily so. Just as verbal language can be deceptive, so can the language of dress. Individuals can assume disguises to deceive the observer. Such a disguise usually involves dress, but requires correlation of dress with other style-of-life symbols. We can seldom be fooled by people we know, but we can be deceived by strangers because we depend almost entirely upon external cues of dress and grooming, facial expression, tone of voice, and conversational style, plus props such as automobiles or furnishings in living quarters to identify them.

Not all disguise via dress is deception: in the theater, players deliberately dress to fit a role, choosing costume that helps the audience identify the age, social class, sex, or occupation of the character being portrayed, and the audience knows that the dress used is intended to transform the actor temporarily into the stage character and obliterate for the moment the real-life identity of the person playing the part.

Beau Brummell remains a classic example of someone who used clothing and other props purposely to establish a role for himself in a situation that was not make-believe or deceptive. The careful way in which he prepared the setting for his entrance into society suggests that his arrival as leader of the fashionable elite of London was more than fortuitous circumstance (Franzero 1958). Brummell's education at Eton and the opportunity to meet the Prince of Wales helped him establish a foothold in society, as did a modest inheritance from his father. But more important was the astuteness with which he chose his acquaintances and put his inheritance to work. He bought several good horses in order to transport himself in "correct" style. He chose his apartment carefully so that it would be in the "right" location. He hired a cook who could prepare exquisite meals for dinner parties and invited groups of carefully chosen guests. Within the security of the "right" setting he practiced the art of personal dress to its fullest and established a unique image for himself in a position between the florid elegance of the earlier part of the eighteenth century and the neglect in dress affected by some fashionable Englishmen in the latter part of the century. The lingering legend of Beau Brummell after more than a century is proof that his uniqueness aided him in establishing his role as fashion leader.

In times of great social unrest and rapid change, an individual's approach to dress is likely to reflect general social upheaval. The hypothesis that variability in dress reflects conflict concerning content of social roles (Bush and London 1960) appeared to be substantiated in the late 1960's and the early 1970's. Racial roles, the roles of rich and poor, the roles of male and female, were questioned and efforts made, particularly by the young, to articulate new roles within all these categories, and to wear dress that reflected these new roles. Sometimes during a time of testing new roles the language of dress becomes a jumbled code, difficult to decipher. For example, a study of college students in the late 1960's showed that variation in style of dress was a weak indicator of radicalness of political ideas, even though the general public was interpreting forms of dress that deviated greatly from the traditional as indicating political radicalism (*Life* 1970).

ADORNMENT AS STATEMENT OF SOCIAL WORTH

Evaluations of social worth are often made on the basis of personal adornment. In some societies valued kinds of adornment are widely available to all, with perhaps some restrictions placed on age. Among the Andamans, when studied by Radcliffe-Brown (1933) scarification was a mark of added value generally available to all boys and girls who were at the threshold of adulthood. The kind of value it bestowed and the incentives to acquire them were thus described:

> The explanation of the rite [scarification] would therefore seem to be that it marks the passage from childhood to manhood and is a means by which the society bestows upon the individual that power, or social value, which is possessed by the adult but not by the child. . . . The individual is made to feel that his value — his strength and the qualities of which he may be proud — is not his by nature but is received by him from the society to which he is admitted. The scars on his body are the visible marks of this admission. The individual is proud or vain of the scars which are the mark of his manhood, and thus the society makes use of the very powerful sentiment of personal vanity to strengthen the social sentiments (1933:315).

In societies with sharp social divisions of caste or class, adornment that represents the most desirable symbols of social worth may be exclusive to an upper-class elite. The elite maintain a monopoly on these symbols as long as they maintain a monopoly on wealth, for lack of economic resources prohibits lower classes from adopting adornment that could proclaim for them a social worth equal to that of the upper class. However, when wealth becomes more available to the common man, as happened in the Late Middle Ages, the upper classes cannot automatically keep "fine dress" exclusive to their class. Enactment of sumptuary law is one way a social group may try to stave off obliteration of the outward distinctions of class that exclusive access to finery provides them. In the late seventeenth century in Nuremberg, where four ranks of society were recognized, the paternalistic government regulated the amount that citizens of all ranks could spend on clothes, weddings, christenings, and burials. Regulation on dress included top-to-toe specifications. Specifically, a late fourteenth-century Nuremberg ordinance indicated that "no burgher, young or old, shall wear his hair parted; they shall wear the hair in tufts as it has been worn from of old" (Greenfield 1918:109). An order of the mid-fifteenth century directed cobblers "on pain of a definite penalty henceforth to make no more peaks on the shoes" (1918:110). Equally intriguing is that even horses had differential access to adornment, for they also had to abide by the sumptuary laws that bound their masters. In the upper class the horse that drew a bride's coach might have his forelock, mane, and tail tied with a colored ribbon; in the second class only his forelock and tail; in the third class nothing but his forelock (1918:128).

Earlier in origin, much more explicit and detailed, and more restrictive, were sumptuary laws in Japan (Hearn 1904:183–185). However, they reached their peak at about the same time as in Europe, that is, about the seventeenth century. During the Tokugawa period (1600–1867) the regulations for the farmer classes varied according to their income and described in great detail the limitations placed on the exact length of houses, the kinds of foods to be served, and the fibers to be used in the thongs of sandals. In the family of a farmer worth 20 *koku* of rice, no one was allowed to wear leather sandals: only straw sandals or wooden clogs were permitted and throngs of the sandals or the clogs were to be made of cotton. In the family of a farmer assessed at 10 *koku* the women of the family were required to wear sandals with thongs of bamboo grass.

When wealth is widely enough dispersed for lower classes of people to afford finery in dress similar to that worn by those in the upper classes, but they are prevented from doing so by strict enforcement of sumptuary laws, they may spend money on adorning themselves in ways unique to their own social level and not competitive with other classes. Some regional dress in Europe is such a phenomenon, and represents a phase in the long transition from feudalism to capitalism. Davenport (1948:376) suggests that much of European regional dress emerged in the sixteenth century when the bourgeoisie costume became differentiated on the basis of provinces or sometimes cities. These differentiations became a basis for the later peasant regional costume. As the well-to-do bourgeoisie climbed the social ladder to become gentry, the peasantry were also rising, and well-to-do peasants could afford to adopt the regionally unique costume of the former bourgeoisie.

ADORNMENT AS INDICATOR OF ECONOMIC STATUS

Adorning oneself can reflect connections with the system of production characteristic of the particular economy within which one lives. Clothing worn at work can identify the productive, that is, occupational role of an individual. A uniform and badge indicate services expected from a policeman; a pin, cap, and white uniform the services expected from a nurse. Other costumes place individuals in general occupational categories: white-collar apparel (suit with shirt and tie) is, for example, associated with many levels of office work and the professions. Blue-collar apparel of denim or work twill is associated with some kind of manual labor.

In America, women's dress is generally more ambiguous in its symbolism of occupational role than is men's. This ambiguity stems partly from the tendency of industrial societies to recognize only occupational roles that produce money income and partly from traditions established during the nineteenth century. Thus, because they do not receive money income for work, the large number of women who are exclusively homemakers, performing many productive tasks within their households and communities, do not have clearly perceived positions within the American occupational structure, and correspondingly no form of dress that clearly distinguishes them as belonging to a particular occupational category. However, persistence of nineteenth-century traditions concerning male and female roles is probably what more strongly limits symbolic association between women's dress and occupation; for nineteenth-century society developed an expectation of women to indulge in personal display through dress, contrasted with an expectation of men to eschew such display and to garb themselves in somber symbols of the occupations provided by an industrializing society. In the twentieth century, women continue to fulfill the display role, exhibiting a great deal of variety in their dress, as they are homemakers and also as many of them are workers in a number of different occupations. Among white-collar women workers, who represent the largest percentage of women in the labor force, relatively little consistency in dress has developed to symbolize the occupational category, despite occasional drifting in that direction. At the turn of the century, for instance, a costume consisting of a dark skirt and a shirtwaist seemed destined to become a standardized type of dress for female white-collar workers since it was widely used by them and in a general way resembled the type of dress that had become standard wear for male white-collar workers. But, as time passed, competing forms brought variety into the dress of female white-collar workers and the shirtwaist and skirt did not emerge as long-lasting symbols for the group. A trend in the 1970's toward use of so-called career clothes by female as well as male workers in some business institutions such as banks may indicate that occupational dress symbolizing white-collar work for females has simply been slow in coming, or it may represent one more drifting toward consistency that will disappear as variety reasserts itself.

As far as economic symbolism is concerned, women's dress probably indicates ability to consume more clearly that occupational role since consumption is dependent on money available, no matter what the source. This is not to say that type of work, and the skill with which it is done, does not affect dress, for occupation affects income, and income, in turn, directly affects ability to consume, hence the opportunity for both men and women to indulge in personal display. In some societies, because of religious conviction or moral precept, conspicuous display in dress is at a minimum no matter what level of income. In others display is confined to class levels that can afford it. In still others ability to display is widely available and actual display largely a matter of personal values and philosophy.

ADORNMENT AS POLITICAL SYMBOL √

Adornment has long had a place in the house of power. It may show the position of a person in a hierarchial system of authority; it may be visible proof of affiliation with a particular political party, or dedication to one political ideology and opposition to another. If political power passes from one ideological group to another, sometimes the entering group will adopt the symbolic dress of their predecessors. Napoleon reintroduced types of dress that were symbols of state from the old regime to support the legitimacy of his empire visually and to unite the old and new elite. At other times a group will institute its own symbols of dress, as did Castro and his followers when they adopted drab fatigue uniforms. At yet other times, subtle modifications in dress, rather than radical change, may occur among the politically sensitive. For example, the military coups in Nigeria in the 1960's resulted in de-emphasis of the Nigerian "national" dress among the Ibo politicians and civil servants of eastern Nigeria, because the "national" dress symbolized the peoples of the west and north, that is, their political opposition.

An occasional political figure may have unique adornment that helps set him apart in his elevated position of leadership. Moshe Dayan, defense minister of Israel in the 1960's and 1970's made a black eye patch more than a cover: it was his particular ornament and mark of identification. The brown derby was the personal identification mark of Al Smith, New York politician and Democratic party leader, who ran for president of the United States in 1928, whereas the ten-gallon hat symbolized Lyndon B. Johnson in the 1970's.

Traditional ceremonial costume of royalty has become less common in the world, but the investiture of Prince Charles in 1969 as Prince of Wales gave opportunity for traditional costume to mix with the contemporary. Queen Elizabeth dressed in twentieth-century fashions but her son, the prince, was bedecked in eighteenth-century splendor. The 1970 wedding of the crown prince of Nepal was another occasion for much traditional ceremonial display. In both cases fineness in dress indicated the elevated political status of the participants (*Newsweek* 1970).

Military and police uniforms with various kinds of ornamentation call attention to those who stand ready to exert force in maintaining social order according to the authority delegated to them by those in positions of power. Police uniforms adorned with brass buttons, badges, buckles, and insignia announce the policemen whose job is to help with law enforcement. Identification of police uniforms as symbols commanding

respect was sometimes challenged in America in the 1960's, as sentiments were expressed against what was considered the dehumanized,
impersonal nature of police authority within America's mass society. This
loss of respect for the uniform sometimes encouraged its abandonment,
apparently in the hope that removal of the uniform would also remove
hostility it might symbolically stimulate in encounters between police and
the public. In 1969 *Newsweek* reported that a growing number of police
forces were moving into civilian clothes in an effort to reduce a military
image which had become unpopular and to encourage people to regard
policemen as "friends" (*Newsweek* 1969).

Decorative emblems frequently accompany planned political
activities. Pins, badges, armbands, and hats often declare political affiliation and support. American political conventions are usually made colorful by these kinds of identification. In protest marches against the war in
Vietnam in 1969, black armbands identified those voicing their protest.

During the reign of Queen Anne in Britain in the early years of the
eighteenth century, preferences for political parties could be indicated by
beauty patches. Whig women patched the right cheek, the Tories the left,
and those who were neutral, both cheeks. Out of either vanity or political
fervor, one woman in 1771 stipulated in her marriage contract that she be
permitted to patch on the side she pleased no matter what her husband's
political stand was (Andres 1892:192).

The seriousness with which people may take the ideological symbolism
of dress was probably never so clear as during the French Revolution,
when fine dress and powdered hair identifying the aristocracy placed
them at the risk of being arrested by the revolutionaries (Davenport
1948:653). Trousers also were an important symbol of political differentiation: to be a *sans-culotte* was to be a revolutionary who wore tubular
trousers; knee-breeches (*culottes*) belonged to the aristocracy.

Powdered hair lasted longer in England than in France but there, too,
met political opposition. When a flour shortage hit England, anyone
using hair powder was required to purchase a license at one guinea per
year (Ashton 1885:60–61, 73). In angry opposition to the legislation, the
Whigs in 1795 entreated men to abandon hair powder. Some organized
the Crop Club, a group that cut off their hair and made a ceremony of
combing out the powder.

A twentieth-century social movement with strong political intent is the
women's liberation movement that gained momentum toward the end of
the 1960's. The members of this movement did not have physically
restricting dress to protest against as did their nineteenth-century predecessors, but they followed in the spirit of their feminist forebear by
protesting against the social restraints of their clothing. Rejection of
cosmetics, elaborate hairstyles, foundation garments, and of the practice
of removing body hair was a symbolic demand for freedom from customs

that placed women in a position of dependency upon rather than equality with men.

ADORNMENT AS INDICATOR OF MAGICO-RELIGIOUS CONDITION

An individual's approach to self-adornment may reflect affiliation with a religious sect or denomination. In addition, it may show position within a religious group and possibly indicate the intensity of a person's religious participation. Some dress showing religious affiliation or position was once common, fashionable dress of laymen, but, as the dress of the laymen changed, the dress of the religious did not — perhaps as a symbolic reinforcement of belief in the everlasting value of the tenets of the religion to which they subscribed. Sometimes the dress used was formerly the clothes of the poor people, at other times the dress of the well-to-do. In either case, the antique appearance of forms of dress characteristic of an earlier time sets apart the religious individuals or groups who are wearing them so that they can readily be distinguished. The Roman Catholic church has retained examples of dress that typify the poor and the rich of bygone days — some of the vestments of the priests take their form from the everyday costume of well-to-do Romans. From the fourth century, while Roman dress changed steadily, church dress changed little if at all. The male monastic orders, however, adopted and kept the everyday dress of the poor people of the Middle Ages. For example, St. Benedict, in the sixth century, prescribed the scapular, which had been a farm-laborer's apron, as the work garment of his monks (Davenport 1948:99; Norris 1947:172). The women's orders, evolving later than the men's, wore tunics or frocks similar to those worn by the male orders but with added draped head coverings similar to those of widows and married women of the Middle Ages.

The dress of the Roman Catholic clergy shows how clothing can indicate position and rank within a religious structure, with different dress prescribed for different clerical ranks such as priest, bishop, cardinal, and pope. Outstanding distinctions in clerical dress are the tiara of the pope and the scarlet costume of the cardinal. These items and others identify relative positions in a hierarchial system of prestige, responsibility, and power.

The dress of the Hasidic Jews is considered by them to be apparel once worn by all Jews (Poll 1962:65). Since most present-day Jews dress similarly to non-Jews, the costume worn by the Hasidim is an exclusive symbol of their sect. Hasidic men and women in America utilize systems of dress related to other American dress but with distinguishing differences. The dress of the Hasidic men indicates for them their degree of religious intensity. The greater the number of rituals and the more intensely these are observed, the greater the esteem accorded a person, and costume makes known to the individual and to others this degree of intensity. The less the fervor of a man's religious observance, the more his appearance resembles that of a man in modern Western dress. The most religious class, the Rebbes, have the greatest quantity of Hasidic elaborations in dress. The Yiden class wear the fewest of the Hasidic symbols and are the least religious and also least ritualistic (Poll 1962:59–69).

The relation of adornment to the individual as a religious figure may differ. Adornment may protect the religious individual in his encounter with the supernatural; it may prepare him to act as celebrant of a religious rite; it may symbolize his leadership in acts of petition or meditation; and it may also be a means for his assuming the power of the supernatural, as he puts on the clothes of God.

ADORNMENT AS A FACILITY IN SOCIAL RITUALS

In many rituals of social life, such as weddings, funerals, feasts, and dance, dressing up in garb with more fineness than that used in routine day-to-day existence is expected. Dress used for such events may range between the best dress one has to a very explicitly prescribed type of dress. Donning the dress generally marks "putting on a mood": ritual cheerfulness and gaiety or ritual sadness and gloom may, for example, be required. In Western society the traditional black garb of the widow identifies her as the chief mourner. How well an individual can assume the required mood may determine how socially at ease the person will be in the ritual situation.

ADORNMENT AS REINFORCEMENT OF BELIEF, CUSTOM, AND VALUES

Adornment, or rejection of adornment, may serve as a means for symbolically tying a community together. Agreement on bodily adornment reinforces common consciousness and a common course of action that holds people together in a closely knit group. This unifying function of adornment is easier to identify in a small, homogeneous society than in heterogeneous mass society, because not all groups within the latter type of society have the same beliefs, attitudes, and values. In the small Amish community, for example, a very clear-cut symbolism can be observed within their very restricted definition of finery (Hostetler 1963:131–148). Amish dress admits individuals into full participation with the society of the Amish and clarifies the part each plays. Hats thus distinguish the Amish from outsiders, but variations do exist in hats for young boys, bridegrooms, grandfathers, and for bishops. Their dress stands as an ever-present reminder of the Amish position in society and of the individual duties associated with Amish life.

The Hasidim are also aware that their religious dress may protect them from the disunifying effect of outside influences, as illustrated by the following remark of a Hasidic Jew:

With my appearance I cannot attend a theater or movie or any other place where a religious Jew is not supposed to go. Thus my beard and my sidelocks and my Hasidic clothing serve as a guard and a shield from sin and obscenity (Poll 1962:65).

ADORNMENT AS RECREATION

For people who have leisure time available as well as the opportunity for display, acquiring materials for personal adornment or adorning oneself may be recreational activities, that is, they may provide respite from regular routines, responsibilities, and work. As the recreational purpose is achieved, however, other functions may also be served. For instance, in societies where leisure is a scarce resource monopolized by a social elite, personal display that is recreational may become an indicator of social class.

During the nineteenth and twentieth centuries American society has generally allotted more discretionary control of time to women than to men; therefore, dressing as a recreational activity has been more characteristic of the former. For the same reason — available time — male and female adolescents in the twentieth century have used dress as a recreational outlet more often than older age groups. An aspect of the entertainment value of dress was also identifiable among the youth in the 1960's and early 1970's who used unique adornment to authenticate that they were "doing their own thing" — really joining in a popular search for identity.

ADORNMENT AS SEXUAL SYMBOL

Male and female have historically been differentiated by their dress. However, bodily adornment of the sexes has not only been used to distinguish one sex from the other but also for the purpose of sexual enticement. Obviously, emphasizing the genital area by special ornamentation or type of clothing focuses attention on that area. The codpiece, a decorated covering for the male genitals, is one example. The "pasties" over the nipples of a burlesque dancer is an example for females. Padding of men's shoulders and women's breasts and hips emphasizes differences in male and female body contours.

Dress used to entice members of the opposite sex may be considered within two settings: private and public. Private or intimate settings are best exemplified by the bedroom or boudoir where undergarments, sleeping garments, or lack of garments, are used to lure one's spouse, lover, or momentary companion into sexual involvement. These liaisons may represent legal or illegal relationships between the sexes or between members of the same sex. Historically, adorning the body has been an integral symbol of sexual enticement. Public settings such as the street, restaurants, and theaters are places where dress can be a public announcement of sexual identity and an enticement to private settings. Prior to enticement, whether for heterosexual or homosexual involvement, sexual identification must occur. Dress and ornamentation may emphasize body characteristics and mannerisms that have been culturally defined as symbolic of sexual enticement. Emphasizing body characteristics beyond what the mode in dress prescribes has often provided the additional variable necessary for enticement. Thus, micro-miniskirts during the time of the miniskirt, the tightest sweaters during the era of the sweater girl, or the most sleekly fitting trousers for males, may publicly announce the availability of the wearers for sexual pursuits. Films have stereotyped the dress of the prostitute in Western society so that red high-heeled shoes and a matching handbag worn with tightly-fitting clothing and heavy makeup are common symbols.

In countries, ordinarily tropical, where a completely or partially nude body is the norm in public, the nude body with its obvious sexual distinguishing characteristics is seldom used for sexual enticement purposes, while ornament may. In special nude enclaves within clothed societies, such as in Europe and America, nudist-colony members claim the nude body is less enticing than the clothed body. Some analysts of behavior in these colonies explain the differences as essentially cultural. Interaction patterns are altered among the nudists so that more controls are placed on touching and looking at each other and on verbalization with sexual references than among nonnudists (Weinberg 1968:217–219).

SUMMARY

Adornment is a communicative symbol that serves crucial functions within human lives. Individual satisfaction may be derived from pleasurable emotional experiences prompted by both display and observation of the adornment provided by dress, whether extensively or minimally developed. Adorning oneself supports the individual in his endeavors to speak as a unique individual and provides him a way of expressing, reinforcing, initiating, or camouflaging mood. At the same time that adornment offers a way for individual expression and for dealing with life aesthetically, it serves a number of useful functions within society. It can be used to indicate social roles, to establish social worth, as a symbol of economic status, as an emblem of political power or ideological inclination, as a reflection of magico-religious condition, as a facility in social rituals, and as a reinforcement of beliefs, custom, and values. Furthermore, adornment can be elaborated into a recreational activity and utilized in sexual enticement.

REFERENCES

ANDRES, WILLIAM
1892   *Bygone England.* London: Hutchinson.
ASHTON, A. JOHN
1885   *Old times.* London: J. C. Mimmo.
BUSH, GEORGE, PERRY LONDON
1960   On the disappearance of knickers: hypothesis for the functional analysis of the psychology of clothing. *Journal of Social Psychology* 51:359–366. (Reprinted 1965 in: *Dress, adornment and the social order.* Edited by Mary Ellen Roach and Joanne Bubolz Eicher, 64–72. New York: John Wiley and Sons.)
DAVENPORT, MILLIA
1948   *The book of costume.* New York: Crown.
FRANZERO, CHARLES MARIE
1958   *Beau Brummell: his life and times.* New York: John Day.
GREENFIELD, KENT ROBERTS
1918   *Sumptuary law in Nürnburg: a study in paternal government.* Baltimore: Johns Hopkins Press.
HEARN, LAFCADIO
1904   *Japan.* New York: Macmillan.
HOSTETLER, JOHN A.
1963   *Amish society.* Balimore: Johns Hopkins University Press.
Life
1970   Which would you pick up? Guess again. *Life* 68 (March 13): 61–62.
Newsweek
1969   Out of the blue. *Newsweek* 74(13):79. September 29.
1970   Nepal: "Come, let us marry." *Newsweek* 75(11):14–15. March 16.
NORRIS, HERBERT
1947   *Costume and fashion.* London: J. M. Dent and Sons.
POLL, SOLOMON
1962   *The Hasidic community of Williamsburg.* New York: Free Press of Glencoe.
RADCLIFFE-BROWN, A. R.
1933   *The Andaman Islanders.* Cambridge: Cambridge University Press.
WEINBERG, MARTIN S.
1968   "Sexual modesty and the nudist camp," in: *Deviance: the interactionist perspective.* Edited by Earl Rubington and Martin S. Weinberg, 217–219. New York: Macmillan.

Uncovering the Secret Vice: Toward an Anthropology of Clothing and Adornment

RONALD A. SCHWARZ

Clothing is a subject about which anthropologists should have much to say, yet remain mysteriously silent. While anthropologists always include language and tool making as distinguishing characteristics of man, adornment receives little systematic consideration. Indeed, descriptions of clothing are so rare in some texts of social anthropology (Beattie 1964; Lienhardt 1964; Mair 1965) that the casual reader might easily conclude the natives go naked. In their silence they are, although perhaps for different motives, like the Big men in New York for whom clothing is an important yet unspeakable topic.

... the secret vice of ... custom tailoring. ... Practically all the most powerful men in New York ... are fanatical about the marginal differences that go into custom tailoring. They are almost like a secret club insignia for them. And yet it is a taboo subject. ... They don't want it known they even care about it (Wolfe 1965:256–257).

Why should anthropology bother about clothing? Because around the globe, Man, the naked ape, does something to adorn or clothe himself.

While the question of why anthropologists have not given dress the same attention as other aspects of culture is of some concern in this article, the major goal is to review what has been said on the subject, and to develop a foundation and methodological approach for the anthropological study of clothing and adornment.

One of the unsettled issues in the discussion of clothing in the social sciences is that of definitions. Adornment, clothing, ornament, dress, and attire are frequently employed as general terms. Also there are practices such as head deformation, scarification, cosmetics, body painting, and hairdressing, all of which are a form of bodily modification. Since I do not wish to enter into an extended discussion of the merits and weaknesses of

terminology at this time, I use clothing, adornment, and dress interchangeably and will mean them to refer to all forms of bodily modification from an earplug to a hand-tailored suit.

THE ORIGIN AND FUNCTIONS OF CLOTHING

> Man is born naked but dies and is put away
> with his clothes on.
> H. and M. HILER, *Bibliography of costume*,
> p. xiii

In *The origins of art* Hirn (1900:214–227) discusses the origin of self-
decoration. After a careful examination of the available ethnographic
evidence, and a review of theories of the origin of adornment, he concludes there is no possibility of deciding with any certainty the question of
why man began to decorate himself. The search for the origin of ancient
customs is no longer seriously engaged in in anthropology and little has
been said in the past 73 years which could cause us to modify Hirn's conclusion. Though one must acknowledge that we can never *prove* that a
particular complex of sentiments gave rise to the practice of adornment,
it would be unfortunate if we let logic interfere indefinitely with our
disposition toward raising such basic issues.

Adornment: Evidence from the Apes and Archeologists

There is solid evidence that the disposition to decorate the body has its
roots in our primate heritage. Chimpanzees, at least those in captivity,
seem to enjoy decorating themselves with strings and rags, painting their
bodies, and prancing around to display themselves. There is not, however, any evidence for either regular use or stylistic continuity of adornment among primates. Thus, though we may owe a sentimental debt to
our prehuman ancestors, clothing, like language and tool fashioning, is a
uniquely human product.

The first archeological evidence of adornment is found on bones in
mid-Paleolithic Neanderthal burials where ocherous clays were apparently used. Textiles could not survive in early deposits and teeth, bone and
shells do not appear until the Aurignacian period, together with mural
drawing. The first eyed-bone needles date from this period and may be
taken as evidence of sewing. Female figurines with exaggerated feminine
characteristics and adorned with bracelets are also found in these Aurignacian sites. Textile garments and the evidence for weaving do not appear
until the Neolithic (Beals and Hoijer 1959:383–384; Benedict
1931:235).

Most theorizing about the origin of adornment is based on the study of its use among primitive and tribal societies (Benedict 1931; Bliss 1916; Bunzel 1931; Crawley 1931; Dunlap 1928; Flugel 1929, 1945; Harms 1938; Hiler 1929; Hiler and Hiler 1939; Hirn 1900; Sanborn 1926; Thomas 1909). A few authors argue for a particularly theory, however, most agree that a combination of environmental, psychological, and sociocultural factors are involved in the origin and evolution of clothing, and that motives for continued use of an item may be rather different from those which led to its adoption.

PROTECTION FROM THE ENVIRONMENT. This position holds that the origin of *clothing* (not simply ornamentation or decoration) is a human response to environmental conditions and the need for protection from elements which cause discomfort.

While there is an intimate relationship between clothing and ecological conditions in some areas, there are regions where one would expect to find protective garments, for example the freezing regions of Tierra del Fuego and Australia, but where such items are absent. It should be noted, however, that though the Fuegians and Australian aborigines are without outer garments, body painting is common to both groups.

PROTECTION FROM SUPERNATURAL FORCES. Several authors (Hirn 1900; Spencer and Gillen 1899; Frazer 1890) suggest the origin and main function of primitive adornment may be traced to man's need to defend himself from malevolent spiritual powers. Hirn (1900:217–219) summarizes some of the early anthropological evidence for this theory. He states:

It is probable . . . that there are many primitive tribes which, in the same way as the aborigines of New Hebrides, cover themselves in the most scrupulous manner, "not at all from a sense of decency, but to avoid Narak, i.e. magic influence," the sight of even another man's nakedness being considered as most dangerous (1900:217).

And in addressing himself to those writers of the time who would place the disposition to "morality" or modesty as generating man's tendency to cover the genitals, he has this to say:

. . . it is evident that even before any such transformations to moral institutions and moral feelings took place, regard for public safety may have induced the males to conceal the seat of so dangerous an influence.

Belief in the power of supernatural forces to cause illness, death, and pregnancy, is as common as the use of adornment. Spirits to which these powers are attributed are often associated with natural phenomena such as the wind, rain, rivers, lightning, the sun, and the moon. In short, there appears to be sufficient evidence for asserting that the use of adornment to protect oneself and the community against harmful spirits is a common motive for its use in primitive and tribal societies.

THE SHAME HYPOTHESIS. The shame theory of bodily covering is rooted in biblical lore in Eve's seduction by the serpent, and parallels are found in American Indian folktales. According to this theory, clothing was adopted to conceal the genital organs out of a sense of shame or modesty, and that from the figleaf more complex types of clothing evolved (Dunlap 1928:64; Sanborn 1926:2).

This theory has been thoroughly demolished by most authors (Hirn 1900; Westermarck 1891) and its popularity was due more to the moral climate of the nineteenth century than ethnological evidence. Dunlap 1928:66) puts the relationship between modesty and nudity in its proper perspective when he states:

Any degree of clothing, including complete nudity, is perfectly modest as soon as we become thoroughly accustomed to it. Conversely, any change in clothing, suddenly effected, may be immodest if it is of such a nature to be conspicuous . . . Clothing itself has not modesty or immodesty.

THE ATTRACTION HYPOTHESIS. This is perhaps the earliest serious theory put forth by anthropologists regarding the origin of adornment. Ellis (1900) and Westermarck (1891) maintain that the original purpose of clothing was to attract attention to the genitals and their erotic functions thus increasing the observer's sexual interest in the wearer. This position is consistent with the theoretical views of Simmel (1950) and Goffman (1956) who emphasize that concealment and privacy stimulate interest, whereas familiarity results in indifference.

A modified version of the attraction theory was later advanced by Bick (1968). He suggests that all persons past the age of puberty may be treated as consumers and objects of consumption in the "sexual market place" (1968:3). In this context, adornment

. . . can be seen as a symbolic system which provides a major indication of the individual's willingness to participate in this market, at any particular moment, as an object of consumption . . . Adornment then, to paraphrase McLuhan, is the frequently unconscious medium for each individual's sexual message (1968:3).

The desire to draw attention to oneself, or to communicate the state of one's availability or nonavailability in the sexual marketplace are important aspects in the complex of sentiments surrounding the origin and use of clothing, but like the other hypotheses discussed above they are inadequate to serve as a general theory.

THE STATUS AND RANKING HYPOTHESIS. This is the position that the origin or principal function of clothing is to differentiate members of a society into age, sex and class or caste, and is only secondarily related to erotic matters. Support for this view is found in the use of adornment, especially scarification and circumcision, in age groups. While there is a general association with sexual maturity and the erotic possibilities that this implies, the ceremonies signify more than sexual availability. Indeed, some of the participants in such ceremonies reach puberty several years before the event is held.

It may be that the earliest form of adornment were items obtained in the hunt and used for display by the successful hunter:

In the feather crowns of the Xingu chiefs . . . we may thus see only a later development of proudly arranged spoils of chase, by which a successful hunter proclaims his achievements (Hirn 1900:221–111).

Benedict (1931: 236) observes that:

on the plains of North America men's dress is a heraldic display of war counts, and on the Northwest coast a man's hat will be built up in cumulative units to designate his rank.

Clothing and adornment also play an important role as indicators of a person's status as a member of a particular tribal or ethnic group. A Nuer, for example, is identified by the absence of the lower incisors, and among males, by six cuts on the brow (Evans-Pritchard 1940:123). The blue veil identifies the Tuareg, and in the Guatemalan highlands the Indian population is divided into territorial and ethnic groups each of which uses a distinctive mode of attire.

WHAT HAPPENED TO THE CLOTHES?

The search for origins and the study of social functions of adornment was clearly a matter of concern to anthropologists in the early decades of this century. During the ensuing years there have been a few attempts to discuss clothing and adornment in a systematic fashion. Most ethnographers, among them Bunzel (1952), Parsons (1936), Lewis (1951), Redfield (1930), Reichel-Dolmatoff and Reichel-Dolmatoff (1961), and Vogt (1969), include descriptive sections on dress in their monographs, usually under the rubric of material culture.

Along with the ethnographies which continued to be written, two major trends characterized anthropology during the forties, fifties, and sixties: one a holistic study of social institutions and their functional interrelationships; and another, toward specialization within a single institution (for example, kinship). Often the latter involved an integration of anthropological data and theory with those of other disciplines such as economics, clinical psychology, politics, and art. The study of material culture, which traditionally included clothing, evolved into a systematic investigation of technology and cultural ecology which hardly touched on dress. Anthropologists interested in art and aesthetics focused on specific "art" products: carving, sculpture, painting, music, and dance. This is illustrated by the contents of three volumes dealing with the anthropology of art and aesthetics (Helm 1967; Otten 1971; Jopling 1971). The books contain 65 articles published between 1949 and 1970 and only one deals with clothing (Sturtevant 1967). Contributions by anthropologists are included in Roach and Eicher (1965), which deals with clothing, adornment, and the social order. It is however, an eclectic collection of excerpts and articles. There is no critical analysis of the field nor do the editors attempt to develop a general theory. In short, during the past thirty years we have increased our knowledge of the technology, psychology, social organization and art of the naked ape, but we have made little progress in understanding his refusal to remain naked. In our rush toward specialization and new forms of integrating anthropology with other sciences, clothing was left hanging in the closet.

GETTING CLOTHING OUT OF THE CLOSET

The easiest way to indicate the importance of clothes to society is to reflect on what would occur if they were absent:

What would Majesty do, could such an accident befall in reality; should the buttons all simultaneously start, and the solid wool evaporate, in very Deed, as here in Dream, *Ach Gott*! How each skulls into the nearest hiding-place; their high State Tragedy . . . becomes a Pickelherring-Farce to weep at, which is the worst kind of Farce; . . . the whole fabric of Government, Legislation, Property, Police, and Civilized Society, *are dissolved*, in wails and howls.

Lives the man that can figure a naked Duke of Windlestraw addressing a naked house of Lords? Imagination, choked as in mephitic air, recoils on itself and will not forward with the picture (Carlyle 1869:59–60, original emphasis).

Clothes do more than just indicate a person's sex, age, occupation, and position in a social hierarchy, they are associated with a complex of sentiments and serve to channel strong emotions. Like other symbols, clothes also have a conative aspect — they move men to act in prescribed ways. Among the Fon of Benin, for example, a village chief wears one hat when acting in his capacity of chief, another when performing his duties as head of a lineage, and another when acting as head of his family. One of the best examples of the way use of clothing to communicate emotional as well as social aspects of a situation is found in Murphy's discussion (1964) of social distance and the veil among the Tuareg. He quotes Lhote on the uses and psychology of the veil:

The style of wearing the veil, of placing the different parts about the head, may vary from one tribe to another and some individuals give their preference, according to personal taste, to certain local styles . . . But beside these different fashions, there is also the turn, the knack which makes it more or less elegant. Similarly there is a psychology of the veil; by the way in which it is set, one can gain an idea of the mood of the wearer just as among us the angle of the cap or hat permits analogous deductions. There is the reserved and modest style used when one enters a camp where there are women, the elegant and *recherchée* style for going to courting parties, the haughty manner of warriors conscious of their own importance, like the whimsy of the blustering vassal or slave. There is also the detached and lax fashion of the jovial fellow, the good chap, or the disordered one of the unstable man of irritable character. The veil may also express a transient sentiment. For example, it is brought up to the eyes before women or prestigeful persons, while it is a sign of familiarity when it is lowered. To laugh from delight with a joke, the Tuareg will lift up the lower part of his veil very high on his nose, and, in case of irritation, will tighten it like a chin strap to conceal his anger (Murphy 1964:1266, translated from Lhote 1955:308–309).

This aspect of clothing, its ability to express (and conceal) certain principles and emotions, and move men to act in the culturally appropriate manner, may be called its symbolic or rhetorical power. Through their capacity to symbolize a social order, what is and what should be, clothes are related to social action and communication in a dynamic way.

TOWARD AN ANTHROPOLOGY OF ADORNMENT

This section outlines some ideas about a foundation for an anthropological study of clothing. The main purpose is to present issues and outline principles, rather than draw conclusions. There are two broad areas of query between which it is useful to distinguish for analysis: clothing in relation to men, and clothing in relation to Man. On the one hand there is the role of adornment in particular societies and in Society. On the other hand, there is the relationship between Nature, Man, Clothing, and Culture.

As the basis for an inquiry into the status of clothing, we must undress man and place him firmly in a naturalistic context, not just an ecological one. Man's relationships are not only with what is "out there" but with himself in a biological and philosophical sense. What he produces, be it a spear, a house, a law, a poem, or a pair of shoes, reflects the choices he makes within an environment only partially produced by him and with which he interacts. Following the philosopher Buchler (1955) we may distinguish between three modes of human production: doing, making, and saying, and consider them as alternative ways in which an individual establishes his relationship to the world. Note that these are presented as *alternative* modes of production, and there is no implication of a hierarchy among them.

The mode of production which characterizes objects of material culture such as clothing, is "making." As Buchler states:

When a man carves in stone, determines his wardrobe, composes music, or arranges the dinnerware on the table, when in short, he makes, he is ordering materials in accordance with an established or an evolved disposition. He is judging a natural complex by contriving its structure or by modifying an existing structure within it. He is adopting one order and ignoring or discarding another (Buchler 1955:12).

How a man orders his materials, no less than what he says about them or describes them to be, reflects the direction of his self and defines the character of something in his world. The properties of things are defined by being brought into relation to us. This is accomplished not only by *saying* something about them, but by *doing* something to them *and/or*, *making* something out of them (Buchler 1955:12–13): "It is not the mind that judges, it is the man" (1955:29).

Modes of judgment, according to Buchler, are also modes of communication. We communicate by acting and making as well as by stating. Furthermore, the communicative aspect of what we produce is not limited to the meanings stated by those who make the judgments.

The communicative power of products may far surpass the communicative intent of their producers. Becoming communal possessions, they affect conduct and understanding . . . The communicative power of a product is in no way dependent on the mode of its production, nor on the merit or moral quality of its utterance (Buchler 1955:30)

Buchler's assertion that all three modes of judgment are effective in communicating follows a position in modern philosophy suggested by George Berkeley, and expanded on Charles Peirce and Josiah Royce, that anything whatever may function as a sign: "Anything is subject to interpretation and is therefore a possible vehicle of communication" (1955:30).

The purpose of presenting this philosophical exposition is twofold: first, to put material culture into what I consider a more fitting relationship or balance with verbal behavior and social action; and second, to anticipate those critics who may say that anthropologists should limit interpretations of signs and symbols to what informants say about them (see Nadel 1954; Wilson 1957).

Taking the position that what men *make* may be as important as what they *say* in defining a relationship with their environment (sociocultural as well as natural), the study of clothing and adornment becomes rather significant as an anthropological enterprise. It is not just the fact that only humans adorn themselves, but that *more than any other material product, clothing plays a symbolic role in mediating the relationship between nature, man, and his sociocultural environment*. In dressing up, man addresses himself, his fellows, and his world.

Natural Contexts and Adornment

The notion that to understand symbols one should look first to the body and environment is not new in anthropology. Hertz (1960), for example, provides substantial evidence to demonstrate that the dualism expressed in the opposition of the left and right hand is used to distinguish between cultural phenomena in many societies. And others, notably Douglas (1970), Lévi-Strauss (1963), Needham (1960), Faron (1962), and Turner (1967, 1969) have employed the concept of "handedness" in examining the relationship of values to social divisions and other aspects of behavior. Douglas takes the matter beyond that of handedness and states that "Most symbolic behavior *must* work through the human body" (1970:vii, emphasis added). And she goes on to suggest that once social categories are established, they modify the experience of the body and sustain a cultural framework for viewing social relations (1970:65).

Another "given" which, like the body, exhibits structural stability and processual regularity, is the natural environment. Ecological conditions as well as anatomy provide opportunities and obstacles for the person and present a natural basis for classifying social units and relationships between them. This environment should not, as Hughes notes, be left unexamined:

The concept of "environment" should not be a residual category, the unanalyzed foil against which the complexities of the individual organism are held, or unexamined ground against which the figure of the human personality is illuminated. For the environment itself is prefigured, has points of saliency, of structure, of all-or-nothing emphases which function as coercive and orientational frameworks for the perceiving organism ... it [the environment] is ... a background of *structured* opportunity and obstacle in both physical and social terms (1965:11).

Since the natural order provides the raw materials for adornment as well as a potential classificatory framework which may be reflected in how man conceptualizes his body and what he wears, it too invites serious consideration.

In short, to develop an anthropology of clothing not only should the social contexts and uses be examined, but also contexts provided by the human body and the natural environment.

Clothing and Structural Models

One of the earliest systematic studies on clothing was done by Richardson and Kroeber (1940) on changing styles of women's dress. In suggesting that modes and styles of clothing reflect social conditions and are affected by the flow of events, they conclude:

... the basic features of style as distinct from more rapidly fluctuating mode, being taken for granted at any given moment, are largely unconscious in the sense they are considered axiomatic (1940:148).

Though Richardson and Kroeber refused to consider psychological explanations (1940:150), Lévi-Strauss interprets their findings as evidence for the operation of laws underlying phenomena which might be superficially judged as arbitrary. He asserts,

These laws cannot be reached by purely empirical observation, or by intuitive consideration of the phenomena, but result from measuring some basic relationships between various elements of costume (1963:58).

Analyzing clothing at this level takes on the same character as a problem in structural linguistics and the natural sciences. The empirical problem is to identify the basic components, patterns, and systems of relationships (communication systems) among elements taken individually and as clusters or groups. The issue is not simply whether clothing may be studied by methods and concepts similar to those used in linguistics, but, as Lévi-Strauss phrases it, "whether they do not constitute phenomena whose inmost nature is the same as that of language" (1963:61).

The best example of an approach to the study of clothing using a linguistic model is in the work of Bogatyrev (1971), who did his work before Lévi-Strauss suggested that such an enterprise might be useful. Though Bogatyrev does not go so far as to suggest there might be structural homologies between the system of language and the system of clothing, he does assert that,

In order to grasp the social functions of costumes we must learn to read them as signs in the same way we learn to read and understand languages (1971:83).

For Bogatyrev the "function of a costume is an expression of the attitudes of the wearers" (1971:93):

The function may relate to the costume itself (as an *object*) or to the various aspects of life which the costume (as a *sign*) is indicative of (1971:80, original emphasis).

Thus Bogatyrev challenges us to consider in addition to the formal structures of clothing their ethical role in society. In order to do this, however, we need information beyond that provided by the clothing itself. He notes,

A costume is like a microcosm where one finds mirrored in their relative intensities the aesthetic, moral and nationalistic ideals of those who wear it. In order to fully comprehend the role of costume as an expression of folk ethics, we must recognize the ethical ideals reflected in a costume's form (in such things as the restrictions as to who may wear it) and we must have knowledge of the *general* ethical ideals of the people as well. Otherwise we might miss or fail to understand certain expressions of such ideals in the functions of the costume (1971:93, original emphasis).

To illustrate some of the concepts discussed above, the following section presents a case study of the clothing of an Andean Indian society. It is based on information collected during several years of research over a ten-year period.

A STRUCTURAL ANALYSIS OF CLOTHING: THE GUAMBIANOS OF COLOMBIA

The Guambianos inhabit the western slopes of the central cordillera in southwestern Colombia. There were more than a hundred tribes in the area before the Spanish conquest but warfare, disease, and colonial institutions resulted in the elimination or acculturation of most. In contrast to this general pattern, the Guambianos have maintained much of their native culture, including language and a distinctive mode of dress.

On the basis of an analysis of Amerindian languages (Matteson et al. 1972) the Guambiano, previously believed to be part of the Chibchan family (Rivet 1946), are now considered unclassifiable or as an isolate (Matteson et al. 1972:22). Over the centuries, Paez, Quechua and Spanish words have been added to the vocabulary and today most Guambianos are fairly fluent in Spanish.

There are approximately 7,500 Indians living on the reservation of Guambía. The territory is approximately 6,000 hectares, about half of which is suitable for cultivation. Reservation land ranges from a low of about 2,600 meters in the western section and continues to a high of almost 4,000 meters in the east. It is roughly divided into three ecological zones: (1) a cold, damp, relatively flat forest and grassland (the *paramo*) in the high eastern part, which is poorly suited for farming but used for grazing animals — it is considered a dangerous area populated by a wide range of spirits associated with natural phenomena — women are particularly susceptible to these malevolent powers, but all Guambianos ritually "cleanse" themselves before climbing there; (2) the *middle zone*, consisting mostly of sharp inclined slopes and used for growing potatoes, ullucos and onions; and (3) the *lower western* region, used mostly for the cultivation of corn, wheat, barley and beans. Most of the land is too steep for plowing by draft animals and the Indians cultivate with metal-tipped digging sticks and shovels.

During this century the reservation population increased from 1,500 (in 1900) to about 7,500 (in 1973). In the early part of the century there was a surplus of land and forest resources; today all farmland is parceled out. Guambianos live in neighborhood clusters (*veredas*), most of which have between twenty-five and ninety households. Descent is bilateral, and postmarital residence is patri-virilocal. During the period for which a model of their clothing is presented, the 1920's and early 1930's, neighborhoods were small and men obtained their wives from outside their *veredas*. Agricultral activities are shared by both sexes, and women cultivate household gardens in addition to their work in the fields. The division of labor emphasizes the female's role in the home; cooking, caring for the children, and weaving skirts and ponchos. Males spend part of their time in politically sponsored activities (care of trails, building of bridges), caring for animals and weaving hats. Reciprocal labor exchange and cooperative work (*mingas*) is common.

Political affairs of the reservation are managed by an Indian council (*cabildo*) in which all residential areas are represented. Only married males are eligible to participate, and officials serve for a one-year period. High offices are almost always filled by individuals with previous experience in a lower position. Serving in the cabildo is a sacrifice of time and money but there are no financial prerequisites to occupying a position. Cabildo officers adjudicate disputes, supervise the distribution of land, organize community projects and sponsor religious festivals.

The Guambiano world view is a part mixture, part blend of Spanish and Indian beliefs. Guambianos are baptized, married and have funeral services in the Catholic church. Native ceremonies, however, follow church services in the latter two events. They acknowledge the power of a wide range of supernatural beings and engage in frequent rituals to avoid contamination which might lead to illness and death. Women and children are especially susceptible to spirits and during menstruation women are prohibited from performing many normal activities.

Two major themes characterize Guambiano culture and operate as guiding principles in a wide range of situations. One is that of "equality" (*latá-latá*) and the other is accompaniment (*linjab*). Equality is the ideal of how things should be, while accompaniment reflects the notion of doing things with and for others, and implies hierarchy and reciprocity.

Guambiano Dress and Social Structure

Guambiano dress has undergone continuous modification. Although major changes are few, each generation seems to add its own distinctive touch to the costume and it is impossible to designate a single mode of dress as characteristic for the whole society at any one time. For example, during my first visit to the reservation in 1962, there were still some older men who continued to use the white shorts which were typical of eighteenth- and nineteenth-century clothing. Once a new item is introduced, however, the tendency is for most of the population to accept it. A dramatic change in dress styles occurred about the turn of the century when the men began weaving flat, circular hats which take on a slightly conical shape when placed on the head. Both sexes adopted this style of hat. Another dramatic change was the adoption, by the men, of blue kilts worn over the white shorts. This occurred during the 1920's and the cloth was the same as that used by the females for their shawls.

The basis of the model (Figure 1) is the style of dress used on the reservation during the 1920's and early 1930's. There are several reasons the dress of this period is selected as the basis for formal analysis: first, the adoption of the blue kilt by the men represents a change to an item which, according to some accounts, was used before the conquest; second, the low profile, four-surfaced, conical style of hat is unlike those worn by any other South American Indian group; and third, the period was one in which the Guambianos were under pressure from townspeople to divide the reservation and adopt a western style of clothing. During this time they vigorously defended their territory and the right to dress as they wished. For them, clothing was an important symbol of their Indian status they strongly desired to maintain. Finally, their dress as a whole has a truly distinctive combination of elements which clearly sets them apart from other Indian societies.

The following section describes and analyzes the clothing of the Guambiano Indians; the elements of clothing are considered and a model using the basic items and stylistic features is presented. Reference is made to natural contexts, and homologies among ecological, anatomical, social, and adornment structures, are cited. It is only a partial analysis of the Guambiano system of dress, and is intended to be suggestive of a method, not a comprehensive statement.

Figure 1 depicts the major items of Guambiano clothing. The position of the male on the right and female on the left follows their principles of sexual and spatial orientation; East is the cardinal direction. In addition, there are differences between head and body levels, and within the latter, above and below the waist. The upper level is a profile of the hat and indicates a triangular design in the lower portion and a circular design

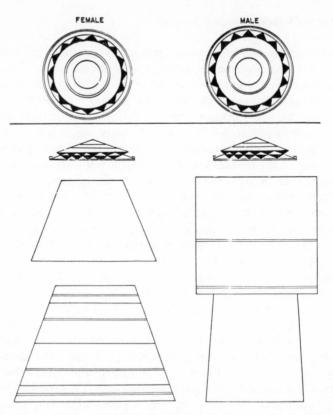

Figure 1.   A model of Guambiano clothing. Top and back views of a Guambiano couple

above. In the female's skirt, the design consists of an odd number of horizontal lines symmetrically arranged from top to bottom. Above the skirt is a blue *manta* made of commercially produced blue cloth. To the right of the manta is a sketch of the male poncho. The design consists of two horizontal stripes, or groups of stripes, arranged asymmetrically below the center. Below the poncho is a kilt made of the same blue cloth women use for their mantas. The hats are made by the men and no aspect of construction or design denotes sexual differentiation. Garments worn below the neck are woven by the women.

At the level of intercultural communication, the clothes of the Guambianos distinguish them from other Indians in the area and the white world. There is a clear difference between men's and women's body garments, but the use of similar color and design features tends to reduce the contrast, as do the similar hats. Except in cases of extreme poverty it is difficult to tell the economic and social status of a Guambiano from the clothing worn. Older garments are used in the fields and everyone has at least one good set of clothes for ceremonial events and going to market.

Women's beads and jewelry provide some basis for differentiation but there is a limit to how much can be used without becoming ostentatious. Furthermore, through inheritance, gifts, purchase, and borrowing, even poor females obtain beads in sufficient quantities.

This apparently egalitarian emphasis exhibited in their dress is related to social changes following the Spanish conquest. Before Spanish dominance was established, Guambiano males served as warriors, and a two-class system of nobles and commoners existed. Afterwards, when the warrior role ended, class distinction was gradually reduced, their inferior position in the regional social structure was stabilized, and policies which threatened their social and cultural integrity were instituted. As Turner (1969:175) indicates, such conditions frequently result in an emphasis on the egalitarian dimension of social relations and generate symbols associated with equality, homogeneity, and community.

The general uniformity of clothing styles in Guambía, and its lack of symbols associated with class hierarchy, suggest that at one level their clothing is an expression of their structural inferiority within the larger social system. At another level, however, it serves to mask the individual differences of wealth and power and "bodies forth" the principle of equality.

Figure 1 and Table 1 indicate that along various axes Guambiano clothing is marked by dualisms. The women weave body garments for themselves and the men. Men make the hats worn equally by both sexes. Left and right are opposed as are female and male, lower and upper, line and circle, odd and even, symmetry and asymmetry.

Table 1.   The dualisms of Guambiano clothing

Maker	Item	Feature	Left/female	Right/male
Male	Hat	Shape	Conical	Conical
		Design	Circles, triangles	Circles, triangles
Female	Poncho,	design	Horizontal lines	Horizontal lines
	Skirt	No. of lines	Odd (7, 9, 11)	Even (two or groups of two)
		Pattern	Symmetrical	Asymmetrical

The patterns exhibited by the major items of Guambiano dress may be divided latitudinally into left and right corresponding to the female–male dichotomy, and altitudinally into two major regions, upper and lower, head and body. The lower, or body region, can be further divided into parts below and above the waist. While the skirt and poncho use similar colors and horizontal lines as design elements, there are differences in the number of lines used (odd–even), the pattern of arrangement (symmetrical–asymmetrical), and the position on the body (below–above). Terms used for these items indicate the below–above contrast has significance as part of a body–space hierarchy. One of the meanings of the morpheme *lend* is "down" or "below", and *lendik* is a word for the female skirt. This contrasts with *tur*, meaning "upper" and "head", and *turí* the Guambiano term for the male poncho. Thus even without taking the male-made hat into account the association of female with left and below, and male with right and above, is evident.

At the upper level are the male-made hats, which are the same for men and women. Circles are always used on the top, and the lower parts contain triangles. At the level of heads and hats, left and right are equal, and aesthetically, the hats contribute to the symmetry and unity of the costume as a whole.

Turning to social relations and dividing activities into those primarily concerned with: (1) "bodily" functions (subsistence production and reproduction); and (2) the maintenance of order among social groups (politics) and humans and spirits (religion); we find that structural principles guiding relationships in these situations are homologous to those exhibited in Guambiano clothing. To begin with, productive and reproductive activities basically involve the middle and lower parts of the body, they occur in the middle and lower parts of the reservation, and are organized in a fashion which unite men and women in some activities and divide them in others. Men and women often work together in the fields, unite for sexual purposes, but are divided with respect to hunting, a male activity, and cooking, weaving cloth and giving birth — female activities. Insofar as inequality exists at the "lower" level it is the female side and lower region that has greater importance. And it is the females who produce the body garments and give them to the men. This asymmetrical pattern is balanced by the structure of symbols and social roles related to levels of authority and activities directed toward the maintenance of order.

Males make the hats and give them to the females. They symbolically unite the couple, making no distinction between left or right, female or male. The opposition of hats and body garments exhibit a symbolic structure similar to that of the human body where below the neck, not above, significant anatomical differences occur. The men weave the hats and at the institutional level it is the men who fill political positions in the cabildo. The function of this organization is to maintain unity among spatially separated neighborhood units and not, incidentally, to build bridges between them. Besides, politics is "heady" business, men's business! Men with the most prestige and power in Guambía are those who "understand" and speak persuasively. Insofar as political power has spatial location, it is toward the upper, eastern part of the reservation. Over ninety percent of the reservation governors during this century lived in the upper section. Thus, as the right to left flow of hats contributes to the aesthetic unity of clothing, so does the flow of political power from right to left, upper to lower, east to west, serve to maintain the political unity of the reservation.

Another area of social relations where the male role, and symbolically the hat, have special significance, is religion. Here I refer to the structure of authority between human and spiritual beings. Within the Guambiano social and spatial framework these are inversely related to one another — human control is most direct at the lower levels and decreases as one moves up to the higher regions of the reservation and beyond. In the higher parts, fetishes are used to protect crops, and the *paramo* is inhabited by wild animals and supernatural forces dangerous to humans. It is especially dangerous for women who may be impregnated by spirits located there. Religious action directed at mediating relations between the human and supernatural world is performed solely by males. Thus, the hat may be viewed not only as a symbol of men's political status, but also their position as curers and diviners.

In short, the items of Guambiano clothing and their relationship to parts of the human body exhibit a pattern similar to that which characterizes the structure of their social relationships. The result may be considered as a transformation of the principles of Guambiano social logic to the level of clothing. Aesthetic and ethical order are an arrangement of binary units structured along opposed but complementary axes. Females produce items worn at the lower level of the body which exhibit both unity and opposition of left and right, and a hierarchy of male above female (poncho above skirt). Similarly, social roles in relation to production and reproduction establish the greater importance of women, yet the authority of men remains. In contrast, men weave the hats used equally by both sexes. Their authority over females occurs in all areas of life and men serve as politicians and shamans to maintain political and religious order. In a rhetorical sense the hat symbolizes the unity, equality, and symmetry of society and links it with men. It reflects the hierarchy explicit in head above body; sky, rain and spirits above earth, and male above female . . . at least that is what it appears to do.

There remain a few unexamined aspects of Guambiano clothing and society which suggest the analysis is not yet complete. Focusing briefly on *internal design features*, we see in the *female skirt* the horizontal lines are arranged *symmetrically*, the same number above and below the center. In contrast, the *male poncho* has two lines (or groups of lines) placed *asymmetrically* below the center. Turning to decorative features woven into the hat we find *circles on top* and *triangles below*. Circles and triangles are symbolically important in other contexts and, not surprisingly, the women are associated with the circles and men with the triangles. Thus the message communicated by decorative aspects of clothing seem to reverse the one expressed in the overall positioning of the items. Now it is the females who are linked symbolically with symmetry, men with asymmetry, and the women (the circles) are above the men (the triangles).

Can these principles be tied in with culture and social structure in Guambía? Yes, but at the level of what Lévi-Strauss (1953:526) refers to as "unconscious models", and which I prefer to call the "not-spoken-of-too-often" models. At this level, men are linked with division in space, time and structure, and the women with unity. For example, neighborhood groupings in Guambía are neighborhoods of patrilaterally related male kinsmen, a pattern sustained by the norm of patri-virilocal residence and female exogamy. These groups are united structurally through the communication of women between them. With respect to the role of women in maintaining temporal or historical unity, and their position above the men, the explanation is rather straightforward. Mama Manuela Caramaya is the legendary mother of the two men, Tumiñá and Tombé, from whom the modern-day (Catholicized) Guambianos are descended (Hernandez de Alba and Tumiñá-Pillimué 1949), and it is the women who have the children.

Reconsidering Guambiano dress and social structure in light of the above, the symbolic role of clothing in the dialectic of social life is more fully revealed. While clothing is often "taken for granted", it is an essential part of communication: it helps define a situation by emphasizing certain principles while serving to conceal or maintain ambiguity about others. While clothing and adornment vary in what, when, and how they symbolically relate to behavior, they are always, even in their absence, part of the process and structure of action. Just as woof threads may be woven into cloth to conceal those of the warp, a society may weave a social fabric which publicly exhibits one set of norms while masking other structures. In Guambía, the rhetorical function of the hat is to communicate a message of unity and hierarchy and link it with the men. Yet we find in the decorative elements the very principles the hat is designed to cover up, circles above the triangles, women above and the men below.

NATURE, CULTURE AND CLOTHING

Murphy makes the following observation about the present state of anthropological theory: "We do not just fail to return to basic questions — we have forgotten what they were" (1971:71). An understanding of how and why man gets dressed, as well as what happens once he does, is a move back towards the basics. Since clothing is universal among human groups it seems proper to raise the question as to its role in Society as well as in societies. One answer which has the advantage of avoiding motivational arguments such as modesty versus immodesty, is that the use of adornment has something to do with man's image of himself in relation to the world he experiences. In adornment we see a use of nature (the material component) to reject or distinguish oneself from nature (animals and human nakedness) and to affirm the human or cultural aspect of life. Ogibenin, referring to body appearances as well as clothing, suggests that both merit consideration:

... since ... they [body appearances and clothing] are used in human societies as signs, they constitute a boundary area which provides illustrations of transitional phenomena between nature and culture. In this area, perhaps ontogenetic (with reference to a given culture) analogies of precultural behavior of man viewed in phylogenetic perspective could be sought, for in this area the psycho-biological and the psycho-social stimuli provoke different reactions, both resulting in a formation of a complex entity object-sign which belong to the level of the intersection of nature and culture (1971:14).

An example of the use of adornment to make this transition can be seen in the face-painting of the Caduveo. Lévi-Strauss (1963:176) writes that for the Caduveo,

The face-paintings confer upon the individual his dignity as a human being: they help him to cross the frontier from nature to culture, and from the "mindless" animal to the civilized man.

A similar theme is implied in the creation myth of an Amazonian tribe:

In placing men on earth the sun distributed among the groups tools, weapons, a basket, a mask, and loincloths, although to the Desana he gave only a piece of string (Reichel-Dolmatoff and Reichel-Dolmatoff 1961:27).

Face-paintings, loincloths, hand-tailored suits, all clothes, may be viewed as material expression of man's judgment about himself as a "cultured" being, different in a fundamental way from the rest of nature.

THE ANTHROPOLOGIST AND THE BIG MEN

I began this paper asserting that social anthropologists have paid little attention to the role of clothing and adornment. It seems, therefore, proper to conclude by raising the question of why clothing is so rarely the object of systematic query. We delve into clitorectomy and ambiguity, sorcery and profanity, patrilineality and locality, but dress — only in passing, unless it leaps out at us in a chief's costume or ceremonial robe. Normally the strange clothing of the natives fades quickly into the background only to be revived at a cocktail party when we bring attention to ourselves through the use of items acquired in the field. Our houses too are often filled with strange artifacts, emblematic of our ambiguous status within society and the academic community. The contrast in the way we relate the material culture of societies we investigate to our writing and personal lives suggests to my mind a paradox of the anthropologist's position. In what we materially exhibit we mark ourselves off from the society to which we belong, yet in refusing to consider seriously the clothing we collect, we unintentionally reveal the extent we are, perhaps, part of the Big-men subculture. Among the Big men, clothing "is a taboo subject. They don't want it known they even care about it . . . Sex, well, all right, talk your head off. But this, these men's clothes" (Wolfe 1965:257).

REFERENCES

BEALS, R., H. HOIJER
1959   *An introduction to anthropology.* New York: Macmillan.
BEATTIE, JOHN
1964   *Other cultures.* New York: Free Press.
BENEDICT, RUTH
1931   "Dress," in *Encyclopaedia of the social sciences,* volume five. Edited by Edwin R. A. Seligman et al., 235–237. New York: Macmillan.
BICK, MARIO
1968   "What's on, what's coming off?: notes on a theory of adornment." Paper presented at the sixty-seventh annual meeting of the American Anthropological Association, Seattle, November 23.
BLISS, S. H.
1916   The significance of clothes. *American Journal of Psychology* 27:217–226.
BOGATYREV, PETR G.
1971   *The function of folk costume in Moravian Slovakia.* Translated by Richard G. Crun. Approaches to Semiotics 5. The Hague: Mouton. (Originally published 1937.)
BUCHLER, J.
1955   *Nature and judgement.* New York: Columbia University Press.
BUNZEL, RUTH
1931   "Ornament," in *Encyclopaedia of the social science,* volume eleven. Edited by Edwin R. A. Seligman et al., 496–498. New York: Macmillan.
1952   *Chichicastenango: a Guatemalan village.* Seattle: University of Washington Press.
CARLYLE, THOMAS
1869   *Sartor resartus: the life and opinions of Herr Teufelsdröckh.* London: Chapman and Hall. (Originally published 1831.)
CRAWLEY, ERNEST
1931   *Dress, drinks and drums: further studies of savages and sex.* Edited by Theodore Besterman. London: Methuen.
DOUGLAS, MARY
1970   *Natural symbols: explorations in cosmology.* London: Barrie and Rockliff.

DUNLAP, KNIGHT
1928   The development and function of clothing. *Journal of General Psychology* 1: 64–78.
ELLIS, HAVELOCK
1900   *Studies in the psychology of sex*, seven volumes. Philadelphia: F. A. Davis.
EVANS-PRITCHARD, E. E.
1940   *The Nuer.* London: Oxford University Press.
FARON, LOUIS C.
1962   Symbolic values and the integration of society among the Mapuche of Chile. *American Anthropologist* 64(6): 1151–1164.
FLUGEL, JOHN CARL
1929   Clothes symbolism and clothes ambivalence. *International Journal of Psycho-Analysis* 10: 205–217.
1945   *Man, morals and society: a psycho-analytical study.* New York: International Universities Press.
1950   *The psychology of clothes.* International Psycho-Analytical Library 18. London: Hogarth Institute of Psychoanalysis. (Originally published 1930.)
FRAZER, JAMES G.
1890   *The golden bough: a study in comparative religion,* two volumes. London: Macmillan.
GOFFMAN, ERVING
1956   *The presentation of self in everyday life.* Edinburgh: University of Edinburgh Social Research Centre.
HARMS, ERNST
1938   The psychology of clothes. *American Journal of Sociology* 44:239–250.
HELM, JUNE, *editor*
1967   *Essays on the verbal and visual arts: proceedings of the 1966 annual spring meeting of the American Ethnological Society.* Seattle: American Ethnological Society.
HERNANDEZ DE ALBA, GREGORIO, FRANCISCO TUMIÑÁ PILLIMUÉ
1949   *Nuestra gente "Namuy misag": tierra, costumbres y creencias de los indios Guambianos.* Popayan, Colombia: Universidad del Cauca.
HERTZ, ROBERT
1960   *Death and the right hand.* Translated by Rodney and Claudia Needham. London: Cohen and West.
HILER, HILAIRE
1929   *An introduction to the study of costume: from nudity to raiment.* London: W. and G. Foyle.
HILER, HILAIRE, MEYER HILER
1939   *Bibliography of costume.* New York: H. W. Wilson.
HIRN, YRJO
1900   *The origins of art: a psychological and sociological inquiry.* London: Macmillan.
HIRNING, L. CLOVIS
1961   "Clothing and nudism," in *The encyclopedia of sexual behavior,* volume one. Edited by Albert Ellis and Albert Abarbanel, 268–283. New York: Hawthorn.
HUGHES, CHARLES C.
1965   Under four flags: recent culture change among the Eskimos. *Current Anthropology* 61:3–69.

JOPLING, CAROL F., *editor*
1971   *Art and aesthetics in primitive societies.* New York: E. P. Dutton.
LÉVI-STRAUSS, CLAUDE
1953   "Social structure," in *Anthropology today.* Edited by A. L. Kroeber, 524–535. Chicago: University of Chicago Press.
1963   *Structural anthropology.* Translated by Claire Jacobson and Brooke Grundfest Schoepf. New York: Basic Books.
LEWIS, OSCAR
1951   *Life in a Mexican village: Tepoztlān restudied.* Urbana: University of Illinois Press.
LHOTE, HENRI
1955   *Les touaregs du Hoggar.* Paris: Payot.
LIENHARDT, GODFREY
1967   *Social anthropology.* New York: Oxford University Press.
MAIR, LUCY
1965   *An introduction to social anthropology.* London: Oxford University Press.
MATTESON, ESTHER, *et al.*
1972   *Comparative studies in Amerindian languages.* The Hague: Mouton.
MURPHY, ROBERT F.
1964   Social distance and the veil. *American Anthropologist* 666:1257–1274.
1971   *The dialectics of social life.* New York: Basic Books.
NADEL, S. F.
1954   *Nupe religion.* London: Routledge and Kegan Paul.
NEEDHAM, RODNEY
1960   The left hand of the Mugwe: an analytical note on the structure of Meru symbolism. *Africa* 30(1):20–33.
OGIBENIN, BORIS L.
1971   "Petr Bogatyrev and structural ethnography," in *The functions of folk costume in Moravian Slovakia.* By Petr G. Bogatyrev, 9–32. The Hague: Mouton.
OTTEN, CHARLOTTE M., *editor*
1971   *Anthropology and art.* American Museum Sourcebooks in Anthropology. Garden City, New York: Natural History Press.
PARSONS, ELSIE CLEWS
1936   *Mitla: town of the souls.* Chicago: University of Chicago Press.
REDFIELD, ROBERT
1930   *Tepoztlán.* Chicago: University of Chicago Press.
REICHEL-DOLMATOFF, GERARDO, ALICIA REICHEL-DOLMATOFF
1961   *The people of Aritama.* London: Routledge and Kegan Paul.
RICHARDSON, JANE, A. L. KROEBER
1940   Three centuries of women's dress fashions. *Anthropological Records* 5(2):111–153.
RIVET, PAUL
1946   Le groupe Kokonuko. *Journal de la Société des Américanistes* 33:1–61.
ROACH, MARY ELLEN, JOANNE BUBOLZ EICHER, *editors*
1965   *Dress, adornment, and the social order.* New York: John Wiley and Sons.
SANBORN, HERBERT C.
1926   The function of clothing and of bodily adornment. *American Journal of Psychology* 38:1–20.
SIMMEL, GEORG
1950   *The sociology of Georg Simmel.* Translated and edited by Kurt H. Wolff. Glencoe, Illinois: Free Press.

SPENCER, WALTER B., F. J. GILLEN
1899   *The native tribes of central Australia*. London: Macmillan.
STURTEVANT, WILLIAM C.
1967   "Seminole men's clothing," in *Essays on the verbal and visual arts*. Edited by June Helm, 160–174. Seattle: University of Washington Press.
THOMAS, WILLIAM I.
1909   *Source book for social origins*. Boston: R. G. Badger.
TURNER, VICTOR
1967   *The forest of symbols*. Ithaca, New York: Cornell University Press.
1969   *The ritual process: structure and anti-structure*. Chicago: Aldine.
VOGT, EVON Z.
1969   *Zinacantán*. Cambridge, Massachusetts: Harvard University Press.
WESTERMARCK, EDWARD A.
1891   *A history of human marriage*. London: Macmillan.
WILSON, MONICA
1957   *Rituals of kinship among the Nyakyusa*. London: Oxford University Press.
WOLFE, TOM
1965   "The secret vice," in *The kandy-kolored tangerine-flake streamline baby*, 254–261. New York: Farrar, Straus and Giroux.

The Very Human Arts of Transformation

JUSTINE M. CORDWELL

The anthropological analysis of clothing and adornment should be based on the assumption that mankind, from earliest times, has probably regarded the human body as the primary form of sculpture — and not been particularly pleased with what he has seen. Why then, if that were not the case, would he have spent tens of thousands of years painting, daubing, plastering, pinching, cutting, pricking, dyeing, and distorting this body in the name of beauty, dignity, virility, fecundity, and so on? One of the best answers, and the most simple, came from a dignified East African, who said "... Because it shows we are human beings" (Faris 1972). Certainly no other member of the animal kingdom can claim a need for, or create, such a bewildering variety of transformations as can *homo sapiens*. As Eicher (1972:516) has pointed out,

In analyzing the aesthetics of dress, we are concerned with the body as an art form, the body as plastic, the body as an art gallery. . . . Greatest virtuosity in aesthetic expression via display of the human body is managed through use of a wide variety of media, textiles and cosmetics being the most common. . . . These media either act on the body plastic and reshape it or they create the illusion of reshaping, or they are simply added to the body with little regard for basic body form.

Portions of this paper appeared in 1976 in *Cosmetic Journal* 8(4). Washington, D.C.: Cosmetic, Toiletry, and Fragrance Association. I wish to thank my fellow editors in this series, Sol Tax, Ronald Schwarz, Paul Hockings, and Charles Reed, for their invaluable suggestions, references, and unpublished information that would be helpful to students. Special gratitude is due to Paul Lazar, Chairman of the American Medical Association's committee on cosmetics, who started my interest in cross-cultural studies on cosmetics, and who took time from a grueling schedule to educate me at least to a small degree in the basic facts of the anatomy and physiology of the human skin. I also wish to thank Yvonne Damien of the library of Loyola University, Chicago, and the librarians and assistants of the Field Museum Library, Chicago, for their kind assistance in expanding the bibliography so that it would be more useful to the interested student of cross-cultural cosmetics. All illustrations in this article are by the author.

Forbes (1955:202) in his history of paints, pigments, inks, and varnishes, says "In fact the oldest paint support was probably the human body."

The term *cosmetic* can be used in several ways; as a noun it can refer to media of pigmented paints, powder, oil, and scent (Eicher 1972:516), or as an adjective, as in the cosmetic reshaping of the body to fit some aesthetic, cultural norm. Customarily our Euro-American culture has taught us to think of cosmetic transformations occurring mostly from the neck upward and as being temporary in nature, except for instances of cosmetic plastic surgery and tattooing by a few. Indeed, we sometimes flatter ourselves that such cosmetic changes are the epitome of "civilization". But if all mankind in time and geographical space were surveyed, we would find ourselves to be rank amateurs in these arts. Indeed, one is hard put to find cultures in which there has not been some form of the cosmetic arts of transformation. It would seem that human beings have spent a long time considering the bodies with which they have been forced to live, and that the members of at least eighty percent of the societies in the world decided that they either could not, or would not, leave well enough alone in letting nature take its course with their bodies. As Shapiro once wrote (1947):

so universal is this urge to improve on nature that one is almost tempted to regard it as an instinct. Aside from such fundamental drives as those for food, love, security, and the expression of maternal solicitude, I can think of few forms of human behavior that are more common to mankind as a whole. Perhaps it is precisely because part of its motivation is involved with sexual attraction that this impulse to draw attention to the body finds an outlet among the civilized sophisticate equally with the untutored savage.

Hundreds of thousands of years ago, as humans spread out over the world from what appears to be their African place of origin, they seem to have carried with them not only a liking for self-decoration, probably with mineral colors, but also a mystical feeling for the life-imitating properties of the color red in particular. In Neanderthal burials at Spy (Belgium) and Chapelle-aux-Saints the bones are covered with red ochre (iron oxide or hematite) in such a way that it would seem to indicate that the bodies were painted with the pigment: perhaps a testimony to their belief system — a futile but touching gesture of giving the color of life to the dead. However, it has recently come to light[1] that the reason many societies rub iron oxides on hides they are tanning is less aesthetic or traditional than it is practical. Without actually knowing how the process worked, early man may have stumbled on the phenomenon that ferrous oxides destroy the enzyme produced by bacteria on the skins, and which, unchecked, would break down the protein in them, causing them to deteriorate by the

---

[1]   In conversation with Lawrence Keeley of the Anthropology Department, University of Illinois, Chicago Circle.

process of digestion. Cro-Magnon burials too evince the same painting of the body, but with a thicker layer of ocher (Forbes 1955:202). In some African societies south of the Sahara, camwood is ground up and painted on the body of the deceased to absorb liquids and prevent odors in what would appear to be the same type of aesthetic, religious, and hygienic ritual of cosmetic decoration practiced by our early ancestors.

Evidence of the personal adornment of the Paleolithic peoples comes from archeological sites in cave floors of Europe. These have yielded bone and antler containers with stoppers in which have been found the remains of cosmetic pigments mixed with fats, yellow and red ferrous oxides, and black manganese oxides. Lumps of ocher have been found in ancient burials in both the Old and New Worlds. Arroyo de Anda, Aveleyra and Eckholm (1966:43), describing the burials of hundreds of Maya from the Classic and post-Classic period on the island of Jaina off Yucatán, mention that some of the bodies must have been painted with red ocher, which later settled on the bones.

An even more impressive clue to the antiquity of this human concern with self-appearance is provided by the South African paleoarcheologist and physical anthropologist, Raymond Dart (1974). The evidence he presents is almost beyond the comprehension of contemporary man because of the immense time depth involved as well as the eerie implications concerning the self-image of some hominids. Adjacent to the site containing the bones of a number of australopithecine individuals Dart found a strange, rounded dark stone that was waterworn or polished from generations of handling. There are two pitted holes in the stone and lines that appear to have occurred naturally, rather than having been scratched on it. When the stone is held in certain positions, with the light source from the side, there appear on its sides not one, but four, apelike faces — all with the low brow of this early hominid. The bones of the individuals in the site are dated at *two-and-a-half million years before the present.*

We also owe the discoveries of the great age of hematite and specularite mines in southern Africa to Dart's suspicions that these mining operations for cosmetic and medicinal ochers and manganese oxide belong to the Middle Stone Age rather than to the much later dates of the Neolithic that were being assigned to them without carbon-14 dating. Dart encouraged anthropologists and geologists to investigate the mine sites in Swaziland, Rhodesia, Zambia, and Cape Province, South Africa. Appealing to the national pride of pragmatic mine-owners, he persuaded them to hire these scientists, and through other sources found the funds to have the carbon-14 dating done on charcoal and bones of gazelle and zebra found at different levels in the floors of caverns in the Bomvu Ridge in northeastern Swaziland. These remains of meals or offerings to earth spirits, and of the dolomite Middle Stone Age tools of these miners have been given a confirmed date of 43,000 B.P. — proof of the oldest known mining operation in the world (Dart and Beaumont 1971). What were these ancestral miners digging out of the earth? Glittering, sparkling specularite; the soft, greasy-feeling cosmetic hematite; or ocher worn by chiefs and priests among the Africans of the nineteenth and early twentieth centuries. The black version of this glittering ferrous oxide lies close to the surface and occurs in some outcroppings, but the red specularite is deeper in the earth and must be mined, with appropriate propitiation to the spirits living deep in the earth whose bones and children the miners are disturbing. The Africans call the black specularite the "male" ore, and the deeper ore of red, the "female".

Whether specularite or the more ordinary red, black, and yellow ochers, the demand for cosmetic and medicinal ores grew greater as populations grew larger. The surface sources were gradually used up and men were forced to learn to "read" the clues offered by the rocks and mineral outcroppings in order to find the right places to mine. But persons of other lands and cultures, besides the Africans, used and desired cosmetics, and when they ran out of their sources went on searches for them (Dart 1969).

One of the cosmetic and medicinal ores mined by early Africans, in what is now Zambia, was manganese oxide of black color. The Broken Hill mine of this century in Zambia is there because of this manganese. Thirteen kilometers away at Chowa, a prospecting miner named Bush accidentally discovered psilomalene, the ore of manganese, in outcropping ridges that were only six or seven centimeters high; yet these, because of their hardness, should have been the highest outcroppings on the Chowa Ridge. As Bush put down some trenches beside these psilomalene low ridges, he found the earth came out very easily, and that what he had discovered was an ancient mining operation that had been filled in with loose mined ore of psilomalene. Along with the ore fill there were broken muller and grinding stones, broken perforated stones, and a polished stone ax. All these finds were similar to Nachikufu II artifacts at similar mines near Mumbwa and Solwezi dated to the fifth millennium B.C. (Dart 1953:94–95).

Dart reasons that, since the Africans were not using the hard psilomalene ore for cosmetics, and were returning it to the earth after the difficult labor of mining it, it cannot have been that they were after. The real prize was manganese dioxide (pyrolusite). Because the Africans had used manganese oxide for cosmetics and medicines, exploring traders had traced the source. These were foreigners who were not interested in the cosmetic aspects of the manganese, but in the fact that where there are rich deposits of manganese oxide there may be psilomalene, the harder ore — and in psilomalene may be found the purest forms of manganese dioxide, pyrolusite. Only this substance can explain the hard, sustained labor of mining into the psilomalene lodes, and the thousands and thousands of tons of that ore that was returned to cover the quarries and trenches dug by ancient Africans. Pyrolusite occurs in some manganese deposits às purple crystalline inclusions or as a soft black amorphous mineral within the psilomalene.

At the time these mines were worked, pyrolusite had significance only to people who understood pigments. These would have to be people who knew how to color and tint glazes and glass and how to dye woven fabrics. Perhaps they also already knew the value of pyrolusite as flux in smelting of other ores, such as silver and lead. None of these techniques were familiar to the Africans, but they were known to the Phoenicians, and perhaps to the Egyptians, Sumerians and Indians of that period, the fourth millennium B.C.:

Of itself, manganese gives, according to the quantity used, the whole range of regal colour from amethyst through amber, violet, purple and brown, to black in glazes and glass. Being also a most powerful oxidizing agent, it washes out the greenish and brownish tints that cannot otherwise be excluded from ordinary glass, and thus renders glass colourless (hence the name *pyrolusite* or fire-washer), a discovery of great antiquity attributed to the Phoenicians. Even more magically to its ancient empirical employers, the oxidizing power of manganese modifies the reds and yellows produced by ochreous iron pigments into the lighter hues of pink and cream, and it also transforms the blues and greens of copper pigments into more delicate pastel shades. . . . It dyes itself and acts as a mordant or fixative for other textile dyes (Dart 1953:95).

Evidence from these ancient mining operations has caused scientists and historians to reexamine the rock paintings of southeastern Africa, the paintings that thirty-five years ago the Abbé Breuil had declared were serious evidence of the passage of other races from alien cultures, along trade routes of which we were historically unaware. Dart (1953) as well as Beaumont and Boshier (1972) believe that those who scoffed at the idea that Caucasians, Phoenicians, Chinese and Indians could have passed through that part of Africa may be forced to change their minds. Certainly the rock paintings of the Massif of Tassili in southern Algeria show bearded, capped, and robed light-skinned peoples of the Mediterranean and their ladies riding oxen, far from their seaport homes (Davidson 1966:53).

Cosmetic and paint pigments played a large role in exploration and trade in the ancient world; and it was this search for the precious commodities by entrepreneurs that played an important part in the growth of man's inventory of culture. But in the instance of the African miners working for foreigners, we must close the trade circle by asking what desirable commodity could have induced the miners to work so hard and for so long for strangers who are shown in supplicant poses in the rock paintings, not with weapons and show of strength. If we take the factors that the Africans used red and yellow ochers cosmetically on their bodies, and that ancient man also used red ocher on animal skins he wore, then it is possible to advance the hypothesis that two commodities that would have been treasured by the Africans and readily accepted into their lifestyle as highly desirable would be *oil*, to warm the skin and act as cosmetic base (instead of animal fats), and *textiles* receptive to dyeing with red ocher. This would be the incentive to labor, and it would set these into a cultural inventory that would last for thousands of years.

Archeologists are also becoming more aware of the importance of cosmetic needs and their relation to migrations of early societies. A new valley with water sources, grasses with seeds, berries in abundance, and ample game, though closer to an old home, is not as much a lure to migration and resettlement as is one that is closer to cosmetic sources, even though it might be contiguous with the territory of an unfriendly people. An example from the nineteenth and twentieth centuries is that of the Australian aborigines, who would travel a hundred kilometers through enemy territory to mine materials for paints used in special ceremonies. Another example is the ground malachite on one of the cattle paintings on the rocks of the Massif of Tassili in the center of the now arid Sahara. This green stone comes from far to the east, but arrived at the spot where it was used most probably from Egyptian trade sources. The Egyptians used this green, ground stone under their eyes to cut glare from dry earth as well as on the lids for eye shadow. However, its toxic properties must have gradually become apparent, because there is no evidence from paintings or burials of its use after 1500 B.C.

Having established a great time depth for the use of cosmetics, let us examine some of the motivations for cosmetically transforming the human body, other than the more obvious one of sexual attraction. There are, for example, utilitarian reasons for cosmetic transformations by members of some societies in Southeast Asia, on Pacific islands and in Japan, as in the case of tattooing displaying symbols of social status in conjunction with clothing styles and their elements. In the religious ceremonies of other societies, the ritual use of transformations blends cosmetic change with other added media, such as feathers, beads, shell, textiles, resins, grasses, and fur, to transform mere humans temporarily into supernatural beings. Belief systems may dictate the need for protection against unseen, malevolent forces, with the resultant production of cosmetic amulets on the skin, some permanent by scarring and tattooing, others temporary in paint or dye. In some instances, cosmetic designs function as both curative and preventive medicine.

Whatever the basic functions of cosmetic decoration of the body, the ends are achieved by either *temporary* or *permanent* means. The temporary methods are those most familiar to us — the application of cosmetic pigments in a fat base, water or oil-based paint, powder, or temporary dyes. The colors of the pigments chosen are dependent upon the culture of the individual using them, for each society has its own historically established aesthetic tastes in this line. Those cosmetics most universally used are the earth minerals; the ferrous and manganese oxides; stibium, antimony and galena; and finely ground semiprecious stones or minerals for greens, blues and lavenders. Vegetable dyes yield colors too, and the most widely used in the Old World are saffron, henna, and indigo.

Permanent cosmetic effects have until recently been the monopoly of other cultures around the world. *Permanent* refers to the permanent coloring of skin by tattooing or to permanent "aesthetic" deformation of parts of the body, such as flattening the heads of infants by cradle board attachments, binding their heads into sugarloaf shapes, filling and inlaying of teeth with jewels, stretching lips or ears by the insertion of labrets or plates in small slits, or enlarging the lobes with progressively larger inserts of wood, metal, or stone. For example, Arroyo de Anda, Aveleyra and Eckholm (1966:43), remarking on other burials in the Maya cemetery on Jaina say,

The skeletons . . . indicate that these people followed the usual ancient Maya custom of deforming the skull—a method of modifying the shape of the head by the application of pressure during infancy—and that tooth mutilation was in vogue. The incisors were filled in various ways; sometimes their outer sufaces were inlaid with small disks of iron pyrites or of semi-precious stones.

To all these cosmetic affectations the Maya also added the use of labrets and stone inserts in the earlobes, which dragged them downward.[2]

Only a few of our own cosmetic transformations fall into the category of permanent body decoration, probably because it seems the most alien and unacceptable to Euro-American cultures. It intrigues us, however, even as we might shudder at effects that we know must be very painful to achieve. Relatively few individuals in our society submit to them when compared to the millions of others who do without them. Some such practices surface dramatically, as when a prominent member of a legislative body decides that exposure of his hair transplants is unavoidable. Other processes remain more discreetly private, such as permanent hair removal, or cosmetic plastic surgery: a little tuck here, a little tuck there, for an illusion of the partial renewal of youthful lines. What matter if it be somewhat painful in the process? The reward would seem to be worth it to many.

Of all the forms of permanent cosmetic adornment, tattooing is pos-

---

[2] The Maya also hung little, light balls of resin by string from the forelocks of their children, so that it would swing between the eyes. The peering at this irritating object strengthened inner eye muscles to produce the envied "Maya squint". Rulers and wealthy merchants, and perhaps priests, if not endowed with the cultural ideal of a very high bridged nose, would fastened on false noses for special occasions.

sibly the most artistic, since fine lines and detailed designs are possible. Though it was once considered an acceptable ornamentation by certain socioeconomic groups and generally among sailors, tattooing in Western societies has gradually faded as an art form on living flesh. The reaction of people in Euro-American cultures to Rod Steiger's effective portrayal of a man completely covered with tattooed designs in *The illustrated man* (Smight 1969) demonstrates our contemporary, learned distaste concerning this particular type of cosmetic expression. This same shocked reaction, however, astonished the Japanese of the nineteenth century; they could not understand the revulsion shown toward tattooing when Victorian British and Americans visited the islands after they were opened to foreign trade and visits. It was practically a fine art in Japan, and was used to cover a great deal of the body. Tattooing was considered to be in good taste by lower and middle-class Japanese, but the upper class and nobility did not use it. Once the shock of the visitors was felt the emperor outlawed tattooing. In climates such as Japan's, where outer clothing is a necessity for a large part of the year, one would be tempted to theorize that the purpose of tattooing might be to function as erotic surprise. On the other hand, there is the practice of public bathing: what better way to display one's social rank and one's aesthetic tastes, semiclothed in tattoo designs, in such a socially leveling situation as the baths.

Extensive tattooing of the body seems to have been at one time a pattern for a very large region of the world. This particular type of body decoration ranged from tattooing from foot or knee to the waist or thorax, and in a few areas within this region from the soles of the feet to the crown of the head. The total geographical area in question covers most of Southeast Asia, Polynesia, and Japan. The antiquity of the art seems to go back to the early Ainu, prehistoric Eskimo, and the early historical dynasties of China. Originally tattooing in this region may have belonged exclusively to the ruling classes and served as indication of social status and rank. While this remained one of its functions, it became an art form for a wider range of people within each society using it.

According to Bouteiller (1953:517–523), the most beautiful and artistic virtuosos of the tattooing art were the Burmese. Their artists utilized almost every existing color in the past, but in this century confine themselves to indigo (blue), cinnabar or mercurous oxide (red), and resinous soot (black). Their designs of Buddhist and Brahmin themes have traveled from India by way of religious teachers, tracts, and small colored illustrations printed in India.

The all blue-black tattooing of the Thai was a sign of prestige and virility — part of the respectable costume of Thai males. The introduction of red in tattooing art came from Burma. While those who could afford to do so tattooed from waist to soles of feet, the lower class added tattooed, magical signs on heads and shoulders for good luck.

Cambodians were distinctive with red ink designs, while Laotians favored blue and black. Favorite themes of artists in these two culture areas today are elephants, lions, tigers, and leopards in designs that cover the subject from waist to knees, *comme culotte*. The principal reason for this permanent cosmetic addition to the body, in spite of a textile wardrobe that hides most of it, is to conform to the cultural concept of virile dignity, to provide identification of social status or profession, and to provide artistic amulets or magical protection.

The Dyaks of Borneo gradually add tattooing designs over the years, until the body is covered from neck to ankles with symbolic artistic designs that show clan, genealogy, status, ranks passed through, and achievements — an aesthetic walking billboard of one's lifelong accomplishments — a male prerogative generally. For a man to die without having achieved even partial tattooing would be for him to leave the world without truly becoming a human being.

Samoan tattooing is performed on young men with an adzelike tool, the striking edge of which may have European needles bound together in a row by tightly wound thread. The needles are dipped in an inky substance made from the soot of burned *lama* nuts and water, then sharp, steady taps on the skin create bands around the waist up to the thorax region, around the hips, and around each leg to the knees (Figure 1). This is done in several sittings, and while the young man is being tattooed his friends comfort him by singing, "When it comes to pain, women must bear the

Figure 1.   Body tattoos: young Samoan men bathing (after Sutter 1971:45)

children, and men must be tattooed." As a final consolation, he is reminded that unlike shells and other types of necklaces, the tattooing cannot be lost in any way or lessened by his daily acts of bathing.

The Tonga islanders embellish their arms, and lower legs as well, while the Hawaiians used to practice a simpler form of banded lines and simple geometric designs. Emory (1948:235) maintains that the Hawaiians lost the more intricate arts of tattooing in their geographical isolation, for mummified bodies found in caves on the Hawaiian islands show much more elaborate body tattoos. It is Marquesas islanders and the Maori of New Zealand, however, who once practiced an elaborate tattooing that covered almost the entire body of males. It has been said that some men shaved back into the natural hairline of the head in order to expose even more skin for further designs. The artistic, curvilinear, and circular patterns common to this area of the Pacific contained the genealogy of their tattooed owner, as well as his earned ranks and social status. Without these designs, the individual was a commoner, a social nonentity, who had achieved nothing in his lifetime. Thus the play between cosmetic art form and psychological security becomes apparent, as it does in Southeast Asia. The tattooed designs, because of their curvilinear character, conformed to the features of the face and head, accentuating them.

Though display of rank, achievement, and sexual attraction may have been three of the purposes of this tattooing, a fourth one became evident during war dances and in the subsequent storming of an enemy stronghold. With glaring, pop-eyed effect, mouth ajar and tongue protruding as far as possible, with horrible yells and brandished war clubs, these perambulating art galleries stormed ashore on an enemy's beach. It was enough to cause the surrender of those adversaries who had not already fainted behind the beach palms.

Herman Melville's description of tattoo art in *Typee* makes nineteenth-century Polynesia come to life, and gives dramatic meaning to the wooden arms, legs, and heads, covered with model tattoo designs, that are to be found in museums in Europe and the Americas. Occasionally, one finds trophy heads there as well, preserved intact with the tattoos on the dried skin: mute testimony that someone was outbluffed and outfought. Robley (1896:1–2), who collected his drawings of Maori tattooed heads from the period of the 1864–1866 campaign in New Zealand until his retirement, reports that Abel Tasman visited New Zealand in December 1642, and that in his detailed description of the people there is no mention of tattooing. Yet Captain James Cook returned to London from the South Seas in 1771, after his first voyage, with detailed sketches of such tattooing from the Maori. This would seem to indicate the rapid development of the art, probably from contact with voyaging Marquesas islanders.

More detailed work on the tattooing of the Pacific may be found in

Emory (1948); Handy and Handy (1924); Mead (1928) which compares Samoan, Tahitian, Maori, and Hawaiian tattooing; and Robley (1896). Hambly (1925) is one of the few general works on the subject, but reflects a diffusionist point of view. Von den Steinen (1925) is a classic field study on tattooing in the Marquesas. Occasionally the researcher comes across descriptive accounts in the papers of the Church Missionary Society published in London. For example, there is one account of an interview in New Zealand with a tattooed Maori chief who was converted to Christianity (Church Missionary Society 1816). The interviewer must have wished to share his culture shock with his gentle readers, for there is included a sketch of a wooden bust of the chief, made by himself, illustrating his own tattooed designs for posterity.

The second great region of tattooing in the Old World ranges from Afghanistan, through Iran and Iraq, Turkey and the whole Middle East, the Arabian peninsula, Egypt, and the Maghreb of North Africa, in other words, much of the Islamic world. The standard work on the body arts of this vast area of Southwest Asia and North Africa is that of Henry Field (1958). He and his assistants, who were women, were able to record in great detail the designs and placement of the scattered tattoo designs, done mostly in indigo or soot black, of both men and women. The field-workers were able to gather the names of designs, and also to some extent their purpose, but there is a lack of depth in the exposition of the real function of these in relation to religion, magic, and sexual attraction. Many of the designs draw on a common Islamic symbolism, but it is apparent that most have their antecedents thousands of years before the arrival of Mohammed. These designs are also found in the rugs and embroideries of societies living a thousand or more miles apart today, so they represent clues to contact by migration or trade that may go back to the Neolithic period. For example, one can see predynastic Egyptian designs from painted, clay figurines (Keimer 1948) in Field's drawings. There are good luck motifs that are the same, though separated by hundreds of miles, simply because they are Islamic. Some Arabic women closer to the Mediterranean cultures go to great lengths when they are still young to have garland tattooing done around their waists and around each breast. A more common type seems to be simple geometric designs done from pubis to thorax, and on the thighs and ankles. Sometimes these run from ankle halfway up the side of the leg, resembling the clock of a stocking.[3]

Facial tattooing in this area on both men and women may be at almost any spot on the face, but is usually found predominantly on the temples, on the forehead between the eyebrows, on the cheeks, or in a goatee effect on the chin. Done in indigo with sharp needles, these decorations of

---

[3] Islam, in this instance at least, opened up a profession to females, for all this intimate tattooing was done on women by women tattooers.

the skin seldom serve as cosmetic beauty marks: some of them are talismans to keep a love; some serve as preventative medicine against headaches; and some as amulets against what Field was constantly being told was the evil eye.

The tattooing of arms and legs of men seems to have been done to prevent and cure disease, such as the depiction of a snake to make one immune to snakebite, or a design around the wrist and ankle to give strength in the work of harvesting, walking, or even irrigating. No matter how prosaic its ultimate purpose, however, the tattooer seemingly cannot resist making the design to the best of his ability, and to compliment the body of the tattooed.

Tattooing among the American Indians was once so widespread that it was found over two continents, even though not practiced by every tribal group. Even Captain John Smith managed to include in his accounts of the New World a description of the colored marks beneath the surface of the skin on the chests of Indians with whom he came in contact (Smith 1883). Andean pottery reveals that tattooing was used by people of the valley cultures of pre-Incan times and by the Incas as well. Hambly (1925) suggests a Pacific Polynesian contact might have introduced this cosmetic trait with others such as panpipes, but the widespread use of this permanent cosmetic in the New World from the Eskimos south to the Amazonian Indians would seem to favor a much earlier introduction. Archeological sites in Alaska have found prehistoric burials with evidence of tattooing (Van Stone 1974) and today the practice continues (Leechman 1951) much in the manner described by Hambly. This cosmetic skin art of the Eskimo utilizes lignite, charcoal from birch or willow, or soot from pots as a black base which is mixed with water. A sinew is soaked in this substance, then a selected area of the skin on the face is pinched together and lifted up, an awl is punched through it, and the sinew's one dry end is threaded through the hole and pulled through leaving the black "ink" in a line under the skin. By proper placement of the second hole, opposite to the first puncture, a straight or curved line is achieved. The designs are made up of a series of parallel bands, with smaller geometric designs dotting the spaces between them. If one is a good bear killer a band may be worn across the nose.

The permanent, cosmetic scarification or cicatrization, unlike tattooing, is based on the reaction of the epidermis and dermis to slashing and to the introduction of irritants into the wounds in order to slow down healing and promoted the development of keloid scar tissue. Decoration by raised scars is found primarily among peoples of very dark skin, where the art of a tattooer would be lost against this background. Most of the practice of this cosmetic art form is found south of the Sahara among the peoples of West Africa and the Sahel and eastern Sudan. Some of these peoples are not content with the simpler cutting and irritant process, and so add soot and herbs to darken the scars, or as in the case of the Sokoto Fulani, who have lighter skins, rubbing indigo into the wounds to produce permanent blue welt designs on the face. The subtleties of this three-dimensional cosmetic art can be quite beautiful within their cultural context (see Figures 2 and 3).

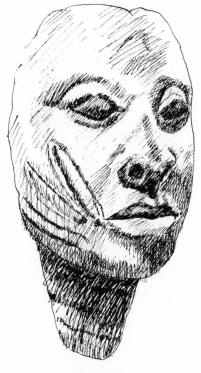

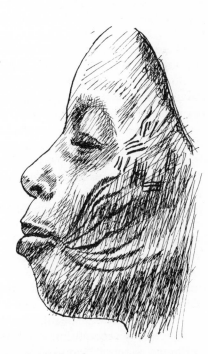

Figure 2.   Ancient terra-cotta head with facial scarification, Ife, Nigeria (after W. Fagg, *Nigerian images*)

Figure 3.   Gobir Hausa woman with facial scars, Niger (after Abercrombie 1972:28)

The purposes for which cicatrization is done are much the same as those for tattooing. In West Africa, the use of cicatrized tribal marks on children became extremely important in the eighteenth and nineteenth centuries as internecine warfare, sparked by slave wars and migrations, made it imperative that a child stolen in infancy would at least know his or her antecedents. Sometimes keloidal symbols were added later in life indicating achieved rank or steps upward in social status. They were almost universally done on the "canvas" of the face and upper body. Trans-Saharan diffusion of designs occurs, as when a young woman of the Ivory Coast shows off a keloid pattern of a sunburst around her navel, while a Moroccan girl may have one tattooed in indigo in the same place. The borrowing of aesthetically pleasing scar designs can sometimes lead to some local confusion when such cosmetic transformations act as a visual language. Clifford (1944:109) records a case in point in central Nigeria where the Bassa-komo have borrowed many elements of the Igbirra culture, their neighbors:

> There is a marked tendency on the part of both sexes to adopt the Igbirra markings which consist of keloidal squares, lozenges, and dotted lines — in the case of the women the pattern is elaborate and extensive and by no means unattractive; a compound of powdered antimony and palm oil is rubbed into the incision which heals in two or three weeks. Work is done by itinerant Hausa.

This latter piece of information is a clue to the diffusion of Islamic designs throughout West Africa, the Sahel and the northern Congo basin.

Sometimes a change in skin color can lead to a shift from keloid designs to tattooing. One could hypothesize that such a gene shift in a population would lead to this, pointing to the historical disappearance of Bini cicatrization marks that were once recorded on bronzes made in Benin City, Nigeria in the period before and during Portuguese contact. These consisted of small welts on the forehead which seem to have denoted membership of a chiefly family. They survive in the iron and ebony (modern) inserts on the foreheads of ancestral heads (*uhum-elao*) found on the altars of hereditary chiefs in Benin City. A considerable portion of the population of this city today is what the Africans call "yellow".[4] This refers to the fact that their skin color is a light yellow-brown. It is possible that these people represent a homozygous portion of the population bearing genes brought by the Portuguese, who, after many years of trade with the Bini, were expelled from the kingdom. No Europeans were allowed in until the Dutch sent emissaries to the *oba* [king] nearly a hundred years later. The introduction of new genes and their subsequent isolation may account for this particular phenomenon, but the result, a different color of "canvas" for aesthetic, cosmetic decoration caused these people of lighter skin to use blue, tattooed, tribal markings in which they evince great pride. An interesting conjecture is whether or not this was the impetus for the disappearance of the keloid scars of the forehead.

Temporary changes and transformations of cosmetic nature rarely

---

[4]   The skin color of West Africans varies greatly, both within gene pools representing one ethnic group, and collectively over many such groups. The Yoruba and Bini, for example, recognize the existence of yellow, red, brown, and black people, and have descriptive terms for each.

injure the people using them. If there were any such dangerous materials and methods used, their victims are no longer with us, and the innate good sense of other members of their society would not have allowed the perpetuation of such well-known use of arsenic as a powder by ancient Romans to render a complexion fashionably pale, a practice revived in Europe during the eighteenth century, much to the sorrow of those using it, who evidently did not read history in Latin or in translations. For thousands of years kohl or antimony (stibium or galena are other terms) which has a lead base, has been worn by peoples of Mediterranean littoral, southwest Asia, India, and West Africa. Local infections, lead poisoning, and possible blindness do not deter its users (some as in Morocco, have sensibly substituted a soot-based substance). Its users insist this eye cosmetic is medicinal as well as aesthetic, and of course the intelligent, disease-bearing flies avoid it, so there is no infection from that source.

Westerners have altered their bodies painfully in the name of fashion over the centuries by means of corsets and pointed shoes, but most of the more permanent, extreme reshaping of the body has been avoided, except for ear piercing, in which they have shown remarkably little imagination. Today's cosmetic surgery, though painful, is defined as a return to aesthetic "normalcy", an attempt to correct nature's mistakes and to slow aging. It cannot be compared to the deliberate distortions of the human body, such as the Chinese bound foot, done for a "swaying flower" effect. A mishap occurring during a temporary, drastic transformation, such as the creation of a tiny waist by a corset, can be remedied quickly by a slash of confining corset laces in the case of fainting. However, a Chinese bound foot turned gangrenous or tattoos and cicatrization poisoned by infections cause ugly deaths instead of aesthetic enjoyment. The persistence of human beings in their pursuit of permanent cosmetic transformations, in the light of the inconvenience, agony, and possible death caused by these forms of cultural beautification, is a truly amazing phenomenon.

Euro-American societies emphasize temporary transformations, and we seem to consider these to be minor in character, even though we are supporting a very large cosmetic industry that caters to our desire to alter that with which nature has endowed us. For most of us the epitome of the extreme use of cosmetics is the clown in a circus or a mime in a theater. We extol as artists of transformation those makeup specialists of Hollywood who create Draculas and Blackulas, the Phantom of the Opera, Boris Karloff's monsters, and even Fred Gwynne's amiable Herman Munster. We accept the exaggerated makeup on the actress playing the Madwoman of Chaillot but the same transformation worn on the street would repel us by its inappropriateness.

Strange, that growing up in the age of such traditions in theatrical license, we hate to admit to our own little cosmetic body transformations. And, they are "little" since, as we have already noted, we seem to have concentrated most of our efforts on the head. The most we allot our bodies is tan from the sun or ultraviolet lamps if we are white, or a little lotion, oil, or lubricating stick for glistening highlights if we are black. The most daring suggestions from beauty editors of slick-paged magazines in the past few years have been on how to shadow the female cleavage (fore and aft), how to rouge the ears, or how to submit daringly to small painted designs simulating tattoos on a bared shoulder or exposed thigh in a slit dress. Those familiar with the history of Mediterranean or Southeast Asian cosmetic practices know that these practices have been around for at least five or six thousand years, and probably longer.

While there may be a certain elegance possessed by those individuals who have undergone painful body deformation or cosmetic skin decoration to achieve cultural standards of cosmetic beauty (see Figures 4 and 5), the majority of human beings over the centuries and around the world have chosen the quicker, painless, and by far the more colorful route to

Figure 4.   Ubangi woman, Central African Empire
(after Jefferson 1974:fig. 148)

Figure 5.   Suyá Indian, married man with lip plug,
Amazon basin, Brazil (after Schultz 1962:119)

cosmetic transformations, temporary means of self-decoration. It is the term *color* that is the key to much of the human pleasure in cosmetic self-decoration, though mankind has never repudiated either black or white for dramatic touches. One of the ranks achieved by Aztec noblemen included the right to paint the entire body black, against which colored feathers and bright textiles must have been magnificent. Not so magnificent was the sacrificial victim made up in the same cosmetic, but without the contrasting finery. On the other hand, the very dark brown and blue-black Nuba of southeastern Sudan cover their young male wrestlers with a mixture of water and lime-talc. Often negative designs are created by wiping off the mixture in lines or patterns, or making little block prints in oil or water from carved stamps. A black eye-liner, kohl, is used universally in southwest Asia, India, and North and West Africa (see Figures 6 and 7).

Figure 6. Priest or actor applying black makeup, Classic period, A.D. 600. Drawn from painted Maya vase in the Anne Whipple Collection, Chicago

Figure 7. *Kabuki* actor in white, black, and red makeup (after Shor and Launois 1960:739)

However it is color with which man is not endowed that has most intrigued human beings in cosmetic transformations. Earth minerals and dyes from all manner of plants have yielded almost every hue that people can see in rainbows and in water drops, and in the natural world around them. Not all of the colors and pigments they found were as suitable for tinting the human skin such as cinnabar or mercurous oxide, used in Indonesia. Dressed skins used for clothing were probably stained or painted, sometimes in designs, partly because the colors could remain permanent, rather than fading or washing off as they would on human skin. Paleolithic man must have felt a great sense of discovery in this, and its logical consequences must have been the dyeing of spun fibers and cording. In the Neolithic period these were to become the knotted, hooked, and woven textiles of mankind.

Why is mankind so fascinated by the color red? Its use is so ancient that its original symbolism is something at which we may only guess. Is it an imitation of the life-giving properties of blood, of fire and warmth, of its intensity as a hue, or its seeming dominance in any refraction of light? But, how natural for humans to be attracted to the one hue that is the most recognizable at great distances. As discussed earlier in this paper, its deliberate use by man, for which we have evidence, began in the middle Paleolithic.

Red ocher, and other ferrous oxide colors, such as orange and yellow, probably are the most widely used red cosmetic pigments in the history of mankind (Figures 8 and 9). Essentially a dry substance, it can be applied to the human body, first by grinding it to a powder, then applying it in

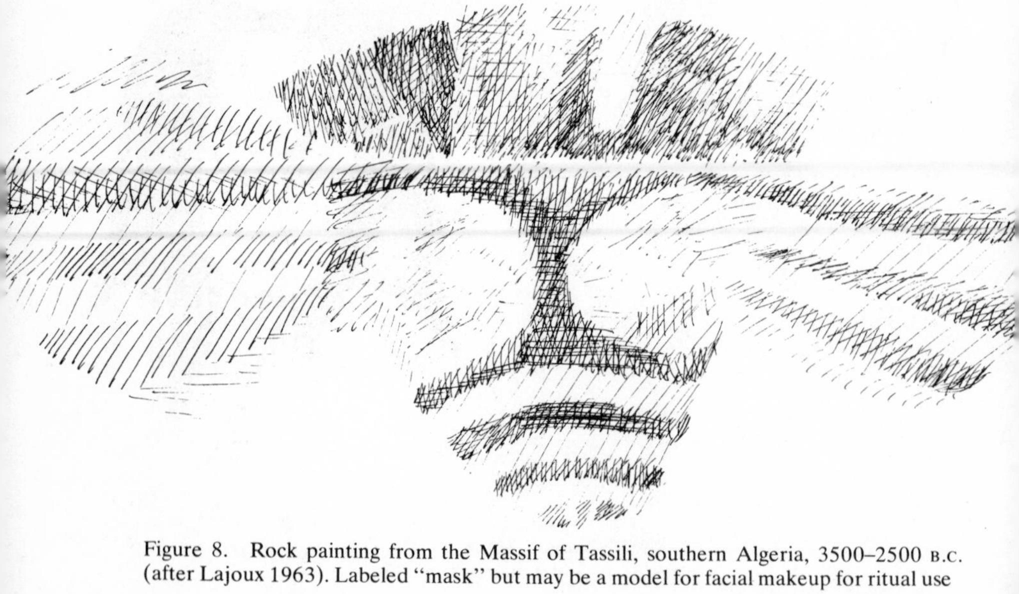

Figure 8.   Rock painting from the Massif of Tassili, southern Algeria, 3500–2500 B.C. (after Lajoux 1963). Labeled "mask" but may be a model for facial makeup for ritual use

Figure 9. Ritual dancer from Toulépleu, Ivory Coast, with ocher facial paints (after Darbois 1962:78)

one of the following simple techniques: mixed with water, milk, or urine, painted on and allowed to dry; mixed with animal fat or oil, to be rubbed on for good adherence; or, mixed with oil and painted on, then coated with oil to bring out highlights of body form, increase intensity of hue, to prevent the surface cracking when the body moves, and to provide better adherence of the pigment. Many peoples of the world still use these minerals applying them as described, and have improvised and created new shades of red when no red ocher was available to them. This may be done where yellow ocher occurs by the process of pulverizing it and heating it to as high a temperature as possible, thereby turning it into ferric oxide, which is a rosier hue than the orange red of red ocher or hematite (Faris 1972:61).

Limitations of space preclude any extensive description of the various uses of ochers by less complex societies. However, the joyous use of such colors by peoples whose lives may seem hard and deprived (to those accustomed to comfortable material standards of living) makes it most appropriate to include some of the cosmetic practices of two societies of the Pacific area and two of East Africa.

We picture the Australian aborigine in "the bush" living in a world of dust, of brassy haze and merciless sun, surrounded by no colors but unending shades of brown, tan, and faded rust. The reality is often far from this, in the blue shade of great rock outcroppings and hills, on rolling grassy slopes and the shade of dark green eucalyptus trees. With the red, yellow, and black ferrous oxides they mine, along with pipe clay (Mountford 1969), they create designs that reveal in these colors they treasure their complex world view of the quintessential spirits of every living thing. Their palette is from the earth and their canvases are cave walls, bark, and wood, but the primary canvas is the human body in a celebration of both life and the unseen world.

It was Margaret Mead (1928) who brought to our attention the richness and diversity in the many societies in New Guinea. But the Second World War and postwar explorations of the hidden mountain valleys have revealed peoples that again force us to dispense with preconceptions of rainy, forest-filled ravines, and frightened peoples too busy alternating head-hunting with trying to keep dry to attempt any cosmetic decoration to cheer themselves or their environment. Explorers of the New Guinea mountain highlands have provided everything from ethnographic works, ethnological comparisons and films, such as *Dead birds* (Gardner 1963), to books that are simply accounts of travel through the perilous and unexplored regions (Saulner 1963). Thanks to those who photographed in color, such as Robert Gardner, *Gardens of war* (Gardner and Heider 1968) — stills from the village used in *Dead birds*; the National Geographic Society; and Saulner (1963), we have opened before us some of the most artistically successful and creative use of earth colors in combination with many other materials, such as shell and bone for septum ornaments that extend cosmetic facial designs, as any that have ever existed. Not only is everyday cosmetic use of great artistic importance to New Guinea dandies but their ritual transformation into spirits and deities by cosmetic and costume means transcends or at least equals the work of some of the most imaginative of theatrical designers in Euro-American cultures. The most successful transformations are primarily of New Guinea men, though in some small societies women take part in rituals while using cosmetic decorations of a more elaborate kind than normally found. The blending of extreme facial and upper body cosmetics with coiffure and headdress for ritual transformations is done so well and so imaginatively that optical illusions created by cosmetic color, hair, seeds, clay, and feathers literally seem to turn the human being into a strange spirit of another world, or perhaps a bird with a human body.

In the body arts of the Nuba (Faris 1972), and to a lesser extent in those of the Pokot, Turkana, and Samburu peoples of northern Kenya (Cole 1974) there is found a different approach to cosmetic art using ochers. In both the Nuba society and those of the northern Kenyans there is a kind of celebration of the aesthetic attractiveness of a healthy, well-built body. The Nuba use their ocher cosmetics over the entire body in elaborate, original designs, clothing themselves in color, and leaving the elders to cover bodies no longer perfect with cloaks and wraps. The Samburu, Pokot, and Turkana use the ochers as cosmetic supplement to the beads and leather and textile cloaks of their costume — particularly the Samburu in dressing the elaborately structured, braided hairstyles of their warriors. Among these three peoples all adornment, particularly beads, seems to be designed to draw attention to specific parts of the body, such as powerfully developed back muscles, or arms and the percussive assistance and visual movement of beads is most apparent in the social dances they love. Cole's chapter in this volume elaborates on the importance of ocher cosmetics and adornment in the life-style of the Samburu, so in our discussion here we will summarize Faris' analysis (1972) of Nuba body painting.

To the Nuba the human body is the ultimate — the only — art form. It is not that they are obsessed by their bodies, but they use them as an expression of everything important to them in aesthetic values and changing social status. The body becomes a means of visual communication. On the other hand, body painting, with ocher pigment as the medium of the cosmetic, is not universal, but is used for those between puberty and thirty-five or forty years of age. However, the attitude toward exposure of the attractive body pervades the entire society. No clothing is worn, except by those who have not shaven off their pubic hair, who wear shorts; or by elders, who wear cloaks; and women past childbearing who assume a skirt wrap.

It is the men who create and wear the painted body designs, which are vivid and asymmetrical. These are crowned with the finishing touch, a coiffure that combines shaving and painting part of the scalp, adding wax to the remaining hair, and the addition of feathers. Some of these dandies create an entirely new design each morning, relying on a special friend to complete designs on his back and head that he cannot reach himself. The completed "dressing" is far more striking in effect than many elaborate textile costumes. The women "clothe" themselves in solid ocher colors of red or yellow; their truly aesthetic presence being due to the cicatrization designs that are worn in sets, with a set being added for each elevation to higher statuses, such as puberty, age grades, marriage, childbirth, and widowhood. The highlights and shadows play from these raised designs, depending on the ocher color worn and the enameling of an outer oil layer.

The application of cosmetic color by the Nuba is always done over the daily oiling of the body, except for the limestone talc and water mixture done before bracelet and stick fights. Oiling is also done as a daily cosmetic ritual simply for the health of the skin in the dry heat of the southeastern Sudan. Oil also functions as a source of warmth, protecting the skin in colder seasons. The paste of earth and other colors is made by water and clay being painted, patted, and rubbed, building several layers to assure the pigment sticking to the oiled skin for at least two days. Without oil the effect is chalky. The application of all this cosmetic color takes approximately an hour. Oil and ocher is usually added to the outside as a final, glistening, enamel effect. The decoration is removed by mixing mud and spreading it on the body where it is allowed to dry and absorb the oil, then the whole cosmetic decoration easily washes off. The oil that is used can come from several sources: in the indigenous world it is either vegetable, from roasted and ground sesame seeds, or animal fat from pigs or other animals. The Nuba now buy cotton seed or peanut oil either from local markets in small amounts or in four-gallon tins from Arabs in markets sometimes forty miles away. When the latter is done, the purchaser sells the oil in his own village to friends and neighbors in small amounts.

The red ocher that is admired so much is not found locally, so the women grind the yellow ocher and fire it at a high temperature to create a red ferric oxide that is darker than the normal red of hematite found naturally. The talc white is chalky limestone, but another source for white is freshwater clam shell (Faris 1972:61).

Sleeping with makeup one hopes to preserve is a problem the world over. Our only worry is whether or not the hair dye, lipstick, and mascara will come off on the pillowcase. The Nuba have solved this problem by constructing sleeping racks for beds. They lie in one position all night to save their cosmetic body decoration, and the young men go so far as to sleep with their neck on the edge of the bed so that their coiffure will hang out into space. Since the sleeping racks drip with pigment and oil — and there are strict regulations about who may sit on them, it is easy to see who has broken the rule (Faris 1972:64).

Evidence for the use of red cosmetics in the New World is found in eyewitness accounts of conquistadores and the Catholic priests who followed in their wake. From them and from the archeological research of almost a hundred years we have learned of the complex world views of even the least complex of Indian societies; and of the most complex societies, the civilizations of Central America and the Andes, we have had revealed to us the grandeur and beauty that staggered the first Europeans to view it. Early accounts by European chroniclers give valuable descriptions of textiles and clothing, body decorations, both permanent and temporary, along with that of jewelry, in which they were particularly interested. The color red, and its usually most available cosmetic base, hematite, was almost universally used. Lumps of it are found in ancient burials of the northeast woodlands in North America, and it was found on the skin of mummies from caves high in the Andes. It was not the exclusive source of the color red, however, for the American Indians were ingenious in discovering and domesticating plants of every kind that could yield either food or dyes. They even put beetles out to pasture in Central America when they discovered cochineal. Fray Bernardino de Sahagún speaks of some cosmetic customs of the women of New Spain (Mexico):

Their faces were painted with dry, colored [powder]; faces were colored with yellow ochre, or with bitumen. Feet were anointed with an unguent of burned copal incense and dye. They had hair hanging to the waist, or to the shoulders; . . . or the hair [twisted with black cord and wound about the head. . . .] It was cut and dyed with black mud . . .; it was dyed with indigo, so that their hair shone. The teeth were stained with cochineal; the hands and neck were painted with designs. . . . The stomach and breasts were also painted. . . . They bathed in the sweat house and with [soap and] water (de Sahagùn 1950–1963: vol. 8, pp. 47–48).

The past tense in which this priest describes cosmetic usages of red would seem to indicate that in Mexico, as elsewhere in North and South America, the church had much to do with condemning and suppressing the use of body arts and cosmetic use of color. Except for ceremonial occasions very little body paint is found today in North American Indian societies. Tribes with relatively little or no contact with Europeans or peoples of European stock living in their territories continue the use of tattooing, colored body decorations, red ocher, or vegetable dyes in cosmetic self-adornment. The majority of these are found on the eastern slopes of the Andes and in the Amazon basin.

We know more about the body painting of the Maya and the Aztecs than almost any of the more complex societies. Von Hagen (1960:34) drawing on de Landa's descriptions (1864) writes that painting of the face and body was general among Maya men. Black was used by young, unmarried men, and by those enduring a fast. Red was used by warriors, which at least kept bleeding wounds in key with their makeup. The priestly caste and those about to be sacrificed painted themselves blue. The use of red and black designs together was considered particularly elegant. Almost any social positions could be indicated by the color of their cosmetic paint. Women tattooed their bodies, but not their breasts; they had their teeth filed to points and painted their faces, usually red. This red, unlike a hematite-based paint, seems to have been a red stain or dye from the seeds of the *achiotl* plant, and symbolized blood. For cosmetic use it was mixed with *ix tahte*, a liquid, amber-colored resin from *conifera* (also burned as incense). This was a very sticky cosmetic, but it was also supposed to be prophylactic against sun and insects. Beside the writings of de Landa and de Sahagún there are the few Aztec and Mixtec codices that were not burned. These, coupled with the delightful clay figurines of Jaina, on which many colors were painted, still tell us graphically of the exuberant use of body cosmetics as they were keyed into costumes and accessories. At their theatrical best in state ceremonies they must indeed have represented the ultimate in the art of cosmetic transformations.

Plant dyes, such as henna, have certain advantages when used as cosmetics. Applied correctly to the skin, the color can last for many days, despite the domestic chores of women and the labor of men. The most famous of red dyes, henna, has been in use for thousands of years, and predates anything known in this color except hematite. Henna comes from a plant called *Lawsonia*, which grows to shrub size. There are two kinds of henna plant: one, *Lawsonia alba*, which has beautifully scented blossoms that always have been prized more than roses in the Middle East, spiny, and is both the *camphire* of the Bible and the mignonette of Jamaica; the second is the spineless version, *Lawsonia inermis*, the seeds of which, as well as the leaves, are crushed and ground into a paste to make the familiar red-orange dye.

Henna was introduced into French fashions in the 1890's and has become familiar to Europe and the Americas as a hair dye. It has come and gone in popularity on the hairdressing scene, but is enjoying a new vogue that is probably inspired as much by a return to "natural" ingredients as anything else. With this emphasis on hair in Euro-American culture, we do not always consider the other dye uses to which this plant was put for thousands of years, just as it is today in the Islamic world. Here in the societies that geographically stretch from Morocco to Afghanistan, depending on local cultural customs, henna is used to dye the soles of the feet, the nails, the hair, and even beards. Hands are dyed as well, for special occasions, such as the rites of passage of marriage or circumcision in some societies, such as in Tripoli, or among the Hausa of northern Nigeria.

When henna is used for the hair on the head, it produces aesthetically desired auburn shades in the dark brown hair of the peoples of the

Mediterranean littoral, particularly the eastern Mediterranean areas. But to accentuate dark hair, turning it blue-black, a henna pack is done first, then the hair is dyed with indigo. In Iran bushy black beards were once much admired: men would wash and dry their beards several times a day, then every night they would dye them. In some cultures henna was believed to have medicinal properties: in Afghanistan, the hair was dyed red if one had a bad headache, in hopes of curing it (Field 1958). Respectable Hindus did not use henna in India; the Muslims, however, used it on nails and on beards. In fact, though henna was the favorite color for cosmetic use on beards it is recorded that they were also dyed green or blue, or bleached white (Field 1958).

Greeks, Romans, and Egyptians used henna and bleaches, sometimes spending inordinate amounts of time turning dark brown hair to blond or light auburn. The latter effect was achieved with the leaves and stems of the henna plant, while darker colors were effected by an infusion using alfalfa leaves, with vinegar and alum as mordants.[5] The Egyptians used to dye the manes and tails of white horses with henna. The ancient Chinese used henna on their fingernails, perhaps as a precursor to lacquer. Its migration from the Mediterranean world can probably be explained by the contact the Chinese had with Greece when the Greeks had trading centers along the north shore of the Black Sea.

There is another type of red dye that came out of northern India in early historical times, and the use of which spread outward over at least two thousand years. The ancient civilization of northwest India seems to have been seminal for many of the cultural traits that have spread down that great subcontinent, and for ones that have traveled both to the east and the west. One could almost trace the diffusion of these traits by watching for the appearance of the particular red dye that seemed to follow them. Literature mentions this red coloring as *kum kum*, but specific botanical information seems to indicate that the reference is to *kesar, kum kuma,* or *zafron*, which is *shafzifran* or saffron, from the crocuses of northern India. Saffron is the intensely colored, yellow pollen of the crocus; however, at the tip of the stamen there is found inferior pollen that is orange-red. This can be mixed with fats to make a cosmetic paint for marking the foreheads of women. Very little of it in water can beautify the hands and feet by tinting them red, which is done by the temple dancers of Thailand. Saffron was imported by Rome from India, and it was in Rome that it was discovered that certain mordants could be added to saffron dissolved in water to turn it into blue and green dye for fabrics.

[5]   Mordants are usually mineral salts, such as alum or sodium chloride or soda, that "set" a dye color into whatever is being dyed, i.e. textiles, skin, hair, and so on.
[6]   Portions of the information on saffron came through conversations with botanists at the Field Museum of Natural History, Chicago. I am grateful for their interest and kind assistance.

There is an effect of bleaching, the removal of color from black hair, that is used cosmetically. Bushy, rust, and orange hairstyles are found in portions of Melanesia, such as New Ireland. The custom is dying out, but is still used sometimes in mourning a deceased family member. This effect on the hair is achieved with lime, usually from burnt shells, and lasts until the hair is grown out. The presence of red hair in populations of Africa south of the Sahara is due not to bleaching and dyeing, but to gene factors in the population, and is a natural occurrence.

Kohl, that seemingly simple cosmetic used to create the "houri" eyes of the Islamic world, must have one of the widest distributions of any cosmetic of the Old World, from Morocco through the Maghreb to the Middle East, Iran, India, and some of Southeast Asia. When used by predynastic Egyptians it was made from ground sulphide of antimony and manganese oxide, but today's Egyptians use vegetable substances mixed with zinc oxide, lead, copper, and sulphide of lead, but rarely sulphide of antimony. This mixture is not used by all the women of the Maghreb, for the Algerian women use a simpler compound of lampblack and oil, or burnt nutshells and oil. Antimony is also found in Asia Minor, Iran, and possibly Saudi Arabia. The length of the trade route probably had a great deal to do with substitutions for such a cosmetic before the twentieth century. Thus, although the harmless lampblack may not have kept away the flies and the diseases they carried, the people using that variety of kohl avoided more serious long-term problems of infected glands about the eye and a type of lead poisoning.

The Roman women used kohl, probably because the Greek women had used it. It was called *stibium*, sometimes *stimni*; another mixture called *collyrium*, with somewhat the same base was used as a medicinal ointment for such things as boils, and sometimes doubled as eyeliner. Kohl is applied by means of a small stick, which is dipped in the substance, then the tip is run along between the eyelashes when the eyes are closed. Several exquisitely carved applicators made of ivory appeared in the traveling exhibition of Pompeiian art — except that they were labeled "hair ornaments". With kohl now being imported into Europe and the United States (under Food and Drug Administration regulations), it is becoming one of the newer cosmetic "fads", and places selling it have to search out Indian and Arabic ladies to demonstrate the technique of application.

In examining the case for other colors used as cosmetics, we find that blue is not generally used as a temporary body paint, but is common in tattooing as a permanent color. In fact, with the exception of eye shadow in our own society, blues and greens have been comparatively rare in the palettes of the world since the very ancient Egyptians. Two instances of blue as temporary body color come to mind, only because they have become legend by reason of recorded history and travelers' accounts. The first is that of the ancient Britons, the Picts, met by the Roman legions. The islanders painted themselves with blue vegetable dye to frighten their enemies in battle, but from the manner in which the Romans were able to conquer them, the effect would appear to have been more puzzling than terrifying. The second instance of blue body coloring seems to have been accidental, rather than planned. The blue men of the Sahara have been known for centuries in the legends of other cultures. These are the Requibat Bedouin or the "blue" Berbers of northwest Africa. These racially mixed wanderers wear robes and turbans dyed very dark blue with indigo, with the result that their flowing, enveloping robes have served to rub the indigo onto the bodies of men and women alike, and their hands have changed in color from their natural brown to dark blue, from the constant adjusting and wrapping of the dyed textiles of their clothing. That which was accidental at first has become a constantly renewed cosmetic coloring, a successful cosmetic symbol reinforcing their identity as a people.

Temporary coloring and body decoration by more permanent means has been used by so many people in so many cultures, for so very long, that looking back on this encapsulated survey one might have the impression that all the members of each society mentioned were equally involved in cosmetic usage. In reality these transformational materials might be used only by specific individuals or subgroups, by only one sex, or by only a few individuals on special occasions for particular rituals.

Whatever the rationale people give for their desire to change themselves, the very long history of their search for the cosmetic means to do it defies all logical, rational explanations, which is exactly why one may say that these are indeed the very *human* arts of transformation.

REFERENCES

ABERCROMBIE, THOMAS J.
  1972   The sword and the sermon: an American Moslem explores the Arab past. *National Geographic* 142(1):3–45.
ARROYO DE ANDA, LUIS AVELEYRA, GORDON F. ECKHOLM
  1966   Clay sculpture from Jaina. *Natural History* 74(4):40–46. (Reprinted 1971 in: *Anthropology and art*. Edited by Charlotte Otten, 311–317. American Museum Sourcebooks in Anthropology. Garden City, New York: Natural History Press.)
BEAUMONT, PETER, ADRIAN BOSHIER
  1972   Mining in South Africa and emergence of modern man. *Optima* 22(1):2–12.
BOUTEILLER, MARCHELLE
  1953   Le tatouage: technique et valeur sociale ou magico-religieuse dans quelques sociétés d'Indochine (Laos, Siam, Birmanie et Cambodge). *Société d'Anthropologie de Paris: Bulletins et Mémoires* 10(4):515–534.

CHURCH MISSIONARY SOCIETY
1816   Account of the New Zealanders. *Missionary Papers* 3 (Michaelmas).
CLIFFORD, MILES
1944   Notes on the Bassa-komo tribe in the Igala division. *Man* 44(95):107–116.
COLE, HERBERT M.
1974   Vital arts in northern Kenya. *African Arts* 7(2):12–23, 82.
DARBOIS, DOMINIQUE
1962   *African dance: a book of photographs.* Text by V. Vašut. Translated by A. Jappel. Prague: Artia.
DART, RAYMOND A.
1953   Rhodesian engravers, painters and pigment miners of the fifth millennium B.C. *South African Archaeological Bulletin* 8(32):91–96.
1969   The bloodstone source of metallurgy. *Ethn. Facüldade Ciencias do Portugal* 21(1):119–129.
1974   The waterworn australopithecine pebble of many faces from Makapansgat. *South African Journal of Science* 70(6):167–169.
DART, RAYMOND A., PETER BEAUMONT
1971   On a further radiocarbon date for ancient mining in southern Africa. *South African Journal of Science* 67(1):10–11.
DAVIDSON, BASIL
1966   *African kingdoms.* Great Ages of Man. New York: Time-Life.
EICHER, JOANNE BUBOLZ
1972   "African dress as an art form," in *A current bibliography on African affairs*, volume 5, series II.
EMORY, KENNETH
1948   Hawaiian tattooing. *Occasional Papers of the Bishop Museum* 18(17):235–270. Honolulu.
FARIS, JAMES
1972   *Nuba personal art.* Toronto: University of Toronto Press.
FIELD, HENRY
1958   *Body-marking in southwestern Asia.* Papers of the Peabody Museum 45:1. Cambridge, Massachusetts: Peabody Museum.
FORBES, ROBERT J.
1955   *Studies in ancient technology*, volume three. Leiden: Brill.
GARDNER, ROBERT, *director*
1963   *Dead birds.* Color film, 83 minutes.
GARDNER, ROBERT, KARL G. HEIDER
1968   *Gardens of war: life and death in the New Guinea stone age.* New York: Random House.
HAGEN, VICTOR W. VON
1960   *World of the Maya.* Mentor Books. New York: New American Library.
HAMBLY, WILFRED D.
1925   *The history of tattooing and its significance.* London: Witherby.
HANDY, E. S. CRAIGHILL, WILLOWDEAN CHATTERSON HANDY
1924   *Samoan house building, cooking and tattooing.* Bulletins of the Bishop Museum 15. Honolulu: Bishop Museum.
JEFFERSON, LOUISE
1974   *The decorative arts of Africa.* London: Collins.
KEIMER, LOUIS
1948   *Remarques sur le tatouage dans l'Egypte ancienne.* Mémoires de l'Institut d'Egypte 53. Cairo: Institut d'Egypte.

LAJOUX, JEAN-DOMINIQUE
1963   *The rock paintings of Tassili.* London: Thames and Hudson.
LANDA, FRAY DIEGO DE
1864   *Relation des choses de Yucatàn de Diego de Landa.* Paris: Auguste Durand.
LEECHMAN, DOUGLAS
1951   Beauty's only skin-deep. *The Beaver* September, pp. 38–40. Winnipeg.
MEAD, MARGARET
1928   *An inquiry into the question of cultural stability in Polynesia.* Columbia University Contributions to Anthropology 9. New York: Columbia University Press.
MELVILLE, HERMANN
1846   *Typee: a peep at Polynesian life.* New York: Wiley and Putnam.
MOUNTFORD, CHARLES P.
1969   *The aborigines and their country.* Adelaide: Rigby.
ROBLEY, MAJOR-GENERAL HORATIO GORDON
1896   *Moko, or Maori tattooing.* London: Chapman and Hall.
SAHAGÚN, FRAY BERNADINO DE
1950–1963   *Florentine codex: general history of the things of New Spain,* twelve volumes. Translated by Charles E. Dibble and Arthur J. O. Anderson. Santa Fe, New Mexico: School of American Research/ University of Utah.
SAULNER, TONY
1963   *Headhunters of Papua.* Translated by M. Shenfield. New York: Crown. (Originally published 1961.)
SCHULTZ, HARALD
1962   Brazil's big-lipped Indians. *National Geographic* 121(1):118–133.
SHAPIRO, HARRY
1947   *From the neck up.* Man and Nature Publications, Science Guide 131. New York: American Museum of Natural History Press.
SHOR, FRANC, JOHN LAUNOIS
1960   Japan: the exquisite enigma. *National Geographic* 118(6):733–778.
SMIGHT, JACK, *director*
1969   *The illustrated man.* Film. Warner-Pathé.
SMITH, JOHN
1883   *The adventures and discourses of Captain John Smith.* London: Cassell.
STEINEN, KARL VON DEN
1925   *Die Marquesaner und ihre Kunst,* volume one: *Tatauierung,* Berlin: Dietrich Reimer.
STONE, JAMES W. VAN
1974   *An early archeological example of tattooing from northwestern Alaska.* Fieldiana, Anthropology 6:1. Chicago: Field Museum.
SUTTER, FREDERIC KOEHLER
1971   *Samoa.* Honolulu: University Press of Hawaii.

You Dance What You Wear, and You Wear Your Cultural Values

JOANN W. KEALI'INOHOMOKU

This paper explicates two propositions. The first proposition is that costumes affect the shapes of movements, especially as exemplified by dance movements. The second argues that behavior reflects cultural values and, therefore, costume-shaped behavior visually manifests cultural values.

YOU DANCE WHAT YOU WEAR

Some years ago I was a member of a class in Japanese dance offered at the University of Hawaii in Honolulu. It was a summer class, and most of the nearly thirty students in the class were elementary schoolteachers who had come from the United States mainland, to find ways to enrich their teaching. Most of these students were Caucasian women who were tall when compared with most Japanese women, a fact that became significant.

The class members had to provide themselves with the necessary dance equipment: a parasol, a fan, and most important, a kimono and belt. The kimono needed to have sleeves that were long enough for the dancing student to hide her hands while grasping the torso side of the sleeve ends for certain gestures. When ready-made kimonos at local shops proved to be designed for women who were shorter in stature and limbs than many of the students in the class, some female students solved the problem by buying kimonos in the men's departments, and some got busy with a sewing machine, but most settled for kimonos that were too short. When they grasped the fabric of the sleeve ends, they had to contract their shoulder muscles and flex their elbows in broken-wing fashion. It was evident that these students would never achieve the correct "line" in their dancing, no matter how hard they tried.

The examples used in this paper are drawn from the author's own empirical research.

Even more disturbing was the fact that the students looked as if they were wearing bathrobes over their shorts or jeans, and they had to wear shorts or jeans for modesty's sake because their kimonos kept flapping open below the belt.

Our teachers, a husband-and-wife team, followed traditional Japanese dance instructors' methods in that they never gave us verbal instructions or criticisms. Rather, they repeated the correct movements again and again while we students kept trying to copy them. But despite our repetitions, we always looked wrong and we did not know why. In fact, we were an amusing sight because our knees kept poking through the kimonos.

Believing that a clue to our troubles was contained in those kimonos, I one day handed my kimono and belt to the lady teacher and asked her to dress me. She did this, and the results were startling. The fabric was firm and taut around my legs. The kimono did not flap open. And, I discovered that I *had* to move differently. The rest of the class followed suit, and when we learned how to bind our kimonos properly, we began to move more correctly, and of course we began to have a more appropriate "look" when our knees were hidden by the tightly bound kimonos. I believe this was as instructive to our teachers as it was to us. It was, apparently, the first time they had taught a group of kimono-ignorant persons. For me this experience shocked me into deeper realization of how truly clothing can shape movement.

I had already known that clothing can shape movements, and had many times instructed my own students of dance to pretend they were wearing Restoration dresses with their arms resting on the panniered skirts to help them achieve the rounded, poised arms that I wanted them to use with a stylized "modern-dance" walk. But, there is a difference between knowing and deeply realizing, and the experience with the Japanese kimonos crystallized a principle for me.

Looking at several dance cultures we can see how this principle works. For example, the Korean woman court dancer, who dances with sleeves that hang to the floor, moves with elegant thrusts of the wrists to project those sleeves so that they neither drag on the floor nor touch any of her headdress. Practice sleeves are used in rehearsals so that the dancer responds kinetically to the fabric weight and length. The teacher continually reminds the pupil to fling the sleeves far enough with sweeping gestures over the head, because the real dance costume will include a delicate crown that must not be disturbed by those sleeves. The sleeves determine the way the dancer moves, and in fact, become very real extensions of the arms.

The Arabian belly dancer, who attracts focus on her abdomen, not only because of its rippling movements but also because the clothing permits that focus, would not move freely if she was tightly belted or wore extremely heavy clothing. Neither would the effect be the same if she moved under a tent-shaped Mother Hubbard dress.

The Pueblo woman, with her bulky wrapped boot-leggings, cannot move her legs and feet in the way a barelegged, barefooted woman might. There are several inches of padding between her calves, and her leg movements tend to rock from side to side, or pump up and down in a line that extends from the width of her hips rather than move with the ankles and knees close together. The resulting movement style seems to be so accepted that the Pueblo woman continues to dance *as if* she was wearing padded boots in those Pueblo dances where she does dance barefooted.

The *taupo*, or ceremonial hostess of a Samoan village, is constrained to hold her head quietly and poised in order to wear her large headdress appropriately. The bulky *tapa* [barkcloth] wrapped around her lower torso affects the way she sits on the ground for body-percussion dances. Barkcloth does not drape softly, and it will not fall modestly between her thighs when she sits cross-legged. She must sit down and arrange the tapa carefully, and while vigorously moving her flexed knees up and down, she must be conscious of keeping it modestly in place.

The Burmese woman dancer who wears a longer-than-floor-length skirt must keep nudging the skirt fabric out of the way while she loco-motes from side to side or forward and back. The clothing exacts this nudging, or the dancer would soon be entangled in her costume. Similarly, in some Spanish dances a skirt is worn that has a long train to be kicked out of the way as the dancer changes her line of direction. Of course the Burmese dancer or Spanish dancer could avoid the need for the kicking action by avoiding locomotion or pivoting. She could also avoid it by having shorter skirts. That they are not avoided indicates that the interactions between the movement and costumes are considered desirable. Indeed, the relationships between movements and clothing manipulations have become distinctive features of these dances.

Footwear is important in shaping movements. For instance, the supple slippers of the Scottish dancer permits foot articulations and extreme foot extensions. The clogs of the Irish dancer create "shoe music" so that dance-contest judges can sit under the performance platform and concentrate solely on the percussive sounds. Blocked "toe shoes" of the Western ballerina, shape her entire body alignment as well as actual foot movements. The hard high heels of the Spanish flamenco dancer not only make the movements audible, but they also permit the feet to withstand percussive stamping that would be painful to bare heels. Again, the Black United States male ballroom dancer, who slides his feet as if he is skating on ice, is able to do this because he is wearing slick, snug shoes on a hard floor. Bare feet on sand would never permit replication of those movements. Obviously, the total dance environment, especially the hard floor in this case, also shapes the movements, but the clothing is of prime importance because it is part of the body. Clothing is an extension-shaper of the dancer-self. The costume becomes part of his person.

Headdresses and masks shape movements also. The Aztec dancer who wears a huge fan-shaped headdress simply cannot move as he would without that balance problem on his head. A pragmatic reason for Hopi Kachina dancers to follow unmasked leaders is that vision is impaired by the masks and by the sweat that pours from their brows into their eyes. Accoutrements, especially those that are manipulated, often become the inspiration for movements and stance. The Tahitian woman dancer who holds a tassel in each hand moved the tassels rather than articulating her fingers. The dancer from the Philippines or Southeast Asia who balances candles or wineglasses on her hands and head must have absolute control over her balance and breathing.

Clothing can function to constrict movements, as the Japanese example shows, or to extend body movements, as in the Korean court dance example. Clothing can reveal body movements and thereby encourage movement styles, as exemplified by the Arabian belly-dancer costume, or determine movement styles that change the shapes of the natural body as exemplified by the ballet dancer's blocked shoes.

Over and above the importance of costumes as indicators of culture, status, tradition, or genre; over and above their decorative or artistic enhancement, costumes are important because they determine movement styles. Actually, most dance makers are choreographing costumes made animate. Without the awareness of how costumes shape movements, those movement analyses which treat bodies *as if* they were unclothed, and likewise, those notation systems which treat movements *as if* moving bodies had no body extenders or shapers, are ultimately inappropriate. This principle is of extreme importance to the dance ethnologist (see Prost 1975).

YOU WEAR YOUR CULTURE

All students of other cultures should be aware of this second principle, whether or not they focus on dance ethnology. What is signified by this correlation of movement to costume? We must deduce that costumes are most likely to shape body movements where motor behavior itself, in some way, reflects cultural values.

The most obvious and seemingly universally valued patterns are those that distinguish behavior between the sexes, and these are always revealed in costume. One does not need to turn to affective forms, such as dance, to find these distinctions. For example, in Western societies, formally dressed women usually wear skirts, and men typically wear trousers, and that clothing shapes walking and especially sitting behavior.

The woman who wears a short skirt cannot with impunity sit with her legs akimbo or with her hands clasped over the crotch, although a male wearing trousers typically does both.

The Japanese woman wears her kimono more tightly bound than the Japanese male. Indeed, Japanese males often wear trousers or a long pleated skirt, and these garments permit greater freedom in stance and leg gestures. In the binding of kimonos, Japanese women dancers are visible models for everyday feminine behavior. But in other respects Japanese dance behavior becomes more than a model for ordinary behavior. It becomes a stylization of idealized essence. The Japanese female dancer, as exemplified by the geisha, gently shifts her head from side to side, subtly reminiscent of a *kokeshi* doll. The sparkling, dangling appendages to her coif also sway delicately and add to the dancer's delicate appearance. This head-shifting is not everyday behavior: it is special behavior enhanced by special costume effects. It accentuates idealized femininity, and it contrasts with the idealized masculinity of Japanese male dance behavior, which includes a stance of deep second position plié, and dynamic gestures of arms and hands. When the Japanese woman dancer (who may be a female impersonator) poses in arrested movement, her legs, torso, and head assume a posture that forms a curving S silhouette. This silhouette is the antithesis to the H shape of the male pose. The costumes not only enhance the silhouettes, they literally make them possible.

Arabian belly-dancer movements seem to reflect the epitome of femininity within the appropriate culture. There are two functionally contrastive occasions for belly dancing to be performed. One is for the commercial dancer who performs for her own gain by "giving pleasure" to men. She is the professional dancer for whom the sanctioned norms held for the "respectable" wife and mother do not apply. The other occasion is for the "respectable" wife and mother to belly-dance for other women as a pastime. To while away the social hours, groups of exclusively female friends and relatives take turns dancing, singing, and playing musical instruments for one another. They make sure they are well hidden from male eyes. The values associated with the desirable Arabian woman can be inferred, whether she professionally dances for men and for men only, or socially dances for women and women only. The movements and apparel seem to show that a woman is considered a physical, sexual being with the power to excite. Both men and women need to be protected from this. This is controlled by polarized solutions — either openly performing outside the pale of polite society, or revealing oneself to other women only. The belly dance is primarily a solo dance that expresses the individual style of each performer. Likewise, for all that the belly-dance costume has certain predictable features, the dancer's individuality is expressed in her choices of costume details, colors, and ornaments. Just as her movements are individualized, undulating, and focus on the mid-torso, so also her costume is individualized, but always reveals movement flow while focusing on the mid-torso, usually by lack of clothing in that area. Arabian line dances for males, however, contrast to women's dances by their emphasis on rigid and terse bodies, and on uniformity in movement and clothing. It is a dance to show masculinity through controlled strength and the solid unity of the male group. The torsos are quiet, and the men clasp one another's hands as they press against one another's sides to locomote in unison with emphasis on dynamic footwork. Whether they wear Western clothing or traditional clothing Arabian male line dancers are austerely covered with little, if any, variations in clothing from one man to the next.

Values expressed in Korean court dances are different from those expressed in other Korean women's dances, because the court dances are imbued with a special refinement. The lusty Korean farm woman would probably never dream of identifying with ethereal-appearing court dancers who seem to float in their full organdylike dresses and long sleeves that effectively hide the real body. Court dancers even appear to have no hands, which are the means for doing work. This otherworldly quality reflects one stratum of a traditionally highly stratifed society. The court is not for common people, and it has its own aesthetic standards. It is the special set-off quality that surrounds the activities of the royal court that reinforce the court's glory, and, ultimately, the power base for the kingdom at large. Though today the monarchy is no longer a Korean reality, the memory of those days and the elegance surrounding them continue in affective culture forever to remind the Koreans of a glorious past tradition. Considering the fact that the Koreans were so often political pawns between China and Japan, the glorious tradition becomes even more precious for maintaining ethnic identity and pride. Court dancers today no longer dance in a real royal court; they are specially trained dancers who perform on gala occasions to evoke its memory.

The Pueblo Hopis are ideally egalitarian, and they do not tolerate self-aggrandizement in their dances. The uniformity of dance costumes, the impassive facial expressions, and the square-cut bangs that may well extend over a girl's eyes, make this clear in women's dance. Dance clothing for females matches the feminine ideal of being the stalwart mainstays of Hopi society. In the sturdy boot-legging, the bulky untailored handwoven dresses, the amorphous shape of covering capes, and the squared tablita headdresses, their movements are not soft nor fluid nor seductive, and neither are their costumes. Hopi female dance movements and costumes are direct, angular, and circumscribed. They always wear dresses while dancing, unless they are clearly mimicking a man in transvestite-type clowning that sometimes precedes the annual dances of the women's healing societies. Feminine dance behavior is always more circumscribed than male dance behavior. Hopi men's dances also reflect the value placed on self-effacement. Though their movements are wider and more active, they too have uniformity of costume, though the costumes may dramatize a greater variety of characters than the women's costumes do. In unmasked dances the men also maintain impassive expressions on their faces, and in masked dances their personal identity is completely obscured.

The Samoan taupo does not regularly wear her tall headdress and the bulky tapa swathing: she wears them when she is functioning specifically as the taupo as required on state occasions for dancing and *kava* rituals. At such times she must be distinguishable from the other women of her village: her studied and dignified behavior serve to set her apart and so does her costume. As we have argued, costumes and behavior are mutually reinforcing. The values reflected here go beyond simple sexual distinctions because they reveal the Polynesian focus on rank.

CONCLUSIONS

Behavior is often shaped or reinforced by costumes, and this is especially noticeable in affective expressions such as dance. From the examples given in this paper, which could be multiplied indefinitely, it becomes evident that dance behavior as shaped by costumes only sometimes directly reflects everyday models, and often explicates much more than male and female distinctions. Behavior during performances of affective culture often becomes exaggerated, stereotyped, or specifically directed to indicate status or role.

Costumes that shape behavior apparently do so in direct correspondence to values that indicate cultural focuses. The study of costumes as movement-shapers that make values explicit is vital for the understanding of a society. A linguistically based ethnoscience research plan could never, by itself, get to the crux of this issue because costumes and behavior alike are visually perceptible phenomena. It is impossible to ask the right questions of informants until the visible milieu is observed and analyzed also.

REFERENCE

PROST, J. H.
    1975   "Filming body behavior," in *Principles of visual anthropology*. Edited by Paul Hockings, 325–364. World Anthropology. The Hague: Mouton.

SECTION TWO

Signs, Symbols, and the Social Order

Living Art Among the Samburu

HERBERT M. COLE

The artistic energies of pastoral and nomadic peoples are often focused on their own persons, to celebrate and ornament their bodies. The Samburu of northern Kenya are such a people; indeed like many other pastoralists, they have virtually no visual art other than personal decoration. Nor is there any question here that the people are motivated to self-embellishment for aesthetic reasons — some tribes, and certainly the Samburu, are as self-conscious about their appearance at certain age levels as the most fastidious starlet of the West. Hours upon hours are occupied by men and women in shaving or hairdressing, preening, jewelry making, the application and reapplication of pigments. Minor changes in the decorative ensemble are made often, while major ones signal important changes of status.

The Samburu are a nomadic, Maasai-speaking group of cattle herders.[1] Their country, a vast expanse of thorn-strewn semidesert, occasionally relieved by partially forested mountains, is stark and barren, but very beautiful. Water and grass are major preoccupations in this rather harsh environment; women often must walk five miles and more for water,

I worked among the Samburu for two short periods in March (in Wamba) and May 1973 (in Barseloi), an aspect of wider research for a forthcoming book on African body decoration. This fieldwork was supported by a fellowship from the National Endowment for the Humanities and grants from the Academic Senate, University of California, Santa Barbara. I am grateful for the support of these institutions. I would also like to acknowledge the generous scholarly help of Jean Brown, then of the Kenya National Museum, as well as the logistical support cheerfully given by Father Peter Tallone and Father Aldo Vettori, of Wamba and Barseloi, respectively.

[1]   See Spencer (1965, 1970, 1973) for the fullest anthropological studies of the Samburu. Although his works do not emphasize material culture or personal decoration, he does record several customs relating to ornamentation. Ceremonial usages are omitted from this study because I did not personally witness any important ceremonies. Samburu personal arts relate closely to those of the Maasai and the styles can easily be confused.

herds of cattle (and smaller ones of goats, sheep, and camel) are more or less constantly moved in search of water and graze. Cattle, in fact, are the major factor in Samburu life, which is largely ruled by their needs. Cattle in turn supply most human needs: milk, the daily staple; blood, drawn less frequently and mixed with milk for food; and still less frequently, meat; skin for clothing; and "money" for exchange and bridewealth. Cattle are the prevailing topic of conversation, the reason for wars or raids (common fifty years ago but still occurring occasionally in the 1970's), and the means to wealth and status.

The domestic compound (*ngang*) especially reflects the centrality of cattle in Samburu life. It is a corral defined by encircling branches of acacia thorn and containing domestic houses and smaller corrals, the whole area being "paved" with dung. Architecture is simple, as befits a seminomadic pastoral life. The domed house (*ngagi*) is comprised of light withies bent and lashed, then covered with fiber mats, animal skins, and/or a dung and earth cement. People quite literally live with their animals and with flies, which are a basic characteristic of Samburu life.

In dress and ornamentation, however, cattle are secondary. The human body itself is the armature for sculptural masses of beads (women) and for numerous ornamental accents and bands (males) which in turn reflect age, status, and, of course, tribal aesthetic preference as well as personal taste. For both sexes personal ornamentation can be graphed from a minimum during infancy through a crescendo of weight and visual intensity in the prime of life, then to a falling off, in middle and later years, when dress ceases to be a major preoccupation. Ornaments are sometimes the same for men and women, but generally, as the illustrations reveal, both uses and styles are distinct and can be treated separately. I will examine first the general types and meanings of male ornamentations, then female. In conclusion I will compare and interpret the two, placing Samburu personal art in a larger context.

No self-respecting Samburu is ever without some kind of personal embellishment. Within several weeks of birth children of both sexes obtain waist, sometimes neck, wrist, and ankle beads provided by the parents (or grandmother) and strung by the mother or an older sister. If a newborn child is sick, medicinal beads, strings, or amulets will be tied on to cure and protect him. Yet most of the beaded strands acquired in childhood are decorative and carry no great significance other than that the child has been started on the traditional road to increasing personal ornamentation. His or her socialization to traditions of dress has begun, however, as has an acute consciousness of personal decoration. For boys the road leads to being a *moran*, to warrior status, which time is perhaps the apotheosis of male personal art in East Africa among several peoples. Until a youth is circumcised and initiated as a moran, however, there are restrictions in his dress and decoration. Boys and men need mobility for herding, running, and fighting, and they prefer fairly discrete bands, of beads, leather, and plastic, to the overall and more cumbersome, more restrictive decoration of females. A boy in the premoran stage generally wears relatively little (Plate 1). He will pierce his ears but can only wear a wooden lobe plug, as ivory is exclusive to moran. He may effect tubular plastic ear "wings" and a few bracelets or necklets, but overall his decoration is restrained. He may never decorate with oil and red ocher (though he is allowed to use charcoal); he may not braid his hair or grow it long; he may not wear the kinds of jewelry restricted to moran. A boy (or anybody for that matter) often wears one or more amulets or charms, as prescribed by a native doctor, to cure or prevent diseases.

Plate 1.   Premoran boys with restrained personal decoration

After his circumcision and ceremonial induction into the warrior age grade however, a young moran turns to artistic preoccupations, spending vast amounts of time and energy to make himself beautiful, attractive to young women to whom he may now openly pay court. Much of a moran's ornamentation and ostentation, in fact, stems from his relationship with his girlfriend/mistress, and her decoration depends on him as well. His girlfriend (*ntito*) will make some of his necklets, armlets, bracelets, belts, and other beaded articles for him with materials he provides. These may be simply beads on a string, while more elaborate belts and armlets consist of beads sewn onto a hide base, the dominant color being blue, with accents of several other colors. Many of these things are virtually mandatory for a well-appointed moran. To enumerate them all here seems unnecessary; most proclaim, in striking visual terms, that a young man is a *moran*, thus one apart from other males and from society as a whole.

What decorations moran provide for themselves and each other are, if anything, more important. Each moran wears a pair of ivory earrings made from elephant tusks, which in the old days were probably the products of communal hunts linked with induction into warrior status. In former times, too, a moran who had killed an enemy had the privilege of wearing four brass bracelets on his right arm, the same type worn still by women in long coils, and commemorative scars made on his right shoulder, which could well be called "the marks of pride". But hair remains the most important, prestigious symbol of moran status, and thus of manhood, which it typifies. Upon circumcision he begins to grow and ocher his hair.

The significance of braided, dressed hair to a Samburu male is signaled by the fact that moran often spend twelve to fourteen hours or more in its preparation (Plate 2). A European doctor told me that one warrior, having been seriously mauled by a lion, refused to enter a hospital because he would have been required to have his long hair cut off prior to treatment. Like Samson, the moran sees his hair as giving him strength, courage, and masculinity. If it rains he will protect his hairdo with a skin

Plate 2.   Moran hairdressing. The three-pigtail style on the right is much cultivated and sought after

hat (*nkaranda*) while his body remains uncovered. Hair, indeed, is important to all Samburu, who must shave it off if a close relative or age-mate dies. Such occasions are then doubly distressing to a moran who may have been growing and dressing his hair for more than ten years. But he shaves it, if reluctantly, because of the belief that *not* to do so would bring misfortune upon friends and kin. Leach (1958) draws attention to "magical hair" which Spencer discusses in the Samburu context (1965, 1973) in some detail. The concern with and elaboration of hair among moran then, has deeply rooted emotional, psychological, and social dimensions.

The goal of nearly all Samburu moran is to grow hair long enough to fall, when braided, to the middle of the back or below. This style when arranged in one pigtail terminating in a wooden arrow-shaped pendant, is called *suroro*. But there are many other styles, each named, and these fashions change over the years. Even relatively short hair, not yet braidable, can be shaped into the *kub* style which is quite impressive when saturated with red ocher and fat. A style with short braids on the back of the head (*sakara*) is an intermediate step before the hair is long enough to gather into pigtails (Plate 3). Once hair is long enough to work, it is parted across the head into "back" and "forehead" hair. Forehead hair is arranged today in one of two prevailing styles: it is twisted, with these dozens of thin strands gathered and tied together under a button in the center of the forehead, or, if not long enough for that, it is twisted and shaped over a piece of leather or other stiff material, cardboard, for example, in what can be called the "visor style". Other variants have been

Plate 3.   Intermediate style with six short pigtails

recorded;[2] different styles move in and out of fashion in various Samburu areas, and may, like other forms of decoration, be specific to certain clans. The important thing is that hair be dressed, and meticulously so.

Shorter back hair which can be gathered into pigtails is usually so worked, for pigtails, the longer the better, figure in flirtatious dance gestures when a moran more or less casually but deliberately throws his pigtails, with wooden pendants, over his head to strike the bare head of a girl dancing opposite him. Here we see that hair is an active, mobile aspect of Samburu life, that it is actually *used*. No doubt the aesthetic dimension of hair in motion, in the characteristic leaping dances and head-thrusting dance gestures of the Samburu, is important. Indeed the years of moranhood are the most important ones for dancing, and beautifully dressed hair is dramatic in this context.

The processes and ambience of personal decoration are interesting. The moran will assemble under "their" tree, if living at the main settlement, or anywhere in their compound if living in the bush or a cattle camp, to embellish themselves and each other. Here they shave all body hair, which in contrast to a moran's hairstyle (*lmasi*) is considered unattractive. They paint their own faces with delicate lines and spots in orange, yellow, or white (in 1973) — a form of decoration known curiously as *balu*, adopted from the European word *blue* and ultimately from Reckett's washing blue which was presumably used in earlier days. Orange or white *balu* is however more striking and hence a more appropriate contrast to the rich brown skin color of Samburu men. They also apply quantities of vivid red ocher (from iron-rich stones or earth) to their hair, often to parts of faces so as to frame the features, and over the neck and shoulders in a continuous plane, usually ending in a large triangle on the chest. Animal fat is the base of such painting, and its application makes the body glisten. Among males only moran paint with red ocher on a regular basis, although elders do so in a more restrained and less self-conscious manner for special events such as initiations, their own weddings, and so forth. These preening and decoration sessions of moran are times of heightened self-awareness approaching narcissism; mirrors are passed from hand to hand; men admire their own decorations and work on improving them. The Samburu place great emphasis on physical beauty, and a moran may become quite embarrassed should his hair get messed up or his painted patterns smeared.

Moran commonly help one another in hairdressing (Plate 2). An individual completed coiffure is often the product of five or more sessions with as many helpers. All moran know the intricacies of twisting and shaping, but those who can fashion the most elegant, flowing, and

---

[2]   Joy Adamson (1967:147, 345–349) illustrates hairstyles which vary somewhat from those I describe. Spencer (1965) also shows a few variants.

"danceable" styles are naturally more in demand. For these "pigtail" styles the back hair is divided horizontally into several parallel sections. Work begins on the lower one, with other hair tied up on top of the head. Sixty or more "braids" may be made from one section an inch or so high, running the width of the head. These are not in fact true braids, for two small strands are twisted tightly together with red ocher and animal fat. In any case, one moran may have upwards of four hundred thin strands. These may be lengthened somewhat to conform with others by twisting in thread or fiber (in the case I witnessed, thread unraveled from a cloth). These braids are grouped and tied onto a pointed wooden pendant, which is often beaded as well. Several sessions and a good many working hours later the finished coiffure will be proudly displayed. During the period in which it is being worked and perhaps at other times (simply to protect it), the hair is covered by being tied up tightly in a piece of cloth or animal skin.

Although moran are unable to marry usually until their late twenties or early thirties, they are acutely woman-conscious and their cosmetic art is meant to attract admiring girls and married women. The social pressure within their own male group is also strong. To be a Samburu moran is to be carefully and artistically dressed, coiffed, and painted. And this was as true in 1973 as it was in 1900. Moran traditionally had a subculture of their own, largely separated from the main settlements so as to protect them, and hedged about by numerous social and ritual restrictions which, it is fair to say are advertised by their distinctive decoration in general and fancy hairstyling in particular.[3]

When a moran marries or becomes an elder (these occur at about the same time), however, he more or less abruptly returns to a less flamboyant style of dress. His hair is cut short; he takes off most of his beaded ornaments, replaces ivory earrings with smaller, more discreet metal pendants, and seldom applies any pigment at all to his head or body (Plate 4). He wears a longer wrapper of a darker color. As a man of respect and dignity he no longer postures, preens, and decorates. Because he is married he no longer need appear so elegant before women and girls. He spends much of his time among fellow elders discussing cattle, when the next rain will come, or when the settlement should be moved.

The same abrupt acquisition and diminution of embellishment does not occur in the female world. A girl begins to acquire beads when very young, building up her collection over the years (Plate 5); she never gives up the practice of self-decoration although as an older woman she becomes more casual about it. The most crucial years for a woman are

[3] The period of moranhood, lasting from twelve to sixteen years, has been called by Spencer (1970:131) one of "social suspension" between boyhood and elderhood, when they marry and make the most important decisions. In a sense, then, their distinctive dress marks this long liminal period.

Plate 4.   Two moran with different hairstyles; an elder, with few decorations, on the right

Plate 5.   A group of unmarried girls of various ages

from just about the onset of puberty through to the early years of marriage. Yet at the age of seven or eight, a girl begins to receive presents of beads from a moran admirer. Many of the girls' ornaments are given by moran; she is also sometimes given beads by married sisters and older women. A girl's major preoccupation is with her collection of neck beads. She normally keeps her head shaved so as to show off this massive accumulation as well as her decorative headband and pendant earrings. Nubile girls, who have become the serious girlfriends and lovers of moran (though they very rarely marry one another) are as conscious of their beauty as are moran. They quite constantly keep their upper bodies and heads covered with red ocher and animal fat, the essential cosmetics which often overlay their neck bead ensembles so as to obliterate their colors. Neck beads are complemented by shiny brass armlets, preferably four by the time she marries, one on each upper and lower arm. Leather skirts too are decorated with beads in narrow linear patterns which are apparently not symbolic, and pendant earrings of certain kinds may be worn, others being reserved for married women. Young or pubescent girls also may acquire decorative scars on the abdomen, and often around the waist and onto the back. These patterned keloidal reliefs, for both males and females, contrast with lighter, barely visible scars made at any age for protective and medicinal purposes. The decorative scars on the lower torso are primarily beauty patterns, and are optional; they are stimulating to both sight and touch. In this regard it is notable that a moran will sometimes give his lover a twisted beaded bandolier, worn at the neck or over the shoulder, ending with an eagle or crow claw. The lovers will play with this, marking and scratching each others' flesh on the back, chest and more intimate places, another example of love play involving tactile as well as visual sensations. This can be considered a type of transient and private scarification lasting some hours or at most a few days.

A number of girl's ornaments, too, are calculated to make sounds, especially in the dance. In jumping dances even neck beads made an audible "whoosh" as they flop up and down (Plate 6). More dramatic are the sounds of the girls' large iron anklets, clanking rhythmically as they walk or dance. Two different kinds of audible back pendants are worn, one suspended from neck beads to about buttock length, the other from waist nearly to the ground. Each terminates in metal rattles, small squares or iron, bottle caps, CO_2 cartridges, rifle shells and the like. These, given to girls by their moran friends, have particular and individual sounds by which a girl can be recognized as she walks in the dark.

The most significant changes in female personal art occur when she marries, and these decorations make it easy to differentiate married women from unmarried girls even of similar ages. The "wedding band" is an iron circlet worn on the right wrist, but characteristic neck beads and

Plate 6.   Girls dancing

earrings also distinguish married women, as does a new beaded skirt made by her mother. The most important acquisition is *mparo*, an integrated set of necklaces, made from thin dark slivers of flexible wood or elephant tail, each with a frontal and central red bead (Plate 7). I have counted more than a hundred red beads on one mparo, and this assemblage invariably overlays a substantial number of "ordinary" varicolored beaded necklaces and stiff circular shoulder pieces. Altogether it is not uncommon for a woman to wear ten or more pounds of beads and other ornaments. To make room for the black and red mparo bundle, at the time of her marriage, a girl will remove roughly half of her neck ensemble which she distributes among her younger sisters and friends. The moran who gave them to her no longer has any claim either on the girl or her beads, although earlier, before the girl marries, she can break off her relationship with a moran at any time by returning the decorations he gave her.

Women's earrings are among the more fanciful and imaginative of Samburu personal arts, and a woman may wear as many as three or four pairs of them at one time. Coiled brass circlets, hung pendant from each ear but supported by a string over the head, are all but mandatory for married women, and proscribed for the unmarried. Large rectangular beaded leather pendants are common but optional; girls also may *not* wear them. Openwork, beaded ovals and circlets of several styles, strung on stiff wire, are in widespread current use by girls and women alike.

Plate 7. A married woman. Note the ivory amulet in the lower center of her neck ensemble, and the even row of red *mparo* beads above

These, like a number of other embellishments, are in more or less constant movement as woman walks or turns her head, and are clearly designed with this "mobile" and projecting quality in mind.

The number of earrings, neck beads, brass or iron armlets or other smaller ornaments are a fairly clear indication of a woman's status — that is, of the wealth and generosity of her husband, who takes over from her moran friend the task of providing his wife with jewelry. This is not to say that a poor woman will have very few beads or ornaments, for unvoiced laws, or better perhaps, codes of egalitarianism, as well as a woman's own property in cattle, and thus her own wealth, cause even a poor one to meet a certain standard. But a poor or poorly married woman will be less sumptuously laden; she will have fewer expensive items, such as coiled brass or iron armlets, than a wealthy one.

Although the rate of conformity to basic items and colors in the scheme of female decoration is quite high, as it is among moran, scope is provided for individual preference to such an extent that no two women look exactly alike — despite an outsider's first impression of uniformity. And the Samburu themselves are of course much more sensitive to nuances and variations than foreigners will be. There are even some subtle, regional, clan, and class preferences which are hard for an outsider to discern. Nearly all items in the glossary of decoration have varying sizes, color combinations, shapes, and styles, and each bead shape and size is likely to have a specific name. Many items too are optional, and individual spiritual and medical histories account for further variations. Several different sorts of charms against infant mortality can be worn as jewelry. Many pregnant women wear strings of green and black beads in their hair to insure safe delivery. Varying types and colors of beads, too, are held and spat upon, as a sanctifying act, in prayer to the high god *Nkai*. The evident centrality of beads in Samburu life was graphically revealed to me by a women who had inadvertently sold me three white beads on a string of old red ones. When I gave them back I asked why they were so important. Her reply (loosely translated) was this: "Our ancestors had just those beads when Samburu started [that is, at the beginning of time]. They were white stones which they found on Mount Muele [a sacred volcano] growing on stalks of grass. We use them for praying."[4] Some women pray with white beads, some with the highly valued old ones (the type on *mparo*), and still others with green and black ones. My data are not sufficient to interpret the variables; I can only suggest, without much confidence, that prayer beads may be a matter of personal choice. What is perhaps more important is the fact that beads, the cornerstone of female jewelry, are found in creation myths and that some beads are highly sacred and valuable as well as decorative. Color symbolism in beadwork seems indirect and associational rather than explicit: green for cattle-sustaining grass; blue for the sky and god, Nkai; white for milk and purity; red for blood which is the staple food.

Imported glass beads have long been an intensively traded commodity in East Africa and indeed are among the few necessities of life which are *not* available in the local environment. As items of exchange beads seem to have been second only to cattle as Samburu "money". It is not surprising, perhaps, that women can give a fairly good accounting of the time and circumstances of acquiring as many as fifty or sixty strands or circlets of beads, most or possibly all of which have minor individualizing features. I do not believe it is a mistake to suggest that a woman's personal decoration, in contrast to a man's, is a graphic autobiography by which she can accurately recall or retell the events of her life. Although I did not

[4]   The beads in question were neither very old nor were they stone. They were white plastic ones which I can only assume resembled those of the myth, which was corroborated by my Samburu interpreter as common knowledge.

actually record such a "bead-biography", I had several hints that this interpretation is correct.

This biographical notion of women's decoration is substantiated by the beads and practices of older ladies. If they are more casual and less self-conscious than younger women, they are by no means unconcerned. As women age they begin to remove certain strands or groups of strands and give them away — some or all of their wedding beads, *mparo*, which are expensive and rare today, to one or more daughters at their marriages; other strands to younger women as presents and perhaps to relieve themselves of weight; and certain strands to their grandchildren. The latter practice particularly shows the biographical nature of at least some jewelry. The strands which she gives to her son's children are the ones which she began to wear when that son became a moran. For every moran son a mother will wear proudly, pendant between her earrings, two strands of alternating dark blue and white beads ending with a few inches of green beads and finally a cowrie shell (Plate 8). My data are not clear

Plate 8.   Older woman with a diminished neck ensemble and two double strands indicating two sons as moran

whether she gives those very beads to the child or ones like them newly purchased, although the latter seems more probable; otherwise, the woman's strands would not remain with her long. It is notable in any case, that a man can be a moran, without marrying, for about fifteen years, so she would still have a fairly long period for wearing these "badges". I have seen women with eight such strands, indicating four sons who had become moran. More commonly, on the other hand, a woman disburses her beads rather than accumulating more, unless the new ones commemorate a specific event. After she stops having children, too, an older woman will remove the lower strands of white beads on her headband; she has worn these since childhood but now certain sanctions (which are not very clear) prohibit her from bright (or white) strands, although strands in which white alternates with a dark color are acceptable.[5] In fact an older woman's ensemble of decoration tends toward darker colors, as well as larger beads, than those of younger women. The latter may simply reflect what beads were available from traders at the time of purchase, but the former I believe to be an artistic principle, and not simply arbitrary. There is in fact a notable progression from the uniformity of bead sizes and overall red ocher colors characteristic of married girls toward greater contrast and variation in colors and ornament types as a woman grows older.

The ornamentation discussed here is worn all the time, day and night. A significant if obvious fact is that nomadic, pastoral peoples own little more jewelry than they wear. To some extent people actually wear their portable wealth (other than stock) presumably to keep their movable property to a minimum. Some special forms and styles of ceremonial dress exist, but the bulk of ornamentation and that illustrated here is worn daily — in contrast to the codes of personal ornament among West African sedentary agriculturalists who are able to store quantities of decorative jewelry and other items for infrequent usage.[6]

Implicit above is the contrast between Samburu male and female aesthetic preferences which are in fact shared by several other pastoralist peoples of Kenya, Uganda, and southern Ethiopia. Rendille, Dorobo,

[5]   The verbal data collected are sometimes in conflict with visual patterns observed. There may exist (or have existed) an authorized ideal which in real life is honored in the breach, perhaps for aesthetic reasons, possibly because of what bead types and colors are available for purchase at any given time.

[6]   Since I attended only one Samburu ceremony, a wedding, I cannot explore types and styles of ceremonial dress beyond observing that red ocher is extensively used and that many "special" ornaments worn are in fact "ordinary", but for different people. Both the bridegroom and his father, for example, wear certain types of beads and dress normally worn by women, and feathered crests are worn by moran at some of the six *ilmugit* ceremonies undergone in their transition from boyhood to elderhood. Some of these decorations are mentioned by Spencer (1965, 1970, 1973). Settled agriculturalists in Kenya seem to have largely adopted the dress and ornament types (if not the styles) of nearby pastoralists. One reason for this, according to Jean Brown (personal communication) is that pastoralism is the ideal of even agriculturalists, thus their ornamentation is also revered.

Turkana, Pokot or Suk, Karamajong, and especially Maasai decorative schemes relate to those of the Samburu while having distinctive features of style, that is, of color, shape, and texture, enabling a person conversant with individual dress "grammars" to spot a person of a particular tribe at some distance. Ethnicity in dress, as in language and other customs, is a means of identification to other peoples, to members of one's own group who will understand finer nuances, and to the self in that specific items have personal significance. As in virtually all African arts, that of personal adornment carries critical cultural messages which are not otherwise explicit. Dress is in fact a message system of some complexity and subtlety as well as a culturally-specific expression of aesthetic values.

Differences in Samburu male and female ensembles, in shape, texture, and accent, therefore both express and reinforce sexual and age-grade differences. Uninitated boys are held to restrained dress styles which change abruptly after circumcision and initiation to moran status. The long period of moranhood, when men remain unmarried but sexually active in spite of their real and figurative separation from main settlements, is a time of extraordinary pride in the body and its decoration, the image of masculinity. Bodies are banded and accented and coiffures are elaborate; physical mobility for dancing, running, and fighting is preserved. Indeed masculinity is exaggerated by moran body arts. Adornment by elders becomes somber again; they are married and occupy themselves with decision making and administering the tribe. They do not need to show off.

Women marry early and are sought after still earlier. Their aesthetic self-consciousness at the age of ten or eleven is equal to that of a twenty-year-old moran. Ever-expanding bead ensembles, along with heavy armlets and skirts, alter their natural shapes and restrict their mobility. Whereas moran highlight their bodies for display, adolescent and young married women partially cover and bulk them out, both to define and reinforce their beauty. When physical beauty wanes at middle age and after the birth of children, preoccupation with elegant dress wanes too, even if significant social markers remain visible. For both males and females, then, there is an internal logic to the aesthetic system which squares with the messages it conveys.

It is evident that this form of art lives and moves. It cannot be stationary, as it is defined by the human armature which it in turn both beautifies and defines within the social system. Surely there are elements of fashion and fad in Samburu arts, but much more as well. Dress, cosmetic, and hair ensembles reach into and express vital dimensions of social, spiritual, and economic life. They are sometimes flamboyant but never superficial for in being so alive and multifaceted, it is safe to say that if or when the arts were taken away, a Samburu person would no longer feel like a human being.

REFERENCES

ADAMSON, JOY
1967   *Peoples of Kenya.* London: Collins and Harwill.
COLE, HERBERT M.
1974   Vital arts of northern Kenya. *African Arts* 3(2):12–33, 84.
1975   Artistic and communicative values of beads in Kenya and Ghana. *The Bead Journal* 1(3):29–36.
LEACH, EDMUND R.
1958   "Magical hair," in: *Myth and cosmos.* Edited by John Middleton, 77–108. Garden City, New York: Natural History Press. (Originally published 1958. *Journal of the Royal Anthropological Institute* 88(1–2):147–164.)
SPENCER, PAUL
1965   *The Samburu: a study of gerontocracy in a nomadic tribe.* Berkeley: University of California Press.
1970   "The function of ritual in the socialization of the Samburu moran," in *Socialization: the approach from social anthropology.* Edited by Philip Mayer, 127–158. London: Tavistock.
1973   *Nomads in alliance: symbiosis and growth among the Rendille Samburu of Kenya.* London: Oxford University Press.

Beads and Personal Adornment

ILA POKORNOWSKI

Beads have become such a part of peoples' dress that they are usually thought of as interesting, but hardly of great importance. However, many anthropologists, archeologists, and art historians today agree that the study of beads as an "intimate" part of culture has a highly significant value both in the reconstruction of material culture and tracing trade contacts and in the study of bead adornment as a visual language (Cohn 1959:77). This paper was undertaken in order to investigate the value of bead research, first by locating and surveying the general literature on the subject, and then by concentrating on the history, production, and function of beads in one particular culture, the Yoruba of West Africa. For the purposes of this paper, beads will be defined as small objects of various shapes, of more or less regular form, made of both naturally occurring and artificial materials, with some provision made, generally by perforation, for their use on clothing or adornment of the body, by stringing or attaching them in a series.

THE UBIQUITOUS BEAD

The use of beads for adornment of self or of clothing probably began in the Neolithic period, but the practice was based on the much more ancient use of shells, teeth, and vertebrae of fish, reptiles, and mammals, and designs worked in flint or obsidian by pressure flaking. Strung on plant fibers or sinews that crumbled with time, deliberate arrangements in these media are sometimes found in burials and silently indicate the pleasure in creating this particular form of adornment.

The pervasiveness of beads in African cultures presents the student of this medium of artistic expression with the unique opportunity of examining what is almost the full range of materials selected by mankind over thousands of years. Not only is there a full range of forms made from natural media such as teeth, vertebrae, cowrie shells, ostrich shells, nuts, and ivory, as well as drilled and shaped stone, but there are indigenous copper, brass, silver, and gold beads. Archeological sites at Ife in Nigeria have revealed that glass was being produced locally before European contact. But it is the "trade bead" of glass from European and Middle Eastern sources that Africans seized upon and used with consummate skill in both art forms and self-decoration. The archeologist van Riet Lowe (1955:3) has said that "Africa was sprinkled with them [beads] daily, in hundreds of thousands."

Literary references document the geographic extent and the duration of the use of beads in trade in Africa. The writer of the famous *Periplus of the Erythraean Sea* mentions the trade in beads in East Africa around A.D. 60 (van Riet Lowe 1955:2). Ibn Battuta, traveling to Mali in 1352, said that a traveler in that country carried only salt, aromatic goods, and beads for barter (Ibn Battuta 1929:317, 322). Andrew Battell, trading in Benguella in southwest Africa in 1600, bought cattle, with each priced at fifteen one-inch-long blue glass beads (Battell 1901:17).

No matter what the material of which they were made, beads were used for a wide variety of purposes. In Zulu society, beads marked changes in status through life of both males and females (Twala 1968:366). In the past, Zulu who wore beads reserved for royal use without the king's consent were put to death (Schofield 1958:194). Among the Lovedu, beads played a part in the rites of ancestor worship, and so important were they that capricious ancestors might cause an illness to a loved one as a reminder that their beads were to continue being worn to assure their continued prestige in their afterlife (Krige and Krige 1968:63). The Kikuyu used a sacred bead in the ceremony of oath-taking, for perjury was believed to result in the death of the perjurer and serious harm to his relatives (Hobley 1922:241–242). Among the Thonga, as soon as a child had cut his incisors, a white bead was tied to one of the hairs above his forehead to help the rest of the teeth to come through normally. If this were not done, it was believed that the child would not become intelligent (Junod 1927:vol. 1, p. 51). The Thonga also wore large white beads in the hair, or sometimes hung short strings of small beads from the head to indicate possession by spirits (Junod 1927:vol. 2, p. 480).

THE VALUE OF BEAD RESEARCH

Because of this widespread geographical and chronological use of beads, it would appear that research concerning them could be valuable in a number of fields. Beads found in ancient ruins could aid in dating those ruins, and shed light on the technological development of the people who made them (van Riet Lowe 1955:12), or provide evidence of migrations, trading activities, and culture contact. Beads can indicate the aesthetic tastes of those wearing them (Eisen 1916:1); for example, the sculptures of both the Nok and the Ife cultures depict large numbers of beads in a similar arrangement of heavy ones and small ones, indicating an aesthetic and cultural connection (Willett 1971:73). Beads could further our knowledge of the social aspects of a culture, for example, the Ingombe Ilede site in what is now Zambia contains burials with gold-decorated skeletons contemporary with much simpler burials, indicating considerable social stratification (Davidson 1972:97–98).

Eisen (1916:1) commented that bead study "has been much neglected"; Beck (1928) developed a classification system which remains the standard work on the subject; and Caton-Thompson says of her material on beads originally published in 1931, that it was a "pioneer attempt to get them taken seriously as a potential aid to chronology before the days of carbon were even imaginable" (Caton-Thompson 1971:13). In spite of the promise which many people felt was held by bead study, subsequent advancement has not been rapid. Raymond Mauny wrote in 1952: "The whole study of African beads still remains to be done" (quoted by Fourneau 1955:17). And Ryder said in 1969: "A . . . general and cooperative approach is needed to elucidate the mysteries that at present surround the bead trade of medieval Africa" (1969:60, footnote 3).

PROBLEMS OF BEAD RESEARCH

Studying beads from written records means using many incomplete and scattered observations from unprofessional observers who did not consider beads important: terminology for bead types changed over time (Schofield 1958:187–189); and there are great problems with inaccurate translations of references to particular beads (van Riet Lowe 1955:15). Using traditional sources within a culture may result in varying and confusing information; people may use a single word for quite different beads; Schofield even found that an important part of current bead identification was the manner in which the beads were strung (1958:183, 190–191).

Working with actual beads has its own set of problems. Even proper description is difficult, for instance, there can be great color difference within the same bead (Beck 1928:52) and between opaque and transparent glass even when colored by the same chemical (van der Sleen 1967:50). To be useful, data about a bead must include other information. Method of manufacture is important. For example, the Bantu-speaking peoples, using iron tools, made ostrich eggshell beads in a slightly different way from the people whom they displaced, enabling the distinguishing of the earlier beads from the later ones (Schofield 1958:182). Date and origin should be indicated (van der Sleen 1967:51), both difficult questions, for once a bead became a favorite, it persisted and was often imitated. Arkell (1936:305) has reported a still active bead factory in Cambay, India, which has been in operation for a time span which van der Sleen interprets to be at least seven thousand years (1967:18, 69). Research in a geographical area believed to have been the source of particular beads may not be useful, for a bead type may never have been used in the culture of its origin (van Riet Lowe 1955:6, 15).

The key to value of specific material on beads is the ability of the investigator to interpret the findings. Beck (1931:236) comments that the lack of stone beads in an excavation may be due to a taboo on wearing stone, or possibly an inability to make them. Because beads "are subject to [so] many vagaries of custom and fashion" each area has to be analyzed separately before generalizations can be made (Schofield 1958:228). Data on the Yoruba that was researched for this paper will help substantiate this point.

THE YORUBA

The Yoruba, one of the three largest ethnic groups in Nigeria (Bascom 1969:1), seem never to have constituted a single political entity but a common origin and cultural heritage are indicated by their language, even with its many dialects, and by a cycle of myths and legends, such as the following myth of origin, with similar basic traditions (Smith 1969:10, 11).

Myth of Origin

Olorun, the sky god, gave to Orishala a five-toed chicken, a chain, and a snail shell containing some earth, and told him to go down and create the world. However, Orishala stopped at a party and became intoxicated. His younger brother, Oduduwa, having heard the instructions, went to the edge of heaven, descended the chain, and threw the dirt on the water. The chicken scratched the earth, spreading it in all directions to the end of the world (Bascom 1969:10). When Orishala awoke and claimed the earth, the two brothers fought. Olorun gave to Orishala the power to form human bodies and he became the creator of mankind. Oduduwa, creator of the earth, was given the right to own and rule over it. He became the first king of Ife (Bascom 1969:10) and later sent his sons to found kingdoms for themselves. He gave each son a beaded crown with a fringe which partially concealed the wearer's face (Smith 1969:109). This myth validates many elements of the customs and beliefs of the Yoruba (Bascom 1969:10), including the importance placed upon beads.

The Relationship of Beads to the Supernatural

Special colors and types of beads are associated with particular Yoruba gods, a practice begun by the deity Obalufon (Thompson 1971:8/1). The wearing of these beads varies according to locality (Frobenius 1913:194).

ODUDUWA. Worshippers of Oduduwa, creator of the Earth, wear no beads (Bascom 1969:81), but his priests wear necklaces of white beads (Talbot 1926:vol. 2, pp. 33–34).

ORISHALA. Worshippers of Orishala, creator of mankind, are distinguished by necklaces of many strings of small opaque white beads (Bascom 1969:81).

ORUNMILA. Orunmila, the god of divination, transmits and interprets the wishes of Olorun to mankind. His priests, (*babalawo*) wear distinguishing marks of office: "a wristlet of palm fibre, or of variously coloured beads round the left wrist" (Farrow 1926:104); the beads, according to Lucas (1948:180), would be white, blue, and red; according to Bascom (1969:80), usually alternating opaque tan and light green; or according to Thompson (1971:2/2), green and yellow, which the priests call "*tutu ati opon* – lit. cool and red (orange)".

ESHU. Sacrifices prescribed by the *babalawo* are taken to Olorun by Eshu, the divine messenger, whose worshippers and priests are identified by a string of small opaque maroon or black beads worn around the neck (Bascom 1969:79).

SHANGO. Another series of gods and goddesses exemplifies the relationship between deities and beads. The priests of Shango, god of thunder, wear necklaces (Ellis 1894:96) or wristlets of black, red, and white beads (Lucas 1948:181); his worshippers use red and white beads (Forde 1951:82). His priests demand the *Otutu* and *Opon* beads as part of the fee to initiate people into the mysteries of Shango worship (Johnson 1921:34).

OYO. The followers of Oyo, wife of Shango and goddess of tornadoes and thunderstorms, are distinguished by tubular maroon beads worn in strings around the neck (Bascom 1969:88).

OSHUN.   The worshippers and priests of Oshun, second wife of Shango, wear her "distinctive necklace of transparent amber-coloured beads" (Farrow 1926:65).

YEMOJA.   Yemoja, the mother of Shango, and the goddess associated with water, wears blue beads (Ellis 1894:44) or small crystal glass beads around the neck (Bascom 1969:88). Worshippers wear necklaces of small clear glass beads (Farrow 1926:47).

OLOKUN.   At Ife, Olokun is goddess of wealth, particularly of the glass beads which were manufactured there in great quantity. Among the southeast Yoruba, Itsekiri, and so on, he is the god associated with the sea and of imported wealth, especially Mediterranean coral beads (Fagg 1963:13).

SHOPONO.   The insignia of Shopono, the small pox, believed to be a demon who infests the world (Johnson 1921:28), are cowrie-shell bracelets and necklaces of small black disk beads made of palm-nut shells (Bascom 1969:92). His priests bury victims of the disease and demand as payment the green and yellow beads called *Otutu* and *Opon* (Johnson 1921:28).

YORUBA RELIGION IN CUBA.   Among the Yoruba in Cuba whose ancestors were taken there as slaves, the gods became identified with the Catholic saints, but beads of the proper colors continued to be worn by the worshippers. St. Barbara is Shango with red and white beads as her symbol; St. Teresita is Oyo who wears long maroon beads; Our Lady of Mercy is Orishala whose beads are white; the Virgin of Regla is Yemoja with crystal or blue beads; yellow beads belong to Oshun who is the Virgin of Cobre. These African traditions were strongest and purest in large urban centers where there were more worshippers and more money to carry on the ceremonies properly (Bascom 1951:14, 15, 19).

The Relationship of Beads to Political Status

The myth of creation with its account of the dispensation of beaded crowns provides the Yoruba with a sense of unity through common origin (Bascom 1969:10), validates the authority of the kings to rule, explains the primacy of Ife, the use of the beaded crown as a symbol of authority, and the distinction of rank between kings. Only those who allegedly derive from the sons sent out by Oduduwa may wear beaded crowns with fringes (Willett 1972:210).

It is not possible to determine how many crowned kings there were before the intertribal wars of the last century. Many kings assumed that status during these wars or were granted it by the British. Recently, for payment or favors, even town chiefs have been given the privilege of wearing beaded crowns. Formerly, if a town chief had worn a beaded crown without permission from the Oba to whom he was subject, it would have been considered treason (Bascom 1969:12). Restrictions had extended also to other beaded objects such as slippers and gowns (Forde 1951:20). The point is that it is the ambition of each Oba to wear the fringed crown, a strong visual sanction of his authority, and is considered to be powerful in its own right (Willett 1972:210).

THE OBA'S CORONATION.   The coronation and installation of a Yoruba Oba, considered to be sacred or divine, were solemn and lengthy rites (Smith 1969:110). The Alafin of Oyo, head of all the kings of Yoruba, was crowned at the shrine of Shango. Here he received the state dress: the royal robes; a special sword; a staff covered with small multicolored beads; and the *Ejigba*, a knee-length string of costly beads which represented the chain of office: "chains they say are for captives, hence they use beads." The crown was "artistically done" and "made of costly beads such as coral, agra, and the like, which in this poor country stands to the people instead of precious stones" (Johnson 1921:42–45, 51).

For a new Oni of Ife, a new crown was made, incorporating some beads from his predecessor's crown to preserve the link with Oduduwa (Bascom 1969:30). Nowadays crowns are made of multicolored beads of imported glass; formerly they were made of larger red beads of carnelian and jasper which came from Ilorin (Fagg 1963:26), or coral, tubular beads from the Mediterranean.

THE OBA'S DRESS.   Surviving bronzes and terra-cottas found at ancient Ife show kings with elaborate regalia. Dress was simpler than it is now, but personal ornaments were more elaborate with bead anklets and bracelets and a wide variety of flounced headdresses apparently of beads. The larger beads were usually painted red, evidently to represent the treasured jasper beads. Strings of small black beads suggest a possible veil of beads over the face. Paired badges, probably made of beads, appear. These are probably similar in function to the ones worn by chiefs in Ife today, although they are different in form (Fagg and Willett 1960:27, 28, 31).

Descriptions of actual dress which indicate the significance of beads to Yoruba rulers appeared in the nineteenth century. Clapperton (1829:37, 322) described the king of Oyo as wearing three strings of large blue cut-glass beads and trousers and cap ornamented with coral beads. The king requested a gift of large coral to be brought from England (1829:59).

Campbell, in the mid-1800's, said the king of Oyo wore a strand of large corals around his neck and always wore a crown of coral when he showed himself to the public. He described the Alake of Abeokuta as wearing a "costly necklace of coral and a double strand of the same ornament about his loins" (Campbell 1861:28, 29, 31, 95). A royal burial dated around the third quarter of the century contained the body of an Oba wearing a necklace of red stone beads and another of mixed blue glass and red stone beads (Willett 1960:10).

In the early 1900's, the headdress of a ruler of the Yoruba-related Ijebu is described as a tiara, formed of coral beads mounted on chamois leather. Coral was so greatly prized that the ruler wore a number of long strings of beads, and even coral on his legs in a style similar to the grieves of former ages (Lloyd 1960:62). In 1904 the Alake of Abeokuta visited London, wearing a crown covered with "thousands of multi-coloured beads", footgear "studded with beads", and carrying a scepter "covered in gaudy pattern with variegated beads" (Elgee 1905:393–394). Talbot (1926:vol. 3, p. 569) speaks of the Alafin of Oyo's traditional *Ejigba* and "high conical crown formed mostly of blue beads, some of which hung over and concealed the face".

THE OBA'S RELATIONSHIP TO THE TOWN.   The two institutions which domi-nated the precolonial political life of the Yoruba, the Oba and the town, were closely related (Smith 1969:107). Usually the town radiated out from the palace of the Oba. The status given a Yoruba town depended more upon the traditional prestige of the ruler than it did upon the size and population of the town. Differentiation was made between "crowned" or "capital" towns whose rulers wore fringed crowns and "subordinate" towns whose rulers could not (Krapf-Askari 1969:4, 26).

Beads in Relation to Age, Sex, and Status Roles

Beads were also significant in age, sex, and status roles among the Yoruba, but data is sparse and scattered.

STATUS.   While bodily decoration and clothing, according to Bascom (1969:99), were available to all who could afford them, beaded clothing was reserved for the king:

The wearing of beads distinguished chiefs and Obas in an unmistakable manner from the non-titled person, . . . Significant too was the part of the body on which the beads were worn. Crowned Obas not only wore beaded crowns with fringes but also strings of the barrel-shaped and round beads around the neck, wrists and ankles. A village chief was not entitled to wear a beaded crown but might wear beads around the neck, wrists and ankles. Many ordinary chiefs wore beads around the neck and wrists only, the number of strings and the shape reflecting their rank (Ojo 1966:259).

Clapperton says court etiquette allowed town chiefs who appeared in front of the king of Yoruba (Oyo) to wear "no beads, no coral, or grandeur of any kind" (Clapperton 1829:47). Among the Ijebu, the quality and size of coral beads was a sign of rank and wealth: important men would wear necklaces of one to four strings which reached to their navels; the king had a great many (Lloyd 1960:62).

By custom, when a slave was sold, his beads and clothing had to be removed and returned to the old master within twenty-four hours; otherwise the former master had a right to a part of the labor of that slave (Ajisafe 1971:64).

AGE AND SEX. Johnson (1921:100) said that both boys and girls under eight wore no clothes, but he does not mention ornament. According to de Negri (1962:10, 12), girls wore only waist beads until puberty, when they would be presented with a garment to be worn with the beads. At the present time waist beads are not so commonly worn, except by children.

Beads played a significant role when a woman was old enough to marry, forming a substantial part of her dowry and remaining an important part of her property (Johnson 1921:99). When she was married her parents would take her to the bridegroom's house dressed in costly clothes with "beautiful beads around her neck and waist" (Dennett 1910:166). If as a bride she satisfied her husband, presents were sent to her parents and she herself was covered with corals, other costly beads, and gold necklaces if obtainable (Johnson 1921:115).

Beads in Relation to the Economy

Limited information is available about local production of three types of beads and about the bead embroiderers.

PALM AND COCOA NUTSHELL BEADS. On the hip next to the body, women wore belts almost a meter in length, consisting of rounded beads made from the hard exteriors of oil-palm nuts (Hambly 1935:432). Cocoa nutshells were also used but valued less. The manufacture of beads from these was an important female industry (Johnson 1921:125) with some women devoting much of their spare time to their making (Fadipe 1970: 152). Each disk was flattened to a thin piece, then "rounded, perforated, and smoothed by rubbing on a stone covered with sand and water" (Hambly 1935:432). Oyo and Lanlate were prominent specialist towns (Ojo 1966:260).

STONE BEADS.   Evidence for red bead manufacture in ancient Ife is scanty (Ojo 1966:259–260), but data about their more recent production in Ilorin is available. The quartz was brought by traders from French territory, carried down the Niger by canoe, and then brought by head load or railway to Ilorin. The stone was gripped by the toes of the operator firmly against a cloth pad, chipped roughly into shape, drilled through with a palm-oil lubricated drill first from one end and then the other until the two met, rubbed across the grinding stone, and finally polished on a smooth board. Flaws were repaired with gum. The workers, all Yoruba, say their ancestors came from Old Oyo, their ancient capital. Clarke (1938:156) says men produced the beads but Daniel (1937:7–8) says the beadworkers were of both sexes.

Formerly these beads were very popular. Clarke (1938) describes an unbored plug to be worn in the earlobes, a pendant, and four types of beads, each having its own distinctive name. But demand for these indigenous beads diminished, which Clarke sees primarily due to a change in feminine fashion caused by the introduction of Christianity, which fostered a contempt of things connected with the old days, but both Wass (this volume) and Cordwell (1952) point out that changing modes of dress are inevitable among the Yoruba. By the 1930's the finished article was of little value, considering the extremely laborious process involved in making it. The guild in which the workers were organized broke down with the economic decline (Daniel 1937:8; Clarke 1938:156–157).

GLASS BEADS.   Glass beads were made in ancient Ife (Fagg and Willett 1960:27). Frobenius, the first European to report this possibility, had heard of a legendary old town, founded by Olokun, who had buried extremely precious beads in large jars for the people of Ile-Ife so they might grow rich and give greater sacrifices to the gods than did the rest of mankind (Frobenius 1913:306–307). With permission from the Oni of Ife to dig, Frobenius discovered bits of glaze and later entire jars glazed inside and out (1913:93), possibly used as crucibles in which to melt glass. Inside these were "glass beads, rings, irregular bits of glass tube, and always at the bottom a mass of fused bits of glass", in colors of "light green, greenish white, dark red, brown and blues" (1913:309). This glass might represent a completely indigenous product or reprocessed Portuguese or other European bottle scrap brought north from the coast and melted down (Cordwell 1952:341).

Glass bead manufacture seems to have been an important industry in Ife, for fragments of the crucibles are found all over that town (Willett 1967:106). The industry seems to have been long discontinued, the nature of the crucibles forgotten, and a supernatural significance attached to them. A complete crucible had been used to store beads at one shrine, and another was said to have been the drum of the creator of the Earth.

The discovery of these bits of glass led to the foundation of a new industry in Ife. The pieces were drilled to make beads (Fagg and Willett 1960:29).

BEAD EMBROIDERY. Bead embroiderers produce the crowns, caps and other beaded articles used by the kings and the *babalowo*, although some *babalowo* produce their own beadwork. The bead embroidering is done by men (Bascom 1969:102), perhaps because if women were allowed to do it, daughters might introduce it into the countries of their husbands. Workers carefully guard their beadwork designs, doing it either in the chief's palace or in the privacy of their own homes. It is believed that unauthorized workers would become deaf and blind (Mellor 1938:154). Cordwell, who interviewed three Yoruba beadworkers (1952:222–224), found that even though their income might be lower than that of other creative specialists, their aesthetic motivation was great. She suggests the beadworker's implied and expressed pleasure in their work might be based on the social recognition given them, for it is the beadworker who is sought by the chiefs to produce the work and it is he who arbitrates individuals' rights to use the work in particular forms.

The traditional style of crowns, of the Obas vested with the rights of the sixteen original kingships of the Yoruba, is a tall conical shape, with the bead designs on them appropriate to the ceremonies attended by the Oba. Thus one king may have as many of these traditional shapes as his office can afford; one with mask designs for the *egungun* festival (worship of spirits of individuals having supernatural or psychic powers when alive); one with birds marching up four sides of it, representing spirits of the mothers (see Drewal, this volume) or birds whose proverbs make a powerful protective medicine, or state crown designs for anniversary ceremonies — all with a veil of beads over the face. For modern, everyday use, the basic styles of these crowns have been a close-fitting cap, a pillbox form worn by some chiefs of Muslim faith, and another variation showing influence of Roman Catholic prelates. Deviations in the conical forms and in everyday crowns appear to have resulted from contact with European styles of headgear (see Cordwell 1979). The materials used in these crowns varied: cowrie shells, red jasper, coral, German glass beads, and small Czechoslovakian trade beads. The substitution of the valuable red jasper for cowries, which served as money and therefore represented wealth, may signify the retention of the association of power with richness of material (Cordwell 1952:218–222).

This manufacture of beaded crowns and coronets, the emblems of royalty and chieftaincy, is still practiced (Forde 1951:8), probably the only exclusively aristocratic art left in Ife (Willett 1972:213).

SUMMARY AND CONCLUSIONS

Because beads have been used by man for such a long time and over such a wide area of the world, their study can be very valuable in furnishing information about a culture: dating of finds, technological development, culture contacts, religion, aesthetic preferences, and social organization. Unfortunately this same pervasiveness also causes difficulties. Quiggin has said, "an extensive trade in beads spreading so widely, and over so many centuries makes identifications and dating peculiarly difficult" (Quiggin, 1963:41). Modern science is developing techniques which can be expected to contribute: microscopic analysis (DuToit 1965:12), spectrographic analysis (Fourneau 1955:16), and chemical analysis (Schofield 1958:181). Because of the variation in the usage of beads, each culture needs individual study to utilize fully the information which becomes available from authorities in different fields.

Among the Yoruba, beads serve many functions. Local bead production played a definite role in the economy. The individual expressed his or her personal, aesthetic preferences within cultural guidelines. The symbolism of beads: their color, material, size and shape, and area where worn on the body, helped the individual to communicate nonverbally his religious beliefs, either as worshipper or priest, and to establish identity, indicating sex, age, wealth, and status. Society used beads as symbols to provide a feeling of unity to the various subgroups; to validate the authority of the king; and to explain the differences in rank among the rulers and confirm their succession.

The changes in the shape and material of the symbol of Yoruba ruling power, the crown, indicate the "receptiveness to change and the emphasis on wealth and status, which are basic to Yoruba culture" (Cordwell 1952: 221–222).

REFERENCES

AJISAFE, A. K.
  1924   *The laws and customs of the Yoruba people*. London: George Routledge and Sons.
ARKELL, A. J.
  1936   Cambay and the bead trade. *Antiquity* 10:292–305.
BASCOM, WILLIAM R.
  1951   The Yoruba in Cuba. *Nigeria* 37:14–20.
  1969   *The Yoruba of southwestern Nigeria*. New York: Holt, Rinehart and Winston.
BATTELL, ANDREW
  1901   *The strange adventures of Andrew Battell*. Edited by E. G. Ravenstein. London: Hakluyt Society.

BECK, HORACE C.
   1928   Classification and nomenclature of beads and pendants. *Archaeologia* 77:1–76.
   1931   "Appendix I: Rhodesian beads from the 1929 excavations," in: *The Zimbabwe culture*. Edited by Gertrude Caton-Thompson, 229–243. Oxford: Oxford University Press.

CAMPBELL, ROBERT
   1861   *A pilgrimage to my motherland, an account of a journey among the Egbas and Yorubas of central Africa, in 1859–60*. New York: Thomas Hamilton.

CATON-THOMPSON, GERTRUDE
   1971   *The Zimbabwe culture*, second edition. London: Frank Cass. (Originally published 1931. Oxford: Oxford University Press.)

CLAPPERTON, HUGH
   1829   *Journal of a second expedition into the interior of Africa from the Bight of Benin to Soccatoo*. London: John Murray.

CLARKE, J. D.
   1938   Ilorin stone bead making. *Nigeria* 14:156–157.

COHN, J. C.
   1959   The bead collection of the archaeological survey, Johannesburg. *South African Archaeological Bulletin* 14(54): 75–78.

CORDWELL, JUSTINE M.
   1952   "Some aesthetic aspects of Yoruba and Benin cultures." Unpublished doctoral dissertation, Northwestern University, Evanston, Illinois.
   1979   "Human imponderables in the study of African art" in: *The visual arts*. Edited by Justine M. Cordwell. World Anthropology, The Hague: Mouton.

DANIEL, F.
   1937   Beadworkers of Ilorin, Nigeria. *Man* 37(2):7–8.

DAVIDSON, BASIL
   1972   *Africa, history of a continent*. Spring Books London: Hamlyn.

DENNETT, R. E.
   1910   *Nigerian studies*. London: Macmillan.

DU TOIT, A. P.
   1965   A preliminary survey of the beads of Ingombe Ilede, Northern Rhodesia. *Man* 65(3):11–15.

EISEN, GUSTAVUS
   1916   The characteristics of eye beads from the earliest times to the present. *American Journal of Archeology* second series 20(1):1–27.

ELGEE, C. H.
   1905   Ensigns of royalty in West Africa. *Journal of the African Society* (16):391–396.

ELLIS, A. B.
   1894   *The Yoruba-speaking peoples of the slave coast of West Africa*. London: Chapman and Hall.

FADIPE, N. A.
   1970   *The sociology of the Yoruba*. Ibadan: Ibadan University Press. (Originally published 1939.)

FAGG, WILLIAM
   1963   *Nigerian images*. New York: Praeger.

FAGG, WILLIAM, FRANK WILLETT
   1960   Ancient Ife: an ethnographical summary. *Odu* 8:21–35.

FARROW, STEPHEN S.
1926   *Faith, fancies and fetish or Yoruba paganism.* London: Society for Promoting Christian Knowledge.
FORDE, DARYLL
1951   *The Yoruba-speaking peoples of south-western Nigeria.* Ethnographic Survey of Africa, Western Africa 4. London: International African Institute.
FOURNEAU, J.
1955   Ancient glass-paste beads from Zanaga (Middle French Congo). *South African Archaeological Bulletin* 10(37):15–19. (Original French publication 1952. *Bulletin de l'Ifan* 14(3). Dakar.)
FROBENIUS, LEO
1913   *The voice of Africa,* two volumes. Translated by R. Blind. London: Hutchinson.
HAMBLY, W. D.
1935   *Culture areas of Nigeria.* Field Museum of Natural History Anthropological Series 21:3. Chicago: Field Museum.
HOBLEY, C. W.
1922   *Bantu beliefs and magic.* London: Witherby.
IBN BATTUTA
1929   *Travels in Asia and Africa 1325–1354.* Translated by H. A. R. Gibb. London: George Routledge and Sons.
JOHNSON, SAMUEL
1921   *The history of the Yorubas.* London: George Routledge and Sons.
JUNOD, HENRI-ALEXANDRE
1927   *The life of a South African tribe,* second edition, two volumes. London: Macmillan. (Originally published 1912.)
KRAPF-ASKARI, EVA
1969   *Yoruba towns and cities.* Oxford: Oxford University Press.
KRIGE, J. D., E. J. KRIGE
1963   "The Lovedu of the Transvaal," in: *African Worlds.* Edited by Daryll Forde, 55–82. London: Oxford University Press International African Institute.
LLOYD, P. C.
1960   Osifakorede of Ijebu. *Odu* 8:59–64.
LUCAS, J. OLUMIDE
1948   *The religion of the Yorubas.* Lagos: C.M.S. Bookshop.
MELLOR, REV. W. F.
1938   Bead embroiderers of Remo. *Nigeria* 14:154–155.
NEGRI, EVE DE
1962   Yoruba women's costume. *Nigeria Magazine* 72:4–12.
OJO, G. J. AFOLABI
1966   *Yoruba culture: a geographical analysis.* London: University of Ife and University of London Press.
QUIGGIN, A. HINGSTON
1963   *A survey of primitive money.* Northampton: John Dickens. (Originally published 1949. London: Methuen.)
RIET LOWE, CLARENCE VAN
1955   *The glass beads of Mapungubwe.* Archaeological Survey, Archaeological Series 9. Pretoria: Government Printer.
RYDER, A. F. C.
1969   *Benin and the Europeans 1485–1897.* New York: Humanities Press.

SCHOFIELD, J. F.
1958 "Beads: South African beads and their relation to the beads of Inyanga," in: *Inyanga, prehistoric settlements in Southern Rhodesia.* Edited by Roger Summers, 180–229. Cambridge: Cambridge University Press.

SLEEN, W. F. N. VAN DER
1967 *A handbook on beads.* Liège: Musée du Verre.

SMITH, ROBERT
1969 *Kingdoms of the Yoruba.* London: Methuen.

TALBOT, PERCY AMAURY
1926 *The peoples of southern Nigeria,* four volumes. London: Oxford University Press.

THOMPSON, ROBERT FARIS
1971 *Black gods and kings: Yoruba art at UCLA.* Occasional Papers of the Museum and Laboratories of Ethnic Arts and Technology 2. Los Angeles: University of California Press.

TWALA, REGINA G.
1968 "Beads as regulating the social life of the Zulu and Swazi," in: *Every man his way: readings in cultural anthropology.* Edited by Alan Dundes, 364–379. Englewood Cliffs, New Jersey: Prentice-Hall.

WILLETT, FRANK
1960 Recent archaeological discoveries at Ilesha. *Odu* 8:5–20.
1967 *Ife in the history of West African sculpture.* New York: McGraw-Hill.
1971 *African art: an introduction.* New York: Praeger.
1972 "Ife, the art of an ancient Nigeria aristocracy," in: *African art and leadership.* Edited by Douglas Fraser and Herbert M. Cole, 209–226. Madison: University of Wisconsin Press.

Symbol and Identification in North American Indian Clothing

EVAN M. MAURER

Amongst the native peoples of North America clothing has always served a complex function that is at once practical and highly symbolic. Articles of dress woven from native plants and animal hair or created from the prepared skins of animals were used throughout the continent to provide some protection against the elements, and to make the people's lives more efficient and comfortable in the variable climates in which they were forced to live and work at all seasons of the year. These native peoples were nonliterate communal groups who, through centuries of social development, came to utilize clothing as one of their principal means of visually communicating information about the groups to which they belonged as well as about themselves as individuals.

The concept of clothing as a principal vehicle of social and personal information presupposes a common level of understanding among the audience to whom the communication is being made. When a non-Indian audience is confronted by a beautifully detailed warrior costume from one of the hunting cultures of the Great Plains they usually admire the ensemble for its color, grace, and general bold effect. But few if any will have an idea of the many levels of direct and extensional information that such a costume contains about the spiritual beliefs and personal history of the individual who wears it. While general levels of symbolic information were sometimes shared by the various tribes of a particular region, we cannot assume even that a member of one Plains tribe would give the same interpretation to a common symbolic form as would one of their neighbors. Color symbolism is a good example of this strong degree of variability, as even closely related tribes such as the Lakota and the Cheyenne used different colors to denote the four sacred directions — one of the key forms of their symbolic code of visual communication.

The clothing produced by the tribal groups of North America must be conceived of as operating on several levels of symbolic information. A costume might indicate the specific tribal affiliation of the wearer and might also show if he belonged to a specific military or social group. Often the same garments could simultaneously provide specific information about the personal achievements of the individual as a warrior or as the recipient of unique and powerful sacred visions. On still another level the same costume could also convey a great sense of the wearer's pride and prestige as related to the fineness of his appearance. This last aspect of social prestige gained from the visual beauty and symbolically charged effect of a garment would also reflect great honor and peer status on the person who made or decorated the piece of clothing. Often the act of making a garment was believed to be under the guidance and protection of sacred powers who taught the people techniques such as weaving, or sent them inspiration for the conceptions of decorative forms and the perfection of their execution. In this system therefore, the maker as well as the wearer of a garment might share in the spiritual power and blessings that it represented.

The physical vastness of the North American continent and the great diversity of its natural environment is reflected in the cultural variation of large regional groups, tribes, and subtribal organizations that proliferated in all geographic areas of the country. Further complicating the task of organizing and tracing the development of styles and general motives of clothing and its decoration among these highly differentiated groups is the fact that must take into account the many regional migrations and frequent intertribal contacts that apparently had been going on long before Europeans invaded the Americas. As an example, one could cite the history of the Cheyenne nation which was forced from the western section of the Woodlands area around the early seventeenth century. The move meant adaptation to a new physical environment and, accompanied by their mastery of horses introduced by the Spanish, led to a new and rich culture as migrating big game hunters. This change also encouraged the development of a mobile warrior society whose courage and brilliant costumes became a romantic ideal of the white world from the mid-nineteenth century to our own time.

Any consideration of the nature of North American Indian clothing must acknowledge the large role played by the interaction with the invading white European culture. Like most preliterate, nonindustrialized societies, the world of the hunters and farmers of North America was greatly affected by the introduction and swift adoption of European materials and technology. Where peoples had for thousands of years clothed themselves with garments of their own making, the introduction of European woven cloth very quickly supplanted the use and eventually even the knowledge of how to prepare certain materials of native dress. The most obvious example of this phenomenon involved the tribes of the southeastern region of the United States. By the early 1830's, when McKinney and Hall produced their fascinating pictorial survey of Indian portraits from the Woodlands and southeast areas, the majority of the tribesmen illustrated wore garments of European cloth cut and sewn in imitation of European or white American models. The principal exceptions to this change in favor of the European style were the continued manufacture and use of fingerwoven sashes and garters (although utilizing imported wool) and the maintenance of traditional headgear and the soft-soled moccasin sewn from native tanned hides (Plate 1).

While the variance in style and basic look was often great, the general clothing types most commonly found among the tribes of North America can be reasonably organized into a small number of categories. Headgear in all areas of the country is usually limited in its use and almost always relates to male status in the community. Otterskin turbans with side drops are first illustrated on the warriors of the Mississippi cultures of the southeast around A.D. 1200–1600 and then became popular with the fighting men of the Woodlands and southern Plains three hundred years later (Plate 1). The common use of bird feathers in a wide variety of head decorations led to its becoming the iconographic symbol par excellence of the American native. As with the previous example cited, use of feathers was very often related to the status and achievements of males in the community (Plate 2).

The robe made from prepared animal skins or the blanket woven from animal hair or plant fiber is possibly the most ubiquitous garment of the North American tribes. It was worn by both men and women and often constituted the principal item of an individual's wardrobe. Skin robes are found in most parts of the country and could be made from deer or elk, or sea otter on the northwest coast, but most commonly were of buffalo hide left whole for winter use or used with the thick hair removed in the warmer seasons (Plates 3 and 4). Robes and capes of the wolf, bear, or mountain lion, however, were reserved for use by warrior societies or as symbols of a special power or medicine received in a dream or vision.

Shirts were worn by men during the colder months or for special ritual purposes usually associated with war. They were most often constructed from two skins of an antelope or deer. The natural shape of the skin was utilized in the garment so that the rear legs were sewn to make sleeves while the forelegs hung below the hem of the shirt as a decorative fringe. Decorative panels of the dyed and woven quills of the porcupine were often applied to the outer sleeve seams, down the front of the side seams, and in isolated motifs on the chest and back. Human and animal hair, furs, shells, and natural pigments were also utilized in the decoration of these impressive garments. Later, as in all elements of native dress, objects of European origin such as cloth and colored glass beads were used in combination with or in place of the natural decorative elements (Plate 2).

The most archetypical item of male dress was a simple breechclout worn between the legs and secured with a belt around the waist. It was considered a symbol of masculinity and is even worn by many Indian males today as an undergarment because of its intense cultural meaning (Plate 5).

Leggings of skin and later cloth were worn in the Woodlands, southeast, Plains, and Plateau regions and usually follow the same special uses and types of decorations that were described for shirts. While men's leggings were long and most often attached to the belt (Plate 5), women's leggings were knee length and were tied with decorated garters just below the knee.

The early European explorers recorded observations of native American women in dresses of one or two pieces that were either supported by straps or sewn over one shoulder. Such garments were reported from the east coast to the southwest, but in the northwest and west they were not used, as the women of those regions seemed to favor a skirt of skins or woven bark or grasses. Decorated versions of these garments often served as major symbols of female social prestige and in some cases personified important aspects of female sacred power (Plates 6 and 7).

The moccasin, a sewn, native tanned hide shoe with or without a hard rawhide sole, was the primary footwear of the American Indian. As was the case with all clothing types, the items used for everyday wear were usually unadorned, while dress or ceremonial moccasins could be highly ornamented with fringing, woven quills and later beads, fur, metal cones or tinklers, cloth, and natural pigments. Like other articles used also for ceremonial dress, the moccasin's decoration could carry symbolic information pertaining to its wearer. Along with the moccasin, the sandal was also in use in two very different areas of the country. In the southwest the ancient Pueblo peoples wove intricately patterned sandals in varied colors, while the tribes of the Pacific northwest coast were first reported to have worn open sandals made from the bark of the cedar tree — a natural fiber also used in capes, skirts, and hats.

To these basic types of clothing were added various accessories that completed the costume for both sexes. Major items among the many that could be included in this category are sashes, belts and garters, bags and pouches, and jewelry consisting primarily of hair ornaments, earrings, necklaces, armbands, bracelets, and rings. During the precontact epoch these items were produced from such natural elements as copper mined in its metallic state, seeds, dried hooves, feathers, stones, and varieties of shell both natural and worked. This last decorative element was one of the major trade items in ancient North America, sometimes being transported thousands of miles along trade routes that stretched from the Gulf of Mexico to the Great Lakes.

This utilization in clothing of elements from the animal, vegetal, and mineral worlds is an example of the extent to which the everyday life of the North American Indian was interrelated with the phenomena of their natural environment. They conceived of the natural world as being vitalized by spiritual forces equal to and in many cases more powerful than their own. Their spiritual goal was to live in harmony with the other elements of the natural universe by following long-established practical, moral, and social codes of their people. Respect for the earth and its forces was the foundation of their lives and communication with its motivating spirits meant life and power. This conceptualization of the elemental interrelationship of the sacred and the mundane worlds is reflected in the way native Americans incorporated natural elements in their costumes (Plate 8). When seen in full ceremonial clothing covered with direct and extensional symbols of spiritual power, the American Indian was truly a *Gesamtkunstwerk* in honor of man's harmony with the sacred forces of nature.

Among many North American tribal groups clothing has been used to indicate membership and rank in religious societies that have responsibilities on an individual and tribal level. In the Woodlands area around the Great Lakes the principal spiritual and healing complex is known generally as the Midéwiwin or Midé, a multigraded medicine society around which is centered the spiritual and physical well being and healing of the people. Each major grade of the Midé has its own animal symbols that appear on articles of clothing and accessories used in the group's rites and ceremonies. These can range from hats to breechclouts in the basic forms of clothing but are more commonly found on the many bags and pouches that hold the magical paraphernalia used by individual Midé members. The bags are carried during the ceremonies and thus by extension must be regarded as an integral part of the costume. One of the traditional forms of the bag is the pelt of the animal associated with the society grade level, the most common of which was the otter (Plate 9). The entire animal was used with decorations applied to its nose, paws and tail. Along with this direct use of an animal form as grade symbol there evolved a similar system of decorated skin pouches with woven and embroidered porcupine quill designs and bags woven of nettle fiber with designs in contrasting yarn made of dark brown buffalo wool. The two sacred animals most commonly depicted are the thunderbird, an eagle-like avian creature of great power, and the underwater panther, a horned feline who combines powers of both the earth and the waters. In all cases the bold, graphic design is arranged frontally in outline form. When worn or carried these decorated containers convey an important message proclaiming the status and power of the individual. By extension they are as well the visual symbols of the social, mythic, and spiritual structure of the tribe and as such confirm the essential role of the individual in the cosmic plan.

Plate 1.   Group of Sac and Fox chiefs, *circa* 1874–1877. Photograph by W. H. Jackson, Edward Ayer Collection, Newberry Library, Chicago. These Woodlands-Prairie men wear a combination of traditional and European clothing that shows the effects of material acculturation. The chief seated on the left wears a headdress made of a woven yarn sash, a deer hair roach and feathers. The hide leggings and moccasins are decorated with brightly colored floral beadwork with the large flaps characteristic of this tribe. The bearclaw necklace is the emblem of a proven warrior of great bravery and the cane, a cross-cultural status symbol. The chiefs to his left and on the far right wear otter fur turbans decorated with glass beads and silk ribbons. The leggings worn by the man seated second from the right demonstrate the movement of clothing items from one tribe to another either as gifts or war booty. They are not Sac and Fox in style or cut, but are most likely Pawnee, as indicated by the bottom tabs, hair fringe, and large panels of black and white bead decoration. The man on the far right wears a loosely fitted cotton shirt decorated with silk ribbon, a style still used by Woodlands and Prairie peoples today. Their blankets are all woolen trade items as are their shirts, or at least the cotton cloth used to make them

Plate 2.   Wiyakasha (Red Plume), Blackfoot, Lakota, photograph by W. H. Jackson, *circa* 1874–1877, Edward Ayer Collection, Newberry Library, Chicago. The eagle-feather war bonnet and hair-fringed shirt are hard-won symbols that proclaim this man's experience and success as a warrior and leader. He carries a wooden stemmed pipe and pipe bag across his lap which is covered by a buffalo robe decorated with lines of colored porcupine quills and tufts of woolen yarn. His painted face decoration could symbolize power received in a dream or vision, or maybe an aspect of secular, personal decoration

Plate 3. Group of five Pawnee chiefs of the Republican band. Photograph by W. H. Jackson, *circa* 1874–1877, Edward Ayer Collection, Newberry Library, Chicago. The man on the left wears a fingerwoven head sash also popular in the Woodlands. His blanket, and those worn by the two men on the left, are commercial trade items. The chief second from the left is wrapped in a buffalo robe and wears hide leggings decorated with beaded panels, probably of a dark blue background with yellow bear-paw motives, the symbol of one of the major Pawnee military societies. He and the last man on the right have loom-beaded garters tied below the knee. The central chief wears a headpiece particular to the Pawnee that may derive from the southeastern turban tradition. The bearclaw necklace is symbolic of great prowess and bravery as a warrior. His buffalo robe is painted with what is probably a boxed feather motif

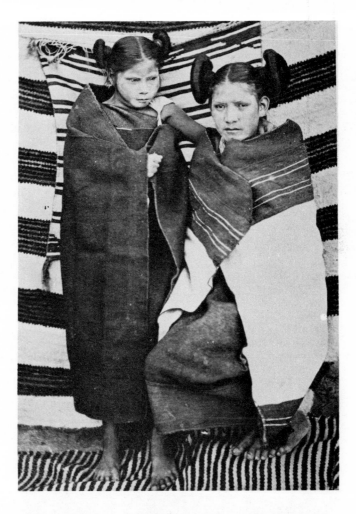

Plate 4. Two young Hopi Girls, *circa* 1885. Edward Ayer Collection, Newberry Library, Chicago. The premarital status of these girls is indicated by their double chignon hairstyle. They wear traditional Hopi dresses attached over the right shoulder and Hopi-style blankets

Plate 5.   Plenty Horses, Cheyenne, *circa* 1875. Edward Ayer Collection, Newberry Library, Chicago. This warrior wears the basic male costume of the Plains, breechclout, leggings, and moccasins. The former are made from stroud, the English woolen cloth manufactured specifically for the Indian trade since the seventeenth century. Leggings, pipe bag, and moccasins are decorated with another common trade item, the colored glass bead. He also wears armbands, bracelets, and rings made either from a copper alloy or nickel silver. Around his neck is hung a presentation peace medal struck with the image of one of the American Presidents

Plate 6. Dress, Lakota, *circa* 1860–1875. Logan Museum of Anthropology, Beloit College, Beloit, Wisconsin. This Plains woman's dress is adorned with a full yoke of blue, yellow, red, and green glass beads. The central design element at the bottom of the yoke represents Grandmother Turtle, an animal familiar in Plains mythologies associated with the powers of the earth. It is a basic symbol of female sacred power and is shown at the water's edge represented by the multicolored line above it. The large field of light blue symbolizes the lake with elements of the sky reflected in it

Plate 7.   Navajo woman, Juanita, *circa* 1875. Photograph by W. H. Jackson, Edward Ayer Collection, Newberry Library, Chicago. The southwestern woman wears a traditional two-piece woolen dress, which like her blanket is made from wool raised by her tribe. The colors of the dress are black and red while the blanket would be black, red, and white. Her necklace is most likely of turquoise and shell and she wears a leather belt decorated with Navajo-made silver ovals called *conchos*

Plate 8.   Pomo woman (California), *circa* 1890. Courtesy, Field Museum of Natural History, Chicago. This costume indicates the woman's wealth and status in the community. Her hat is of basketry, woven from grasses, fern, and other natural fibers. The major costume element is the hide skirt hung with long leather fringing. The body of the skirt is decorated with rows of clam and abalone shell, juniper seeds, and grasses reflecting their two main sources of food, the earth and the sea

Plate 9.   Midé bag, Winnebago, *circa* 1800–1820, Cranbrook Institute of Science. This exceptional example of the Woodlands area medicine society emblem is embellished with tabs of blackened buckskin decorated with colored porcupine quills, ribbon and small brass bells.

The Midé and its clothing concentrates to a large degree on individual rank, knowledge, and action, but other Native American groups' rituals subsume the single person into the whole. This is primarily achieved by the wearing of standard types of traditional costumes including elaborate masks which hide the individual's identity and complete their transformation from men into gods and sacred spirits. This phenomenon is best illustrated by the ceremonial life of two very disparate groups, the Pueblo farmers of the southwest and fisherman–hunters of the northwest coast.

Both groups have specific seasons when the great costumed public performances are held. In many agricultural communities of the arid southwest seven major ceremonies are conducted each year with the express purpose of assuring rain and the fertility and growth not only of the crops but also of the people and of the world itself. These ceremonies mark the appearance of the Kachinas, a large group of spiritual beings who represent almost all the important forces in the life of the people.

These beings are often associated with the Hopi people of northern Arizona, where, as in other Pueblo cultures, they are personified by members of male secret societies that are the principal ritual groups of the culture (Plate 10). Each of the approximately 260 Hopi Kachinas is recognizable by the specific details of a costume that generally includes a native woven cotton or wool kilt, shirt, sash, and belt (Plate 11). Body paint, hand-held objects and different costume accessories collectively help to differentiate one Kachina from another but the principal identifying factor is the painted mask worn by most Kachina dancers. Usually fabricated from leather or cloth it is often articulated by wooden facial features, additions of fur, feathers, branches, and most important, paint. Kachinas often appear in groups and it is not unusual to find fifty to seventy dancers in the same costume, their slow, repetitive dance filling the town plaza with the power and comfort of timeless ritual. Here the individual identity of the participants is forgotten as the community acknowledges their role and responsibility in performing the sacred rites that assure the harmony and continuance of their world.

In the area of the northwest coast the tribes were blessed with abundant food sources from the land, rivers, and sea. Their major tribal ceremonies were held during the winter months after the harvest had been gathered and stored. This was the time for the presentation of elaborate costumed dramas that depicted a complex of mythological stories about the creation of the world and the powers of the many spirit forces that affected the lives of the people. While these ceremonies held important secular meaning, their prime motive was the public performance of the sacred myths. In the great clan houses of tribes like the Kwakiutl (see Holm 1972) dancers would don the elaborate costumes and masks and thus be transformed for the ritual drama that stood at the very center of tribal life (Plate 12).

In an even more formalized manner the social structure of the northwest coast peoples is based on intricate forms of clan and family lineage regulated by both birth and wealth. Rank and privilege were proclaimed by song, speech, and costume in tribal cultures where relative status in the community was of prime importance. Whole costumes from headgear to leggings were decorated with a readable heraldic system based on familiar animals associated with clan symbolism, and personal, often inherited, spiritual relationships (Plate 13). Costumes were worn at the social and religious events that expressed their highly differentiated and formally structured society. As a new rank was achieved or a fresh honor bestowed upon an individual the concurrent rise in prestige and status was often marked by that person's right to wear another highly specialized symbolic garment. In this way the ownership and display of ritual clothing was literally the visual fabric of the social order.

Clothing as a symbolic form of group identification is also seen in the

Ghost Dance, a messianic, revivalist religion that became a strong force among the Prairie and Plains tribes from around 1872 to the early 1890's. At this time these people were coming under intense pressure from white settlers, herders, and miners who were the relentless vanguard of white America's political and economic expansion. During this period the tribes were brought under white control and restricted to reservation areas which effectively ended their traditional way of life. The Ghost Dance promised a last judgment when the Great God would punish the whites and drive them from the earth. At the moment of triumph the ancestors would be reborn and with them the great herds of buffalo, their staff of life, which had nearly been exterminated by the white hunters. This return to the days before the intrusion of the whites was symbolized by a return to the old ways including the abandonment of the dress and tools of the white world. The believers gave up wearing store-bought shirts, dresses, and trousers in favor of traditionally styled garments made from native tanned hides. Because the game that provided the hides was so scarce, many used white muslin cloth to create shirts and dresses in the traditional shape adorned with the fringing that was such a common early feature (Plate 14). Often these Ghost Dance garments were decorated with the images of animals and other natural forms that related to the prophesies and visions of the revival priests. Thus when faced with the crisis of losing the basic elements of their spiritual way of life the people sought a return to the old ways and symbolically expressed their return through the vehicle of clothing.

Clothing as group identification was not a new concept to the Plains tribes who had developed specific styles of dress and decoration that can be divided generally into regional areas, and for the most part into individual tribal styles (Maurer 1977). On an intratribal level there were even distinctions made among the various military societies that organized the vital hunting, police, and war activities of the people. These groups often wore or carried special garments or accessories that identified them as a member of a specific group (Plate 3). Amongst the Oglala branch of the Lakota tribe members of the Kit–Fox society wore necklaces and headbands made from the totemic animal as part of their "uniform". The same concept was followed in the Bull society of the Mandan where the men of the ranks wore a buffalo scalp with horns while the elite members of this graded organization wore helmet masks utilizing the complete buffalo head.

It is clear that in the complicated social systems of the native American peoples a symbolic garment could simultaneously stand for clan or other group association as well as for individual privileges and honors, for the two concepts were in many ways united. However, it is among the warriors of the Prairie and especially the Plains tribes that the concept of clothing as a vehicle of personal information is most strongly represented.

The men of these tribes were superb hunters and warriors whose prowess on foot and especially on horseback was the very basis of the survival of their people. This system evidenced a great deal of communal responsibility and work, but above all it glorified the achievements of the individual. Being preliterate societies these tribes, like all the peoples of North America, relied on the spoken word and the image to convey the essence of both myth and history. Just as a warrior would recount his successful adventures in great detail through oration and song, so would his clothing, its decoration, and his personal adornment proclaim these valorous actions (Powell 1977). Pictographs describing these important war encounters were drawn upon shirts, robes and even tepees and their interior liners (Plate 15). A general system of symbols that represented honorable activities such as leading successful raids against the enemy, stealing their horses, or receiving battle wounds were often applied to the clothing of warriors in much the same way as battle ribbons and medals are worn by contemporary soldiers. These decorations were a means of proclaiming a public message that brought honor to the individual as well as his family.

While the preparation and decoration of specialized warrior society gear was undertaken by the males, usually in association with their warrior society fellows, the production of decorated robes, garments, and even tents for holy men or sacred societies was restricted to female guilds (Marriot n.d.). Membership in these groups was only available to women of high moral standing whose skill at applying quilled decoration was inspired by sacred powers which they alone shared. Women of these guilds had great respect in the community and the production of each specially decorated robe was a signal event that brought new prestige and was in many ways treated with the same ritual honors afforded to acts of great courage performed by the warriors.

For all the tribes of North America the harmony of the natural and the human world was the essence of their being. This harmony was also a basic foundation of their social order, and it found an eloquent and beautiful expression in the magnificent garments which were the visual symbols of the structure, honor, and sacredness of their lives.

Plate 10. Sivu-i-giltaga Kachina, Hopi, *circa* 1950, Barry Goldwater Collection, Heard
Museum, Phoenix, Arizona. This carving represents a Kachina dancer in full ceremonial
costume. The small wooden figures are traditionally made for Hopi girls as part of their
religious training

Plate 11. Hopi man and boy, *circa* 1885, Edward Ayer Collection, Newberry Library, Chicago. The Hopi both wear the cotton and wool kilt and sash that the Hopi still produce for their own use and for sale as ceremonial costumes for other Pueblo peoples. The colors are white, black, red, and sometimes green. The smaller blanket behind them is also of Hopi design and weave

Plate 12.   Northwest coast (Kwakiutl) man in costume of the Hamatsa ceremony. St. Louis World's Fair, 1904. Courtesy, Field Museum of Natural History, Chicago. The major element of the costume is the large carved and painted wooden mask with movable lower jaw that represents the cannibal bird of this winter ceremonial. The rest of the costume consists of long, twisted strands of cedar bark

Plate 13.　Man modeling traditional northwest coast heraldic garb, (Tlingit), St. Louis World's Fair, 1904. Courtesy, Field Museum of Natural History, Chicago. This man's headgear is covered with white ermine fur and topped by walrus whiskers. The painted wooden frontlet is carved with the clan image of a raven and two anthropomorphic faces. The design woven into his blanket carries symmetrically arranged animal forms. In his hands he carries a wooden rattle carved in the form of ravens and a frog. The staff is also a status object and presents crests in the form of a sea lion, killer whale, devil fish, and dogfish

Plate 14.   Ghost Dance shirt, Arapaho, *circa* 1890. Kansas City Museum of History and Science. The form of this muslin shirt is directly copied from hide shirts worn in the prereservation days. The fringing itself is made of native tanned hide. The painted images relate to Ghost Dance visions of a return to the old days. The symbols are eagles, bear paws, trees, stars, and crosses

Plate 15. Painted buffalo robe, Pawnee, *circa* 1870. Edward Ayer Collection, Newberry Library, Chicago. This beautifully painted Plains robe portrays the combat triumphs of the warrior who owned it. The details of costume, hairstyle, and accessories are the visual symbols that proudly conveyed this warrior's personal history to all who saw it

REFERENCES

The Art Institute of Chicago
   1964   *Yakutat south: Indian art of the northwest coast.* Chicago.
BOAS, FRANS
   1895   "The social organization and the secret societies of the Kwakiutl Indians," *United States National Museum Annual Report*, (2):311–738.
CATLIN, GEORGE
   1973   *Letters and notes on the manners, customs and conditions of North American Indians*, 2 vols. New York: Dover. (Originally published 1841).
CONN, RICHARD
   1974   *Robes of white shell and sunrise.* Denver: The Denver Art Museum.
DORSEY, GEORGE A.
   1905   *The Cheyenne: ceremonial organization.* Field Columbian Museum Publication 99, Anthropological series 10 (1). Chicago.
FEDER, NORMAN
   1964   *The art of the Eastern Plains Indians.* The Nathan Sturges Jarvis Collection. New York: The Brooklyn Museum.

1971   *American Indian art.* New York: Henry A. Abrams.
FLINT INSTITUTE OF ARTS
1973   *Art of the Great Lakes Indians.* Flint, Michigan.
GUNTHER, ERNA
1966   *Art in the life of the Northwest Coast Indians.* Portland: The Portland Museum of Art.
1972   *Indian life on the Northwest Coast of North America as seen by the early explorers and fur traders during the last decades of the eighteenth century.* Chicago and London: University of Chicago Press.
THE HEARD MUSEUM
1965   *Kachinas: the Barry Goldwater collection at the Heard Museum.* Phoenix, Arizona.
1976   *Navajo textiles from the Reed Mullan Collection.* Phoenix, Arizona.
HOLM, BILL
1972   *The crooked beak of heaven.* Seattle: University of Washington Press.
HONOUR, HUGH
1975   *The new golden land.* New York: Pantheon Books.
HOWARD, JAMES H.
1976   Ceremonial dress of the Delaware man. *The Bulletin of the Archeological Society of New Jersey* 33.
LANDES, RUTH
1968   *Ojibwa religion and the Midewiwin.* Madison: University of Wisconsin Press.
MARIOTT, ALICE L.
n.d.   *The trade guild of the southern Cheyenne women.* Oklahoma Anthropological Society.
MAURER, EVAN M.
1977   *The native american heritage.* Chicago: The Art Institute of Chicago.
MINNEAPOLIS INSTITUTE OF ARTS
1976   *I wear the morning star: an exhibition of American Indian ghost dance objects.* Minneapolis, Minnesota.
POWELL, FATHER PETER J.
1969   *Sweet medicine. The continuing role of the sacred arrows, the sun dance, and the sacred buffalo hat in northern Cheyenne history.* 2 vols. Norman: University of Oklahoma Press.
1976   "They drew from power: an introduction to northern Cheyenne ledger book art," in *Montana: past and present.* Los Angeles: The William Andrews Clark Memorial Library.
1977   "Beauty for new life: an introduction to Cheyenne and Lakota sacred art," in *The native American heritage.* Chicago: The Art Institute of Chicago.
SHOTRIDGE, LOUIS
1919   War helmets and clan hats of the Tlingit Indians. *The Museum Journal* (University Museum, University of Pennsylvania) 10(1–2):43–48.
THOMAS, DAVIS AND KARIN RONNEFELDT
1976   *People of the first man: life among the Plains Indians in their final days of glory.* New York: The Viking Press.
WATERS, FRANK
1963   *Book of Hopi.* New York: The Viking Press.
WILDSCHUT, WILLIAM AND JOHN C. EWERS
1959   *Crow Indian beadwork: a descriptive and historical study.* Contributions from the Museum of American Indian/Heye Foundation 16.

Badaga Apparel: Protection and Symbol

PAUL HOCKINGS

In a society where all arts are either verbal or musical, dress takes on a peculiar significance as one of the few arenas in which the culture makes a visual statement about its social values. So it is with the Badagas: it is true that they have houses and temples, but these amount to a most rudimentary architectural statement, being in the one case utilitarian two-room huts and in the other mere copies of their ancient ancestors' square temples. Furthermore, what little painting and sculpture adorn their temples is the work not of Badagas, but of commercial artists or the Boyar stonecutting caste from the Madras plains. It is only in the distinctive costume of this refugee community that we find some sort of visual symbol of Badaga social history.

The Badagas first went to the Nilgiri plateau in South India late in the sixteenth century, following the collapse of the Vijayanagar empire. Their ancestors had been subjects of that empire while they were still living in the plains of southern Mysore, but political and economic conditions forced a move. Later more family groups took the same route to the hills, the final migrants settling there in the eighteenth century, during the Mysore wars and the associated ravages of Haidar Ali, Tipu Sultan, and their Muslim armies.

The Badagas' apparel (*parte*) offers a marked contrast with both the dress of their Hindu ancestors in Mysore and their tribal neighbors, the Todas (cf. Emeneau 1937). Tattooing and costume styles have been used by the community both to give it a distinctiveness and to change its identity for reasons of security.

The work on which this paper is based was supported in the field by the American Institute of Indian Studies. The author is also indebted to Whabiz D. Merchant for her critical comments. Photographs are by the author with the exception of Plate 3 by Bryan Alexander.

Clothing fulfills a number of functions in any culture — a fact that is repeatedly stated in this volume — and for southern India we may mention the following seven functions: to give warmth, to protect from sun and rain, to conceal the genitalia, to express the distinction between the sexes, to decorate the body, to express status and other social distinctions, and to give employment to those who elaborate and tailor clothing. In the latter part of this paper, I will postulate an eighth function: to symbolize affection, protection, and superiority, when clothing is presented to a relative or associate.

There may be as many as five phases in the production of clothing, that number depending on its material and elaboration. First, the raw material has to be killed, gathered, or cultivated, as the case may be; then it has to be processed, for example by decortication, maceration, or carding and spinning; next it may be woven into a cloth, and perhaps dyed; then it might be tailored; and finally the tailored garb can be decorated by embroidery, beadwork, or similar artifice. We should try to keep these stages in mind as we examine the ethnohistory of dress in this particular community of ancient Hindu refugees, even though the last two stages hardly enter into the preparation of their apparel.

It is said that before they left Mysore the Badaga women wore *saris*, several meters of cloth draped round the body, and men wore *dhotis*, shorter lengths wrapped around them as loincloths. These at least are the traditional clothes of men and women in the Indian plains, now worn with such extras as blouses, shirts, underwear and shoes. But only in the twentieth century have the Badagas reverted to this plainsman style of dress, and that in combination with certain European influences too.

Once on the Nilgiri plateau the settlers found themselves to be a social remnant, a few scattered families from farming castes (primarily the Okkaligas), and their immediate neighbors were the pastoral Toda tribe and the agricultural Kota tribe. The hierarchy of castes that they had known in the Mysore plains was no longer represented; indeed the caste and lineage units which had formed the framework of marriage arrangements were no longer viable, and new clan units had to be constituted within the Badaga community. At the same time one simple solution to the problem of finding spouses on the Nilgiri plateau was never attempted: namely intermarriage with the vegetarian Todas or the carrion-eating Kotas. The three communities have maintained their distinctiveness to this day, and are characterized by strict endogamy, separate languages, different economies, varying settlement patterns, and distinctive styles of dress.

According to legend the settlers in the eighteenth century, at least, fled to the hills because they were being pursued by Muslim soldiers who wanted to marry Badaga girls, some of whom were unusually fair and attractive. To avoid such a dishonor befalling a Hindu family, these refugees adopted a style of female dress that was seemingly copied from that of the low-status Kota tribe, and also tattooed the woman's brow (Benbow 1930:1–3; Karl 1945:1; Kariabettan 1958:6). This was not the only change in costume to be stimulated by the Muslims however; it is said of Tipu Sultan that, "seeing a Lingayat woman selling curds in the street without a body-cloth, he ordered the cutting off of her breasts. As a result of which act the wearing of long garments came into use among the whole female population of Mysore" (Thurston 1903:191). Word of this change in fashion, and of the fanatic prudery of Tipu, undoubtedly reached the Badagas, some ten percent of whom were Lingayats too. Yet they may have begun covering the breasts even before this gruesome event, simply on account of the cold weather at five to seven thousand feet.

TRADITIONAL APPAREL

For at least the past two centuries the dress of Badaga women has consisted essentially of three cloths. One is a triangular headcloth tied across the brow and behind the ears, and falling down behind over the hair and neck. It is worn by all married women. A second cloth is a loincloth folded over double, wrapped around the waist and falling to a few inches below the knees. Their dress is completed with the third cloth, half the size of the loincloth, which passes over the breasts but under the arms, and reaches to the waist: this cloth is kept in position by two red bands, two inches in width, one (*oḍekaṇṇi* or *sate*) passing over the upper chest and under the arms, the other (*puka:su*) going round the waist. Both are tied tightly, leaving the shoulders bare and creating a baggy effect in front below the bosom (Plate 1). One scurrilous folktale of the Todas has it that the Badagas are descended from a marriage with a female black langur, and that their women therefore have to carry a supply of leaves under these baggy upper cloths for their food supply. The cloths are nowadays of white cotton, although one occasionally sees a sky blue headdress, and forty years ago red ones were in fashion. A woman's adornment is traditionally complete if she has a small tattoo in the middle of her brow, a gold ring in one nostril, a pair of large gold earrings, and a gold chain round the neck which indicates her married status (Plate 2). Heavy brass bangles formerly adorned the upper arm, while bracelets and toe-rings of silver are still common (Ward 1880:lxxii; Shortt 1868:60; Rhiem 1900:508–509; Francis 1908:130; Thurston 1909:81; Tignous 1911:116; Benbow 1930:13–15; Verghese 1963:419).

In the 1930's a small number of women, who had been to high school or who had cultural contacts with Tamil women from the plains of Madras, began giving up this traditional white dress for multicolored saris. Today

Plate 1.   Badaga women in traditional dress

only the older Badaga women can be seen in their traditional dress. In the 1940's high-school girls began wearing jackets. Today at the English-language private schools in the Nilgiris one occasionally meets Badaga girls in full English school uniform, including a short skirt; and the word *miniskirt* has actually passed into the Badagu language, even though the article has never been seen in their villages. Since 1950 blouses covering the upper arms and shoulders have become popular. Another innovation is underwear: since the 1950's all young women have worn brassieres, and underpants are worn by all schoolgirls.

The basic dress of the men is a loincloth (*muṇḍu*) worn over a breech-clout that is kept in place by a string around the waist; the doubled-over loincloth reaches to the ankle, but is commonly pulled up to the knees. A cloak or blanket is wrapped around the upper part of the body, and a turban of cotton or silk sits loosely around the head (Plate 3). Tradi-tionally no footwear was worn, for fear of offending the deity they walked upon; but in the nineteenth century men began wearing leather boots and sandals which had been purchased. Men's shoes came into use early in the present century. A distinctive pair of gold earrings, perhaps a silver

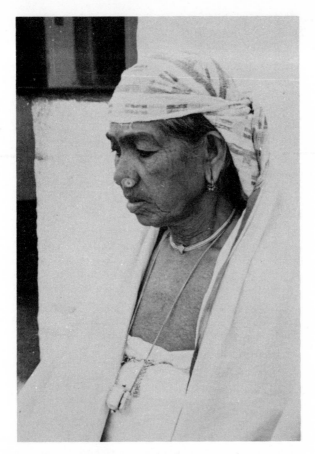

Plate 2. Lingayat woman wearing *ta:li* and *liṅga*

finger-ring, and an umbrella or walking stick complete the men's apparel. The elaborately embroidered Toda cloak, *pu:txuḷi* in Toda, *pugaru si:le* in Badagu, is also favored by older men, and is virtually a mark of office for village headmen. At the turn of this century men started wearing European-style jackets and trousers; but before that they had adopted shirts, which hang outside the loincloth (Plate 4); Kashmir shawls in red, orange, green, or blue wool have also been popular with the men since the 1920's. "Pork-pie" caps, colored nightcaps, and "Gandhi" caps have likewise been fashionable alternatives to the turban for some time. By mid-century the pubic-cloth was giving way to cotton shorts or Western-style underpants, except among older men (Ward 1880:lxxii; Shortt 1868:60; Grigg 1880:220; Francis 1908:130; Thurston 1909:81; Tignous 1911:116; Vivekanandam Pillai 1937:247).

This account of Badaga appearance will not be complete without some

Plate 3.   The Badaga paramount chief

further notes on body ornaments. Men as well as women usually wear gold earrings, which are still made from melted gold sovereigns. Women also have gold nose-rings, always worn in the left nostril. Gold, silver, or brass armlets may be worn by women just above the right elbow. Numerous silver, gold, or glass bangles will be on the wrists; men too wore a silver bangle and silver or copper toe-rings until fifty years ago. Silver or steel rings are worn on the fingers of both sexes (Thurston 1909:81–82). Necklaces of great variety are also favored by girls. In general, where gold ornaments are too costly, women wear them in filigree silver, brass, copper, iron, or steel instead (Grigg 1880:220). Badagas believe that if a person wears gold, the length of his lifetime will be greater. One might think that wearing gold invited theft, but in fact it seems that this did not often occur amongst the Badagas. Throughout the nineteenth century men, when traveling from village to village, carried a walking staff with a small ax head in lieu of a handle, for protection. When, however, they were to walk to the plains on a trading expedition, prior to 1825, they would first divest themselves of all ornaments, including even their silver waistbands and any richly made cloak. They were clearly very much

Plate 4.   Normal town dress for men

afraid of brigands, even though the men traveled in groups of up to a hundred.

This still does not complete the list of ornaments, however. Priests wear a silver ring during each festival. Some of the headmen wear gold or silver "rings of office" on their fingers, given their ancestors by East India Company officials or even earlier chieftains of Mysore. The headman of Ke:ti wears one called *sinaganige*, which his ancestor seems to have taken from another Badaga headman after a hand-to-hand fight. It is now worshipped in his home every Monday. Such rings can always be given as security against a fine, and are conventionally worth a thousand rupees in gold coins. Women who go barefoot — still the great majority today — wear silver rings on three or four toes of each foot (in Southern India slippers are associated mainly with Muslim women and Hindu dancing girls).

Until the 1930's it was the custom for men to carry noncollapsible umbrellas made of palm leaves on a cane frame (such umbrellas can still be seen in Kerala occasionally). Since the Nilgiri plateau is very wet for part of the year, these or their more recent Western equivalents often substitute for a walking stick. Until very recently it was thought disrespectful to the men for women to carry umbrellas, so they did without. Conversely men, particularly on formal occasions, carry umbrellas to emphasize their respectability; and men supervising festivals carry staffs to help achieve the effect of authority.

THE SUPPLY AND CARE OF CLOTHING

Each person was thus wrapped in a total of eight to ten meters of cloth. Where did it come from? The Badagas themselves did not have specialized castes: there were no weavers, blacksmiths, washermen, or other craft specialists, as one usually finds in caste society, for all were farmers. Even so, the lowest of the phratries of the Badagas, a group called Toreyas, are reputed to have woven cloth in the nineteenth century (Harkness 1832:31), and before that time, that is, before the British opened up markets in the area, cloth was being woven in certain other Badaga homes. But this was not the only cloth available, for trading expeditions went to the market towns of the plains once or twice a year and bought calico, the local cotton. When political conditions made such expeditions too dangerous, however, the homemade cloth was always a stopgap. It was made from the fibers in the large aloes' leaves, or the fibers of two Nilgiri bushes, hoary basil, *Ocimum canum*, and more commonly the harmless nettle, *Debregeasia velutina*. The possibilities of this latter plant were well known, for its fibers were widely used in South India for fishing lines and bowstrings. It is said that the people of Nañjana:ḍu used to specialize in making the cloth, perhaps because they had access to the necessary bushes, and that they used to barter it to other villages in return for grain. Even when markets had opened up and cotton cloth could be bought, some Badagas still continued to use this fiber for stitching old clothes. The fiber, called *mañji*, lent its name to the cloth made from it. Even today, when no one would dream of going to the trouble of preparing such cloth, a small piece of the fiber is still given as a ritual present to a dead woman by her father or brothers during the funeral.

The *mañji* fibers were obtained by decortication of the bark or maceration of the aloe's leaf. Four pegs were then driven into the ground, fibers stretched from one to the other to form a rectangle, and then on this simple frame a warp was laid in one direction and the weft threaded in from the other. The cloth was thereby woven without a mechanical loom (Belli Gowder 1923–1941:2, 3, 9).

The concept of starching clothes to make them stiffer and resistant to rain has long been known to the Badagas, and was probably first used by them as a means of strengthening their *mañji* cloth (Ward 1880:lxxii; Grigg 1880:220). Before Badagas could get soap, in the nineteenth century, they used to boil their clothes in a large water-pot, adding ash and some kind of mud to the water. Later the clothes lay on the grass to dry, while a starchy paste was made; some little millet, *Panicum miliare*, was boiled in water, and stirred with a stick, till the sticky residue could be sprinkled on the clothes that were drying in the sun. Large cloths such as cloaks would be stretched out by two women while a third applied the paste, and girls would at the same time be given instruction in these techniques. No boards or other ironing equipment were used.

There are numerous rules governing the wearing of clothes. One is raised to the formality of a proverb, with many implications: "If you wear your brother's cloth, it is as if you dressed yourself up in a tiger's skin." Less comprehensible perhaps is the rule about wearing new clothes on a Tuesday. If some special occasion obliges a person to wear his new cloth on a Tuesday, he will at least briefly put it on the day before too. Otherwise, it is said, he will not get another new cloth until this one is torn or completely worn out: Tuesday is not in general an auspicious day.

Prior to the education and higher standards of the present century Badagas changed and washed their clothes each Monday, the weekly holiday. Women generally change their clothes in a diminutive bathroom; men change wherever they wish to, even outside their houses. In early days when very poor women had no change of clothes, they would wash one body-cloth first, dry it, then put it on and wash the cloth it replaced. The women may wash the clothes of both sexes, but Badaga men only wash male items. Men's and women's dirty cloths, other than menstrual clothing, may be mixed together, and even the latter items may be carried home along with men's clothes once the washing is completed.

LIFE-CYCLE RITUALS

Childhood Rituals

Badaga apparel changes to some extent as the individual passes through the various phases of a lifetime. The need for clothing for infant warmth is emphasized by a proverb: "The child will grow fast by old rags, and the buffalo will grow fast by dung." It means that a child needs only rags to keep it warm if it is to grow, whereas a buffalo needs the dampness of an uncleaned pen to grow up in. For this reason a woman keeps all old rags for her child, even from the third month of pregnancy, otherwise they are kept for use at menses, or as bandages. For the first six months, before the baby begins to crawl, it is kept bundled up in rags: cotton cloth folded to eight or ten thicknesses for greater warmth. It is thought that if the child's temperature is kept high he can lower it, but if it gets too low he cannot raise it. In the past poor boys wore nothing at all until they started school in their seventh year; and similarly girls went nude until their fifth year. Thereafter both sexes would wear at least a loincloth, although they would still sleep naked. At an early age however the boys of wealthier families were given a loincloth made of half a cloak. A half-cloak (*o:gutu*) might even be worn by very poor adult men: it was made by splitting a cloak lengthwise down the middle. Only old cloth is used for small children, and if someone were to give a child a new cloth it would first be worn or rubbed on a parent's body "to make it old": this apparently reflects a widespread belief that death can be cheated if the infant looks like "rubbish". Today girls and boys wear vests and pants or long skirts from the age of one or two years. Even so, it is clear that all children have become social beings — have been through a naming ceremony which *inter alia* entitles them to a funeral — before they don any clothes. At that ceremony the mother's brother or else the mother's father gives the infant a pair of gold, silver, copper, or iron bangles. Another iron bangle is given for the left wrist by the Kota tribesman associated with that family. A rich mother's brother will also give the baby a pair of anklets, a chain necklet, and a waistband of silver or gold thread. For a baby girl there will be a flat, leaf-shaped silver pendant hanging down from the band to cover her pudenda; possibly this is a relic of female dress in ancient times. The first clothing a child receives, other than the rags he has been bundled in since birth, is a gift from the mother's brother at the naming ceremony: it is minimally a towel or kerchief — as a proverb points out, "It is a turban, whether it goes once or ten times round the head."

Small children go through an ear-piercing ceremony. Sharp earrings of gold or silver, also given by the child's mother's brother, are thrust through the earlobes by one of his parents, after the rings have been touched by the oldest male relative present and then by the mother's brother — who is considered the child's spiritual adviser. This ceremony is commonly done, for convenience, on the same day as the first shaving of the child's head: both should be done to children of both sexes.

Badaga children traditionally had a distinctive haircut, which set them apart from childen of other Nilgiri communities. The entire crown of a girl was shaved, but with long hair left hanging down the sides of the head; after the age of ten her hair was allowed to grow back. Boys grew hair on the crown, but had it trimmed off the sides (Thurston 1909:75; Tignous 1911:119; Benbow 1930:15). Women grow their hair long, and knot it loosely on the nape of the neck, where, once they are married, it is usually covered up by the ends of their headcloth (Shortt 1868:60).

Since we have been describing for the most part traditional Badaga appearance we should perhaps make mention of female tattooing. This was a matter of some historical importance, since according to legend the tattooing was adopted by Badagas when they fled into the hills from

Muslim pursuers: it was felt that the tattoos would make the women look like tribals, and not the caste Hindus they certainly had been previously, and so they would cease to be tempting to Muslim men. While this may well have been the case, tattooing subsequently became a mark of female maturity; young women today rarely have tattoos, however, in part because of the pain involved but more because of the "backward" implications. Tattooing marked the fact that a girl was approaching marriageable age. Today when girls may wait till sixteen or eighteen before marriage it no longer has such a relevance, and is seldom performed.

No ceremony is involved in tattooing. It is done to girls aged eight to eleven, whenever convenient for a tattoo artist — often an itinerant woman from another caste. The designs are stereotyped, but may vary with a girl's wish. Essentially though they form a cluster of simple marks in the center of the brow, and a horizontal line beside each eye. Sometimes a design is added to the back of the hands; and in earlier times it was usual to have double rows of dots around the upper arms, clusters of dots on the shoulders, stars or other devices on the right forearm, a spot on the chin, and a double row of dots across the upper chest (Jagor 1876:195; Grigg 1880:220; Rhiem 1900:504; Thurston 1909:81–82). Although tattoos are now done with a needle and ink, the traditional material was a mixture of soot and rust scraped from the bottom of a cooking pan, to which water was added, perhaps with some millet starch (Thurston 1909:82). Before needles were readily available in the villages, a spine of the Bengal currant (*Carissa spinarum*), or the common Nilgir barberry (*Berberis tinctoria*), was used to puncture the epidermis.

Boys are not tattooed. There is nonetheless one situation in which their bodies are permanently scarred. At about the same age that girls are tattooed, boys are branded on the shoulder and forearm, this being believed to give them strength in their future milking and churning activities (Thurston 1909:83).

About a tenth of the Badaga population is Lingayat, that is, adherent to a sect which worships Shiva as the supreme deity, and reverences him in particular in the form of a *liṅga*, a phallic emblem which Lingayats, unlike other Hindus, wear on their bodies. Vegetarianism and extreme personal purity are expected of those who in effect become vehicles of the god by wearing this emblem.

A *liṅga* is given to a Lingayat boy at about his thirteenth year — or certainly an odd-numbered year, and on the night of the Śivaratri festival. This is not the place to go into details of the initiation ceremony, but some salient features should be mentioned (cf. Natesa Sastri 1892: 758–760; Miles 1933:73). The small personal liṅga, made of four sacred substances, is wrapped in a cloth at the time of the initiation and tied around the youth's neck. For a year thereafter the liṅga is worshipped morning and evening, and worn in this cloth. During that period the youth may not marry. But after a year he can wear the emblem in a silver or gold case (*karaṭakke*) which is hung on a string around the neck. There are in fact two types of case, differing in shape, which are intended for the two sexes. Women are often not given a liṅga until menopause, however, and do not go through the initiation ceremony just mentioned (see Plate 2).

One Badaga clan, the Kaggusis, think of themselves as Lingayats but are not accepted as such by the others. Instead of a liṅga, which is manufactured at a Lingayat monastery in Mysore, and which would not be supplied to the Kaggusis, they wear a sacred thread on which is strung one *rudrakśa* bead, the hallowed fruit of *Elaeocarpus ganitrus*. To this they do worship in the usual way each morning and evening. All boy Kaggusi babies receive the bead and string at the annual Great Festival (*doḍḍa habba*) held in the first year of their lives. It thus does not indicate initiate status so much as membership in the Kaggusi clan.

Marriage Rituals

A girl's maturity is marked by physical changes rather than a ceremony of initiation; unless one were to think of her marriage as a kind of initiation ceremony. Since Badaga villages had a menstrual hut, and some still do, a girl would go thither at the first signs of menstruation. After remaining there three days she should take a bath, throw out her old clothing, put on a set of fresh clean clothes and cut her fingernails (Belli Gowder 1923–1941:3–4). The girl should only enter her home after seeing the stars in the sky, on a Monday, Wednesday, or Friday evening; as she crosses the threshold she puts the right foot down first — all this to promote auspiciousness. She enters the house as an adult woman, and the mark of this is that now, for the first time, she is wearing the woman's headcloth. Modern girls using a sari put the end of it over their heads on this occasion. The new clothes are a gift from the girl's father (Samikannu 1922:32; Miles 1933:73–74).

The Badaga wedding, like any other, is an occasion for distinctive dress for the young couple and new dresses for all of the other participants. The ceremony is quite a complex one, but here we need only mention those aspects relating to the appearance of the people involved. The betrothal is signaled when a woman from the fiancé's party ties an ornament (*uṅgaramane*) around the betrothed girl's neck. Minimally, for the wedding, the bride puts on clean white clothes of the kind a woman normally wears, and traditionally she would have added a turban. But she is also given jewelry and several new cloths or saris by her parents, her mother's brothers and mother's mother. In walking to her new home the bride wears her father's present, but carries her old dress in a bundle and gives it to her husband's mother.

This wedding is not the only major rite in a marriage, for it is followed by a second ceremony about seven months later, once it is clear that the bride is pregnant. This is done on an auspicious day, usually a Wednesday or Sunday, and again the bride and groom put on new clothes. From this time the bride wears the marker of a wife, for her husband asks her father thrice if he may tie the *ta:li*, and then places this gold marital necklet around her — which she wears ever afterward. He is provided with the necklet by his mother. During this ceremony the groom wears a turban, "otherwise people will consider it a funeral". In other words, the groom is not removing his turban out of respect to anyone. His turban, shirt, and loincloth, and perhaps a wristwatch, are gifts from the bride's father.

It used to be the rule that until this "seventh-month" ceremony, the girl's father supplied all of her clothing requirements; but that afterward it was her husband's duty. The meaning is clear: the bride can be returned to her father's house if she does not produce children, and she would not be bringing anything of her husband's back with her. A curious feature of such a divorce, for that is what it is, is the financial transaction involved. The groom's family pay a nominal "bride-price" of two hundred rupees, in gold, which has to be returned to them in the event of a divorce. If that money is returned, however, the sum of 1.25 rupees, five small silver coins, is deducted from the bride-price as the nominal cost of the clothes the girl has brought to the groom's home.

A similar return of apparel occurs if a young widow wishes to return to her parent's home or to remarry. She must then pay a visit to her former husband's family, wearing a *savari* in her hair. She returns the *savari*, a bundle of human hair 50 to 75 centimeters long, and also all of her jewelry, to the dead man's family, even though at least some of it was given by her own father. Her affines bless her, give her a meal, present her with some new clothes, and often say she can keep the jewelry. In a similar fashion a widower has to present a turban to his former wife's family and obtain their blessing before he can remarry (Harkness 1832:115–116; Rhiem 1900:504–505; Tignous 1911:119; Samikannu 1922:32–33; Belli Gowder 1923–1941:5–6; Benbow 1930:17; Ranga 1934:3).

With the transfer of clothing gifts at the time of a wedding, we get to a point in the lifetime of an individual where his position in Badaga society is being clearly defined, albeit through the symbolic offer of protection and adornment that these obligatory gifts seem to represent. Figure 1 shows the principals at a wedding, with broken lines representing the flow of clothing or jewelry.

These prestations make a statement about status differences within the Badaga family that are crucial. In each case a gift of clothes or adornment passes from someone superior to someone inferior, either by reason of sex (mother's brother, father, husband's father) or of generation level

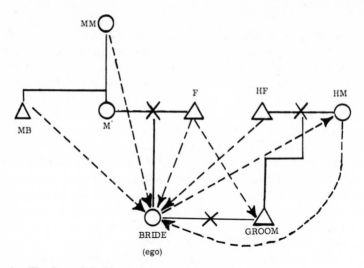

Figure 1.   The flow of clothing and jewelry at a Badaga wedding.
Key: F, father; M, mother; MB, mother's brother; MM, mother's mother; HF, husband's father; HM, husband's mother

(bride's mother's mother, bridegroom's father), or of both (bride's mother's brother, bride's father): these are the major determinants of status in the society. The only seeming anomalies in this pattern involve the husband's father's gift to the bride, and her return gift of old clothes to his wife. Let us therefore look at these items more closely.

The groom's family, that is, the husband's father, gives an *uṅgaramaṇi*, a gold necklet, to the bride-to-be. This is worth two hundred rupees, and is not exactly a bride-price: informants told me they wanted the bride to enter the groom's house looking suitably affluent, and hence made the gift — gold, be it remembered, brings health and good fortune to its wearer. Since the necklet is to be returned if divorce occurs, it is little more than a loan to the bride by her affines. But what of the old clothes given to her husband's mother by the new bride, seemingly a most demeaning present and one that is in no sense equivalent to the gold *ta:li* that passes in the opposite direction by way of the groom? It will be remembered that a newborn baby is wrapped in cloths that cannot be new. I postulate that the intention of the bride's gift is to signify that a baby is to follow, and the husband's mother should keep these old clothes to swaddle it in: it is she, after all, who will nurse it much of the time. Probably these are the clothes for which the 1.25 rupees are deducted from the two hundred rupees returned at the time of a divorce.

One last point remains to be made about this pattern of marriage prestations: a father is not obliged to give his son anything when the latter marries. This has to be seen against the fact that marriage is patrilocal: a son brings his bride from her village to live thenceforth under his father's roof. Traditionally Badagas have lived in a patrilineal joint family system. But if the father gives his son nothing at marriage, no reciprocal inferiority-superiority relation is then expressed; and that surely is the essence of the marriage: the son is the social equivalent of his father, wears a turban in the house in his presence, and indeed by this marriage ensures the persistence of the patrilineage for another generation. He will take over his father's position in due course, and inherit some of his property too.

The gift from the mother's brother to a bride marks the penultimate phase of a long and close relationship. All children, of either sex, regard their mother's brother as their guru or spiritual guide: in this sense he becomes a kind of father to them, although he is in their matrilineage. The gift he makes at a niece's marriage amounts to a debt which she has eventually to repay; and she begins to do so at a short once-in-a-lifetime ceremony.

Once the former bride has some children she can be considered permanently settled with her husband. She can then think about doing the ceremony for the eldest living mother's brother who was her guru; but as often as not the matter is left too late, and the now aging woman performs the ceremony with her guru's son instead. About eight days beforehand she sends a message to the guru or his son that she is coming; then she dresses up well, and walks to his village, taking at least one of her male children with her. Interestingly, a barren women still takes a boy, perhaps a stepson borrowed from a junior wife, to signify that she is permanently in her husband's household. When a woman was a child, she called the mother's brother guru; now that he is old and she married, she calls him *ma:va* [uncle]. On arriving, she must give him a token gift (*ka:ṇike*) of 1.25 rupees, and may also add an extra five or ten rupees as a more substantial voluntary gift. She is also obliged to bring him at least one piece of cloth, generally a turban, loincloth, or cloak. This does not end the exchange however, for the mother's brother must in return give a piece of cloth to his niece and another to her son. If he can afford it he will give the woman a costly dress, or perhaps a pair of earrings, a calf, or even a cow. The imbalance created in the past by the man's giving of guidance to the little girl and cloth to the bride is thus not righted by her gift; yet this ceremony is commonly the last formalized relation between the two until the woman attends her uncle's funeral.

What is the meaning of maintaining this imbalance in gift-giving? It is probably to be explained by Badaga marriage patterns. The Badagas favor cross-cousin marriage, and the best arrangement is considered to link a man and his mother's brother's daughter. An acceptable alternative would however be a mother's mother's brother's son's daughter. From the point of view of the boy who is taken by his mother to exchange gifts with the old man — or equally his son — that boy is being introduced to a lineage where he could find just such an acceptable marriage partner in the near future. His taking of a girl in marriage from that matrilineage could be seen as righting the imbalance in the next generation by taking the girl off her parent's hands. The various gifts made on this occasion are not returnable at a later time: they are a type of prestation called *summu*. Its amount can clearly vary, the prestige for the uncle's family being higher if something really valuable is given to the woman. As an example, I may mention that an informant's wife was to visit her guru when he was a poor man. Prior to the visit, therefore, my informant arranged with his wife's uncle that she would present him with a magnanimous 101.25 rupees, a turban and a loincloth; and in return for all this the guru would give the woman an unfortunate cow worth only sixty or seventy rupees.

Funerals

We now come to consider by far the most complex of all Badaga ceremonies, the funeral; and again will dispense with a description of the public display of the corpse and the cremation that follows. For purposes of the present study, we must concentrate on the various items of adornment and clothing that are given to the corpse, and on the relationships of the donors to the deceased individual. There are in fact four types of material goods that are presented to the dead during a funeral: clothing, jewelry, tools or weapons, and foodstuffs.

If the deceased is male, he is given new clothes for the funeral by his own family; if it is a woman, she is given a new loincloth, upper cloth, head cover *and* turban by her brother, father, or a more distant agnatic relative. While both sexes are covered with a cloak, only female corpses receive a *banna:*.

The banna: cloth, even if only a small piece, has to be provided by the brother of a dead woman, or else by her father if he is alive. It must be of colored cloth, for it symbolizes the saris the women used to wear before coming to these hills (Belli Gowder 1923–1941:8). It is torn a little way down the middle so that it will pass over the head and the two ends fall over the shoulders. It is said the cloth is worn to signify that even in the place where the woman is cremated, or buried, as is the Lingayat practice, she has a consanguine relation. In preparing the female corpse, an embroidered cotton cloak (*pugaru si:le*) is wrapped around the body and over the ends of the banna:, but previously the cloak has been torn in two, and one half, which is left on the cot where the corpse lies, is later taken as payment by the man who carries this cot back to the village when the cremation is over. Since it is considered more important than the cloak, the latter must not be given until the banna: has already been presented to the corpse; the male donor takes precedence over the female in clothing the deceased.

This cloak is supplied for the funeral by the daughters of the dead person, and their husbands, thus several may be brought, although it is essential only for the eldest daughter to do so. More usually they will split the cost, or else agree that one daughter brings the requirement for one parent, another for the other one. There is no taboo against a man seeing the cloak his daughter has obtained for him; indeed, if it is a nice example of Toda embroidery, she might bring it to her father when he is sick, and tell him he can keep it if he gets well and she will obtain another for his funeral. An important distinction however is that the end of the cloak with an embroidered pattern (cf. Emeneau 1937) must hang over the legs of a living person, but be inverted and cover the head of a dead person. This cloak should be made by the neighboring Toda tribe, usually with quite shoddy embroidery because it will be burnt, but often today a simple length of cloth is bought in a shop to serve the purpose. A female corpse, like a male, should be wearing a turban; and although the practice is rarely seen today, a girl should also wear a turban at her wedding: these are the sole occasions when she does so.

For a dead man his affines provide a cloth called *muććuku si:le*, which may indeed become a very costly token of their relative affluence. The act of giving this cloth not to the corpse but to his widow is said to represent a second marriage of the widow to the deceased. It is for this reason that, at a man's funeral, his widow is well dressed, almost as a bride. Covering her head with this cloth, she is led to the corpse by some of her agnates and a band of Kota musicians. After going anticlockwise, an inauspicious direction, around it once, she is allowed to sit with the corpse of her husband for the first time.

The corpse of an old lady must be given a waist cord (*puka:su*), but to merit this gift she must have a grandchild, by either her son or her daughter, who makes the presentation. Interestingly, it could be given to a woman who died young, provided her husband had grandchildren by another wife.

Other items for a dead woman can be worn only by a corpse. The *sa:vukaṇṇi*, for example, is a cord about half a centimeter in diameter which is made of cotton, dyed red, and has four conical bone buttons on each end. This cord, about a meter long, is tied around the head of both male and female corpses, over the top of the head and under the chin: obviously it is to keep the mouth closed during the ceremony. Another string, some 75 centimeters long, is the *oḍekaṇṇi*, tied above the breasts of a female. Unlike the cord worn there in life, it has ten beads attached to each end, and over them is a blue cotton thread. The cord is of double thickness, the two parts being bound together at three points by blue cotton. The *kaćće* is a strip of white cotton cloth, about 20 centimeters wide and 1.80 meters long, with a colored geometrical pattern along one side. The ends are embroidered in black and red. This item, specially woven by the Chetti traders who are associated with the Badaga villages, is tied around the waist of a female corpse. Two strings of beads, made by these same Chettis, are also given to a female. *Kaikattu maṇi* are cylindrical red beads that are strung around her wrist; *kakila maṇi* are tiny black beads tied around the female's neck. A *savari* is a bunch of human hair given her with a comb: it is knotted with the hair of the corpse and the comb on the back of the head. This, the *kaćće*, and the two strings of beads, are given to the dead woman by her mother or her brother's wife. Every female, even a small girl, must wear a silver ring on the finger at her cremation.

Before the cremation begins, all of the most valuable clothing and jewelry, except for a man's silver waistband, is removed from the corpse and handed over to male relatives — women in fact are not allowed to be right at the cremation place. A *puka:su* and other minor items may also be removed at the last moment, particularly if they are at that time difficult to obtain. It is clear that in earlier times more wealth was burnt with the corpse, in a mild kind of potlatch reminiscent of Toda cremation

gold or silver rings for finger and ears, silver chains which are wound around the neck and waist of the corpse, some money which is tied in his upper clothing, boiled rice and clarified butter which are poured on the wood, a kind of flute, a bow with an arrow as weapons of defence on the journey to the realm of the dead, a small gourd vessel filled with clarified butter which has been tied to a twenty-foot pole for the journey, then sugar, peas, lentils, and boiled rice tied in a bundle. These are all necessary for the journey to heaven (Mörike 1849:105).

With a Lingayat corpse, the *liṅga* is taken from the neck and tied in a cloth to the left upper arm, if a male, or the right upper arm if a female. For a younger dead woman, this would probably be the first time she received a liṅga.

There are numerous other aspects of the Badaga funeral that involve apparel in one way or another. For one thing, a man's favorite clothing, flute (*buguri*), walking stick, or umbrella may be burnt beside him on the pyre. His entire body is covered at the time with the embroidered cotton cloak (*pugaru si:le*).

The widow wears a special nose-ring that hangs below the nostril. At one point in the complex ceremonial the right and then the left earring of the widow or widower are removed; and in the case of a surviving widow, she breaks her bangles; her nose-ring and necklace are also removed, and then her *ta:li* is broken to indicate that her marriage is now broken: an important gesture, because Badagas permit the remarriage of widows. These various actions are carried out by a senior man of the dead person's family, or in the case of a dead woman, of her husband's family. The jewelry is given to another man of the dead person's family. Then the person who took the jewels off a widow thrusts short sticks of the false bog myrtle (*Dodonaea viscosa*) in the holes in the ears and nostril; or similarly for the holes in a widower's ears. Immediately the widow or widower takes the sticks out again, and puts them into the pocket of the cloak — together with the thread from a widow's *ta:li*, as a sort of forget-me-not (Ward 1880:xxii; Natesa Sastri 1892:836). One copper coin, as a minimum, should be put in this pocket (*go:te*): it is seemingly to pay for a passage to the afterworld, and is provided by an agnatic relative.

As an index of the maleness of the corpse, his former Kota associates bring model bows and arrows, knives, and so on, to cremate with him, if he were a meat-eater. For vegetarian Lingayats who are buried, a hoe and crowbar are brought which will later be used to dig the grave. For dead women the Kota associate brings two iron rings, one for each second toe. Furthermore, the natal family brings a winnow, a model pounding-stick, a sieve, and a wooden ladle, as well as baskets of parched barley, crude sugar, tobacco, chick pea and wheat cakes to present to the corpse of their former sister or daughter. A sackful of millet is put inside the bundle as the corpse is being wrapped up. As we have already mentioned, a piece of *mañji* fiber is given for use of the dead, who is thought to need it for sewing in the afterlife. It must be accompanied by, but not attached to, a needle (*su:ñji*), which is stuck through one of the baskets offered. As might be expected, this too is only given to a female.

Next, the sister of the deceased should cut some hair from her head and tie it to the right toe, or both big toes, of the corpse, whether male or female. She then circles round the cot anticlockwise, falling down four times as she does so. Shortly afterwards the procession leaves to begin the cremation, and the corpse, still on the cot, is preceded by this same sister, now shaking a loose part of her upper cloth from side to side as she walks. This complex set of symbols is to be understood in combination with another part of the following procession, where the oldest male relative of the deceased holds a raised hatchet above his head. This hatchet is a ceremonial object, and sometimes has half a dozen separate blades welded onto it; the central blade has a half of a lime stuck onto it during the funeral. Early reports speak of men appearing to be wrestling with demons in front of the procession. The meaning of all this symbolism is that it is hoped any evil spirits or ghosts hovering around the cremation ground will not possess the vulnerable people in the procession. The woman is flicking them away with her cloth; and the old man is both discomfitting the spirits with his blades and intending that the juice of the lime get in their eyes. The pieces of hair tied to the corpse are a decoy: it is hoped the spirits will enter these hairs rather than the living body of the woman, or others in the procession. That one of the ghosts most feared is that of the dead man himself is suggested by the fact that his wife and illegitimate mistresses are also reported to cut off locks of their hair and put them inside the pocket of the cloak (Thurston 1909:113). This seemingly farfetched interpretation becomes less so when one learns that ghosts are commonly induced to leave a woman's body during an exorcism by persuading them to enter one of her hairs, which is then corked into a bottle, cut from her head, and buried. Women are thus not uncommonly possessed by the ghosts of departed lovers, particularly suicides. We are now in a position to summarize the pattern of prestations that centers on the newly deceased (Figure 2). Except in the unusual situation where a woman's father is still alive when she dies, all necessary gifts come from siblings or from descendants. This is only to be expected from the commonplace fact that old people die and are mourned by their younger siblings and descendants. What seems to be achieved by the pattern of prestations is the acknowledgement of a tie between the several descent groups that have perhaps been sundered by the death. The reason it is important to "heal these wounds" with formal presents at the funeral is in a general sense to perpetuate the integration of Badaga society; but more specifically it is to maintain kin relationships that will probably become pertinent again after some years, when a young man is to marry his mother's brother's daughter, his mother's mother's brother's son's daughter, his father's sister's daughter, or perhaps some other more distant cousin.

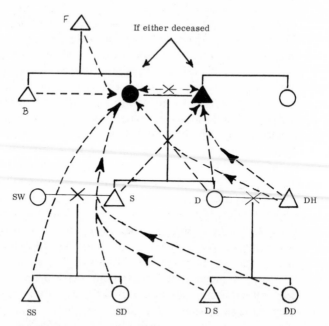

Figure 2.   Prestations at a Badaga funeral.
Key: F, father; B, brother; S, sons; D, daughters; SW, sons' wives; SS, sons' sons; SD, sons' daughters; DH, daughters' husbands; DS, daughters' sons; DD, daughters' daughters

Relatives sense a certain ambivalence in their status when at a funeral. For one thing, as Hindus, the Badagas feel polluted by the proximity of a corpse, and are ritually impure until they cleanse themselves afterwards. And being impure, they are vulnerable to possession by ghosts and evil spirits — for which reason suckling infants, the most susceptible of all people, do not attend funerals. At the same time, great reverence is expressed for the deceased, and especially so by a number of formalized gestures that again involve clothing in a variety of ways.

Dancing is one gesture of respect. The Badagas have a special dress for this, consisting of a carelessly pleated skirt and, in former days, a large red turban, both of which are worn by male relatives and visitors from other villages as they dance in a circle near the corpse (Plate 5). It is essential that men who give a pugaru si:le and a banna: to the corpse should dance at least briefly in the dress. Women, with rare exceptions, do not dance in

Plate 5.   Men dancing at a funeral

public; but men and boys sometimes imitate women in these dances (Mörike 1849:103; Natesa Sastri 1892:834). This is a kind of licensed behavior, and because it is very funny it would only be considered appropriate at the funeral of a very aged person. Although such dancers are allowed to wear turbans during their performance, this too is exceptional behavior; otherwise during a funeral the only people who may wear a headdress are the commune headman, men of the superior Lingayat phratry called Woḍeya, and of course the corpse. As men first come into the presence of the corpse they remove their turbans; even the women, whose heads are supposed to remain covered throughout, do take their headdresses off while offering grain to the corpse. Shoes also have to be removed by both sexes as a gesture of respect, both when paying their formal respects to the corpse and later, while standing on the cremation or burial ground, and in the former of these two situations men should properly be bare from the waist up — although I have rarely seen them so. This is seemingly the correct dress for men in any hallowed situation, since it applies during the sowing ceremony, while taking an oath at a temple, when acting as a priest, and even when in the inner, more sacred room of a house (Plate 6).

Plate 6.   Lingayat priest being revered during a burial

During the nineteenth century, the widow's suicide on the husband's pyre was an event in the remembered past of the Badagas, and was still occurring elsewhere in India. Observers were able to note then that,

at the present day . . . the widow merely pretends to rush towards the blazing pile to sacrifice herself with her husband's dead body, and is pulled back by her friends, who throw her robe on the funeral pyre instead, and she herself commences a new lease on life with new clothing (King 1870:21; cf. Harkness 1832:107, footnote, and 134; Sherring 1881:172).

Today not even this vestige of sutteeism remains; but it was doubtless a major factor in stopping all women from entering the cremation ground. By 1900 the practice had stopped, but the modern burning of twigs snatched from the widow's ears and nose and put in the pugaru si:le pocket is probably a vestige of the ancient custom (Rhiem 1900:506–507). The widow nowadays wears a white sari on the eleventh day after the death, at which time the soul of her husband is leaving the earth finally; but the next day she can put on a colored sari and jewelry once more, and no longer thinks of having her head shaved. At least one male relative must remain bareheaded until the corpse has been completely disposed of. As a sign of his special mourning status, however, he drapes the end of his cloak loosely over his head.

Two other uses of cloth — but not clothing — during the Badaga funeral may be mentioned. One is in the construction of the catafalque (*gudikattu*) under which the corpse lies. This complex wooden structure (cf. Thurston 1907:frontispiece; 1909:facing p. 119) is covered in flags and large quantities of cotton sheeting, and topped with a ball of cloth covering hay, over which an umbrella is poised (Plate 7). The cloths, which have been supplied by the bereaved family, are taken afterward by the Kota tribesmen who built the catafalque, and by the commune Toreya (Harkness 1832:133).

Another use of cloth is confined to the Lingayat burials. Once the corpse has been placed in the grave it is "made into a *linga*" by the recitation of certain formulas. It thus becomes holy instead of polluting, and so while the last *pu:ja* is being offered to the corpse a cloth is stretched above the grave to protect it from inauspicious or impure matter, such as bird droppings, that might chance to fall in. The cloth must be a new one bought by the agnates of the deceased.

CLOTH IN THE LARGER SOCIETY

We have so far shown that clothing, as well as being a cover for the Badaga body, is an important item of prestation, which passes between relatives on ceremonial occasions and thereby helps cement valuable kin

Plate 7.   Catafalque in use during a funeral

ties. That does not exhaust the social utility of clothing, however, since gifts can equally unite different sectors of the Badaga community, and are even extended to members of other tribes who have ritual and economic links with the Badagas. But although the range of circumstances in which clothing is given is a wide one, there is seemingly a common factor underlying these situations: clothing is given to people who, no matter how prestigeful they may be, are at the time in a serving capacity *vis-à-vis* the donors of the gift. In other words, a kind of superiority–inferiority relationship is present.

Thus, to take a simple example, an old lady who was a respected midwife and herbal therapist never charged people for her services. Nonetheless, her patients generally gave her a cloth of some kind after their treatment. When I spent some weeks interviewing this lady about the Badaga medical system it was suggested that I should give her a costly shawl.

There are other situations where unrelated Badagas exchange cloth for services rendered. Priests in general are members of the agricultural community, and the priesthood is only an avocation for them. They are remunerated for their services by goods such as cotton cloth, by retaining a half of each coconut offered in *pu:ja*, and also by keeping the silver coins that form a part of many temple offerings. Priests wash their own clothes with ash and water, but do not use soap as it might contain animal fat. Woolen clothes are not permitted inside a temple, not so much because of their origin on living animals, as because it is too difficult to keep them clean and hence unpolluted.

The Ancestress festival (*Hette habba*) is one occasion where cloth gifts become of central importance. Its major celebration is at the northerly village of Be:eragani, where a special small building called the Weaving House comes into use only during the festival, at the end of December. A weaver of the Chetti weaving caste walks up from the nearby Madras plains with a hand loom and works in this building for a week. Before starting he purifies himself by bathing, and then offers worship to the loom and other materials. The Badaga villagers thereupon present him with a piece of cloth and some money, and ask him to weave a shawl (*tuppati*) and two *kaćće* strips for the ancestress-goddess Hette:

Until the last day, they are not permitted to set eyes on the god Heththeswāmi [Hette]. On the morning of the last day, the pūjāri[priest], accompanied by all the Badagas, takes the newly woven cloths to a stream, in which they are washed. When they are dry, all proceed to the temple, where the idol is dressed up in them, and all, on this occasion only, are allowed to look at it (Thurston 1909:96).

The image is in fact also bedecked with waist and neck ornaments and an umbrella, offered money, rice, fruit, and even buffaloes for the temple's herd, and then cajoled with the following prayer: "May all good acts be remembered, and all bad ones forgotten. Though there may be a thousand and one sins, may I reach the feet of God" (Thurston 1909:97). It is worth noting that the priest who acts as an intermediary between the village and this goddess is fed for the entire year by the community, receives a quarter-rupee coin given by each household to the goddess, and also a turban and his simple clothing requirements (he is in fact a mere boy). This priest, who offers worship to Hette twice daily through-out the year, as well as during her annual festival, is clearly being remun-erated for services rendered.

Badagas eschew the flagrant display of differences in wealth: an osten-tatiously rich man, it is realized, would be constantly plagued with requests for loans. Even so, the quality and variety of a family's clothing do signify something about its wealth. Until this century the poorest people, generally landless laborers, had real difficulties in getting clothing, and would therefore beg the castoffs from richer families. A woman who thereby obtained a cloak might even tear it down the middle, to create two *o:gutus*, one for herself and the other for her husband. Her misfortune is even enshrined in a proverb: "The sorrow of an old woman is over rags; the sorrow of a virgin is over marriage." This offhand charity was not without its social consequences: when the donor family got themselves into a feud or factional dispute, they could count on such poor clients as they had helped to swell the necessary numbers of their supporters.

The Toreyas, the lowest Badaga phratry, were reputed once to have been weavers of a "coarse kind of sackcloth" (Harkness 1832:31). More generally though they have served as servants to the village headmen, and thus as messengers for the rest of the Badaga community, especially when a funeral is being organized — for it is a public, not a family ceremony. It is however one particular Toreya family in each commune that has this function: "He removes his turban, so that the very sight of a Toreya without a turban on his head is a sign that he is bringing tidings of death, and the people gather round him at once and hear the news" (Natesa Sastri 1892:834). After a funeral the head of the family, referred to as "Commune-Toreya", is given two large measures of rice, five rupees, and some of the cloths from the catafalque. Given that economic discrimination and backwardness in education have made the Toreyas poorer than other phratries in general, such funerary prestations were important in meeting their clothing requirements.

CLOTHS AND INTERTRIBAL RECIPROCITY

The Kota tribe, living in seven villages scattered among the Badaga ones, are another group who are closely tied to all Badagas by a service relationship. Carpentry, building, ironworking, jewelry manufacture, pottery, and leather-curing were the main crafts for which Badagas depended on Kota trading partners. Although the Kotas were primarily paid for all this labor with a suitable portion of the Badaga harvest, there were other occasions when they received clothing too. The Kotas wove nothing themselves. During the annual Kota festival for the god Kambattaraya, Badagas still make gifts of clothing to their Kota partners, and also lend them jewelry and dance dresses for the occasion. Traditionally, though, most Badaga jewelry had been made by the Kotas in the first place.

Relations between the two communities were largely broken in 1930, and have been quite attenuated since then. But even before that they were not always amicable. On one occasion a group of Kotas dressed themselves in a ceremonial manner, "in new waistcloths, wore shoulder cloths in the fashion of high caste men, and painted on their foreheads the red and white trident of Vishnu" (Mandelbaum 1941:235):

They were told to go to a certain Badaga village to demand tribute for the Kotas and their gods . . . The temerity of these Kotas in adopting dress and symbols sacred to the Badagas [even though the latter are not actually devotees of Vishnu] and coming to levy tribute to boot, so aroused the villagers that a mob intent on trouncing the four soon collected (Mandelbaum 1941:235).

In this case clothing was a clear index of social status. The Kotas are viewed by all Badagas as distinctly inferior, and no claim to anything else was going to be countenanced.

Another tribal group whom the Badagas considered inferior to themselves was the Kurumbas. These people were much feared for their sorcery, and one of their number was appointed for life to protect each Badaga commune from the sorcery of other Kurumbas. The entire family of guardian Kurumbas was fed for as long as they stayed in a Badaga village: they were also given a quarter of a rupee per month and a share of the grain harvest. Their clothing was simpler than the Badagas', but they normally obtained it all from the Badaga commune they were connected with: its headman would collect grain from each household, then convert this into cash to buy the cloth that had been requested. By about 1950 the fear of Kurumba sorcery had passed, and with it this exchange system. Its origin is adumbrated in a Badaga legend about a man out hunting, who met a Kurumba "with leaves on as his cloth. He offered his cloth to the Kurumba and made him his servant . . ." (Belli Gowder 1923–1941:30).

Yet another tribe is closely linked to the Badagas, and again cloth is one important commodity that passes between them in both directions. The Todas are buffalo pastoralists, and because they are vegetarians, they occupy high ritual status in the Badaga view. The Toda dress is essentially the same for both sexes, an embroidered cloak or *pu:txuṭi* worn over a loincloth (Emeneau 1937). Until the Second World War Badaga headmen wore the same item, which they obtained from Toda trading associates; in Badagu it is called *pugaru si:le*. There was no confusion however about who was a Badaga and who a Toda, because the Badaga headman always wore a distinctive turban and earrings too. And when, late in the last century, a few Todas adopted turbans, they were still distinguishable because only the Todas had beards. So important is the Badaga's turban as a distinctive social marker that Todas sometimes refer to Badagas as "they who wear the turban" (Rivers 1906:574; Walker 1965:38).

The clothing requirements of all Todas used to be met by their Badaga associates. The cotton cloth actually originated with Chettis in the Madras plain, but Badagas obtained it from them for the Todas. The Toda women emboidered it, and sewed two lengths together to create a rectangular cloak. Although normally made for the Todas themselves, it could be returned to a Badaga or Kota headman for his own use. Other cloaks were very shoddily embroidered for use in the Badaga funeral.

Another dark grey cloth was obtained from Badagas to make the *tüny*, a small loincloth that is the required clothing of Toda priests. According to legend, it was the ancient clothing of all Todas before they acquired the cloaks. The same cloth was also used for wrapping a Toda corpse (Rivers 1906: 103, 236–237, 342, 633). It is this dark grey cloth that was reputedly woven by Toreyas, one of the Badaga phratries. In the nineteenth century the Todas were already using English needles and imported blue and white thread, but for ordinary sewing and repair work they used the same *mañji* as the Badagas (Macleane 1893:905). This is not the place to describe the complex Toda funeral (cf. Rivers 1906; Hockings and Walker i.p.); but we should mention that Badagas may take part in it. At one funeral in 1963 the Badaga women mourners were given some *sa:vukaṇṇi* cords that hung above the doorway of the hut where the deceased lay; these would later be used in Badaga funerals.

There are other ceremonial situations where members of the two communities meet and exchange cloth. Once in a lifetime a Toda should visit the married daughter of his Badaga associate and give her a young female buffalo. In return she presents him with at least one article of clothing, generally an embroidered cloak.

Accessories and skills also changed hands on nonceremonial occasions. Todas and Kurumbas used to supply their Badaga associates with umbrellas made out of cane and leaves until early this century. Todas have recently taught Badagas to make walking sticks, and to carve decorations on them. They have also taught a few Badaga men to embroider. Thus the two visual arts of the Nilgiri plateau that were distinctively Toda have in recent decades been diffusing into Badaga culture slightly.

Since the Todas were — and are — buffalo pastoralists, their relations with the Badagas have often involved herding. They used to exchange buffaloes with each other: for example, two good animals for three not-so-good ones. In this kind of barter, any difference in value that remained outstanding after the exchange was paid for by the Badagas in cloth, grain, or gold and silver ornaments, and by the Todas in wood or basket products. Cloth and grain might also be given to a Toda who grazed his Badaga partner's animals with his own during the summer months. In a dispute involving a Badaga and a Toda, the maximum fine that could be levied on the Badaga would be two cloaks, and on the Toda two female buffaloes. The values expressed in all of these fines and barter arrangements clearly refer to a time when coinage did not circulate on the Nilgiri plateau as it does today.

One other community is in a close economic relationship with the Badagas: it is the Chettis of the adjacent Madras plains. There people are weavers in their home villages, but once a month a Chetti tours through a group of Badaga villages selling clothes, dancing dresses, lamp wicks, ornaments, and other knickknacks, including the various beads and strings needed for the Badaga funeral. He also used to supply the cotton thread (*nu:lu*) with which men of the Ha:ruva clan made their sacred threads. In earlier days they were paid in millet and honey; today they take cash.

This completes our summary of those intertribal relations that involve the exchange of cloth. We can see that the following pattern (Figure 3) emerges: it shows how the Badagas occupied a key position in the circulation of cloth on the Nilgiri hills, especially before local markets opened up in the mid-nineteenth century.

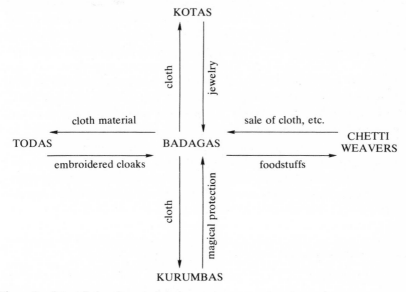

Figure 3.   Intertribal exchange of cloth

CONCLUSION

So, in a paper devoted to the ethnography of apparel, we find we have also been considering the same subject as did Marcel Mauss in his classic essay: ". . . to isolate one important set of phenomena: namely, presta-tions which are in theory voluntary, disinterested and spontaneous, but are in fact obligatory and interested" (Mauss 1966:1). Because we observe the gift being made at one point in time, we tend to think of it as a mark of friendship or familial affection; yet viewed over a span of years these isolated incidents become a system of prestations: "The form usually taken is that of the gift generously offered; but the accompanying behaviour is formal pretence and social deception, while the transaction itself is based on obligation and economic self-interest" (Mauss 1966:1).

Cloth, with the Badagas, is one of the commonest items of ceremonial exchange. It is particularly suited to achieve the ends of self-interest to which Mauss refers, for it is the one most visible aspect of every individual when it is worn; it is clearly differentiable according to degree of newness and cleanliness, especially as the favored color for Badaga clothing is white; it is easily used according to occasion by different members of the family who vary by size and by sex, since none of the clothing is tailored; and the degree of affluence of a donor can easily be signaled by clearly perceptible degrees of ornamentation or variations in the quality of the cloth material. And since it burns easily, cloth is an ideal gift to destroy at the funerary potlatch. It is certainly the most widely offered gift, being given even more extensively than food on formal occasions. The cloth, being of cotton, is a pure vegetable product and does not carry any pollution when it is new. It is easier both to store and to carry than food is, and can be presented to very high-status people such as Woḍeya priests, who would not under any conditions accept any kind of food from the lower Badaga phratries. While food and other artifacts are given by Badagas, notably during funerals, cloth is seemingly the one most commonly preferred ritual gift in this society.

Apparel, in short, is much more than a cover for the Badaga body; it is a symbol of complex and enduring relationships that hold the society together, and also help stabilize its relations with the useful neighboring tribes. What Marcel Mauss said about the nature of a total system of prestations is thus applicable to the specific social situations in which Badagas acquire apparel:

These phenomena are at once legal, economic, religious, aesthetic, morphological and so on. They are legal in that they concern individual and collective rights, organized and diffuse morality; they may be entirely obligatory, or subject simply to praise or disapproval. They are at once political and domestic, being of interest both to classes and to clans and families. They are religious; they concern true religion, animism, magic and diffuse religious mentality. They are economic, for the notions of value, utility, interest, luxury, wealth, acquisition, accumulation, consumption and liberal and sumptuous expenditure are all present, although not perhaps in their modern senses. Moreover, these institutions have an important aesthetic side which we have left unstudied; but the dances performed, the songs and shows, the dramatic representations given between camps or partners, the objects made, used, decorated, polished, amassed and transmitted with affection, received with joy, given away in triumph, the feasts in which everyone participates — all these, the food, objects and services, are the source of aesthetic emotions as well as emotions aroused by interest (Mauss 1966:76–77).

REFERENCES

BELLI GOWDER, M. K.
    1923–1941   "A historical research on the hill tribes of the Nilgiris." Unpublished manuscript, Ketti.
BENBOW, JESSIE
    1930   "The Badagas — beliefs and customs." Unpublished manuscript, United Theological College, Bangalore.

EMENEAU, MURRAY B.
1937   Toda garments and embroidery. *Journal of the American Oriental Society* 57:277–289.
FRANCIS, WALTER
1908   *Madras district gazetteers. The Nilgiris.* Madras: Government Press.
GRIGG, HENRY B., *editor*
1880   *A manual of the Nîlagiri district in the Madras presidency.* Madras: Government Press.
HARKNESS, HENRY
1832   *A description of a singular aboriginal race inhabiting the summit of the Neilgherry Hills, or Blue Mountains of Coimbatoor, in the southern peninsula of India.* London: Smith, Elder.
HOCKINGS, PAUL, ANTHONY R. WALKER
i.p.   "Toda secondary funeral ritual," in *Main currents in Indian sociology*, volume five. Edited by Giri Raj Gupta. New Delhi: Vikas.
JAGOR, ANDREAS F.
1876   Die Badagas im Nilgiri-Gebirge. *Verhandlungen der Berliner Gesellschaft für Anthropologie, Ethnologie und Urgeschichte*, 190–204.
KARIABETTAN, N.
1958   Atikārikaḷ [On the Atikari clan]. *Malai Nāṭṭu Kural: Nīlakiri*, (Ketti. India), July:9.
KARL, WILLIAM V.
1945   "The religion of the Badagas." Unpublished bachelor's thesis, Serampore College, Serampore, West Bengal.
KING, WILLIAM ROSS
1870   The aboriginal tribes of the Nilgiri Hills. *Journal of Anthropology* 1(1):18–51.
MACLEANE, CHARLES D.
1893   *Manual of the administration of the Madras presidency, in illustration of the records of government and the yearly administration reports*, volume three. Madras: Government Press.
MANDELBAUM, DAVID G.
1941   "Social trends and personal pressures: the growth of a culture pattern," in *Language, culture, and personality: essays in memory of Edward Sapir.* Edited by Leslie Spier, Alfred I. Hallowell and Stanley S. Newman, 219–238. Menasha, Wisconsin: Sapir Memorial Publication Fund.
MAUSS, MARCEL
1966   *The gift: forms and functions of exchange in archaic societies.* Translated by Ian Cunnison. London: Cohen and West. (Originally published 1924 as *Essai sur le don.* Paris: Presses Universitaires de France.)
MILES, ARTHUR (GERVÉE BARONTI)
1933   *The land of the lingam.* London: Hurst and Blackett.
MÖRIKE, E. G. C.
1849   Eine Todtenfeier auf den blauen Bergen. *Evangelische Heidenbote*, 102–105.
NATESA SASTRI, S. M.
1892   The Badagas of the Nîlagiri district. *Madras Christian College Magazine* 9:753–764, 830–843.
RANGA, NAGAYYA G.
1934   *The tribes of the Nilgiris (their social and economic conditions).* Bezwada (Vijayawada), Andhra Pradesh: Vani.
RHIEM, HANNA
1900   Die Badagas. *Allgemeine Missions-Zeitschrift* 27:497–509.

RIVERS, WILLIAM H. R.
1906 *The Todas*. London: Macmillan.
SAMIKANNU, C. PAUL
1922 Function of religion among the Badagas. *Madras Christian College Magazine*, n.s. 2:26–38.
SHERRING, MATTHEW A.
1881 *Hindu tribes and castes; together with three dissertations: on the natural history of Hindu caste; the unity of the Hindu race; and the prospects of Indian caste; and including a general index of the three volumes*, volume three. Calcutta: Thacker, Spink/London: Trübner/Bombay: Thacker/Madras: Higginbotham.
SHORTT, JOHN
1868 *An account of the tribes on the Nellgherries, by J. Shortt ... and a geographical and statistical memoir of the Neilgherry Mountains, by the late Colonel Ouchterlony*. Madras: Higginbotham.
THURSTON, EDGAR
1903 Deformity and mutilation. *Bulletin of the Madras Government Museum* 4:180–201.
1906 *Ethnographic notes in Southern India*. Madras: Government Press.
1909 *Castes and tribes of Southern India*, volume one. Madras: Government Press.
TIGNOUS, H. P. J. A.
1911 In the Nilgherries. *Illustrated Catholic Missions* 26:99–102, 116–119, 154–157.
VERGHESE, ISAAC
1963 An evaluation of the position of Badaga woman of the Nilgiri Hills through proverbs. *Folk Lore* 4:418–425.
VIVEKANANDAM PILLAI, T. H.
1937 The Badagas. *Journal of the Madras Geographical Association* 12:246–250.
WALKER, ANTHONY R.
1965 "Toda social organization and the role of cattle." Unpublished bachelor's thesis, University of Oxford, Oxford.
WARD, BENJAMIN S.
1880 "Geographical and statistical memoir of a survey of the Neelgherry Mountains in the province of Coimbatore made in 1821 under the superintendence of Captain B. S. Ward, Deputy Surveyor-General," in *A manual of the Nílagiri district in the Madras presidency*. Edited by Henry B. Grigg, lx–lxxviii. Madras: Government Press.

SECTION THREE

Man, Masks, and Morals

Analysis of an African Masked Parade

SIMON OTTENBERG

The *njenji* [masked parade] of Afikpo is unusual for Africa in that it is a masquerade with very little musical accompaniment and dancing. It is, in fact, a parade; the majority of the players form a line, which shows off their skillful manner of dressing and masking, their styles of movement, and the contrasting arrangement of the various types of masqueraders. I will describe the event briefly and then I will comment on its aesthetic and symbolic qualities.

The term njenji literally means "walk-walk". Because word duplication in the local tongue is used for emphasis, the very term suggests that this is no ordinary walk, and indeed it is not. It is presented in November and December, on the first day of *ɔkɔci* [the four-day dry season festival], by each of the twenty-two villages of the Afikpo, an Igbo people in south-eastern Nigeria (Ottenberg 1968, 1971a). Some villages hold this festival on the same days; if so their parades are held at the same time. Other settlements have theirs at different times.

The festival marks the first major appearance of the masqueraders during the ceremonial season; they appear again in a number of other ceremonies during the next three or four months. During the four-day festival girls visit their female relations and friends in neighboring villages while those villages are holding their feasts; they, in turn, are visited by their friends and relations at the time of their own festival. Adult men feast their daughters and visit their sisters and other female relatives living elsewhere. The visitors make a practice of bringing presents of yams

Research was carried out at Afikpo between December 1951 and February 1953 with the aid of a Social Science Research Council Area Research Fellowship and the help of a grant from the Program of African Studies, Northwestern University, Evanston, Illinois. Further research was done between September 1959 and June 1960 under a National Science Foundation grant.

and other foods in order to eat well with their hosts. In addition, on the last day of the festival wives perform a rite, carried out at their husbands' ancestral shrines, by which they ceremonially rebind themselves to their husbands and to the sexual rules of the patrilineal grouping with which they live.

It is also at the time of this festival that a new village age set, composed of men, who are roughly in the same three-year age group in their late twenties, is formed or has just completed its formation (Ottenberg 1971a). This occurs in a village about every three years. In those years when a new age set is formed, it takes part in and directs the masked parade, which is then usually larger and finer than it is in other years, although of the same nature. It is this larger form that I shall describe below. In such a parade all men of the new age set as well as younger males, who are members of the village secret society, are required, by a rule of the village elders, to take part; in a large Afikpo village there may be as many as one hundred and fifty masked players.

In some villages secret rehearsals are held before the parade; in others, however, nothing is done until the day of the event. In either case the players spend several days preparing their costumes and determining who shall dress in what form. Age and size are probably the most decisive factors in the latter consideration. The performers borrow strings of plastic beads, cloth, necklaces, and other items of dress from their wives, girlfriends, mothers, sisters, and other relations.

On the morning of the performance the players dress in the village center, an open common, which is then closed to females and to boys who are not secret society initiates (every adult male is). Some older men, who no longer participate in the parades, help the other men dress; this process can take a while because some of the costumes are quite elaborate. At this time an *ekwe* [small wooden gong] is beaten to announce that the preparations are in progress and to stimulate the performers. When all is ready, shots are fired by hired gunman from old, long Danish guns and the drumming stops. The common is then opened, and women, children, and men come out, sometimes in something of a rush, to see the paraders move around the village before they go on to other settlements.

The gunmen repeat their actions in each village that is visited by the players; in fact, the actions of all *njenji* performers are much the same in each settlement they pass through. In addition to the paraders and the gunmen, there are also from two to six hired singers, the parade's only musicians. Some of these singers proceed at the front of the parade singing the praises of the entire group of players, the age set involved, and prominent individuals in the audience, who give them presents out of pleasure and also sometimes for fear that the singers will deride them in song if they do not. Although the gunmen are unmasked and usually wear white shirts and waist cloths, the singers wear net masks and gnomelike costumes of brown raffia that cover them from head to foot.

Following along with the praise singers are small groups of net-masked players; each group wears a slightly different costume and each has its own form of movement. These groups do not proceed strictly in the line, and sometimes they fall beside or behind the main column of maskers. Some of the maskers move in a special style, responding to the voices of the singers.

The costumes of the net masqueraders are probably ancient dress forms of Afikpo and the central Cross river area of Nigeria. They seem less popular than they used to be, and it is harder now to find persons willing to wear them; the wooden masked forms, on the other hand, seem to be increasing in popularity. Made from native string, the net masks are prepared by tight looping and are variously colored in black, dark brown, and white. These masks blend with the raffia of the costumes, while the wooden masks are more prominent. Usually two masqueraders wear ɔteghita, one of the net forms, which consists of a black top hat with red-and-white cloth bands on it and a raffia skirt. They dance together in a slow and controlled style. Others also wear the ɔkpa eda, in which the net mask is held forward by wooden cross-pieces. The raffia-skirted players, often adolescent boys, carry knives or machetes. Another player wears *egbiri*, a net form marked by its elaborate headpiece with modern mirrors on it, and carries a dark horsetail in his right hand which contrasts nicely with the light raffia body piece. One or two other masqueraders may wear other types of net forms, each type generally moving separately from the others. Afikpo has had a rich net-masking tradition, although it is less of interest. These players, as other maskers, represent *mma*, a generalized kind of spirit, which is associated with *egbele*, the secret society spirit which is also known by other terms. Mma, in their masked form, are generally not considered harmful but are rather playful.

The main column is headed by some five to twenty players, who wear *igri*, long, relatively large wooden masks. They dance about intensely and enthusiastically, and represent virile young adulthood. The mask itself is said to be the mask of madness; when someone dons it, he can act eccentrically. The player carries a symbolic form of shield in his left hand and a machete is tied into the waistband of his raffia skirt. The igri players are often drawn from the age set that is immediately younger than the one honored by the festival. They also protect the column and may have to ward off an occasional playful male attacker as they pass through some village other than their own.

Either before the igri or with them there is usually a man dressed in old brown or khaki clothes and wearing an ugly, dark wooden mask with a distorted face. He carries a gun and sometimes a large cloth sack to represent a bag of cowries, an old form of money, over his shoulder. This masker represents a powerful slave trader of a type known in the area as *Aro* (Ottenberg 1958). Sometimes a second player represents a slave who carries the bag for the slaver. The appearance of these players, the only ones to wear this form of costume in the parade, contrasts nicely with the other performers. Representing power and evil from former times, they perform a scene in which the Aro dealer prevents the passage of the column until he selects a masked boy from the back of the parade line to be his "slave". The boy is actually returned to his place to take part in the event. This cameo is enacted at the start of the parade in the home village and may be repeated upon entering other villages. The Aro player is usually older than the age set and is sometimes paid some money to perform the role. Although the audience watches him with delight, his wife usually thinks him foolish, and may not, at a later date, give him the present that is given to the other players by their female friends or relatives.

Following the Aro and the igri come maskers richly dressed as adolescent girls (adolescence is the traditional time of marriage among the Afikpo for females). Usually fifteen to twenty-five tall men, drawn from the age set that is forming and the one below it, dress in this manner. They appear to be the main center of attention for the entire parade, wearing white masks representing female faces; each mask having a small child sitting on top of it. In addition, these maskers wear elaborate women's ceremonial headdresses usually decorated with numerous glass mirrors, colorful shirts, necklaces, plastic waistbands, and many colored cloths that hang from their waists to form a sort of skirt. The *agbɔghɔ mma* [girl-spirits] walk in longish strides with their bodies quite straight, carrying canes, the only pieces of male attire they use, in their right hands. There is considerable competition among the age set members for the first position in the line of "girls." This is not the only occasion at which men dress as females at Afikpo, for it also occurs in other masquerades and always attracts attention.

Behind the *agbɔghɔ mma* come paraders dressed in a modern form of costume. Usually there are five to fifteen of these players, younger than those who precede them but still adults, dressed in modern European style with dresses or shirts and skirts. They also wear brightly colored wooden masks that are rounder than most Afikpo styles and originated among the Ibibio people who dwell some distance to the south. These players carry modern ladies' handbags and, unlike most of the performers, who go barefoot, they wear shoes; many also have elaborate forms of headdress (Plate 1). Representing young married women, they contrast strikingly with the more elaborately dressed "girls" in front of them.

The remainder of the line is made up of a large number of players of decreasing size and height. They wear a variety of wooden mask forms and again are in modern or "foreign" dress. Many of the paraders

Plate 1.   An adult couple followed by men in a variety of costumes

proceed as couples: sometimes husband and wife, sometimes two men walking side by side, sometimes two adult women together (Plate 2). They represent schoolteachers, European missionaries, civil servants, clerks, and schoolboys. A few also dress as Muslim men with long colorful gowns. The players may hold canes or walking sticks (even a shooting stick has been seen) or they may carry books, perhaps bibles, and even be reading from them as they pass by. There is delightful variation in dress and a sense of style here; unlike the whole groups that appear earlier in the line, whose members wear the same costumes, individuals who appear at this point in the procession display the creativity they used in designing their own (Plate 3). The very young secret society members, some no more than five or six years of age, come near the end of the line and also attract interest; for some of them, this may be their first experience in the njenji.

At the very rear of the column are the *ekpo afam*, one or two men of the age set directing the proceedings, who pull up the rear, keep the stragglers going ahead, and characteristically wear wine red shirts and the brass *ikpo* bells used in wrestling ceremonies at their waists.

The procession is most impressive as it moves through a village. As the players approach a settlement, people hear them coming and come out to the common to view them. The igri cavort and the Aro gambols about. Drinks of native gin are offered to the elders watching the event by

Plate 2. Adult couples parading by

Plate 3. Young men in the parade, the first three dressed as Europeans. Note the canes and the shooting stick

players or by unmasked helpers who follow along with them. As a rule, the performers do not go through all twenty-two Afikpo villages, but only the ten or so closest ones. The others are simply too far to visit in one day. In the evening the performers return to their home settlement, where they parade again, sometimes moving through the village compounds, or past the secret society priest's house for a blessing. Afterward, the common is closed to noninitiates; the men change into ordinary clothes and spend the night there and in the adjoining men's rest houses. They generally eat, drink, talk over the happenings of the parade, and sleep, but they may also dance, drum, and sing secret society songs. The next morning they disband, returning to their home compounds in the village.

The parade is pleasant to watch, but it seems light in symbolism and aesthetic intensity compared to some other Afikpo masquerades (Ottenberg 1971b, 1972). The audience is, perhaps, not as large nor as demonstrative as at other events, although many men, women, and children do turn out for it. Nevertheless, much can be said about its meaning. Let me begin with some sociological comments. The parade is a statement about age: persons dress and behave according to their years, and in general the older ones are at the front of the line and the participants' positions in the line recede as their ages decrease. And, of course, the age set that is forming or has recently been formed plays a central directing and acting role, as has every age set before it and as every one will after it. The parade is a test of the ability of the age set to organize and to do something well, (other tests connected with its formation are also given to the age set, and it must carry them out). All of this is not surprising in a society in which age and authority are so heavily intertwined and in which age determines the order in which men take part in many activities (Ottenberg 1971a).

Sociologically the parade also reflects behavior associated with the dry season festival. This involves members of both sexes visiting other villages and receiving visits in return. Symbolically the paraders bring their young marriageable "girls" to be viewed by other villages. In fact, girls traditionally marry at about that age, and often marry into the villages that their players visit: some are in the audience watching their hometown boys, men, and brothers pass by. The festival has a sexual quality about it: visiting girls may use the occasion to establish or renew acquaintances and liaisons. The sexuality in the parade is expressed in the virility of the igri and the beauty of the adolescent "girls" who follow them. The four-day festival period is seen as largely female, while the parade has a strong element of masculinity in it. The event, therefore, nicely mirrors some of the dry season festival activities.

At the level of village organization several comments can be made. One is that as the players pass through the home village, the audience consists of much of the village, the players the rest. It is a community affair, locally sponsored and directed, using local masks and costume elements, and associated with the village men's secret society. Only the hired gunmen, the singers, and some members of the audience are likely to be from the outside, because individuals with these skills are not always available locally. Thus the play involves the whole village. The competition and arguments associated with the parade that involve players vying for the leading one or two positions among the adolescent "girls" may also mildly reflect divisions in the village. This sometimes takes on the form of competition between members of different patrilineages of the village, but the successful contender or contenders often seem to come from the older village patrilineages. On the whole, however, the play cuts across traditional village rivalries and unites all. The real competition is actually an informal one, between the villages; each tries to show the others, through its visits that it has the best dressed and organized maskers. As a result, villagers are pleased when their men put on a fine performance and upset when they do not.

At the cultural level certain simple points can also be made. The play is about Afikpo history. At the front are the masqueraders, wearing traditional types of net masks, and the igri players. The *agbɔghɔ mma* probably represent a transition — they combine traditional costume elements with modern cloth, plastic beads, and mirrors. But after them come those dressed in modern clothing. This last part of the parade has a nice satirical quality to it; the masqueraders are poking fun at modern clothes and social roles by dressing up so finely in them. This is especially evident from the fact that they also wear masks, which represent a contradiction to the forces of modernity that generally abhor traditional masking. In contrast, the net maskers at the front of the line are delightful, but traditional and not satirical.

It is interesting to note that there seems to be no mythology associated with the parade, nor is there any strong religious feeling. It is not an enactment of a myth, nor is it associated with a sacrifice or a religious ritual. The spirit of the village secret society is certainly behind it, but it is not omnipresent, dangerous, or demanding. Like most Afikpo masquerades, the display element is foremost; this feature is characteristic of many masked performances among the Igbo (Jones 1945).

The parade also symbolizes the values of young adulthood through the virile igri and the adolescent "girls". Even the players that follow the latter represent young or middle-aged adults, not old women or male elders. The oldest player in the production, in fact and in representation, is the Aro slave trader, a singular contrasting case. The theme of strength is also demonstrated in the power of the Aro trader, in the machetes and knives of the *ɔkpa eda* net-masked players, and the physical abilities of the igri dancers. Both these groups wear brass bells associated with wrestling, a major Afikpo sport, tied to their waists. The theme of strength runs through Afikpo life; it is found in wrestling, whipping contests, canoeing, fishing, farming, and formerly in warfare. It is strongly tied to concepts of male identity.

We have to ask why it is that the men of the age set that is celebrating its formation do so through the act of dressing up and moving about as adolescent girls, an act that can hardly be considered manly in a society which stresses the separation of the sexes and the belief among men that women need to be kept in their place. As part of their "initiation" as an age set, the members feed the elders a large and impressive feast, and they may perform some act of labor, such as rebuilding a farm path or a bridge. These are, however, manly deeds, as is the very act of directing the njenji parade. But what about dressing as girls? I believe that the act of appearing in this fancy manner, seemingly funny and a bit ridiculous, is a way of reiterating their maleness, which is represented by the igri who precede the "girls" and protect them. The role reversal is a statement of maleness, as it is at other masked events where it also occurs in different forms. At another *rite de passage* involving certain forms of secret society initiation, we again find a stage where boys are dressed, symbolically, as girls; this phenomenon therefore, seems to be tied to some conception of a change in life status for males at Afikpo.

At the psychological level little needs to be said other than to rephrase information already presented and to make one new point. We see both the interest in and the hostility toward modernity in the appearance of the "modern" players near the back of the parade line. We also note the adolescent girls are a mockery of real ones by their overdressed condition; this probably reflects the hostility of males toward females at Afikpo as well as some insecurity among men about their own roles *vis-à-vis* women in the society, especially under conditions of social change that make men feel that it is more difficult to control females than formerly. Psychologically, also, the men become spiritual forces, a role normally held by the elders in the villages and the village group who are seen as being closest to the spiritual world. The new point is that boys, before they are initiated into the secret society, have from the time they are five or six years old, their own imitation secret societies, based on compound, ward, and village membership, and having their own shrines, masquerades, and costumes. Because some boys are not initiated until their late teens (the age is going down rapidly nowadays), youths have often had a full and rich experience with these children's societies. The adult play, then, is probably in some ways a return to childhood pleasures and delights, although it is done in a different social context and not in a childlike way; it can also be seen as a continuity with childhood experience, rather than as something entirely different from it. The continuity continues within the secret society, for as the initiate matures he moves up the line in the njenji parade, playing older roles. By the time he is thirty he has played most of them. This is true in other masquerades as well.

Aesthetically we have a performance that emphasizes dress and de-emphasizes technical movement. It consists of players flowing past the audience at a fairly steady rate, and it is a contrast of costumed segments, each with its own colors and style, the igri against the "girls", the net maskers with raffia dress against one another and against the cloth-draped wooden maskers, the young adults at the front against the youths toward the rear, modernity in contrast to antiquity. A segmentally contrastive fashion parade without much mixing or interaction between the different groups of players, it is an event without a real climax. The moderate increase in interest on the part of the audience that occurs as the igri appear reaches its peak when the adolescent "girls" go by; but because the audience is largely nondemonstrative, this is difficult to tell. It is at this latter point that the humor seems finest, and it is also at that point where there is the greatest range of social, psychological, and cultural symbolism (Ottenberg 1973). It is, of course, the point at which the men of the new age set appear. After this segment, there is still strong audience interest, but it seems to be somewhat diffused because individuals are attracted by different characters as they pass by.

Finally, there is a nice contrast between the relative freedom of movement of the front part of the line — Aro, net maskers, igri, gunmen, and praise singers — and the back of the parade where persons remain much in line and appear thus somewhat constrained in contrast. It is as if there is a sense that the old days at Afikpo were freer, the new ways more confining. This is probably true for children, who nowadays are burdened with school, but for adults the reverse seems so; warfare and slave trading restricted activities of individuals, and there were fewer occupational possibilities in former times. So the contrast in the parade reflects real historical contrasts at Afikpo, either in actuality or in reverse order.

The parade form at Afikpo, without much music or dance, seems to be unusual both for Igbo country and for traditional Africa as a whole. I do not know its history at Afikpo; I can only surmise that originally it took less the form of a line than the form of groups of differently costumed individuals moving through village after village, and that as the initiation age became lower and more children joined the group, the more formal line evolved for the modern elements at the back of the parade. In any case the njenji is rich in meaning, and it is more than a simple display. It is a series of statements, which we have broken down into general analytical categories, and it is also an aesthetic event, with humor, satire, and finery.

REFERENCES

JONES, G. I.
1945 Masked plays of south-eastern Nigeria. *Geographical Magazine* 18(5):190–200.

OTTENBERG, SIMON
1958 Ibo oracles and intergroup relations. *Southwestern Journal of Anthropology* 14:295–307.
1968 *Double descent in an African society: the Afikpo village-group.* Seattle: University of Washington Press.
1971a *Leadership and authority in an African society: the Afikpo village-group.* Seattle: University of Washington Press.
1971b "The analysis of a traditional play," in: *Annual museum lectures, 1969–1970,* 50–60. Accra: Ghana Museums and Monuments Board.
1972 "Humorous masks and serious politics among Afikpo Igbo," in *African art and leadership.* Edited by Douglas Fraser and Herbert M. Cole, 99–121. Madison: University of Wisconsin Press.
1973 Afikpo masquerades: audience and performers. *African Arts* 6(4):32–35, 94–95.

Pageantry and Power in Yoruba Costuming

HENRY JOHN DREWAL

Among the Yoruba of Nigeria and Benin, cloth is an important means of expressing one's station in life — occupation, training, status, wealth and well-being. The Yoruba proverb *omo l'aso eda* [children are the clothes of men] suggests the importance of cloth in equating it with the Yoruba's most valuable possession, children.[1] Clothes, like children, are what a man shows to the world, and society judges him accordingly (Lindfors and Owomoyela 1973:19). Attire also often defines a person's member-ship in social, religious, or economic groups within the community and substantial amounts of money are devoted to *aso ebi* — outfits worn by all members on ceremonial occasions. Thus during the Efe/Gelede cere-monies, the principal performer praises a women's society (*Omo b'ori owo*, literally "child over money") by referring to its society cloth:

Aso t'eda ma be gba mu o e.
E wu t'eda ma ti lo wa la waju.
Aso igba ye o lo-ni-gba ma da o.
Aso t'eda lo wa o.
Eo ma fi pon'mo ni.

This study is based on fieldwork conducted among the western Yoruba groups in Benin and Nigeria (Anago, Ohori, Ketu, Egbado, and Awori) in 1970, 1971, 1973, and 1975. I wish to thank the Institute of African Studies, Columbia University, New York, the Institute for Intercultural Studies, New York, and Cleveland State University, Cleveland, Ohio, for their generous financial assistance; the Institutes of African Studies at the University of Ife and the University of Ibadan, and the Nigerian Museum in Lagos for many courtesies extended during the course of the field research; and most especially Margaret Thompson Drewal for her insights and assistance in all aspects of this study. Above all, I wish to thank my informants for sharing their knowledge of masquerading and costuming traditions in Yoruba culture. With the exception of Plates 3, 4, and 5, by Margaret Thompson Drewal, and Plate 24 by Howard Wilman the photographs are all by the author. This study was submitted for publication in 1975.
[1] This proverb also serves as the basis of an Efe song performed at Emado Quarter, Aiyetoro, northern Egbado in 1971: *Jengenden, rengen, omo l'aso/Owo ni ngo ni, omo l'aso/Jengenden, rengen, omo l'aso* [Jengenden, rengen, a child is like cloth/Money I will have, a child is like cloth/Jengenden, rengen, a child is like cloth].

[Your clothes are fitting for the season.
Your garments are the most fashionable.
You are the owner of the clothes which are in style.
Your clothes are made fashionably.
You are using them to carry your child (on the back).]
(Emado Quarter, Aiyetoro, 1971)

The society members are honored not only because their clothes are "fashionable" but also suitable for supporting another sign of prosperity and well-being, children. The cloth is thus an outward expression of participation and responsibility in a larger group. Conversely, the absence of clothing for the Yoruba indicates the *lack* of social responsibility. Nakedness is frequently used in definitions of different types of insanity (Bascom 1951) and a most effective way to shame someone is to remove his clothing in public. For example, in one Efe song, the performer challenges his audience in saying:

Oruko meje l'Esu ije o.
Ani bi ng ba ka a bi o ba pe,
Egbe gbogbo k'o bo mi l'aso.
Ogba o gba mi ni sokoto.

[There are seven names of Esu.
And if I fail to enumerate them correctly,
Let cult members take away my clothes.
Let men of my age group remove my trousers.]
(Olabimtan 1970:195, 202)

Only children are allowed to go about with little or no clothing until they approach the age of responsibility.

Clothing, while important as an indicator of social roles and responsibilities, is also valued for its aesthetic qualities as *ohun eso* [ornament] (Lawal 1974:245). Clothing is said to add (*buyi kun*) to the person and, in Yoruba fashions, it literally does. Large and heavy cloth wrapped around or draped on the body provides voluminous folds that add substance and massiveness. Yet the extravagance of the cloth enhances only when it meets another important aesthetic criterion, appropriateness. Yoruba say "the head wrap is good only when it fits" (*gele o dun bi ka mo o we, ka mo o we, ko dabi ko ye ni*). Thus one who dons expensive yet inappropriate garments is said to *aro'gi l'aso* [wear cloth like wood] (Lawal 1974:245).

This last image suggests that aesthetic evaluations of costume are somehow different from those applied to sculpture. This distinction seems to involve the kinetic qualities of cloth, the way it echoes in a unique way the movements of the wearer. It is not rigid wood, rather a flexible material which constantly responds to movement, weight, and air. The Yoruba are keenly aware of this difference and capitalize upon it in their fashion modes. The layers of cloth soften shapes and provide substance to enhance personal presence. The movement becomes more subtle as the multiple folds "soften" and "smooth" the angularity of certain gestures. The wrapper (*iro*) of traditional female fashion requires constant retying. This action becomes performance as the female uses the occasion to display the extent, texture, and quality of her cloth while providing a fleeting glimpse of her often brightly colored undergarments (*tobi, yeri*) and petticoats.

Male fashions offer similar opportunities for display. The large gown (*agbada*) which often extends beyond arm's length is spread outward and then folded over the shoulders in a distinctive arm, shoulder, and upper torso gesture which draws attention to the cloth and wearer as it reveals the full and elaborately embroidered sleeves of the shirt (*buba*). When a young dancer imitates an elder's dance without an *agbada*, he realistically performs the characteristic gestures of folding the cloth on his shoulders as an integral part of the danced pantomime.

Ritual, even more than social or secular occasions, demonstrates the importance of cloth in Yoruba culture. Through elaboration and specialization, attire defines specific roles within cult groups. At festivals, members without official roles may wear garments used for other important secular occasions such as births, naming ceremonies, and marriages. The addition of emblems of their devotion to a divinity (beads, bracelets, and so on) mark their cult membership. Cult officials, however, are designated by the distinctive apparel and regalia used in ritual contexts. Such persons may adorn their heads in special hairstyles, *idirun onisango*, *agogo*, or the conical projection of Osun priestesses, or elaborate headgear such as the peaked hats of Oluorogbo and Obatala priests in Ile-Ife, the stemmed caps of Ondo cult officials in Pobe (M. Drewal 1975) and the beaded crown with veil of Yoruba kings.

A progression toward increased concealment and transformation in the costuming generally appears among those most responsible to and in closest proximity with spiritual forces. In ritual context, appropriate attire seems extremely important. An incident at a sacrificial ceremony to prepare the way for the annual Efe/Gelede performances in Aiyetoro, Northern Egbado, graphically illustrates the point (Drewal 1973:65). At the outset, the newly installed *abore* [the one who presents gifts] neglected to remove her head wrap before beginning the invocation. The following exchange occurred:

Cult member (to *abore*): Open your head wrap!
Abore: I had forgotten.
Another (to *abore*): Tie your head wrap around your waist.
Another: It is forbidden. You must stretch it and tie it around your waist.

She immediately removed it, tying it about her waist as a sash (*oja*). Several initial responses from the gods being negative, there seemed to be general agreement that these might have been due to inappropriate attire on the part of the *abore*.

Most of the preceding examples of personal adornment in ritual contexts focus on the head (*ori*). The head as the site of man's intelligence, destiny or fortune, is also an object of a cult. It is the "place" where the spirit of a god enters or mounts (*gun*) the devotee during rites of possession. Incisions made in the heads of cult initiates receive substances which bind them spiritually to their god. The importance of the head requires that it be altered in various ways — painted, covered or uncovered, shaved — to be prepared appropriately for important ritual tasks.

In most instances, the head is covered and extended by means of headdresses. These headdresses affect not only the top of the head but, in the case of the sacred king's veiled crown, the eyes as well. The custom of averting one's eyes in the presence of one's elders out of respect and reverence is widespread. Covering of the eyes suggests other beliefs as well. The veil of the beaded crown as Robert Thompson notes "diminishes the wearer's individuality so that he . . . becomes a generalized entity. Balance between the present and the past emerges. No longer an individual, the king becomes the dynasty. . . . The crown becomes a mask" (1970:10). The crown as mask visually unites the realms of living king and ancestors, the very function of the sacred king. Thus masking, whether in veiled crown or other type of concealing headdress, makes visible the philosophical "blurring" of cosmological realms by distorting or transforming human features and qualities into sacred, supernatural ones (Cole 1970:7–8; H. Drewal 1975). The beaded veil also shields ordinary people from the allegedly powerful stare of the king, for those of special powers are often called "the owners of four eyes" (Abraham 1958:462; I. O. Adeleye, personal communication, April 6, 1971). The covering of head and eyes finds its richest expression in masquerades directed toward powerful spiritual entities, the gods and ancestors. Two such masquerades among western Yoruba groups are Egungun and Efe/Gelede.[2]

EGUNGUN

The Egungun cult honors the ancestral males (specific individuals or the collective ancestors of specific lineages) in stunning displays of cloth (Morton-Williams 1954, 1960; Beier 1956, 1958a; Adedeji 1972; dos

---

[2]   The discussion of Egungun and Efe/Gelede is based on western Yoruba practice. Egungun, being generally a pan-Yoruba phenomenon, may vary significantly in other areas. Efe/Gelede is traditionally found in western Yorubaland. Variations within this area are noted in the text (see Map 1).

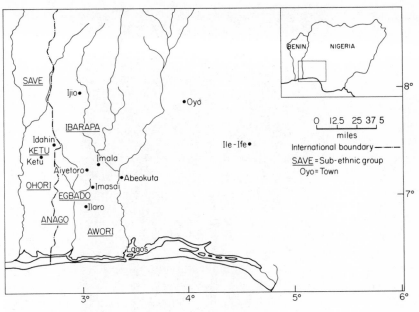

Map 1. Yorubaland

Santos and dos Santos 1969; Thompson 1971, 1974). Numerous myths concerning the origins of Egungun stress the singular importance of cloth as the major transforming medium in honor of the deceased (Thompson 1974:219; Idowu 1962:33–34). One version, contained in the Ifa verse *osa meji*, describes how the cloth of Egungun (*aso Eēgun*) became the prerogative of men. The myth traces the development of the Egungun cloth from ordinary (*aso lasan*) to a special masquerade ensemble with a netted veil which speaks in the altered voice of the ancestors (Verger 1965:212–215).

Thus myth establishes the preeminence of cloth, cloth which proclaims the devotion of the descendants by its exquisiteness. The community judges the status, wealth, and commitment of a lineage by the fineness of the costuming (Plate 1) as well as the "power" elements added to it. Thus,

> the *egunla* . . . are paraded. These are the principal *egungun* of the lineage groups, each named after an illustrious ancestor. Their costumes are elaborate and costly, and their display is competitive, reflecting the resources of their owners. Some I have seen with velvet trains sixty feet long; one from a royal lineage is complete with beaded crown, finely worked in tiny gold-coloured beads, the garments elaborately embroidered (Morton-Williams 1954:95).

The *egunla* are but one type of Egungun. Other categories have their own distinctive costuming formats. In one elaborate funeral commemoration

Plate 1. Egungun displaying richly appliquéd and embroidered cloth, monkey hair, shells, and a carved headdress depicting a leopard. Pobe, Benin, 1973

witnessed in Ilaro, Egbado, four varieties performed.[3] The first is the miracle worker (*onidan*), Aiyelabola [We-meet-wealth-in-the-world] a large, round, single piece of costly velvet covering the masquerader. As it whirls around, the cloth spreads outward like an enormous umbrella. Aiyelabola is regarded as female because in the course of the spectacle, she "gives birth" to a vast array of miracles (*idan*).

The *idan* form a second category of Egungun. Unlike most Egungun, the *idan* do not represent individual or collective ancestors, rather they demonstrate the marvelous magical powers of Aiyelabola and, by extension, the power of the ancestors. The Ilaro performance included a large snake, a crocodile, a leopard, a dancing mat, a palm-wine drunkard (*elemu*), a harlot (*asewo*), a bride and groom, and a burial shroud representing death (*oku*). The *idan*, an entertaining or theatrical aspect of the Egungun cult, are yet another expression of "mysteries" concealed in magical cloth.

[3] Subsequent to the submission of this manuscript, further research in Ilaro was conducted in 1977–1978 and published in a special issue of *African Arts* 11(3), 1978, devoted to the arts of Egungun among Yoruba peoples.

The third type, by far the most numerous, is *alabala*. Worn by young boys and men to represent specific ancestors, the *alabala* is in the form of a large rectangular sack with leggings, that completely envelopes the wearer. An assortment of material is used to create the costuming, including *aso oke*, a traditional, prestige strip cloth woven by men and used for its strength, velvet used for its elegance, and various cotton cloths of bright and assorted colors. The material is cut into triangles and sewn together, which "brings one color next to another in order to make it shine" (R. Taiwo, personal communication, October 13, 1975). The visual effect of many brilliantly colored triangles covering the surface does make it "shine" and dramatically distinguishes it from ordinary dress. Two other features complete the ensemble. The first is a cloth netting (*awo*) which allows the wearer to see. It is mentioned in the Egungun origin myth cited above. The second is a tuft of wool above the netting. It represents the tuft of hair (*osu*) seen on the heads of certain cult initiates, which marks the place where spiritual medicines have been inserted into the skin. The *alabala*, their arms obscured by the sack of cloth, manipulate their garment forward and backward, up and down to alter color/cloth combinations and shapes. While dancing to the staccato rhythms of the *bata* drums, they execute rapid, large-amplitude movements and thrusting kicks.

Elegba is a fourth type of Egungun present at Ilaro. Just as Elegba serves as unpredictable mediator/messenger between men and gods in Yorubaland, Egungun Elegba accompanies and assists Aiyelabola during the performance by maintaining the proper distance between audience and performers and unexpectedly burst into provocative dances which were described as "bombastic" by one informant. The costume is a tight-fitting garment sewn in different materials and surmounted by a carved head with the Elegba-like tailed headdress.

Another structural format of Egungun costuming is the multilayered panels (Plate 2). Informant testimony (Thompson 1974:219) continually stresses the mystical importance of the panels; their sawtooth fringes (*igbala*), which may be related to the triangles of color in Ilaro; and the color red. In motion, primarily whirling, the panels fly outward on the wind, extending the ancestral apparition in space and, in effect, fanning the surrounding audience with the unseen purifying and protecting powers of the afterworld. Other Egungun, executing rapid, large-amplitude shoulder movements, radically alter costuming shapes (Plates 3 and 4).

The Egungun, regarded as *ara orun* [spiritual beings] or literally "people from the afterworld",[4] must not be touched or approached by the

---

[4] *Orun* has been defined or discussed by several writers (Crowther 1852:238; Abraham 1958:527; dos Santos 1967:97). It is an important and sometimes confusing concept which has been inadequately translated as "sky" or "heaven". It seems more appropriate simply to convey its meaning as the cosmological realm of spiritual forces, gods and/or ancestors.

Plate 2. Egungun for a deceased hunter dressed in rich panels with sawtooth edges (*igbala*), and ram, monkeys' and birds' heads carved on a platform headdress. Idofoi quarter, Aiyetoro, Nigeria, 1971

uninitiated. The ancestral garments, which totally conceal the wearer and transform his human features, stress the separation between realms and at the same time demonstrate their interpenetration (Plate 5). Transformations are a trademark of certain types of Egungun performances. At Pobe and Ilaro, masqueraders alter their shapes totally by manipulating and changing their garments in exciting displays of dexterity. Attendants accompany the most powerful Egungun carrying sacred whips or staffs (*işan*) to guide and control the ancestor and maintain a safe distance between performer and audience. They perform a dual role in protecting both: the returned ancestor from being adversely affected by the presence of negative forces in the community; the audience from inadvertently touching a spiritual force which could destroy or diminish them. These "separation" procedures thus emphasize the gulf between realms and at the same time the spiritual force that binds them together.

Plate 3.   Egungun executing vigorous shoulder movements in dance. Pobe, 1973

EFE/GELEDE

Egungun, judged by the exquisiteness of its cloth, stresses lineage, solidarity, and strength. By contrast, Efe/Gelede[5] places emphasis on communality, for as informants from the various areas of western Yorubaland state "Gelede is the remedy for communal distress," that is, epidemic, drought, locusts, and so on. Costuming reflects Gelede's communal nature in the procedures of "borrowing" cloth. The borrowed material generally forms an assemblage of pieces that are tied, bound, or wrapped, rather than purchased, tailored, and sewn as in Egungun. A cult elder from Aibo Quarter, Aiyetoro, makes the following important distinction:

[5]   This ritual complex is frequently called simply Gelede in the literature and by some informants. Nevertheless the Yoruba clearly distinguish between Efe and Gelede ceremonies while recognizing their unity. Elderly informants claim "there can be no Efe without Gelede, and no Gelede without Efe." The shorthand expression, Efe/Gelede, reflects these beliefs.

Plate 4.   Same Egungun with accompanying *bata* drummer

You will never hear an individual say "my Gelede will dance today." Gelede belongs to the town. If you have money, you can buy cloth, as many kinds as your money can buy to make an Egungun, but you will never see a person owning Gelede (Adepegba, personal communication, April 3, 1971).

And another, from Ketu Quarter, commented: ". . . [Gelede] was the one that went about collecting cloths. It was a day collector of cloths" (A. O. Akinwole, personal communication, April 19, 1971). Murray (1946) notes cult officials are charged with controlling the dresses because the cloths are "usually borrowed, not bought". The lending of cloth, by members in the cult, serves as a vehicle of community cohesion, binding people together, despite lineage and political ties (Drewal 1973:49–51).

Gelede pays tribute to the spiritual powers of females, whether elderly, ancestral, or deified, which can affect positively or negatively the entire community. The most important Efe/Gelede ceremonies occur in response to some communal disaster. The artistic displays of song, masquerade, and movement stress traditional mores, social continuity, cohesion, and stability — themes calculated to please these spiritually powerful women, also known as *orisa egbe* [the gods of society].

Plate 5.   Various Egungun at annual festival. Pobe, 1973

A number of myths suggest the overriding concern of the living in their efforts to "pamper" the mothers through the transforming arts of masking. One elder, from Ilogun Quarter, Aiyetoro, said, "before there were masks, they used calabashes to make people enjoy and to make the dancers perform well. They could not dance as they should have if they did not cover their heads" (A. Bankole, personal communication, April 3, 1971). The elderly king of Aibo Quarter offers another: "The masquerades that our ancestors did, instead of carrying sticks and dancing with them stretched up, they thought of carving something which they wore on the day following Efe night. This was known as Gelede" (M. Oni, personal communication, March 24, 1971). Another account by an elderly priestess, from Ketu Quarter, states: ". . . these masks are an ancestral rite that the ancients did in the past which they called *eso* [a thing done with carefulness]. . . . They must not do it in an uncovered way. They must not dance nakedly to allow people [especially the destructive mothers] to see their eyes" (". . . *ere yin da gegebi ase ti awon agbalagba ti se koja lo ti won pe gegebi eso nitori won ko gbodo jo nigbangba. . .*") (A. O. Akinwole, personal communication, April 19, 1971).

A more elaborate text from the ancient Ifa verse known as *osa meji* recounts the mythic origin of Efe/Gelede masquerading:

Pele ni ns'awo won lode Egba
Pele ni ns'awo won lode Ijesa
A da f'Orunmila, o ns'awo re Ilu Eleiye

Won ni ko ru Aworan, Oja ati Iku
O gbo, o ru, o de Ilu Eleiye, o ye bo
O wa nsunyere wipe—
"Mo ba'ku mule nwo ku mo
Iku, Iku gboingboin
Mo b'arun mule, nwo ku mo
Iku, Iku gboingboin"

[Prudence was their secret among the Egba
Prudence was their secret among the Ijesa
Ifa told Orunmila when he was going to the grove of the witches,
He must put on a mask, a head wrap and leg rattles.
He obeyed, he put them on, he arrived at the grove of the witches and he was safe.
He rejoiced in dancing and singing—
"I have covenanted with Death, I will never die.
Death, Death no more
I have covenanted with sickness, I will never die.
Death, Death no more."]

(Beyioku 1946)

Orumila, the deity associated with Ifa, put on an image or mask (*aworan*), head wraps (*oja*), and leg rattles (*iku*) — the three essential elements found in all Gelede costuming — to protect him from the destructive propensities of the mothers.

Another version of Efe/Gelede origins links the cult's beginnings with the life of Adebiya, a former king of Ketu (Moulero 1971:11–19) who was also known as Edun, (a name given to an elder twin). The throne was disputed by the younger twin, Akan, and Edun fled with the help of a friend, first to Issale and then to Ilobi. At Ilobi, Edun planned a ruse to frighten his rival. He gathered a large number of shells and strung them on two long cords. Then he placed two posts on either side of the path leading to his hiding place and tied the cords to them. In the middle of the strands of shells he placed a tree trunk on the top of which he sculpted the face of a man. As clothing, he covered the sculpture with dried banana leaves. Then taking a calabash, he carved a mask, painted it with kaolin, and crowned the statue with it. When all was ready he gathered his followers and taught them the following song:

Afudelude ero Ilobi
Ilobi ni ise olude

[Strikers of brass against brass, people of Ilobi
It is Ilobi that possesses brass]

When Edun's rival came at night to capture him, he raised the alarm and quickly pulled on the cords. The noise frightened Akan and his followers and they fled, falling down in the dark, knocking their heads on trees and breaking arms and legs. After his victory, Edun returned to Ketu and the throne. Later the people of Issale came to ask how he had fooled his brother at Ilobi. Edun taught them the ruse and told them to do it only at night for it was *oro-efe* [a joke], and its other name was *olokun-ajaro-okoto* [owner of the sea who fought with the sound of shells]. Thus those at Issale performed it at night according to Edun's instructions. It was only later that they began to do it during the day.

Despite certain inconsistencies and possible folk explanations, several themes emerge: the use of sound to frighten and protect (whether by shells or brass); a masquerade using a garment (banana leaves), a mask (calabash), and rattles (shells) and the mention of Olokun, goddess of the sea associated with the mothers in certain areas (Thompson 1971:ch. 14; Beyioku 1946).

The concept of covering thus persists in all the preceding accounts. The means may differ but the notion of concealment as an expression of caution and indulgence runs like a leitmotif throughout. Specific references to covering the eyes and head are also echoed in a series of important verses about the history and imagery of the mothers collected by Pierre Verger (1965). In two of these, the primordial mother (Odu) explicitly prohibits others from looking at her face (i.e. her secret enclosed within the interior of her sacred calabash, *igbadu*) or suffer the dire consequence of being struck blind (1965:153–154, 208–209). According to Fadipe (1970:303–304), a penetrating glance is characteristic of the mothers: ". . . people . . . seen greedily devouring with their eyes the food another person is eating . . . are often considered as witches . . . and are supposed to have the evil eye." Masquerading indulges the mothers and provides protection from their "devouring eyes".

It is not surprising, then, that Efe/Gelede cult organization reflects this mythic preoccupation with concealment. The cult, striving for perfection in performance, is generally organized into two broad categories: (1) the performers, and (2) those who assist the performers (Drewal and Drewal 1975:38, 78, note 2). Among the assistants specifically concerned with the masquerade ensemble are the carvers (*agunwa*), painters (*amuti*, literally "holder of the bird's feather"), and costumers (*agberu*, literally "carrier of the loads"). In the Awori cult at Lagos there are also assistant costumers (*iya agberu*) as well as "controllers of the dresses" (*iya alarun*) with two assistants, *otun* and *osi iya alarun* (Murray 1946).

Given this mythic and organizational framework and the concepts of communality and borrowing, let us consider the rich program of masquerades which constitute the spectacle of Efe/Gelede.[6] Efe, a nocturnal rite, traditionally occurs in the main marketplace — a major setting of

[6] The following description is based on Efe ceremonies observed in Ketu and Idahin. Variations in ritual procedure and visual elements in other areas are noted in the text and described in Murray (1946), Beier (1958b), Harper (1970), Olabimtan (1971), Moulero (1971), and Drewal (1973). Masquerading in Efe/Gelede portrays both males and females but all the performers are male.

social, religious, and economic activity involving primarily women. It is thus most appropriate for a ritual which seeks to gather together all segments of the society in order to pay homage to the special powers of women. And in an Ifa verse collected by Verger (1965:168–169), the placation of the mothers occurs in the market. The marketplace (*oja*) is also a metaphor for the world (*aiye*). The proverb *aiye l'oja, orun n'ile* [world is a market, afterworlds is home] stresses the idea that existence on earth is like coming to market to do business before returning to the realm of the ancestors (Lindfors and Owomoyela 1973:23).

At one end of the area, Efe/Gelede cult members construct a small enclosure and double-arched entrance made of palm fronds through which the principal performer, the masquerade singer, Oro Efe, emerges. Between nine and ten in the evening men, women, and children begin to gather bringing lamps, food, mats, and chairs. They arrange themselves in a large circle with the double-arched entrance on the edge of the performance area (*agbo*) often sitting together in age-group societies (*egbe*) — see Figure 1. Families with titled elders (especially women) and other important personages take preferred positions along the front edge of the circle. This mass of people, sometimes as large as a thousand to fifteen hundred, includes Efe/Gelede cult members, a small percentage of the total audience; local inhabitants of various religious faiths, Muslim, Christian, and traditional; their relatives living in other towns; and "strangers". These strangers, known as "people of the world" (*omo ar'aiye*), are spiritual beings who can cause harm if displeased, but whose

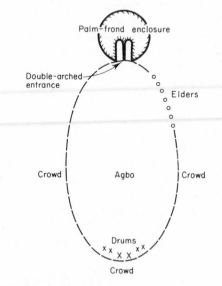

Figure 1.   The Efe/Gelede performance area

presence at Efe indicates approval of the ceremonies and good fortune.[7]
As people continue to arrive and arrange themselves around the *agbo*, a
colorful array of masqueraders perform in succession, preparing the way
for Oro Efe, whose repertoire of songs will last until the light of dawn.

The first masquerader, Ogbagba, emerges. Ogbagba represents
Esu/Elegba (Moulero 1971; Beier 1958b:9). He is the messenger who
facilitates or complicates communications between man and the gods
(*orisa*) and must therefore be honored first. The cult chorus sings his
praises as he moves through the performance area.

Arabi Ajigbale comes next. The masquerader, covered completely in
raffia palm and cloth and wearing anklets (*iku*) literally "sweeps" into the
arena as the crowd sings:

Arabi ajigbale
Aso alaso dun igbale
Arabi ajigbale
Aso alaso dun igbale

[Arabi, the one-who-sweeps-every-morning
The cloth of another is good for sweeping
Arabi, the-one-who-sweeps-every-morning
The cloth of another is good for sweeping]

(Moulero 1971:36–43)

Palm leaves and the act of cleaning, "sweeping" the way, suggest associations with Ogun, god of iron. In fact Ogun often appears in conjunction
with Esu/Elegba as powers that "open" the way (Beyioku 1946; S. Osubi,
personal communication, April 22, 1973). Another masquerader,
Agbena [carrier of fire], follows, bursting upon the scene with a pot of fire
upon his head. He rapidly traverses the area, forcing the crowd backward
as sparks fly and the crowd sings:

Ko pa na njako
Oloko l'adugbo

[The fire in the bush starts without warning
Farmers with fields near the bush, beware]

(Moulero 1971:46)

Agbena, disappearing as quickly as he appeared, is immediately followed
by Apana, the "extinguisher of fire":

---

[7] One informant, a king from Iboro, remarked, ". . . we realize our prayers have been
answered when strangers visit during the night. Young children, grown-ups, and old people
will come and then disappear at daybreak" (A. Bakare, personal communication, April 16,
1971). See also Idowu (1962:177–178) for his discussion of *omo ar'aiye*. Spiritual strangers,
also referred to as guests (*alejo*), are generally thought to be malevolent (dos Santos
1967:69–70). They include various forest beings like *aroni*, as well as *abiku*, children who
plague their mothers because they are "born to die". Such negative forces are closely
associated with the destructive mothers (*aje*), hence their presence at Efe/Gelede
ceremonies.

Owner of fire, kill your fire!
The hoopoe [bird with decurved bill] is coming,
Put down your load,
Because one does not light fires
To regard the bird of the night.

(Beier 1958b:9–10)

The performance enters a new phase as all lights are extinguished. The "bird of the night" refers to the impending appearance of the most sacred of Efe/Gelede masks, the face of the Great Mother, Iyanla (Drewal 1974d). Recalling the myths which refer to the primordial mother's prohibition against gazing upon her "face" (Verger 1965:154), all lights are extinguished.[8] The concealment of the Iyanla mask correlates with beliefs about the covert qualities of feminine powers clearly indicated in the following:

Mother who kills animals without striking. . . .
My mother kills quickly without a cry. . . .
Great mother whose body we dare not see. . . .
Mother of secret beauties. . . .

(Beier 1958b:10–11)

Old bird did not warm herself by the fire.
Sick bird did not warm herself in the sun.
Something secret was buried in the mother's house.

(Drewal 1974a:60)

The mothers operate mostly during the hours of darkness, transforming themselves into nocturnal creatures to "kill without striking".

Female covert powers have a creative dimension as well (Drewal 1974b). She possesses the secret of creation, for, as many informants remark, "it is women who gave us birth." She has an assuasive power captured in the proverb *owo ero lowo obirin* [soothing are the hands of the female] (Odugbesan 1969:211). She also possesses *iroju*, the inner power of endurance, patience, and perseverance (Crowther 1852:157; Lawal 1970:130). Such attributes usually place female deities within the category of *orisa funfun* [gods of whiteness]. This particular pantheon is identified with the color white as the color of coolness, calm, purity, and creativity. Sacrificial offerings to these gods must be of this color, clear, or bloodless, indicative of the soothing quality inherent in these substances.[9]

---

[8] Concealment of the mother's face persists in shrine context as well: Older Iyanla masks on a raised earthen mound are covered by a white veil and the shrine for the earth mother, Onile, in Ogboni lodges is covered by cloth (Williams 1964:141).
[9] Murray (1946) was told about a sculpture for the Great Mother (Iyala/Iyanla) in the Lagos cult founded by Ketu immigrants: ". . . the secret part of Gelede which non-members may not see. This is a very 'beautiful' carving of a woman about four feet high which is called Iyala — the great mother. Sacrifices made to Iyanla include gin, kola, beans, and especially snails, . . . for they are peaceable creatures and Iyanla is a woman of peace."

In the darkness the Great Mother comes in whiteness. Her white face, a massive and starkly rendered head with protruding forehead, deep-set eyes, and projecting board below the chin is covered with an enormous white cloth which trails on the ground (Figure 2). The chorus and crowd sing:

It is sweet to trail on the ground
Another person's cloth
It is sweet to trail it on the ground.

(Beier 1958b:10)

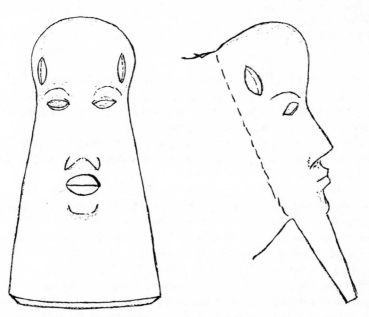

Figure 2.   Great Mother mask. Ofia, Benin (after Moulero 1971)

A similar song among the Ohori Yoruba says:

Aso alaso dun iwole
Aso alaso dun iwole
Ososomu [Iyanla] ko ni kan

[The cloth of another is good to trail on the ground
The cloth of another is good to trail on the ground
Ososomu has none]

(S. Osubi, personal communication, Iwoye, 1973)

The cloth is the major focus of these sung praises and, according to Beier (1958b:10), refers "to the huge white cloth which was bought by the joint effort of the Gelede members". Once again, the communal nature of the costuming, created by the contribution of all, stresses cooperation and cohesion among the "children of the mothers".

Iyanla moves slowly through the performance space, bent over, sometimes leaning on a staff or cane and people sing:

Orisa nla [Iyanla] a e!, o de o.
Ori e pekete pekete
Ososomu ku jegue
Ara lila l'o de

The Great Goddess, the goddess has come
The one with the enormous head
Ososomu must not be slow in coming
It is her pride that makes her do it

(Moulero 1971:47)

Her movement evokes images of age, wisdom and omnipotence. The cloth signals awesome covert powers cloaked in the whiteness of creation and protection. Thus her appearance assures the beneficence of the mothers for the performances to come.

Among Egbado Yoruba, the masquerade of the mothers occurs at the finale of the afternoon Gelede performances. Myths collected in Northern Egbado in 1971 focus upon the female progenitor who, finding life-giving water, assures the prosperity of the community. The ancestress, her sacred water, and her deity become the focus of worship for descendants. In certain areas, this founding ancestress/tutelary deity is Yemoja, or Olokun (Thompson 1971:ch. 14), while in others it is Odua. Cool white is the color of Yemoja's and Odua's cloth.

In the Egbado towns of Igan Okoto, Joga Orile, and Imasai, the mother comes from the sacred stream surrounded by her "children" who wear lengths of white cloth and wave branches in salutation. The masquerader, dressed predominantly in white, moves in a slow and stately manner with ritual rattle (aja) in his hand. Some masks are surmounted by a ritual vessel, a reference to her life-giving waters (Plate 6). Prominent earplugs recall ancient ritual regalia thus blending ancestress, priestess, and deity into one image.[10]

The mother manifestations of Egbado all project images of age by means of white hair, ancient regalia, and slow, stately dignified movement. Age evokes ideas of pride, inner strength, endurance, and above all

---

[10] The mother mask phenomenon seems to survive among Yoruba descendants in Akutown, Sierra Leone. Two informants whose grandparents were leaders of the cult described a special female masquerader known as Mama Sofi, representing one of the cult's early female elders. She shares certain traits with the mother masqueraders in Northern Egbado. She only appears on special occasions and unlike the normal Gelede who dance in pairs, Mama Sofi comes alone at the conclusion of the dance performances, moving slowly, bent over, leaning on a cane to depict her legendary age (M. Akinsulure and E. Frazer, personal communication, August 27, 1972).

deep wisdom which recall the awesome covert spiritual powers of the mothers and their knowledge of human and agricultural fertility. The prevailing whiteness, color of creativity and calm, and the mother's appearance during the daylight hours seems to stress her beneficent attributes and minimize her mysterious and frightening nocturnal activities.

Plate 6.   Great Mother mask showing ritual bowl, white hair, ear plugs, and ritual bell (*aja*) in lap. Joga-Orile, Nigeria, 1971

The first singing mask, the female Tetede, appears soon after the departure of Iyanla. Tetede [the one who comes before] is a name given to the first of twins, regarded by the Yoruba as the younger because it comes to test the world for the elder who follows (T. Moulero, personal communication, May 15, 1971). Tetede performs such a function for the principal performer, Oro Efe, for she first clears the way for him through chants honoring the gods, ancestors, mothers, and elders and then calls him to appear and perform. Tetede, being a female masquerade, is also called the "wife" of Oro Efe who, informants explain, represents "the most beautiful woman who pleases the witches" (Harper 1970:78). It may be that Tetede "pleases the witches" because she is one of them, for Lawal (1974:239–240) notes that "extremely beautiful women" are often thought to be witches or spirits in transformed state.

Tetede performs a series of songs as she dances. The mask superstructure consists of a spiraling open-work head wrap surmounted by a large bowl. The thrusting wooden breastplate draped with a long cloth panel flutters with the dancer's movements, while rattles echo the rhythm of the drums.

Upon the call of Tetede, two attendants of Oro Efe come into the area before the double archway and kneel. They are two young girls, virgins, called *arugba*.[11] On the head of one is carried a miniature statue of Oro Efe and on the other, a long rectangular box carved in the form of a popular game board known as *ayo*. These images represent special medicines which accompany and protect Oro Efe throughout his performance (T. Moulero, personal communication, May 15, 1971). With everything in place and ripples of expectation and excitement running through the crowd, the drums fall silent and Oro Efe, accompanied by a flute (*fere*) replies to Tetede singing:

Nigba t'o pe mi l'ekini
Apa l'o ran mi l'ise
Nigba l'o pe mi l'ekeji
Iroko l'o be mi l'owe
Nigba l'o pe mi l'eketa
Mo je fun rerere apela l'ai p'agba
Bi o ba pe mi tan, maa lo.

When you called me the first time,
I had been doing a task for the *apa* tree.
When you called me the second time,
I was providing service for the *iroko* tree.
But when you called me the third time,
I answered in a clear, resounding voice.
Now that you have finished calling me, go home.

(Moulero 1971:53–56)

From the area in front of the entrance the female cult head and her assistant, both completely dressed in white in honor of the gods of whiteness (*orisa funfun*) and the Great Mother, strike sacred four-sphered bells (*aja*). They ritually call Oro Efe to the world, announce his coming, and insure his protection. Next a flute player appears. His short bursts of music praise Oro Efe, call him by name, and silence the crowd. Oro Efe appears in the double-arched darkness of the entrance (Plate 7).

---

[11]   See Lawal (1970:30) for a discussion of *aruaba* and their role in Yoruba worship and art. The miniaturization of Oro Efe, like the companionship of Tetede, as younger twin/wife, and the pairing of Gelede masks and dancers suggest a possible symbolic correspondence between doubling and duality in the imagery of the mothers (see Drewal and Drewal 1975:41).

He slowly sways, majestically swinging the whisks in opposition. The slow, insistent beat of the leg rattles announces his coming. With his first high, piercing note, the flute ceases and the crowd falls silent. All attention focuses upon Oro Efe as he carefully honors deities, ancestors, the mothers, and elders. His sharply inclined torso and slow methodic stamping express reverence for these spiritual powers. Upon completion of this important devotion he emerges fully, rises to full stature, and moves toward the center of the performance space where he delivers a song of self-assertion. His majestic costuming reinforces the extraordinary quality of his tense and piercing voice. While singing, he paces up and down the space, flashing the whisks as a way of greeting and blessing the assembled community. The songs, which can be grouped into basically four categories (invocation, social commentary, history, and funeral commemoration), touch upon the major concerns of the community.

Plate 7.   Oro Efe in performance at Ketu, Benin, 1971

After Oro Efe offers a song in solo, the performance enters its second stage — choral repetition. A chorus made of male and female cult members moves through the crowd and repeats the song. Like a spokesman for the king, the chorus makes public the sacred utterances. The chorus, supported by the rhythms of a drum ensemble, continues to sing until the entire audience learns the song and joins in the performance in a united and joyful manner. This full participation implies acceptance of and support for the opinions expressed by Oro Efe. Some songs may of course be more popular than others, but without exception, the community joins in singing. This united expression of public opinion has power both to strengthen the communication with superior beings (*orisa*, ancestors, the mothers) as well as the practical power to compel antisocial individuals to mend their ways or face public ridicule, ostracism, or total banishment. The weight of public opinion, voiced by Oro Efe and intensified by communal assent, is believed to have the power to affect the future, the power of *ase*.[12]

The ultimate impact of Efe derives from the interpenetration of verbal, visual, and kinetic arts. Oro Efe gives voice to the concerns of the people. He carefully honors the owners of powerful *ase* and insures their benevolent intervention in the affairs of the community by reinforcing traditional values and attitudes. Oro Efe, majestically attired and spiritually and socially sanctioned to strengthen the bonds among the living, ancestors, and deities, is truly the monarch of the night. Much of his grandeur is displayed in a complex costume that is assembled in a specific way.

Oro Efe first puts on leggings (*ibose*) which go over the feet and up to the knees.[13] Cords tied around the ankles and just below the knees secure the leggings. He places *iku*, iron idiophones worn as anklets, over the leggings (Plate 8). Approximately six are placed on each leg and supported by padded cloth (*agbeku*) wrapped around the ankles. He then puts on a short jacket or arm wraps (*ibopa*). He suspends a large bamboo hoop (*agboja*) horizontally from his shoulders with straps. Several layers of brightly colored (red, yellow, green), richly embroidered and appliquéd cloth panels (*gberi*, or *apa*) are placed over the hoop and tied (Plate 9). An outer jacket with sleeves, usually red, may be added over the cloth panels and tightly tied with another piece of cloth. The body of Oro Efe grows massive with the addition of each item. His height increases with the placement of the large mask which covers the upper part of his head

[12] The concept of *ase* is fundamental to Yoruba belief. *Ase* is the vital force, energy, mystical power, and potential which is present in all things (persons, objects, ancestors, gods) in varying amounts and differing manifestations (Drewal 1974a:26–27; Lloyd 1962:15; Crowther 1852:47; Abraham 1958:71). Bowen (1858:173–174) refers to the same concept without mentioning the Yoruba term. Verger (1964:15–19) provides the fullest exposition of *ase*.

[13] Lasisi Ogundipe, who created his own costume, was kind enough to allow the documentation of the procedure in his compound. Normally, this preparation would take place in the cult house (*ase* Gelede) or the palm-frond enclosure at the performance area during the night of Efe. The headdress was carved by the Ketu master, Alaiye Etuobe, in 1970.

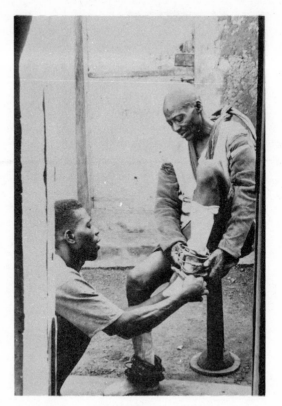

Plate 8.   Oro Efe putting on leg rattles, *iku*. Ketu, 1971

and is secured by means of cords (*igbagbon*) tied under his chin and at the back of his head (Plate 10).

The headdress is composed of three parts (Plates 11 and 7): (1) the suspended veil; (2) the main head or face; and (3) the superstructure. The veil, made of cloth or other materials, obscures the wearer's face while allowing him to see. The main head portrays a formal, frontal human face rendered in stark, cool white. The clarity of the sculptured facial features, especially the pierced eyes and the mouth, are given further definition by the use of dark colors set in whiteness. The superstructure, in contrast to the simplicity of the main head, is a complex composition of curving, spiraling masses and spaces in several layers. The curving, circulating forms of pythons and turban wraps (*lawani*) contrast with sharply defined vertical cutlasses which extend downward at the sides. Behind is a sculpted rendering of a leather panel (*laba*) with an interlace motif. In front, a white crescent moon crowns the brow of the face. Animal motifs (lion, leopard, panther, mongoose) occasionally command the summit of the superstructure, but more frequently birds perch on top. Colors — blue,

Plate 9.   Tying panels (*gberi*, or *apa*) over the bamboo hoop (*agboja*). Ketu, 1971

yellow, green, and especially red — delineate surface patterning and offer a contrast to the whiteness of the main head.

The visual impact of Oro Efe's masquerade ensemble creates images of status, power, and royalty. The expansion of the chest and torso by means of the bamboo hoop amplifies the grandeur, importance, and stature of the wearer as it intensifies his physical presence. The elaborate embroidered and appliquéd panels suspended over the hoop display a profusion of motifs. Several contain crosses, stars, and chevrons in square or rectangular areas with straight-edged borders. Some panels have sawtooth borders, very similar to the *igbala* of Egungun costuming (Plates 7 and 2). Moulero (1971:24–26) records a song by an Oro Efe describing himself as the Egungun of the king (Egun Oba). Still others display elaborate interlace motifs which echo the sculpted *laba* with interlace that adorns the back of Oro Efe's headdress. The display of this voluminous, elaborate cloth with royal and ancestral imagery implies wealth and superior status.

Oro Efe maintains his pacing movement at the generally slow and

Plate 10.   Placing headdress on head of Oro Efe. Ketu, 1971

dignified tempo appropriate to his status and age. Appropriateness, an essential aesthetic aspect in dress, extends into the realm of movement, for an elder who dances like a youth is called *agbalagba akan* [shameless] while a youth who dances like an elder is regarded as a weakling (Lawal 1974:247). Oro Efe terminates each line of paces with a turn that causes the panels to flutter outward on the wind. The image of "flying" panels seems most appropriate for the panels are known as "wings" (*apa*) and the padded jerkin with open sides worn by Oro Efe in some areas, is known as *agbe akalangba*, a name derived from two species of birds with "puffed-up plumage" of brilliant colors (Abraham 1958:27, 56; Harper 1970:78, 93). Such bird attributes associated with Oro Efe costuming suggest additional references to his role as the major manipulator of feminine powers within a supremely masculine garb.[14]

[14]   See the variations in Efe performances discussed below where Oro Efe perches on the rooftop like a bird.

Plate 11.   Oro Efe, Lasisi Ogundipe, in full regalia. Ketu, 1971

Images of power proclaim both physical and spiritual attributes. The lion, leopard, and snake symbolize strength (and royalty).[15] The knives suspended from the superstructure suggest masculine prerogatives. This same imagery connotes a spiritual dimension. Osumare, goddess of the rainbow, is linked with the python. Soponnon, god of smallpox, contagious diseases, and earth, and Ogun, tutelary deity of hunters and god of iron and war, are associated with knives.[16] The red paneled skirt is similar to the ritual regalia of some Egungun masqueraders and to the skirts of Sango priests which fly outward in ritual dances (Plate 12). The interlace motif on the carved *laba* in the superstructure is a royal prerogative. Such *laba* are also reserved for use by priests (Abraham 1958:400).

[15]   See Palau-Marti (1964:170–176). The Yoruba say of the leopard, *akamo ekun o ni iyonnu* [it is difficult to encompass a leopard] (Crowther 1852:94).
[16]   The use of raffia palm fibers (an Ogun-related material) on Efe headdresses in some areas, the predominance of the color red, and the role of the god of iron as "messenger" of the mothers (Thompson 1970:ch. 14) are other Ogun dimensions which enrich the knife imagery in this particular headdress.

Oro Efe's leg rattles (*iku*), besides providing rhythmic punctuation for his songs, also suggest spiritual protective power. In form they are similar to those worn by an *abiku*, a child who is "born to die". The sound of the rattles put on the child's ankles frightens away certain spiritual forces which seek to destroy him (Morton-Williams 1960:35; Crowther 1852:4). In much the same way, the *iku* worn by Oro Efe protect him by providing a sound context that purifies by scattering negative forces. The protective sound of the rattles which parallels the "voiced power" of Oro Efe, is a central element in the origin myths provided by Murray (1946) and Moulero (1971) and the songs commemorating the creation of the masquerade at Ilobi by the "strikers of brass against brass" (Lasisi Ogundipe, personal communication, April 25, 1971).

Plate 12.   Shango priests in midst of dance. Ede, Nigeria, 1971

The cloth veil and mask which obscure the wearer's face add a further element of spiritual power. As one female elder of the cult remarks "they [Oro Efe and Gelede masqueraders] must not dance it uncovered to allow people to see their eyes" (A. O. Akinwole, personal communication, April 19, 1971). And the covering of the eyes occurs in the myth of Orunmila putting on a mask, head wrap, and anklets for protection as he was going to the grove of the destructive mothers. The veil of netting in one Oro Efe ensemble with sawtooth-edged panels also recall the Egungun costuming format and the myth of how a male deity, Orisanla, added netting to the cloth of the ancestors when he took it from the control of the women (Verger 1965:212–213). Despite the masking, the identity of Oro Efe is generally known and frequently announced by the drummers or by himself in the course of his song performance. He thus occupies a removed and spiritually elevated position distinct from the masses, while still being recognized as a specific individual in much the same way as sacred Yoruba kings (*oba*) who wear veiled beaded crowns.

The crescent moon (*osupa*) may also refer to supernatural powers. Ogundipe (personal communication, April 25, 1971), in talking of the moon on his own headdress, first explained that the moon and the turban wraps (*lawani*) serve to identify him as a Muslim.[17] However further discussion revealed another function, for the moon: "allows everyone to see clearly and enjoy." This comment recalls the Yoruba saying that "the moon over Oyo helps the Alafin [king] in Oyo to know what is going on in the provinces" (Crowther 1852:225). The monarch, his all-seeing powers symbolized by the moon, knows and exposes all sorts of plots, scandals, or disorders within his realm, exactly what Oro Efe does in the course of his performance.

Perched at the top is the supreme symbol of spiritual power — the bird of the mothers. The mothers, also referred to as "owners of birds" (*eleye*), can, by using their spiritual power, transform themselves into birds of the night in order to fly to their victims. On this mask, the bird's long white beak grasps a scorpion. Inquiries about this imagery evoked a riddle: "Can a bird take a scorpion in its mouth?" to which was replied "No"; in other words only a bird of supernatural powers, the bird of the mothers, can perform such a feat.

The visual imagery of Oro Efe combines status and power with suggestions of royalty. Animal imagery, paneled skirts, and rattles refer to physical/spiritual powers. The cloth veil, frontal head and crowning birds of Oro Efe's headdress closely parallel the major iconic elements of some royal beaded crowns (Thompson 1970:10). The assemblage of royal motifs becomes even more explicit when Oro Efe, in one of his opening songs, collected at Aiyetoro, says "I have become the king of Efe; all youths prostrate before me." The final additions are whisks (*iruke* or *irukere*), placed in the hands of Oro Efe as he begins his performance. They are accoutrements of elders and kings, made from the tails of buffalo, monkey, antelope, and most commonly horse, and serve a function analogous to that of the fan used by the unmasked Oro Efe in some Northern Egbado areas. The whisks purify as they serve to greet and provide blessing for the assembly. They also suggest the heritage of the past, the ever-present ancestors, for Beyioku (1946) notes they are "emblematic of heredity — *b'esin ba ku a f'iru de'le. Omo eni ni ns'ehin*

---

[17]   Harper (1970:78) received a similar explanation at Ijio.

de ni [the horse dying leaves the tail behind. The children survive the parents]."

Efe masquerade ensembles vary significantly throughout western Yorubaland. Thompson (1971:ch. 14) notes that some Efe masks are worn with palm fronds. Murray (1946) describes Efe in Lagos as wearing a "big male helmet mask and dressed in raffia." In Ilaro (Olabimtan 1970:194) the headdress is called *ate Efe* [the tray of Efe]. The face of a man projects from the center: "Round the edge of the tray-like mask are hung strings of cowries and small mirrors; through the slit gaps between these the Efe is able to see his way about." At Ibara Quarter, Abeokuta, the Efe headdress is an image of man's head painted white. Raffia fiber attached to the rim covers the wearer's face. At Otta, among the Aworn Yoruba, the headdress has a circular disk or tray carved above a mask which fits over the head of Oro Efe. In Ohori Yoruba areas, the night masks, known as *akpasa*, are painted white and have elongated ears and a flat boardlike projection below the chin. In some Northern Egbado towns, several Oro Efe may perform in order of seniority, most senior last; they are not masked or elaborately costumed, rather they wear wide-brimmed white woven hats (*akete*) and a flowing white gown, *agbada*. They perch on the peaks of roofs on the edge of the market area. They sing Efe songs to the chorus and crowd below using a large square fan (*abebe*). According to a Sala Orile chief, their rooftop position recalls numerous stories of the birds of the mothers perching on the roofs of their victims (A. Orobiyi, personal communication, March 23, 1971). The fan, besides serving as a baffle to direct the performer's voice, provides spiritual protection. Ritual fans are attributes of mystical power for the act of fanning is believed to placate and dispel negative forces, to purify and prepare an area for a ritual. Thus an Oro Efe at Ketu sings:

Mo f'abebe be nyin o
Mo f'abebe
B'oru mun abebe ni be
Mo f'abebe be yin

[I take fan to beg you
I take fan
If there is heat, it is fan that begs it
I take fan to beg you]

The Gelede masquarade dances take place in the late afternoon on the day following Efe. While the crowd gathers at the main market, the dancers are preparing in their compounds. The male costuming is essentially the same as that of Oro Efe, only somewhat less elaborate (Plate 13). The masks are generally more simple. The embroidered and appliquéd panels of Oro Efe are usually replaced with layers of different head

Plate 13.   Male Gelede masquerader. Idofa, Nigeria, 1971

wraps (Plate 14) although some male Gelede have panels similar to those of Oro Efe (Plate 15). Both male and female Gelede dress in their lineage compounds, borrowing the head wraps and wrappers necessary to complete the ensemble. The masks, however, according to several informants, are traditionally kept in the cult house (*ase Gelede*) and are regarded as the property of the cult as a whole. In Lagos, the dressed but unmasked dancers procede to the *ase Gelede* with "a cloth over their faces . . . to have their masks fitted" (Murray 1946).

The costuming of the female Gelede has some elements in common with the male such as the leggings, arm wraps, and idiophones. However, other elements give a decidedly female form to the costume. In contrast with the bamboo hoop of the male which produces width and bulkiness in the torso, the female has several strips of cloth tightly wrapped around the torso from waist to chest, giving the impression of a narrow bodice (Plate 16).[18] The layered panels (*gberi*) of the male are replaced by the wrapper

[18]   This costuming convention is found primarily in the Ketu region. Female Gelede in Northern Egbado appear corpulent from a profusion of dangling and wrapped cloth about the torso.

Plate 14. Tying head wraps (*oja*) on the bamboo hoop (*agboja*) in male Gelede costuming.
Idofa, 1971

Plate 15. Pair of Gelede with elaborate appliqué panels over *agboja* and whisks in hands.
Idahin, Benin, 1971

Plate 16.   Female Gelede with tightly wrapped torso, protruding hips and buttocks, and wrapper (*iro*). Ketu, 1971

(*iro*) in the female. It is tied around the waist and descends to about mid-calf. The hip and buttocks area are built up by means of either wooden sticks (*bebe*) or a cylindrical spool which is tied around the waist and covered by the wrapper. This construction creates the impression of large, ponderous, and protruding buttocks and is also reminiscent of the shape created by a baby's legs when carried on its mother's back. The other distinctive element in female costuming is the wooden breastplate (*omu*) which is tied around the dancer's chest above the tightly wrapped bodice. These may be elaborately carved with figures (Plate 17) or in the form of statuettes (Plate 18) or simply rendered with a cloth draped over them (Plates 19 and 20). The final step in costuming involves the mask. Cloth known as *aso* Gelede is attached to the lower edge of the mask by means of wooden pegs or nails in order to cover the face of the dancer. The mask is then placed on the head, angled forward slightly over the forehead, and tied under the dancer's chin and the back of his head with cords (*igbagbon*). With the mask properly affixed, the dancer is handed horse-tail whisks, one for each hand, and emerges from the house to make his way to the market.

The first to appear in the afternoon performances may be children in the dancing lineages of the cult. Their costuming often indicates their neophyte status as performers (Plate 21). Frequently they wear poorly carved masks or simply painted calabashes with cloth suspended from the

Plate 17.   Female Gelede with elaborately carved breasts showing lizards and monkeys. Imasai, Nigeria, 1971

mask to cover their faces. As they progress in their training, wrappers, arm and leg wraps, and leg rattles may be added. The addition of the hip/buttocks construction and wooden breastplates in female Gelede, and the bamboo hoop and head wraps in male Gelede, signal their maturity as performers.

The primary purpose of the costuming is to embellish, amplify, and define the sexual character of the masquerader. In the male, the girth, width, and impressiveness of the chest and torso are greatly emphasized by means of the bamboo hoop (*agboja*). Prestige, pride, and stature are expressed in the many-layered strips of cloth or panels which cover the hoop and create the impression of solidness and substance (Plate 22). This costuming mode does not imitate normal fashion, yet it produces the same effect — that of enlarging and enhancing the stature of the wearer through a display of wealth of cloth. The male masquerade ensemble creates an image which by its height (the elevated overriding head and superstructure) and width in all planes (the hoop covered with layers of cloth) transcends reality.

Plate 18.   Female Gelede with breasts carved in the form of twin figures (*ibeji*). Joga-Orile, 1965

Plate 19.   Female Gelede with cloth draped over breastplate. Ketu, 1971

Plate 20.   Female Gelede displaying cloth panels in dance. Ketu, 1971

Plate 21.   Two young Gelede dancers. Sala-Orile, Nigeria, 1971

Plate 22.   Male Gelede with elaborate hairstyle. Idahin, 1971

Female costuming embellishes sexual attributes. A breastplate creates protruding, often elaborately carved breasts which thrust forward from a narrow, tightly wound bodice. Below and behind, a wooden construction covered in thick layers of cloth produces broad hips and massive buttocks. The exposed wooden breasts and massive hips and buttocks simply embellish further these physical characteristics thus defining in visual terms the essence of femaleness.

Cloth attains its ultimate effect when in motion. The importance of costuming to create "moving" illusions is evidenced in the ver-bal/rhythmic phrases (*eka*) provided by the drum ensemble which deter-mine the masquerader's steps. A number of these *eka* focus on the manipulation of cloth and costuming. For example: "Elewele ileke mo'birin so'di sesesesese" ["Body beads make woman put out her but-tocks (sound of leg rattles)"] (Adepegba, personal communication, Aibo quarter, Aiyetoro, April 19, 1971). The *eka* refers to the body beads (*ileke*) worn by small girls and women around their hips and usually covered by *iro* [a wrapper] (de Negri 1962:10, 12). When the dancer hears this *eka* he thrusts out the buttocks in time with the rhythm and although he does not actually wear *ileke*, the construction of the costum-ing as described above allows the cloth to be flipped outward as if the beads were making it bounce. The movement accompanying this *eka* consists of a series of very rapid, rhythmically complex, small amplitude jumps which are performed with such force that they literally tear up the ground. The dancer's torso is inclined forward from the hips, drawing attention to the buttocks region, the action alluding to bouncing body beads. This kinetic motif is very common in female Gelede dancing. Another *eka* is: "Sango ntu, ye ye ye" ["Sango fly outward (sound of cloth in air)"] (Adepegba, personal communication, April 3, 1971). The lead drum beats the phrase as the dancer enters the market. The onomatopoeic "ye ye ye" refers to the sound created by the action of cloth flying outward as the dancer turns. The allusion is to the dance of Sango priests whose ceremonial skirts fly outward during sudden turns which characterize their choreography (Plate 12).

The female Gelede dance is characterized by highly stylized and regulated movement, generally in a predetermined sequence and within the framework of two motifs — stamping and jumping. The stamp is done at moderate tempo with a high energy level and an emphatic downward stress at the end. The arms, extended by the flashing whisks, move in fully realized curves and sweeps that recall fanning gestures. The stamp, a crossing of the leg over the midline of the body, reflects and reinforces the narrowness of the female Gelede bodice, tightly wound head wraps, her narrow stance and directed use of space (Drewal and Drewal 1975:42). In Idahin, a pair of female Gelede entered the performance area in the stamping pattern and radically reversed their forward-inclined torsos. They executed a backward arch and stamp. The chest and belly were clearly presented as the movement caused the breasts to swing upward and thrust outward.

Jumping is characterized by a series of very rapid, rhythmically complex, small-amplitude steps which are so powerful as to dig up the earth. The intricate footwork on the balls of the feet is punctuated by the bouncing buttocks or, more precisely, the activated costume. The thrusting wooden breasts bob provocatively. The dancer displays the cloth draped over the breasts by stretching it between extended arms (Plate 20) as often seen in women's dances (Plate 23). In Ketu, a pair of female Gelede entered with a backward jumping combination, aggressively presenting the hips and buttocks to the audience by focusing attention on the exaggerated costume construction protruding in the rear. The costuming and the manner of execution of the steps emphasized the buttocks which plays a prominent role in the dances of Yoruba women (Lawal 1974:247). Subtle variations in rhythm and weight transferal alter the action of the buttocks from bouncing up and down to swaying from side to side.

The male Gelede, using basically a stamping motif, develops his choreography in the way he uses space, manipulates his upper torso, and relates to the audience. Costuming enhances forceful movement. The bamboo hoop suspended from the shoulders circumscribes the chest just under the armpits. The strips of cloth dangling from it

form a cylinder around the torso. This structure is particularly important in the Ketu area where there is a great preoccupation with manipulating the bamboo hoop which gives the illusion of a massive chest
(Plate 24). The structure of the costume and the style of the dance are
interrelated. By manipulating the suspended hoop with his hands, either
by rotating it as the body twists, bouncing it as the body rocks, or by
jumping it in time with the shoulders, the dancer greatly enhances and
extends his movement. With an explosive attack, the male fluctuates from
twists to rocks to jumping shoulders, appearing continually agitated and
erratic. The cloth panels suspended from the hoop fly outward, bounce,
and sway in constant motion. As excitement builds, the dancer turns
around and around, panels swirling, and sometimes he twirls with such
great force that he is nearly carried off the ground. In Pobe, a male must
turn so fast and strongly when the drums play *igbeni* that he sometimes
falls on the ground. Thus costume enhances and punctuates movement
creating a powerful illusion that cannot be achieved by dance alone.

Efe/Gelede exhibits a keen sensitivity and knowledge of costuming and
the manipulation of materials to create powerful images. The dances of
female and male Gelede create a powerful illusion of humanity that

Plate 23.   Woman manipulating and displaying cloth in dance. Ila-Orangun, Nigeria, 1971.

Plate 24.   Male Gelede gripping and manipulating the bamboo hoop during dance. Idahin, 1971

transcends reality. The dances are displays of power, both physical and spiritual, for the male performers externalize the vital natures of men and women, projecting an image of vital life force, *ase*. Costuming contributes significantly to the transcendental illusion of males and females by creating superhuman images with the layers of variegated cloth, the extended height and width in the male, and the exaggerated narrowness of the torso contrasting with prominent breasts and massive buttocks in the female. These images in cloth, in combination with the distinctive choreography of female and male Gelede, express the inner power and vital potentiality of *ase* and through it, deeply held beliefs and attitudes about the nature of the sexes and their respective roles in Yoruba culture.

CONCLUSION

For Yoruba peoples, cloth is a way of expressing both aesthetics and allegiance. Club or society cloth, while enhancing the stature and presence of its wearer, communicates social responsibility and involvement. In Egungun, fabric is transformed into ancestral apparition. Elegant, vibrant cloths, purchased and tailored by lineage members, proclaim a family's solidarity and stature within the community, while power substances alert spectators to the extraordinary potency of spiritual beings that cannot be approached or touched. In contrast, Efe/Gelede masquerades, as ensembles often made of cloths borrowed from a large number of households, stress communal harmony more than lineage identity. Efe/Gelede assures the pleasure of the mothers by encouraging the involvement of all their "children," the community. Gelede masquerades, unlike Egungun, are closer to the living than the afterworld. As such, they project transcendent images of males and females rather than materializations of supernatural forces. Despite such differences in focus, the stunning displays of cloth in both Egungun and Efe/Gelede attest to the richness of Yoruba thought and artistry.

REFERENCES

ABRAHAM, R. C.
   1958   *Dictionary of modern Yoruba.* London: University of London Press.
ADEDEJI, J. A.
   1972   The origin and form of the Yoruba masque theatre. *Cahiers d'Études africaines* 12(2):254–276.
BABALOLA, S. A.
   1966   *The content and form of Yoruba ijálá.* Oxford: Oxford University Press.
BASCOM, W. R.
   1951   Social status, wealth, and individual differences among the Yoruba. *American Anthropologist* 53:490–505.
BEIER, H. ULLI
   1956   The egungun cult. *Nigeria* 51:386–392.
   1958a The egungun cult among the Yoruba. *Présence africaine* 18–19:33–36.
   1958b Gelede masks. *Odu* 6:5–23.
BEYIOKU, A. F.
   1946   "The historical and moral facts about the gelede cult." Unpublished letter, Nigerian Museum archives, Lagos.
BOWEN, T. J.
   1858   *Meroke: missionary life in Africa.* Philadelphia: American Sunday School Union.
COLE, HERBERT, M.
   1970   *African arts of transformation.* Santa Barbara: University of California Press.
CROWTHER, S.
   1852   *A vocabulary of the Yoruba language.* London: Seeleys.
DREWAL, HENRY JOHN
   1973   "Efe/Gelede: the educative role of the arts in traditional Yoruba culture." Unpublished doctoral dissertation, Columbia University, New York.
   1974a Efe: voiced power and pageantry. *African Arts*(2):26–29, 58–66, 82–83.
   1974b "Gelede imagery," in: *African art as philosophy.* Edited by Douglas Fraser, 99–107. New York: Interbook.
   1974c Gelede masquerade: imagery and motif. *African Arts* 7(4):8–19, 62–63, 95–96.
   1974d "Iyanla: mask for the mothers of western Yorubaland." Paper presented at Third Triennial Symposium on African Art.
   1975   Masked theatre in Africa. *Mime Journal* 1(2):36–53.

DREWAL, MARGARET THOMPSON
1975   Gelede dance of the western Yoruba. *African Arts* 8(2):36–45, 78–79.
DREWAL, MARGARET THOMPSON, HENRY JOHN DREWAL
1975   Gelede dance of the western Yoruba. *African Arts* 8(2):36–45, 78–79.
FADIPE, N. A.
1970   *The sociology of the Yoruba*. Ibadan: Ibadan University Press. (Originally published 1939.)
HARPER, P.
1970   The role of dance in the Gelede ceremonies of the village of Ijio. *Odu* n.s. 4:67–94.
IDOWU, E. B.
1962   *Olòdúmaré, god in Yoruba belief.* London: Longmans.
LAWAL, B.
1970   "Yoruba Sango sculpture in historical retrospect." Unpublished doctoral dissertation, Indiana University, Bloomington.
1974   Some aspects of Yoruba aesthetics. *British Journal of Aesthetics* 14(3):239–249.
LINDFORS, B., O. OWOMOYELA
1973   *Yoruba proverbs: translation and annotation.* Athens: Ohio University Center for International Studies.
LLOYD, P. C.
1962   *Yoruba land law*. London: Oxford University Press.
MORTON-WILLIAMS, P.
1954   "The egungun society in south-western Yoruba kingdoms," in: *Proceedings of the third annual conference of the West African Institute of Social and Economic Research.* Edited by Philip Dark, J. W. Williams, and K. A. Busia, 91–103. Ibadan: University College of Ibadan. Mimeographed.
1960   Yoruba responses to the fear of death. *Africa* 30(1):34–40.
MOULERO, T.
1971   "Le guelede." Unpublished manuscript, Porto-Novo, Benin.
MURRAY, K. C.
1946   Unpublished notes in the Nigerian Museum archives, Lagos.
NEGRI, E. DE
1962   Yoruba women's costume. *Nigeria* 72:4–12.
ODUGBESAN, C.
1969   "Femininity in Yoruba religious art," in: *Man in Africa.* Edited by M. Douglas and P. M. Kaberry, 199–211. New York: Tavistock.
OLABIMTAN, A.
1970   "An introduction to Efe poems of the Egbado Yoruba." Mimeographed staff seminar papers and subsequent discussions, School of African and Asian Studies, University of Lagos, Lagos, 192–216.
PALAU-MARTI, M.
1964   *Essai sur la notion de roi chez les Yorubas et les Aja-Fon.* Paris: Berger-Levrault.
SANTOS, D. M., DOS
1967   "West African sacred art and rituals in Brazil: a comparative study." Mimeographed seminar paper, Institute of African Studies, University of Ibadan, Ibadan.
SANTOS, J. E., DOS, D. M. DOS SANTOS
1969   Ancestor worship in Bahia: the Egun-cult. *Journal de la Société des Américanistes* 58:79–108.

THOMPSON, R. F.
  1970   The sign of the divine king. *African Arts* 3(3):8–17, 74–80.
  1971   *Black gods and kings: Yoruba art at UCLA.* Occasional Papers of the
         Museum and Laboratories of Ethnic Arts and Technology 2. Los
         Angeles: University of California Press.
  1974   *African art in motion.* Los Angeles: University of California Press.
VERGER, P.
  1964   "The Yoruba high god: a review of the sources." Paper prepared for the
         Conference on the High God in Africa, Ibadan, December 14–18.
  1965   Grandeur et décadence du culte de *iyámi òsòrògà* (ma mère la sorcière)
         chez les *Yoruba. Journal de la Société des Africanistes* 35(1):141–243.
WILLIAMS, D.
  1964   The iconology of the Yoruba Edan Ogboni. *Africa* 34(2):139–165.

Mende Secret Societies and their Costumed Spirits

LORETTA R. REINHARDT

A great deal of work has been devoted to the study of Mende religion or cosmology, principally Hofstra (1937, 1940, 1942); Little (1954, 1967b); Harris and Sawyerr (1968). Due to the secrecy attached to many aspects of Mende belief there still, of course, remain areas which out-siders cannot know or understand. However, a general outline, at least, can be understood.

Much of what has been written on this area of Mende culture has been phrased in terms of the "supernatural" (e.g. Harris and Sawyerr 1968:3). Little, however, notes the difficulty of answering the question, in respect to Mende perception, "Where, aside from western definitions of the matter, do 'natural' phenomena end and 'supernatural' phenomena be-gin?" (1967b:216). Although this is a problem whose answer should benefit from the method of cognitive systems analysis, I would suggest, on the basis of the literature and on impressions received from informants, that the main division in Mende cosmology fall into two main cat-egories: things that are "natural", that occur in nature, and those that are made by man (cf. Little 1976b). Thus, what Westerners would refer to as supernatural, the Mende would lump with, or at least consider only as a subdivision of, the natural world. To take, for instance, the case of *nɔmɔli*, Westerners would see them first as archaeological artifacts, or as works of art, and then as having "supernatural" connotations in Mende thought.

The field research on which this paper is based was supported by a grant from the United States National Institutes of Mental Health and by a fellowship from Southern Illinois University. In Sierra Leone the work was sponsored by the Institute of African Studies, Fourah Bay College, Freetown. I am most grateful to Dr. Philip Dark for a very thorough criticism of an earlier draft of the paper and also to Miss Mary Jackes for helpful suggestions on parts of the text. Would that I had been able to solve all the points they raised! I am also of course very grateful indeed to the many Mende who were willing to spend time talking to me and trotting around with me.

The Mende do not consider them as either archaeological artifacts or works of art, and they certainly do not consider them manmade; *nɔmɔli* are considered by the Mende to have been made by spirits, and are found through instructions given by a spirit in a dream. Nor do I think that the Mende consider them or their helpful effects toward human and agricultural fertility beyond the realm of nature as they conceive it. As one older man said to me, when we were discussing the problem of sorting out fake nɔmɔli in museum collections: "if you could show them to me, if I could see them, I could tell you which are natural and which are not" (cf. Alldridge 1910:289). Further, as one of Little's informants said: "The (Poro) *ngafa* [spirit] was made by God and not by man" (1954:114).

Although the problem of distinctions between types of phenomena as the Mende view them is far from solved, nonetheless, I think it worth raising for consideration. This is not to say that there are no aspects of the Mende world view that could not be described as dealing with the supernatural, as understood in Christianity or used in general anthropological literature, but only that the Mende themselves do not seem to classify things in a way that is coincident with European classifications.

In any case, one category of Mende belief that has great importance is that of spirit beings, *ngafanga*. There are two main categories of spirits, ancestral and nonancestral, each of which has two or more subdivisions (Hofstra 1940, 1942; Little 1954:114–115). We are concerned here with those nonancestral spirits, called cultic spirits, associated with the various secret societies, and which are represented in material form.

One of the more perplexing problems in the study of the arts of the western Guinea coast region is the situation described by Vandenhoute (1948) and Harley (1950) for the peoples of the Haut-Cavally and hinterland Liberia areas. Vandenhoute, speaking of the striking development of masking as a feature of these societies, writes:

Although at least to a certain extent this "profitable" character already accounts for the abundant number of masks and even for the abundant differences in format, it does not give us further information about the extent of the morphological heterogeneity. Since, except for some rare exceptions, a clearly defined function of a mask, either of a high level or a low level (when having a merely recreative nature), does demand a mask of a type or color that is rigidly fixed. On the other hand, morphology does not at all show us the actual function of the mask, other than in exceptional cases. We can therefore say that a morphological or stylistic classification is completely independent of a classification based on the spiritual functions of the masks (1948:3).

Certainly, an impression gained from most of the literature on the Mende since the late nineteenth century, and also from a preliminary impression in Mende country itself, seems to suggest that a similar situation must prevail there. One reads and hears of scores of different "devils", and even during the space of a relatively short time in Mende country, may see very many. The difficulty of discerning order in such heterogeneity is not difficult to understand, as has been noted elsewhere:

There has never been any adequate treatment of the ubiquitous raffia devils in the literature on West Africa. This is most likely because both the European researchers had a peculiar interest only in more conventional sculptural forms such as woodcarving and because indigenous peoples, holding many such devils sacred, made them less than easily available (Dark et al. 1970:4).

Also noted in the same report was that a stylistic survey of masking among the Mende and neighboring peoples should be given the highest research priority, because of the perishability of wood and the fact that the ranks of old, knowledgeable, carvers are fast thinning (1970:4). While such a program will enhance understanding of the relations among the masking traditions of the area, it now seems to me important to stress that a full understanding of the meaning and functions of masking and devils cannot be achieved by a study of one type (wooden masked) excluding other types (composite masked). The importance of this point will become clear in the ordering of the Mende masked spirits, ngafanga, below.

Confusing as the original impressions may be, on closer observation, a meaningful order does begin to appear. Its overall outline appears to be based on the opposition between sacred and profane — perhaps secular would be the better word here (Durkheim 1915). The rules for the maintenance of the order appear to be fairly clear and simple, too. Nonetheless, I must stress that this ordering is tentative, and I would expect it to be amended on the basis of fuller work. But I do not think that the basic outline will change.

In support of the discussion of the spirits themselves, I also wish to give a brief description of each of the major secret societies. For the Mende as a whole there are four: Poro, Sande, Njaye and Humɔi; the Wunde is delimited to the Kpa-Mende. Certainly Sande and Poro are the best described of the Mende secret societies. Information on Njaye, Humɔi and Wunde is much sparser. This holds for the costumed spirits of Njaye and Humɔi too. However, there is enough information to fit them in the outline. As for Wunde spirits which may be represented in material form, present evidence does not allow any definite statement.

THE PORO SOCIETY

Little (1967b:240) has aptly termed the secret societies, "cultural arbiters" and this is especially to the point in the case of Poro. All males must undergo initiation into the society in preparation for their roles as adults. Anyone who does not is looked upon as a boy, and may not marry. In the old days initiation periods were rather infrequent, but of long duration. Nowadays they are virtually an annual occurrence, and for those boys who attend school may occupy only a few weeks during the dry season in the Christmas vacation period. Poro and Sande initiation sessions may not be held in the same town at the same time (cf. Alldridge 1910:220), and the bush, or sacred grove of each is located at opposite ends of the town.

Little (1967b:118–126) has described the initiation ceremony at some length. Considering that Poro secrets are restricted to men, one of the notable features of the initiation is the prominent part played by the *Mabɔle*, the only woman official of Poro, whose position is hereditary (McCulloch 1950:31), and who also sits in the "inner circle", or highest council of Poro. Throughout the session, and at its close, the initiates are repeatedly impressed with the importance of Poro secrets and oaths, which, if divulged or broken, will result in pain or death.

Poro's authority ultimately rests on its access to the powerful ancestral spirits of its hereditary officials, and on their control of powerful medicines (*hale*). However it is also backed up by the fealty owed it by the secular authority, the chief. In addition, in the old days Poro had its own armed band of masked members which dealt with those who flouted Poro dicta (Little 1965:353). It is easy to understand, then, how this authority effectively extended not only through the religious and social spheres, through rules laid down in initiation, but also to political life and to economic matters as well. In respect to the last case, Alldridge (1901:133) considers that the rules made supported the apportionment of wealth to the powerful. But one gathers from Hofstra (1937:110) that the rules may have worked to the opposite effect at times; prohibiting harvesting of palm kernels at periods of heavy farm work would have protected smaller households from larger ones which could spare members to preempt this lucrative work.

The internal organization of Poro remains a problem, as Little has noted in his review article (1965). Various authors have suggested levels or ranks of membership ranging from three to ninety-nine. In general, decisions are made in Poro by its "inner circle" or senior hereditary officials. According to Little, the head of Poro among the Mende is the *Gbeima*, or most senior; second in rank is the *Sowa* (Innes 1969:134, s.v. *sowo*), who, with the Mabɔle, moderates the initiations (Little 1965:360). Lower-ranking Poro members do not have a voice in decision making, their duty being to abide by and carry out dicta given by the inner circle.

The Poro Spirits

SACRED.   Our first problem arises in considering the sacred ngafa of the Poro. This spirit is called *Gbeni*, and may not be seen by noninitiates. Thus there is no visual documentation of it specifically for the Mende. Wright, in a general article (1907:423, plate 8, no. 1), published a picture of a "Bundu" type of mask and described it as worn by the "porro 'devil', a spirit who may not be seen by women or non-members . . ." This mask is now in the British Museum (No. 191288), and a similar one in the same collection, double-janus (No. 200094B), is annotated by Warren d'Azevedo (1970) as being a *Jobai* entertainment mask in the Gola Poro. Wright gives no provenience for the mask he illustrates other than "the interior".

Little first describes the Gbeni as follows: "The Gbeni's costume consists of cloth and leather. He wears a leopard skin, and carries medicines, including Arabic writings, and glass accoutrement, in addition to his leather mask" (1967a:246). He later comments on the "apparently secular nature of this particular 'spirit'", receiving the answer already quoted above: "'The (Poro) *ngafa* was made by God and not by man'" (1954:114). In his 1965 article, however, he describes the Gbeni as having a "wooden mask", apparently absentmindedly following this with an incorrect reference to his earlier work, the first cited in this paragraph (1965:360). On the face of it, we may take these statements as normal absentmindedness one may have in dealing with topics having no special interest. On the other hand, they may indicate a confusion between Gbeni and *Gɔbɔi* (Innes 1969:22, s.v. *gɔbɔ*), which will be discussed further below.

SECULAR.   The most important secular spirit of Poro is Gɔbɔi (Plate 1). The several Gɔbɔi ngafanga which I documented follow Little's description of Gbeni given above fairly closely. The headdress is a squat cylinder composed of various materials, such as leather, fur, cloth, shells, beads, and mirrors. Materials and their colors may vary from one headdress to another, although the basic form is constant. The cylinder fits around the wearer's head, with two small flaps projecting in front, forming an opening of ten centimeters by fifteen centimeters; through which the dancer may see. From both the top edge and base of the cylinder extend flaps decorated with the above-mentioned materials. There is a full shoulder mantle and an ankle-length cape of raffia. The dancer's body is covered in country cloth with ruffs of raffia at his wrists and ankles, the arm length being exaggerated. The clothing is necessary, since, in the strenuous dancing, the dancer's body would otherwise be evident, and this would not be proper in the representation of an important spirit.

Plate 1.   Gɔbɔi, rushing

The front of the costume is covered by a large leather apron, sometimes decorated, and usually falling to about knee length. At the back of the costume is a large panel containing miniature prayer boards made by Muslim Mori men. Down the center of this panel runs a large spinal hump covered in colored fabric.

Gɔbɔi's approach is heralded with great ceremony and a considerable retinue. Its attendants (Plate 2) are the same as the *mboleisia*[1] described by Little for Gbeni: "The followers wear head-ties, headdresses of animal skin, and a head tie is wrapped round the body in the form of a tunic: short trousers of country cloth are also worn" (1967b:246). The Gɔbɔi is also accompanied by other ngafanga; in the area in which I worked these were usually the *Falui* and *Nafalie* (see below). Its performance is marked by heavy, low grunts, as if to emphasize its being a spirit from the bush, and by alternate steps on each foot with the full weight of its back, causing the miniature prayer boards to clack heavily (Plate 3).

[1]   Innes's term for the attendants is *magbebla* (1969:18).

Plate 2. Gɔbɔi's attendants

The attendants spend great effort in controlling the dancing spirit, for it rushes and charges, dispersing the audience, who regard the performance with more awe and less amusement than they do that of other, minor Poro spirits. The attendants also give great attention to picking up even the most minute pieces of raffia that may fall from his costume. Although I received no definite confirmation on this point, the explanation for this procedure would appear to parallel that given for the same service performed for the Sande spirit (see below).

If Little actually did not confuse Gɔbɔi with Gbeni, others have (e.g. Alldridge 1910: plate facing p. 197; Eberl-Elber 1936:190), and there is certainly reason to do so.[2]

[2] Nor is the problem illuminated in Migeod's recorded description. The materials for the "image" are described as *Kolo* — bark or skin (cf. Innes 1969:50, s.v. *kɔlɔ*), which would indicate a Gɔbɔi costume. Later, when the young men ask the big men the name of the spirit, they are told first that its name is Goboi; another name is Povuli, which contraction means Poro himself; and, his other name is Gbeni (Migeod 1916a:107–108).

Plate 3.   Gɔbɔi's miniature prayer boards at back of costume

Other points relating to this confusion may also be mentioned. On the occasions when conversation did come round to the Gbeni, my informants were vague and often very ill at ease. This I took as a polite refusal to continue the conversation. However, it may have represented a true lack of knowledge or genuine confusion. "I have heard of it, but I have not yet seen it", is a typical response. One of my most knowledgeable informants, an important elder, showed considerable ambiguity concerning Gbeni–Gɔbɔi, until I loaned him, at his request, a copy of Little (1967b). Thereafter he clearly differentiated the two. A younger man emphasized that Gɔbɔi is a chiefdom devil and must be treated with great respect; nowadays, he said, there may be two or three Gɔbɔis in a chiefdom, but in "ancient times" there was only one. The costume was made in the bush with great secrecy and care before being presented to the public.

In addition, an anthropologist working elsewhere among the Kpa-Mende said that the people there called Gɔbɔi, slides of which I showed him, Gbeni (Gerald Johnson, personal communication, 1968).

The resolution of this confusion is difficult on present evidence. Little notes that the Gbeni no longer comes out in the larger towns because of the disturbance that would be caused by the flouting of Poro rules by literate people (1954:136). He also often remarks that it is to be expected that there will be local variation in the structure of Poro. Thus we may conclude that the process Little noted in 1954 has changed, and that by coming out, Gbeni has become secularized, assuming that Gbeni and Gɔbɔi are of the same form. Or we may conclude that since Wunde is so important for the Kpa-Mende, they either lack Gbeni or identify Gɔbɔi with it. Or we may conclude that Gɔbɔi is simply an extra special Poro minor spirit, despite the aura of awe surrounding it. I incline toward the last conclusion for three reasons, first, Gɔbɔi may be seen by noninitiates; second, there are two different terms and descriptions in the literature, despite the confusion; and third, Gɔbɔi has a composite headdress and not a wooden mask, and so parallels other minor spirits in its formal composition.

There are many other secular spirits of the Poro. Two which are most often seen are Falui and Nafalie (Plates 4 and 5),[3] and these are also the two which are most often copied by children.

The Falui wears a hat, in the form of an elongated cone surmounted by a tuft of bush cock feathers, just beneath which a small bunch of miniature prayer boards may dangle. The hat is usually decorated with horizontal and vertical bands of cowrie shells and is covered with colored material, often red. The wearer's face is covered with a country cloth hood, and over this, depending from the edge of the hat is a good-sized ruff of black monkey fur, which the wearer can manipulate so that he can see from beneath. His shoulders are covered by a large mantle of raffia. The rest of the body is covered by a full country cloth robe, usually having a cowrie shell appliqué decoration at the level of the left hip. The robe has one sleeve which completely covers the wearer's right arm and hand, in which he usually carries a stick. The left sleeve is cut off, barely suggested, the cut sometimes emphasized by a band of cowrie shells. When I once asked a Falui why it had no left arm, I was answered, "Because I was too friendly with the English!" — it may be noted that a number of the wry jokes and riddles told by entertainment devils are at the expense of the white man. The Falui also wears ruffs of raffia at the ankles. This type of costume appears widely among peoples of this area of the western Guinea Coast.

The Nafalie wears an oval hat, somewhat like a squat bishop's miter. In terms of materials and colors the decoration may be very simple or quite complex. A cloth hood covers the wearer's face, often having holes cut in it for the wearer to see through. The body is completely covered in a

[3]   Innes defines *nafale* as "a devil, similar in appearance to *ngafagɔtui*, that appears on ceremonial occasions, usually following *gbeni* or *wujei*" (1969:89). He defines *ngafagɔtu* as "a devil of the Gbonji society which appears at the ceremonial celebrations of important men" (1969:100). My own information is simply that Nafalie is the word the Kpa-Mende use, and Ngafagɔtui is the term the Ko Mende use. Likewise, while Falui is the more general term, Kpa-Mende generally call this spirit *Yumaiyumie* (cf. Innes 1969:138, s.v. *yomayoma*).

Plate 4.   Falui, center right; Nafalie, left foreground; Gɔbɔi, center rear

Plate 5.   Nafalie, posturing

country cloth suit, with raffia mantles depending from the shoulders and waist, and ruffs of raffia at the ankles and sometimes at the wrists. A stick is carried in each hand.

These two spirits, as I saw them, functioned as part of the retinue of Gɔbɔi and, to some extent, as clowns, posturing and telling riddles. Still, they are not "complete clowns"; there is restraint in their actions, and I was told that in olden days they used the sticks they carry to beat bad people. Indeed, at the Kenema fair, which draws huge crowds for its displays of devil dancing, when the police had no luck in pushing the crowd away from the dancing area, a Falui and Nafalie approached, waving their sticks, and the crowd moved back as a single body.

Two other Poro devils of fairly general occurrence are Jobai (Plate 6), described by Innes or "a boy's devil" (1969:35), and *Yavie* (Plate 7). The Jobai's headdress is in the form of a squat cylinder divided into panels of mirrors alternating with colored decoration. From its top ascends a delicate structure of sticks wound round with colored crêpe paper. Pompoms of the same material sit at the tops and bases of the sticks. The body of the dancer is hidden in an immense haystacklike cover of raffia. From the bottom edge of the cylinder depend four long flaps decorated with colored material; these lay over the raffia costume. The Jobai will envelop little boys in its dress after which they will pop out with great merriment and excitement.

Of the two Yavie which I saw, one wore a headdress similar to that of Jobai in form and materials of decoration. The other had a decorated

Plate 6.   Jobai, dancing

Plate 7.   Yavie, posturing

cone rising above the cylinder, as well as decorated sticks. Both had frontal openings guarded by flaps. A raffia mantle covered the shoulders. The rest of the raffia costume consisted of a suit of sheared layers of raffia. Four flaps of colored material fell from the base of the headdress and lay over the shoulder mantle. One of the Yavie wore a frontal apron of colored cloth.

Yavie's costume is generally greatly appreciated, one man saying, "It is the finest devil of all." This is because the costume is very full, and it is appreciated that the layered shearing of the raffia takes a great amount of work: "When it spoils it is very hard to fix; you need many people to get raffia." Regardless of the elegance of its dress, its dancing is not considered particularly interesting. Its movements are slow and cumbrous, and it, again, functions as a satellite of Gɔbɔi.

THE SANDE SOCIETY

Sande is the women's society which parallels Poro. It is known as "Bundu" by neighboring tribes who have it, and the Mende also use this term, too, at times. All females must undergo initiation which trains them for their roles as adult women, wives, and mothers. Very often, girls are married immediately upon completion of initiation, the betrothal having been arranged beforehand. As with Poro, initiations are nowadays of relatively short duration, especially for girls in school. Major descriptions of Sande initiations are given by Alldridge (1910), Little (1967b), and Margai (1948). Unlike Poro, no man plays any role in Sande initiation;

nor may he enter its bush, nor approach any of its girls, during the period of initiation. Sande secrets may not be divulged to nonmembers, and men prefer not to show any particular knowledge of its workings, although, as Little notes, most adults have a general knowledge about all the societies.

Sande's internal organization appears to differ to some extent from that of Poro. Contrary to some earlier authors (e.g. Alldridge 1910), Little considers that Sande has neither quite the cohesion nor the extent of authoritative power that Poro has:

Like the Poro society, the Sande is under the control of a number of senior officials, consisting of older women, who have attained the higher grade. These senior women are distinguished by the white head tie they wear in public, and they are known as *Sowoisia* (pl. of Sowo). It is a status that must be achieved: that is to say, no initiate can proceed to the higher rank without undergoing a further period of training. This applies even to the daughter of a Sande leader, though as the latter's heiress she has the advantage of the various secret medicines. The principal official is the *Majo*.

The Sande is convened for initiation purposes about the same time as the Poro, but in a less formal way. Individual Sande women make themselves responsible for the institution and develop what might be described as a personal connection with various households and compounds within the local community. This means, in effect, that there may be as many as five separate Sande "schools" within the same town. Occasionally, a fresh Sande group is started by some woman who is popular in the town. She must, of course, possess the necessary seniority and qualifications for the task. Quite often, the prelude is a dream in which the woman concerned learns of the whereabouts of certain important herbs and thus receives a "call" to the work.

As this and succeeding paragraphs indicate, there is a fairly close similarity between the Sande school and the European type of "finishing school" (1967b:126).

This, then, gives a picture of a much more diffuse structure than that of Poro. Nonetheless, my own experience suggests that there may be a wider underlying structure paralleling that of Poro more closely than Little would suggest. The Kpa-Mende dialectic variant for *Majo* is *Tajo*. Such a leader may be found in even a very small village in the area where I worked, as leader of the local Sande society. On the other hand, Paramount Chief Madame Mabadja of Bagbe chiefdom, was recognized as the principal Sande leader of a four-chiefdom area and had the power to call in members and masked dancers from all of the area when a big occasion warranted, although she no longer took part in directing initiation schools. In the 1920's, some thirty years before becoming paramount chief she had already established herself as a big Sande woman. (Although her own mother had been paramount chief in the years of the British arrival, a considerable period intervened during which a rival descent group supplied paramount chiefs.) Madame Yoko's rise to ascendancy in the late nineteenth century, albeit on a far grander scale, gives much the same picture (Easmon 1958).

Although I have no information which would contradict Little's view that high Sande offices are achieved rather than hereditary, it does seem strange that out of the four major Mende secret societies, three are reported to have hereditary high officials, and one does not. As a solution, an alternative hypothesis might be that, whatever the entrepreneurial aspects in the establishment of local and Sande schools, there might be a guiding body of an hereditary nature on a wider geographical basis. Again, this, as other aspects of Mende social organization, may bear further study.

Further, the postulation that female paramount chiefs, who gain their office through hereditary, may also have hereditary leadership in Sande (they would also, ex officio, be members of Poro), again raises the question of the relationship between secular and sacred authority. Little's view, in essence, is that they are quite well separated (1960:204–205). Harley (1941), with other earlier authors (e.g. Alldridge 1901:131) saw them as closely integrated. This problem will be discussed further in the later section on Poro-Sande interrelations.

The Sande Spirits

SACRED.   The sacred ngafa of Sande is the *Sowie* (cf. Innes 1969:135, s.v. *sowo*). The mask alone, without the costume, is called *soowie*. In addition to the black wooden mask characteristic of other sacred ngafanga, the Sowie's raffia costume also is dyed black (Plate 8). Nowadays the raffia costume may be embellished with brass or crotals, and with cloth streamers. Wright (1907:424) mentions "jingling seeds attached to the waist". As with other spirits, no parts of the dancer's body may show. For the Sande dancer this is managed by wearing very long sleeves or socks over the arms and socks or boots over the feet.

There are quite a large number of *soowesia*, or "Bundu masks" scattered in museum collections throughout the world, the British Museum holding one of the fullest collections (Dark et al. 1970:1). This corpus, allied with documented field examples, should eventually allow very useful statements about areal and temporal variation. One thing, however, that is very striking in viewing any range of such masks, is the great and imaginative variety shown in the treatment of its hair or headdress area. The virtuosity shown in the carving of this part of the soowie is one of the principle criteria used by Mende in an aesthetic evaluation (Reinhardt 1973).

The Sowie is accompanied by a principal attendant, or "interpreter", for it cannot speak or be spoken to directly in ordinary Mende by anyone. There are also other attendants, one of whose jobs it is to pick up even the very smallest pieces of raffia that may fall from the costume. The reason

Plate 8.   Sowie. Mask carved by the late Pa Jobu of Bagbe chiefdom

given for this is that if a man unknowingly should step on such a strand of the sacred costume he will contract genital elephantiasis. Several authors mention this also as a punishment brought down on a man who spies on Sande matters (e.g. Harris and Sawyerr 1968:104). Harris and Sawyerr also report that in former days the Sande women would disable the genitals of any man they caught spying (1968:104).

In addition to these attendants, other Sande women sing and accompany the dancing with *segbulesia* [calabash rattles]; men play the *kili* [small slit drum] and the *sangbe* [large slit drum] in accompaniment.

Wright gives the term *normeh* for a "Bundu devil" (1907:424), and this may compare with the term given by Innes, *nɔwɔ* (1969:117). However, other authors give the term normeh, or *normah*, as designating the second grade of the society, to which the "devil" belongs (Alldridge 1901:141; Wallis 1903:251). Although I did not get specific information on Sande grades, it seems possible that normeh/nɔwɔ may refer to the second grade of the society which must be attained before a woman is allowed to dance with the spirit. It was earlier noted that the senior members of the society, the sowoisia, are distinguished by wearing white head-ties on ceremonial occasions. So too, do some of the devils when they dance, thus it may be that the levels are designated in this manner when they dance: a sowo will have a head-tie wrapped around the upper part of the mask; a nɔwɔ will not.

This view is supported by statements averring that the head-ties designate "older" and "more important masks" which take precedence over the others. On the other hand, it is not given support by statements that the head-ties are "just for decoration", or by the explanation given by a carver, that the head-ties are wetted to help keep the mask from cracking in the sun, and that they may be used to hide small cracks in the mask.[4] It may also be noted that the head-ties on the masks are not always white: various colors and materials occur, probably because of their wider availability nowadays. It may be observed too, that while, during a day-long exhibition of dancing, several masks may appear, the costume and dancer remain the same, judging the latter by leg proportions and so on. Thus, during the breaks between dances a new mask is affixed to the costume. And finally, it may be observed that head-ties are not reserved for the oldest masks. In one dance I observed, what at least appeared to be the oldest mask did not have a head-tie, while a newer one did. The above statements are not totally contradictory, rather they depend on the particular individuals' points of view, which further study should reconcile.

As to the ownership of the mask itself, it would be best to say that, once treated with the society's medicine, the mask belongs to the society. It is kept in the society house or in that of the society leader. She has control over it, but she does not *own* it in an exclusive sense. Masks may be acquired in different ways:

The leader will buy a mask for the society. It is hers, but, of course, it is attached to and used for the society. The society has different levels. It is a special privilege to dance with the devil. Such a woman will often buy a mask. It is hers, but the leader of the society has the say over when it will be used. The women buy the mask, but they get the raffia and other necessary things to make the devil themselves. The devil receives dashes when it dances. These go to the society leader, but the woman who owns the devil will receive part.

This may be one purpose in displaying the dash when it is received.

If my mother owns a mask, and I have risen to the level of a dancer also, when she dies, I will inherit it. If I have shown no interest, then it goes back to the society.

That is, it becomes the virtual property of the leader. Other information also indicates that Sande women may get masks as gifts from their husbands or "friends".

---

[4]   Water is also poured over other raffia devils to protect them from the sun and the dust during dancing.

In concluding a discussion of a long and involved court case involving the illegal sale of some Bundu masks to a Guinean trader, the man who had settled the case made the point that:

A society mask is not the personal property of the leader or anyone else. She does not have the right to dispose of it on her own. Nor should a chiefdom official try to force her to do so. The use of the masks is decided on by consultation among the big women. Nor does the leader even go to "unlock" the mask by herself, but a number go together. So that, in case something should go wrong [about the medicine], there will be strength in numbers.

SECULAR.   The secular or amusing spirit of Sande is the Gɔndi (Plate 9). This term is not given in Innes's dictionary, nor has any attention heretofore been given to the two different kinds of Sande spirits in the literature, except in the paper by Phillips (1972).

Simply, the Gɔndi is a spoiled Soowie. When a Soowie cracks so badly that the crack cannot be hidden by a head-tie, it can no longer be used to

Plate 9.   Gɔndi. Mask also carved by the late Pa Jobu

represent the sacred ngafa. It is then smeared with white paint, or covered with pompoms or other decoration, and used with a very sparse raffia costume, not dyed black, to which various rags may be attached. No attempt is made to hide the dancer's features: hands and feet are not covered, and she may even part the raffia and peer out so that one may see her face.

As one informant said, "The Gɔndi is a funny Bundu devil. She can speak even to you, not through an attendant. You can tell the Gɔndi because she has rags in her costume and you can see her naked head." When I asked if this was a new devil, the answer was that "we have always had Gɔndi, even years ago."

This would certainly appear to be so, judging from the following passage, which, although it does not name the Gɔndi, clearly describes it:

A sixth devil, who appeared to be rather skittishly inclined, sat alone and was now and again admonished for her hilarity, one or two of the other devils striking her with the twigs they carried. She seemed to be what they locally termed "funny", as she adorned her fibrous costume with all kinds of oddments in the way of shells, and was altogether a very peculiar young person, although she was certainly a favourite with the people generally.

Her great desire was to get up to me, which after a time she succeeded in doing by a series of spasmodic gyrations in which she informed me that she was hungry and wanted food. That no doubt was only a ruse to obtain from me a bright new shilling, but after receiving it she was immediately pounced upon and the money taken from her closed fist. She continued to dance before me for a few moments, and was then borne along by the Bundu party and the crowd (Alldridge 1910:225).

THE NJAYE SOCIETY

Njaye has been compared with the Sherbro Yassi society (McCulloch 1950:37), the latter described by Alldridge (1901) and Hall (1938), among others. It is a curing society, concerned with certain kinds of mental illness, and also with agricultural fertility. Its membership therefore is open not only to its hereditary members, but also to anyone needing to be "washed" with its medicine, man or woman, provided he or she has already received Poro or Sande initiation:

Insanity, and other forms of mental complaint, are put down to breaches of the rules of the Njayei society. The complaint results from the sufferer having trespassed on Njayei bush, or from his having seen the dead body of an important member of the society before it was ritually purified. In such circumstances, initiation is the only cure, unless the person is already a Humui member. In that case, he undergoes treatment without initiation into the Njayei. There are reciprocal arrangements between the two societies, and the members address each other as "brother" and "sister". This is not surprising in view of the fact that the respective functions of the two societies overlap in certain respects. For example, the Njayei deals, along with the Bongɔi section of the Humui, with persons who have broken the prohibition on sexual intercourse in the bush.

Membership of the Njayei, like that of the Humui, is also gained when the person concerned dreams of the Njayei medicine, or "wrongs" one of its elders. . . . In addition to treating the mentally sick, the society supplies medicines for making the farming bush fertile. Sometimes its services are employed by the Chiefdom Council for this purpose . . . certain Njayei ingredients can increase a person's self-confidence and develop his "personality"; hence their use in elections for the chieftainship. If the successful candidate is already an Njayei member, he may then spend some time afterwards, secluded in the Njayei house, in order to confirm and consolidate his future chances of luck and prosperity (Little 1967a:249–250).

The hereditary office of leader is filled by a woman, called *Magba*, who is usually assisted by a man, called *Lomba* (Dawson 1966:26; cf. Innes 1967:74, s.v. *magba* and 72, s.v. *lɔmba*). It may be noted that in Sherbro the Yassi headwoman was "*ex officio* a leading figure in Poro and is entitled to Poro burial" (Little 1965:357).

The Njaye Spirits

SACRED.　　The sacred ngafa of Njaye, illustrated in Plate 10, is the *Njokui* (cf. Innes 1969:114, s.v. *njayekɔi*). Its mask is of blackened wood, about three feet long, and is worn horizontally, or, more accurately, diagonally, with a half helmet cupped over and somewhat behind the wearer's head. It is ornamented with strips of aluminum, cowrie shells around the crown above the face, and bush-cock feathers of black and ultramarine surmounting the crown. Although not dissimilar in form to some of the Kongoli entertainment masks, it carries a much more powerful impact, an intended effect. Various aspects of its form: the facial schema, its axis, suggest comparison with masks of surrounding peoples such as the Toma and the Baga. Its costume is of undyed raffia; a cloth mantle is worn around the shoulders.

One informant described it as "terrible, with teeth like an alligator. It can go under a river, like the Sewa, for a week." Needless to say, this description, plus published pictures of the Baga *Banda* mask (e.g. Leuzinger 1960: plate 15), and masks in the British Museum similar to the Banda, listed as having been collected from the Mende, made me doubt the authenticity of the example carved for me by Pa Jobu. As he said, however, "This is the way we carve them around here", later that day taking me to see the one shown in Plate 10. When I showed him the plate in Fagg and Plass (1966:121), he identified it as the *Landa* mask of the Kissi. The Njokui, I was told, is called out in only "very serious cases". But when it comes out, anyone can see it.

Plate 10.   Njokui

SECULAR.   The secular ngafa of Njaye (Plate 11) is *Fakoi* (cf. Innes 1969:9, s.v. *fakɔiɔ*). Dawson (1966:21, 26) mentions Fakoi, but not Njokui. The Fakoi shown in Plate 11 was photographed at the Kenema fair devil dancing display. Its costume conforms with that of other amusing ngafanga in having a composite headdress rather than a wooden mask. Nowadays cloth replaces leather as the main constructional material for such headdresses. The formal blocks of the headdress are set off by bands of cowries: at the base of the cylinder, at its top, and at the top of the cone, from which rises a bunch of black raffia. It carries sticks in its hands.

THE HUMƆI SOCIETY.   The primary function of the Humɔi society is the regulation of conduct between the sexes. Breaches of its rules amount to *simɔɔngama*, which is roughly the equivalent of the western notion of incest, although the rules cover a much wider range of action than just that (Little 1967b:145–149). Membership in the Humɔi, as with Njaye,

Plate 11.   Fakoi

is not only hereditary, but is open also to transgressors of its rules, since transgressors must be washed with its medicines and so initiated into the society in order to guard its secrets (cf. Little 1967b:249).

Humɔi is also held in general regard as a curing society: "The bush sacred to the Humui serves as a kind of hospital in this respect, and small children may be taken there for treatment" (Little 1967b: 250–251).

It may also be involved with meanings connected with fertility other than those strictly related to rules for conduct between the sexes, judging from Migeod's description (1917:156) of an Humɔi dance: "It dances, it grows, it rises to a great height. And it became small again. It dances, it bears children." As also noted for Njaye, the head of the society is a woman, called *Kpeke*, and she attains her position by right of heredity.

The Humɔi Spirits

SACRED.   Fortunately Migeod, during his work in Sierra Leone in the early part of this century, did document the Humɔi ngafa (1917, 1926). He viewed the Humɔi spirit as "a fetish or medicine personage in the Poro Society" (1917:156). He also wrote that the society had a male and a female branch (1926:254). Of the male branch, he writes:

> They have as outward and visible sign a dancer. He appears as a short man and extends himself to a height of about eight feet. He is completely clothed in long fibre like a bear, and wears a mask on the top of his head, and when he lengthens himself he has so much "fur" on him that still no opening is visible. The fibre expands naturally, and so is evidently made to fit his figure when at full length, and contracts when he shortens himself. When short he is below the normal size of a man. Probably he stoops when in the short position, which is the normal one for moving about. When lengthening he either pushes his head up with his hands or with sticks concealed inside his garment (1926:254).

On the facing page of the same work the dancer described is shown (1926:254, plate 6). Although the photograph is vague, it is clear that the mask is similar in form to a soowie, or Bundu mask. The raffia costume has three layers: the first depending from the base of the mask; the second, appearing to be a skirt, must depend from the dancer's shoulders; the third consists of raffia leggings.

A description of its dance given has already been quoted (Migeod 1917:156). This article also describes the commissioning of the carving of four Humɔi masks, one "like a big Sowo mask". The other three are described as: "like a deer's head, with four horns on one head; with hippopotamus teeth on it; like a leopard head. You put four teeth this side, you put four teeth that side" (1917:154). The same account later describes dyeing the raffia and country cloth costumes with camwood and *baji* [satinwood] to make them reddish-brown and yellow, respectively. The Humɔi head is described as being dyed first with baji, then with indigo, to make it black. Another head is also dyed black with indigo; the other two heads were dyed red (1917:155). I cannot say how far the account given Migeod is reliable, since wooden masks are not dyed black with indigo (*njaala*), but with *njui*. I have not seen in the field, or in collections, Mende masks like those described here, but that is not to say that such may not exist, or may not have existed in the past, since so little is known of Mende masking. We have here another problem which needs further study.

I also was informed that the Humɔi ngafanga mask is like a soowie, but I was not able to see one. Since this information was given without any question on my part that could be regarded as "leading", and since I am sure my informant was in no way familiar with Migeod's articles, I regard the two descriptions as safely independent and mutually supportive.

SECULAR. A further problem is that I did not come across any composite-headaddressed ngafanga, or "entertainment devils" of the Humɔi. And considering Migeod's description of spirits other than the soowie-type example, the question certainly remains open, and vexing.

THE WUNDE SOCIETY

Regarding the Wunde, Little says only that it is "concerned largely with military training, is popular among the Kpa-Mende, but appears to owe its origin to the Timne neighbours of the latter" (1967b:240). Even on this relatively small point there is disagreement in the literature. Addison (1936:207) quotes a detailed and characteristic legend purporting that the Wunde was introduced to the Kpa-Mende from the Kono. On the other hand, Sahr Matturi, an important and knowledgeable Kono elder, vigorously denied that the Kono had anything to do with the Wunde.

McCulloch summarizes the information on the Wunde, saying "Little is known about its purpose and organisation; it is said to have resembled the Poro, which it may have rivalled in power in this area in the past. It appears to function today mainly as a dancing society" (1950:37).

Certainly my own impression, gathered from various people, is that it continues to rival the Poro, as far as the Kpa-Mende are concerned. As one man said, when early on in my fieldwork I asked if this area could be considered Sewa-Mende, "No! We are Kpa-Mende here. We have the Wunde." Others also indicated that for the Kpa-Mende, Wunde is *the* important society; Poro is secondary. However, I am not sure whether universal initiation among the Kpa-Mende into Wunde is considered as necessary as it is into Poro (cf. Addison 1936:208), but it is clear that advancement for a Kpa-Mende closely correlates with advancement in the Wunde.

McCulloch (1950:37) cites four grades, or levels of advancement in the Wunde:
1. *Ngambublesia*, or senior members;
2. *Kamakwesia*, who dress like women and act as peacemakers in the fire dance;
3. *Lahlesia*; and
4. *Kuriblesia*, the latest initiates.

This may be compared with Addison's enumeration of the grades in the same society (1936:208):
1. *Fambu* or *Ngombublesia*, the fire men with long sticks;

2. *Kamakwesia*, who dress themselves like women and wear a large
   bunch of feathers as a headdress — they sing, dance, and make peace;
3. *Kabong* or *kuriblesia*, who hold a short forked stick; and
4. *Lahwa*, who hold a long staff and lead the dancing.

My own information on Wunde grades comes from two principal
sources, the first, a group of men who outlined the levels as follows:
1. *Fambos*, who gather all the dancers and dance with a bunch of sticks;
2. *Kamakowesia*, who dress like women, wear headdresses like birds and
   shoulder-arm strands like wings;
3. *Kabon*, who dance with a long stick;
4. *Laa*, who dance with forked sticks;
5. *Ngɔmbuwasa*, heavy fire men, very bad men, of whom people are
   afraid; and
6. *Lawas*, the heads, the most important members.

The second source, independent of the first, was a man who had just
joined the ngɔmbuwasa, and was receiving hearty congratulations all
round. He confirmed that there are six grades, but added that there are
grades within the grades. Thus there are three main grades within the
ngɔmbuwasa, and also grades within the lawas, although he declined to
talk about the latter, since he was not a member of that level, and
therefore could not "really know about it".

As far as this information goes, it correlates fairly well with the corresponding terms found in Innes's dictionary (1969), although his definitions are, of course, more general: *fambo*, junior member of Wunde
society (1969:10); *kamakɔwɔ*, Wunde member who dances in women's
clothing (1969:39); *kagbɔg*, Wunde member who can take the position of
kamakɔwɔ, *laandèkpè*, or *ngɔmbu wepe* (1969:38); *Laa*, junior official in
Wunde (1969:69); *ngɔmbu wa*, a high official in Wunde society
(1969:109); *laa wa*, senior member of Wunde (1969:69). His definitions
for *kamakɔwɔ* and *ngɔmbu* both indicate dressing in women's clothing
during the dance. However, it may be noted that the basic definition for
ngɔmbu is "fire". *Laandèkpè* and *ngɔmbu wepe*, mentioned in the definition for *kagbɔg*, are simply defined as Wunde officials, the latter a minor
one.

Thus the terms he gives: *laa*; *laa ta hu*, senior member of Wunde,
(1969:69); *laa wa*; and *laandèkpè*, may all refer to grades within the *lawa*
(*laa wa*) level. Likewise, *ngɔmbu wa* and *ngɔmbu wepe* may refer to
grades within the level *ngɔmbuwasa*. Here as elsewhere the problem
would benefit from further study, although detailed information on
Wunde is no easier to come by than other comparable information among
the Mende.

Obviously the positions are defined primarily in terms of the function
they play in the dance, whatever their other functions may be. My
information is that the dance is performed on three kinds of occasions:

initiations, funerals, and "other celebrations", such as the visit of a district commissioner or other dignitary (cf. Addison 1936:208). I have witnessed the dance as given on the latter two kinds of occasions, and Addison described the initiation dance. While some say that the funeral dance is supposed to be more solemn, others say rather that it is "to cheer people up". I could not see any functional differences of this kind. The differences among the Wunde dances I saw seemed related to scale and to the general spirit, or lack of it, of the dancers.

The Wunde dance always starts after dark, around a huge fire, in which nowadays sometimes tires soaked in kerosene are used to augment the blaze. The different grades are called in according to a set of traditional choruses. The fambos are the first to enter the scene dancing in a circle around the fire, rhythmically beating their bundles of switches against their ankles. The other grades enter subsequently, forming new circles, with the lawas led by the chief wielding the *hembe*, a circular fan, in figure-eight motions. After the mock battle, the call *"Ah masende, masende, bawa mu ndo yalei"* ["Ah, women, come and join us to dance"], brings all the women into the ring, and after them the children, too. While there is an order in the calls to dance, and in the part each group of performers plays, it is very hard for an outsider to follow, because of the constant interweaving of the different circles, each trying to cut through the other, and the chief with the hembe forcing them all to change directions at his will. The dance may last all night. To quote Addison's account of what is indeed an impressive rite:

Then comes the great event of the night. In the centre of the dancing ground we make a great fire. Without fire life would cease to exist. Around this form the *Ngombublesia* in a circle to guard it from attack; another circle forms round them and they are the *Lablesia*; another circle around these two circles is made up of the *Kuriblesia*, the men and boys who have just joined the society, or who are the youngest members. The circles move round while the drums beat and the women sing. Presently they all begin to dance as they move round the fire each circle keeping to its circle. Then, suddenly, the *Kuriblesia* will try to push the *Ngombublesia* into the fire with their short forked sticks, but the *Lablesia* will try to stop them, and the *Ngombublesia* with their longer rods will strike at the attackers to beat them off. There is great excitement, singing, dancing, drums beating, the fire roaring, the moon shining, the circles shouting and struggling; a very fine sight to see. The *Kamakwesia* then join the revolving circles and make peace between the defenders of the fire of life and those who wish to destroy it and them. Nobody is hurt. All the pushing and striking is fun.

Peace taking the place of the tumult around the fire of life, men and women, boys and girls, then mingle in one great throng and dance and sing until the sun begins to rise, and then the dance ends. The fees taken from those who have been initiated, and those who have desired to rise in grade are then divided between the senior members of the Society, and everybody returns home to await the next summons for the Wunde men and boys to meet (1936:209).

As indicated above, there may be a closer relationship between the secular and sacred authority of the Wunde among the Kpa-Mende than is the case with Poro elsewhere. In one chiefdom I knew of, the chiefdom speaker, most likely next in line of succession to the chieftainship, was head of the Wunde, and in another chiefdom, the paramount chief apparently played the same role in Wunde there.

A further question relates to the place of women in Wunde, but the evidence is inconclusive. One account quoted by Addison states that "women were not admitted because of the inability of the sex to keep a secret." On the other hand, in another account given him, the woman who had the dream which originated the society is named Masandi (1936:207). Innes defines *masende* as a "women member of Wunde" (1969:80). Beyond the use of the same term in the final chorus of the Wunde dance quoted above, I have no information. But one wonders if there may not be an office in Wunde corresponding to that of Mabɔle in Poro. Migeod's statement that, "apparently one single female initiate is allowed . . . called Masendi" (1926:249), certainly lends support to the possibility that there is such an office.

The Wunde Spirits?

Whether costumed spirits are associated with the society is a further open question. I did not see any, but it is possible that they are sometimes represented, for in the same account given Addison which refers to Masandi, reference also is made to a "devil" which her husband encountered: "The devil, Fanjawa, however is continued in the Wunde Bush, but not as a devil. . . . We cannot get Fanjawa the devil to be here to-day, but we dress up a man to look like him, an awful figure, but very funny" (1936:207). The closest corresponding term to Fanjawa that I can find in Innes's dictionary is *fowa*, "a devil" (1969:14).[5]

SUMMARY

Poro-Sande Interrelations

As may be seen in the paragraphs concerning the Poro and Sande societies, there are parallels in their function and organization. Where possible, elements of complementation and opposition have also been noted, and should certainly receive further study.[6]

---

[5]   One informant suggested that the Nafalie is a Wunde devil, but I do not give his information much weight.

[6]   Migeod (1926:100) reports that in mourning the death of a Sande leader, the women "wore a cloth round their middle and drawn up between their legs like a man's. . . . It is rather curious that in many of their celebrations the women should either wear their waist

Although Little is concerned with dealing with each society rather in isolation, he does cite the work of earlier authors who tended to view the societies as being more closely connected:

... according to Harley ... it was also customary for the head woman of Sande to confer with the leader of Poro. The latter was overlord of Sande and so the men's society had indirect supervision of the girls' training as well as charge of the boys. Mary Kingsley, who also mentions the Sande head woman's practice of attending Poro meetings, goes even further in this respect, claiming that the boys' and girls' initiation schools represent two sides of the same institution ... (Little 1965:356).

He further notes (1965:359) that,

Harley came to doubt if the pinnacle of power, represented by the inner circle, was *within* the Poro. He suggests that it was within the cult of the masks of which the Poro was the most highly developed form for manifesting the power of the ancestors toward the people.

The precise word for Poro in Mende is, according to Little, *Poe*, meaning literally "no end" (1965:354; cf. Innes 1969:126, s.v. *pcc*.) One of Schwab's literate Mano informants gave him a translation of *Bo* (Poro in Mano) as "earth": "of the earth, pertaining to or having to do with the earth or ground. Schwab's conclusion in this respect is that Poro is an elaborate modification of earth-mother worship" (Little 1965:354).

Butt-Thompson (1969:239) refers to one legend of the origin of Bundu, claiming it to be the "Mother of Poro; this being founded on a misunderstanding of why the Head is an honorary member of the Poro council." Although it is hard to trace Butt-Thompson's information, due to lack of citations, I mention this passage in connection with Schwab's view, and also with reference to the carver Sonah's account of the origin of Bundu masks (purporting that they were the first masks carved). When I asked him if before this they had not carved masks, he said no, and was quite strong on the point. In all tact, I simply could not go any further on that point with him. Of course, the legend itself may be viewed as a "just so" story, but it was supported, at least in part, by different information gained from other informants.[7]

---

cloth like a man's, or wear knickers like a man. In ordinary life they would not do so." Thomas (1916:180) writes that "women sing Poro songs and men sing Bundu songs during an eclipse", although it is not clear in this case whether he is referring to Mende or Temne practice.

[7] In Little's experience, the most widely occurring accounts of the origin of Poro report the murder of the first Mende chief, or "big man", and his head wife and daughter, and the appropriation of his wealth and power by a band of rival big men, who pretended that he still lived and was attended by the wife and daughter in the bush. The big men then used this deception to further their own power and aggrandizement. This account, as Little notes, recapitulates various institutional features of the society, for example, the office of Mabɔle equals the wife of the original man (Little 1967b:242–243).

As with virtually all discussions of the structure and interrelationships of Poro and Sande the above is tenuous and based on data from several peoples, mostly Liberian. As Little notes (1965:356), comparable information is almost nonexistent for the Mende. This of course is because of the extreme secrecy with which the Mende surround society matters of any importance. Nonetheless, taken together with what we do know of the Mende societies they are suggestive of something more than a simple functional analogy between the two societies. Insofar as a structural interrelationship goes, it would be extremely helpful if we could acquire definite evidence as to whether or not there is conference between leaders of Poro and Sande among the Mende.

As to the male-female opposition and the putative primacy of the female element, that, too, must remain an open question for the present.

General Interrelations Among the Societies

With the exception of the Wunde, which appears to overlap in its functions with the Poro among the Kpa-Mende, the structural relationships among the societies may be expressed as follows:

1. Poro and Sande are universal in membership, with Poro as the ultimate arbiter.

2. There is the possibility of conference between the leaders of the two societies and the possibility of membership in Poro for the Sande leader.

3. Membership in Humɔi and Njaye is dependent on prior initiation into the two former societies.

4. There is a close functional and social–symbolic relationships between the two latter societies.

Overall, what are the functions and importance of the secret societies? Little likens them to medieval Christianity:

Through their staff of hereditary officials, masked "spirits", and rituals, the secret societies canalize and embody supernatural power. Collectively, they provide an institutional structure which bears resemblance to the medieval church in Europe; but with one or two important differences. Like the medieval church, they lay down various rules of conduct, prescribe certain forms of behaviour, and are the sole agency capable of remitting certain sins. On the other hand, both their control over supernatural power and their regulation of lay conduct and behaviour is, to some extent, departmental and even a matter of specialization. That is to say, particular fields of the cultural life and their regulation tend to fall within the exclusive province of specific societies. The combined effect, however, is a pattern of life which is influenced very largely by the secret societies (Little 1967b:240–241).

He later summarizes their functions as:

(a) General education, in the sense of social and vocational training and indoctrination of social attitudes.

(b) Regulation of sexual conduct.

(c) Supervision of political and economic affairs.

(d) Operation of various social services, ranging from medical treatment to forms of entertainment and recreation (1967a:248).

It is now, with some regard to the last-named functions, entertainment and recreation, that I return to a consideration of the masked spirits of the societies.

Outline and Discussion of the Masked Spirits

The outline presented here is based on a selection of the major types I documented in the field, supplemented by a reexamination of some of the older literature as well as by verbal information concerning two types I did not have the opportunity of documenting. Although a few problems will be noted, the "fit" appears to be good. The division between sacred and secular is marked formally by the use of wooden masks for sacred ngafanga, and the use of composite masks (or headdresses) for the secular. This division applies to each of the four major masking societies discussed (see Table 1).

Table 1. Masked spirits (ngafanga) of Mende secret societies

	Poro	Sande	Njaye	Humɔi
Sacred	Gbeni	Sowie	Njokui	Humɔi
Sacred/secular?	Gɔbɔi			
Secular	Falui	Gɔndi	Fakoi	?
	Nafalie			
	Yavie			
	Jobai			

The obvious criterion in this classification is formal: the sacred ngafanga wear black wooden masks (*pace* the indecisive information on the Gbeni; the secular ngafanga wear composite headdresses) *pace* the varicolored wooden ones mentioned by Migeod (1917). Even if the major division is accepted, there still remains an anomaly, as anyone familiar with Mende masked devils will note. This is the *Kongoli* (Plate 12), ubiquitous in the Kpa-Mende area. The Kongoli wears a rough, unpolished, black wooden mask with grotesque features. The raffia costume is undyed and very scant; the wearer's body is scarcely concealed. The Kongoli is a complete clown, a buffoon; anyone can talk to it, and it will answer or propose riddles, sometimes of a racy nature. Its dancing

Plate 12.   Kongoli

lacks any degree of the stateliness which characterizes that of the other devils: it sometimes rolls on the ground, does somersaults, and so on. In many ways it is like the Gɔndi, but it does not seem to "fit" with the other devils. It may dance at most celebrations, but I was told that it does not dance in the Poro bush. Again, I was told: "Anyone can make it, not just a carver"; "It is just for amusement and making money." One man averred that "The Mende got the Kongoli from the Sherbro. A Sherbro man came up here dressed in one once, and so the Mende began to make them." This is quite possible, considering the movement of carvers and entertainment troupes throughout the larger region. However, I do not know anything of the present-day occurrence of Kongolis in Sherbro country.

It may be noted that the Kongoli does not occur in the Ko-Mende area. Its analogue there is the *Jobuli* (Plate 13), which also wears a black wooden mask, with features that are, if not as grotesque as those of the Kongoli, still quite heavy. Its raffia costume is of a very full haystack form, strips of which are sometimes indigo-dyed. It also tells riddles and sings

Plate 13.   Jobuli: note crown carved on forehead

songs, but, probably due to its heavier costume, its dancing lacks the abandon of the Kongoli — so much for the "exceptions to the rule".

Another, less obvious, but important, supportive criterion in the classification presented is essentially functional, and depends on observation of audience reaction in the context of the dancing performances of the different spirits. Little's remark on the "apparent secular nature" of the Gbeni (1954:114) has already been noted above. I cannot remark on the performance of the Gbeni, not having seen it, but it is true that all the other spirits do give dancing performances during celebrations, and that these are in the way of entertainment. Thus they all have a secular aspect in this respect. However, close observation of audience reaction shows that a different reception is given the dancing of the sacred, or more important spirits, for instance Sowie and Gɔbɔi, than is given the lesser ones, the simply amusing spirits. There is more reserve, sometimes awe, in the appreciation of the dancing of Sowie and Gɔbɔi; the appreciation centers on the excellence, the virtuosity, of the dancing. As for the lesser spirits, *amusing* is an apt term, while here, too, there is appreciation of excellence in dancing, the reception of their joking and cavorting is in a much lighter vein. I do not think this difference could be easily caught without repeated observation and consideration. This is particularly the case with regard to the various Poro spirits. When Gɔbɔi makes one of its uncontrolled rushes, the crowd scatters wildly, but the crowd will also back away if Falui or Nafalie advance menacingly with their sticks. However, Gɔbɔi will never posture or cavort in the manner of the other secular Poro spirits, and certainly not in the manner of Kongoli. The same applies to the difference between Sowie and Gɔndi. When Sowie appears alone, the reception is more reserved. When Gɔndi appears with Sowie there is more "audience participation" and abandon (Plate 14).

Plate 14.   Dancing with Gɔndi and Sowie

Another difference between the sacred, or more important spirits, and the secular, or amusing spirits, is that the former needs interpreters, whereas the latter can be spoken to directly. In addition, there is the dogma of "found" masks. It was noted above that the Mende find nɔmɔli when digging their farms, and consider them to have been put there by spirits. Likewise, Sonah's narrative mentioned above, concerning the origin of the soowie, indicates that the original one was found by an old woman after instructions in a dream. Even now, he said, some masks are found, but not as much as before. Another person made an attempt to explain the dogma more fully to me:

In fact, all the [sacred] masks are originally found. A person has a dream, and suffers much. When he awakes, he goes to the place and finds the mask. This mask, the original one, is like clay. It is heavy to wear. Only society members can see it. So the mask is washed and the carver is washed with the same medicine. Then he carves a substitute mask for public appearances.

This certainly ties in everything neatly, as far as the Mende are concerned, regardless of the empirical problems of the researcher! It also helps explain the difficulty in getting attributions as to the carver of a particular mask: not only are people probably genuinely vague about this, particularly if it is an old mask or was traded into the area, and so on, but it would seem that they also are not willing to admit to this "flaw" in the dogma. As far as I know, it is only sacred masks that are found in this way.

However, all the spirits have medicine as part of their accoutrement. It is the medicine which activates the costume as a spirit and makes it very wonderful and dangerous at the same time (*masubɔngowa*). Even children, when they are making their imitation devils, will get leaves from the bush to put in the headdress, to serve as "medicine". A further point here is, that while Westerners would speak of the person dancing in the costume as impersonating the spirit (cf. Little 1967b:251), the Mende phrase it differently: "It is a special privilege to dance with the devil."

The secret society ngafanga appear on four principal kinds of occasions: (1) initiations; (2) funerals of big men; (3) visits of dignitaries or other civil celebrations; and (4) to punish infractions of society rules. On the three former sorts of occasions various devils may appear and there is music, singing, and dancing. The last occasion would seem to be different in tone, judging from accounts given me, and from Alldridge's description (1901) of Sande operations in the apprehension and judgment of a violator of that society's rules. He writes that there is no music when the devil makes an "arrest" (1901:143). Likewise, although I had no opportunity of observing such proceedings, my information is that the Njokui or the Humɔi will sit in state in the town center to make judgment: they do not dance on this occasion.

For most celebrations nowadays, as I observed them, both Poro and Sande spirits will dance, not together usually, but alternately. However, on one occasion I observed, a Nafalie caroused around dancing Sowies, causing considerable commotion, but more amusement than any real consternation. Some people said that in the old days Poro and Sande spirits would not dance at the same time: "When the Poro boys were pulled, their devils dance, and the Bundu devils danced for the Bundu people." Nowadays it is different, said one young man, with mild sarcasm, "because of the increased cooperation".

A final note should be made concerning the "life expectancy" of masks and costumes. It varies. I have seen masks that were a good thirty years old and still in perfect condition, though the more delicate carving was somewhat effaced by constant rubbing with palm oil. On the other hand, I have also seen masks less than ten years old riddled with insects, nibbled by mice, especially around the mouth where they are fed, or simply cracked, so that they were no longer fit for public use. The raffia costumes have a much shorter life expectancy, probably no more than five or six years, if that, depending to some extent on frequency of use. Thus, the life expectancy of masks and costumes presents a problem in terms of changing social conditions. In the old days, when initiations and other celebrations were less frequent, the schedule probably better fitted the life expectancy of the costumes. A major effort could have been made every five or six years to outfit all the necessary figures. Now, with initiations an annual occurrence, and other celebrations too, probably more frequent, there is more call for the appearance of the ngafanga, but there are fewer young adults remaining in the villages to make and dance with the costumes. Thus the richness and pomp of ceremonial life is waning.

In conclusion, I should again like to emphasize that the classification presented here is tentative. The primary criterion used is a general formal one: media differences in mask construction signify different types of spirits. The classification proposed on this basis is further supported by observation of contrastive variation between the two main types of costumed spirit in similar functional contexts, and by statements of informants. It is likely that fuller application of similar criteria will lead to a refinement of the classification, but not all such similar criteria will be found to have differential significance. For instance, while it is very likely that there is some color symbolism operating, as in the black of the traditional costume of the Sowie, the great variety of color used in the decoration of the secular or entertainment devils is probably just an effect of new colors and materials available in the markets in recent times.

As stated at the outset of this paper, there still remain areas of Mende thought and culture which outsiders cannot yet know or understand. Nonetheless, after nearly a hundred years of secondary and partitive attention to the problem of Mende masking, this paper does present a possible basis for the understanding of one of the most complex masking systems in West Africa.

REFERENCES

ADDISON, W.
1936   The Wunde society: Protectorate of Sierra Leone, British West Africa. *Man* 36 (273): 207–209.
ALLDRIDGE, THOMAS J.
1901   *The Sherbro and its hinterland.* London: Macmillan.
1910   *A transformed colony.* London: Seeley.
BUTT-THOMPSON, F. W.
1969   *West African secret societies.* New York: Argosy-Antiquarian.
DARK, P. J. C., A. GERBRANDS, L. REINHARDT HILL
1970   Report for the National Institute of Mental Health on Small Research Grant MH13353–01: Survey for Ethno-Aesthetic Research. Mimeo.
DAWSON, J. L. M.
1966   Traditional concepts of mental health in Sierra Leone. *Sierra Leone Studies*, n.s. 18:18–28.
D'AZEVADO, WARREN L.
1970   *The artist archetype in Gola culture.* Preprint No. 14. Nevada: Desert Research Institute, University of Nevada.

DURKHEIM, EMILE
1915   *The elementary forms of the religious life.* Translated by J. W. Swain. London: George Allen and Unwin.

EASMON, M. C. F.
1958   Madame Yoko, ruler of the Mendi confederacy. *Sierra Leone Studies*, n.s. 11:165–168.

EBERL-ELBER, RALPH
1936   *West Afrikas letztes Rätsel: Erlebnisbericht über die Forschungsreise 1935 durch Sierra Leone.* Berlin: Bergland.

FAGG, WILLIAM, MARGARET PLASS
1966   *African sculpture: an anthology.* London: Studio Vista.

HALL, H. U.
1938   *The Sherbo of Sierra Leone.* Philadelphia: University of Pennsylvania.

HARLEY, GEORGE W.
1941   *Notes on the Poro in Liberia.* Papers of the Peabody Museum of American Archaeology and Ethnology, Harvard University 19(2). Cambridge, Massachusetts: Peabody Museum.
1950   *Masks as agents of social control in northeast Liberia.* Papers of the Peabody Museum of American Archaeology and Ethnology, Harvard University 32(2). Cambridge, Massachusetts: Peabody Museum.

HARRIS, W. T., HARRY A. E. SAWYERR
1968   *The springs of Mende belief and conduct.* Freetown: Sierra Leone University Press.

HOFSTRA, SJOERD
1937   The social significance of the oil palm in the life of the Mendi. *Internationales Archiv für Ethnographie*, 34(5–6):105–118. Leiden.
1940   Ancestral spirits of the Mendi. *Internationales Archiv für Ethnographie* 39(1–4):177–196. Leiden.
1942   The belief among the Mendi in non-ancestral spirits and its relations to a case of parricide. *Internationales Archiv für Ethnographie* 40(5–6):175–182. Leiden.

INNES, GORDON
1969   *A Mende-English dictionary.* Cambridge: Cambridge University Press.

KINGSLEY, MARY H.
1899   *West African studies.* London: Macmillan.

LEUZINGER, ELSY
1960   *The art of Africa.* Baden-Baden: Holte.

LITTLE, KENNETH
1954   "The Mende in Sierra Leone," in: *African worlds.* Edited by C. Daryll Forde, 111–137. London: Oxford University Press.
1960   "The role of the secret society in cultural specialization," in: *Cultures and societies of Africa.* Edited by Simon Ottenberg and Phoebe Ottenberg, 199–213. New York: Random House.
1965   The political function of the Poro: part I. *Africa* 35(4): 349–365.
1966   The political function of the Poro: part II. *Africa* 36(1): 62–71.
1967a   "The Mende chiefdoms of Sierra Leone," in: *West African kingdoms in the nineteenth century.* Edited by C. Daryll Forde and P. M. Kaberry, 239–259. London: Oxford University Press.
1967b   *The Mende of Sierra Leone,* revised edition: London: Routledge and Kegan Paul.

MARGAI, MILTON A. S.
1948   Welfare work in a secret society. *African Affairs* 47(189):227–230.

McCULLOCH, M.
1950   *Peoples of Sierra Leone*. Ethnographic Survey of Africa, Western Africa 2. London: International African Institute.
MIGEOD, F. W. H.
1916a   The Poro society: the building of the Poro house and making of the image. *Man* 16(61):102–108.
1916b   Mende songs. *Man* 16(112):184–191.
1917   A Mende dance. *Man* 17(102):153–156.
1926   *A view of Sierra Leone*. London: Kegan Paul.
PHILLIPS, RUTH
1972   "The Vai women's society mask." Paper presented to the Manding Conference, School of Oriental and African Studies, University of London, June.
REINHARDT, LORETTA R.
1973   "A preliminary statement on Mende aesthetics." Unpublished manuscript.
THOMAS, NORTHCOTE W.
1916   *Anthropological report on Sierra Leone*, volume one: *Law and custom of the Timne and other tribes*. London: Harrison and Sons.
VANDENHOUTE, P. J.
1948   *Classification stylistique du masque Dan et Guéré de la Côte d'Ivoire occidentale*. Leiden: Brill.
WALLIS, C. BRAITHWAITE
1903   *The advance of our West African empire*. London: T. Fisher Unwin.
WRIGHT, ARTHUR R.
1907   Secret societies and fetishism in Sierra Leone. *Folklore* 18:423–427.

Hortelanos: *An Investigation into a Masking Tradition in a Changing Society*

JANET BRODY ESSER

It is customary in the city of Uruapán, in the Mexican state of Michoacán, for the various *barrio* [district] fiesta parades to be led by a ragtag group of men whose disguises are completely individualized and highly inventive. This group comprises the masquerade of the *hortelanos* [gardeners]. Although the participants share strong linguistic, family, and *compadrazco* [fictive kinship] ties with the surrounding Tarascan villages, they have entered the milieu of urban life and are likely to be employed as mechanics and mill-workers.

In general the masks are constructed by the participants themselves who in most cases have no other contact with maskmaking. In contrast to other masquerades in the area, which adhere to prescribed visual forms, the *hortelano* masks tend to be fanciful in the extreme and the usual practice is for each such nonexpert to vie with his fellows in the invention of fantastic apparitions. These are not begun until shortly before performance and stress the use of ephemeral and indigenous materials.

Masks are discarded and left to rot after the fiesta although a few may reappear in succeeding years until suffering a natural demise. No attempt is made to preserve them. At the most their lifespan is three years, and it is considered preferable to apply oneself to fresh inventions. This is a departure from the careful preservation of masks and headdresses observed in other masking traditions in the region. Although stock characters and repeated forms do emerge in the hortelanos, the emphasis would appear to be on novelty, individuality, and spontaneity — qualities which are all antitraditional. These appearances, however, are highly deceptive.

The plates in this paper were photographed by the writer during the fiesta of la Magdalena on July 23, 1972. The subjects are participants in the masquerade of the hortelanos and are all residents of the Barrio de la Magdalena, Uruapán, Michoacán.

The form of the hortelanos, no less than that of the other masquerades, is determined by tradition, and ostensible spontaneity is hedged around by the limitations of a highly structured function. Implicit in this function is the need to provide a transition from the world of ordinary experience to the intensified one of the fiesta. Thus the hortelanos proclaim the specialness of what is to follow: they provide for a bursting release of built-up tensions while at the same time serving as a focus which seeks to attract and manipulate the attention of the spectators.

In addition to this specifically aesthetic role, the hortelanos offer a channel whereby ideas may be examined on a nonthreatening level. By presenting a series of satiric and often bawdy commentaries, some of which are traditional and others topical as perceived by the community, they are able to absorb and reflect changes in the greater world while at the same time maintaining a traditional integrity.

Barrio fiestas in Uruapán honor the patron saint of the community and are generally observed for two days. The first day is barrio-oriented, while the second seeks to display the community's accomplishments to the city at large (Weiner 1971:3–6). It is in the middle of the second day of the fiesta that the parades which the hortelanos lead are held. This masquerade includes a wide variety of representations, among them *espanta-pájaros* [scarecrows]; grotesques and fanciful creatures; film and television personalities; and *maringuillas* [women enacted by men].

The city of Uruapán lies in the *tierra templada* [temperate zone] of Michoacán some seventy kilometers from the Carapán junction of the Guadalajara-Morelia highway (West 1948:4). The route which leads through the sierra past several Tarascan-speaking communities, including Cherán and Aranza, has for years provided a convenient detour for tourists wishing to visit the volcano, Parícutin. Recently a highway connecting Uruapán and Pátzcuaro has been completed, offering spectacular scenic views and serving to link Uruapán further to the main tourist centers of attraction. The city has a population of approximately 70,000 people, many of whom find employment in the local cotton mills. The Cupititzeo river, which originates here, provides the source of power to local industry and has created a rain forest of singular beauty, the national park, donated to the nation by its late owner, the poet Eduardo Ruiz. The center of the city teems with commercial activity and vehicular and pedestrian congestion. A large middle class is busily engaged in trade and services. Adjoining the principal plaza is a central market which attracts people from the surrounding sierra villages, many of them, presently or in the recent past, Tarascan speakers. An important network of transportation is established by the existence of frequent and inexpensive bus services. Cargo trucks also make forays into the Tarascan *meseta* [upland] region, the substandard quality of whose roads all but precludes ordinary automobile travel.

Uruapán is subdivided into a number of barrios, each with a strong sense of community identity, especially among the poorer members who form a majority of the population. The binding factors are forged from a shared heritage of rural origin, customs, family, and compadrazco ties, as well as by common residence.[1] A sense of territorial exclusiveness runs high, and young men of one barrio may be considered to have trespassed when entering another, and be subjected to hostile encounters. Those barrios which lie on the outskirts of the city exhibit rural tendencies in house construction, ownership of *milpas* [maize fields], and tenacity of ritual observances. Many of these barrios were in actuality separate villages and were incorporated into the urban structure only recently. In physical appearance they offer a wide range of aspects: some of the streets are paved and the houses form a continuous wall broken occasionally by barred windows and small, sparsely stocked, shops; others are country lanes gutted with craterlike chuckholes and exhibit homes in the form of wooden *trojes* [granaries] identical to those constructed in the surrounding Tarascan-speaking communities (Beals et al. 1944:figures 1, 2; plate 3). Cows, pigs, and chickens are commonly raised within compound walls.

The barrios occupy an anomalous position with regard to generally accepted distinctions between Indian and mestizo societies (Beals 1967:95–96). Structurally the barrios have much in common with Indian communities in terms of attitudes toward residence, outsiders, public works, obligations, and so on. Marriage patterns in previous generations have tended to maintain strong bonds with the surrounding rural villages and although Tarascan is not spoken, many Tarascan words and customs are preserved. Physical and mental patterns which might serve to distinguish Indian from mestizo traits are often ambiguous. An individual may be employed in some form of rationalized industry, be conversant with policies of the *sindicados* [labor unions], and continue to cultivate his *milpa.* His wife may wear city dress, have her hair permanent-waved, and kneel on the dirt floor of her kitchen to grind corn on the *metate.* The same person may define himself as Indian or mestizo depending upon context or circumstance. The barrios are changing but the process is not unilineal, rather, the phenomenon of change is dynamic: old customs are retained with modification; new ones are accepted, again with modification. The resulting amalgam is new and fluid, with consequences which, as yet, are not completely understood.

Each barrio celebrates an annual fiesta which coincides with the day of its patron saint as recorded in the Roman martyrology. The semiritualistic form of the fiesta permits the acting out of shared traditions, beliefs,

[1] Physical residence does not in itself constitute full membership in the barrio community. An individual who lacks the proper family and compadrazco alliances may spend most of his life in the barrio and still be regarded as an outsider.

and ideals. Produced by the community, it reaffirms a sense of well-being and displays to the outside world an image of united purpose. The fiesta is composed of various *cargos* [burdens]: the responsibility for the making of masks, decorating the streets, refurbishing the *santos* in the barrio chapel, instructing dancers in traditional choreography, and the hiring and housing of bands of musicians. Each *cargo* has one or more individuals who serve as *carguero* [sponsor] (Plate 1). In usual practice the assumption of responsibility in the annual fiesta is an avenue to greater leverage within the community and results in increased status. Indeed, refusal to participate may be deemed *egoismo*, a form of antisocial behavior, and community pressure is likely to be applied to the miscreant. The mechanism of the fiesta would seem to insure that wealth not be individually hoarded but plowed back into the group in the form of shared ritual.[2] In addition to augmented social standing accruing to the individual contributor, each barrio takes pride in the quality of its fiesta and a strong sense of competition exists among the barrios.

Plate 1. Three cargueros (front row) of the hortelanos relax after the parade. The man in the white hat (center) is *algaucil*, or constable, of the barrio and does not participate in the masquerade. His activities as sponsor consist in providing meals and advice to the participants. Because of the respect accorded to his position his presence is thought to lend dignity to the proceedings

---

[2] The concept of "limited good" as propounded by Foster (1948, 1965) for the people of Tzintzuntzan is operant also in the attitudes toward fulfillment of obligations and redistribution of material wealth in the barrios of Uruapán.

The Barrio de la Magdalena is neither the richest nor the largest barrio in Uruapán but it is known for the lavishness of its annual fiesta, which is held on July 22 and 23, and has been increasing in complexity with a greater number of the inhabitants participating. Satisfaction has been expressed by involved citizens who have voiced the hope that the barrio will become famous on this account. Each year the fiesta includes three masquerades: the *negritos*, who are dressed like colonial overseers and accompany the children's dance; the *viejitos* who are young boys masked to represent old men; and the hortelanos.[3] The masks for the negritos and the viejitos are provided by two professional mask makers, part-time specialists, who, as highly respected residents, are consulted also on matters of barrio policy.

In the 1940's a priest issued a citywide ordinance against fiestas because of alleged violence. The ban was rescinded after a hiatus of eight years at the instigation of another priest who was more sympathetic toward them. It was reported that before the ban all of the barrios produced fiestas as elaborate as that of the Barrio de la Magdalena is now. Some of the barrios never resumed the celebrations and a number of masking traditions were abandoned at that time (although closely related forms continue to be performed elsewhere in the region).[4] Many of those that did survive did so with considerable alteration as to kind of mask employed and the age of the participants.[5] The barrio members insist that their fiesta celebrations emerged from the hiatus with renewed vigor and that the components are all of traditional form with only minor modifications. In the Barrio de la Magdalena the masquerade of the hortelanos was resumed in 1957 at the instigation of the barrio's two professional mask makers who that year made all of the masks themselves.

The hortelano masquerade is considered to be a *cargo*, and its sponsorship generally involves a number of men, some of whom are also participants. While the cargueros donate time and offer some direction, monetary contributions are not required. In this the hortelanos departs from usual practice because in all other *cargos* the donation of money or

[3]   In Uruapán and in the villages of the meseta, *negrito* [black one] dances are often held in conjunction with fiestas. One version described by Beals is (1946:144–147, plate 6) is still practiced in Cherán on Christmas Day, New Year's Day, and Epiphany. The negrito masks of Uruapán today are shiny black, often with forked beards, aquiline noses, and pursed lips. The *viejitos* [little old men] are danced in the villages near Pátzcuaro, where the maskers are adult men, and in the Barrio de la Magdalena, Uruapán, where in recent years the performers have been boys ranging in age from seven to fourteen. The masks of the viejitos in both regions present wrinkled, light-skinned visages with toothless, senile grins.

[4]   Prior to the hiatus negrito dances similar to that of Cherán were performed in the Barrio de la Magdalena and in the Barrio de San Francisco of Uruapán. The maskers wore dark business suits, black gloves, and bland, beardless masks.

[5]   The viejitos, for example, were formerly danced by grown men, and individuals from nearby villages have objected to the barrio's present practice of using boys. These critics suggest that the decrease in the age of the participants reflects a lessening of the devotion with which the *cargo* is regarded.

valuable goods is considered to be an inherent part of participation. Generally two men undertake the responsibility of the hortelanos and ask others to join with them. These initial cargueros make their commitments during the fiesta of the preceding year. As with all other aspects concerning the fiesta, the business of deciding upon individual sponsorship is usually attended to in a fairly informal manner: there is no central steering committee; during the course of a fiesta most responsibilities for the next year's undertakings will have been assumed on a voluntary basis. Suffused with the positive mood generated by the ambience of a fiesta one individual may ask a friend to share a burden with him. His knowledge of this friend is accurate and he is rarely refused. It sometimes happens that second thoughts occur but the original commitment is always honored and, in the case of the hortelanos, discharged with enthusiasm. It has been reported that at times cargueros of hortelanos emerge in a seemingly casual manner — those who are most enthusiastic assuming positions of leadership. Since these leaders are highly respected by virtue of repeated participation in this or other fiesta functions they are assured of the approval of the group.

The structure of the hortelanos allows much more latitude for individual interpretation and does not seem to require the kind of sustained direction which is necessary for other masquerades. Each masker provides his own disguise and the responsibilities of the cargueros generally are discharged by providing dressing houses, squiring participants to places of assembly, addressing some words by way of formal admonishment concerning deportment, and suggesting a few dramatically potential situations. After the parade the carguero holds open house and the participants relax while discussing each incident of the morning's activities. It is customary for such a group to be photographed by an itinerant professional and the resulting picture becomes a cherished momento (Plate 2). One informant, who is himself a carguero for the hortelanos as well as for the viejitos, reports that the cargueras tend to perform from a sense of camaraderie rather than a sacred obligation.

All of the barrio fiesta parades in Uruapán are led by hortelanos, but nowhere is the number of participants nor the variety of masks and disguises as great as in those produced by the Barrio de la Magdalena. Although the disguises of the hortelanos are varied and individualized a number of themes serve to bind them together visually and conceptually. To a lesser or greater degree all of them are in ragged dress in marked contrast to the splendor of the maskers who follow them in the parade. Old, torn, and ill-fitting clothes are mandatory and accoutrements include "ready-mades" which would delight the heart of any dadaist.[6] It

---

[6]   "Ready-made" was a term coined by the artist Marcel Duchamp to describe his use of manufactured objects in unusual contexts. Dadaists are subscribers to an antiestablishment art movement founded in Zurich in 1915.

should be noted here that the plethora of discarded objects to which we are accustomed does not exist in Mexico in general and certainly not among the poor. Paper cartons, bits of wire, string, plastic, and so on, are carefully hoarded and their liberal inclusion in the attire of the hortelanos is not as nonprecious as might appear at first consideration (Plate 3). Nevertheless, the kinds of materials used are very different from those of the other masquerades. Instead of silk, embroidery, sequins, and braid, the raw materials include baling wire, masking tape, old gunny sacks, and interlinings from overcoats (Plate 4). Ephemeral and indigenous materials are emphasized. Cabbages and onions adorn masks made of calabashes (*huaje* in Tarascan, from the Nahuatl), palm trunks, banana leaves (Plate 5), animal skins (Plate 6), cardboard boxes, tortilla baskets, and even fragments of soccer and other playing balls (Plate 7). In some instances the application of cosmetics is an acceptable alternative to the use of a face mask. The emphasis on variety and the ingenious use of humble materials actually generates its own sense of plenitude analogous to the luxuriance of the other masquerades.

A number of constant or stock characters begins to emerge from the assortment of disguises exhibited in the repertoire of the hortelanos. In addition to a scattering of celebrities (e.g. Topo Gigio, a sort of Mexican Mickey Mouse, who may be represented in flapping huaje mask, and Cantínflas, who has appeared complete with suitcase — Plate 8), *espantapájeros* [guerrillas] (Plate 9) and animals are represented. An important subgroup is that of the maringuillas (Plate 10), transvestite characters who conceptualize the role of women in the masquerade: various aspects of womanhood are invoked, including the maternal, seductive, pious, and dignified. With the exception of the maringuillas some overlapping of categories is common, as guerrillas may incorporate animal masks into their disguises and espantapájeros put on negrito or viejito masks (although here the context is completely altered). Antique masks weighty with dignity acquired by virtue of having been danced once long ago are brought out to dance again. Horrific images or grotesques of all kinds abound: mummies and animal-headed figures (Plate 11) swinging dead chickens or rats are recurring themes. Medical treatment, especially, is parodied with graphic horror. Even the ubiquitous tourist and his omnipresent camera is represented, his *gringo* freckles exaggerated into plague spots.

Although a number of boys and youths may participate in the hortelanos, in general, the masquerade is composed of the young married males of the community with leadership assumed by a few respected enthusiasts of early middle age. It is reported that the pressing obligations of married men prohibit their attendance at the many rehearsals required by the more structured masquerades. The viejitos, for example, practice almost every afternoon at the home of their carguero for a period of about three weeks prior to the fiesta. Although almost everyone in the barrio is adept at all of the traditional dances only the best dancers are chosen to perform. Rehearsals seek to instill errorless group interaction. In contrast to these masquerades, the kinds of efforts which are demanded of the hortelanos are less rigorous in terms of time since most preparations are made at the last minute.

The masks and accoutrements of the hortelanos are usually the invention of the individual participant who, in the overwhelming number of instances, is not a professional mask maker. Even in the few cases where the services of the professional are sought, as, for example, by his son or close friend, the mask maker departs dramatically from his normal style and choice of materials. One mask maker whose work includes negrito masks, examples of which are included in the collections of the regional museum in Morelia and the anthropology museum in Mexico City, makes masks of gourd with bits of wool glued on and a nose made from the gourd's stem (Plates 12 and 13). Another, the carver of the viejito masks, is a habitual leader of the hortelanos and usually constructs for himself a disguise comprising a number of gourds combined with animal skins (Plate 14).

Plate 2.   Copies of group portraits are eagerly sought by participants in the hortelano masquerade. Groupings generally emerge on the basis of compadrazco and *pandilla* ties. The masks portrayed here are made of gourd, cardboard and soccer-ball fragments

Plate 3. Cardboard masks, such as the three on the left, are usually constructed at the dressing stations on the morning of the day of the parade. The simplicity demonstrated in the design of the mask on the left is rare, but nonetheless effective

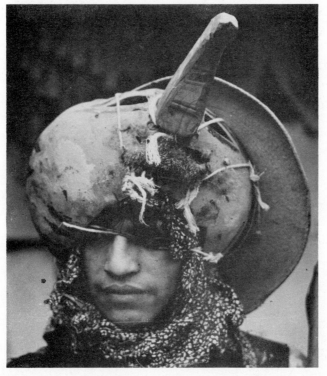

Plate 4. Mask of large pumpkin-shaped squash worn on top of head during moment of relaxation. The squash has been painted blue and a carved wooden nose added as well as scraps of fur. Remnants of overcoat interlining protect the masker's head and throat

Plate 5.   Masker emerges from foliage behind dressing house. Mask is constructed of dried banana leaves wrapped around bamboo frame. Headdress is piece of cut plastic street decoration and shirt has been smeared with red paint

Plate 6.   Neighbors press close to observe hortelanos in the barrio. Masks are of gourd, cardboard, and animal skins. Masker on right has added false nose and spectacles of plastic

Plate 7. Masks are often worn tilted back when the participant is resting. For a functioning view of the same mask see Plate 2, second row, third from left. Rubber playing balls and vegetable fiber were used for its construction. Remnants of burlap were used for the vest

Plate 8. A masker disguised as the popular Mexican movie star, Cantinflas, emerges from the dressing house carrying a suitcase.

Plate 9. Guerrilla in animal-skin mask and old felt hat. Bullet hole may be observed in crown. The hat, which is of very thick felt, belonged to the masker's great grandfather, who, it is claimed, saw duty with Pancho Villa

Plate 10. Maringuillas (front row center and right) in street in front of dressing house after staging of mock *robo*

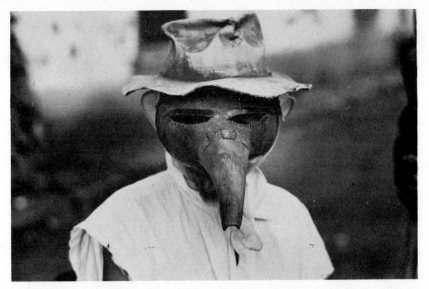

Plate 11. This red-painted gourd mask was made by a barrio baker with no previous experience as a mask maker. The movable nose is the gourd's top and is attached to the face portion with yarn

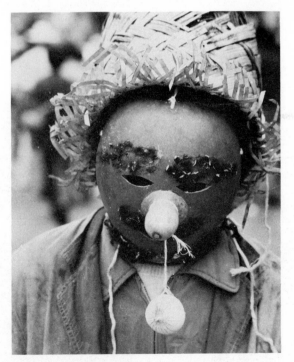

Plate 12. This gourd mask was made by one of the barrio's two professional mask makers. The nose is the stem of the gourd and the hat (added by the masker) is a frayed tortilla basket. This was the second annual appearance of the mask which was then discarded at the end of the fiesta

Plate 13.   This gourd mask with attached gourd cap was also made by a professional mask maker. The beard was made from vegetable fiber

Plate 14. This gourd and animal-skin mask was made and worn by the second professional mask maker who resides in the barrio. He was also a carguero of the hortelanos

Despite the seeming "hellzapoppin" quality of the hortelanos the *cargo* is undertaken with an air of seriousness. The participants gather together on the morning of the second day of the fiesta at one of the homes previously designated as dressing stations. Here they are exhorted by an older barrio resident to conduct themselves with the kind of dignity befitting their roles as emissaries of the barrio. These admonitions include warnings against molesting any bystanders along the parade route. The participants begin to arrive at the dressing houses at about eight in the morning and masks are often assembled at this time. In addition to mutual aid in dressing provided by the maskers themselves, supplementary aid is proffered by the owner of the dressing station and his household. Officially the inside of the house and its yard are forbidden to nonparticipants although small boys do enter and leave at will. In contrast to the hilarity with which the disguises are later greeted the atmosphere in the dressing houses is quite restrained. Food is not served and the participants do not dine until about three in the afternoon after they have completed their physically taxing circuit of the city. Spirits are imbibed in small amounts; a more abandoned attitude toward drinking is postponed until the afternoon.

At about ten or ten-thirty in the morning the disguised hortelanos begin to emerge singly or in small groups from the dressing house (Plate 15). A small crowd of spectators, composed mostly of young boys, eagerly anticipates their appearance. In the daylight the hortelanos gravely inspect each other and often return to the house for minor adjustments or to offer additional aid to those who have not yet completed their costumes.

Disguises are conceived of individually, two or more members never teaming to present a tableau. From the time the hortelano leaves the dressing house until the termination of the parade the participant remains in character. He is not simply a man in costume; every gesture and attitude of posture supports his assumed characterization. Even the quality of his voice is changed as he affects either guttural or falsetto tones. His identity has been transformed and he no longer responds to his own name. Nor is this interpretation of character static. Again, from the moment of completion of disguise, whenever there are spectators in attendance, the hortelano acts out a series of dramatic situations either alone or with a changing cast of partners. If, as is customary, some of these situations have been suggested by a carguero earlier, it will have been in a desultory manner without a definitive sequence in mind. Other situations are thought out by the individual alone or result from discussions with one or a few of his fellows. Cooperation in the Barrio de la Magdalena is often enlisted from one's *pandilla* [agemates] and dramatic presentations among the hortelanos may be enacted by those thus related. Since the participants are well known to each other and most of the situations are of

Plate 15.   A participant disguised as an espantapájero in a dried banana-leaf mask poses in front of one of the dressing houses

a traditional nature, a minimum of cues results in successful interaction. Thus, what appears to the outsider to be spontaneous is in reality an interpretive treatment of an internalized stock of shared patterns. Although these patterns exhibit variety, resultant behavior is far more stylized and conventional than would appear to those not acquainted with the corpus. Still, despite yearly repetition, changes in content do occur, reflecting that which has caught the imagination of the populace. So it is that characters from cinema and television enter the repertoire. In the barrios close by the national park tourists are in constant attendance and, not surprisingly, are parodied in the annual parade. Fads and fashions are reflected in the choice of satirical subjects. A few generations ago masks representing the bourgeois, fat and officious, were common, as were pirates and "wild Indians". These have passed from favor to be supplanted by carabineros and cartoon characters. In the midst of all this variety a degree of cohesion is provided by the incorporation, in almost all instances, of vegetables into the costumes — however incongruous (Plate 16).

The term *hortelanos* is said in the barrio to refer to the divine gardeners who advised Mary Magdalene that Christ had risen from the tomb. They are also said to represent those who cultivate vegetables, especially

Plate 16. This espantapájero is wearing a mask made from a soccer ball. The hair is of cut-plastic street decoration and blue spots have been daubed on his arms with a paint brush

tomatoes, and the majority of the participants, regardless of disguise, do carry as a badge of occupation long poles or crooks such as are commonly employed in horticulture (Plate 17). These poles are used to comic advantage and serve as flexible props during the performance of the masquerade. Thus it would appear that a sacred theme is combined with a profane one just as in the fiesta itself concerns of ostensibly religious nature are melded, sometimes imperceptibly and sometimes quite jarringly, with the secular.

An elderly resident of the Barrio de la Magdalena, father-in-law of one of the two professional mask makers, described the masquerade of the hortelanos as he remembered it from his youth.[7] All of the participants

---

[7] As this informant is about seventy-seven the events described would have been coeval with the period of revolution.

Plate 17.   The poles carried by the hortelanos are like the ones used to remove fruit from trees. The mask in the center was made of mens' undershirting stretched over a bamboo frame

made their own masks of huaje, dressed themselves in old trousers and jackets, and prepared long poles with hooked ends. Their first concerted performance took place in the atrium of the local church.[8] A series of situation comedies which varied a little from year to year were staged. A sequence was established and adhered to which was much less flexible than that in evidence today. First they pretended to be truck gardeners and with their poles searched for hidden chilies near the feet of the spectators. This not only delighted the onlookers but served the very practical and still essential function of keeping the crowds from pressing too close. Next, they shouted, "to war", and, wielding their poles like spears, clashed them together, making a great racket while many of the participants executed pratfalls. A sudden shift in scene had them working on a magazine, and a giant notebook was brought out, the poles now being understood to represent huge pencils, These hortelano journalists went from person to person among the spectators asking for names so they could be written down. Next, one hortelano announced that he had discovered a deserter and the locale was transformed to a mock court-

[8]   It is customary in Uruapán and in the villages of the meseta and lacustrine region for masquerades to be performed in the churchyard immediately after Mass on the first day of the fiesta. In recent years, perhaps because their performance takes place on the second day, the hortelanos have omitted this observance.

room, complete with judge. During all of these scenes the poles continued to be flourished with decidedly scatological intent. Now the prisoner was summarily tried and condemned, and a mock priest heard a scandalous confession. When the time arrived for absolution, all stops were pulled and everyone, participants and bystanders, ended by being doused with water. Thus, using a flexible cast and a minimum of props in a manner which would make the most "experimental" of our contemporary theatrical techniques appear staid, these villagers laid waste the most sacred of institutions, the press, the military, the law, and the church.

Of the stock of characters included in the masquerade of the hortelanos, one of the most enigmatic is that of the maringuilla, who is a young man who is masked or made up to look like a woman (Plate 18). Considering the cult of *machismo* among the mestizos of Mexico, it is perhaps startling to find that even among ostensibly mestizoized popula-

Plate 18.   Two maringuillas; the one on the right, seated on a burro and carrying a broken parasol, is the son of a respected barrio elder

tions such as those residing in the barrios of Uruapán, the custom persists. My elderly informant recalled a separate group of twelve maringuillas, dressed in long *huípiles* [smocks] covered with many colored sequins, who followed the band of hortelanos.

In Uruapan, today, the maringuilla is occasionally referred to as a *malinche*, a name deriving from that of Cortes' Indian mistress and interpreter, Malinztin.[9] Whether this is a reference to woman as quintessential betrayer (Eve, Delilah, and so on) is not at all clear. Other sources in the communities report that since women do not dance in Masquerades and since their role *vis-à-vis* the horticulturalists is so important (bringing them food to eat in the fields, and so on), homage is paid them by surrogate inclusion in the parade. Middle-class informants in Uruapán find the institution of the maringuilla repugnant and claim it is a sign of degeneracy on the part of the *indios*.[10] The barrio residents, however, maintain that there is no stigma attached to the performance and that the obligation is undertaken with a sense of dignity and sacrifice. No slur on the participant's manhood is implied.

The maringuillas do not dress with the other hortelanos: one or two dressing houses are reserved for this function and the men are helped by their sweethearts and sisters. Again, small boys are the only ones permitted unlimited access to the interiors of the dressing houses. The availability of cosmetics in the city has led to the abandonment of masks for this characterization although maringuilla masks continue to be employed in the Tarascan-speaking towns.[11] The young men are padded and elaborately made up. This, plus the recent introduction of naturalistic wigs, lends a startling credibility to their impersonations of pulchritude. It is possible that it is this naturalism, as opposed to the more stylized image which must have been achieved with masks and fiber wigs, which has led to the accusation of degeneracy by the middle class. The young men conduct themselves with the utmost seriousness and despite the presence of the aforementioned small boys there are no catcalls nor insulting remarks at this time nor at the time of emergence from the dressing house. Indeed, some of the results are so gorgeous that the impact upon the crowd is one of awe. The maringuillas are by no means standardized. Some emphasize maternal aspects and carry baby dolls in their arms on whom they lavish attention. Others are pious and dour in appearance. Still others are outrageously flirtatious, dressed in miniskirts and even bathing suits. Another, draped in a *rebozo* or shawl and holding an

[9]   Kurath (1967:167, 170) reported *malinche* and *maringuilla* as signifying a transvestite portrayal. Although *malinche* is readily understood by the populace, *maringuilla* is the generally accepted designation throughout Uruapán, the meseta and lacustrine region.
[10]   The term *indio* is used as one of disparagement throughout this region.
[11]   A mask in the Pátzcuaro museum, reported to date from the nineteenth century, depicts a maringuilla from the lacustrine region.

umbrella, rides on a burro and strikes a pose reminiscent of a Goya print. During the parade, each maringuilla has at least one "masculine" escort with whom he often walks arm in arm. The escort's role is protective in the extreme in such burlesques as attempted purse-snatchings. The maringuilla may playfully provoke a spectator during the course of the parade, asking if he wants a kiss. Before the spectator has time to recover from his embarrassment, the escort rushes to the "defense" behaving most ferociously to the delight of all. The role of maringuilla is not repeated by the same performer in succeeding years but there is no lack of willing participants.

Feelings of exclusiveness with regard to territory are keenly experienced by adolescents and young adults in Uruapán and might be summed up in the statement: "The women of our barrio are forbidden to the men of your barrio." Before the hiatus of the 1940's this rivalry between barrios was formalized by the staging of a mock *robo* [abduction]. At some point during the fiesta a group of men on horseback from a different barrio would enter and seize one of the maringuillas, carrying him off. The concept of robo as a forcible and undesirable alternative to a proper church wedding still causes much anxiety in the minds of Uruapán parents including those of the middle class.

At present the robo as enacted in the Barrio de la Magdalena is intrabarrio (Plate 19). After leaving the dressing houses the two or three

Plate 19.   A maringuilla in a bathing suit poses with other hortelanos during the enactment of the robo

groups of hortelanos converge upon the house containing the largest number of maringuillas. This house is distinguished by being centrally located and festooned on the street side with pine ropes and ribbons. A crowd of barrio residents has been assembled expectantly for some time. A cry of "Dance *hortelanos*" is heard and a band strikes up traditional music whereupon the maskers begin a crowded dance singly, in twos, or small groups. The movement of the dance is a sort of shuffling two-step but the enormous variety and ingeniousness of the masks and costumes impart to it tremendous impact. After the dance a series of mock duels ensues (Plates 20 and 21) followed by cries, directed toward the house, of "We want the woman", and, "We demand the woman!" These grow more insistant until finally the house is stormed, and the gate opens, admitting the hortelanos. No one is admitted into the house compound except the *hortelanos* — inside the maskers relax, tilting back their headdresses while waiting for the maringuillas to complete their toilettes and for tension to mount again in the crowd without (Plate 22). Finally hortelanos and maringuillas rush from the house out into the street where, after the disguises of the maringuillas have been enjoyed by the crowd, a fresh series of duels and burlesques are staged. These succeed each other in rapid profusion. Again the bystanders call for a dance and, to the rhythm of a *pirecua*, a traditional Tarascan folk melody, both hortelanos and maringuillas commence dancing vigorously.

Plate 20.   The poles of the hortelanos are employed in a mock duel while awaiting the arrival of the maringuillas

Plate 21.   One hortelano menaces another with his forked pole. The gourd mask on the left has an animal-skin beard and a paper tongue. The center figure shows typical swathing of the masker's head and neck for purposes of comfort and disguise

Plate 22.   The maskers are relaxing within the house compound of the maringuillas' dressing station. On the left, a cardboard box mask is worn tilted back

Shortly after this, at about noon, the hortelanos, including the marin-guillas, assemble at the entrance to the barrio near one of the principal avenues where the parade is to start (Plate 23). At the head of the parade, in all their variety, are the hortelanos. Barrio residents say their function is to make people laugh. Next comes a band, then the viejitos another band, then the *yuntas* [flower-bedecked yoked oxen] with their *mayor-domos* on horseback and on foot, next the young women in *huaris* [traditional Tarascan finery] twirling heavily laden trays of fruit, and another band, followed, at the end, by a coterie of men on horseback and burros. Interspersed with all this are strolling barrio residents, adults, and children. The parade route leads from the barrio to the central plaza, where performances are offered before the municipal palace, and back home again. The peregrination, which proceeds at a leisurely pace, requires one-and-a-half to two hours to complete its circuit and during the entire time the hortelanos perform without ceasing. Improvisations continue during the parade — as in the case of one masker who was swinging a cleanly dressed animal skin. As he turned a corner he spied a dead rat lying near the curb and quickly exchanged this more grisly artifact for its milder counterpart and began to exploit its potential with rich effect.

Plate 23.   A carguero of the hortelanos is disguised as a guerrilla in a mask constructed of gourd and skin. The *jicara* [gourd] slung over his shoulder is painted in the traditional manner for which the region is known. Also traditional is the fact that it is filled, for the fiesta, with tequila

In the meseta villages surrounding Uruapán masquerades similar to the hortelanos are danced at Christmas time. In Capacuaro, a Tarascan-speaking village some sixteen kilometers from Uruapán, a maringuilla mask was carved recently by a local mask maker for use on Noche Buena. This mask, however, was made of *tzirimú* [carefully cured wood] and painted with synthetic enamels. A tradition which more closely approximates that of Uruapán may be observed in San Juan Nuevo, a town settled in the 1940's by refugees from the then active volcano, Parícutin. There a masquerade called the *cúrpites feos* is danced on January 8. The *cúrpites* is a solemn masquerade danced in Angahuan and San Lorenzo which utilizes delicately carved masks with long bleached horsehair wigs said to represent wise old men. The cúrpites feos, however, is a burlesque danced by married men dressed in old rags. The masks are made of rough, unpainted wood, and the participants claim to be "having fun". In return for dancing they are fed at many individual houses.

In the meseta fiestas are celebrated on a village-wide rather than a barrio base, and parades are dispensed with. It is only among the barrios of Uruapán that the hortelanos have the function of advertising the strength of the barrio to the world at large. It is felt in the barrio that the more hortelanos there are participating, especially as it is their function to lead the parade, the better the impression that will be made on the outside world. Participation denotes a sense of caring about the welfare of the barrio, and the community desires greatly that this concern be broadcast.

The masquerade of the hortelanos is part of a larger complex of activities wherein communally shared values are afforded ritual expression. The very fact that we are aware of the aesthetic richness of the masks, costumes, and accoutrements, even when we know nothing of their functional context, makes it imperative that we turn our attention to the motivations which give rise to these forms. That amateurs appear to be capable, year after year, of successfully sustaining a high level of dramatic and visual intensity, and that participation is volunteered enthusiastically, raises questions concerning the dynamics of art's relation to the cultural matrix. As with other masking traditions in the area the concerns of the hortelanos are inseparable from those of the community fiestas on whose behalf enormous reserves of energy and resources are expended.

In general, the splendor exhibited by the masking traditions in Uruapán and in the surrounding Tarascan villages is viewed in the nature of an offering — something poor people are capable of providing through extraordinary effort — which will please the saint or patron. There need be neither direct nor analogous reference to religion in the form of the masquerades, although peripheral patterns may imply either vestigial remains of such references or a desire to capitalize upon tokens in order to tie the secular into the religious framework. For example, one of the dance figures of the viejitos involves the formation of the performers into a Latin cross. This is always greeted with a hushed response on the part of the spectators and its anticipation accounts for a high degree of tension. This figure is referred to as *la cruz*, and the viejitos are said to dance in honor of the Virgin only at Pátzcuaro, and the Magdalene at Uruapán. And yet, the viejitos have no prototype in Christian iconography and as strong a case could be made for the cross representing the four cardinal points and for the little old men to be representing tribal elders rather than the twelve apostles as was suggested by one informant. Similarly, the *moros* [Moors] in dances performed in a number of surrounding villages have long ago lost their Christians, and while the glitter and sumptuous-ness of their dress is said to be pleasing to St. James, in whose honor they are danced, the inclusion of horses in the dance is said not to be in imitation of that saint's equestrian attribute.[12] The statue of Christ crucified which stands over the altar in the church at Zirahuén is fes-tooned with wooden spoons and bowls of local manufacture. It would appear that religious devotion is expressed by the act of offering the best and most costly items which the community can produce rather than by parable or iconography. An Uruapán mask maker who is much admired in the Barrio de la Magdalena for his contributions of labor, skill, and valuable goods, gives voice to shared belief when he states that the donation of a rich man is essentially effortless, while that of a poor man is understood by God to be in the nature of sacrificial devotion. Poor people manage any number of "miracles" during a fiesta. The multitudes of visiting musicians are housed and fed; those who ordinarily are garbed in the drabbest of dress suddenly appear in silk and velvet encrusted with reflective materials; plow oxen are transformed with adornments of flowers and loaves of bread; and bakers and garage mechanics produce masks for the hortelanos powerful in revealed creative energy. Excess is certainly the order of the day and the joyful noise referred to by the psalmist includes a reaffirmation of human abilities.

Art, according to the dicta of our Western technologically oriented society, is that which is housed in a museum. This location in space is also a commentary on the function of art as perceived by our culture. In the museum the art object is tastefully displayed in static isolation. It is in this abstracted setting that we view art when we go, as on a pilgrimage, to pay it homage. We admire and respect but we do not interact. On the rare occasions when interaction is required we may be affronted or possibly even delighted, but we ask at once: "Is it art?" For art in our society is purely visual and stationary. It is meant to be observed as it remains,

---

[12]   In none of the several lacustrine and meseta villages where I have observed the dance of the moros is there any mention by the residents of Christians ever having been included.

according to our expectations, quietly on its wall or pedestal. How strange, then, that the works produced by peoples who consider art to serve a very different function should be so immediately accessible to our aesthetic appreciation. How much this fact attests to the power of these works to move us! And how much our own persistent image of the role of art compels us to twist the products of other cultures out of context as we nail to the wall that which was meant to move!

We deem that to be art which is passive, monumental, and has endured the ravages of time. That which has survived is art, we say, thereby debasing all that is ephemeral. And yet there are whole complexes of activities in which participation and change, building and destruction, are central to that orchestration of tensions which results in the aesthetic experience. One such activity has been described — a fiesta masquerade produced and performed, awaited and enjoyed, by a group of people whose material means are, by our standards, quite limited. As a vehicle which gives ritual expression to shared beliefs the hortelano masquerade is existential in nature rather than static. Although visual, it moves through time as well as space and as with other temporal arts, the performance itself is one of its vital dimensions. Thus, anticipation and repletion are essential facets of the total experience. Repetition of the masquerade at regular intervals, in addition to providing for both continuity and modification, is in itself part of the aesthetic whole. In the small community described social roles are clearly demarcated and the limits of experience ordinarily circumscribed. The factor of disguise inherent in the masquerade greatly expands the number of possible roles permitted and through resulting transformation ordinary reality is transcended. As an art form the hortelanos involves the auditory and kinesthetic as well as the visual and includes elements of drama and social commentary. Above all, it is an art form which grows out of life activities and is considered of sufficient import to merit meaningful sacrifice.

REFERENCES

BEALS, RALPH L.
   1946   *Cherán: a sierra Tarascan village.* Publications of the Institute of Social Anthropology, Smithsonian Institution 2. Washington, D.C.: Government Printing Office.
   1967   "Mesoamerica: remnant heritage," in: *Indian Mexico past and present.* Edited by Betty Bell, 87–99. Los Angeles: University of California Press.
BEALS, RALPH L., PEDRO CARRASCO, THOMAS McCORKLE
   1944   *Houses and house use of the sierra Tarascans.* Publications of the Institute of Social Anthropology, Smithsonian Institution 1. Washington, D.C.: Government Printing Office.

FOSTER, GEORGE M.

    1948   *Empire's children.* Publications of the Institute of Social Anthropology, Smithsonian Institution 6. Washington, D.C.: Government Printing Office.

    1965   Peasant society and the image of limited good. *American Anthropologist* 67(2):293–315.

KURATH, GERTRUDE PROKOSCH

    1967   "Drama, dance and music," in *Handbook of Middle American Indians.* Edited by Robert Wauchope, 158–190. Austin: University of Texas Press.

WEINER, JANET E. (JANET BRODY ESSER)

    1971   The compleat fiesta. *Terra* 10:3–11.

WEST, ROBERT COOPER

    1948   *Cultural geography of the modern Tarascan area.* Publications of the Institute of Social Anthropology, Smithsonian Institution 7. Washington, D.C.: Government Printing Office.

SECTION FOUR

The Cloth of Culture Change

Siona Clothing and Adornment, or, You Are What You Wear

E. JEAN LANGDON

> The *Yagé* people come dancing and singing.
> Like us they are, dressed in *cusmas*. Their
> faces and clothing are full of designs, and they
> wear strands of beads about their necks. On
> their arms they have sweet smelling herbs.
> A SIONA INFORMANT

Browsing through any fashion magazine or taking notice of the hundreds
of clothing, jewelry, and cosmetic advertisements filling other periodicals, no reader can miss the suggestion that a person seeks to express his
identity through the clothing he wears. Different clothing styles represent
different interests and capabilities in sports, business, sex, and other
facets of one's personality. The use of clothing to express a person's
identity also has historical references in Western culture. Adam and Eve
put on clothing to mark their loss of innocence. Using the same logic,
missionaries throughout the world attempted to clothe the seminude
savages as a sign of their transformation to civilized Christians. The idea
that "you are what you wear", however, is not unique to Western culture,
and perhaps it is one motive that lies behind the countless hours and
efforts spent in every culture to modify and alter the body's natural state.
This paper will explore the use and choice of clothing among the Siona
Indians of South America. The first part will examine the relationship
between power relations and choice of clothing; the second will explore
the symbolic aspects of clothing in order to demonstrate the relationship
between clothing and meaning.

The data upon which this work is based were gathered during eighteen months of fieldwork
in Colombia between 1970 and 1972. The study was supported in part by the Tulane
University International Center for Medical Research grant AI–10050 from NIAID, NIH,
United States Public Health Service.

SIONA HISTORY

In order to understand the relationship between power relations and clothing, it is first necessary to examine briefly three major time periods in Siona history: precontact, 1700–1925, and 1925 to the present. These periods are characterized by different forms of social structure as well as different styles of clothing and adornment.

The Siona are a small acculturated group of Western Tukanoan speakers scattered along the Putumayo river in southern Colombia. Traditionally they have been a horticultural group whose diet of manioc and other cultigens was supplemented by animals, insects, and plants from the jungle. The indigenous social structure was characterized by homogeneity and egalitarianism. Leadership was informal. Although there was generally a recognized leader of each community, the position was neither hereditary, a full-time occupation, nor permanent. From among the various elders in each community having shamanistic knowledge, the one considered to have the most knowledge and power assumed the role of directing certain community activities, including the decision-making process based on general consensus and the rituals involving the hallucinogen *yagé*. Although the shaman leader was accorded certain respect, his economic position and life-style did not differ significantly from the rest of the community.

Within recent years the Siona have had increasing contact with Colombian society and national culture. First contact with Western culture occurred during the seventeenth century, but was confined to the sporadic and isolated missions established by Franciscan priests. Although the missionaries induced several changes in their culture and social organization, the Siona remained essentially isolated from the mainstream of the Colombian economy and society. The Franciscans left the Putumayo in the nineteenth century, and the Siona were virtually isolated for a hundred years except for an occasional trader entering the area. This was changed, however, with the twentieth century. The Putumayo became an important strategic and economic region for the nation. The rubber boom during the first twenty years, the Peruvian conflict in the 1930's, and the discovery of petroleum in the 1950's stimulated development and colonization of the former Siona territory in a way that has altered the Indians' lives drastically. The once numerous and widespread tribe has been reduced to a few small communities totalling not more than 250 individuals. The small remaining enclaves of Siona are surrounded by colonists from the highlands. Puerto Asis, the nearest town, boasts of many modern conveniences and is becoming an important commercial center in the region. The Siona themselves are rapidly assimilating into the Colombian peasant culture: year by year they rely more heavily upon cash crops to supplement their livelihood and purchase manufactured goods, abandoning their traditional artifacts and customs of living. Most have adopted Western clothing, architecture, and utensils. The younger generations prefer speaking Spanish instead of their native tongue. Schooling has recently become available to all the children, and the traditional social organization based on the role of the shaman has collapsed as the Siona attempt to understand national politics and establish the community government organization outlined by the Office of Indian Affairs.

THE LOCUS OF POWER: MYTH AND PRESENT REALITY

Although Siona social structure was homogeneous and egalitarian, the cosmological and ritual system is concerned with an animistic and stratified universe whose beings are ordered by the power they have to influence events.[1] According to Siona tradition, the universe is composed of five flat disks that are ordered vertically (see Figure 1). Each disk is populated by animals, people, and spirits. The lowest level is called the "underworld" and is populated by the underworld people and animals. The second level, designated as "first heaven", is where the Siona reside as well as animals and countless spirits. The next level, the "second heaven", is populated by hundreds of spirits, including the sun, the moon, and the thunder being, and their respective followers, called "people" by the Siona. The third and fourth heavens are smaller than the first three layers and are less numerously populated by spirits.

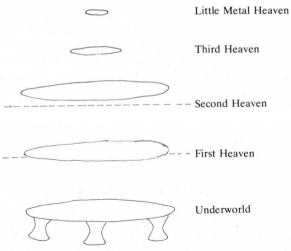

Little Metal Heaven

Third Heaven

Second Heaven

First Heaven

Underworld

Figure 1.   The Siona universe

[1]   For a similar cosmological system among other Amazonian Indians, see Weiss (1972).

The activities of the spirit beings are very important to the Siona, for their actions influence all events that occur in the Siona's world. They are responsible for maintaining the natural rhythm of life as well as for causing disruption in the form of misfortune, serious illness, or other disastrous events. In general, the spirits are neutral and can exercise their power for benefit or misfortune. They must be persuaded to use their powers, and it is the shaman who attempts to influence their actions. He acts as an intermediary between the spirits and the people of his community. When wishing to ensure sufficient game or fish, abundant harvests, or good health for his people, the shaman must contact the spirits. In the same way, when wishing misfortune or sickness upon individuals or other communities, he asks them to exercise their destructive powers.

Contact with the spirits is generally made through visions induced by yagé, a hallucinogenic brew made principally from the vine *Banisteriopsis*. Through the visions, the shaman travels to other levels of the universe and contacts the various spirits. Most of the spirits are elegantly dressed and beautifully adorned. They wear tunics (*cusmas*) decorated with delicate and intricate designs of many colors. Their faces are also painted with delicate designs. Thousands of beads, and feather and seed necklaces adorn their necks and chests. Fragrant herbs are attached to their arms. The different spirits are distinguished both by different motifs painted on their faces and clothing and by their garments' predominant colors. For instance, the Sun People of the summer wear red; the Yagé Mother wears white; the Thunder People wear blue. Occasionally a spirit may be described as wearing articles of Western clothing, such as the motormen on the Sun's canoe, who wear shirts, pants, and caps.

Some spirits serve as allies to help the Siona shamans contact more powerful spirits. The Yagé People figure as possibly the most important spirit allies a Siona may have, for they are the ones who first appear in the novices' visions and serve as his instructors during most hallucinogenic visions.[2] They introduce the Siona to the different spirits and realms in which they live and transmit their knowledge of the universe and its beings to them. As the shaman serves as an intermediary between his people and the spirit world, so the Yagé People serve as intermediaries between the shamans and other powerful spirits.

Although there is not a strict correlation of cosmological level with power, it is evident that there is a stratified system of differential access to power that is related in part to the different levels. As mentioned, the level below the Siona, the "underworld", is populated by the underworld people and animals. They are on the bottom of this stratification of power and have very little effect, if any, on the Siona's lives, for it is said that the

[2]   Robinson (1972) reports this phenomena among the Kofan Indians, whose shamans often perform the yagé ritual with the Siona.

underworld people consider the Siona to be their Yagé People. The shamans of the underworld people drink yagé to rise and see the Siona. When they return to the underworld, they tell their people how the Siona dress and live, so that they may copy Siona customs. In turn, the Siona admire and seek to emulate their allies, the Yagé People, who reside in the level above the Siona in the second heaven. It is through the visions that the Siona see how they dress and attempt to copy them.

Access to power is not totally dependent on one's position in the levels. There are varying levels of power among the beings of one level. Different spirits are more powerful than others: this is true within the Siona community itself. The common man or woman, called "only a man", with no experience in shamanistic training has little ability to influence events in his life. He must depend on a shaman to intercede on his behalf. The shaman's power comes from training and experience with yagé. Through apprenticeship with a master shaman, the novice comes to know the different spirits, at the same time building up a substance of power within himself. This power, called *dau*, is often equated with "knowledge" and is the most important element of a shaman's ability to influence events. Since shamans vary in their power, the people sought to associate themselves with the shaman they considered most powerful. Such alliances with the shamans formed the basic principle of traditional social organization before it was disrupted by the influx of missionaries and colonists in this century. There are four or five communities built around the powerful shamans, who were regarded as competitors. Many Siona tales of the past attest to the competition for power and followers that went on between these shamans. Much of the conflict took the form of witchcraft in which the Siona interpreted any misfortune as an act of sorcery performed by shamans of opposing factions.[3]

This conception of the stratified universe with differential access to supernatural power has been changing as the Putumayo region has been drawn into national interest and increasing activity from the outside. The increased interest and activity has had a major effect on the ritual and ceremonial system surrounding the use of yagé and consequently upon the belief system and cosmology which relies so heavily upon the hallucinogenic experience. With the introduction of schooling and a market economy, young men have ceased to train for the role of shaman. Without the knowledge gained by years of such training, one cannot prepare the hallucinogenic brew nor lead others in its experience. The Siona will not drink yagé without such an expert present. Thus, when the last shaman died in 1960, no survivor had sufficient knowledge or confidence to replace him, and from that time the indigenous political and social structure ceased to operate. Traditional knowledge about the nature and order

[3]   See Langdon (1974) for a complete description and analysis of former Siona social organization.

of the universe has become confined to only a few elders, and it is safe to
say that with the passing of the older generation, the knowledge of and
interest in the vast, complex, stratified world of the spirits and in supernatural power will be gone. On the other hand, concern and interaction
with the complex and stratified society of the national culture will continue to increase, as the younger Siona participate more actively in the
market economy. Access to supernatural power is no longer the concern,
for the younger Siona seeks his place in a stratified system based on
differential access to economic resources.[4]

Within the class order of Colombian society, the Indian figures on the
lowest level. With regard to prestige, he is held in low esteem by many
Colombians who consider the Indian at worst a savage or animal to be
shot and at best a poor ignorant and stupid individual who can easily be
cheated in commercial dealings by underpaying him for his product or by
shortchanging him when he makes purchases. Within the economic system, he is part of the lowest and most exploited sector of the economy, the
small farmer who has no control over the prices received for his crops and
who must always pay what is asked when making his own purchases. The
Siona are well aware of their position within this class hierarchy. They
often stress the need for schooling so that they can "defend" themselves
in their dealings with the Colombians. Some claim at times to have been
paid lower prices for their crops compared to whites. Moreover, when
dealing with non-Indian strangers, they are often timid and withdrawn;
they hesitate to enter strange stores in Puerto Asis, fearing possible
expulsion. Several times when making purchases in small shops in Puerto
Asis, I was noticed by a passing Siona. If he wished to greet me or speak to
me, he would stand outside the doorway and speak to me from there. If
we were walking together and I entered a shop or restaurant where they
traditionally did not deal, only at my urging would the Siona enter.

They have resolved this problem of fear and distrust of the whites in
Puerto Asis by singling out a few businessmen whom they trust, and it is
with these few traders that the Siona almost exclusively deal. Although
recent growth in the town has meant the opening of many more stores, the
Siona continue to patronize the familiar shops, although their prices may
be higher. Ties with these shops have been strengthened many times by
establishing the link of "coparenthood" (*compadrazco*) with the owners,
that is, the Siona parents will ask the owner to be godparent to their child.
Once this relationship is established, the Siona will then often rely on the
"coparent" (*compadre*) to act on his behalf with other Colombians either
in Puerto Asis or in other regions in the nation. A clear example of this

[4] It is interesting to note that Siskind (1973:146) describes differences in the spirits'
clothing as seen by the different generations of the Sharanahua. While the elders see them
dressed traditionally the younger generations envisage them in Western clothing. Since
younger Siona rarely take yagé. I have no comparative data on the visions they see.

intermediary function is the situation in which the Siona couple asks their coparent to find their daughter a position as a domestic servant either in Puerto Asis or elsewhere. The Siona would scarcely think of traveling or working outside their region without having established some contact in the strange location. Most often the contract is made through their co-parents' ties.

HISTORY OF SIONA CLOTHING: A DESCRIPTION OF CHANGING STYLES

Different styles in Siona clothing and adornment correspond with the three major time periods outlined above: precontact, 1700 to 1925, and 1925 to the present.

The Precontact Period

The Siona themselves have little recollection of their dress prior to their first contact with the Franciscans. However, a journal written by an early missionary (Santa Gertrudis 1970) stationed on the Putumayo river during the seventeenth century describes certain aspects of their dress. According to him, both sexes wore little more than a G-string or similar form of sexual covering fabricated from barkcloth. Their bodies and faces, however, were elaborately adorned with black, red, and violet paint, feathers, fragrant herbs, and necklaces of nuts, seeds, feathers, bird bones, and animal teeth. He notes with humor that the men painted their feet and ankles to the midcalf with red from the anatto seed and then glued puffs of cotton on the calves, giving the appearance of polka-dot stockings. No mention is made that differences in clothing reflect differences in social status.

First Contact and Ensuing Isolation

The Franciscans viewed the nakedness of the Siona as evidence of their "savagery"; consequently, clothing them became a major goal of the missionary activities. Through the sale of jungle products collected by the Indians, the missionaries purchased cloth for them. Although the style of clothing introduced by the Franciscans is not mentioned in their journals, it must be assumed that it was the tuniclike *cusma* described by travelers on the Putumayo during the nineteenth and early twentieth centuries. The cusma consists of a long piece of cloth folded crosswise in the middle. A slit is made in the horizontal fold for the head, and the sides are sewn up, leaving openings for the arms near the fold that crosses the shoulders. Red and blue threads are used to sew the seams in a cross-stitch pattern. Often the lower edge and neck slit are embroidered with the same two colors. Both sexes wore the cusma with a variation in the neck slit (Hardenburg, 1912:79), which was cut horizontally for the women and vertically for the men. Today a few of the elder men continue to wear the cusma. They have added trousers underneath the tunic, which reaches below the knees.

The cusmas are made of purchased muslin. Some elders recall that long ago they were made of barkcloth or homespun cotton, probably during the nineteenth century when there was so little contact with the outside world that cloth became scarce. The present Siona dye some of their cusmas black; one elder reports that in his father's time they were also dyed a violet-pink color and red. He also reports that the cusmas had designs on them inspired by hallucinogenic visions, and although none of them today have such designs, the motifs can be seen in Siona pottery, face painting, and other art forms (Figure 2).

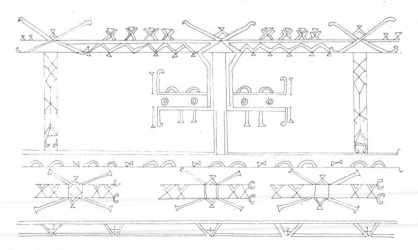

Figure 2.   Example of designs inspired by hallucinogenic visions, drawn by Estanislao Yaiguaje

Throughout this period the Siona maintained customs of elaborate ornamentation that probably date back to the precontact period and incorporate some Western elements such as glass beads and metal coins. One elder male practices these customs today. All eyelashes and eyebrows were plucked out and elaborate designs were painted on the face with red *bixa orellana*. On festive occasions, two other colors were added, a violet and a dark red, both made from unknown plants. The lips were stained black by chewing a leaf, *Calatola columbiana*.[5] The septum and earlobes were pierced. Bones or long macaw feathers were inserted in the pierced septum; bones, feathers, or slender sticks with feathers attached with red and blue thread in the ears. Often flattened metal triangles made from coins hung from the sticks. At the turn of the century both men and women had loose hanging long hair, but the missionaries soon introduced a "bowl cut" for the men.

Neck ornamentation for both sexes consisted predominantly of hundreds of strands of beads tied in choker fashion about the neck; on ceremonial occasions these were so numerous that they covered it entirely. The favorite color was royal blue, interspersed with red, lavender, yellow, and green beads. For ceremonial occasions loose hanging necklaces of feathers, bones, seeds, small nuts, and other plant products were added. Some cut diagonally across the body, from one shoulder going under the opposite arm. Elder males and shamans added necklaces of jaguar or wild pig canines.

Body adornment consisted of fragrant herbs (*Cyclanthus bipartitus* and others) and painting. The herbs were attached to the upper arm and wrists by long woven bands made from red and blue string.[6] Long strands of bleached plant fibers were often attached to the upper arm. Red and black body paints were applied for festive occasions, and the "polka-dot" socks continued to be in vogue until the early 1900's. Today no elder paints his body, but some still paint their faces and use fragrant herbs and beads.

In general, no form of everyday clothing or adornment reflected status differences. However, during ceremonial times, particularly during yagé ceremonies, the elders and shamans were distinguished by the addition of certain articles that indicated their yagé experience. They wore tooth necklaces made of jaguar canines, which through association with the powerful animal spirits implied that the wearer had power. Feather crowns were worn by most participants in the ceremony, during the height of which the shaman was distinguished by a very elaborate crown.

Finally, evidence indicates that the shamans' face designs were perhaps more elaborate than those of the common men, for their knowledge of the spirit world acquainted them with more elaborate designs (Figure 3). During the fieldwork I became aware of the important role of visions in inspiring Siona face motifs. In the early stages of fieldwork, I began to make copies of all the motifs my major informant employed on his face.

[5]   Plant identifications used in adornment were made by Homer Pinkley (1973) in his study of the Kofan ethnobotany. Since the two neighboring tribes share similar cultures, dress patterns, and ecological habitats, it is assumed that the same plants are being used. Voucher specimens are located in the Oakes Ames Herbarium of Economic Plants, Botanical Museum, Harvard University, Cambridge, Massachusetts.
[6]   These bands are woven by attaching five strings to the large toe of one foot and passing them back and forth between the fingers in a manner resembling a cat's cradle game.

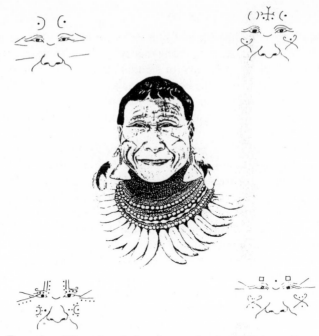

Figure 3.   Examples of Siona face designs (center drawing by Rebecca Beverly Film)

He was not taking hallucinogens during this time, nor had he done so for at least a year or two. At one point, he spent an extended time drinking yagé with a shaman of a neighboring tribe. When he returned from their visit, there was a marked increase in the complexity in the motifs on his face. Not only were the designs more intricate, but also two colors were employed instead of only the one previously used. Other informants remarked that in the old days, when he drank yagé regularly, his designs were even more elaborate. With the passing of the yagé ceremonies and rituals, the designs are now disappearing among the others and he is the last survivor to use them consistently.

1925 to the Present

By the 1920's the missionaries had fully resumed activities in the Putumayo. The Siona children were forced to attend the mission schools, where strong pressure was exerted upon them to abandon their native language and clothing in favor of Spanish and Western fashions. At this time, most Siona boys adopted the trouser and shirt of the white man (Plate 1), and this style has been the predominant one for many years. The women adopted the skirt and blouse. Most women wore a style of blouse with a yoke and a loose full bodice gathered under it, still used by the older women (Plate 2). The eldest Siona woman occasionally wears

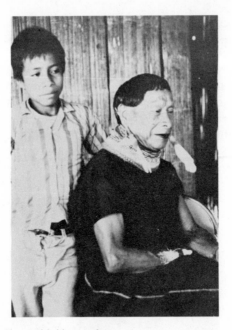

Plate 1.   An elder Siona with his grandson

Plate 2.   An elder Siona woman

an earlier version, which is simply a rectangular piece of cloth that is passed under one arm and tied above the opposite shoulder.[7] It is not possible to determine the origin or age of this style.

Since the 1920's, Siona clothing reflected increasing adoption of western styles. Only a few elders maintain "traditional" dress, while those under thirty reflect the style trends and fashions of the dominant society. At parties or special occasions very "modern" styles may be sported, such as gaily colored shirts on the young men and tight miniskirts or slacks on the younger women (Plate 3). Most adults, however, dress in conservative, comfortable, and more functional Western clothing.

Plate 3.   A young Siona couple

ANALYSIS

The Meaning of Clothing

In discussing the relation between culture and clothing styles, I will limit myself to two styles of clothing: traditional and Western. For the traditional I will consider the cusma and body ornamentation described for the 1700–1925 period, and still worn by a few elders in the community. I suspect that much of what I say also applies to the precontact period, but I

[7]   See Mallol de Recasens (1963) for a drawing of this blouse as well as ceremonial dress of the shamans. Vickers (1975) includes excellent pictures of Siona-Secoya clothing in Ecuador, which is similar to that of the traditional Siona style in Colombia.

will not speculate about values and relationships that date far back with so little evidence available. The postcontact adoption of the cusma introduced a new standard of modesty but little more. The Western style refers to clothing that has been adopted since the 1920's and reflects changes in manufactured clothing and national tastes.

Culture and Traditional Styles

In discussing with various informants their choice of dress and in examining mythology it is obvious that there is an underlying feeling within the culture that "you are what you wear". They stated that their dress was an attempt to copy the Yagé People so that they too would be beautiful and attractive — attributes that are helpful when dealing with spirits or other people. Similar reasoning, linking one's identity to one's clothing, is seen in the descriptions of visions and in mythology. The Siona shaman is able to transform himself into jaguars, anacondas, and other beings. When describing the act of transformation, the Siona say that he "puts on the *cusma* of the jaguar (anaconda, etc.)". In their mythology, they describe the transformation from man to animal as "putting on the *cusma* of the animal". Mythological animals such as the buzzard or collared peccary are said to take off their cusmas of wool and dress in cotton cusmas when appearing as humans. Some elements of the human clothing that they assume contain within them hints of their animal characteristics, for instance, when in human form, the collared peccary wears a large amount of strands of blue beads about the neck. In the middle of the strands there is one single white strand which is said to represent the "collar" of the pig. The red tapir appears in visions and dreams as a fat woman dressed in red. Another example is the appearance in dreams of shamans dressed in the priest's habit. The Siona often say that the shaman is god's representative among the Indians in the same way that the priest is among white men. From such examples it can be concluded that traditional clothing was considered to be a form of social identity.

There is more to the meaning of clothing, however, than social identity. The meaning of clothing is also linked to a pervasive symbolic system found throughout Siona culture. In other articles I have developed the idea that the Siona world view entails a conception of two forces operating in life, a growth force and a destructive force. The growth or positive force is conceptualized in ideas and symbols expressing a state of living, freshness, greenness (both in color and state of maturity), fatness, and good health. The destructive force is associated with rottenness, bad odor, black, dark colors, thinness, sickness, and death. Looking at the role of dress in visions and dreams, we can see these same symbols. In visions or dreams, an evil spirit is often described as wearing a black

cusma, signifying his destructive intent. He may also be described as thin
and bony. On the other hand, most ally spirits and the Yagé Mother are
characterized by white or pale green clothing. They are fat and healthy.
Their fragrant odor contrasts with the bad or rotten odor associated with
destructive forces. In dreams relating to the onset of illness, the Siona sees
himself in a wet or dirty cusma, associating clothing symbolically with the
destructive forces. On the other hand, when a Siona dreams that he is to
recover from an illness, he puts on a dry or clean cusma, a cusma symbolic
of the positive force that now brings good health.

Finally, in examining statements Siona make about choice of clothing,
it is possible to conclude that clothing was likened to the perception of the
social order in which they lived. As stated earlier, Siona society was
basically egalitarian, but they considered themselves as living within an
ordered universe populated by beings possessing different amounts of
power to influence events. The Siona sought to emulate and obtain the
help of spirits having more influence than they in this ordering of power.
In particular, they tried to be like the Yagé People, their intermediaries
with the other spirits. In the same way, the underworld people are said to
emulate the Siona, since they are the Yagé People for the underworld.

Western Clothing and Social Order

While the adoption of the cusma probably did not mark a major transformation in perception of the social order or cultural values, the adoption of Western clothing most certainly did. Not only did the missionaries
discourage the use of traditional clothing and language, they also discour-
aged the young Siona from entering into apprenticeship relations with
shamans, which led to the breakdown of the traditional leadership. This
also meant that the contact with the spirit world that had been continuously maintained through yagé ceremonies was now broken. While the
youth of today have little experience and knowledge of the vast and
complex spirit world that their grandfathers knew so well, they are more
familiar with the national social structure and economy. They are well
aware of the Indian's position within Colombian society and know the
negative effects of Indian identity in economic transactions. While the
elders maintain pride in the traditional ways, the youth seek to understand and emulate a different world and find their place in a different
social structure. No longer do they seek to reflect the clothing and lives of
the supernatural powers governing their lives. Instead, they choose to
emulate the white man with whom they have economic relations. By
having white "coparents", they attempt to gain them as allies in the same
way that their fathers sought allies among the Yagé People.

Choice of clothing reflects the changing perception of the powers that govern their lives. Today, as in the past, they try to emulate those who have influence over their lives, perhaps in order to draw a favorable reaction and to become more like them. Certainly they have not abandoned the idea that "you are what you wear", but the cultural values and changing perception of the social structure have altered what they want to be.

REFERENCES

HARDENBURG, WALTER E.
1912   *The Putumayo, the devil's paradise: travels in the Peruvian Amazon region and an account of the atrocities committed upon the Indians therein.* London: T. Fisher Unwin.

LANGDON, E. JEAN
1974   "The Siona medical system: beliefs and behavior." Unpublished doctoral dissertation, Tulane University of Louisiana, New Orleans.

MALLOL DE RECASENS, MARIA ROSA
1963   Cuatro representationes de los imagenes alucinatorias originadas por la toma del *yagé. Revista Colombiana de Folclor*, second series 3(8):59–79.

PINKLEY, HOMER V.
1973   "Ethnoecology of the Kofan Indians." Unpublished doctoral dissertation, Harvard University, Cambridge, Massachusetts.

ROBINSON, SCOTT
1972   "Shamanismo entre los Kofan," in *Actas y Memorias del XXXIX Congreso Internacional de Americanistas*, Lima, Peru, 2–9 de agosto, 1970, volume four: *Historia, etnohistoria y etnologia de la selva sudamericana*, 89–93. Lima: Instituto de Estudios Peruanes.

SANTA GERTRUDIS, FRAY JUAN DE
1970   *Maravillas de la naturaleza*, four volumes. Biblioteca Banco Popular 10–13. Bogota: Kelley.

SISKIND, JANET
1973   *To hunt in the morning.* New York: Oxford University Press.

VICKERS, WILLIAM
1975   El mundo espiritual de los Sionas. *Periplo* 4 (July–August): 12–23. Ecuador.

WEISS, GERALD
1972   Campa cosmology. *Ethnology* 11(2):157–172.

Sexual Differentiation and Acculturation in Potawatomi Costume

MARGARET THOMPSON MILLER

The forest band of the Potawatomi Indians, who reside in northern Wisconsin, are one North American tribe which can look to present-day museum and private collections for many examples of its traditional dress. On the basis of examination of the literature and of the extant artifacts themselves, one can identify and categorize Potawatomi clothing artifacts with reasonable accuracy and make deductions as to similarities and differences among the clothing artifacts of men and women. Further, one can determine changes in form, meaning, and function of elements of Potawatomi dress over time, and can examine the influence of various non-Indian groups affecting these various changes.

Traditional clothing artifacts of the Wisconsin Potawatomi Indians can be grouped according to the regions of the body in which they are worn: the head region, the neck region, the region of the torso and arms, the waist region, the region of the lower body, and the feet. For men, these artifacts included fur turbans, roach headdresses, sash turbans, feather bonnets, various types of necklaces, hide robes and fabric blankets, shirts of buckskin, beaded garters for both arms and legs, vests, belts and sashes, leggings, breechcloths and aprons, and moccasins. For women, traditional clothing artifacts included loom-beaded headbands, hair ties and braid ornaments, various types of necklaces, woven blankets, ruffled blouses and skirts of fabric, dresses of buckskin, short leggings, jewelry (silver brooches and pendants), and moccasins.

A closer examination reveals several similarities and differences among the clothing artifacts of Potawatomi men and women. For instance, there appears to be a greater variety of head coverings used by men than by women. Hair ornaments for women were purely decorative in purpose, while those for men, for example the roach headdress (Plate 1) and the Plains-type bonnet (Plate 2) communicated status as a successful warrior in addition to providing decoration of the head region. Head protection for men was in the form of a fur hat (Plate 3), while women probably protected themselves from the cold and rain by draping the blanket robe over their heads. Only slight evidence in the literature indicates that Potawatomi women wore other head protectors, such as little bonnets, and cowls attached to their dresses (Kinietz 1965:313).

Plate 1.   Roach headdress from Madison, Wisconsin, side view

Plate 2.   Feather bonnet (Plains type) from Mole Lake, Wisconsin (Shallock Collection)

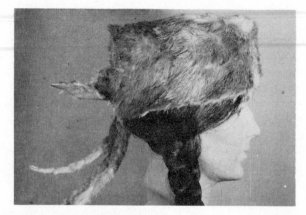

Plate 3.   Otterskin hat from Madison, side view

Both sexes wore similar types of garments: shirts and blouses, leggings, and moccasins. However, a definite distinction was evident among certain garments as being appropriate for one sex and not for the other. For example, though both men and women wore leggings in the nineteenth century, women never adopted the trouser leg covering that the men later did (at least, not until the Potawatomi women adopted white women's fashions for everyday wear in the early twentieth century). The blouses of the women and the shirts of the men were both long-sleeved, collarless garments, but men's shirts were usually decorated with beads (Plates 4 and 5); while women's blouses were decorated not with beads but with silver brooches and silk ribbons (Plates 6 and 7). Both sexes wore the same basic types of moccasins; however, slight evidence exists that the women wore more heavily beaded moccasins than did the men, especially for ceremonial occasions or for formal portraits.

From earliest times, both sexes used hide robes, but with the onset of the fur trade, the hide robe was replaced by a woven blanket robe which remains in use today on ceremonial or formal occasions for women but not for men. The women's blankets in photographs taken during the twentieth century are almost always decorated with ribbonwork, while the men's blanket robes are less conspicuously decorated, if at all.

Plate 4.   Buckskin shirt from Wabeno, Wisconsin (Pichotta Collection), front view

Plate 5.   The same buckskin shirt, back view

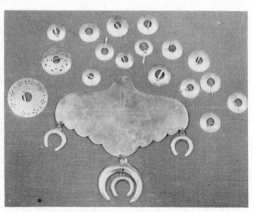

Plate 7.   Silver brooches and pendant from Wabeno,
(Pichotta Collection)

Plate 6.   Unidentified woman wearing
Potawatomi-style ruffled blouse

Neckwear for both sexes was similar and even interchangeable in some cases; however, the men came to wear certain pendant necklaces which communicated a very special status, (for example, Indian leadership, as shown by the wearing of silver gorgets and Indian peace medals).

Both sexes showed a great affinity for costume elements that either moved or sounded with the movement of the wearer. Examples of the former among men's clothing artifacts are seen not only in the heavy tasseling of such items as sashes, garters, and bandolier bags, but also in the flowing, hanging ornaments used on head apparel. Examples are the hanging feathers and ribbons used on both the roach and the Plains-type feather headdress, and the tassels and dangling ornaments used on beaded shirt ornaments. In women's dress, hair ties (Plate 8) and braid ornaments (Plate 9) also belong in this category.

Items in the latter category of costume elements favored by the Potawatomi, those that created sound as the wearer moved, were conical tinklers, hanging coins, strung beads, and thimbles which were attached to items of clothing such as jackets, headdresses, leggings, and sashes.

Though the Potawatomi had many animal totems that indicated clan membership, these totems do not appear on either men's or women's clothing, nor is there evidence in the literature to indicate that the Potawatomi dressed to resemble various totems for ceremonial purposes.

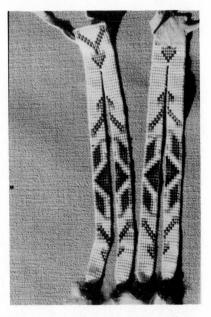

Plate 8.   Hair tie from Madison

Plate 9.   Modern braid ornaments from Partridge Lake, Wisconsin

The Potawatomi had many design motifs in beadwork and ribbonwork that were very similar to those of their proximate Indian neighbors, and which occur with some consistency among the artifacts available in present-day collections, but it is difficult to select any particular design motif as being exclusively Potawatomi or for the sole use of one sex or the other.

Although both men and women of the Potawatomi tribe held the offices of chief and shaman at some time or other, the literature does not indicate that these two offices were marked by the wearing of any special clothing items. The marks of these important offices were perhaps the possession of clothing accessories and tools, such as medicine bundles and special feather fans, rather than clothing worn as body covering.

One general trend in both male and female clothing form was from simplicity to complexity, in kinds of clothing forms used, in numbers of garments worn at one time, and in surface decoration. The change in forms used was more marked in men's costume than in women's, and was from loose, wraparound (buffalo robes) and semifitted, suspended forms (breechcloths, leggings, necklaces) to fitted clothing (shirts, trousers, suit jackets). Moreover, the change was from one or two layers of clothing (breechcloth and robe) to several layers (shirt, yoke, necklaces, vest, waist sashes, leggings, and apron worn over trousers) all worn simultaneously. These changes appear to be related to the introduction of new materials and new techniques for making clothing, as well as to easier access not only to materials for making clothing but also to ready-made items of clothing (calico shirts, trousers, shoes and stockings, jackets and coats).

The change in form of women's costume was not so marked. The dress of the Potawatomi woman, originally two skins attached at the shoulder, evolved into various shapes, numbers of component parts, and was made of different materials, but it remained a skirted garment (Plates 10 and 11). There was no adoption of a bifurcated outer garment for women until the twentieth century, by which time Potawatomi women had largely adopted the white woman's fashions of the day for everyday wear.

Plate 11.   The same buckskin dress, shoulder-covering portion

Plate 10.   Buckskin dress from Madison, underdress portion

Greater complexity in surface decoration applied to clothing artifacts became evident as delicate painting of buffalo hides with curvilinear designs and painstaking porcupine-quill work gave way to flamboyant and extensive application of ribbons and beads on clothing of both men and women. Whereas in precontact times, adornment was applied to the body itself in the form of body paint, by the eighteenth century decoration had been transferred to the extrabody forms of clothing introduced by the fur traders, for example beading was used to decorate vests (Plates 12 and 13), while sashes and garters were loom-beaded in colorful designs and used as costume accessories (Plates 14–17).

Plate 12.   Beaded vest from Wabeno
(Pichotta Collection), front view

Plate 13.   The same beaded vest,
back view

Plate 14.   Loom-beaded sash from Shawano, Wisconsin

Plate 15.   Loom-beaded sash from Madison

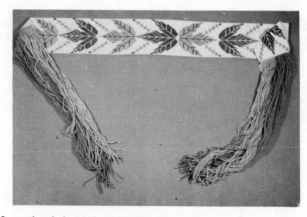

Plate 16.   Loom-beaded sash from Milwaukee, Wisconsin

Plate 17.   Detail of loom-beaded sash from Wabeno, (McGraw Collection)

Changes in the function of Potawatomi clothing artifacts — more evident for men's clothing than for women's — may also be noted. The early Potawatomi man spent most of his time during the fall and winter months on hunts that took him far away from the shelter of the mat-covered houses and fires of his home camp. On the hunt, the Indian's heavy buffalo robes that he carried day and night were his only protection from the elements, and his main means of maintaining body temperature. However, in post-fur trade times his clothing was only one of several protections and insulations in the form of increased layers of clothing, plus permanent shelters along established trapping lines and trade routes. Thus as the form of Potawatomi men's clothing changed over the years from one or two garments to several layers of clothing, clothing came to play only a supplementary role in fulfilling the function of protection from the elements and maintenance of body temperature. For women, these functions were from earliest times performed by fires and the shelter of mat-covered houses as well as by clothing, since the woman traditionally spent most of her time in camp.

Another function of clothing is communication of status within the society, and a change in this function may be noted for clothing of Potawatomi men. A distinction made among early Potawatomi was related to age. Older men cultivated long hair and beards while younger men, dancers and warriors, respected for their feats of bravery, were characterized by shaven heads and the roach headdress. As contact with the white man increased, the role of the successful warrior declined in value, and that of the successful hunter and trapper increased as the tribal economy became more and more dependent upon delivery of pelts to the white man in return for his trade goods, and all Potawatomi men came to adopt the shorter hairstyle of the white man.

Another status distinction of early times was that a chief demonstrated his high position by giving what he had to others of his tribe. This generosity included the distribution of his own articles of clothing, and he became distinguished by his poor and scanty raiment. In later years, as the British, French, and United States military began bestowing gifts of such clothing items as military coats, silver gorgets, and Indian peace medals on certain Indian leaders, and as the Potawatomi economic system became more and more dependent on the fur trade and on cooperation with the white man, the kinds of clothing given by the white men became symbolic items of high status. The new types of Indian leaders, the recipients of these clothing items, then became distinguished by the numbers of items which they owned and wore, rather than by the numbers of items that they distributed among others of their tribe. Change in the communicative function of the headdress eagle feathers that distinguished the warrior also took place. These prized "coup" feathers were won as a result of some feat of valor or of special skill. As the main activity of the tribe turned to the trapping of furs for economic gain, the position of warrior declined, and with it the prestige associated with the wearing of an eagle feather.

There was not so much evidence of the function of clothing as a means of communication of status for the women, because the literature presents no evidence that such clothing items as medals or military coats were distributed to Potawatomi women in an effort to gain their cooperation or political allegiance, thus the clothing of the women did not reflect the shifting political positions of the wearer, as did the clothing of the men. As among many woodland tribes, women were noted for, and gained prestige for, their talents in domestic duties, including fine beadwork and clothing construction, but this occupational status was never as highly regarded as the status available to men.

Men's clothing also changed by becoming more indicative of the wealth of the wearer. Different measures of wealth as manifested through the elements of body covering were introduced. Such items as beads, buttons, silver brooches, and coins (for their decorative value), plus appliquéd silk ribbons and necklaces, became an index of the wealth of the wearer, whereas past indexes of wealth had been horses, blankets, and other household goods. A kind of wealth was also indicated by the great yardage of fabric needed for the ruffled "Potawatomi-style" blouse and floor-length skirt.

Thus it is clear that there were several changes in form, function, and in the meaning communicated by Potawatomi men's clothing elements through time. Though there appears also to have been a change in form of women's costume, there was not as much change in function or in communicated meanings of individual clothing artifacts as there was for men. These various changes in form, function, and meaning of clothing elements were affected greatly by non-Indian as well as Indian groups with which the Potawatomi were in sustained contact. Such non-Indian groups as explorers, Jesuit missionaries, fur traders, United States government Indian agents, Indian boarding school staffs, researchers, and tourists all had some influence on Potawatomi costume.

The earliest groups of white men to come into contact with the Potawatomi were explorers and Jesuit missionaries, whose effect upon their costume was negligible. However, the Indians may have received iron tools from the explorers, which could have been used for cutting or piercing hides. The only comment of the Jesuit missionaries around 1667 on the appearance of the Potawatomi was on the modesty they found among the women and girls of this tribe: *modesty* probably meaning a substantial amount of body covering (Thwaites 1896–1901:27). While missionaries have altered the course of costume evolution among other groups of Indians by preaching increased body covering, for instance among the Eskimos, the Jesuits found no cause to do so among the Potawatomi.

The effect on Potawatomi costume of the French and American fur traders was considerably more important, since the Potawatomi endeavored to become, and to maintain themselves as, middlemen between the traders and the various outlying Indian groups (Lurie 1969:4–5). This effort can be seen as the natural outcome of two characteristics of the Potawatomi: (1) they considered themselves superior to all other surrounding tribes, and set themselves up as arbiters for all the other tribes around Green Bay (Kinietz 1965:312); and (2) they knew well the mechanics of trading, as they and the Ottawa had supplied the Illinois and the Miami with porcupine quills long before the fur trade became a functional reality (Kinietz 1965:176).

The middleman position in the fur trade probably had a tremendous impact on their costume, for they undoubtedly controlled the flow of and acquired more of the trade goods that could be used in clothing manu-facture and clothing decoration than could any other tribal group. A listing of clothing-related trade goods that appeared in the journal of an early trading post owner includes such goods that "are proper for the Savages" as:

Shoemakers Awls. Caps of blew (*sic*) Serge. Shirts made of the common Brittany Linnen (*sic*). Wolsted Stockins, short and coarse. Coarse white Thread for Nets. Sewing thread of several colours. Pack-thread. Vermillion. Needles, both large and small. Venice beads (cited in Douglass 1949:9).

This list could be expanded to include looking-glasses, combs, paints of various colors (which could be used as body paints), brass bells, cloth, and ribbons (Overton 1940). By 1800 red and blue trade cloth was rapidly taking the place of buckskin as a basic material for Indian clothing. A profusion of gay satin ribbons, dumped on the American market in 1790 by the French after the revolution, were quickly adapted by the Indians for decorating the surface of their costumes (Underhill 1953: 137).

Some trade goods were not intended to be used as personal adornment, but were adapted as such by the Indians: the heavy brass and iron kettles, after they became worn and worthless as cooking vessels, were broken up to make conical dangling ornaments; thimbles were also used as conical "tinklers", and coins became more important for their decorative and musical value than as a medium of exchange (Douglass 1949:10). It was not just the gross form of Potawatomi costume that changed with the introduction of ready-made shirts, hats, chemises, stockings and military coats: the decoration the Indians applied to both traditional garments and to the newly-adopted ready-made ones of the white man was also greatly changed. The introduction by the traders of glass trade beads, steel needles, and thread, used to attach beads to garments or as string for necklaces, had a noticeable long-range effect on the appearance of Potawatomi traditional clothing. Before the introduction of beads, fabric decoration had been achieved chiefly through painting, attaching of shell beads, and embroidering dyed porcupine quills onto fabric surfaces. The latter process was a most time-consuming one; by contrast, glass beads needed no long preparation for application after they had been procured, and their method of application to hide or fabric was physically much easier than the application of quills to hide had been. Porcelain and glass beads retained their color every bit as well as quills had, but many more colors were available in beads than had been available in quills. As a result, patterns of two or three colors used before the contact period were elaborated to many more colors, eventually developing into designs incorporating as many as ten to twelve different colors and shades.

The beadwork designs applied to clothing artifacts can help to date any particular piece. At first beads were scarce, and design motifs were only outlines of figures. As the fur trade progressed, they became more generally available, and design motifs incorporated both outlined and filled-in figures. Very late in the fur trade appeared the bandolier bag (Plates 18 and 19), a large square fabric pocket suspended from a shoulder strap about four to six inches wide. The strap and fabric pocket were completely covered with beads. By the nineteenth century, bandolier bags were a sign of wealth for both men and women, because of the great number of beads needed to make them. A proud owner of two bandolier bags would wear both of them at the same time, one over each shoulder. Though the most obvious function of bandolier bags was purely decorative, they were also used for carrying personal belongings during dances and ceremonies.

Plate 18. Beaded bandolier bag from Milwaukee

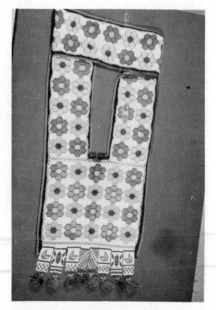

Plate 19. Beaded bandolier bag from Milwaukee

Another result of the contact between Indians and the fur traders was intermarriage between Indian maidens and white men involved in various aspects of the fur trade. Such a marriage strengthened the position of a white man in the fur trade, for it increased his individual influence over some Indians and improved his ability to procure more furs (O'Kelliher 1932–1934:42). Such a marriage could have implications for Indian clothing form: for example, a new Indian wife was sometimes outfitted in the garb of the fashionable white lady of the day. She then brought this clothing influence to family and Indian friends in home territory (O'Meara 1968:190).

The traders themselves influenced clothing worn by Indian men. The overall pattern seems to be that the Indian men adopted white men's clothing faster than the women. This adoption may have begun with the giving of gifts, including clothing, to the Indians by early traders, who wished to win the good will and cooperation of the Indians. As the fur trade became well established and trading posts appeared in outlying areas, an Indian was able to obtain various articles of white man's clothing as well as other supplies on credit for his winter hunting and trapping trips. A trader's outfit for one year, especially in the latter years of the fur trade, was available to Indian and white trappers alike:

A personal outfit consisted of a corduroy round-about pants and vest, four striped cotton shirts, four pair of socks, and four "two and a half point blankets" sewed up in the canvass — with two pairs of blankets to cover — forming a bed and bedding (O'Kelliher 1932–1934:43).

The extent to which the Indians used such "whiteman's gear" in place of the hide garments and woven blankets of his ancestors is not clear in the literature.

The total extent of influence on Potawatomi clothing artifacts exerted by the French and British military sources is hard to determine. However, several specific clothing items adopted by the Potawatomi as clothing accessories are directly traceable to military sources: these are the silver gorgets, Indian peace medals, and the fingerwoven sashes.

There has been documentation of silver gorgets being distributed among certain chiefs of the Great Lakes Indian groups by British military leaders. These gorgets were a very prominent kind of silver pendant used to establish imposed rank among Indian groups and to show alliance of Indian leaders — and thus Indian tribes — with the British. Adoption of widespread use of these pendants clearly shows manipulation of Indian social structure through clothing, since the leaders on whom the silver gorgets were bestowed were not necessarily the leaders chosen by the Indians themselves. Furthermore, Indians were chosen as recipients of the silver gorgets for different reasons than those for which the Indians had traditionally chosen their leaders. The manipulation of Indian social structure through the bestowing of these silver gifts disrupted systems of relationships and had a devastating impact, partly because the Indian economic system had already been irrevocably changed and weakened as a result of the fur trade.

Silver medals, known as Indian peace medals, were also distributed among Indian chiefs and warriors, as tokens of friendship and symbols of allegiance to the government of the United States or Britain. A medal was bestowed only on an influential person, and different-sized medals were given to principal village chiefs, principal war chiefs, and to less-distinguished chiefs and warriors. In addition a medal was always bestowed with a certain amount of formality, the occasion being the signing of a treaty, the visit of an Indian leader to Washington, D.C., or the tour of some Indian territory by some federal official. The use of such medals became essential to any dealings with Indian leaders as the years went by (Prucha and Carmony 1971:xiii).

According to some authors, long fingerwoven sashes of yarn woven in an arrow design (Plate 20) were probably copies of the "Assomption" sashes made by early French Canadians (Underhill 1953:120). The role of the French military in transmitting this weaving design idea is not clear.

Plate 20.   Fingerwoven yarn sash from Madison

Another non-Indian group that directly influenced Potawatomi clothing were the various Indian agents and other United States government employees and researchers from museums and universities who dealt with the Indians in some way. The United States government learned from the time of first interaction with Indian groups the importance of bestowing presents on the Indians in return for friendship, allegiance, or cooperation (Prucha and Carmony 1968). These presents were often clothing items or other items of bodily adornment, for example pendants, buttons, or jewelry.

The practice of giving presents in return for information was also well-established among researchers and used by them as late as the 1920's and 1930's. In 1932 Schoewe indicated that an important factor in collecting artifacts from the Indians was

. . . an intimate acquaintance with them; moreover, one should be kind and sympathetic towards them and make the usual gifts of food, clothing, and money . . . (Schoewe 1932:149).

A scrapbook compiled in the 1920's by Gerend, as he was gathering information for a history of the Potawatomis, contains several letters from Indian informants. In each of these the informant divulged the requested information on his tribal history only after an introductory appeal for clothing needed by his family or friends (Gerend n.d: 46, 53).

The United States government Indian boarding schools were a direct influence on Indian children's clothing because all clothing worn by children attending such schools was furnished by the Indian Service (Smith 1925:72). The source of this clothing is not indicated, but it may have been secondhand or perhaps purchased ready-made by the Indian Service. Some clothing was made from materials purchased by the service: at least the iconographic collections at the State Historical Society in Madison, Wisconsin contain photographs of Indian girls at the boarding schools sewing clothing for their own use. Potawatomi youths were sent to boarding schools until this system was abolished in 1930, and the reaction of the Potawatomi children to enforced wearing of only white man's clothing may well have been similar to the reaction of a young Lakota boy around the turn of the century:

Our second resentment [the first was the cutting of the boys' hair] was against trousers, based upon what we considered the best of hygienic reasons. Our bodies were used to constant bathing in the sun, air, and rain, and the function of the pores of our skin, which were in reality a highly developed breathing apparatus, was at once stopped by trousers of heavy, sweat-absorbing material aided by that worst of all torments — red flannel underwear. For the stiff collars, stiff-front shirts, and derby hats no word of praise is due, and the heavy, squeaky, leather boots were positive tormentors which we endured because we thought that when we wore them we were "dressed up". Many times we have been laughed at for our native way of dressing, but could anything we ever wore compare in utter foolishness to the steel-ribbed corset and the huge bustle which our girls adopted after a few years in school? (cited in McLuhan 1971:103).

Other government agencies are also involved in distribution of clothing forms to the Potawatomi. In times of severe economic necessity, such as the early 1950's in northern Wisconsin, county welfare departments issued appeals for secondhand clothing specifically for distribution to the Indians (Bartlett n.d). This clothing was used as it was received, and not decorated or changed to reflect the taste of the new Indian owner.

Individual Indian agents of the Bureau of Indian Affairs also personally affected the form of Potawatomi clothing, especially in the earlier days of the United States Indian Service, to the extent that they fulfilled their duties of "going among the Indians to teach them to spin, weave cloth, and live like white people, among other things" (Blair 1911–1912: vol. 2, p. 180).

The tourist trade in the twentieth century has not only affected the form of Potawatomi clothing, but it has also to some extent affected the form of the clothing of the white tourists. One thing the tourist trade has done is encourage maintenance of knowledge of traditional crafts such as beadwork and fingerweaving, in that these crafts are used in the manufacture of items to be sold to tourists (Plate 21). Smith reported in 1925:

The women and even the men make many tourist articles for sale during the summer. . . . Most of the women also make buckskin moccasins which are usually beaded in Potawatomi fashion and sell for from two to six dollars a pair, depending upon the character of the leather used. Moccasins from winter hides are thicker and higher priced. They make all sorts of beaded articles, from a simple bandeau to elaborate beaded blouses (1925:73).

Plate 21.   Modern beadwork from Wabeno (Pichotta Collection)

In 1941, Vandenburgh took note of the articles sold at the Milwaukee midsummer festival:

Some fine beadwork was represented in the form of flags, miniature moccasins, rosettes, dolls, all souvenirs which could be pinned to a coat, jacket, or dress (1941:17).

In the late 1940's, Ritzenthaler found that "some of the women sell handicrafts, such as moccasins and beaded lapel pins, to the stores in town which deal in tourist souvenirs" (1953:116). To the extent that the white tourists purchased such items as moccasins and beaded blouses and wore them, their form of costume was affected.

On the other hand, the tourist trade affects the form of Potawatomi traditional clothing because of the powwows which are put on for tourists at Lac du Flambeau: the Indians dress in traditional costume especially for participation in these and other powwows and dances around the United States. Participation in these events is documented for the Potawatomi throughout the twentieth century: Smith (1925) cited Wisconsin Potawatomi participation in powwows, some of which were put on for tourists, at various dance grounds in the neighborhood of Forest County. The Forest County Potawatomi in the 1970's dance occasionally at the powwows at Lac du Flambeau, but their costumes do not necessarily reflect what has traditionally been considered Potawatomi dress. Young Potawatomi boys can be seen dancing with feather fans on arms, back, and head, such as are seen among Plains Indians groups; and families adapt costumes for these tourist dances using elements of costumes from various tribes.

This "pan-Indianism" in costume extends to that worn for everyday as well. In the summer of 1971, several members of various woodland tribes of northern Wisconsin were observed wearing turquoise jewelry, usually considered typical of the Indians of the southwestern United States. The trend may be to wear certain elements of clothing that reflect a basic "Indianness" rather than affiliation with one particular tribe.

Thus it is clear that much information about sexual differentiation and acculturation can be gleaned not only from the Potawatomi dress artifacts which remain, but also from evidence in the literature and in collections of photographs. The changes in form, meaning, and function of clothing elements throughout Potawatomi history were different for men than they were for women, and some of these changes were affected directly and indirectly by various non-Indian groups with which the Potawatomi were in sustained contact. The influence of non-Indian groups on Potawatomi costume and the evolution of traditional Potawatomi dress continues to the present day.

REFERENCES

BARTLETT, EDITH
  n.d.   "Scrapbook on Indians." Unpublished scrapbook, Public Library, Galesville, Wisconsin.
BLAIR, EMMA HELEN, *editor*
  1911–1912   *The Indian tribes of the upper Mississippi valley and region of the Great Lakes as described by Nicolas Perrot, French commandant in the northwest; Bacqueville de la Pothèrie, French Royal Commissioner to Canada; Morrell Marston, American Army officer; and Thomas Forsyth, United States agent at Fort Armstrong*, two volumes. Cleveland: Arthur H. Clark.
DOUGLASS, JOHN M.
  1949   Cultural changes among the Wisconsin Indian tribes during the French contact period. *Wisconsin Archeologist*, n.s. 30(1):1–21.

GEREND, ALPHONSE
  n.d.   Untitled, unpublished scrapbook, Division of Anthropology, State Historical Society of Wisconsin, Madison.
KINIETZ, WILLIAM VERNON
  1965   *The Indians of the western Great Lakes, 1615–1760.* Ann Arbor Paperbacks. Ann Arbor: University of Michigan Press.
LURIE, NANCY OESTREICH
  1969   Wisconsin, a natural laboratory for North American Indian studies. *Wisconsin Magazine of History* 53(1):2–20.
McLUHAN, T. C.
  1971   *Touch the earth: a self-portrait of Indian existence.* New York: Outerbridge and Dienstfrey.
O'KELLIHER, MARJORIE
  1932–1934   "Oconto scrap book." Unpublished scrapbook, Oconto County Historical Society, Oconto, Wisconsin.
O'MEARA, WALTER
  1968   *Daughters of the country: the women of the fur traders and mountain men.* New York: Harcourt, Brace and World.
OVERTON, GEORGE
  1940   Trade goods: Grignon-Porlier post. *Wisconsin Archeologist*, n.s. 21(4):71–73.
PRUCHA, FRANCIS PAUL, DONALD F. CARMONY
  1968   A memorandum of Lewis Cass: concerning a system for the regulation of Indian affairs. *Wisconsin Magazine of History* 52(1):35–50.
RITZENTHALER, ROBERT E.
  1953   Potawatomi Indians of Wisconsin. *Bulletin of the Public Museum of the City of Milwaukee* 19(3):105–174.
SCHOEWE, CHARLES E.
  1932   Uses of wood and bark among the Wisconsin Indians. *Wisconsin Archeologist*, n.s. 11(4):148–152.
SMITH, HURON H.
  1925   Among the Potawatomi. *Milwaukee Public Museum Yearbook* 5:68–76.
THWAITES, R. G., *editor*
  1896–1901   *The Jesuit relations and allied documents: travels and explorations of the Jesuit missionaries in New France, 1610–1791*, volume fifty-one. Cleveland: Burrows Brothers.
UNDERHILL, RUTH MURRAY
  1953   *Red man's America: a history of the Indians in the United States.* Chicago: University of Chicago Press.
VANDENBURGH, MARY M.
  1941   Milwaukee's midsummer festival Indian village, 1941. *Wisconsin Archeologist*, n.s. 22(3):15–18.

Yoruba Dress in Five Generations of a Lagos Family

BETTY M. WASS

Dress in any culture is a means of communication. It conveys messages when members of a society who share a given culture have learned to associate types of dress with given, customary usage. Through this customary association, certain types of dress become symbols for either specific or class or social roles, with this symbolism changing over time in different social and ethnic contexts.

It was interest in the change of dress symbolism over time that became part of the stimulus in planning field research that could demonstrate graphically the dynamics of change in dress. The fieldwork, which ultimately resulted in a study (Wass 1975), was based on the dress worn by one Yoruba extended family residing in Lagos and the associations attached to that dress from 1900 to 1974. Within the study, the associations between dress and role expectations linked to age, sex, education, occupation, religion, marital status, and occasion for the use of the dress were investigated. Variations of status were considered within each of three time-periods identified by changing political conditions in Nigeria.

Two hypotheses guiding the study were developed by Bush and London (1960), who stated that messages conveyed by dress were related to both social roles and self-concepts, and further proposed that *changes* in modes of dress corresponded to changes in social roles and self-concepts. Although these hypotheses were developed in American society, they appeared to be testable in another cultural setting. Because Nigeria as a country and Lagos as its major city have been subjected extensively to forces of change over the past two centuries, it was decided that this city would provide a dynamic setting for a study of changing forms and meanings of dress, relative to changing social roles and self-concepts.

ORGANIZATION OF THE STUDY

The original study had two main sections: an historical perspective of Lagos and of the family, and an analysis of dress.

First, the social setting of Lagos preceding and coinciding with the residence span of the study family (1850 to 1974) was described, then, by using published historical accounts in periodicals, books, bulletins, and newspapers, dating from 1900 onwards, it was possible to extract changing additional directions in Nigeria for the period since then. Time-span divisions were identified as (1) 1900–1939, a period when a low degree of sentiment favoring nationalism was evident; (2) 1940–1959, a period when movements backing nationalism became increasingly stronger; and (3) 1960–1974, the period of postindependence.

It could not be determined in historical perspective whether or not implied attitudinal directions for each period accurately depicted the actual attitudes and opinions of individuals. However, it is assumed that pervading attitudes affect social roles and self-concepts during historical development at any point in time. Attitudes are linked to self-concept as a component of intrapersonal resolution among those cultural elements within one's environment. Self-concept within the context of this study is the sociopolitical image of the Yoruba as a group relative to inchoate Nigerian nationalism during the designated time periods. Out of necessity, however, individual self-concepts mirrored in dress were precluded from the study.

According to both popular and academic writers of Nigerian history, a general shift away from emulation of foreign culture to reaffirmation of the indigenous cultural heritage occurred during the course of the twentieth century. One dimension of this shift was dress. However, when writers treat all individuals as one homogenous group, they overlook the differentiating choices made by groups of people of dissimilar statuses. This study investigated the use of Western or indigenous dress at various occasions by persons in varying status groups, those being sex, age, education, occupation, religion, and marital status. The variables divide persons into groups associated with differing social role expectations.

The characteristics of the study family place them, as a whole, among the Nigerian elite, for they have a long history of five generations of Western acculturation and education, with an accompanying rise in social status. Although family members do not refer to themselves as elite, they exemplify the upper-class ranks (Smythe and Smythe 1960). Criteria for elite status have changed over the years, but because of their education, a continuing critical component for elite status, members of the study family have been in civil-servant or professional positions from the first generation onward: positions acknowledged as part and parcel of the

Nigerian elite. Educational levels and occupations were identified for almost 70 percent of the 607 subjects of the study.

SOURCES OF INFORMATION

The figure of 607 subjects is somewhat misleading, if one is picturing interviews with that many informants. The actual number of informants involved in personal interviews was seventeen: the remainder of the subjects, many long deceased, were to be found in approximately a thousand photographs available from the Yoruba family of the study. It was these photographs that provided the primary data, which was augmented and reinforced by personal communication from the unit family and their relatives. In these pictures the dress of family members, relatives, and friends could be closely examined, and 607 photographed subjects who were fully garbed for assorted occasions were selected for analysis. Those subjects in photographs who were not completely visible from head to toe were eliminated.

The unit family, who provided information concerning the dress and other characteristics of the people depicted, were a household consisting of a mother, three children (two of whom were away at school much of the time), two children of relatives (who lived in the household while attending schools nearby), and an elderly female relative who supervised household help. Ten other subjects, aunts, uncles, and cousins who visited frequently, all cooperated generously in describing and interpreting various meanings of dress and in providing information about deceased family members pictured in the photographs. The researcher lived with the unit family household for six weeks while collecting the data for the study.

The photographs yielded information about forms of dress worn, which was necessary to determine modes of dress. Modes were interpreted as statistical modes and defined as combinations of body covering and adornment worn most frequently during the specific time periods. Consequently, the dress norms for various status groups mentioned above were delineated within the three divisions of the total time period.

CHARACTERISTICS OF DRESS WITHIN HISTORICAL PERIODS

1900–1939

Within the analytical context described previously, nationalistic sentiments appear at a low ebb from 1900 to 1939. In 1900 Nigeria officially became a country within the British Empire and the chief port of Lagos quickly developed as the point of concentration for colonial activity. The era brought higher wages, more and better jobs, and a chance at a new kind of prosperity for West Africans with the right skills. Because the focus of Nigerians was on adjusting to the new system of government, no strong movements advocating independence were pervasive at this time.

Occupations were closely intertwined with religion and education since schools were run by Christian missions and anyone formally educated in these schools was more or less guaranteed a clerical or professional position. Naturally, citizens of Lagos quickly learned to covet education as a catalyst to social mobility although ultimate power in business or government rested exclusively with colonial administrators. By the early nineteenth century, literate Nigerians began to emerge as a new status group distinct from the common people and the old line elite. This educated class emulated the British in many ways while simultaneously retaining Yoruba values.

Family members in the study were part of the population in Lagos that is more than eighty percent Yoruba. Individuals in the family acquired appropriate skills for jobs in the new system and, consequently, were beneficiaries of colonialism. First and second generation family members living in Lagos since the mid-nineteenth century received a Western education and became Christian converts prior to 1900, and this pattern continued throughout the next generation. Third generation family members growing up in the early 1900's took advantage of all the Western education available in Lagos at the time. However, this third generation retained old Yoruba practices such as giving deference to elders beyond the expectations of Western societies.

As for dress, Western styles were common. Persons wearing Western dress, repatriates, missionaries, and businessmen, had been in Lagos since the mid-nineteenth century. The repatriates from Sierra Leone were among the first to emulate foreigners. Christian missionaries, whose dress was dictated for the most part by their religion, and European businessmen, eager to sell imported goods, were all a part of the Lagos scene before 1900. Western dress items comprise about two thirds of the total in the 110 photographs of the period from 1900 to 1939.

In this first period, photographs also show a tendency among the family to wear totally Western clothes or totally indigenous clothes. Mixing and matching items with differing cultural associations in the same outfit was rare; only four percent of the outfits were of this type. Status conveyed through dress is one explanation for this lack of mixed outfits. Formally educated Christian individuals, however, were expected to appear in Western dress. Isaac Delano (1945) noted that the Bible and the tie appeared simultaneously. It follows, then, that nonliterates were associated with indigenous dress and that people were reluctant to mix symbols conveying differing statuses.

The photographs verify that individuals with the maximum amount of education available in Lagos in this period wore more Western dress than the rest of the population. Considering principle garments, that is, those covering the largest area of the body, as the crucial items in determining the cultural character of an outfit, 82 percent of the dress of those with formal education is Western. Generally, more males than females were educated, but in the study family both boys and girls were formally educated after 1900. Thus, it seems reasonable to assume that dress of both sexes would be similar in cultural association. In fact, however, a larger percentage of males (89 percent) wore Western dress than did females (60 percent), displaying a possible sexual difference in use of Western dress. Occupations are an explanation for this difference because educated men moved on to Western-type occupations while educated women were expected to remain in the traditional spheres associated with trading, crafts, and child care. Whether men were actually required to wear Western dress to work is unknown, but their dress did emulate the dress of foreigners in superior positions there.

An example of modal Western dress, dress worn most often, from 1900 to 1939 is shown in Plate 1. For females the items were a dress, shoes, bracelet, earrings, stockings, and neck chain, while for males modal dress including a shirt, long trousers, jacket, shoes, and necktie. Indigenous modal dress is seen in Plates 2 and 3.

Plate 1. 1930: males and female wearing modal Western dress items of the first period (1900–1939).

Plate 2. 1900: male and female traditional Yoruba dress, the male's attire exemplifies male modal dress of the first period (1900–1939)

Plate 3. 1920: female wearing traditional modal dress items of the first period (1900–1939). The fabric of the *iro* [wrapper] is *adire eleko*, a traditional handcrafted textile

According to the Yoruba historian, Samuel Johnson (1921), males were dominant in patrilineal and patrilocal extended families of traditional society and their status was symbolized in the quality and quantity of male dress. These differences did not show up in the small sample of indigenous dress examined from this period. For the most part, females wore more items in an ensemble of indigenous dress than males and any differences in quality were not obvious. Possibly the authority of the male decreased in Lagos due to changes in housing patterns, disappearance of the extended family compound, and changes in the nature of occupations, wage labor replacing farming and crafts. At the same time, women's dress seems to have become comparable to men's dress in quantity and quality.

Johnson also described distinctions in indigenous modes of dress between married and unmarried females. Certain hairstyles and use of a shawl (*iborun*) were said to be the privilege of married women.

In the family population, hairstyles were not visible on twenty-two of twenty-three women wearing indigenous dress in the first period, their hair being covered with headscarves. Nor could definite conclusions be drawn about the marital status of those who used the shawl because, while all women who wore it were married, it was seen on only three photographs in this period.

The photographs suggested age–role differences, for the children's dress was primarily Western. Prior to the Western influence, children wore nothing if boys, and waist beads if girls, until they reached an age near puberty. Western notions of modesty probably became instrumental in dressing children, and Western items of dress were adopted since the jewelry mentioned above was then the only indigenous item for children. Eighty percent of the dress of persons younger than sixteen was Western, whereas those sixteen and over wore 67 percent Western dress (see Table 1). Western dress at that time also symbolized child/adult social differences along European lines. For example, baby boys wore dresses until age two or three when they switched to knickerbockers and eventually, at a later age, to long pants. Western, rather than indigenous, dress may have been adopted for children because wearing Yoruba dress in Yoruba culture implied maturity. In a novel about a Yoruba girl, an aunt tells the girl who is soon to be married,

... English frocks do nothing for your figure. They are neither up nor down, and they allow you to look younger than your age (Johnston 1973:71).

Relaxation in rules relative to dress was evident in photographs of children. Only six outfits in all the photographs from 1900 to 1939 fit neither the Western nor the indigenous mode and five of these were worn by children. Adults were either more conscientious in adhering to the rules of dress for themselves than for their children, or there were rules for children which were not apparent to the researcher due to the relatively small number (36) of children in the population for this period.

Special occasions in all periods call for variation on modal garments in features such as color, texture, or stylistic details. Consistently, however, all persons photographed at special occasions in the first period wore Western dress with one exception, that being a child. The special occasions designated by informants included betrothals, weddings, naming ceremonies, christenings, confirmations, birthdays, housewarmings, retirement parties, funerals, and memorial services.

1940–1959

The second period is characterized by increasing nationalistic sentiment. During the late 1930's, organized political parties arose in Lagos to direct Nigerian desires for self-determination. Students returning from study abroad demanded that Africans be given a greater voice in government.

During the 1940's, nationalism became the lodestar of all the Nigerian political parties, and the Second World War fueled the movement's momentum by raising Nigerian self-confidence when Nigerian soldiers fought as ably as their white allies. Additionally, Nigerians began producing more and more of their own products due to wartime shortages. When Britain attempted to put controls on Nigerian resources to meet wartime needs, Nigerians responded by boycotting imports. The rejection of foreign goods evolved into a cultural renaissance which persisted throughout the second period. Political activists enlisted the backing of the general public in the movement which crested during the following decade in a pervasive desire for independence.

The fourth generation of the study family were young adults during this period. All of them went as far as possible with their education in Nigeria. Six out of seven went to college and five of them studied in England. Education qualified them for elite status, but, as the number of college graduates in Nigeria has increased, the relationship between higher education and superior status has become less assured. As a result, the occupations of the fourth generation could be described as ranging from semiskilled to professional.

The family members were not political activists in the nationalist movement, however, the key informant related nationalistic zeal in that her personal objective upon returning from study in England was to teach students how to use and respect Nigerian products. Nigeria had indigenous fabrics, for example, that were equal in quality to those found anywhere in the world but many people had learned to prefer European goods, because of variety in patterns and lower cost.

In the second period, use of indigenous dress by the study family increased. Based on the cultural identity of main garments, 1940 differing markedly from 1950, indigenous dress composed almost half (46 percent) of the dress worn. In 1940, 36 percent of principle garments worn were indigenous but in 1950 the amount increased to 55 percent. Whether the family adopted indigenous forms during an earlier or later stage than the nationalist leaders is unknown, but in the decade preceding independence the family's increased use of such dress mirrors identification with the national movement that urged renewed respect for African heritage. Western dress had indicated educated, urban, Christian affiliations during the first period, but some time around the beginning of the second period, it lost these meanings. However, several members of the study family appeared conservative regarding change to indigenous dress.

Individuals in the photographs who had the maximum amount of education or had studied abroad used less indigenous dress than the remainder of those pictured. Forty-six percent of the garments worn by the total population of the study were indigenous whereas the dress of the more educated group was 42 percent indigenous. Since the more educated group included the immediate family, perhaps lesser use of Nigerian dress corresponds to noninvolvement in political activities.

Along with the trend toward wearing more indigenous dress, there was another trend toward mixing indigenous and Western. Eight percent of the ensembles worn were indigenous-Western hybrids in this period, twice that of the previous period.

The use of indigenous dress by women in the population showed only a negligible increase from 40 to 46 percent, but the percentage of indigenous dress worn by men jumped from 11 percent in the first period to 36 percent after 1940. These increases were obviously allied to the Nigerian political movement. Male and female statuses were changing in that both sexes were gaining or anticipating gaining authority at their jobs. However, relative to one another, roles were not changing perceptibly. Men's work remained something separate from women's work and women, but for rare exceptions, did not have opportunities to fill high-status positions. Change in men's dress, then, seemed to correspond more to change in self-concept as a group than to change in role. Nigerian men anticipated increased status and power in decision making when their nation gained its independence. Possibly there was hope that male status, which had suffered within the extended family when the society moved from an agrarian toward an industrial society, would be compensated for in increased public political power. This different mode of dress corresponded to a changing self-concept for men as a group.

During the second period a dramatic increase occurred in the average number of items of dress worn in all modes, whether male or female, Western or indigenous. In these decades prosperity increased; the increase in number of garments worn may have been an economic indicator. For women, neck jewelry became an additional item in the traditional mode, supplementing arm and ear jewelry (Plate 4). Footwear, not modal with traditional Yoruba dress during the first period, became part of all modes. Handbags were added to items in the female Western mode (Plate 5).

Plate 4.   1940: female wearing modal traditional dress of the second period (1940–1959)

The largest increase in average number of items used occurred in the female indigenous mode. Articles like the shawl, the second wrapper, and extra jewelry enhanced indigenous dress making such outfits increasingly elaborate. One article disappeared from the female modes however. Stockings, which satisfied Western notions of formality, modesty, and sexual attractiveness were unavailable during the Second World War. They disappeared and never reappeared in the postwar years.

Relative to age distinctions during this period, adults wore more indigenous dress while children wore more Western dress. Persons over

Plate 5. 1940: female wearing modal Western dress items of the second period (1940–1959) with the addition of a hat and rings

sixteen wore 50 percent indigenous dress, an increase from 33 percent in the previous period. Children's dress became more Western, increasing from 80 to 92 percent Western. Children's increasing use of Western dress failed to reflect participation in the nationalistic movement central to adults.

For special occasions, both Western and indigenous dress were worn. Contrasted to the earlier period when special occasion dress was Western, for the study family indigenous dress now comprised 41 percent of the dress worn for special occasions. In comparison, a similar amount of indigenous dress, 46 percent, was worn by the total population for all occasions. In the second period, the question of wearing Western or indigenous dress was evidently not associated with particular occasions.

Generally, two differences in modes of dress are quite obvious during the second period. First, indigenous principle garments were worn more than Western principle garments in the decade preceding independence and, second the group which expressed differences more visibly by their dress were the men. They tripled their use of indigenous dress after 1940 (Plates 6 and 7).

Plate 6.   1940: male wearing modal
traditional dress of a second period
(1940–1959)

Plate 7.   1950: male wearing modal
Western dress of the second period
(1940–1959)

1960–1974

In 1960 Nigeria gained its independence, an event which introduced a
third period relative to dress. The population of Lagos swelled in the
decades prior to independence as individuals from around the country
sought the jobs created by rapid social and economic developments.
Nigerian ethnic groups formed individual organizations to help their
people adapt to urban life in Lagos by providing cultural refuges that
contributed to preservation of ethnic identity. The political parties
founded during the 1930's also had foundations in ethnic allegiances that
were maintained throughout the second period. Amoda (1972) states
that following independence in 1960, the only remaining function of
these political parties seemed to be exploitation of ethnic interests. The
eventual outcome was the destructive civil war lasting from 1966 to 1970.
Ethnic loyalties remain strong as an aftermath of the war, but the need for
unity seems to be acknowledged, at least in theory, throughout the
country. Lagos was spared the carnage of that war and has continued to

lead as Nigeria's most economically advanced city with a population estimated at nearly a million in the 1970's.

Family members in the third period maintained the patterns of education, occupation, and religion of earlier generations. The children attended Nigerian universities, adults had professional occupations, and the family was Christian. Their lifestyle exemplified the Nigerian elite outlined by social scientists (Smythe and Smythe 1960) relative to housing, household help, leisure activities, and dress.

The number of indigenous dress items used by the population from 1960 to 1974 was slightly greater than the period before (Plates 8 and 9). Forty-four percent of the principal garments were indigenous in this period, compared to 43 percent in the second period. While the percentages for the two periods are nearly equal, western–indigenous mixtures almost doubled again in the third period to include fifteen percent of the outfits.

Plate 8. 1970: female wearing modal traditional dress of the third period (1960–1974) with the addition of a choker as neck jewelry

Plate 9. 1960: male wearing modal traditional dress of the third period (1960–1974)

Individuals with the most education wore more indigenous dress than the total population, a reversal from the previous period. Women used about the same amount of indigenous dress in the third period as in the second.

Surprisingly, the dramatic increase in men's indigenous dress during the second period was not maintained. The amount of indigenous apparel worn by men dropped from 36 to 29 percent after independence. One explanation for the decrease is found in the popularity of a new style, the conductor's suit. In the study, conductor's suits, an African version of a Western form, were classified as strictly Western. The result was an increase in data under the Western category and, possibly, wrong conclusions. In fact, the conductor's suit is perhaps neither Western nor indigenous, but belongs in a third category, such as modern West African. The conductor's suit evolved for men in roles identified with Western-type industrial development but who at the same time had gained a voice in decision-making which allowed them to express themselves as independent Nigerians. One might assume the bolstering of self-concepts: the modern business or professional man's occupational role is Western in character yet he is Nigerian, so the conductor's suit expresses both qualities.

Improved self-concepts among women as a group may be implied in the third period by the return to Nigerian hairstyles (see Houlberg, this volume). These Nigerian hairstyles which seem synonymous with expressing pride in being African were not seen generally until about ten years following Nigeria's independence. Traditional braided styles are currently popular with all ages and are especially noticeable with Western dress. When indigenous dress is worn in public the head-tie covering the hair is still usually added to complete the outfit and the hairstyle is not visible. Previously the intricately braided hairstyles were publicly seen only on young girls, and when women showed their hair it was straightened into a Western style.

Besides national pride, one other factor may play a part in women's changing dress styles: a change in roles. During the last century Nigerian women have possessed a degree of financial independence through their own occupations such as trading and crafts, but these were seldom positions of high status. Also women did not have much voice in decisions concerning extended families. Today more women are combining the traditional mother-housemaker role with professional careers in formerly all-male domains. Empirical evidence gathered was too scant to make any binding generalizations about role and self-concept differences for women, but several changes implied by dress were suggested in conversations with the informants, as well as in the photographs. Women presently wearing hairstyles that formerly were seen only on young girls is possibly one example of changing self-concept. Furthermore, the second wrapper which added bulk around the middle of the body in a matronly effect is now unfashionable. The wrapper itself has become smaller and less bulky around the torso, and the shawl, indicating marriage seems to be vanishing from the fashion scene, especially among young people. Finally, a woman's *agbada* which bears the same name as the man's voluminous outer garment is currently fashionable. On the other hand, the wearing of fewer garments probably also signals a trend toward informality that began in Western fashions some time after 1940 when clothing became progressively lighter in weight and more comfortable.

Turning to children, more indigenous dress (16 percent) was worn in the third period. The increase corresponds to that of adults who also wore more indigenous dress after 1960. The vast majority of children's dress remained Western, however, and wearing indigenous dress was something "special". Nevertheless, one generally did not see children at special occasions in indigenous dress — it seemed to be reserved for church or portrait photographs.

Following Nigerian independence ethnic diversity was visually symbolized in clothing. Previously a Nigerian Yoruba might have worn Ghanaian or Sierra Leonean dress or the dress of another ethnic group but this phenomenon disappeared during the 1960's. At least in the family under study, Yoruba people wore either Yoruba dress or Western dress.

STABILITY AND CHANGE OVER TIME

All in all, the characteristics of the study family remained constant from 1900 to 1974 while their dress patterns exhibited change. Immediate family members were urban residents seeing themselves as Lagos people, all of them having lived there for long periods of time, if not all their lives. Family members educated after 1900 took full advantage of all education available in Nigeria and, in some cases, more, and it was this initiative that paved the way for high-status occupations. Religion also remained the same, all family members alive after 1900 identifying themselves as Christian.

From 1900 to 1974 the dress of the family and their friends was predominantly Western although indigenous principal garments were worn increasingly after 1940. Interestingly, the garments worn most often by males and females in both the Western and indigenous modes remained the same from 1900 to 1974. Garments which predominated in each of the four modes are the *iro* wrapper (female indigenous), the *sokoto* trousers (male indigenous), the dress (female Western), and the shirt (male Western).

Western dress during the first part of the twentieth century was generally associated with formally educated, Christian persons in Lagos. Such an individual was set off from both the nonliterate population and the traditional elite class who wore types of indigenous dress. Although most of the dress during the first period was Western, even among the Lagos elite some indigenous dress was always worn. Some individuals simply may have preferred it; for others it was a political symbol. Actually as early as the 1890's a Lagos group had shown their anticolonial feeling by refusing to wear European dress. Since English dress was more common in Lagos than in rural areas (Fadipe 1970), intermittently throughout the twentieth century rejection of this type of dress in Lagos was used as a visual symbol of discontent.

In the second period, nationalistic feelings fueled by the independence movement prompted Nigerians to use dress as one means of severing themselves from the colonialists and identifying with their political cause. Along with the independence movement came a renewed interest in Nigerian precolonial customs and manners. The educated elite were recognized as leaders in cultural assertion, the revived appreciation of traditional things. By 1959, Nigerians were congratulating themselves for renewed respect in their cultural heritage and one signpost of that respect was the claim that every Nigerian owned at least one indigenous outfit (*Daily Service* 1959).

Table 1 indicates changes from 1900 to 1974 in the use of indigenous dress by the total population of the study and by members of the population representing various social status groups that imply role differences. Changes in modes were most evident among: (1) adults older than

Table 1.   Percentage of use of indigenous dress by total population and by members of population in social role groupings over three time periods

Social roles	1900–1939	1940–1959	1960–1974
Total population of study	29	43	44
Age			
Under 16	20	8	16
Over 16	33	50	59
Education/occupation			
Maximum education	18	42	54
Occasion			
Adults, special occasion	0	44	72
Sex			
Males	11	36	29
Females	40	46	47

sixteen, (2) the maximally educated group, and (3) adults participating in special occasions. The most-educated group used progressively more indigenous dress starting with 18 percent in the first period, then 42 percent in the second period and 54 percent in the third period. A more marked increase was found among adults at special occasions since they did not wear indigenous dress during the first period. After 1940, 44 percent of the dress worn at special occasions was indigenous and after 1960 this climbed to 72 percent.

Men also substantially increased their use of indigenous dress from 11 percent during the first period to 36 percent in the second period. This was not continued into the third period for reasons mentioned earlier.

INTERPRETATIONS

Data was enumerated in two ways: (1) individual items were counted in Western and indigenous categories and (2) principal garments by themselves were tabulated in the same categories.

Following the first approach of counting each item, there was no confirmation of the anticipated direct relationship between rising nationalistic sentiments and the increasing use of indigenous dress implied in popular and academic writings. The use of indigenous times in the second and third periods was less than anticipated; in fact, the number of indigenous items worn rose from 28 percent in the first period to 33 percent in the second period and to 35 percent in the third.

Several explanations for the negligible differences come to mind. One explanation is selective perception. An overriding sense of nationalism could fog perceptions so that one might perceive use of indigenous dress to be greater than it actually was. Or, items such as accessories, used over a long period of time, may no longer be viewed as Western. The Western handbag, for example, became a part of female indigenous modal dress.

Other explanations revolve around the social roles and self-concepts of the study population. First, the renewed use of indigenous dress was linked to the elite classes since they had generally worn Western dress earlier and some individuals in the photographs wearing indigenous dress during the first period might have been from a different social class since their identity was unknown. As a result, the use of indigenous dress during the first period might have been recorded as greater than it in fact was. Second, though the family resembled the elite for the most part, they were not politically active and, consequently, may not have worn indigenous dress in the period of rising nationalistic sentiments to the extent that others did. Third, academic scholars possibly viewed dress for special occasions, and use of indigenous dress for special occasions increased substantially in the second and third periods. Fourth, the family may not have been entirely representative of the elite group relative to their dress.

Finally, some garments may be more interpretive than others in the communications process and this explanation was accepted to facilitate the study. The cultural associations of dress drawn from impressions of principal garments rather than equal weighting of all garments showed a marked increase in use of indigenous dress from 29 percent in the first period to 43 and 44 percent in the second and third periods.

The results of the study show definitely that fundamental or enduring modes of dress in a society are communicative of change in social roles and self-concepts of members of that society. Roles and self-concepts of groups in the Yoruba study family are differentiated by dress particularly relative to age, education and occupation, occasion, and sex.

REFERENCES

AMODA, MOYIBI
  1972 Background to the conflict: a summary of Nigeria's political history from 1914 to 1964, in: *Nigeria: dilemma of nationhood: an African analysis of the Biafran conflict*. Edited by Joseph Okpaku. New York: Third Press.
BUSH, GEORGE, PERRY LONDON
  1960 On the disappearance of knickers: hypotheses for the functional analysis of the psychology of clothing. *Journal of Social Psychology* 51:359–366. (Reprinted 1965 in: *Dress, adornment and the social order*. Edited by Mary Ellen Reach and Joanne Bubolz Eicher, 64–72. New York: John Wiley and Sons.)
Daily Service
  1959 Article in *Daily Service*. February 20. Lagos.
DELANO, ISAAC
  1945 *One church for Nigeria*. London: United Society for Christian Literature.
FADIPE, N. A.
  1970 *The sociology of the Yoruba*. Ibadan: Ibadan University Press.
JOHNSON, SAMUEL
  1921 *The history of the Yorubas*. London: George Routledge and Sons.
JOHNSTON, RHODA OMOSUNLOLA
  1973 *Iyabo of Nigeria*. Claremont, California: Claremont Graduate School.
SMYTHE, HUGH H., MABEL SMYTHE
  1960 *The new Nigerian elite*. Stanford, California: Stanford University Press.
WASS, BETTY M.
  1975 "Yoruba dress: a systematic case study of five generations of a Lagos family." Unpublished doctoral dissertation, Michigan State University, East Lansing.

Social Hair: Tradition and Change in Yoruba Hairstyles in Southwestern Nigeria

MARILYN HAMMERSLEY HOULBERG

The Yoruba have a strong tradition of visual communication through sculptural forms and, in fact, are acknowledged to be the most prolific wood-carvers of Africa. But their sculptural genius is not confined to wood and other hard media. One of the liveliest of the sculptural arts to be found in Yorubaland today is hairstyling. Hairdressers can be seen performing their art on shaded verandahs or under trees, often seated next to their colorful signs offering a variety of illustrated hairstyles for their customers to choose (Plate 1). The names and forms of the styles reflect aspects of Yoruba contemporary life. Style 6 in the plate, "Face-to-face", takes its name from the fact that it is designed to stay in place during "face-to-face", the colloquial term of kissing.[1] In a more topical example, when Nigeria switched over from driving on the left side of the road to the right in 1972, the Nigerian government slogan "Nigeria drive right" was soon interpreted in hair. Needless to say, the dominant feature of this style was a dramatic projection to the right (Plate 2, style 5).

Hairstyles, in addition to being a popular art form reflecting and interpreting Yoruba contemporary life, also perform the more traditional function of indicating and maintaining social categories. They also are important in rites of transition from one category or status to another. This paper will briefly examine the form and function of hairstyles in both traditional and contemporary Yoruba culture, noting what, if any, characteristics they share.

I am grateful to the Kress Foundation and to the Wenner-Gren Foundation for grants which supported my fieldwork among the Yoruba in 1970–1971, 1973 and 1975. I also wish to thank Klindt Houlberg and Mark Schiltz for their valuable assistance and encouragement and John Brewer for helpful comments on this paper. I also wish to thank Tai and Sheila Solarin of Ikenne for their warm hospitality.
[1] "Face-to-face" has also been taken as the name of a popular soccer pool. In both cases, "face-to-face" refers to the slang for kissing.

Plate 1.   An Ijebu-Ode (Ijebu) hairdresser works outside the window of her house. Her sign offers a variety of styles to her customers: 1, 2: Eko bridge, 3: Ade-ọba [the king's crown], 4: Ogun pari [the war is over], 5: John Kennedy, 6: Face-to-face, 7: Ade-ọba, 8: Macwira with crown, 9: Macwira, 10: Remo carpet, 11: Be back, 12: Be front, 13: Baret, 14: Police cap, 15: Four adeṣe line. The sign is by Bayo Art, 25, Oyo Street, Olorunshogbo, Mushin, Lagos. Photograph: December 10, 1973, by Klindt Houlberg

Plate 2.   Sign belonging to hairdresser Dupe Ṣeṣan, of Ikenne, Ijebu-Remo. Names of styles: 1, 2: Eko bridge, 3: Alhaja (hairstyle for Yoruba Muslim women), 4: Ilekedi, 5: Nigeria drive right, 6, 7: Ogun pari, 8: Mọrinmọ [the sex act], 9: Ikoto, 10: Edabo, 11: Remo carpet, 12: Ogun pari. Note that variations of the same style are offered in the case of "Eko bridge" and "Ogun pari". This sign is also by Bayo Art (see Plate 1). Photograph: June 15, 1975

The first objective will be to demonstrate how Yoruba hair behavior must be analyzed as a total system of visual communication from both synchronic and diachronic points of view. It is a system which only takes its meaning from being analyzed in its social context and one which must be seen as constantly undergoing differential rates of change. The second objective will be to show how Yoruba hairstyles often function as what Victor Turner (1967:50) has termed "multivocal" symbols. Turner defines multivocal symbols as those which are meaningful in many contexts or on many levels. As will be shown, the same hairstyle may convey different but related meanings depending on the context.

MODERN FEMALE YORUBA HAIRSTYLES

There are two main categories of contemporary hairstyles popular among Yoruba women today: (1) *ọlọwọ*, literally "hand done", in which the hair is parted and braided and no thread is used (Plates 3 and 4); and (2) *olowu*, literally, done with thread, in which the hair is parted and each section twisted and then tightly wrapped with heavy black cotton thread or, more recently, heavy black plastic (Plates 5 and 6).

Plate 3. Style: "Koroba" [pail], a braided style of the *ọlọwọ* type which uses no thread. Photograph: November 1973, Ikenne, Ijebu-Remo; by Klindt Houlberg

Plate 4. Style: "Ojo-peti" [rain not enter ear]. This style has been updated through the alternative name of "Ojukwu dǫbalę fun Gowon'', a reference to Ojukwu, the Biafran leader, surrendering to Gowon at the end of the Nigerian civil war in 1970. Ojukwu is represented by the flat braids across the front of the head, Gowon by the topknot. Photograph: November 1973, at Ikenne, Ijebu-Remo, by Klindt Houlberg

Plate 5. Hairdresser Ife-olu Solaru of Ilishan, Ijebu-Remo, creating "Eko bridge" style. The hair has been parted and gathered together in sections. Section by section the hair is drawn out and heavy plastic thread is wrapped around each section until the end of the hair is reached as has been done on the right side. Photograph: June 9, 1975

Plate 6.   The completed "Eko bridge" style shown in progress in Plate 5. Each straight projection was next wrapped around a thin metal rod to coil it. The coils were then all gathered at the top and tied together with the ends of the threads. The knot was neatly trimmed with a razor blade. Time: approximately forty-five minutes. Price: 50 Kobo (about $US0.75). Photograph: June 9, 1975

According to Gwatkin *olọwọ* is the older, more traditional type of Yoruba hairstyle (1971:1). The *olowu*, or thread-wrapped, styles were not introduced until after the Second World War and not generally worn until the sixties. The ethnic groups to the north of the Yoruba, such as the Hausa and the Kanuri, as well as the Yoruba, are traditionally noted for their woven or plaited styles; eastern Nigerian groups, such as the Ibo and Ibibio, are known for thread-wrapped styles. The thread-wrapped style of hairdressing probably thus came to the Yoruba rather recently from the east.

Ọlọwọ: The Braided, Women's Style

Braided styles were usually worn by young girls and older women whereas thread-wrapped styles are more commonly worn by older girls and young women. As one might expect, almost every Yoruba woman can braid hair while the newer and more elaborate thread-wrapped styles are generally done by full or part-time professional hairdressers. Traditionally, the women within a compound braid each other's hair with no money changing hands, while professional hairdressers charge fees commensurate with the amount of time necessary to complete a particular style. A braided hairstyle usually lasts from one to two weeks.

A well-known braided hairstyle that is found throughout much of Yorubaland is *koroba*, which means "pail" (Plate 3). It is said of this style that the bottom of the pail is at the back of the head and that the whole face is like the pail's mouth. Both the mouth of the face and that of the pail are capable of receiving liquid. Another receptacle interpreted in hair is the more traditional basket, which, like hair, is also woven. The basket style, called *ṣuku*, was originally worn only by royal wives (Plate 7).

Plate 7. Style: "Suku" [basket]. Formerly this style was reserved for the king's wives but now anyone who wishes may wear it. Photograph: June 15, 1975, Ikenne, Ijebu-Remo

Another traditional braided hairstyle is *ojo-peti*, meaning "rain not enter ear" (Plate 4). A feature of this style is that the front part of the hair is braided across the head from one ear to the other, ending in the braids cantilevering out over one ear, thus theoretically protecting it from rain.

While this style is well known throughout Yorubaland it is interesting to note that in some areas it has been updated by receiving a name which commemorates a political event, the end of the Nigerian civil war: *Ojukwu dọbalẹ fun Gowon* [Ojukwu bows down to Gowon]. The horizontal braids at the front of the head represent a prostrate Colonel Ojukwu, the leader of the secessionist state of Biafra, capitulating to Major-General Yakubu Gowon, at that time the head of the Nigerian federal government, who is represented by the high top knot.[2] As will be shown, there are other instances where the same style is known by a number of names. The names of hairstyles tend to change more rapidly than the range of styles themselves. Other traditional braided styles are *kolẹsẹ* [that which is without legs] and *ipakọ ẹlẹdẹ* [back of the pig's head]. Kolẹsẹ consists of parallel braids starting at the front of the head and ending at the nape of the neck. Ipakọ ẹlẹdẹ runs in exactly the opposite direction, from back to front culminating in spirals over the forehead resembling pigs' tails.

Olowu: The Thread-Wrapped, Women's Style

These thread-wrapped styles usually last about one to two weeks and are most often done by professional hairdressers. There is regional variation in how women learn this craft. In some areas, such as Ila-Orangun, there is an official hairdressers' union (in Ila it is called Ẹgbẹ Ifetayo) which takes on apprentices who pay fees to learn the trade.[3] The period of apprenticeship varies but is usually a minimum of six months and may continue for several years. Upon completion, the apprentice receives a certificate and as a member will continue to pay monthly dues to the association. In some areas there is no formal instruction and women learn informally from other women, often their mothers.

Professional hairdressers purchase their hairstyle signs ready made from local sign painters or from Ibadan or Lagos. The hairdressers do not specify what styles they want on the sign, for the sign painters simply illustrate the latest fashions and a woman will select the one she likes best. Sometimes the names of the hairstyles are painted directly on the signs, which tends to standardize them. This range of names provides an insight into contemporary life, reflecting the latest developments in popular culture and current events as well as certain aspects of Yoruba religious and political life.

---

[2] In fact, Ojukwu was represented by a subordinate and did not personally capitulate before Gowon.

[3] According to Linda Sprague (personal communication, 1975), in 1975 in Ila-Orangun, the barbers' union and the hairdressers' union were both headed by the oldest barber in Ila, Afolabi Adeoye, who stated that he held meetings for both groups separately.

Many modern engineering and architectural structures of both Lagos and Ibadan in southwestern Nigeria are interpreted sculpturally in female hairstyles. There are a number of versions of Eko bridge, also known as Lagos bridge, including styles 1 and 2 in Plate 2 (see also Plate 6). The openwork in this elaborate style is said to reflect the concrete openwork in the supports of the bridge itself as well as the supports of the cloverleaf approaches. In addition, the braids themselves form a bridge. Cocoa House, a skyscraper located in the center of Ibadan and a prominent landmark is appropriately rendered in a vertical openwork hairstyle. Other standard features of modern cities are reflected in styles such as "Roundabout" with the circular traffic intersection represented by sweeping circular braids, and "Four-lane highway", represented by four parallel braids from front to back.

In a society where wealth and status are so interrelated it is natural that female styles should reflect these concerns. A prestigious, expensive, factory-produced carpet made in the Remo area of Yorubaland has resulted in an interlaced hairstyle "Remo carpet", which repeats the curvilinear pattern characteristic of these carpets (Plate 8). Another

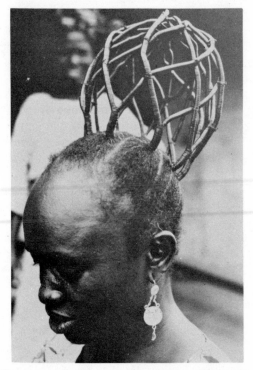

Plate 8.   Style: "Remo carpet". This style echoes the curvilinear patterns typical of the prestigious carpets made in the Remo town of Ilishan. Time: approximately forty-five minutes. Price: 80 Kobo. Photograph: June 29, 1973, Ikenne, Ijebu-Remo

hairstyle, more directly linked with wealth, is "Rockefeller". In 1975, there was a recommendation by the Udoji Commission to double salaries and pay nine months arrears to all civil servants in Nigeria. This event was commemorated in Yorubaland by the "Udoji" style (Plate 9). Even more explicit, concrete celebrations of wealth are the styles using the names *naira* and *kobo*, the currency of Nigeria (Plate 10, styles 2 and 6).[4]

Many names of female styles comprise a lively social commentary on the nature of male–female relations:

1. "Face-to-face" (Plate 1, style 6), the colloquial term for kissing: as previously noted, this style is designed so that it will not be crushed during the act of kissing;

2. *Kojusoko* [Face your husband] may possibly mean either to confront your husband or, based on the preceding style, to kiss him;

Plate 9.   Style: "Udoji". This style commemorates a civil service salary increase, a recommendation made by a commission headed by Chief Udoji. Photograph: May 6, 1975, Ikenne, Ijebu-Remo

[4]   The naira and kobo hairstyle can also be interpreted simply to commemorate the changeover in currency systems from one based on the old British system to the decimal system on January 1, 1973.

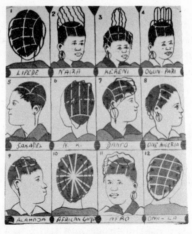

Plate 10.   Hairdresser's sign at Ibadan. Styles: 1: Lipede, 2: Naira (the currency of Nigeria), 3: Kereni, 4: Ogun pari, 5: Sakadel, 6: N.K. (Naira, Kobo, the currency of Nigeria), 7: Danfo, 8: One Nigeria, 9: Alahaja, 10: African Games, 11: Afro, 12. Ona-la. Photograph: August 1974, by Mark Schiltz

3. *Ọrọkọ ko wọti* [The word of husband does not enter ear]: in this style, the braids run randomly all over the head but carefully avoid the ears;

4. "Cut-cut": an expression which refers to the way some women continually cut from one man to the next, never settling down and marrying one;

5. *Agbere asiwo kọrọ* [Harlot stand up]: prostitutes are often satirized and parodied in Yoruba culture, and this style publicly censures this socially unacceptable member of Yoruba society;

6. *Mọrinmọ* [The sex act] (Plate 11): informants in various parts of Yorubaland stated that the multiplicity of the forms and the concentric motion used to form the spiraled projections were a direct reference to the sex act — in 1975 this hairstyle was popular over a large portion of Yorubaland and was worn by young girls as well as by young and middle-aged women.

Of course, social commentary styles listed above do not necessarily relate to the actual state, situation, or behavior patterns of the wearer. These styles function as a mode of social control through publicly censuring certain types of behavior and humorously condoning others. Their names inform us that it is socially unacceptable to be a prostitute, but it is only human for a woman to ignore the words of her husband. These styles also provide a socially approved outlet for personal expression both for the customer and the hairdresser who is free to keep creating new styles and names.

Certain aspects of the popular music scene are a source of some of the

Plate 11.   Style: "Morinmo" [the sex act]. The concentric motion used to form the spiraled projections is said to be a direct reference to the sex act. Photograph: June 22, 1975, Ila-Orangun, Igbomina

names of female styles. In 1975 two very popular albums by Yoruba musician Sonny Ade were also hairstyle names: "Miliki system" (*miliki* is a slang word for "delightful") and "Synchro system". But perhaps the most concrete interpretation of the pop scene is to be found in the style "West African record" (Plate 12), which features the hair coiled into the form of three phonograph records.

The political and religious structure of Yorubaland is also reflected in female styles. The traditional institution of royalty is referred to through names such as *Ade oba* [The king's crown]. Yet the former federal head of state, Major-General Yakubu Gowon, is also represented in styles such as "Gowon: stand up and clap." The religious pluralism of Yorubaland is reflected in certain styles. As many as forty percent of the Yoruba profess themselves to be Muslims and this is reflected in styles reserved for Muslim women. An Alhaja is a Muslim woman who has made the pilgrimage to Mecca, but there are several popular styles called "Alhaja", which apparently can be worn by any Muslim woman, even if she has not been to Mecca (Plate 2, style 3; Plate 10, style 9).

Hairstyles are often just one of the cultural responses to specific events. For example, the Nigerian civil war generated images of various types in many media throughout Yorubaland. Fabrics with printed slogans such as "One Nigeria" and "Keep Nigeria one" were just one of the many

Plate 12.   Style: "West African record". In this style the hair is formed into three phonograph records. Hairstyle by Ife-olu Solaru of Ilishan, Ijebu-Remo. Time: one hour. Price: 1 Naira (about $US2.00). Photograph: September 27, 1973, Ikenne, Ijebu-Remo

responses to the intensive government radio, newspaper, and poster campaigns during the war. Hairstyles took similar names (Plate 10, style 8). The end of the war was commemorated with several styles. One was the previously mentioned *Ojukwu dọbalẹ fun Gowon* which symbolized the Biafran surrender (Plate 4). Another was *Ogun pari* [The war is over], a style which was still popular in 1975 (Plate 13).

Hairstyles, head-tie styles, and fabric patterns commemorated the Second All-Africa Games held in Lagos in 1973, for which a classical Ife bronze sculpture, the Olukun head, was selected as the symbol. A large replica was put at one end of the sports stadium and plastic carry-all bags with its photographic image were sold (Plate 14). Hand-painted imitations of the commercially produced bags were also sold in markets and although quite far removed from the naturalism of the original, retained the vertical projection of the crown. These bags were subsequently carried back to many parts of Yorubaland. Later, a hairstyle called "Second All-Africa Games" featured an exaggerated vertical projection that echoed the crest of the king's crown, the salient feature of the sculpture (Plate 15). A fabric design consisting of a photographic reproduction of the Ife sculpture along with the words "Second All-Africa Games 1973" as well as car decals with the same motif also resulted. Both undoubtedly helped to publicize the event and its symbol and thus, indirectly, to

Plate 13.   Style: "Ogun pari" [the war is over]. This style commemorates the end of the Nigerian civil war (1967–1970). Hairstyle by Ife-olu Solaru of Ilishan, Ijebu-Remo. Time: about 40 minutes. Price: 60 Kobo. Photograph: September 29, 1973, Ikenne, Ijebu-Remo

Plate 14.   A student's school bag, a souvenir from the Second All-Africa Games, Lagos, 1973. It features a photographic reproduction of the Olokun Head, a classical Ife brass sculpture. Photograph: December 5, 1973, Ikenne, Ijebu-Remo, by Klindt Houlberg

Plate 15.   Style: "2nd All-African Games". This style emphasizes the vertical crest of the king's crown of the Olokun Head, the symbol of the games, as shown in Plate 14. Photograph: November 25, 1973, Ijebu-Ode, Ijebu-Remo, by Klindt Houlberg

reinforce the hairstyle. The head-tie style by the same name which commemorated the games, appropriately enough for fabric, to produce the stadium's waving flags (Familori n.d.:5). A many-braided hairstyle, of short-lived popularity, and similar to "Second All-African Games" called "Census" commemorated the Nigerian federal census of November 1973 (Plate 16). This is only one of many examples where very similar hairstyles may have different names, just as we have seen that the very same style may also have different names.

On April 1, 1972 Nigeria switched from driving on the left side of the road to the right, and the publicity attending this event resulted in cultural expressions in many media. Popular songs referring to Ogun, the Yoruba god of iron (and war), were broadcast on the radio. Ogun is the special deity of all those who work with metal and thus is also the deity of drivers. Government reminders to drive on the right were frequent on the airwaves. A popular fabric featured motifs of cars, trucks, and buses along with the slogan "Traffic drive right". The female hairstyle and head-tie style "Nigeria drive right", both featured dramatic projections to the right (Plate 1, style 5). The event was also noted in male styles but without the exaggerated emphasis to the right (Plate 17, style 6). In both of these examples, that of a well-publicized, government-sponsored sports event and of a radical change in a national traffic regulation, we have seen that

Plate 16.   Style: "Census", commemorating the Nigerian federal census held in November 1973. It is similar to "2nd All-Africa Games", a style popular when the census took place. Photograph: December 3, 1973, Ikenne, Ijebu-Remo, by Klindt Houlberg

hair must be studied as part of a larger system of cultural responses to a variety of social stimuli.

MODERN MALE YORUBA HAIRSTYLES

Barbers learn their craft in a similar way to that described for professional hairdressers. They undergo a period of apprenticeship, receive their certificates and set up in business for themselves. Barbers have signs which are similar to those owned by female hairdressers, and sometimes the sign is incorporated into the structure of the shop itself. Whereas most professional female hairdressers work outdoors, either in front of their own homes or in market stalls, barbers usually have shops with several barber chairs and big mirrors on the walls. The barber chairs are sometimes made out of a modified automobile axle and two wheels, one serving as the base of the chair and the other as a rotating seat. Since women most often have their hair done while sitting on the ground between the knees of the hairdresser, an elaborated facility for female hairdressing is not necessary. In addition, since barbers may use electric shavers as well as hand clippers, they may also require a ready source of electricity.

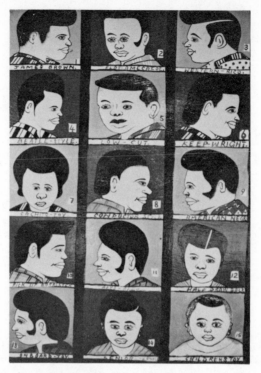

Plate 17.   Barber sign at Ope Barbing Saloon, Ibadan. Styles: 1: James Brown, 2: Flat-Ameca Joe, 3: Western-Rico, 4: Beatle-style, 5: Low-cut, 6: Keep Wright (*sic*), 7: Cachito-toy, 8: Conductor style, 9: American Negro, 10: Pick up barrister, 11: Boy's Afro, 12: Half draw back, 13: Onboard-toy, 14: Senior-Service, 15: Children's toy. Photograph: July 3, 1975

A survey of the names of styles on barber signs reveal certain similarities with those of female styles. However, there is more differentiation according to occupation in male styles: "Army style", "Civil service", "Police partin" (Plate 18, style 10), "Conductor style" (Plate 17, style 8), "Pick up barrister" (Plate 17, style 10). On the other hand, both show a similar interest in pop stars and current events. A barber shop in Ibadan, Ope Barbing Saloon, features styles after two American black performers: "Chubby Checker" (Plate 18, style 1) and "James Brown" (Plate 17, style 1). The Beatles were still popular in 1975 with names such as "Beatles show style" and just "Beatle style" (Plate 17, style 4). That there is an interest in blacks of other nationalities is reflected in names such as "Ghana baby", "Puerto Rico" (Plate 18, style 7), "Western rico" (Plate 17, style 3), "British negro", and "American Negro" (Plate 17, style 9). A male style which exploits the status which comes to those who have been abroad is the style "Have-been-to" with the place unspecified. Two more styles which mirror the typical concerns of young men are

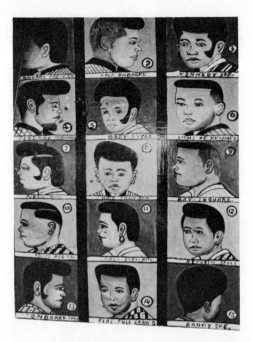

Plate 18.   Barber sign at Ope Barbing Saloon, Ibadan. Styles: 1: Chubby Checker, 2: Half onboard, 3: Kennedy Joe, 4: Federal-onboard, 5: Body style, 6: Light of Kennedy, 7: Puerto-Rico, 8: Half draw back, 9: Bay Toquare(?), 10: Police partin (*sic*), 11: Girls Baby Rico, 12: Republic style, 13: Onboard-toy, 14: Flat full draw B, 15: Boogy Joe. Photograph: July 3, 1975

"Girl follow me" and a tripartite style called, appropriately enough, "Three jolly friends".

Although some hairstyles, or at least their names, are very short-lived, others persist for a long time. For example, hairstyles named after former United States president John F. Kennedy were still popular in 1975, twelve years after his death. They bear names such as "Kennedy style", "Kennedy Joe" (Plate 18, style 3), "Light of Kennedy" (Plate 18, style 6), and "Minister of Kennedy". A Kennedy style with a thread-wrapped form with a side part and a prominent crest is also popular among women (Plate 1, style 5).

Another hairstyle enjoying great popularity throughout Yorubaland is the Afro. While the initial impulse for the Afro came from Africa in the 1960's, it was in the United States that it reached its fullest statement. It then returned to Africa where it is now associated most closely as being an American black style. One barber's sign advertised the Afro by urging customers to "Come here and get your American bush." Just as the Afro is a unisex style in America, it is also worn by both males and females in Yorubaland. However, in addition to the usual American-type Afro where the hair is combed out so as to radiate out fully in a spherical fashion, certain braided styles for women are also called "Afro" (Plate 10, style 11). Since the combed-out Afro requires skillful shaping, often with an electric shaver or clippers, women will go to male barbers for this style. The Afro wig is also popular among young Yoruba women. Some use it in preference to plaited styles and some just to cover their own hair when they have not had time to have it styled. Afro wigs are also used to protect plaited styles when a head tie is worn or as a base to build up a more elaborate head tie. In addition, Afro wigs are also worn by men when they play the part of women during certain ritual occasions (Plate 19) as discussed later in this paper.

Plate 19.   Male dancer dressed as a woman for satirical purposes at the Balufǫn festival, Ikenne, Ijebu-Remo. He wears a black Afro wig. Photograph: September 29, 1973

This brief survey of contemporary Yoruba hairstyles reveals that both the form of the styles, as well as their names, are a lively and thriving popular art. In the next section traditional Yoruba behavior in relation to hair is discussed in terms of an exploration of the extent to which modern practices are rooted in traditional ones.

TRADITIONAL YORUBA HAIR BEHAVIOR

In Yoruba traditional culture, hairstyle is just one of the many visual symbol systems related to the body; other examples are scarification, tattooing, and body painting, which are outside the scope of this paper, except insofar as they relate to hair. It is relevant to note, however, that Yoruba women traditionally use four main cosmetics: (1) red camwood powder mixed with palm oil (*osun*); (2) white chalk (*efun*); (3) ground galena; and (4) indigo.

Efun is worn on the face; osun is rubbed on the body, especially the feet; galena is used to outline the eyes and to darken the eyebrows; and indigo is applied to the hair. Osun and efun are said to have cooling, calming properties and are used in a variety of Yoruba head and hair rituals.

Head hair is especially appropriate as a ritual focus and social indicator since it is so highly visible and as a medium is capable of being modified in an endless number of ways. It can be shaved in patterns or entirely removed. It can be dressed in elaborate sculptural styles, or it can be totally neglected. In a sense, hair can be considered a "process" symbol involving the element of time since it is capable of growth and regeneration. Because of all of these characteristics hair is particularly suitable for indicating temporary changes. This is in contrast, for example, to the permanent changes involved in body arts such as facial scarification, which, in the case of the Yoruba, is used to indicate lineage affiliation, a permanent status for life. Edmund Leach (1967:82) notes that hairdressing is a widespread feature of ritual behavior around the world. The Yoruba are no exception. Among the Yoruba, hair is also considered powerful after it has been removed. Leach observes that "separated" hair derives its power from the ritual contexts under which it is removed. As will be shown, hairdressing and separated hair are both important in Yoruba ritual.

Hair and the Life Cycle

Hair plays an important role among the Yoruba in rites of passage. Van Gennep, in speaking of society in general, has defined these as "rites which accompany every change of place, state, social position and age" (van Gennep 1960). He identifies them as having three stages:

1. *Separation.* A detachment of the individual from a state or social position;

2. *Liminality.* A period of status marginality: this occurs when an individual is, as Victor Turner (1967:93) has termed it, "betwixt and between" statuses, observing that this stage is often characterized by reversals of normal behavior at a variety of levels.

3. *Aggregation* reincorporation into society in a new state or status. The principal rites of passage or transition are birth, marriage, initiation, and death; and to the Yoruba hair is important in each of these rites.

BIRTH AND CHILDHOOD.   According to Bascom, based on material he collected at Ife in 1937, newborn children are first brought out of the house on the day of their naming ceremony, the sixth day for girls and the eighth day for boys (Bascom 1969:56). The child receives a number of names and a large feast is held. It is also on this day that the head of the child is shaved, unless the child is one of several types of sacred children or is considered to have been born through the intercession of a certain deity. In these cases, as is discussed presently, the shaving of the head is done at a later date by special cult officials. After the child's head is shaved, the hair is saved to be used in a charm to insure its good health. This shaving of the head may be considered to mark the separation of the child from its former status as a visitor from the spiritual world. Young children are considered to be close to the spirit world since, according to the Yoruba reincarnation cycle, they have just arrived from heaven. The shaving, as a rite of separation, prepares the child for incorporation into the world of the living, a world marked by culture and kinship affiliations. The shaved hair, removed under the ritual context of the naming ceremony, is a powerful medicine which will insure the continued existence of the child in its new status.

As children grow up they may either continue to wear their hair closely cropped or, if girls, braided in a variety of styles. According to the Yoruba historian, the Reverend Samuel Johnson, writing at the end of the nineteenth century, children at that time either had their heads entirely shaved periodically or, if boys, had all but a central strip of hair running from the forehead to the base of the neck shaved (Johnson 1920:101). The strip was sometimes formed into two circles. While the strip and circular patches are seldom, if ever, worn by Yoruba children today, these styles can be seen in Yoruba woodcarvings dating from this period.

MARRIAGE.   In the nineteenth century marriage was marked by brides wearing an elaborate hairstyle called *agogo*, which was characterized by a high, central crest. The height of the crest was often increased by the insertion of supplementary plaits in a concentric fashion. There are two main variations of agogo. In one, the central crest is flanked by braids radiating up from each ear (Plate 20). In the other, the crest is flanked by two or three braids running parallel to the crest from the forehead to the nape of the neck (see Houlberg 1978:58, figs. 3, 4). According to Johnson (1920:101) unmarried women wore their hair in anywhere from eight to fourteen small braids across the head from the right to the left ear. He emphatically states "a marked distinction must always be made between that of married women and the unmarried; this is a social law which on no account should ever be infringed" (1920:125). However, married women are no longer restricted to wearing agogo and hair is no longer used to demarcate the social categories of married and unmarried among the Yoruba. However, as is shown in Plate 20, the agogo style is still used in a number of Yoruba religious cults, one of which is discussed later.

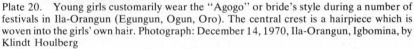

Plate 20.   Young girls customarily wear the "Agogo" or bride's style during a number of festivals in Ila-Orangun (Egungun, Ogun, Oro). The central crest is a hairpiece which is woven into the girls' own hair. Photograph: December 14, 1970, Ila-Orangun, Igbomina, by Klindt Houlberg

Hair plays an important part in initiation rites into Yoruba traditional cults on two levels. First, the head of the initiate is shaved marking a separation from the profane status and an incorporation into the new sacred cult status. Secondly, a specific cult hairstyle may subsequently be worn by the initiate to mark his or her cult affiliation. The role of hair in the Yoruba rituals surrounding several types of sacred children and in the cults of Shango and Eshu is discussed in detail later.

DEATH.   Just as birth is marked by head shaving, so is death. As Bascom has described, when adults die, as part of the burial preparation, the corpse is taken out outside after dark, seated on an inverted mortar of the type used for food preparation, undressed, and bathed using soap, water and a loofah (Bascom 1969:66). At that time the head is completely shaved. If a person is a member of certain cults, the shaving will be done by appropriate cult officials. The corpse is then dressed again, the clothes being put on backward so that the soul will know its way back to earth when it is reborn in subsequent generations. Here again, hair is shaved as a rite of separation, but in this case it marks the separation from the world of the living in preparation for reincorporation into the spirit world, since in the Yoruba reincarnation cycle souls return to heaven to await rebirth. It is also interesting to note the reversal of normal clothing patterns in the liminal period of this rite of passage, a period which is often said to be characterized by reversals of various types. While shaving the head before burial is still done in many areas, recently there have been cases where the hair is simply neatly groomed and, in the case of women, carefully braided.

Secular Hairstyles

In addition to hair functioning in rites of passage related to the life cycle, it is also important in several secular contexts, being used to convey information about political and occupational roles and kinship affiliation.

HAIR AND THE PALACE.   There are a number of special hairstyles and rituals associated with the palace. Traditionally, messengers of each Yoruba king had his servants' heads shaved in a distinctive way so as to be readily identifiable (Plates 21 and 22). The styles varied from area to area. In the Oyo area court messengers called *ilari* wore several styles of hair depending on the particular kingdom. At Oyo, Johnson (1920:62) records that male ilari had alternate sides of their heads shaved every fifth day except for a circular patch on the crown. The term *ilari* means literally "incision on the head", *ila* being the line made by parting or cutting, and *ori* the head. The hair on the circular patch was allowed to grow as long as possible and was braided and dyed with indigo. Each ilari's name was his message. The number of court messengers on hand, and thus the number of ready-made, conventional messages, depended on the size and power of the kingdom. The names generally signified either attributes of the king or indicated his will in particular matters. Thus, a messenger named *Madarikan* [Do not oppose the king] might be sent to a recalcitrant subject. His hair would proclaim his role of palace messenger while his name would proclaim his specific message. Upon the death of a king, his ilari would allow their hair to grow long. Upon the coronation of a new king, a special initiation ceremony would be held for the ilari; their heads would be shaved, medicines rubbed into the new incisions, and they would receive new names.

At Iganna, a kingdom near Oyo, the ilari formerly wore their heads half shaved and with a special braided crest in a style similar to that of Oyo.

Plate 21. Detail of an Egungun ancestral masquerade janus headdress depicting a court messenger (*ilari*) at Iseyin, Oyo. The head is half shaved with a braided crest similar to that shown in Plate 22. Collected at Iseyin in 1961 and now in the Phillip Hitchcock Collection

Plate 22. Egungun ancestral masquerade at Iganna, Oyo, illustrating the court messenger hairstyle called *ǫba gbilę* [servant of the king]. Owner: Ago-Are compound, one of the five compounds of Iganna which is permitted to contribute court messengers (*ilari*) to the king. Photograph: July 24, 1970

Alternative halves of the head were shaved every eighth day by the Osanyin priest who presided over the royal Osanyin shrine within the confines of the palace. Since Osanyin is the god of medicine, it is appropriate that the officials of this cult be charged both with the task of initiating the ilari and with maintaining their hair. As part of the initiation, the ilari lived for seven days in the rooms of the Osanyin shrine in the palace. Their heads were entirely shaved except for two circular patches where the hair was allowed to grow long. Subsequently, their heads were shaven on alternate sides every eighth day and the braided crests were annually rebraided and dyed with indigo during the annual *bere* festival by a woman brought to the palace for that specific task. The *Egungun* ancestral masquerade headdress shown in Plate 22 illustrates this style known as *oba gbile* [servant of the king].[5] This Egungun represents deceased ancestors of the Ago-are compound, one of the five compounds in Iganna allowed to contribute ilari to the palace. As of 1975, the ilari at the palace in Iganna are not wearing their special messenger hairstyles since the present king, who acceded in 1959, has not yet initiated his ilari. In another case where sculpture provides examples of former hairstyles, an Egungun headdress from Iseyin another kingdom traditionally under Oyo, illustrates a similar type of ilari hairstyle (Plate 21). In addition, it is colored black on the half with hair and red (with camwood) on the shaved half, a bilateral polychrome feature also to be seen at Ife.

Bascom (1969:35) reports that at Ife the heads of messengers were shaved on alternate sides every four days in a fashion similar to that described for the Oyo area. In 1937, these messengers, called *emese*, numbered over a hundred. They carried messages and performed errands not only for the king but also for the palace chiefs. Bilateral asymmetry in head shaving was also extended to head and body decoration for certain ceremonial occasions. Bascom records that during the festival for the god Oranmiyan, who is said to have been born half black and half white, the emese paint the right half red in camwood and the left side white with chalk.[6] Bilateral hair and body decoration figures prominently in the hair behavior associated with the cult of Eshu, the messenger god, and will be referred to again.

Hair is truly used as a process symbol in the case of Yoruba court messengers. The regenerative aspects of hair are maximized in the alternate shaving pattern. Yet this careful controlling of hair is contrasted with the practice of letting the hair on one or two circular patches grow as long

[5]   This headdress shows the crest but the half-shaved head feature is not apparent in the photograph, in contrast to the headdress shown in Plate 21.
[6]   To account for the fact that the *emese* paint their bodies red and white instead of black and white, Bascom (1969:83) quotes the town chief Akogun, who was in charge of the worship for Oranmiyan, as saying that black is not used because "no one would wish to be colored black with charcoal." He notes that Eredumi, an Oranmiyan priest under Akogun, stated that Oranmiyan was half red and half white.

as possible. This long hair grows out of the patch which has received the tiny cuts into which medicines have been rubbed. These medicines were said to increase the social effectiveness of the name of the ilari and thus to insure the success of the ilari's royal mission. Hair, magical power, and a verbal designation reflecting a political decision, i.e. the name of the selected ilari, all merge together in the case of the Yoruba court messenger to function as a method of social control. In addition, for the ilari, hair also functions in the rites of transition from the reign of one king to his successor. The heads of messengers are shaved as part of that rite of separation.

Though the messengers of some Yoruba palaces are no longer wearing distinctive hairstyles, in 1975, in the Igbomina kingdom of Ila-Orangun in northeastern Yorubaland, there are some fifty ẹmẹsẹ who still wear their messenger hairstyle. The first-ranking ẹmẹsẹ in Ila, called the *elẹmẹsẹ*, is pictured in Plate 23 wearing an oval patch on the crown, the mark of the Ila messenger. The head is shaved and the patch trimmed every fourteen days. This may possibly be an abbreviated version of a formerly elaborate style.

Plate 23.   An oval patch of hair is the sign of the court messenger (*ẹmẹsẹ*) at Ila-Orangun, Igbomina, here worn by the *elẹmẹsẹ*, the head of the court messengers of Ila. Photograph: June 24, 1975

The office of kingship is more associated with beaded crowns rather than specific hairstyles. However, in some areas the king's wives have traditionally worn the hairstyle called ṣuku, which literally means "basket" (Plate 7).[7] It is à style in which braids are formed from the hairline up to the crown of the head culminating in a small topknot. More recently, however, as the political power of the traditional Yoruba kings has diminished, there has been a corresponding democratization in this hairstyle. All women are now free to wear ṣuku if they wish.

THE HAIRSTYLE OF HUNTERS.   Hunters as an occupational group are also associated with a special style of hair, the main characteristic of which is that the hair is worn long and formed into a tail, most often worn at the back of the head. Based on evidence provided by wood sculpture from the Egba area, hunters may also have worn this tail on the left side of the head (Thompson 1971: ch. 15, plates 1, 2, 3). The hunter's cap is similar in form to the long-tailed hairstyle which it may have been designed to accommodate, having its own long tail, which sometimes extends midway down the back. Traditionally, the cap was decorated with medicine calabashes called *ado* which were meant to protect the hunter from the spirits at large in the bush. His long hair is said to give him added strength and also to protect him in the same way as the ado do. Since the bush is the source of many of the plants and animals which are used to make Yoruba medicines of various types hunters are said to have a great knowledge of these. As will be shown, the hunter's hairstyle and long-tailed cap is important in the cult of Eshu, the trickster god, as one of his aspects is Eshu the hunter.

Thus far, in the overview of the various functions of hair in traditional Yoruba society, hair has been seen to: (1) function as an important element in the rites of passage of birth, marriage, initiation, and death; and (2) convey information indicating marital and political status and religious and occupational affiliation. Hair is also considered to have powerful magical and medicinal properties, both on the head and after it has been removed in a ritual context. An attempt has been made to note the modifications which have occurred over time in some of these traditional practices. Against this background, the form and function of hair in a selected number of religious cults is now examined in detail.

---

[7]   There is regional variation in the hairstyles worn by the king's wives. A photograph taken in August 1974 shows the Orangun of Ila with ten of his wives, all of whom wear an identical tripartite hairstyle.

ETHNOGRAPHIC DATA AND ANALYSIS: HAIR BEHAVIOR IN FOUR YORUBA RELIGIOUS CULTS

Four Yoruba cults have been selected to demonstrate specific examples of how hair and head decoration function, for to examine this adequately for all the cults, with all the variations over time and space, is beyond the scope of this paper. Yoruba religious hair behavior can only be understood when it is viewed in relation to Yoruba secular hair behavior and to both the Yoruba religious and the Yoruba social systems.

Hair Behavior Related to Yoruba Sacred Children

Children undergo initiation into Yoruba religious cults for one of two main reasons. First, they may be considered sacred because of special circumstances surrounding their birth, (or death and rebirth), circumstances which indicate that they require special ritual attention and possibly initiation into a special religious cult. Among the many types of sacred children are *dada* [children born with a full head of hair]; *ibeji* [twins], *aina* [those born feet first]; and *abiku* [those who die in infancy or early childhood], who are considered to be reborn repeatedly to the same mother. The specific cult into which they will be subsequently initiated is indicated by the particular circumstances of their birth, or in the case of *abiku*, their death and subsequent rebirth. However, in some areas, there may not be specific cults for each type of child and they may either be subsumed under a related or more dominant deity or may simply be venerated at the domestic level without a corresponding cult affiliation. As a child may fall into more than one category, parents may consequently become involved in the ritual networks of multiple cults. A child may be born feet first and with a full head of hair; twins may be born with these or other characteristics. Initiation into the relevant cult or cults occurs anywhere between birth and the seventh or eighth year.

The second reason for the initiation of children into a cult occurs when a child is considered to have been conceived due to the intercession of a specific deity. Usually the child will be initiated into the cult of that specific deity some time before the mother gives birth to her next child. Hair plays an important part in the cult initiation rituals of children who are being inducted for either of these reasons.

Children who are born with long thick curly hair are given the proper name Dada and are considered to bring good luck and wealth to their parents. Dada children are said to "bring their names from heaven", as is said also of all the other types of sacred children who receive a standard name related to the particular circumstances of their birth. These standard names, called *oruko amuntorunwa*, are not sexually differentiating

— both boys and girls born with long hair receive the *oruko* [first name] of Dada in addition to their *oriki* [praise names] and *orile* [group-origin name] (Abraham 1958:482, 486).

Dada children are said by some to arrive in this world with their hair already having been braided in heaven. Thus they are considered to have supernatural or divine power in their hair, so their heads are not shaved at their naming ceremonies, and their parents are permitted only to wash the hair but not to comb or cut it. It is said that to do so would cause the illness or even possibly the death of the child. Thus, young children with long matted hair are instantly recognizable as dada (Plate 24). Dada children take their names from the god Dada who is said to have had thick curly hair, and to have been one of the early legendary kings of Oyo who reigned before his brother Shango, the god of thunder and lightning. In the Yoruba divine genealogy, Dada, Shango, and Shopona, the god of smallpox, are all said to be the offspring of Yemoja, a river goddess, and of Oranmiyan. Dada is also said to be the god of vegetables since the parents of dada children must feed them vegetables as part of the periodic rituals honoring them.

Plate 24.   A dada child of about one year at Ikenne, Ijebu-Remo. The hair of dada children can be washed but not combed or cut until after a special ritual has been performed. Photograph: October 18, 1973

The praise names of dada children reflect the wealth that they are said to bring to their parents: *Olowo ori* [one who possesses wealth on the head] *Olowo ade* [one who has a crown of money], and *Olowo ẹyọ* [rich owner of a large cowrie shell].

The linking of hair with money occurs at both metaphoric and literal levels. Dada children are considered to bring good luck in the form of money to their parents. Traditionally, cowrie shells, the former currency of the area, were tied into the long hair of dada children as concrete symbols of the wealth they are said to bring. More recently, Nigerian halfpennies and other currencies with holes in the center are tied to the hair either instead of or in addition to cowries. In the Ijebu area, weekly ceremonies must be held for dada children, consisting of the serving of beans, rice, and other vegetables. Traditionally, drummers were also hired as part of the ceremony to accompany the singing of praise songs in honor of the children.

The heads of dada children are shaved only under special ritual conditions. The act of head-shaving may be said to mark the incorporation of the already sacred child into the world of the living and, more specifically, especially in the Ijebu area, into the cult of Dada. In areas where no Dada cult exists, riverside rituals about to be described are usually carried out by the head priestess of the cult of Yemọja,[8] considered mother of the mythical Dada and also a river goddess associated with fertility and newborn children. Yemọja's priestesses have riverside shrines where the heads of the dada children are shaved. This ritual may take place when the child is anywhere from one to seven or eight years of age, depending on the relative wealth of the parents or the health of the child.

In the Ijebu area at Akio, the Dada shrine is on the west bank of the Aye river, a short walk from the town. When a dada head-shaving ceremony is to be performed, the parents take the child to the head priest of the cult of Dada, pay him a cash fee, and the party proceeds to the riverside shrine where songs of praise are sung before and during the head-shaving. Once the Dada priest has removed the hair, it is placed into a pot or box along with other ingredients and taken home by the parents where a feast will then be held in honor of the child. Whenever the child falls ill the parents make a medicine, consisting of the hair mixed with river water and other substances, which is rubbed on the child's body. Notably, rivers and their cults are closely associated with fertility; the hair removed at the riverside is reunited with river water to form the medicine

---

[8]   They may also be carried out by the most prominent river cult priestess in the area. In the Ijebu-Remo town of Ikenne, dada rituals were conducted by the priestess of the local river cult of Oluweri, *olu* being "chief" and *eri* "river". In other areas of Yorubaland, the shaving of the heads of dada children may be done by elderly dada who have a knowledge of the ritual.

which will be used to insure the good health and life of the child. This curative aspect of the dada head-shaving ritual accounts for the fact that if a child falls sick the ceremony is held as soon as possible. After the head-shaving ceremony, weekly ceremonies featuring the serving of vegetables, especially beans and rice, will continue to be held in honor of the child. This will taper off as adolescence approaches and the survival of the child seems more assured. After the riverside head-shaving ritual, no particular hair behavior is associated with dada children.

Twins, called *ibeji* (*ibi* [born], *eji* [two]) are named according to birth order regardless of their sex. The first born is Taiwo [he who tastes the world] and the second Kehinde [he who follows behind]. Like dada children, twins are considered to bring good luck and wealth to their parents if they are properly propitiated. Twins are given weekly feasts consisting most often of beans and palm oil, both said to be effective in cooling down their anger, for they can be vindictive if not appeased. They are also said to decide to die if they are not properly venerated: a reflection of the high infant mortality rate among twins. In the Ijebu-Remo area, twins do not have their heads shaved at their naming ceremony, this being done at a later date as part of an initiation ceremony into the cult of twins. While in this area there is a twin cult with special officials and a set membership, in other areas the veneration of twins may only be carried out at a domestic level. What follows can only be considered characteristic of the Ijebu-Remo area although similar practices may be found elsewhere in Yorubaland.

In Ikenne, Ijebu-Remo, when twins are about one year old they undergo a twenty-one day ritual called "The making of the twin pots" which serves to incorporate them into the cult of twins.[9] Both head shaving and head decoration are important parts of the ceremony. The preparations begin with the mother of twins going to the house of the *Iya ibeji* (*iya* [mother]), the head of the cult of twins, in order to set a date when the Iya ibeji and her senior cult members will come to her house. At this time she seals the arrangements by making a cash payment, 1.05 naira, in 1973.[10] The office of Iya ibeji is customarily held by the oldest mother of twins in the town, and only mothers of twins qualify as senior cult members. The mother of twins then buys two identical small-lidded pots in the local market, which she then exchanges with household cooking pots of a similar size so that the pots to be used in the ritual will have been hardened through exposure to the cooking fire.

On the morning of the appointed day, the mother goes to the market and buys a number of foodstuffs which will be added to the pots at various points in the ritual. The twins are given their morning bath and the water is saved as it too will be added. When the Iya ibeji and her entourage

[9]   More recently, if the parents are government workers, the ritual is shortened to three days.
[10]   In 1973 one Naira was approximately $US2.00.

arrive, they bring other important ingredients including substances previously gathered at the local sacred river, the Uren: several types of river
plants, river soil, and sacred water from the river itself. First the river
materials and then the symbolic foodstuffs are added to the pots. The
foods include honey, beans, and palm oil, said to be the favorites of the
twins, and bananas, corn, and yam, said to be the favorites of the *colobus*
monkey, the animal sacred to twins. To this is added the umbilical cords
of the twins which were saved at birth. The bath water is then poured into
the pots. At this point, the heads of the twins are shaved by one of the
senior cult members and the hair is also added. The shaved heads are then
decorated with ẹfun, the white chalk, and osun, the red camwood powder
mixture. It will be recalled that both are cosmetics traditionally worn by
women and that osun is said to have an especially cooling effect. The red
osun is dotted in the center of each head and the white ẹfun is spotted
around the edge. Then the heads are washed and the water containing
these controlling ingredients is put into the pots. Every day for seven days
this process is repeated. The heads of the twins are painted in the morning
by any mother of twins, who will be paid a small sum by the mother of the
initiates, and at night their heads are washed and the water dripped into
the pots. On the seventh day, bean foods, *akara, moin-moin,* and *ekuru,*
are served with palm oil stew to all the friends who have been notified
earlier about the coming feast. Drummers are hired to accompany the
singing of the praise songs to the twins and there is dancing. The same
feast is then held two weeks later on the twenty-first day and that
concludes the ritual.

After the concluding day, sacrifices are to be made to the pots in honor
of the twins every seventeen days. If the twins should become ill, the
contents of the pots will be rubbed on their bodies in an attempt to restore
them to good health, just as in the case of the dada children. The twins are
to marry on the same day and on the marriage day, the contents of the two
pots are combined and one pot is discarded. In the event that the misfortune should occur that one of the twins should die, a small wooden
sculpture, *ere ibeji*, is commissioned from a local carver to represent the
dead twin. If both should die, a pair of images are commissioned. One pot
is buried with each twin and a wooden image put in place of each pot on
the family shrine. As twins grow up there is no particular hairstyle or hair
ritual associated with them except that twin girls can often be observed to
wear identical hairstyles, at least until marriage.

There are many levels of symbolism imbedded in this ritual but it
suffices to say here that head shaving and head painting mark two phases
of the initiation ritual. Shaving the heads of the twins, as in the case of
dada children, marks the separation of the initiate from the spirit world in
preparation for incorporation into the world of the living as a member of
the particular cult. In the case of twins, it marks the beginning of a

twenty-one-day liminal period, in which head painting marks the first seven days. The removed hair and the pigments used in the head painting constitute part of the mixture which is subsequently rubbed on the bodies of sick twins in an attempt to prevent the death of these often frail children. The high infant mortality rate, especially among the often smaller and more vulnerable twins, is a partial explanation for the many rituals among the Yoruba which are designed in some way or another to prevent the death of children. This is consistent with the theory that ritual builds up around chance situations. Thus it is to be expected that the liminal phase of the initiation ritual for twins would be of longer duration than that for the more normal-sized dada children: twenty-one days instead of merely part of one day. In the case of twin ritual, the magical curing aspects of hair and the cooling aspects of materials which have been in contact with the head join other controlling materials, such as beans and palm oil; all are designed in some way to prevent the premature return of the child to heaven, i.e. to prevent its death. It is appropriate that much of the ritual should focus on the head, which is considered by the Yoruba to be the seat of various of the multiple souls.[11]

Another hair ritual designed to prevent the premature death of children centers around *abiku*, children who are, literally, "born-to-die". When a mother repeatedly bears children who die in infancy it is considered to be the same child being born over and over. Abiku, before they are born, are said to set a date with other abiku for their return to heaven. Abiku rituals are designed to make the abiku child stay beyond the appointed date, for once that date has passed there is a good chance that the child will survive.

In the Oyo area, according to information collected at Iganna and Iseyin in 1975, when a child is designated through Ifa divination to be an abiku, the *babalawo* will order the parents to do one of three things for a certain length of time in order to make the child stay beyond his or her prearranged death date. The parents may be ordered to put iron bangles (*şaworo*) on the ankles of the child or to shave the alternate sides of the child's head every two weeks or to tie both arms of the child at the elbow joint. In the case of head shaving, this is usually prescribed until the child is four years of age. The Catholic Mission Hospital at Iseyin, Oyo, reports that it is not unusual to treat abiku children who have this distinctive bilateral hairstyle (personal communication, 1975).

Abiku are given special names which indicate their parents' apprehension of their possible early death. A typical female name is *Durorikẹ* [if you remain, you will be petted]. Another name given to both boys and girls is *Kosọkọ* [there is no hoe (to dig the grave)] (Abraham 1958:7). The abiku children whose heads are shaved on alternate sides every two

---

[11]   For a further discussion of the multiple soul see Bascom (1969: ch. 7).

weeks are called *Alalakun* (*ala* [owner], *ila* [parting], *kun* [carved]) or *Ilari Osanyin* (*ilari* [the parting of the head], *Osanyin*, the god of medicine). Both these names concretely link abiku children with the court messengers, the ilari; both wear their hair in the same bilateral style and are related to the god of medicine.[12] In the case of the ilari at Iganna, their heads are shaved on alternate sides every eight days by the head of the Osanyin cult, Baba Osanyin. It will also be recalled that the *ilari* are initiated by him and as part of that initiation medicines are rubbed into tiny incisions made on the head. Abraham (1958:19) notes that the purpose of this is to "imbue the *ilari* with the qualities of the name bestowed on him". However, the medicine may also be considered to protect the ilari while on their royal business and generally to enhance their efficacy. Abiku children are also associated with medicine in that they often fall sick and thus require more medicine than normal children. In the Iganna area abiku and ilari are said both to take the same medicinal leaf internally.

In order to understand more fully the significance of the half-shaved hairstyle in the case of abiku, it is necessary to consider not only ilari but also Eshu, the trickster/messenger god of the Yoruba, who is sometimes shown in ritual sculpture wearing this same half-shaved hairstyle. In some areas, as reported by Drewal (1974:15), in an interesting discussion of ilari hairstyles on Gelede masks, ilari are worshippers of Eshu and thus apparently more linked with him than with Osanyin. Yet this would not seem to contradict the ilari–Osanyin link since Eshu is very closely associated with medicine. His ritual sculptures often show him festooned with ado, medicine calabashes, and he is also said to have a knowledge of medicines.[13] Thus all three, abiku, ilari, and Eshu would seem to be linked by medicine as well as their half-shaved hairstyles. Yet it may also be possible that all three are also "messengers" on one level or another. Abiku travel back and forth between heaven and earth, ilari between the palace and the people, and Eshu between men and the gods (*orisha*). The alternate pattern of the shaving of the head may also reflect the "back-and-forth" nature of being a messenger, of being a link between two entities. In the case of abiku, the asymmetrical, bilateral hairstyle reflects the "betwixt and betweenness" of these children whose sojourn on earth is often so temporary and who seem to be so equally attached to heaven and to earth.

In addition to hair ritual among children who are considered sacred due to circumstances surrounding their birth, there is also special hair ritual

[12] Significantly, a six-inch-high bronze medicine bottle in the author's possession takes the form of a human male figure wearing the half-shaved hairstyle, further reinforcing the link between medicine, this hairstyle, and the ilari.
[13] Osanyin and Eshu are further linked in ritual sculpture in that the priests of Osanyin are also shown wearing a hunter's cap adorned with medicine calabashes (see Carroll 1967: plate 35).

involving children who are considered to have been conceived through the intercession of a particular deity. They have their heads shaved by a cult official of the specific cult, with this act serving to mark the separation phase of a rite of passage of initiation into the cult. For example, in the Oyo area, at Iganna, according to Mark Schiltz (personal communication, 1975), when all the children conceived through the intercession of the god Oro have reached the age when they start walking and when their mothers expect new babies, they must be brought to the Oro sacred grove or bush before the beginning of part of the annual Oro festival.[14] The parents, relatives, and the Oro priests take the children to the Oro bush where a head-shaving ceremony is performed. The same holds true near Ijio, Oyo, where children born through Oyan, a local river goddess, are brought down to riverside shrines on the Oyan river and their heads are shaved by Oyan priestesses. In both cases the hair is saved and used as medicine.

Thus we have seen that shaving the heads of a number of types of children: dada, twins, and children born through special deities, marks the separation phase of a rite of passage, namely the rite of initiation into a specific cult. This can also be considered a passage from a vulnerable spirit status to the world of the living and therefore to the world of kinship and culture. This is also the case with abiku head shaving even though there may not be an official cult. Head shaving as part of children's initiation ceremonies into specific cults in each case has three important aspects. First and of prime importance is *who* shaves the head. The cult personnel make a dramatic public claim of that individual for their own specific cult through the act of hair removal within a ritual context. Second, head shaving serves to mark the transition of the child from a spirit status to a social status, one involving kinship, culture, and a specific cult association. Finally, in some cases, removed hair continues to function beyond the separation ritual. It is considered to be insurance for the continued existence of the child in its new status.

Hair Behavior Related to Yoruba Religious Cults: The Deities Shango and Eshu

A number of Yoruba religious cults use hair both during the rites of passage related to the cult and as an indicator of specific cult affiliation by both priests and members. The form and function of hair in the cults of Shango and Eshu are discussed here as two examples which exhibit a variety of fascinating hair behavior. In both, hair is an element of the

---

[14] According to Schiltz (personal communication, 1975) the particular Oro referred to here is Oro Majẹsin, a cult said to have come to Iganna from the Ijebu area.

sexual role reversal that occurs in the cults when priests become transvestite, as the wives of the god himself; this is best analyzed in relation to Eshu mythology and Eshu's position in Yoruba cosmology.

Shango is the Yoruba god of thunder and lightning who is said to have been the fourth king of the Oyo Yoruba. He is considered a hot-tempered, violent god who punishes thieves and liars by striking them down with lightning, often burning down their houses in the process. On the other hand, he rewards his worshippers with the good things of life, especially children. Shango priests holding both hereditary and nonhereditary titles perform a variety of functions. They officiate over the Shango shrines of the town, rainmaking, cult initiation, and funeral ceremonies, rituals held when lightning strikes, and the town's annual Shango festival. *Magba*, the hereditary priests, do not go into possession or trance states, while *elegun*, nonhereditary priests, go into often-violent possession states when they are being "ridden" by the god during Shango ritual. Elegun are also called *iyawo orisha* (*iyawo* ["bride" or "wife"], *orisha* [god]), brides of the god, and as such become transvestites when out on the god's business (Peter Morton-Williams, personal communication, November 1969). Their female dress consists of a shirt bedecked with cowries and a skirt traditionally made up of *wabi*, appliquéd panels, or just a cotton skirt (Plate 25). They also wear a female hairstyle, and, as brides of the god Shango, it is to be expected that the most dominant hairstyle is agogo, the crested style traditionally worn by Yoruba brides. They wear it in both its variations, of braids radiating from each ear to the crest as shown in Plate 20, and of parallel braids flanking the crest. However, more recently the central crest may be omitted and the *kolęsę* style of multiple parallel braids can be seen to be worn by Shango priests. In addition, *şuku* (Plate 7) is also worn. While Shango priests and devotees of both sexes are never supposed to cut their hair after their initiation into the cult and most generally are supposed to wear it in the agogo style, the priest shown in Plate 25, photographed in 1973, did not have hair long enough to plait in any style. He has simply tied it in little tufts as a generalized indication of a female style. It would seem that there has been a gradual permissiveness in what is considered proper ritual appearance. Shango priests even more recently have been seen wearing imported, women's Afro wigs of the type shown in Plate 19.

Members may be recruited into the cult of Shango either through being born into the cult or advised to join it through Ifa divination. When both male and female members undergo initiation, their heads are shaved by a Shango priest while they are seated on a Shango mortar, marking their passage from a secular to a sacred status. Johnson (1920:35), describing practices of the late nineteenth century, records that tiny incisions were made on the shaved head and magical substances rubbed into them. As priests and members, they are to let their hair grow long and wear a

Plate 25.   Shango priest with his hair tied in tufts to resemble a woman's hairstyle. Photograph: November 21, 1973, in the market at Ikenne, Ijebu-Remo

female style, traditionally agogo and more recently, ṣuku and kolẹṣẹ. When priests and members of the cult die, they will again be seated on the Shango mortar and their heads once again shaved. Shango priests explained to Morton-Williams that this signifies their removal from the cult as "Shango is a cult for the living" (personal communication, 1969), Thus head shaving upon death marks passage from life and cult membership to death and nonmembership.

   Several different female hairstyles can symbolize Shango. A fuller knowledge of the social context of a hairstyle, most notably the sex and full regalia of the wearer, is necessary before one can recognize its symbolic significance. Yoruba hairstyles often function as multivocal symbols, that is, a hairstyle may communicate different information depending on its particular context. Thus, for example, agogo, the bride's hairstyle, can indicate the married status of a woman or membership in the cult of Shango. Agogo itself can communicate this information in two style variations: the central crest is flanked by either radiating or parallel braids. This multivocal aspect of Shango hairstyles is reflected in cult sculpture where cult priests and devotees are depicted wearing various female hairstyles (Thompson 1971: ch. 12, plates 3, 4, 5). These sculptures often depend on hair being just one of a cluster of symbols communicating cult identity such as cult jewelry, clothing, and other cult symbols such as double ax blades and *şere* rattles. In both the ritual and sculpture of Shango, the most important thing would seem to be that the hair is female in style for both males and females.

In summarizing the essence of hair behavior related to the cult of Shango, it can be seen that head-shaving functions in rites of passage and certain female hairstyles serve to distinguish priests and members of the cult. In general, Yoruba hairstyles often function as multivocal symbols, the specific message depending on the social context. However, in the case of Shango priests and members, the essence of the message being communicated is femaleness, and more specifically, bride and wife to Shango.

In the last cult to be discussed, that of Eshu, hair communicates a more complicated, multifaceted message. Eshu the trickster god has many aspects and hair is used to convey various characteristics. Eshu hairstyles must be analyzed in relation to Yoruba secular hairstyles, especially those of the palace, and in relation to Eshu mythology and the position of this deity in Yoruba cosmology.

The characteristics of the trickster god Eshu of the Yoruba have been well described by Wescott (1962). He is said to be the messenger of the gods working in tandem with Ifa, the god of divination, as companion mediators between gods and men. Ifa may be said to represent certainty and order while Eshu introduces chance and uncertainty into man's affairs. Eshu is conceived as a creature of paradox: he is all and one, old and young, tall and short. The Janus-headed dance-hooks which depict Eshu with another face on the back of his projecting hair are said to reflect the fact that Eshu can see into the past as well as into the future (see Carroll 1967: plate 32). His colors, black and white, reflect the extremes which characterize him, although it may also be recalled that black and white were also the colors originally associated with the court messengers of Ife. Eshu is said to be a troublemaker who tricks men into offending the gods. Because men must then make food sacrifices, Eshu is said to feed the gods and thus the spoon is one of his symbols. Eshu is also a hunter, and as such is associated both with the bilateral messenger hairstyle and the long hair of hunters. Since both court messengers and hunters must go outside the town into the bush where the spirits ascend and descend between heaven and earth, both are appropriate and congruent metaphors for Eshu. In the material that follows, the symbolic function of hair in Eshu cult sculpture is discussed first and followed then by an analysis of the hair behavior found among Eshu priests and devotees.

Eshu's libidinal energy and strength is said to reside in his hair which in cult sculpture is often shown dressed in a prominent tailed hunter's headdress or hairstyle. In some cases, the hair of Eshu and his devotees is actually carved in the form of a phallus (Plate 26, Plate 27). Wescott records a praise song for Eshu which links his hair with strength:

He is the one who fights
He is the one who bears a club
He is the smooth-haired one
The one with hair down the back of his head
The one with fullness of hair
Elegba, the strong man, is coming.

(Wescott 1962:338)

Plate 26.   Woodcarving depicting an Eshu devotee holding a bowl. She has her hair dressed in a form resembling a phallus. Photograph: July 1970, in a small Ibarapa town. Height approximately fourteen inches

Eshu cult sculpture sometimes shows the god or his devotees with a curved knife projecting out of the head; Thompson observes that the word for "knife", *abe*, is also used to refer to the penis (Thompson 1971:4/5). Eshu is said to be vain about his hair, and thus combs and mirrors are also his symbols. When Eshu priests are out on the god's

Plate 27.   Woodcarving for the cult of Eshu depicting him as a hunter with a phallus projecting from his head. He is flanked by male and female attendant figures. Height fifteen inches. Collection of Anne and Jay Whipple

business, such as begging for alms in the market, they most often wear a dance hook over one shoulder (Plate 28). The elaborate projection emanating out of the head of Eshu which hooks over the shoulder is sometimes carved as a hunter's headdress, a hunter's cap, a janus head-dress, a curved knife, or as a phallus. While sometimes it is difficult to distinguish between some of these forms, together they convey the notion of omniscience, aggression, and sexual energy. Eshu in his hunter aspect and Yoruba hunters themselves have long hair, often festooned with medicine calabashes. Since they both must traverse the spiritual no-man's-land in their work, they need and use medicines for protection. Both are associated with sexual energy that is not procreative in intent. Long hair and the medicines are equated with strength and serve to protect against potentially malevolent spirits. In light of Eshu myth, which links hair with sexual energy, a link concretized in Eshu sculpture where hair is sometimes carved in the form of a phallus, it is not surprising that some younger-generation Yoruba refer to Eshu as a sex god, although this is an obvious oversimplification.

Augmenting Eshu as hunter is the metaphor of Eshu as messenger. Just as the hairstyle of actual hunters is projected onto the religious plane to convey the aspect of Eshu as a divine hunter, so the Yoruba palace messenger hairstyle, too, is utilized to convey Eshu's messenger aspect. Eshu is said to deliver messages from men to the gods and he can, in turn, bring both good and bad from the gods to the men. In accord with this function, Eshu, when depicted in cult sculpture in his divine messenger aspect, is shown with his head half shaved in the fashion previously described for the royal court messengers.

Plate 28.   Eshu priest in his transvestite role as the wife of Eshu. He wears a woman's scarf since he did not have time to have his hair plaited in a female style as is customary. Photograph: July 1970, Igbo-Ora, Ibarapa, by Klindt Houlberg

Wescott (1962:340–341) recounts an interesting myth which joins this bilateral messenger aspect of Eshu with his devious nature. Eshu was said to have broken up a lifelong friendship of two men who owned adjoining farms. The deity walked down the path separating the farms wearing a hat which was black on one side and white on the other. He also put his pipe at the back of his head and hooked his club over his shoulder so that it hung down his back. After he passed, one farmer asserted that the old man had gone one way and wore a white cap, the other that he had gone in the opposite direction and wore a black cap. Eshu had succeeded again in causing men to quarrel. A variation of this myth, in this case Afro-Cuban and quoted by Thompson, relates in a similar fashion how Eshu used the bilateralness of his hair and body decoration to cause disagreement between two observers on opposite sides of the road (Thompson 1971:4/4). Eshu used the fact that one half of his head was shaved and that one half of his body was painted white and the other black to convince the one person that he had seen a baldheaded white man and the other that he had seen a black man with a full head of hair. Of course, another argument ensued.

One level of explanation for the bilateral hair and body-painting symbolism associated with Eshu observes that aspects of Yoruba social structure, namely that of the Yoruba palace organization, have been projected into the religious sphere. The Yoruba court messenger has been utilized as the metaphor for one half of the divine communication team of Ifa and Eshu. However, the following myth, recorded by Thompson at Ilora, near Oyo, in 1963, attempts to reveal the origin of the bilateralness of the messenger symbolism of Eshu in terms of still further myth rather than by referring to any corresponding aspect of Yoruba traditional life. Ifa, the god of divination, decided to see who his real friend was among all his acquaintances. He pretended to die and many came to put claims on his property. The news of the death of Ifa came to Eshu while he was shaving his head. In tears he ran with his head only half shaved to see his friend Ifa. Ifa said, "You are my real friend. You will be my friend forever more. I have seen you arrive with your hair unfinished. Henceforth, this tuft will remain on your head as the sign of friendship which is genuine "(Thompson 1971: 4/3). In this myth, the myth of origin of the half-shaved messenger hairstyle has been synthesized with a myth of origin of the partnership between Eshu and Ifa. Both refer back to a single point in mythical time.

The myths surrounding Eshu, and especially the one quoted above, exhibit one of the characteristics singled out by Lévi-Strauss as most typical of mythical thought. In *The savage mind*, he likens mythical thought to the act of *bricolage*, the constructing of something by simply using what is at hand, because he notes that new myths are constructed from the constitutive units of the myths already existing in the culture (Lévi-Strauss 1966:16–17). Thus in Eshu myths we have examined related to hair, we have seen that the trickster aspect of Eshu is grafted onto the messenger aspect by myths which tell of how he uses his messenger hairstyle and body painting to play tricks. In turn, the messenger aspect, represented by the bilateral hairstyle, is joined with the Eshu-Ifa alliance through a common myth of origin. While Eshu cult sculpture often refers to the various aspects of Eshu as recounted in myth, Jean Laude's point (1973:26) that art is often more than an illustration of myth and may in fact generate still further myth is well taken in the case of Eshu ritual objects. Lévi-Strauss has likened the artist to the *bricoleur* because he too combines and recombines what is at hand. The Yoruba carver inherits a wide variety of Eshu hair and head symbols. This vocabulary includes the hunter's tailed headdress and tailed hairstyle, the knife, the penis, the messenger, the half-shaved hairstyle, and others. Each iconographic element is related to a cluster of myths and may serve to generate still others. In the case of the cult of Eshu, the art and myth related to hair are engaged in an ongoing dialectic.

There is geographical variation in hair behavior among Eshu priests and cult members. In some areas, Eshu priests, just as in the case of Shango priests, are said to become the wives of the god when they go out on the god's business, especially to beg for alms in the market. An Eshu priest photographed in the Ibarapa town of Igbo-ora in 1970, shown in Plate 28, wears a woman's scarf, earrings, and a woman's dress. He carries out his sexual role reversal to the point of wearing red fingernail polish. He stated that he had not had time to get his hair plaited as a woman so he just used a woman's scarf. He is shown with his Eshu board on which a number of Eshu symbols can be seen: combs and mirrors, a reference to Eshu's vanity, especially about his hair; spoons, both plastic and silver, a sign of the sacrifices he provides for the gods; and coins, both a reminder to give alms to appease Eshu and also a reference to the marketplace where money is exchanged and where Eshu is particularly troublesome. Over his left shoulder is his Eshu dance hook carved in the form of a phallus.

In the Ijebu-Remo area at Shagamu, both Eshu priests and female devotees have been observed to wear the following bilateral variations involving head painting, head shaving and hairstyling: (1) one half of the head shaved and the other braided or just cut short and left unbraided — one half may also be colored black with charcoal and the other red with osun; (2) the entire head shaved with one half colored black and the other red; and (3) a different braided woman's hairstyle on each half of the head, for example, ṣuku, the basket style, may be worn on the left and kolẹṣẹ [without legs] on the right.

Based on hairstyles alone it can be seen that one cannot distinguish a court messenger from an Eshu priest or devotee. Obviously, the bilateral messenger hairstyle is a multivocal symbol as we have seen in the case of abiku children. Its primary message is "messenger", but its fuller context provides additional information. It is only through examining the total social context that the specific message becomes clear. And just as Eshu is multifaceted, more than one hairstyle serves as his symbol.

The broader question of why the priests, and in some cases the priestesses, of Yoruba religious cults cross the sexual boundary in dress and hairstyles, is beyond the scope of this paper. However, there are a number of directions that such an explanation can take in the Yoruba case. One is that when the sexual boundary is a structurally significant one, as it traditionally is among the Yoruba, a visually dramatic social statement is made by crossing it; it may mark a role change from the profane to the sacred. As Max Gluckman (1965:257) has noted, in small-scale societies where people play multiple roles, ritual is often used to indicate the particular role being played. The ritual may include changes in dress and hair as well as the wearing of masks. Gluckman also observes that ritual isolates roles through exaggeration, which "may be carried as far as complete reversal" (1965:257). In Yoruba ritual this extends to reversals of sex roles, and, as noted above, hair plays a prominent part in these sexual role reversals which are an important part of Yoruba religious behavior.

Hair Behavior Related to Balufọn and Egungun

Within the religious system sexual role reversal may also function to parody the role being portrayed. Hair and clothes also feature prominently in these ritual role reversals. An interesting example was witnessed by the author in September, 1973, in Ikenne, Ijebu-Remo, during the annual Balufọn festival. Balufọn is the god of weaving and thus many fine cloths together with especially elaborate hairstyles are worn by women in this festival, said to be held in their honor. The last day of the three-day event featured role reversals in both directions. About a dozen young and middle-aged men dressed as women and flagrantly parodied women's styles of walking and dancing. Many of the men wore women's imported Afro wigs available in most local markets (Plate 19), and some also wore colorful bras of European manufacture, also purchased locally. It was said that any man in the town who wanted to dress as a woman on that day was free to do so and that this was done for the general amusement of the audience. The laughter that they generated increased as their imitations of women became more exaggerated. It is consistent that this transvestism should be featured in a festival which also included social comment on a number of other levels: the songs composed and sung by the women of the various compounds ridiculed certain social offenders of the town, such as those who were licentious in behavior or had not repaid debts — even the king of the town is not immune. It is also a time when certain desired social changes are publicly advocated. One song lauded the efforts of a local educator, Tai Solarin, to obtain state-supported universal education for all children up to the secondary school level. Thus it can be seen that dramatic role reversal during Balufọn, which includes men wearing women's wigs, is consistent in a festival where other social reversals are also taking place. The norms of decorum and circumspection are temporarily suspended when women sing their songs of ridicule and other social comment. It is interesting that role reversal from female to male also takes place during Balufọn: on the last day, the most senior titled woman of the town, who is considered to be the female head of the festival, appeared with her head completely shaved. She was addressed by all as *baba*, literally, "old man". Needless to say she stood out in sharp contrast to all of the other elaborately coiffured women.

Another example of women being parodied by men within a ritual context occurs in the Egungun ancestral masquerades of the entertainment variety. Egungun masquerades are made and worn by men and in the Ijebu area appear at various times during funeral ceremonies. A wide variety of social characters are satirized in these masquerades, including the well-known duo, the prostitute and the policeman. The masquerade shown in Plate 29 depicts a prostitute. The man wearing this bore a leather handbag and wore high-heeled shoes in addition to the elaborate thread-tied hairstyle, of the type called olowu, which can be seen. That thread-tied hairstyles are associated with women making themselves sexually attractive is revealed in the expression "*o korun abẹ lẹ*" ["she tied her hair in wisps with black thread"]. Abraham notes that *abẹ lẹ* stands for *abẹte lẹ* [bribe] and means, "she did her hair in this way to excite sensual desire in her lover when through suckling a child, she is by custom, forbidden sexual intercourse, and will not sleep with him unless he bribes her" (Abraham 1958:319). The Ikenne tailor who made this masquerade has carefully sectioned the hair through the use of contrasting fabrics and has inserted a continuously formed, thread-tied imitation of the sexually alluring olowu type of hairstyle.

CONCLUSION

We have seen that the Yoruba exhibit the full range of hair behavior from the totally untended, free hair, through the careful articulation of it, to the partial or total removal of it. All three make dramatic statements about social categories and changes from one social category to another. The purpose of this paper was to examine the form and function of hair in both traditional and contemporary Yoruba culture, noting what if any characteristics they share. At first glance, a hairstyle consisting of phonograph records or reflecting changes in modern traffic regulations might seem to be a radical departure from the more traditional hairstyles such as those denoting royal messengers or traditional hunters. In fact, both are communicating information in the same visual mode: the content is new but the mode remains the same.

Contemporary hairstyles reflect certain of the changes in social organization which are occurring in Yoruba society today. For example, changes in the occupational structure are reflected in names of hairstyles related to the more recent occupations of the organized military and police forces, as well as the more recent professions such as law. Changes in the political structure from kingdoms to a modern federation are

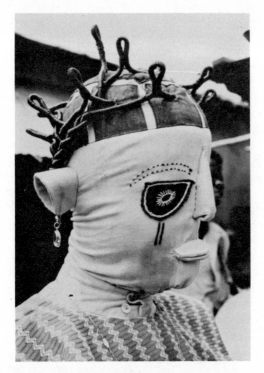

Plate 29. Egungun ancestral masquerade of the entertainment variety which depicts and satirizes the prostitute (*ṣagberi*). The costume is made by tailors and is worn by men. In this example, the hairstyle is of the type considered to be sexually alluring, *olowu*, the thread-wrapped style. A braid emanates from the center of each of the sections, which have been carefully delineated by the tailor. Photograph: October 23, 1973, Ikenne, Ijebu-Remo

reflected in modes of dressing hair. The decline in the prevalence of palace messenger hairstyles corresponds to the declining power of the Yoruba king and his chiefs. Instead we see many styles and names related to the national state, its political activities, and its leaders.

The changing religious composition of the population is reflected in modern hairstyles. Just as we have seen that hair served multiple functions in Yoruba traditional religion, hair also performs certain functions in Islam and Christianity as it is practiced in Yorubaland today. It has been previously noted that certain modern hairstyles are reserved for Yoruba Muslim women. Certain African Christian sects, such as Cherubim and Seraphim, and the Apostolic faith healing sect, Aladura, also have specific hair behavior associated with their faiths: their priests and prophets indicate their sacred state by allowing their hair to go uncut and untended. Thus, just as hair reflected the religious cult composition of traditional Yoruba society, it also reflects the religious pluralism of modern Yoruba society.

The introduction of mass media into Nigeria has had a marked effect on hairstyles as well as on clothing fashions and other types of body adornment. There is more response of a topical nature to current events and popular culture than in earlier times; styles travel more quickly, widely, and uniformly than was the case, although there is still regional variation in names and styles. The hairstyle signs done by the sign painters also are important innovations which assist in the process of diffusion and serve to standardize styles and names.

There have also been certain changes in the mode of production of modern hairstyles. The sexual division of labor which usually exists in Yoruba crafts seems to be breaking down between barbers and hairdressers due to certain technical requisites: women require the services of barbers to shape their Afros. However, since plaited styles for women were becoming increasingly popular in 1975 and the woman's Afro was on the wane, the sexual division of labor may reestablish itself. It is also interesting to note that aspects of Yoruba religion have been appropriated by the crafts of barbering and hairdressing. Just as in the traditional craft system where each craft has a special tutelary god (orisha), in many areas barbering and hairdressing also conform to this traditional practice. Barbers, if they have a special orisha, worship Ogun, the god of iron and war, since they use metal implements in their trade. Female hairdressers, if they have a special orisha, at least in the Ijobu-Remo area, are reported to have Eshu as their special deity because of Eshu's association with sex and hair. It will be recalled that combs and mirrors are his symbols.

The old and the new coexist not only in the craft organization of barbering and hairdressing but in the hairstyles to be seen in Yorubaland today. It is entirely possible that at a twin ritual where the twins have their heads shaved and the contents are put into the twin pots for medicinal purposes, their mother may be wearing "Nigeria drive right". Older sisters may be wearing "Eko bridge" or "West African record". The father may be wearing "Light of Kennedy", "James Brown style", or "British negro". A dada child with coins tied in his long matted hair may be playing nearby. A Christian Aladura priest with similarly matted hair may walk by on his way to the market where a Shango priest with his hair plaited like a woman may be begging for alms. A court messenger with his head half shaved may pass on his way back to the palace. The entire scene may be viewed by a returning Yoruba university student from the United States who sports a full Afro and wears platform shoes known locally as *onilẹ gogoro* ["skyscrapers"]. The traditional and the modern, rather than conflicting, form a continuum. In both cases, hair communicates a wide range of social information: it reflects religious, sexual, occupational, and political categories. As Leach (1967) has stated, in many cultures hair serves to maintain, as well as to cross, social boundaries, and this function continues to be the case in Yoruba hair behavior although perhaps the boundaries are changing more rapidly now than in former times.

If it is true that hair communicates a vast range of social information, it must also be remembered that it is only one element in a complicated system of symbolism related to the body. It is revealing to compare the use of hair with the other symbolic media in terms of social change. Many symbolic systems operate simultaneously on a single individual. Some are related to temporary transformations such as hair, cosmetics, and clothing, and others to permanent transformations such as facial and body scarification and tattooing. The temporary transformations are flourishing among the Yoruba today but the permanent ones are on the decline. For example, face marks denote lineage affiliation and in a society where kinship is providing fewer and fewer rights to an individual because of fundamental changes in the economic and political structure, so these marks are becoming less and less important.

In Yoruba culture hair, as a mode of communication, while serving to reflect social change, in fact may also facilitate it. Yoruba hair forms a symbolic system and as such, according to Turner, serves to help societies become "adjusted to internal changes and adapted to the external environment" (Turner 1967:20). The new rapidly becomes the accepted and familiar through the medium of hair. As we have seen, the Nigerian federal government often uses mass media to promote its policies, programs, and events. The resulting hairstyles and fashions not only reflect the policy or event but can serve to support and reinforce it actively. In addition, both Yoruba and American hairstyles provide yet further examples of how cultures cannot be considered hermetically sealed units. Influences on hair designs have flowed back and forth not only between the Yoruba and contiguous groups but across great distances; American hairstyles bear witness to highly creative influences from Africa (Plate 30). The Yoruba have always incorporated the new with great style, ingenuity, and a lively humor. This characteristic will continue to bring Yoruba culture the world-wide attention it deserves.

REFERENCES

ABRAHAM, R. C.
    1958   *A dictionary of modern Yoruba.* London: University of London Press.
BASCOM, WILLIAM R.
    1969   *The Yoruba of southern Nigeria.* New York: Holt, Rinehart and Winston.
CARROLL, KEVIN
    1967   *Yoruba religious carving.* New York: Frederick A. Praeger.

Plate 30.   An African-inspired American hairstyle. Beads have been strung on the thin braids and the central motif has been formed by attaching a section of braids to a spiral wire. Photograph: New York, July 1976, by Gail Fair

COLE, HERBERT M.
   1970   *African arts of transformation.* Santa Barbara: University of California Art Galleries.
DREWAL, HENRY JOHN
   1974   Gelede masquerade: imagery and motif. *African Arts* 7(4):8–19, 62–63, 95–96.
FAMILORI, FUNKE
   n.d.   *Gele, the Yoruba headtie.* Lagos: Times Press.
GLUCKMAN, MAX
   1965   *Politics, law and ritual in tribal society.* Oxford: Basil Blackwell.
GWATKIN, NINA
   1971   *Yoruba hairstyles.* Lagos: Craft Centre, National Museum.
HOULBERG, MARILYN HAMMERSLEY
   1978   Notes on Egungun masquerades of the Oyo Yoruba. *African Arts* 11(3).
JOHNSON, SAMUEL
   1920   *The history of the Yorubas from the earliest times to the beginning of the British protectorate.* London: George Routledge and Sons.
LAUDE, JEAN
   1973   *African art of the Dogon.* New York: Brooklyn Museum/Viking.
LEACH, EDMUND R.
   1967   "Magical hair," in: *Myth and cosmos.* Edited by John Middleton, 77–108. Garden City, New York: Natural History Press. (Originally published 1958. *Journal of the Royal Anthropological Institute* 88(1–2):147–164.)
LÉVI-STRAUSS, CLAUDE
   1966   *The savage mind.* Chicago: University of Chicago Press.

MORTON-WILLIAMS, PETER
1964   An outline of the cosmology and cult organization of the Oyo Yoruba. *Africa* 34(3):243–261.
SPRAGUE, STEPHEN, MARILYN HAMMERSLEY HOULBERG, *directors*
1975   *When it is time my star will shine: a Yoruba hairdresser in action.* Sound film, 15 minutes, Department of Creative Arts, Purdue University, Lafayette, Indiana.
THOMPSON, ROBERT FARIS
1971   *Black gods and kings: Yoruba art at UCLA.* Occasional Papers of the Museum and Laboratories of Ethnic Arts and Technology, 2. Los Angeles: University of California Press.
TURNER, VICTOR
1967   *The forest of symbols.* Ithaca, New York: Cornell University Press.
VAN GENNEP, A.
1960   *The rites of passage.* Translated by Monika B. Vizedom and L. Caffee. London: Routledge and Kegan Paul. (Originally published 1909 as: *Les rites de passage.* Paris: Émile Nourry.)
WESCOTT, JOAN
1962   The sculpture and myths of Eshu-Elegba, the Yoruba trickster: definition and interpretation in Yoruba iconography. *Africa* 32(4):336–354.

Clothing and Power Abuse

U. R. VON EHRENFELS

Within the framework of tensions that potentially lead to conflicts, minor causes are also worth investigating. The change of clothing habits appears as an altogether negligible and harmless event, disconnected from major complexes of power abuse. However, by analytical study we discover far-reaching consequences pertaining to our theme.

During the first centuries of European colonial expansion, individual acquaintance between newcomers and natives was restricted to the comparatively limited areas of harbors and military centers. At first the European conquerors and immigrants did not dream of propagating, much less imposing, European forms of life on foreign peoples in tropical countries; rather they tended to adopt the latter's styles of life and particularly dress, which they realized were better suited to local conditions. The first British envoys to the court of Delhi, for instance, appeared there in Mogul dress. French Jesuit missionaries in southern India emulated Brahmin dress, and the king of Portugal corresponded in brotherly terms with a king in Zaire who still dressed in local, traditional clothing.

The stationing of resident troops brought a change. Broader, more intimate contacts with local populations began, the more so where "native forces" were formed by colonial governments. Local native soldiers, and especially officers (if any), had to conform to European customs and particularly to the costumes (uniforms) of the conquerors. This form of acculturation was further stressed by military indoctrination on the desirability of imitating the example set by the higher ranks for the lower ones.

Soon European civilians began to feel that native dress was symbolic of disobedience, or at any rate contrary to the demand for submission to the superior colonial power and to Christian demeanor.

Many impulses thus coalesced in the dress complex and became mixed with evolutionist theories about "stages of civilization" from "naked savages" to loosely dressed "barbarians" to tightly dressed "civilized peoples", i.e. Europeans and Americans.

Many national styles of dress in tropical countries left the upper part of the body free from clothing, as Mahatma Gandhi's example illustrated. This was, and partly still is, anathema to certain Christians who perceive in the sight of a half-naked human body the dangers of carnal sensuality.

Not only white-collar workers but also servants in European houses were compelled to put on clothing that covered the entire body so that they would conform to European concepts of being "decently dressed".

The first things black laborers receive on arrival from the "native reserves" in apartheid-ridden South Africa are a pair of pants and a shirt. In the Portuguese "provinces" of Africa, it is not racialism that governs the attitudes toward Africans — provided they have become Roman Catholic, speak Portuguese well, and are dressed in the European style.

Sexual jealousy also seems to have played a not altogether negligible role among the manifold causes that led to the enforcement of specific dress dictates for tropical countries. Particularly in South Asia and East Africa, the nineteenth-century opening of the Suez Canal, with its comparatively fast passenger traffic, made it easier for the European wives and children of colonial officers and civilians to accompany their husbands and fathers. This new situation appears to have further sharpened the taboo on exposure of the upper part of the body, not only for house servants, but even for gardeners working in the open air.

By the time cheap motor transport on buses inaugurated closer contacts between city dwellers and remote rural peoples, European styles of dress had already become prestige symbols among non-Europeans. To be dressed in the new all-covering style had by then become the hallmark of the educated upper classes in East Africa and especially in South Asia.

The spread of air travel initiated a further step along this line. Officialdom and big businessmen travel in dark, "formal dress", sometimes even made of synthetic fibers, thereby setting standards that are meticulously observed. The applicant at a government office or the customer of a bank, whether European or native, is served less courteously and later if not clad in "formal dress" of a type completely unsuited to the climatic conditions of the country.

Western dress, acquired by the proud owner at considerable cost, requires upkeep involving additional expenses for soap, ironing, mending, etc. Besides the often unbearable economic stress put on large segments of the population by the introduction of European clothing styles, it is difficult to know what to think of such fashions in regions where there is sometimes not even enough drinking water. In addition to disastrous harm to physical health, psychic harm is now increasingly recognized. For example, dirty, torn rags cannot fail to have adverse effects on indigenous aesthetics.

Even in the optimal situation, the struggle for more and more European clothing starts a competitive cleavage between the richer, in "better" dress, and the poorer, in lesser states of upkeep. With the dust and heat of equatorial countries, Western-style garments look dirty after even one day's use. Before, anyone could feel pride and dignity through belonging to a given culture or through recognition of one's merits, such as physical beauty or fitness, manual dexterity, prowess at hunting, drumming or dancing ability, or mental gifts; all this is now too easily obliterated by the stern division set by conspicuous dress symbols of wealth and poverty.

This situation also implies changes in the life-style such as subconscious attitudes that find their expression in personal bearing and in all sorts of mannerisms. It has become not only fashionable but an actual "must" to conform to European patterns of behavior, even to the extent of imitating hairdos, beard fashions, and such manifestations of one's personality as forms of relaxation, the use of tobacco and more dangerous poisons, or ways of speaking and laughing.

Chain reactions initiated by foreign clothing styles are not confined to the aesthetic or, generally speaking, to the cultural side of life only. In cotton-growing countries national budgets, as well as private ones, are profoundly upset by the demand for an ever-increasing output of raw material for the clothing industry, while food production often does not meet desperate demands.

However, this socioeconomic aspect of clothing and power abuse is too wide an issue to be included in this paper, which is concerned with the social-psychological and the exclusively psychological aspects of the problem.

Aggression by imitation is a consciously desired goal of hierarchically organized armies all over the world, though to different degrees in different areas. For example, in the Swiss army a minimum of high-ranking officers corresponds with comparatively little martial show. This, however, is compensated for by the free use of military rifles possessed by reserve soldiers, who practice shooting every Sunday, using up at least 700 shots a year. The world over, smart uniforms, conspicuous symbols of rank, and decorations play an important role in the propagation of military agression. The use of European-styled uniforms in colonial armies has added to already existing impulses of aggression.

One could toy with the idea of an imaginary reversed case of dress assimilation. Let us, for a moment, suppose that Nayars, a warrior class of precolonial Kerala, had conquered Portugal in the Middle Ages and that their influence had diffused over the Mediterranean and the Western world. Kerala dress, along with other customs, would have spread. The use of the spotless white *mundu*, an unsewn loincloth, and the unsewn white *vesti* or *angivastiram*, usually folded over the bare left shoulder, would have become high fashion. Here the acculturation symmetry ends. Although costly European dress requires ever-growing expenses for upkeep and maintenance, the simpler Nayar dress in Portugal would have eased, rather than accentuated, economic-aesthetic class differences. The hardships caused by winter cold or rainy storms would have been borne by a Keralized European with the stoicism of a true nobleman, caring little about a discomfort which, after all, touches the mere perishable body only. The acquired dress might have persisted even after the assumed Nayar rule had ended.

But let us return to the actual diffusion of tight-fitting, dark, and highly burdensome cold-country dress into tropical regions. The hygienic effect is adverse. Instead of hardening the body, these fashions make it over-sensitive to the slightest draft. Instead of preparing the wearer for self-control and physical prowess, they tend to make him sluggish through permanent overheating. It has been estimated that a single shirt over the chest deprives one of 70 percent of the cooling effect that perspiration provides naturally. The working and lower middle classes, who are without air-conditioning facilities, bear the brunt of the situation.

Being hot is tantamount to being in a state of mental aggression. It is not mere coincidence that in the midst of a "heated" discussion we admonish an excited partner to "cool down". Warm clothes in hot countries put both a physical and a mental load on the people who wear them. Not only is the thermal equilibrium of the body deeply disturbed, but moreover the use of unsuitable, uncomfortable dress[1] cannot fail to create subconscious aggressive reactions.

Except in a few cases of original thinkers, like Gandhi, dress objects are generally perceived as negligible, if not as actually desirable status symbols. After striving to secure what is mistakenly perceived as a display of progressiveness, the owner, dazzled by possessing it, fails to discern the real cause of discomfort: the object itself, namely, the unsuitable clothing. Instead he searches for, and finds, an emotional substitute, namely, the giver, who is taken to task instead of the given. There is a transfer by a defense mechanism from the given to the giver, who is made the object of distrust and of angry feelings.

Many Africans and Asians profess and actually believe themselves to be perfectly at ease in European dress, that precious sign of dignity *vis-à-vis* foreigners as well as conationals. Still, they are unknowingly affected, both physically and psychologically. This aspect of our theme is

---

[1]   See Putnam and Elisofon 1973: 406, 409, 426; Zaire men are shown wearing Western clothes. The women's dresses, though also foreign, are lighter and easier to bear.

a complex one. We should here also remember that many a Western man, in his own country, is far from having liberated himself from the yoke of overdressing during warm summer days.

The spread of European clothing fashions in the equatorial belt is an example of power abuse. They create dissatisfaction, inferiority complexes, and class tensions. They add to subconscious antagonisms in international relations. They are an economic, social, and cultural aberration, an anachronism in today's world, which has at long last started to see the reverse side of industrial overproduction and to realize the dangers of worshipping "progress" at the cost of an evolutionary equilibrium.

REFERENCE

PUTNAM, JOHN J., ELIOT ELISOFON
1973 Yesterday's Congo, today's Zaire. *National Geographic* 143(3):398–432.

The Garments of the Present-Day Azerbaidzhan Population: Traditional and Modern Elements

A. G. TROFIMOVA

Each historical period features a combination of traditional and modern elements in folk attire. From the historico-social angle, "traditional" is normally understood as all those elements which emerged and consolidated in the previous historical period and continue to exist in modern times. The time span required for an object, concept, or phenomenon to become traditional varies from one period to another, subject to both the socioeconomic pattern of the period and the properties of the phenomenon, concept, or object at issue.

As of now, both traditional and modern elements are discernible in the multiplicity of folk garment styles, including those of the Azerbaidzhan population. In the present study, an attempt will be made to determine the relative proportion of both elements, the reasons for this, and developmental trends.

The folk costume of the Caucasian population, and the population of Azerbaidzhan in particular, of the late nineteenth and early twentieth centuries is currently referred to by many scholars as the ethnic standard for traditional costume (Karakashly 1964:123; Aristova 1966:108–126). It had many features in common with mid-nineteenth-century costume, as is evident from examples both in literature and in museums (Efendiev 1961:8; Trofimova 1971:157–171). Costume styles repeat basic features over and over again, the only differences arise not so much from changes of fashion occurring with time as from the different ethnocultural setups in individual historico-ethnographic zones in Azerbaidzhan.

The folk costume of the Azerbaidzhan population, at its peak in the late nineteenth and early twentieth centuries, was highly developed artistically. This costume contained all the original folk features which are familiar to us and which in the course of time increasingly lost their originality. This is why scholars in Caucasian ethnography often define the costume of the late nineteenth and early twentieth centuries as the traditional one.

Disregarding less significant features of the costume in question, its basic elements can be confined to the following (Kil'chevskaia 1951; Kilchevskaia and Trofimova 1962; Karakashly 1964; Torchinskaia 1971, Trofimova 1971): the female costume set is made up invariably of a *keinek* [tunic-patterned upper shirt] (Figure 1:a, b), *tuman* or *jyuttuman* [skirt-like trousers] (Figure 1:c) of six or more layers of cotton fabric separated with an insert, or narrow long trousers (*darbalag*) of a straight cut and with an insert; on top of these a woman would often wear one or more skirts (*tuman*) also broad and long, and cut from straight cloth. The

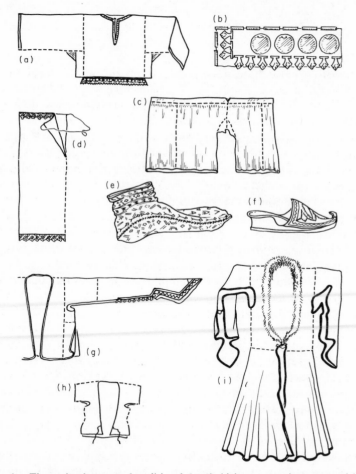

Figure 1.   The main elements of traditional Azerbaidzhan women's costume: (a) upper shirt (*keinek*); (b) a detail of the ornament of the lower part of the shirt; (c) skirt-trouser (*tuman*); (d) head-wear (*tüli*); (e) woolen socks (*jorab*); (f) footwear (*bashmag*); (g) overcoat dress (*arkhalyg*); (h) overcoat dress (*lavada*); (j) overcoat dress (*katibi*)

skirt-trousers and skirt had a tucked-in or sewn-on belt to hold a run-through cord.

Before the Revolution the woman would in no circumstances go bareheaded, except when taking part in specially designated rituals. Moreover, the headgear in combination with a hairstyle had a ritual significance (Karakashly 1964:162–175). Among the most commonly used were two headgear styles (Figure 1:d): a peculiar elongated hood with an unsewn bottom, to cover the whole of the woman's head with plaits (*chutku, chutka, chukhta*) or a special bonnet (*tesek*) covering the hair. Also used were hard frames upon which the headgear rested. To top the headgear, the woman as she left home would put on a shawl, or rather several shawls, on top of one another, one of which was to give protection to the lower part of her face (*yashmag-yashmag*), a custom practiced not only in Azerbaidzhan.[1] The urban Azerbaidzhan and Tat females, particularly those from the merchant milieu would at all times wear in the street a yashmak (*chadra, charshab*) wrapping the whole figure, with a white face cover with an eye-level net (*rubend*) to conceal the face (Kil'chevskaia and Trofimova 1962:121; Guliev 1962:184). The *chadra*-type veil (*charsav*) was also worn by the Kurdish women (Aristova 1966:108).

On her feet the woman wore woolen embroidered socks (Figure 1:e), mostly home-knit, and, when she went out, on top of the socks the footwear then widespread across Azerbaidzhan, resembling shoes with a wedgelike small heel (*bashmag*), usually with an iron heel-tap and a protruding up-turned toe (Figure 1:f).

When going out into the street, and especially in cool seasons, women wore above the gown some outer garment, which varied throughout Azerbaidzhan in cut, pattern, and in nomenclature. Essentially, garments of this type fell into two categories: somewhat shorter jackets either attached at the waist or partly detachable (on the sides and back), which were known as *arkhalyg* (Figure 1:g), *lavada* or *labada* (Figure 1:h), *chepken, don, syvyny* or *zyvyn*, and *nimtene* or *mintene*; and a more impressive costume, usually somewhat longer than the other and, as a rule, detachable at the waist, known as *kjuledje, katibi* (Figure 1:j), or occasionally *chukha*. Both types were the same in terms of their basic cut. Distinctive features of the former are usually a tunic-shaped cut, smaller dimensions compared with the second type of costume, and characteristic protrusions with slits at the hips, these being made more pronounced by a special design feature, such as an edging of braid or fur in the case of the undetachable waist.

Decorations may be worn on the head, neck, breast, hand, or waist. The articles worn on the head served to keep in place or decorate

[1] See M. Tilke's watercolors *Turkic woman from Borchalo, Woman from the Kara-Papakh tribe*, and *Udinka from Nukha*.

headgear. They included chains, stamped plates, coins, and hooks, and clasps made, as a rule, of low-grade silver. Earrings deserve special mention among the head decorations. Neck or breast trinkets took the form of necklaces of tiny pearls or strings of beads of cornelian agate, jade, glass, or paste. Less often the necklaces were made of amber, hollow gold beads, elongated or round, filigree figurines or strings of silver coins held together by tags or chains. Rings were with or without jewels while silver bracelets were made in an unclosed circle and either in sections of stamped plates (gold in well-to-do families), or of silver and gold filigree. An every-present component, particularly in a holiday costume, would be a belt, of leather or cloth with coins sewn on, embellished with metallic adornments, or with pure metal (usually low-grade silver) on hinges.

The male Azerbaidzhan costume of the same period was tailored after the same cut as that of the female. The numerous costume details, and particularly the armaments, conveyed a warlike and austere appearance. The shoulder garment of an Azerbaidzhan male was usually a white calico tunic, normally with a right-hand breast slit (Figure 2:a). Male breeches, worn both as underwear (*tuman*, *dislik*) and outer wear (*shalvar*), had a straight cut, with a medium insert and either a folded or sewn-on waist belt for a run-through cord (Figure 2:b). In some areas with more developed towns, the late nineteenth and the early twentieth centuries saw the emergence in solitary cases of male trousers tailored in contemporary urban style, without the run-through cord in the waist and with a fly.

The outer shoulder wear of males were *arkhalyg* or *don* (Figure 2:c), differing regionally in minor details of cut and finish, but similar in basic pattern: at the waistline the side flaps were always detachable while the frontal ones were usually undetachable. The cut was already somewhat sophisticated, in that it had a shoulder seam and often a rounded arm opening though the sleeve was sewn into it in a manner still unlike the modern style. The second type of garment for outer wear, the *chukha* (Figure 2:d), had the same cut but, like the latter type of female costume, was more elaborate. Also, the chukha was tailored of tougher and thicker fabric (Torchinskaia 1971:143–146).

The basic male headgear styles were the fur hat (*papag*) and the skullcap (*aragchyn*) worn beneath it. Both of these varied, differing in texture, cutting details, and finish. There was also a special hat for summer wear (Figure 2:e). For his footwear a man had woolen socks [*jorab*] usually home-knit (Figure 2:f) and high boots (charyg), or *bashmags* in town (Figure 2:g), not unlike female *bashmags* but of coarser hide and less colorful. Leg protectors (*badysh*) were also worn (Figure 2:h).

Belts were a constant item of the costume. They might be leather, sometimes trimmed, or metallic on hinges, or a broad girdle, or plaited.

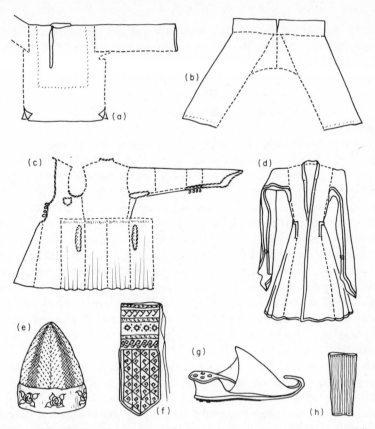

Figure 2.   The main elements of the Azerbaidzhan traditional men's costume: (a) shirt (*keinek*); (b) upper trousers (*shalvar*); (c) overcoat dress (*arkhalyg*); (d) overcoat dress (*chukha*); (e) summer headgear; (f) woolen socks (*jorab*); (g) footwear (*bashmag*); (h) leg protector (*badysh*)

The costume of the Tats in Azerbaidzhan was fairly close to the indigenous Azerbaidzhan style (Guliev 1962:184). Whatever the distinctions, they related merely to the details of costume and adornment. The Tats from the Apsheron peninsula had, toward the end of the nineteenth century, blended completely with the surrounding Azerbaidzhan folk, their male garments being little different even in details from the indigenous clothes.

In the period under consideration the costume of the Talysh minority was also similar in many ways to that of the Azerbaidzhan people (Trofimova 1962:192; Izmailova 1964:93). Yet a Talysh would be easily identified by his headgear, a cone-shaped felt or broadcloth hat. Other articles of male wear differed if only a little, just as the female costume had some minor details of garment or headgear unlike the Azerbaidzhan style. The tuniclike gown was perhaps longer, while in the cold season all women, and in warmer seasons older women, wrapped a shawl around their waists. The Talysh female outer shoulder garment (*arkhalyg*, *bahari*) showed original features in the details of cutting, but it was in the headgear (*dingya* or *chombe*) that the Talysh women showed originality (Izmailova 1964:93; Miller 1930:190) though they relied on the same technique of combining in their headgear several kerchiefs tied with a chain.

The Muslim Kurds also wore clothes resembling in many ways the Azerbaidzhan or Talysh costume (Avdal and Aristova 1962:608–611; Aristova 1966:108–121). Their women would put on a girdled under-garment (*porty*); on top of the skirt there would be a vest and a caftan (*antary*) or another outer wear item, *dalma*. The head would be covered with a skullcap (*arakhchyn*), a special headgear named *dynga*, with either a yellow or green silk kerchief bound on top of these. They were also familiar with the yashmak-type veils (*charsav*). The male outfit was also similar to that of Azerbaidzhan but for a wide sash (*kushak*) and a red cloth fez wrapped with several kerchiefs. This headgear, as often among Azerbaidzhan women, consisted of a rigid frame covered with fabric and coins, with kerchiefs enwrapping it. Among the specifically Kurdish adornments of the past were an ornamental disk-shaped trinket (*karafil*) run through the right nostril, and a silver foot bracelet (*khrkhal*). Similar to the Azerbaidzhan though with some minor differences in nomenclature was the traditional male costume.

This brief description of the male and female folk costume of the population of Azerbaidzhan at the turn of the century cannot cover the whole diversity of costume styles, and there has been deliberate omission of less significant or less popular items.

The Revolution touched off a drive for change in all areas of life and culture, not least in the realm of costume. One of the early changes in the Azerbaidzhan female costume was the elimination of the yashmak and *rubend* symbolizing seclusion and subjugation (*Istoriia Azerbaidzhana* 1963:439). In the 1920's most Azerbaidzhan women ceased wearing the yashmak and *rubend*.

Simultaneously a struggle less explicit but nonetheless earnest was going on to change the accepted type of footwear. This period saw a shift in the footwear styles of most of the Azerbaidzhan urban population from the time-hallowed *bashmag* to markedly urban footwear, such as shoes, boots, low boots, and sports shoes. Women in the villages learned to appreciate deep and cosy galoshes worn on top of thick woolen socks. *Charyg* continued in existence among males as the working footwear. The reason for this change to more modern footwear was that *bashmag* proved to be poorly adaptable to the new living environment: men found it hard to move about and work in a type of footwear in which their feet were not fixed firmly. The *charyg* persisted for a while because of its greater suitability to the living environment in the highlands.

Concurrently, changes occurred in the traditional cuts: collars were added to the tunic-shaped gowns; and modern cuts often replaced the tuniclike cut of some items of outer wear. Thus, the traditional outer shoulder garment of males gave place to coats, military tunics, and field jackets.

The 1930's saw further rapid progress in all spheres of life in Azerbaidzhan. Urban clothes became increasingly current among the urban populace and manufactured fabrics became popular, especially among the people of the Apsheron peninsula. In the countryside the change chiefly concerned male clothes, but the village females too began to give up *en masse* their tunic-shaped gowns in favor of jackets and blouses cut in the modern style. The traditional female outer garments in these years were replaced by and large by modern knitted or sewn jackets. At the time, an estimated twenty-five to thirty percent of the outer female wear followed the traditional fashions. Manufactured modern underwear of knitted and cotton fabrics also became popular.

In the postwar period, particularly in the 1960's, the inflow of consumer goods, including industrial commodities and durables, expanded immensely, paralleling the general improvement of the living standard of the population. This promoted further replacement of the remaining traditional elements in the folk costume of the indigenous Azerbaidzhan people and the other nationalities in the republic. Moreover, this was a time when centers of the new Caucasian vogue were emerging, which resulted in a reconstruction of some elements of the all-union fashion on the basis of the Caucasian vernacular. One such center was Baku, situated at the junction of the Azerbaidzhan and Tat cultures. In the 1950's and the early 1960's there was a trend toward using fabrics of natural silk for female urban daily work clothing. For peasant girls and women, these fabrics were used for their Sunday dresses, with work clothes made, as a rule, of sateen and printed calico. While modern cuts with some vernacular elements were predominant in larger towns, in smaller places similar dresses would invariable feature a long sleeve. Peasant women wore a broad, rather long, gathered skirt and a blouse cut in the European fashion with a long sleeve. Only the old women still wore tunic-like gowns.

The outer traditional female wear continued to survive only for special occasions: it was worn by some women during wedding ceremonies (but never by the brides). The *bashmag* fell out of use. The *chutku* headgear still had some currency if only among older women and chiefly in rural areas. However, the *kalgai* kerchiefs, practical and pleasing to the eye, were widely worn in villages and by a few urban dwellers.

The male clothes in the 1950's and early 1960's had some distinctions

412   A. G. TROFIMOVA

arising mainly from the character of the natural and geographical environment. Thus, on a broader scale than anywhere in the northern towns of the Soviet Union urban residents here in summer wore tussah-silk suits, and jackets of silk cloth. In the country, the overwhelming majority of the population began to wear suits with the modern cut, but in some cases, especially among old men, the traditional cuts of shirts and *arkhaluks* still persisted. Many older men continued to wear traditional high-peaked *papakhas*. Some middle-aged men among those engaged in cattle-grazing wore the traditional *charyg* boots.

The late 1960's and early 1970's witnessed an almost total disappearance of most folk elements from the clothes styles of the rural population. Today one has to take great pains to find in some far-flung villages solitary items of traditional garments, and even these are no longer worn but are kept merely as a memory of the past. In an entire rural district perhaps a handful of older men and women still wear something of the traditional outfit, although some of the rural population still wear broad long skirts with gathers, which are convenient for domestic chores and agricultural work involving sitting on the floor. The head adornments in the form of the *papakha*, among some rural males, and homemade silk kerchiefs (*kalagai*), among many women, are perhaps the most persistent traditional items. Another rare exception is the traditional *charyg* footwear style still worn by shepherds (*chabans*).

Traditional decorative items remain popular among older and middle-aged rural females from the indigenous Azerbaidzhan population. Among these are all kinds of beads, of sard, paste, glass, amber, and hollow gold, usually made up into necklaces. A rare item is the necklace of small pearls strung on several short threads and located only at the front of the neck, with hollow gold beads clasping it behind (among Azerbaidzhan and Tat women of the Apsheron peninsula).

Nearly a quarter of peasant women also wear traditional earrings in the form of a star and crescent, or a hoop with a filigree design on the inside, or two hollow gold balls the size of large peas.

Less popular among peasant women's decorations are rings (silver without stones or gold with stones), and bracelets are almost unknown. Rings may be either silver and in the form of an unclosed flat hoop, or openwork gold in a variety of shapes, to be worn on special occasions.

Urban female clothes follow at present only modern styles, with fewer trinkets than their rural counterparts. Of late, Azerbaidzhan's jewel industry has begun the manufacture of new modern decoration using traditional art motifs. Many similar knickknacks are in demand, too, among urban females. For example, gold filigree with pearl earrings in the traditional style, a product of the jewel factory in Baku, are very beautiful.

Therefore, of the traditional costume of the population of the Azer-baidzhan republic only a small part has survived, yet this small part has a high practical and artistic value in the eyes of modern man.

REFERENCES

ARISTOVA, T. F.
1966 *Kurdy Zakavkaz'ia*: *istoriko-etnograficheskii ocherk* [The Kurds of Transcaucasia: an historio-ethnographic essay]. Moscow.

AVDAL, A., T. F. ARISTOVA
1962 Kurdy [The Kurds]. *Narody Kavkaza* 2. Moscow.

EFENDIEV, R. S.
1961 "Azerbaidzhanskii kostium XVI–XVIII." [Azerbaidzhan dress of the sixteenth to the eighteenth centuries]. Candidates' dissertation, Leningrad.

GULIEV, G. A.
1962 Taty [The Tats]. *Narody Kavkaza* 2. Moscow.

Istoriia Azerbaidzhana
1963 Istoriia Azerbaidzhana [The history of Azerbaidzhan], volume three, part one. Baku.

IZMAILOVA, A. A.
1964 O narodnoi adezhde naseleniia iugo-vostochnykh raionakh Azerbaid-zhana [On the folk costume of the population of the southeastern regions of Azerbaidzhan]. *Izvestia AN Azerbaidzhanskoi SSR, Seriia Obshchestvennykh Nauk* 4. Baku.

KARAKASHLY, K. T.
1964 *Material'naia kul'tura Azerbaidzhantsev severe-vostochnoi i tsentral'noi zon Malogo kavkaza* [The material culture of the Azerbaidzhanis of the northeast and central zones of the Lesser Caucasus]. Istoriko-etnograficheskoe Issledovanie. Baku.

KIL'CHEVSKAIA, Z. A.
1951 Azerbaidzhan zhenzkii kostium XIX veka iz seleniia Odzhek Khal-danskogo raiona [Azerbaidzhan women's dress of the nineteenth century from the village of Odzhek in the Khaldan district]. *Material'naia kul'tura Aze rbaidzhana* 2. Baku.

KIL'CHEVSKAIA, Z. A., A. G. TROFIMOVA
1962 Odezhda i ukrasheniia [Clothing and ornamentation]. *Narody kavkaza* 2. Moscow.

MILLER, B. V.
1930 *Talyshskie teksty* [Talysh texts]. Moscow.

TORCHINSKAIA, E. G.
1971 "Muzhskaia odezhda azerbaidzhantsev XIX-nachala XX v. po sob-raniiu Gosudarstvennogo muzeia etnografii narodov SSSR" [Azerbaidzhan men's dress of the nineteenth and early twentieth centuries according to the collection of the state ethnography museum of the peoples of the USSR], in *Khoziaistvo i material'naia kul'tura narodov kavkaza v XIX—XX vv.* [Articles and materials of Caucasus folk culture of the nineteenth and twentieth centuries]. *Materialy Kavkazs-komu Istoriko-etnograficheskomu Atlasu* 1. Moscow.

TROFIMOVA, A. G.
1962   Talyshy [The Talysh]. *Narody Kavkaza* 2. Moscow.
1971   "Obzor kollektsii odezhdy narodov Azerbaidzhana Gosudarstvennogo muzeia Gruzii im. akad. S.N. Dzhanashia" [Survey of the collection of clothing of the Azerbaidzhani peoples of the S.N. Dzhanashia state museum of Georgia], in *Khoziaistvo i material'naia kul'tura narodov Kavkaza v XIX—XX vv.* [Articles and materials of Caucasus folk culture of the nineteenth and twentieth centuries]. *Materialy k Kavkazkomu Istoriko-Etnograficheskomu Atlasu* 1. Moscow.

The Social Symbolism of Women's Dress

MARY ELLEN ROACH

Women's dress is scarcely a new topic for discussion. Moses (Deut. 22:5) and the prophet Isaiah (Isa. 3:16–24) made their commentaries and recommendations on the subject, as did the apostle Paul (1 Cor. II:15). In the 1970's sociologists, biologists, anthropologists, Marxists, school board members, participants in the women's movement, and writers for the underground press, were among those who contributed their points of view. The subject is, therefore, very familiar, and approached with confidence by people in many walks of life.

Handling the topic can, however, engender uneasiness and inspire one to proceed with caution since the phrase "women's dress" raises the ever-controversial question of whether differences between men's and women's behavior are biologically determined. It is true that a few specific forms of dress have been designed clearly for one sex or the other on the basis of biologically determined characteristics, for example, the sixteenth-century codpiece accommodated the male body; the twentieth-century brassiere the female. In addition, differences in biological functioning of the sexes may encourage or discourage some forms of dress: for instance, it is possible that Western women found skirts generally more convenient to wear than trousers or drawers, especially when taking care of natural functions, until twentieth-century technology provided bifurcated garments that, unlike those of the past, could easily be pulled on and off because of their stretch, elasticity, and easily manipulated fasteners.

But far more important than biological differences in the development of distinct dress for the sexes are social, particularly role, differences. Traditional roles for men and women in Western society have been largely defined on the basis of life patterns developed in its nonindustrial past when women's energies were directed toward nurturing the children they had borne and caring for their homes and men's to sustenance and protection activities requiring considerable physical strength. The dress of each sex tended to be more or less useful in fulfilling these types of roles — at least not so hindering as to prevent role performance. Thus trousers were protective for men and noninhibiting of their body movements as they engaged in physical labor; and skirts and dresses, while inconvenient and sometimes hazardous if they were bulky and long, did not prevent women from taking care of children and managing households.

Once distinctions between the dress of the sexes have existed for a long time, as is true in Western society, their continuation is supported by custom even though the tasks that men and women perform may change. People are simply used to distinctions — they expect men to dress in one way, women in another; they experience shock and social unease if their expectations are not fulfilled. In addition, through time a complex set of meanings becomes attached to the traditional dress of each sex, and sanctions develop that discourage behavior inconsistent with meanings. For example, in Western society where women have long worn skirts, while men have worn trousers, the skirt symbolizes the "proper" woman's role and the behaviors thought appropriate for the woman. Words like "feminine" describe these behaviors as well as the skirt, and a woman accurately portraying her "feminine" role wears a skirt and is gentle, dependent, and nonaggressive. Trousers, by contrast, symbolize the man's role. They are regarded as "masculine", appropriate for males, and their wearing connotes opposite characteristics, that is, forcefulness, independence, and aggressiveness. Children learn these types of distinctions early in life; and their dress serves as an instrument of socialization, reminding them to assume the behavior that people expect from someone wearing the kind of dress that they are wearing. The positive responses of parents and other people given to the female child when she "looks" and "acts" like a girl and to the male child when he "looks" and "acts" like a boy tend to reinforce and continue distinctions between the dress and behavior expected of both males and females.

Consideration of women's dress in the United States from the middle of the nineteenth century to the present indicates that women's dress, symbolically, as well as physically, has operated to limit the social roles of women and thus has helped discourage full participation of women in American society. By mid-nineteenth century styles of dress for men and women had taken very different turns. Men's costumes had become functional for the types of occupations in which they were involved; women's costumes, however, remained consistent with past traditions and were largely for display. Since men in nineteenth-century rural America were in direct confrontation with an environment that required their physical strength for tilling the soil and other heavy labor, they needed sturdy, unencumbering clothes for their work. Laborers in the growing number of factories did also. In a much smaller but expanding group were the middle-class businessmen who became the real style setters in the industrializing society of the nineteenth century. Along with their European counterparts they rejected the elaborate type of dress characteristic of the fashion-setting courts of Western Europe of previous centuries in favor of a drab, sober costume that typically included coat, vest, and trousers of black, grey, or dark blue (or some combination thereof), worn with light shirt and dark tie. In retrospect this rather standard dress, and the rejection of fashion competition that it implied, seems compatible with their roles as no-nonsense businessmen devoting their energies to coping with the organization of resources for the production and distribution of goods and services in a rapidly industrializing nation.

By contrast, women's dress at mid-nineteenth century had not undergone the same kind of metamorphosis, that is, a change from elaborate to plain. Instead, a woman took on, in Veblen's terms, the role of displayer of the ability of the male provider of her household, her husband or father, to pay (Veblen 1953:87–131). Major forms of display for her were her clothes, and, if she were married, her home. Consistent with her display role was participation in fashion changes in ways that might bring recognition of her ability to discriminate among available fashions.

Some courageous American women of the nineteenth century found the type of dress display expected of them to be a burden and began to speak out against a style of dress that made them symbolically, often physically, dependent on men. We find, therefore, accompanying the nineteenth-century feminist movement, a dress reform movement that lasted until the end of the century, even though it went into near eclipse from time to time (Russell 1892). The first organized effort for dress reform was made in 1856 when a Dress Reform Association, which held several conventions, was organized. This effort had apparently spent itself by the sixties, but by the seventies a second dress reform movement was led by the New England Woman's Club. Interest again waned, but in 1891 the National Council of Women, in their first convention, revived the movement by appointing a Dress Reform Committee. This committee's responsibility was described as "this long neglected and despised cause of dress reform, the very mention of which, even now, makes the timid woman shake in her shoes" (Russell 1892:339).

What was the dress like that they wanted to reform? Through the latter half of the nineteenth century a great deal of variation in detail of dress occurred, however, the general characteristics that caused complaints were fairly consistent despite fashion changes. Elizabeth Cady Stanton's remarks of 1857 summarize them rather well. She said:

Woman's dress . . . how perfectly it describes her condition! Everything she wears has some object *external* to herself. The comfort and convenience of the woman is never considered; from the bonnet string to the paper shoe, she is the hopeless martyr to the inventions of some Parisian imp of fashion. Her tight waist and long, trailing skirts deprive her of all freedom of breath and motion. No wonder man prescribes her sphere. She needs his aid at every turn. He must help her up stairs and down, in the carriage and out, on the horse, up the hill, over the ditch and fence, and thus teach her the poetry of dependence.

There is a philosophy in this dependence not so complimentary to woman as she at the first blush may suppose. Why is it that at balls and parties, when man comes dressed in his usual style, fashion requires woman to display her person, to bare her arms and neck. Why must she attract man's admiration? Why must she secure his physical love? The only object of a woman's life is marriage, and the shortest way to a man's favor is through his passions; and woman has studied well all the little arts and mysteries by which she can stimulate him to the pursuit. Every part of a woman's dress has been faithfully conned by some French courtesan to produce this effect. Innocent girls who follow the fashion are wholly ignorant of its philosophy. Women's attire is an ever-varying incentive to man's imagination — a direct and powerful appeal to his passional nature (quoted by Russell 1892:327).

Some of what Elizabeth Stanton said was applicable mainly in her own time. Hers was, for example, the period of the triumph of the grand nineteenth-century courtesan whose dress was copied by royal princesses and by Victorian upper and middle classes alike (Harrison 1971:34–58). Her denunciation of the treating of woman as sexual object, however, has a contemporary ring. In the 1870's, Elizabeth Stuart Phelps further described the "crimes" of women's dress in this way:

[physicians] assure me of the amount of calculable injury wrought upon our sex by the weight of skirting brought upon the hips, and by thus making the seat of all the vital energies the pivot of motion and centre of endurance. . . . I see women's skirts, the shortest of them, lying (when they sit down) inches deep along the foul floors, which man, in delicate appreciation of our concessions to his fancy in such respects, has inundated with tobacco juice, and from which she sweeps up and carries to her home the germs of stealthy pestilences (quoted by Russell 1892:333).

Elizabeth Phelps thus saw women's dress more as a health than a social hazard.

As a result of these kinds of concerns, attempts were made to initiate reforms in dress that would reduce hazards and allow women more freedom of movement. As early as 1851, a short dress and trouser costume was introduced by Elizabeth Smith Miller (Russell 1892:328). Elizabeth Cady Stanton and Susan B. Anthony adopted it; Lucy Stone lectured and traveled in such a costume, and Amelia Bloomer publicized it in her Seneca Falls, New York, newspaper, called the *Lily*, and wore it the longest. As a consequence, she has been immortalized for her efforts by having descendents of the trouser outfit named after her. Most of the women could not stand the censure and ridicule heaped upon them by press and public, and wore the costume for only two or three years. Amelia Bloomer apparently had greater stamina, for she said that she wore her trouser costume for six or seven years. And the generation gap is not new: when Lucy Stone visited Lucretia Mott and Lucretia's daughters begged her not to wear her bloomer costume, and even refused to walk on the street with her, she bought herself a dress to save her friends from embarrassment (Hays 1961:115).

Most of those interested in the dress reform movement saw the bondage of dress as interrelated with a number of factors causing general oppression of women. However, some disagreement existed concerning whether a woman's dress was the cause of or simply the result of her subordination. Lucy Stone, for example, firmly espoused the view that dress reform would only follow reform in social attitudes that reinforced subordination of women, as she said:

I do not expect any speedy or widespread change in the dress of women until as a body they feel a deeper discontent with their present entire position. . . . Her miserable style of dress is a consequence of her present vassalage not its cause (quoted by Russell 1892:328).

However, Gerrit Smith, a supporter of the women's movement and father of feminist Elizabeth Smith Miller, expressed in a letter to his cousin Elizabeth Cady Stanton his belief that a change in dress could be effective in bringing about changes in attitudes toward women by saying:

I admit that the dress of woman is not the primal cause of her helplessness and degradation. That cause is to be found in the false doctrines and sentiments of which the dress is the outgrowth and symbol. On the other hand, however, these doctrines and sentiments could never have become the huge bundle they are now, and they would probably have all languished, and perhaps all expired, but for the dress. For as in many other instances, so in this, and emphatically so in this, the cause is made more efficient by the reflex influence of the effect. Let woman give up the irrational modes of clothing her person, and these doctrines and sentiments would be deprived of their most natural expression (quoted by Kraditor 1968:126).

As she replied, Elizabeth Stanton clearly indicated she did not share Gerrit Smith's confidence that change in dress would lead to other liberating social changes for women. Part of her response was as follows:

When woman shall stand on an even pedestal with man — when they shall be bound together, not by withes of law and gospel, but in holy unity and love, then, and not until then, shall our efforts at minor reforms be crowned with complete success. Here, in my opinion, is the starting point; here is the battleground where our independence must be fought and won. A true marriage relation has far more to do with the elevation of woman than the style and cut of her dress. Dress is a

matter of taste, of fashion; it is changeable, transient, and may be doffed or
donned at the will of the individual; but institutions, supported by laws, can be
overturned but by revolution. We have no reason to hope that pantaloons would
do more for us than they have done for man himself. The negro slave enjoys the
most unlimited freedom in his attire, not surpassed even by the fashions of Eden
in its palmiest days; yet in spite of his dress, and his manhood, too, he is a slave still
(quoted by Kraditor 1968:130).

A review of what followed the nineteenth-century crusades for reform
sheds light on the extent to which all three spokesmen were correct in
their prophecies concerning change in women's dress. By the last decade
of the nineteenth century new laws allowed women property rights in
marriage of which they had previously been deprived — and also rights to
their own earnings. In addition, limited suffrage was extended to women
in a number of states, and women were entering colleges, even coeduca-
tional ones, in growing numbers. The invention of the typewriter brought
jobs for women and encouraged the fashion of the shirtwaist and skirt, as
a sort of female counterpart of the man's business suit; but it was hardly a
liberating outfit, considering its floor length and the corsets worn beneath
it. However, some small breaks with tradition were seen. For example, a
late nineteenth-century enthusiasm for trying to achieve health through
physical culture resulted in the springing up of gymnasiums in towns and
cities across the country; and the despised bloomers, ironically enough,
were given the stamp of approval for gymnastics, as well as for cycling,
which was also thought to provide health-giving exercise.

Not until the First World War brought women into greater numbers of
occupations did really drastic changes in women's dress begin to take
place. First, the many layers of heavy cotton and wool underwear, which
custom had required for so long, were replaced by a few silk or soft,
mercerized cotton garments. Thus women were at last freed from a
tremendous burden of weight. A second revolution, in the amount of
coverage provided by outer garments, came with the 1920's, the decade
that may be better remembered for the stunning change that took place in
women's dress — the uncovering of women's legs — than the fact that
suffrage came to women. American society had never been exposed to
such an exhibition of women's legs before!

As a matter of fact, the comparative freedom of women's dress of the
1920's made the male's dress appear restrictive by comparison. And the
fact apparently did not go unnoticed: in 1929 an Englishman, Dr. Alfred
Jordan, in an article that had both English and American audiences,
pleaded with men to unite in the Men's Dress Reform Party which had as
its goal to ameliorate "the plight of poor, overclothed and suffocated
man." To quote Dr. Jordan:

When women feel dissatisfied with their clothes, why, they try something different, and then go on changing from year to year without asking leave of their man-folks, although more often than not, it is they (the men) who "foot the bill."

Men, on the other hand, are timid creatures, fearful of defying convention and thus inviting chaff. Dissatisfied as they are with their clothes, few men have the courage to change their style of dress (Roach and Eicher 1965:305–306).

But if man's dress, such as his suit, is, as Dr. Jordan says, an enslavement of men, why have twentieth-century women wanted to include a version of his suit in their selection of costumes? This writer inadvertently found some answers to this question in responses that young women made in a discussion of the changing social symbolism of women's dress in the twentieth century. They contributed the following observations:

The pants suit can be used as an example of our women's desire and ability to do any man's job.
     This trend toward women wearing pants . . . would indicate that women wish to take over more of man's role. Woman now has left her happy home in full pursuit of demeaning the superiority of her husband by endeavoring to support the family.

Rather wistfully, it seemed, one young woman said, in referring to the pants suit: "Women, however, are more feminine than ever." Apparently she had some fears that something valued might be lost!

In these somewhat emotionally charged statements the young women revealed their sensitivity to the fact that social prestige is achieved by males through their work. They also perceived a man's suit, or an equivalent thereof, either as a measure of equality with men or as a symbolic demand for freedom from tradition that marks women as inferior or subordinate. It is no accident that men express no similar kind of desire to wear skirts, for psychological gain would not be anticipated. Who wants to adopt the symbols of low status!

Today, a woman has socially approved access to a variety of forms of dress that can provide her more physical comfort and mobility in her various activities than custom allows men. She has lightweight garments for warm weather, bifurcated garments for active sports and work. She can shift her costume to fit her various roles, and has considerable leeway in choosing costume appropriate to a particular role. Her costume, therefore, no longer places her in a physically handicapped and physically dependent position, as it so obviously did in the nineteenth century. But, as Elizabeth Stanton predicted "pantaloons" have not brought her status equal to that of men. Ironically, by their mere variety her clothes, even when a rational adaptation to her surroundings, connote a lower prestige, presumably because males, who have traditionally been the recipients of prestige, do not display such variety. Symbolically her body and her variety in dress, as they reveal and announce her sex, connote subordinate position and will continue to do so as long as American society places less value on roles performed mostly by women, or gives smaller rewards to women when their role performance is equal to or superior to that of men fulfilling the same roles.

Currently some changes in men's and women's fashions suggest that accommodations to a changing role structure are being made. Thus trends to what has been dubbed "unisex" dress, or for men to engage in display in dress as much as women, may be clues indicating that some roles, once assigned exclusively to either males or females, are becoming mutually shared, or what may be called human, roles. For example, late twentieth-century men help with child care, a woman's exclusive task in the nineteenth century. In addition, women as well as men are providers, engaged in gainful employment to help provide for family needs. If, indeed, more social roles are being seen as human roles, dress may be perceived more as dress for human beings rather than as a means of symbolically placing males or females in superior–inferior relationships.

In retrospect, Lucy Stone, Gerrit Smith, and Elizabeth Cady Stanton were all accurate in their predictions concerning reform in women's dress. Lucy Stone was right, for only after a number of legal changes, and accompanying slow shifts in social attitudes, did much reform in women's dress occur. Gerrit Smith was right, for only after women had short costumes and trousered costumes could they actually perform activities that required special physical dexterity. And Elizabeth Stanton was right, for wearing trousers and nonrestricting clothing did not automatically provide either elevated status or greater role opportunities, particularly in occupations, for women.

REFERENCES

HARRISON, MICHAEL
  1971   *Fanfare of strumpets*. London: W. H. Allen.
HAYS, ELINOR
  1961   *Morning star: a biography of Lucy Stone, 1818–1893*. New York: Harcourt, Brace and World.
KRADITOR, AILEEN S., *compiler*
  1968   *Up from the pedestal: Selected writings in the history of American feminism*. Chicago: Quadrangle.
ROACH, MARY ELLEN, JOANNE B. EICHER, *editors*
  1965   *Dress, adornment, and the social order*. New York: John Wiley and Sons.
RUSSELL, FRANCES E.
  1892   A brief survey of the American dress reform movement of the past, with views of representative women. *Arena* 6.
VEBLEN, THORSTEIN
  1953   *The theory of the leisure class*. Mentor Books. New York: New American Library. (Originally published 1899.)

SECTION FIVE

Technology and Textiles

Tablet Weaving by the Jews of San'a (Yemen)

A. KLEIN

In the middle of the nineteenth century, in upper Egypt, a woven linen belt five meters long was purchased. It was blue, red, yellow, and green in color, its intricate pattern and strong weave indicating a very highly developed technical knowledge. This belt, known today as the Girdle of Ramses, and exhibited at the City Museum of Liverpool, was until the first quarter of this century dated 1200 B.C. (Schuette 1956:18). In 1931, Margarete Scharlau-Staudinger, with much painstaking effort, succeeded in reconstructing the Ramses girdle by the ancient tablet-weaving technique known throughout the world (see Kosswig 1967:71). Relying on this reconstruction, Krauss (1931) reestimated the date of the girdle to an earlier period, about 3000 B.C.[1] If the girdle was indeed made by the tablet-weaving technique, as in the method of reconstruction, then this technique has been known for more than 5,000 years.

In the past ninety years, many anthropologists have explored and researched this technique and its geographical distribution. The pioneers were Knapp (1888), who wrote about tablet weaving in Bukhara, and Lehmann-Filhes (1896) who, working from a hint in an old Icelandic poem,[2] recognized an unidentified exhibit in a Copenhagen museum as cards threaded with warp. This helped identify other similar objects, such as those found in Norway: fifty-two wooden cards, prepared for work with linen warp, discovered in the tomb of the Viking Queen Asa (about A.D. 850), now exhibited in an Oslo museum (Kosswig 1970a:6).

The sensation caused by Lehmann-Filhes's demonstration stimulated

---

[1] According to Kosswig (1970a:6). Eighteen years earlier Lee had arrived at this conclusion. Lee (1913) writes that the Ramses girdle belongs to an ancient technique known from archeological finds dating from 3000 B.C.

[2] Freely translating from Bartels (1898a:39): Hunnish maiden/Weaving with cards/Does lovely gold.

much interest in tablet-weaving technique. Researchers started out in search of tablet weavers and weavings. Men and women weaving with the tablet technique were found, in addition to northern Europe, in Egypt, China, the Caucasus, and Turkey (Kosswig 1970a:9).[3] Bartels found in a Moscow museum, in the Caucasus exhibition, threads and cards which reminded him of those found by Lehmann-Filhes. During his trip from the Caucasus to Kutais, Bartels saw a man weaving with cards with gold and silver thread. He tried to establish a connection between the weaving in the Caucasus with that in Iceland (Bartels 1898a:39): do we see here an imported technique, or local development in different places at the same time?[4] La Baume gives an historical survey of weaving in early Europe as well as a long description of tablet-weaving technique (1955:58–59, 64–80, 96–106, 160–163).

Many theories have been advanced about the beginning of tablet and brocade weaving. Flanagan attributes the invention of the loom and brocade work to China from whence it was transported by Sassanian monks to Persia and from there to Europe (1919:167). Robinson maintains that it started in Mesopotamia (1969:10). Lehmann-Hautt sees Egypt as its birthplace (Kosswig 1970a:6). Although this question was much debated around the 1900's, there were no conclusive results.

Many books have been written which have contributed much to the knowledge of weaving and weaving cultures. Heiden (1909) wrote about the weaving technique and its development; Geijer (1964) describes the textile treasures found in excavations at Birka. It is interesting to see the parallels between bands found in Scandinavia and those as given by Kosswig (1970b:plates 11, 12, 15), Schuette (1956:1, 28), and Atwater (1954:illustrations 1, 2, 7).

Tablet weaving in southern Arabia was not researched. However, in the literature about the Jews in Yemen, we find some notes about weavers, but there is little mention of tablet weaving. Interest in Yemenite handicrafts (weaving, embroidery, gold and silver work, and so on) began in this century with the immigration of some one hundred Jews from Yemen to Palestine, which was then under Turkish rule. The difficult economic conditions in Jerusalem during the twenties and thirties created much poverty among these immigrants. Women volunteers created a project called *Shani* which was designed to help them: they supplied the materials and employed the adults in the craft work that they knew. The director of *Shani*, Hadasa Rosenblüth, met with Carl Rathjens, the orientalist from Hamburg, who was then visiting Palestine on his

---

[3]   Kosswig mentions that Professor Ritter reported orally on the existence of this technique in Turkey, still in use at the beginning of the First World War.

[4]   Bartels's question began many arguments among archeologists, historians, and ethnologists. Bartels saw the geographical distance between the Caucasus and Iceland as prohibitive of the transfer of the technique from place to place.

way to Yemen. She asked him to investigate the Jewish quarter in San'a and to purchase examples of weaving, embroidery, and gold and silver work (Rosenblüth 1945:98). Rathjens brought much embroidery and many weavings back with him which today are in the Hamburg Museum. The duplicates in this collection are now in the Israel Museum. The examples that Rathjens bought are important since he is the only person who actually saw these articles in use in Yemen.[5]

Other travelers to Yemen wrote about weaving but did not describe it in any detail. Sapir, who was there in 1854, tells of many villages of weavers (1945:54, 73, 84, 123, 183). Yavnieli who was there in the twenties, gives village statistics according to profession. In his diary we find information about Jewish weavers but he does not specify what kind of weaving.

Two researchers who wrote about Yemenite Jews were Brauer and Goitein. Brauer (1934:203) states that the work of weaving was a very honored profession in San'a. Elsewhere he writes about belts and he classifies them as narrow weavings (1945). Goitein (1955) described the community life of a village of Jewish weavers Al Gades, in Yemen, but not their work. Card weaving among the San'a Jews was mentioned in works by two Yemenite Jews:[6] Kafeh (1961:244) mentions the *Yiška-Tizig*, who is the weaver of *silsulim*[7] narrow bands woven with silver weft threads. The second researcher, Habara, is the only one who gives any kind of description of the weavers themselves and of the weaving technique (1970:345–350). From the description in Habara's book and from supplementary information received in meetings with him, it was possible to learn the method and technique of *Al-Tizig*: the work of weaving bands with silver and gold weft for various uses.

Tablet weaving in San'a as a means of earning a livelihood diminished in the last hundred years, until after the First World War it became the monopoly of a few Jewish families who supplied bands and belts to the Iman's household and the Muslim aristocracy. During this period, the craft suffered three crises, each of which had such severe effects that it nearly disappeared.[8] The importation of embroidery thread (mercerized cotton) from England via Aden, Asmara, or India was the first. The

---

[5]   Rathjens visited Yemen four times during the years 1927–1938. He bought new and used items. He labeled each item with its name and price, the person who made it, who wore it and the specific occasion on which it was worn, whether it was made for Jews or Muslims, and so on.

[6]   Tabib (1931:42) also gives a generalized description of weaving, which was light work for men who were Torah scholars.

[7]   Derived from the Aramaic word *silsula*, which is a braid of bands or narrow belts. These are usually associated with the decoration of women's dress. The weaver of gold and silver threads is called *silsulai*.

[8]   I was told in conversation with elders of the San'a Jewish community who were card weavers in Yemen before emigrating to Israel about the crises which their families lived through in connection with their craft.

availability of cheap ready-made threads popularized embroidery as a craft. Embroidered borders were used as decorative trimming instead of the bands woven of hammered silver and gold thread (this was also the beginning of the process that led to the separation of weaving from gold and silver work).

At the beginning of the century, Yemen was still under Turkish rule. The Turks were interested in a steady supply of local woven goods for their army. They introduced mechanical looms and imported Turkish experts to teach the young people to work them. This was the second crisis: the old people could not learn the new methods needed for these complicated machines. They were, therefore, out of work and had to seek a new trade. Most of them became Torah scribes or small businessmen. When the Turkish army left Yemen after the First World War, the experts left with them. Imports from Turkey lessened and later stopped altogether. Threads, replacement parts, and experts became unavailable. The young people left the Turkish looms, so the older weavers who earlier had left the craft took their apparatus out of storage and resumed weaving. But the old style of weaving existed only in memory. Neither the technique, which demanded great expertise, nor the designs, had ever been written down. Old bands had been used sometimes as patterns, but it depended on the memory of the weaver to conceive and execute them. So, after this long interval of nonpractice, many had forgotten the method. As a result, the techniques which had been passed down through generations were remembered by only a few families.

The third crisis occurred before the Second World War. German industry had been dealing commercially with Yemen since the end of the last century, exporting dyes and threads. When German textile experts arrived in Yemen in the thirties in connection with expanding this export trade, they saw the belts and bands of the Jewish weavers. These interested them greatly and they studied their brocade technique. They brought the technique back to Germany and transferred it from the simple apparatus in Yemen to their modern mechanical looms. With much success they added new designs and a greater variety of colors. They then exported these bands in great quantities back to Yemen. Because of their mass production, they were much cheaper than the handwork and nearly supplanted the local product. This additional blow angered the Jews of San'a who, until then, had considered their profession open to all who wanted to learn. They had not feared local competition because the quality of work had always been the determining factor of the sale.

The families who supplied the Imam's household brought this to his attention. They complained that local production and the families engaged in it were endangered. The Imam responded positively and prohibited the import of belts similar to the work of the Jews and reduced the import of bands in general. From the elders of the San'a Jewish community in Israel, I learned that the Iman's main supplier of bands, Al Sheikh Halevy, swore his sons to secrecy. Now, the profession could not be taught to anyone outside the family.[9]

These three crises, then, helped create the situation that exists today. We know of the craft only from the few remarks in the bibliographic sources mentioned above and the few samples of the belts themselves in private collections, and in the Rathjens collection in the Hamburg and Israel museums.

In Israel, there is now no one among the Jews of Yemenite descent who is active in this weaving either for private or business purposes. There are, however, a few old people who had woven in San'a and still remember how it is done. One of them built a model of the "loom" and reconstructed the work of one of the bands. This apparatus is now in the Israel Museum.[10]

THE APPARATUS AND ITS ACCESSORIES

The apparatus is simple to prepare, easy to assemble, light and portable.[11] No professional skill is required to build it; every weaver can construct his own.[12] It is built from a wooden board called *u'di*, 180 to 250 centimeters long and 15 to 20 centimeters wide. At each end is nailed at right angles a vertical board called *ǧaneb* [hands]. These are 30 centimeters high and the width corresponds with that of the *u'di*. The weaver sits in front of the middle of the *u'di*, with the woven band to his left and the warp to his right. About 15 centimeters in from the right *ǧaneb* there is a wooden pin, attached to the far side of the *u'di*. It is stuck in a hole made in the side of the *u'di* and further fastened by a crude string. This pin functions like the

---

[9] Habara mentions the vow of the Halevy Alsheikh family (1970:348).

[10] Thanks to the initiative of Mrs. Zohar, who is an expert on embroidery, the belt which appeared in Habara's book was reconstructed on a special apparatus which the weaver built for the purpose and which was ordered by Mrs. Lancet-Muller of the Israel Museum.

[11] I prefer to call it "apparatus" even though Shaeffer (1938:542) defines every tool which weaves as a loom.

[12] Card weaving with or without metallic thread can be accomplished by different methods and with various implements. There are several levels of development of the technique: (1) card weaving with two pegs stuck in the earth between which is strung the warp, the work being done with an auxiliary tool (beater, needle, comb): the warp can be as long as five meters (as in Kosswig 1967:191, figure 13); (2) the warp is tied at one end to a nail in a wall or a tree, the other side being attached to the hip belt of the weaver: the tension of the warp is maintained by appropriate movements of the body (Kosswig 1967:105, figure 21); (3) the warp is pulled around pegs which are attached to a board, giving a closed warp of double length (about eight meters); its tension is adjusted by the weaver's knee movements — as Bartels saw in his trip to the Caucasus (1898a:36, figure 1). All the above tools are simple to prepare. They are easy to transport and they can be used out of doors. This is not so with the apparatus described here: because of the heddles it is impossible to work outside.

warp beam on a standard loom. It holds the length of the warp at a given and constant tension (see Plate 1).[13]

Plate 1.   Ǧaneb, the warp's end, and the pin

The Comb

The wooden comb (mušut) orders the warp threads. It is four times wider than the warp: belts six to eight centimeters wide use combs 31 centimeters in length. It is carved finely and precisely by an expert out of a single piece of hazel. Its height is 9 centimeters, the base being five centimeters and the teeth four centimeters.[14] For each five centimeters of comb there are twenty-five teeth, so for a comb 31 centimeters long, there are more than 150 teeth. The base of the individual tooth is one and a half centimeters deep, tapering to the top. Half a centimeter from the top of each tooth there is a hole through which passes a wooden rod which holds the warp threads in place. Through the teeth pass those threads which belong to one card, that is, four threads in each space (Plate 2).

[13]   Looms similar in their basic structure to this one are currently in use on the island of Djerba, Tunisia. One of these is in the Hamburg Ethnological Museum (see Schuette 1956:7). See also the description of a similar apparatus in the chapter on weaving tools in Krauss (1910).
[14]   A comb very similar in its form and size is shown in the figure from Djerba (Schuette 1956:7).

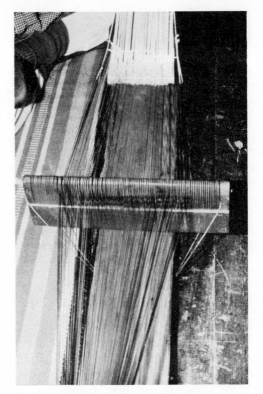

Plate 2.   Comb with the warp inside

The Cards

The cards are called *waraga*. They are square, usually four and a half centimeters, with half a centimeter hole in from each corner. The cards are made of parchment left over from the sheets prepared for the Torah scroll. They were, therefore, of the highest quality, very smooth and thin, only half a millimeter thick, so that in one centimeter there are twenty-one cards. The cards do not bend and do not curl at the edges.[15] When they are not in use, they are tied together with the warp intact. The number of cards is one quarter the number of threads in the warp,[16] and so depends on the width of the band.

[15]   In San'a they prefer to use parchment in spite of its greater cost. Cards are usually made of cardboard, wood, ivory, bone, or hide: parchment is rather rare (Kosswig 1967:67), but it was also found in Morocco (Israel Museum 1973:155).
[16]   In a belt 6 centimeters wide, there are about 300 warp threads and about 75 cards. The Ramses girdle used about 342 cards (Kosswig 1970a:6). The woven belts were usually 6 to 10 centimeters wide.

The Warp

The warp (*sifha*) is prepared without any special tool except for a few nails, on a wall in the room, over which the threads of the warp are passed. The length of the warp is unlimited. Each card is threaded with four threads, one through each hole, according to the scheme of the given design. The warp is fastened to the *ğaneb* by an iron rod one centimeter in diameter which is called the *al-mazqim*. The *al-mazqim* is connected with a single rubber band to the left *ğaneb*. The warp is then pulled the length of the *u'di*, about twenty centimeters above it. The remainder goes around the other *ğaneb* and the warp threads are wound around three wooden sticks. These rest on the far side of the right *ğaneb* and are fastened by the crude string wrapped around the pin (see Plate 1).[17] When the warp and the cards are assembled on the apparatus, the weaver puts the comb through the threads which are then held in place by the wooden rod.

The Heddles

The heddles, *nirim* (in Aramaic)[18] or *fiyam* (in Arabic), are thin wound cotton strings which lift the warp in a predetermined order to get the desired brocade design. Each heddle is tied to a wooden pattern rod above the apparatus, about six centimeters long and one centimeter in diameter. The length of the heddles from the warp to the rod is 60 centimeters. From both ends of the rod a string rises to the ceiling or to a height of two meters from the floor.[19] This is connected at its end to an iron ring. From wall to wall another string passes through this ring parallel to the warp. This enables the heddles to be moved easily along the warp (see Plate 3).

To prepare the heddles, twisted cotton strings 140 centimeters long are folded in two. The middle of the fold is passed over the rod and knotted. We now have two heddles hanging down from the rod. The end of each of these is knotted, the knot being passed under the threads of one card. The two threads of the twisted string of the heddle are separated at a point seven centimeters from the knot and the knot is then passed through it. A loop, called *E'in Hanir* [the mail, i.e. eye of the heddle], is thus formed about four centimeters above the warp. This is an unusual way of prepar-

---

[17]   In the tablet loom from Djerba there is one beam for the weave and two beams which wrap the warp. This maintains the warp tension.

[18]   The *nirim* are mentioned in the Mishnah (Kelim 21:1).

[19]   In the apparatus built for the reconstruction, the strings are pulled up from the sides of the rod. I was told that it is possible to attach it from the middle also, but it is less stable that way.

Plate 3.   Preparation of the heddles

ing the heddle. The mail is steady and does not change its size. It permits easy movement within the warp (see Plate 4).

The number of heddles which are actually worked is the same as the number of the cards, less the threads of the border of the warp (between four and six cards). The heddles are then organized in groups according to the brocade design. In the Star of David design, for example, there are twenty-seven groups. Each group is loosely tied together by a piece of string which then looks like a ring. This ring is called *šalale*.[20] When one group of heddles is raised by pulling the *šalale*, a space is formed in the warp which is called *beit hanir* [shed, i.e. house of the heddle]. The *šalale* represent an improvement on the technique of raising the warp for the pattern. They are prepared beforehand, thereby eliminating the need to count the threads each time. The *šalale* are pulled up and to the side by hand.[21]

[20]   According to what I was told by a Yemenite Jew who had been a weaver in San'a, the work of the heddles predated the work with the cards. The design of the "brocading" used to be done with a needle which helped to raise the threads instead of with the heddles.
[21]   The weaver used to tie the ring to the end heddles in order to make sure that it would not move.

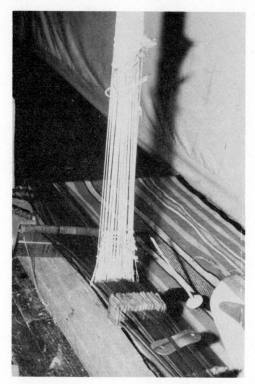

Plate 4.   The order of the implements in the warp: metal thread, shuttle, cards, crossbeams, and comb

The Beater

The beater, *sikin* [knife], is of cast iron, thirty centimeters long. Its form is crude and its surface rough. But the working edge is smooth and blunt so that threads are not caught or cut by it. The straight lines of the weft in the design depend on the tension of the warp and on the smoothness of the well-finished beater (see Plate 5).

The Spindles

There are two kinds of spindles, large and small.[22] One staff is thirty centimeters long with a head diameter of nine centimeters; the second staff is twenty-five centimeters long with a head diameter of six centi-

[22]   The personal choice of the weaver determines which work is done with which spindle, not the size of the spindle.

Plate 5.   Inserting the metal thread and tightening it with a beater

meters. The heads are worked smoothly and symmetrically by a professional woodcarver. There is a hook on the head of each spindle. The larger spindle, *magzal*, is used to wind the threads of the warp and heddles; the smaller, *mabrame*, is used to unwind the imitation metal threads of the brocade (a process not necessary with the hammered metal threads because they are already flat). Kosswig (1970a:24) describes metal threads for brocade which are worked in a similar way. They are unwound to be made flat, but these are the threads of the warp, not those of the weft.

The Shuttle (Spool)

The spool, *malwe*, is carved out of hazel wood. It is ten centimeters long by four to five centimeters wide, and is only half a centimeter thick. Its edges are rounded and smooth. Two centimeters in from each edge is a hole through which pass the silver and gold threads of the weft. The thread is fastened with a knot after one length is threaded. The rest is wound around the width (see Plate 5).

The Thread

The thread of the warp was made of cotton and in earlier times was made entirely at home. The whole family took part in the spinning of the cotton. The weaver prepared the dyes and did the dyeing himself. The dyes were called *dude*, a term which persisted even when commercial ready-made dyes imported from England, Japan, and India were used: these have been available in the market for the last eighty years. The thread of the warp, *nis*, is wound. It is dull, not shiny, with the thickness of normal sewing thread. The colors of the warp were usually black, red, or green; blue was rarely used. The border, of about twenty to twenty-four threads each side, is always different from the warp itself.[23]

The regular weft thread, *sane* or *nahas*, is similar to *moulinée* [six slightly shiny threads loosely plied together]. It is the same color as the warp, but less twisted and thicker. It is wound onto a simple stick.

Gold and silver thread, *šarit*,[24] was brought for the second weft. Originally, hammered pure silver or gold threads were used.[25] Their use has gradually declined in the last hundred years because of the expense of the metals and the ready availability of cheaper imported metallic threads, but it never completely disappeared.[26] The commercial metallic thread is made of two parts, a loosely wound yellow cotton thread, with the metallic thread tightly wound around it. Because *al-tizig* work originated with the hammered metal thread, the weaver must prepare the imitation thread to make it suitable to the technique.[27]

The heddle strings are coarse and thick, about fifteen yarns twisted together. They are similar to fishnet string and chosen for their heavy-duty properties.[28] The ring string is similar to the heddle string. While the heddles are always white, the rings may be in another color, for example red twisted together with white.

WORK METHOD AND DESCRIPTION OF THE BELT

In order to explain the method used in making a *tizig* girdle with gold weft effect I will describe the reconstruction of the work in which a band six centimeters wide with the Star of David design repeated six times was

[23]   Sensitivity to the thinness and uniformity of the warp was great, so it was usual to prepare the threads at home. The weft, which is thicker, was also usually made at home, but they were not so concerned about this. Crowfoot (1931:41) also mentions the sensitivity of the weavers of Egypt and the Sudan to the quality of the warp.
[24]   Rathjens called the gold thread *leonische Faden* (Lancet-Muller 1964:174) and Geijer (1951:66–67) writes that "spun gold thread consists of tinsel wound around a core of silk."
[25]   Concerning gold thread and its preparation, in Yemen, unlike in Europe, India, and other Islamic countries, threads from leather or catgut covered with gold or silver were unknown (cf. Braun-Ronsdorf 1961:5–7).
[26]   Habara (1970:349) states that this is because Muslims were forbidden to wear imitation silver.
[27]   It is interesting that in Kosswig (1970a:24) there is a description of a belt with gold in which the metal threads are worked in a similar way, that is, before weaving they are unwound, not in the weft but in the warp: "Silberumsponnener Seidenlahn fur die Kette."
[28]   See a similar description of the heddles in Crowfoot (1931:43). String of the same width was used also for the borders of the belt.

woven (see Plate 6). This design is called *marbuà* or *sura* and was considered special and expensive. There are 300 warp threads, 75 cards, 75 heddles, and 27 rings or pattern groups.[29]

Before the weaver begins to weave the brocading design, he works a few centimeters with the regular weft. The threads of the warp cover this weft completely. Both sides of the belt, therefore, are the color of the warp. He then strengthens this beginning weave by rubbing melted wax on it. The wax helps prevent the end of the belt from unraveling and ensures its tightness and longevity. After the waxing, he places an iron rod half a centimeter in diameter in the middle of this section. This determines the beginning of the belt. In the same way he distinguishes among the several belts on the warp.

The type of belt the weaver chose to weave for us is called *hazam*, a hip belt designed to hold a short sword called *jambije*. In a belt such as this, the weaver leaves a border about 5 centimeters long to which the buckle will later be attached.

Plate 6.   A sample of a hexagon belt design

[29]   I wish to thank Mrs. Amalia Tidhar, an expert in weaving, for her help in understanding the technique of card weaving and its terminology.

To weave the belt two types of weft thread are used: regular for the basic structure of the belt in the usual manner, and metallic for the brocading. The design appears on the top of the warp and this weft pattern almost completely covers the entire area.

The weaver prepares the metallic threads as he weaves.[30] He sits cross-legged on the floor on a carpet or cushion, takes the smaller spindle (*mabrame*) in his right hand, ties the thread to the staff of the spindle and passes it through the hook (see Plate 7). He places the staff against his thigh and unwinds the threads by rolling the spindle from his thigh toward his knee. The unwound thread he winds onto the staff. He stands up and pulls the thread between his outstretched arms, shoulder height. He then winds it in threes onto the shuttle.[31] Each time he prepares about fifteen

Plate 7.   The preparation of a gold or silver thread and its refinement

[30]   A similar description of the preparation of the thread in this way is given by Schuette (1956:11) of belt weaving with unhammered gold thread in Persia.
[31]   Kosswig (1970a:11, figure 10) describes a belt from Tripoli whose metal weft is prepared from two gold threads. The weaver who demonstrated the work said that three threads are equal to the thickness of the original hammered gold thread.

meters of thread which is enough for sixty rows, about three repeats. He resumes his sitting position and turns the cards through ninety degrees, dividing the warp into two groups. First he passes the regular weft through the shed and beats it down tightly with the beater. He then pulls the appropriate heddle shaft (*šalale*) toward him with his right hand. This isolates the pattern heddles. He lifts these heddles with his left hand to create another shed in the upper part of the warp (see Plate 8). He drops the ring and with his right hand opens this shed wider. With his left hand he then passes the shuttle with the metallic weft through this shed. With the beater he carefully beats the threads together. With each turn of the cards he repeats this entire process, and the threads become intertwined. Because the metallic threads are passed through only the upper part of the warp, the "brocaded" design is seen only from the top. As the metallic weft passes from line to line, it forms a small semicircular loop which extends beyond the border of the warp (see Plate 6).

Those heddles necessary to form the Hebrew letters of the design are grouped together by rings at the bottom, near the warp. Those necessary

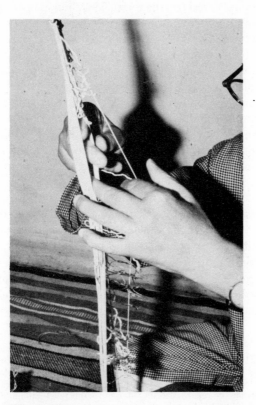

Plate 8. Work with the heddles

to form the Star of David itself are grouped by rings above them, close to the pattern rod. The two uppermost rings divided the heddles into groups of odd and even. Below these come rings, one below the other, in order of their place in the design. The order is the same for the rings on the bottom, that is, each step or line of the design has its own ring.

There are eight steps in the pattern for the letters, and sixteen to form half of the Star of David. These are repeated in reverse order to form the bottom half of the star. An additional row in the middle, between the two halves of the star, row 17, does not repeat. Each repeat is twenty-five rows: eight, sixteen, and one. In an hour the weaver can weave about sixty rows, about fourteen centimeters in length.

The finished product is remarkable in the symmetry and precision of this complicated design. Particularly noteworthy are the letters which are woven along the width of the warp rather than lengthwise as is usual in tablet weaving (Schuette 1956:25; Kosswig 1970b:104, figure 11).

The technique of the heddles, in addition to the cards, offers the weaver opportunities to weave bands or belts which look like the end product of a draw loom. They also enable him to work at a greater speed than he could on the more complicated treadle loom. This then, is not just skilled hands at work. It points to professional knowledge of a high degree.[33]

The belt, at this stage, is not yet ready to be sold. It must first be backed with a leather lining which is sewn to it with leather thong: the portion of the belt not sewn to the lining carries the sewn-in *thouma* [garlic clove], the scabbard of the sword to be held.[34] One end of the belt is finished in a wide V. Two narrow leather straps six centimeters long are sewn to this end, one above the other. The upper one has holes into which the buckle will fasten; to the other end is sewn the buckle. This is the form in which the belt is sold. The purchaser may add various decorations (see Plate 9) such as gold and silver coins, rings, or strips, according to his wealth and rank (Habara 1970:349).

The price of such a belt was between 3 to $3\frac{1}{2}$ rial. If we compare this to the weekly salary of a good tailor in San'a, which was $1\frac{1}{2}$ rial, or that of a goldsmith, which was 2 rial, we see that this was an expensive belt. The weaver's profit, after expenses, would be about $\frac{1}{2}$ rial.

A belt is considered worn out when the metallic threads break and begin to unravel. Once, when the belts were made of hammered metal thread, a worn-out belt would be burned and the metal salvaged and reused. Sometimes, instead of burning the belt, the pieces of metal would

[32]   Lee (1913:92) analyzes the work process of the Ramses girdle and concludes that a belt like this, which has four times more cards than our belt, was done with at least nine heddles.
[33]   According to Schuette (1956:8), "the introduction of a second visible weft thread for brocading may perhaps be regarded as the final step in the development of tablet weaving."
[34]   So-called because of its shape.

Plate 9. Belt with leather lining and *jambije* [sword]

be collected as they broke off the thread.[35] When the belt no longer had any metal left on it, the owner would take it to the weaver and ask for a new belt with the same design. Designs may have included roses, flowers, lines, or geometric patterns (see Plates 10, 11, and 12).[36]

Plate 10. Kerchiefs decorated with the "brocaded" ribbon

[35] I was told that this was the custom in Iraq.
[36] Belts with motifs and geometric forms remarkably similar to these are found in Fez, Morocco, where the work of card weaving is called *mirama* (cf. Israel Museum 1973:154–155). The women used belts to decorate their heads: they added long black silk fringes along the length of the border.

Plate 11.   "Brocaded" hip girdles (*hazam*) in various designs

Plate 12.   "Brocaded" belt for a skullcap

The Star of David design described here was often used by the Muslim aristocracy in Yemen. It appeared not only in woven goods but also in other materials worked by Jews for Muslims, such as carved wooden doors, stone bas-reliefs, coins, and jewelry. This design did not signify to them a Jewish symbol, rather it was a design used by Jewish craftsmen.

CONCLUSION

In the literature about card weaving, tools and products are described. There is also much discussion of "brocaded" belts. But there has never been a step-by-step detailing of the work method used. We have tried, therefore, to give such a description here: that of a weaver who built his loom and wove a belt just as his grandfather used to weave. What is unique about the preparation of a belt such as this by the Jews of San'a is the addition of the heddles. The weave is made with the regular weft, but the "brocaded" design is made with the heddles, which are an improvement bringing about greater efficiency and showing great professional understanding and skill. Weaving supplementary gold weft[37] together with card technique is a very advanced form of weaving.[38] We must accordingly place the achievement of the tablet weavers of San'a on the highest level.

Where or from whom did the Jews of San'a learn this technique? It is hard to say. There are no written accounts of it nor is there any oral tradition referring to it. There is, however, an ancient written source, perhaps the earliest extant, which gives evidence that such work was known to Jews. In the Bible, the Jews are directed to make priestly vestments with hammered silver and gold (Exod. 39:1–3).

REFERENCES

ATWATER, MARY
1954 *Byways in hand-weaving.* New York: Macmillan.
BARTELS, M.
1898a Über das Weben mit Kartenblättern im Kaukasus. *Zeitschrift für Ethnologie* 30:34–39.
1898b Kaukasische Gürtel und Bänder. *Zeitschrift für Ethnologie* 30:329–333.
BRAUER, ERICH
1934 *Ethnologie der jemenitischen Juden.* Heidelberg: Carl Winter.
1945 The agriculture and the arts and crafts among the Yemenite jews. *Shwut Teman* 91–95. Tel Aviv. (In Hebrew.)
BRAUN-RONSDORF, M.
1961 Gold und Silberstoffe vom Mittelalter bis zur Neuezeit. *Ciba Rundschau* 3:1–11.

---

[37] The term *brocade* is not accurate in describing the work with the gold thread in card weaving. In spite of this *brocading* and *brocaded* are commonly used to describe the work of the additional weft of metal in belt weaving (Schuette 1956:8). Forbes (1956:187) says: "The pattern is made by allowing certain threads to pass over more than one thread, i.e. floating either in warp or weft. In the weft this is often called 'brocading'." Emery (1966:171–172) writes: "note . . . that since 'brocading' is primarily a term of weft function. . . ," and "the spools used to carry the 'brocading' weft. . . ," and "the term 'brocading' for example seems to have certain rather widely accepted structural connotations . . . specifically patterning by means of supplementary weft."

[38] La Baume (1955:13) speaks of different levels in the development of weaving and points out that the combination of the technique of card weaving with brocading is "hohere Webtechnik verfahren."

CROWFOOT, GRACE M.
1931   *Methods of hand-spinning in Egypt and the Sudan.* Bankfield Museum Notes 2:12. Halifax: F. King and Sons.

EMERY, IRENE
1966   *The primary structure of fabrics.* Washington, D.C.: Textile Museum.

FLANAGAN, J. F.
1919   The origin of the drawloom used in the making of early Byzantine silks. *Burlington Magazine for Connoisseurs* 34:167–172.

FORBES, R. J.
·1956   *Studies in ancient technology.* Leiden: Brill.

GEIJER, AGNES
1951   *Oriental textile in Sweden.* Copenhagen: Rosenkilde & Bagger.
1964   *Textile treasures of Uppsala cathedral from eight centuries.* Stockholm.

GOITEIN, SH. DOV
1955   Portrait of a Yemenite weaver's village. *Jewish Social Studies* January:3–27.

HABARA, SH. YOSEF
1970   Burden in Yemen and Jerusalem. Jerusalem. (In Hebrew.)

HEIDEN, MAX
1909   *Die Textilkunst des Altertums bis zur Neuzeit.* Berlin.

ISRAEL MUSEUM
1973   Jewish life in Morocco. Jerusalem. (In Hebrew.)

JAVENIELI, SH.
1963   Traveling to Yemen. Tel Aviv: Ayanot. (In Hebrew.)

KAFEH, YOSEF
1961   Customs of Yemen. Jerusalem: Ben Zvi/Hebrew University. (In Hebrew.)

KNAPP, L.
1888   Brettchenweberei in Buchara. *Das Ausland* 61:807.

KOSSWIG, LEONORE
1967   Über Brettchenweberei. *Baessler-Archiv* n.s. 15:71–73.
1970a   *Brettchenweberei und brettchengewebte Textilien im Topaki Saray Museum in Istanbul.* Ankara.
1970b   Carpanacilik ve Istanbul Topkapi Saray müzesinde bulunan carpaner dokumulari. *Türk Etnografya Dergisi* 12:83–109.

KRAUSS, SAMUEL
1931   *Talmudische Archäologie.* Leipzig.

LA BAUME, WOLFGANG
1955   *Die Entwicklung des Textilhandwerks in Alteuropa.* Bonn: Habelt.

LANCET-MULLER, A.
1964   On Jewish embroidery in San'a, Yemen. *Sepher Meir* 7:171–179. (In Hebrew.)

LEE, THOROLD D.
1913   The linen girdle of Rameses III. *Annals of Archaeology and Anthropology* 5:84–96.

LEHMANN-FILHES, M.
1896   Kulturgeschichte aus Island. *Zeitschrift des Vereins für Völkerkunde* 4:376ff.

ROBINSON, STUART
1969   *A history of dyed textiles.* London: Studio Vista.

ROSENBLÜTH, HADASA
1945   *Shani. Shevut Teman* 96–99. Tel Aviv. (In Hebrew.)

SAPIR, JACOB
1945   Travels in Yemen. Jerusalem. (In Hebrew.)
SCHAEFFER, G.
1938   The principle of the loom. *Ciba Review* 2(16):542–545.
SCHUETTE, MARIE
1956   Brettchenweberei. *Ciba-Rundschau* 128.
TABIB, ABRAHAM
1931   The exile in Yemen. Tel Aviv. (In Hebrew.)

Sierra Leone Resist-Dyed Textiles

MAUDE WAHLMAN and ENYINNA CHUTA

Contemporary African textiles are enjoying some success in a United States market eager for handmade rather than machinemade artifacts. This success is due partly to the great range of variations made possible by techniques that capitalize on random designs. The impact of this aspect of African aesthetics on Western appreciation of the arts has not yet been assessed, and perhaps it would be premature to do so before we analyze a system that supports hand-dyed textiles.

Roy Sieber's 1972–1973 traveling exhibition and its accompanying book (Sieber 1972) stimulated a continuing interest in the whole range of African arts, not just traditional wood sculpture. This is especially true of the textile arts which were included in the World Crafts Council exhibition and accompanying book (Paz 1974); in the Field Museum's 1974 traveling exhibition and Wahlman's book (1974); in the African American Institute's exhibition and catalog (African-American Institute 1975); and in the exhibition and catalog by Wahlman (1975).

This paper is an attempt to examine Sierra Leone pattern-dyed textiles from the premise that any artistic endeavor which is successful must be based on or supported by a system with various components which can be studied within the dimensions of technology, economics, and ideology. From a technical point of view we will examine dyers' techniques, dyes, and fabrics. From an economic point of view we will look at dyers, apprentices, customers, and marketing and distribution systems (including the role of middlemen). From an ideological point of view we will look at the design system, which is manipulated by dyers and consumers in efforts to express aesthetic values about textiles and fashion.

By analyzing the interrelationships that exist between the various dimensions in the textile system, we hope to obtain more information about how the system works, about Sierra Leone culture, and about the areas in which information is still lacking.

Many scholars have contributed to the body of knowledge now available on Sierra Leone textiles. Research, some of the results of which are unpublished, has been done by Wahlman in 1970 and 1973, Loretta Reinhardt in 1971 and 1972, Barbara Paxson in 1972 and 1973, Leland Dresser in 1973 and 1974 (Dresser 1974), Nancy Houdek in 1974, and Enyinna Chuta and Miriam Stacy (Chuta and Stacy 1975).[1]

THE HISTORY OF DYEING IN SIERRA LEONE

According to M. A. Tunis, director of the Small Scale Industries Division of the Ministry of Trade and Industry, the art of resist-dyeing of textiles was probably introduced into Sierra Leone in the mid-nineteenth century by Mandinka and Susu peoples who migrated from Guinea into what is now the Northern Province of Sierra Leone.[2] The first pattern-dyed textiles were dyed with indigo, a blue dye made from the leaves of a shrub, *Lonchocarpus cyanescens*, which grows in the Northern Province. Textiles dyed with indigo blue are referred to as *gara* though today the term has a broader meaning and refers to any hand-dyed textiles.

Makeni, in the Northern Province, was the earliest center of textile dyeing. Even today, the bulk of dyed textile production is concentrated in and around this town. By the 1920's dyed textiles were also produced in the towns of Bo and Pujehun, usually by Mandinka women who settled there (see Map 1). Later many dyers moved to Freetown, Sierra Leone's capital and principal port, because it is the largest single market for gara.

Previously, families made their own dyes, and were able to dye enough cloth to meet their own needs and still have some to sell in the local market. This is still true today, but in addition textiles are also produced as a full-time occupation and for a rapidly expanding export market.

DYERS

Chuta and Stacy (1976) interviewed sixteen dyers throughout Sierra Leone as part of a survey of small-scale industries.[3] Of the sixteen dyers, three were men and thirteen women. Though dyeing is traditionally a women's art, it is a family profession; information and techniques are passed along family lines. Women learn how to dye cloth by the time they

[1]   This paper is based mainly on the research done by Wahlman in 1973 and by Chuta and Stacy in 1975, the authors are grateful to the many people who have contributed to the subject, either in print or through personal communication.
[2]   This agrees with Easmon (1924:32).
[3]   Lindblom and Chuta (1976) revealed about 360 small-scale private gara-dyeing establishments, and seven gara-dyeing coooperatives in Sierra Leone, employing about 1,600 people.

Map. 1.   Sierra Leone: towns important to the textile industry

are fifteen years old. Between the ages of five and ten years, girls are sent on errands connected with dyeing, and between ten and fifteen years of age they are taught how to tie various patterns. Today most children are in school, so some dyers take in apprentices who pay to learn dyeing techniques. Two of the thirteen women interviewed had learned the art of dyeing after the age of 25. Of the sixteen dyers twelve had no formal schooling at all, one had finished primary school, and three had some college education.

Traditionally, information about color quality was a carefully guarded family secret. Today, due to the importation of synthetic dyes, knowledge of how dye colors combine to form new colors is based more on experience than on traditional information, formal education, or printed matter. Innovation in design occurs as people try either to copy others' patterns or to develop their own. Information on how to create the designs is not readily imparted to others, so dyers have to copy designs by trial and error, and in the process they sometimes create their own new patterns. Today some tying is farmed out to boys who are paid by the piece (20 cents to $2.20,[4] depending on the complexity of the design). Occasionally tying is done by innovative dyers, or by dyers with free time

---

[4]   All prices are converted from Sierra Leone to United States currency at April 1975 exchange rates.

(such as during the rainy season). Some women specialize in tying patterns, and some tailors create designs with their sewing machines, which are subsequently dyed.

DYEING TECHNIQUES

Three principal resist techniques are used to produce textiles with dyed patterns in Sierra Leone: (1) tie-dye, (2) wax resist, and (3) starch resist. All three methods prevent dye from reaching certain areas of a cloth when it is immersed in a dye bath. Each technique involves a basic step or element which can be repeated either randomly, or in tight configurations, or in combination with basic elements from other techniques. Dyeing techniques are one element in the design system manipulated by dyers and consumers in efforts to express aesthetic preferences concerning textiles and dress. Some textile designs are traditional favorites and are repeated with variations of resist technique, fabric, or dye. Every week new variations on old designs are to be seen in Makeni market square and in Little East Street, the cloth market center of Freetown (Plate 1).

Plate 1.   Little East Street cloth market, Freetown, Sierra Leone. Photograph by James Wahlman, courtesy, Field Museum of Natural History, Chicago

Tie-Dye

Tie-dye can be further classified into at least three techniques called (1) "cloud" (folded patterns); (2) *siti* [sewn patterns]; and (3) *taka* [pleated patterns].

CLOUD PATTERNS.   There are three methods for making the cloud pattern. Kadiatu Kamara, of Freetown, for instance, kneels on the ground to draw a large piece of satin toward her knees (Plate 2), gently folding the cloth with her fingers until it is crushed into a small bundle which is tied with twine. The bundle is soaked in indigo blue dye, unfolded, rinsed, and exposed to the air. As the cloth dries the colors change from greenish to royal blue. This process is repeated for deeper hues.

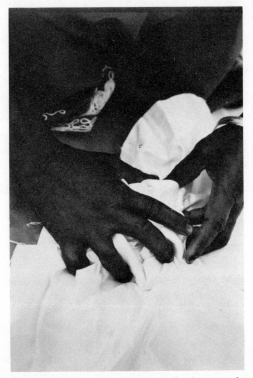

Plate 2.   Kadiatu Kamara folding satin cloth into a cloud pattern for tie-dyeing. Photograph by Maude Wahlman

Hannah Barnet, on the other hand, first soaks the cloth in water, squeezes out the excess, and spreads the cloth over a corrugated iron surface. The material is gathered by hand into a small area and dye is sprinkled over it by the spoonful or handful. After the cloth has absorbed the dye, it is spread out to dry. This method allows for up to forty yards of cloth to be dyed at once. The process is repeated for more elaborate designs, often with more than one color.

A third method for making the cloud pattern is to tie the cloth in loose bunches which resemble clouds. Sewn cloud patterns are crisper than hand-folded examples. Rayon satin is often used for cloud patterns because the satin softens and enhances the random nature of the design (Plate 3).

Plate 3.   Cloud pattern tie-dyed cloth, designed and dyed by Kadiatu Kamara. Photograph by Herta Newton

SITI.   Siti means "sewn" in Mandinka, and refers to patterns created by sewing cloth with thread or raffia in continuous lines of tight tucks which can be arranged in various designs — parallel lines, concentric circles, diagonal lines, and diamond shapes. In 1974 Kadiatu Kamara experimented with siti patterns, all done in traditional diamond-type designs, and with indigo blue and kola-nut brown dyes (Plate 4).

Another type of sewn pattern involves making tiny circles by sewing small individual puffs into cloth. In an overall random design, this is called "cow's eye". When puffs are arranged in circles it is called "record"; smaller circles are called "45 record", while larger circles are called "LP record".

TAKA.   Taka patterns involve pleating fabric and then binding it into a narrow tube. The result is a seemingly simple striped pattern, but when made with two colors, and if repleated between dyes, the result is elegant (Plate 5). The tighter the binding, the sharper the pattern will be. Taka can be made with either parallel or radiating lines, and are often combined with cloud or siti patterns, sometimes in alternating bands. Taka and siti textiles are found throughout West Africa, from Senegal to Nigeria.

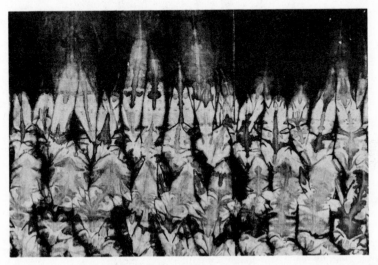

Plate 4. Siti, tied pattern cloth, designed by Kadiatu Kamara. Photograph by Herta Newton, courtesy, Field Museum of Natural History, Chicago

MACHINE-SEWN PATTERNS. Machine-sewn patterns also exist, but they are limited to straight lines and are made by sewing tucks in lines parallel or diagonal to the selvage. If the process is repeated in the opposite direction, the result is a netlike design. Dyers prefer hand-sewn patterns to machinemade ones for several reasons: hand-sewn patterns allow for a greater variety of designs, the double thickness of thread or raffia results in a better resist and thus clearer designs, and hand-sewn threads are easier to remove.

Hand or machine-sewn fabric is dyed by soaking it in cold water for ten to fifteen minutes, then immersing the cloth in dye for fifteen to twenty minutes. The dye is stirred to allow for even penetration of dye through the fabric. Some dyers allow the cloth to dry before untying it. Others loosen part of the fabric while it is wet, retie it, and redye the fabric right away. Sometimes dyers cover parts to be kept white, or parts that have been dyed, with plastic film, to prevent a second dye from changing the white or previous color.

Plate 5.   Taka, pleated tie-dye, designed by Kadiatu Kamara. Photographed by Herta
Newton, courtesy, Field Museum of Natural History, Chicago

Wax-Resist Patterns

Wax-resist patterns, called "candeling", are created in two ways: by
stamping cloth with a wooden stamp that has been dipped in wax, or by
splattering wax on cloth. Ideas for stamped patterns may start with a
drawing on paper — translated into wood by a carver commissioned by a
dyer to make a stamp with a handle. Ready-made stamps can also be
purchased. Some stamped designs are named, just as tie-dye patterns are.

Stamped patterns are created by placing fabric on a table covered with
burlap (to absorb excess wax which will be reused), while a wooden stamp
is dipped in a pot of hot wax kept over a small fire. The dyer stamps the
cloth until most of it is covered with patterns, redipping the stamp into the
wax each time (Plate 6). Care is taken to space the designs evenly over the
cloth, which is then dyed, first in a cola-nut brown if it is to be a two-color
process using indigenous dyes. Fabric may be left in the kola brown dye
overnight to insure a deep rich color. When dry, another pattern is
stamped on the borders and the cloth is immersed in indigo blue dye. The

Plate 6.   Kadiatu Kamara stamping cloth with a wooden stamp which has been dipped into wax. Photograph by Maude Wahlman

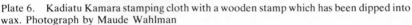

finished cloth has a dark green to black (called "Makeni black") background with white patterns in the center and kola patterns on the borders (Plate 7).

Spattered wax patterns are created by dipping a broom (made of palm leaf ribs tied together) into wax and shaking it over a fabric. The cloth is then dyed, and when dry it can be further decorated with another spattering of wax and redyed. Spattered wax-resist patterns can be combined with stamped wax-resist patterns or with tie-dye patterns (Plate 8).

Starch-Resist Patterns

Starch-resist patterns are made by spreading a cassava or rice flour paste over a cloth, then scraping the wet paste with a comb or the fingers to create wavy designs. The traditional form of this pattern is called *kolinge* [comb] in Mandinka, and exhibits semicircular scallops, similar to fish scales, repeated across a fabric in rows. Each row is offset so that the

Plate 7.   Wax-resist, patterned cloth designed by Kadiatu Kamara. Photograph by Herta Newton, courtesy, Field Museum of Natural History, Chicago

center of the curve falls below the joining ends of two curves in the row above (Plate 9). Kolinge patterns are often done on satin and the cloth may be overdyed with taka stripes.

The various elements of basic patterns used by Sierra Leone dyers can be diagrammed into a taxonomic structure in order to make clearer the overall range of possible pattern combinations (Figure 1). However, another factor in the design system is fabric, for resist patterns can also be applied to a cotton damask cloth which has a textural design woven in. The interaction or balance between fabric type (damask, satin, or plain) and the various dyed patterns is an important factor in the total design system.

All resist-dyed textiles have finishing stages, usually carried out by children or apprentices: stitches are removed by hand, wax is removed by dipping cloth in boiling water, starch is scraped off. Finished fabrics are washed in cold water (sometimes soapy) to remove excess salt, soda, or dye. Then fabrics are rinsed, sometimes in a starchy solution which adds luster to the finished cloth. Fabrics dry before they are pressed, with an iron or by pounding, which is done on folded cloth, placed over a wooden plank, with foot-long clubs, by several young people.

Plate 8. Kadiatu Kamara wearing a splattered wax-resist pattern head tie and holding a stamped, wax-resist cloth. Photograph by James Wahlman, courtesy, Field Museum of Natural History, Chicago

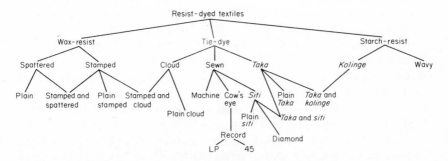

Figure 1. A taxonomy of Sierra Leone resist-dyed textiles

Plate 9.   Kolinge, combed, starch-resist cloth designed by Kadiatu Kamara. Photo by
Herta Newton, courtesy, Field Museum of Natural History, Chicago

DYES

Indigenous dyes (indigo blue and kola-nut brown) were used alone until
the early 1950's when synthetic dyes were first imported. The native dyes
produce patterns in white, a light blue called *fente*, a medium blue called
"butchers' blue", a dark blue, a medium kola brown, a darker kola
brown, and combinations of kola brown and indigo blue which produce a
dark olive green, a dark brown, and Makeni black.

In 1952 two tons of synthetic dyes were imported at a cost of $3,500.
Between 1959 and 1970 the importation of synthetic dyes increased from
three to fifty-four tons annually. In 1971, 57 percent of the imported dyes
came from the United Kingdom, and 42 percent from Germany. The
earliest imported dyes were the aniline type which were not resistant to
sunlight, and thus inappropriate to the tropics.

Attempts to introduce synthetic dyes were promoted by M. A. Tunis
because it was thought that a greater diversity of colored fabrics was
necessary to appeal to the overseas markets in Europe and the United

States. The Small Scale Industries Division assembled dyers from Freetown and the provinces at its Tower Hill office in Freetown, where demonstrations were given on how to use the new synthetic dyes.

The choice of color is up to the dyers, who are influenced by what dyes are available, what sells best, and by special orders from customers. In 1975 synthetic dyes most in demand in Freetown were violet, brilliant green, and brown. Prices for synthetic dyes in 1975 ranged from $16 per pound for blue to $23.65 per pound for violet or brown.

The native dyes are less expensive, but need more time to prepare. Indigo blue dye is made from the leaves of a plant which grows in the Northern Province, especially around Kamakwie and Kabala. The young leaves are collected, pounded, and dried or molded into small balls and then dried. This product is sold directly to dyers or to merchants who market it to dyers in forty-pound sacks.

Indigo dye solutions can be prepared in many ways. One method begins with washing about ten pounds of leaves and throwing away the water. Then the leaves soak in a tightly woven basket for two to four days before being put into a forty-four-gallon drum two-thirds full of water. One tin of soda is added, and the solution ferments for three days. On the fourth day, 44 cents worth of *wanda*, a native root, *Morinda germinata*, used as a fixing agent, is added. The solution stands for two more days, until it is ready, which means it is no longer slippery to the touch.

A second method differs only in that two tins of synthetic blue dye are added during the final stage for a darker blue. A third method starts with soaked leaves, washed in a basket, and then covered with plum leaves, *Spondias monbin*, for three to seven days. The mixture ferments until the seventh day when the leaves are put into a forty-four-gallon drum with 44 cents worth of wanda. Then a solution, made by draining water from boiled tea-bush leaves, *Hyptis suaveolens*; Christmas tea leaves, *Alchornea cordifolia*; rat ear leaves, *Portulaca oleracea*; and a tree bark, *Lophira lanceolata*, is added to the indigo dye bath with enough cold water to fill the drum two-thirds full. Two tins of soda are added and the solution is mixed and allowed to stand for four to five days. Then two tins of synthetic blue are added and the solution is left to stand for another three days. Actually, there could be as many variations for making indigo dye as there are dyers in Sierra Leone.

Each forty-four gallon drum full of indigo is supposed to be good for continuous use for six months. However, the dye is always reinforced by the addition of more soda and more synthetic blue dye.

Kola-nut brown dye is made by pounding entire kola nuts, *Cola acuminata* or *Cola nitida*. Three hundred nuts are supposed to be sufficient to make enough dye for twenty pieces of cloth. The pounded nuts are combined with three gallons of water, which is drained and saved while the nuts are pounded again, again mixed with water, and drained.

The process is repeated; then all the water and nuts are strained through burlap. The dye is then ready.

Climate adds another variable to the technological dimension, for during the rainy season it is difficult to dye cloth. Steady sunlight is needed to dry fabric fast enough to make the process efficient, so most fabric is dyed in the dry season, between October and April, and most of the cloth is sold during this period.

MATERIALS

Many dyers prefer to work with 100 percent cotton cloth, and that which is most in demand is a cotton damask with white-on-white designs that comes in varying widths and qualities (32, 36, 50, and 52 inches are available; the widest is most desirable). Material is sold by the bolt length of 20, 30, or 40 yards. Poplin is also very much in demand, and comes in several colors. Rayon satin is also popular, especially for men's shirts and women's fancy dresses, and is available in white or colors. In Freetown in July 1975 fabric prices ranged from 66 cents a yard for poplin, 88 cents for satin, and $1.37 to $3.02 for damask. More recently corduroy has been available at $2.20 a yard.

Competition is strong among dyers in the Freetown area. The incentive is not only to produce new designs, but also to introduce new fabrics. Dyers search the stock of suppliers for new and different fabrics, and if they find something they like that is suitable, they may buy up all available stock in order to have a monopoly. Competition has led to the use of jersey, toweling, chiffon, corduroy, velvet, lace, and polyester fabrics.

ECONOMICS

The pricing and distribution of the finished piece of cloth from the dyers' workshops to the consumer is now following a more intricate path than the original dyer-in-the-marketplace selling directly to the consumer. Dyed cloth is sometimes sold directly from the dyer's home, but more often by *woko woko* boys and girls who sell cloth on the street from a bundle carried on their heads.[5] Dyed cloth is also sold in Makeni Square, Bo Market, and Little East Street in Freetown (the last a specialized cloth market area). Small businessmen rent shop space or establish themselves at the curb. As everywhere in West Africa, one bargains for textiles, usually getting the best price for buying in large quantity. The average market price for a two-yard *lappa* in 1973, for example, was $3.75.

[5] *Woko* means "go" in Mandinka. *Woko woko* boys and girls are the children of middlemen who buy cloth from dyers, wholesale.

An alternative method of marketing developed in 1971, when the Ministry of Trade and Industry established the Sierra Leone arts and crafts cooperative. By 1974, a small shop was opened for dyers at the peace corps office in Freetown, with the help of Leland Dresser, a Peace Corps volunteer. Staff to run the shop were paid by the Ministry of Trade and Industry.

In 1973, Leland Dresser and his wife studied the economic aspects of selling textiles through this shop. They were kind enough to provide their breakdown of the costs involved in producing a yard of resist-dyed cotton cloth in March 1974, assuming that yard was part of a larger length of material:[6]

Cloth	$1.52
Dye	0.52
Wax	0.07
Soda	0.16
"Powder"	0.04
Wood	0.04
Assistant's labor	0.16
Transportation	0.19
Shop expenses	0.32
Dyer's profit	0.17
	$3.19

So the total was $3.19 a yard or $6.38 for a two-yard *lappa*. Three-and-a-half-yard lengths were also available at $3.19 a yard for dresses.

A brochure was printed in 1973 advertising traditional artifacts, African clothing, resist-dyed textiles, and other contemporary African arts. As listed in this new brochure, the average price for a resist-dyed cloth made with good damask was $6.50. Other prices for two-yard pieces were: poplin $5.20, better damask $7.17, heavy rayon satin $7.20, and light rayon satin $4.55. Bedspreads and wall hangings were also available. Most export orders were from Europe at that time, with some interest from the United States. Since export orders were prepaid by half, the shop could advance dyers enough money for fabrics and dyes. The shop shipped export orders with a slip of paper in each cloth, which identified the individual dyer and gave washing instructions.[7]

---

[6] According to Leland Dresser, in 1974 most dyers could process between twenty and thirty yards of cloth a day. All did not turn out well so the average income per dyer was $1.60 per day. This was considered good since per capita income in 1974 was less than $164 a year (this includes 70 percent unemployment) and skilled labor could earn only $1.87 a day. Chuta (1978) reported that all private gara dyers in Sierra Leone averaged between $880 and $3,300 in annual earnings.

[7] A note on importation: since prices for cloth and dyes fluctuate, and since the Sierra Leone arts and crafts cooperative has begun to add charges for packaging and insurance on export orders, it is best to get a written agreement on costs before ordering large quantities of cloth. The prices are still reasonable since the role of middlemen is minimized. Air freight from Sierra Leone, at $3 a pound for less than a hundred pounds, is very expensive so it is

Cooperatives, however, are not too successful because they have reduced both individual incentive and individual control over buying supplies and selling the product. Seven dyers' cooperatives existed as of February 1978.

Of the one million square yards of gara produced annually, 18 percent is exported to the United States and Europe. Larger quantities than that are traded to such eastern Sierra Leone towns as Koindu and Kailahun, and from there to Liberia, Guinea, and the rest of West Africa (Chuta 1978:19). It is said that a cloth with a new design can travel from a dyer in Sierra Leone to a customer in Lagos, Nigeria, in one week. Dresser (1974) writes that he recognizes Sierra Leone resist-dyed fabrics in the tourist markets of Nairobi on the opposite coast of Africa.

FASHION

Hand-dyed textiles are such an important economic item in West Africa that many people continually compete to make new designs. Others are buying, selling, tailoring, embroidering, and wearing the newest designs, for West Africans are a fashion-conscious people and new designs are important elements in the expression of personal values.[8] Dyed fabrics have long been purchased for use in costume, but since independence in 1961 Sierra Leoneans have worn hand-dyed fabrics as an expression of national pride. The same is true elsewhere in West Africa, and applies also to hand-woven fabrics.

Gara is dyed in pairs (each piece is approximately two yards long) because women traditionally bought two cloths — one for a wraparound skirt (*lappa*) and the other for a blouse (*bakat*) and head tie — or the two pieces of cloth could be sewn into a long formal dress. Often the blouse or the long dress is further decorated with formal geometric embroidery.[9] In this way, the customers further manipulate elements in the design system, by combinations of dyed textiles and embroidery (Figure 2).

---

best to specify that textiles be sent by parcel post, for which one has to allow three to four months delivery time. A Chicago customs official told Wahlman that, when importing textiles into the United States, one should obtain an affidavit from the dyers stating that the textiles were handmade arts. Without such an affidavit, hand-dyed textiles are subject to the import duties charged on all textiles. If large amounts (over $250 worth) are imported, one also needs a letter from a local museum stating that hand-dyed textiles from Africa are considered contemporary African arts. This should not be difficult since these textiles have been exhibited in several museums.

[8]   See Wahlman (1974:14) for aesthetic preferences as of 1973.

[9]   Embroidery is usually applied with a sewing machine (French chain-stitch machines seem to produce the preferred type of stitches), typically by self-employed artisans.

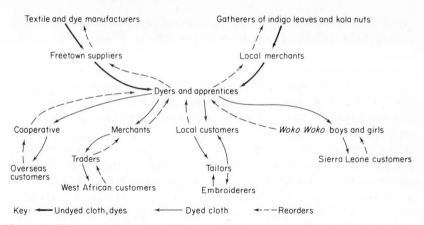

Figure 2. The economic system of Sierra Leone resist-dyed textile production

Men also buy cloth, either by the piece or as ready-made embroidered shirts. Men have the cloth tailored into shirts and pants, sometimes with embroidery and sometimes in the style of Western clothing, without embroidery. Children are often seen dressed in hand-dyed fabrics. Recently Chuta documented the use of identical hand-dyed cloths, in red or blue, as school uniforms worn by the girls of Bo Rosary School.

As the variety and quality of dyed designs increases, and as the market expands, dyed fabrics seem to be utilized and appreciated by more sectors of Sierra Leone and West African society. The dyer Miriam Foray of Freetown was commissioned to produce ceremonial robes for President and Mrs. Tolbert of Liberia in 1974, an indication that contemporary dyed textile arts are beginning to symbolize political consciousness in a way previously reserved for traditional handwoven cloth.

THE DESIGN SYSTEM

Throughout the discussion of techniques, dyes, fabrics, dyers, marketing economics, and fashion, we have referred to design systems, consisting of small pattern elements (fabric types, technique types, and embroidered designs) which are combined with each other in many ways, but according to aesthetic rules which have never been analyzed formally. For instance, some damask patterns are preferred for combination with certain dyed patterns, certain dye colors, and certain embroidered patterns.

Since the damask is imported, while dyeing and embroidering are done by separate entrepreneurs, the coherence of the total aesthetic system seems to rely on some implicit communication. Of all the people in the total textile system, the dyer has a broader range of elements to choose from than anyone else, yet certain combinations are consistently repeated with slight variations. This implies that within the total range of possible design element combinations, certain combinations are repeatedly selected by the dyer, in accordance with a conscious or unconscious cultural ideal for textile aesthetics. One sees this especially in the contrast between textile designs for a West African market, which are very selective and those produced for an overseas market, which exhibit a random combination of design elements.[10]

The design system, or the ideological dimension, is the least explored and needs the most work if the whole textile system is to explain certain aspects of West African culture fully. We need to know, first, the criteria for creating textiles for the local and West African markets, as opposed to production for export. Then, in reference to textiles for the West African market, we need to know which elements are always used together, which types of elements are interchangeable, what the rules are for creating new textile designs, and how the design system allows for innovation.

CONCLUSIONS

Chuta (1978:1, 23) has noted that of all the small-scale industries in Sierra Leone, gara dyeing, dominated by women, has the highest profit rate, the greatest export potential, and a net growth rate of five percent. Furthermore, the traditional dyers who use native indigo dyes earn the highest economic rate of return on capital (1978:29). Recommendations for future growth include: use of extension agents to teach people how to minimize waste of commercial dyes and how to mix them to produce secondary colors, reorganization of cooperatives to allow for greater decision-making by dyers, centralization of international marketing, and rebates of import duty on all cloth and dyes used to produce gara for export.

Several subsystems appear to be operating within a larger system of Sierra Leone resist-dyed textiles. A technological system is at the core, with interactions between dyers, suppliers, climate, and techniques. An economic system includes interactions between dyers, middlemen, apprentices, and customers (Figure 2). An ideological design system is shared by dyers, who manipulate dyes, techniques, and fabrics; and consumers who manipulate dyed fabrics, tailoring, and embroidery.

However, these subsystems are not independent; as dimensions within a textile system, a change in any one affects the others. For example, a technological innovation by a dyer, either with fabric, dye, or resist

[10]   From an information theory point of view one could compare, statistically, the designs selected by the local population with the total range of possible design permutations.

technique, will, if successful, affect not only the cloth and dye suppliers, but also the middlemen who sell cloth, the various markets (domestic and foreign), the customers who wear fabric, and other dyers who may try to copy the innovation. Furthermore, a successful innovation affects the dyer who may have to hire more assistants or send more work out in order to fill new orders.

Conversely any breakdown in the economic system, or lack of effort, can affect the success of a new design and the dyers. If middlemen raise the prices for dyed cloth too much, so that it does not sell well, the dyer may interpret this as a design failure. If suppliers cannot keep in stock certain dyes or fabrics necessary for a new design, it affects production. If quality falls below standard, it also affects the system.[11] If customers' tastes or aesthetic ideas change rapidly, as when a design is only a passing fad, as many are, it affects the whole system.

By examining the total resist-dyed textile system we can see other gaps in our knowledge, besides those already mentioned in regard to the design subsystem. We also need to know more about the social status of dyers, the influence that an overseas market has on dyers in economic terms, the influence Sierra Leone dyers are having on textile aesthetics outside Sierra Leone (in West Africa, Europe, and the United States) and the influence that a dyer's name may have on the demand for his or her textiles. Assuredly there are other gaps in our knowledge. This paper has outlined the hypothesis that Sierra Leone resist-dyed textile production is a system with various dimensions. It is not a static system, but one very much in a state of flux, particularly with respect to an expanding overseas market potential. It is, however, a delicate system, held in balance only by the cooperation of everyone involved.

From this specific textile information not a great deal can be concluded about Sierra Leone culture in general, but one can say that the culture rewards aesthetic innovation, technical skills, and personal enterprise, a continuation of an old West African tradition of reward for these traits. Elsewhere in the world today, technical skill (of this type) and aesthetic innovation are not always rewarded by both the domestic culture and by an export market. Sierra Leone textiles also differ from many West African arts in that they are still commissioned by local people and not made only to sell in airports and to tourists. It is ultimately Africans as consumer-critics who will keep African arts at high aesthetic standards, even if the aesthetic ideology may be constantly evolving.

---

[11]   Chuta reports that cloths which are not up to standard exhibit an uneven distribution of dye, sloppy removal of threads used to tie patterns, or seams. It is cheaper to buy narrow widths of cloth and seam them together to make *lappa*-size pieces, but seams do not appeal to buyers in either the domestic or export market.

REFERENCES

AFRICAN–AMERICAN INSTITUTE
1975   *Sakakke: textile art from West Africa; an exhibition of textiles from Dahomey, Ghana, Ivory Coast, Mali, Niger, Sierra Leone, Togo and Upper Volta, March 19–August 31, 1975.* New York: African–American Institute.

BOSER-SARIVAXEVANIS, RENÉE
1972   *Textilhandwerk in Westafrika.* Basel: Museum für Völkerkunde.

CHUTA, ENYINNA
1978   "The economics of gara (tie dye) cloth industry in Sierra Leone." Working Paper 25, Department of Agricultural Economics, Michigan State University, East Lansing.

CHUTA, ENYINNA, MIRIAM STACY
1975   *A case study of gara technology in Sierra Leone.* Freetown: Njala University College.

DITTMER, KUNZ
1966   *Kunst and Handwerk in Westafrika.* Hamburg: Museum für Völkerkunde.

DRESSER, LELAND
1974   *Sierra Leone arts and crafts.* Freetown: Ministry of Trade and Industry.

EASMON, M. C. F.
1924   *Sierra Leone country cloths.* London: Waterlow.

LINDBLOM, CARL, ENYINNA CHUTA
1976   *The economics of rural and urban small scale industries in Sierra Leone.* African Rural Employment Paper 14, Department of Agricultural Economics, Michigan State University. East Lansing.

PAZ, OCTAVIO
1974   *In praise of hands: contemporary crafts of the world.* Greenwich, Connecticut: New York Graphic Society.

SIEBER, ROY
1972   *African textiles and decorative arts.* New York: Museum of Modern Art.

WAHLMAN, MAUDE
1974   *Contemporary African arts.* Chicago: Field Museum of Natural History.
1975   *Contemporary African fabrics.* Chicago: Museum of Contemporary Art.

The History and Development of Wax-Printed Textiles Intended for West Africa and Zaire

RUTH NIELSEN

A visitor to West Africa invariably would be impressed by the colorful fabrics of intricate design worn by many of the Africans in the large cities or the thousands of small villages, by Africans attending church services, ceremonial celebrations, official functions, or patronizing the sprawling open cloth markets and fabric stalls. As Butler stated:

Many people believe that the African is a person of very simple tastes who is ready to accept all sorts of second quality goods and clearing lines, and crude designs and garish colours, which the more fashionable nations reject. This is far from the truth. It has been the life's work of many merchant converters in Manchester to produce speciality African prints for the people, men and women, "on the coast." The development of a new design for this market normally absorbs more time and effort than is taken over one for the transitory fashion markets (1958:12).

"Speciality African prints" is a broad term used interchangeably with "Manchester cloth" and "African prints" to describe cloth made in Europe for the African market.[1] The cotton fabrics bought and used by the Africans were always an important part of their inherent culture. The designs of the cloth evolved primarily from the indigenous hand and textile industry of West Africa, where the people had a highly developed sense of design, color, and quality (*West Africa* 1950). The exotic-looking fabrics used by the nationals in West Africa and Zaire have been largely unknown to Europeans and Americans, but increased awareness of the cultural heritage of Africa has stimulated recent studies of African dress and textiles. Publications, such as those of Eicher (1970), Plumer (1970), and Sieber (1972), added new dimensions to the existing literature on

---

[1] "Manchester cloth" is a broad term describing all types of printed cloth, produced particularly in Manchester, England. It is used here interchangeably with "African prints" and "speciality African prints".

African dress, but no extensive study had been made to investigate the speciality African prints. Therefore, to contribute to the history of textiles, to acquire a more complete picture of African textile design, it appeared justifiable and logical to pursue a study of printed textiles produced in Europe for export exclusively to Africa.[2]

Printed textiles exported to Africa were of two main types: wax prints (wax batiks) and nonwax prints (fancy or roller prints). An African wax print is a printed cotton fabric of plain weave to which the design is applied with hot wax or resin on both sides of the cloth. It is usually dyed indigo, leaving a blue pattern on a white background after the resin is washed out. Additional colors may be added by either hand-blocking or special printing. Roller prints are ordinary printed fabrics to which the design is applied on one side of the cloth in a continuous process by engraved metal rollers.

This study is limited to the wax prints and restricted to West Africa and Zaire, since these are the regions to which these prints are primarily exported. The African wax prints successfully compete with roller prints probably because they are loaded with tradition, contain expressions of West African culture, and are geared to the tastes and preferences of the people. They are often adopted as the national costume, and acquire the significance of a status symbol, indicating wealth and social prestige. Furthermore, since the nineteenth century these countries have been trading primarily with Europe, and their people were far more traditionally inclined than, for example, the people of East Africa.

A BRIEF HISTORICAL OVERVIEW OF THE TEXTILE TRADE IN WEST AFRICA

Interest in imported textiles dates back to the early West African empires which encouraged trade with foreign markets long before the Europeans arrived on the coast. In the precolonial era, trade routes from the Mediterranean ports of Africa extended across the Sahara and through the rain forest to the West coast. Fabrics were transported on the backs of donkeys and camels, on the heads of porters, and in the holds of river boats (Boahen 1971:185; Davidson 1966:89–92).

Throughout the centuries cloth was consistently a principal trade item and a stimulus to economic production. It served as currency in the marketplace and as barter for slaves; it was exchanged for oil, ivory, and

[2] The incentive to study African prints was partly a result of encouragement and interest by Joanne B. Eicher, of the School of Human Ecology, Department of Human Environment and Design, Michigan State University, and partly a result of eight years of educational work in West Africa where the writer received unforgettable impressions of the variety and beauty of African dress.

gold (Wolfson 1958: 40–54; Davidson 1971:235; Skinner 1964:92; Forde and Kaberry 1967:134; Ryder 1965:204). With the establishment of the English and Dutch East India companies during the late fourteenth and early fifteenth centuries, trade was further promoted and Indian cottons were bought up and traded on the coast of West Africa (de Negri 1966:95–96). From 1720 to 1750 a trade struggle took place between the exporters of Indian prints and the dealers in Manchester cloth. At first Manchester printers provided coarse linen cloth in dull colors, but these did not satisfy Africans who preferred the lighter all-cotton India prints in bright colors. The Manchester cloth, therefore, was modified to suit the African taste, and by 1750 it had acquired a quality comparable to that of the Indian textiles (Robinson 1969a:76). As a further incentive to trade, the Manchester merchants varied their cloth in color and pattern to cater to the different regions in the West African countries, each having its own fashions and tastes and thereby giving rise to a special West African market for the Manchester cotton industry. Consequently, in the nineteenth century the Manchester cloth captured the textile trade on the coast and replaced the more expensive Indian cottons (Robinson 1969a:76). African craftsmen had for some time made starch-resist cloth which was well accepted by the Africans, so to cater to the conservative tastes of the consumer and to attempt to gain a stronger foothold on the West African textile market, the European textile printers made special trips to the west coast to bring back examples of the indigenous cloth, which they copied.[3] During the 1900's there was a considerable increase in the trade of cotton goods, partly due to the following factors: (1) merchants were looking for new and increased markets; (2) cloth was still used as a means of barter; (3) production of special colors and patterns suited for West Africa increased; (4) the quality of cloth improved; (5) cheaper materials brought lower prices; (6) foreign cloth became a status symbol in parts of Africa; and (7) means of communication and transportation improved.

The beginning of the African wax-print market, as it is known today, is somewhat obscure, but it is known that the interest in wax prints can be traced back to the famous Javanese batiks.[4] These were introduced to Holland in the seventeenth century and later spread to other parts of Europe, but due to their exotic appearance they were not readily

---

[3] African prints, inspired by the designs of indigenous cloth, are now held in the Charles Beving Collection in the British Museum, in the Rachel Kay Shuttleworth Collection in Gawthorpe Hall, near Burnley, Lancashire, and in the collection of printed textiles for export to Africa, in the ethnographic museum in Antwerp.

[4] The word *batik* in Malay comes from the sound *tic* derived from the dropping of the wax on the cloth and denotes a certain method of applying resist-dyed patterns to finished fabrics. The special feature of this process is that those parts of a design not intended to take the color in a particular dyeing operation are protected or "reserved" with a coat of wax, resin, paraffin, rice paste, clay, or any other dyeproof substance. This protective coating can

accepted. Interest was aroused for batik fabric, however, when Sir Thomas Raffles in the nineteenth century gave a full description of the processes and uses of batik, and when, at the same time, the European merchants were looking for ways to expand the cloth trade. The merchants began to study the market, the dyes, the procedure, and the best ways of producing machinemade batiks cheaper than the costly hand-printed originals (Robinson 1969a:40). As a result a number of factories were established in Europe to produce machinemade batik for local and foreign markets. These machinemade batiks became known as wax prints and they were introduced to West Africa by various means. C. H. Krantz (personal communication)[5] stated that trade in wax prints to West Africa actually started with the young unmarried European men who arrived in the second half of the nineteenth century. As they settled down to trade, they quickly engaged the African women in their businesses. The women taught them the language and received, in return sewing machines and instruction in how to use them, and before long the sale of the prints flourished. Another beginning was attributed to West African soldiers who were serving in Indonesia (1810–1862). They reportedly brought back Java batiks as gifts for their wives, who soon developed a liking for such cloth (Rodenburg 1967:47). Dutch East India Company merchants trading to Elmina, in Ghana, also played a role in the buildup of local demand for the batik (Beauchamp 1957:209) and by 1893 West Africans had developed a taste for this type of cloth. Flemming, of the Scotch Cotton concern, noticed this interest in batiks, and as a result he had such cloth manufactured by Previnaire in Holland, who had invented a machine that could produce satisfactory imitations of handmade batik. Just as the designs of the Indian cottons were adjusted to African tastes, so were the Java batiks. Thus the African wax-printed textiles became one type of Manchester cloth. E. Voirol (personal communication, 1971) explained that the Basel trading company catering to the various needs of missionaries also supplied them with batiks, and that the Africans eventually adopted the use of wax-printed textiles as a result of the missionaries' influence.[6] It appears, therefore, that traders, merchants, missionaries, and returning soldiers all played a role in introducing the wax prints to the West Africans. Table 1 contains a summary of the important dates.

---

be reapplied to different parts of the cloth for successive dye baths to produce a variety of patterns. Originally this kind of design was accomplished by hand painting (Mattibella Gettinger personal communication with Joanne B. Eicher, Spring 1974; Steinmann 1958:13–15; Irwin and Murphy 1969:6).

[5]   C. H. Krantz is director of Texoprint, the African division of Gamma Holding N.V., Helmond, the Netherlands.

[6]   E. Voirol was director of the Hohlenstein textile printing works at Glarus in Switzerland. This factory closed down in the summer of 1973.

Table 1. A date chart summarizing important trade in textiles with West Africa

Date	Development
1100	Textiles delivered to North African ports, rerouted by caravans to West Africa
14th C.	Trade routes extended to Axim, southwestern Ghana
15th C.	Portuguese sailing ships arrived
16th C.	Expanded trade by ships to West Africa
1500–1800	Cloths used as currency
1553	First British ships began trading
1593	Dutch ships were sent to West Africa
1597	Dutch East India Company began trading
1600	British East India Company was established
17th C.	"Trust" introduced as credit trading
1620	Dutch succeeded in taking over trade from the Portuguese
1621	Dutch West India Company established
1686	D. O'Dapper published list of cloth suitable for West Africa
1700	Trading posts permanently established
1720–1750	Trade struggle between merchants of Indian cloth and Manchester cloth
1750	Manchester cloth became accepted on Africa's west coast; sale of Indian cloth declined
19th C.	Manchester merchants produced cloth appealing to African tastes, capturing West African market
1893	Recorded requests for wax-printed textiles
20th C.	Rapid increase in export of cotton goods to West Africa, interrupted by two world wars
1970's	Cloth continues to be one of chief imports
1974	Wax-printed textiles are still imported, even though they are also produced by indigenous factories

METHODOLOGY

African wax-printed textiles are produced in Japan, Europe and more recently in West Africa. An increasing number of African textile mills have taken up production of wax prints, some of them in cooperation with the European manufacturers. In 1971 the writer visited the three remaining factories in Europe then producing "48" wax prints for West Africa. The factories were located in England, the Netherlands, and Switzerland.[7] The data-collecting project consisted of: (1) a historical overview of the trade patterns of textiles to West Africa; (2) a survey of the origin and development of wax prints; (3) an investigation of the contemporary production and use of speciality African prints; and (4) analysis, description, and comparison of selected designs from the assorted collections. The methodology employed included: (1) inquiries to museums, textile councils and institutes, and wax-print manufacturers; (2) correspondence

---

[7] These were: A. Brunnschweiler (UK) Ltd., Manchester, England; Texoprint division, Gamma Holding N.V., Helmond, the Netherlands; and the Hohlenstein textile printing works at Glarus in Switzerland.

with persons knowledgeable regarding African wax prints; (3) question-naires prepared and mailed to the directors of the factories in England, the Netherlands, and Switzerland; (4) library research; (5) visits to museums and private collections with holdings of African textiles; (6) visits to studios and showrooms of the manufacturers, and observation of wax-print production; (7) taped interviews; (8) photographing the designs; and (9) procurement and classification of two sample collec-tions.[8]

The following may serve as an example of how information on African wax prints was obtained. An article in *The Times* (Butler 1958) men-tioned in passing a famous Manchester design, the "Flying Duck", (Plate 1) that had been produced and sold in remarkable quantities for many years. Letters of inquiry about the "Flying Duck" and other African

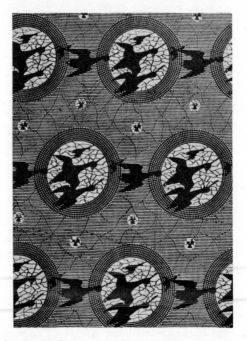

Plate 1.   The "Flying Duck" (I-A-b-1), one of the oldest wax-print designs, traditional because it is old, named, kept, and still in use. The design was acquired from the old Brown Flemming collection and probably dates back to the 1880's. Brown Flemming was one of the first merchants who traded in wax prints for Africa

[8]   Two almost identical sample collections, owned by Eicher and Nielsen, are presently available for examination and additional studies at, respectively, Michigan State University, East Lansing and Andrews University, Berrien Springs, Michigan. Two hundred and twenty-five samples were obtained with 135 different designs. The Nielsen collection contains 117 different samples produced from cotton fibers and constructed in plain weave. The printing method in design application is wax resistant. The Eicher collection contains 108 samples.

prints were sent out. Later, during personal, taped interviews with the three manufacturers, specific questions were asked about the history, sale, and use of the "Flying Duck", which proved to be one of the oldest African wax prints. The discussions led to additional information about other designs, and the writer was invited to observe the designing and production of the prints. Samples of the "Flying Duck" and other designs were obtained, analyzed, described, cataloged, and photographed. Upon request the producers agreed to select an assortment collection, providing samples from various decades, of traditional and contemporary prints, of "best-sellers" and cloth which did not sell too well, of "good" and "bad" designs, of prints with motifs illustrating certain ideas and concepts acceptable to the Africans, and of prints with Javanese influence (Plate 2).

Plate 2.   Alizarine-dyed Java print of a type exported to Africa

DEVELOPMENT AND PRODUCTION OF AFRICAN WAX PRINTS IN THE NETHERLANDS, ENGLAND, AND SWITZERLAND

One of the early wax printers in the Netherlands was Previnaire, who established his print works at Haarlem in 1830 and later on bought several other textile-printing factories. In 1852, assisted by the Netherlands trading society, he invented a machine called "La Javanaise" which was based on the "Perrotine" (W. T. Kroese, personal communication, 1975). This machine could produce prints with the appearance of hand-made batiks, and after having specialized in various types of textiles, the company eventually concentrated on the printing of textiles for Africa. Originally, Previnaire had produced his batiks for Indonesia and other markets, and, according to Rodenburg (1967:46), he was the first to make machinemade batik for West Africa (in 1893). It appears that Previnaire produced the wax prints for the Haarlem Cotton Society, and that Ebenezer Brown Flemming had discovered that the Javanese batik patterns were in great demand on the coast of West Africa (C. H. Krantz, personal communication, 1974) and, consequently, he was able to establish a lucrative trade. During the First World War, the export to Africa stopped and the factory had to close in October 1917. It was liquidated in 1918. The following year a new factory was founded under the name N.V. Haarlemsche Katoendrukkerij (M. A. Bolland, personal communication, 1975), but it was liquidated in 1922 and the machinery was bought by Van Vlissingen at Helmond (Rodenburg 1967:49). Krantz stated that Van Vlissingen at Helmond also acquired the original design collection (personal communication), even though Brown Flemming insisted on his rights to the designs because they were produced in England as well. During the Second World War, under German occupation, the factory encountered various restrictions, but secretely continued to produce African wax-prints. The laboratory director worked day and night to improve his prints and to achieve high standards, while his technicians were successful in concealing the prints between layers of paper so they were never discovered by the Germans. As a result of those efforts the Dutch at the end of the war could send three shipments of printed cloth to West Arica to supply an eagerly waiting market (Krantz, personal communication, 1971).

In 1969 Van Vlissingen, then known as Vlisco, merged with another large textile manufacturer, Hatema, to form one of the largest printed fabric producers in Europe and became known as Gamma Holding N.V. One of its divisions was devoted to the exotic prints intended for markets in Africa, and acquired participating ownership in five overseas print works located in Ghana, the Ivory Coast, Nigeria, and Zaire.

The evolution of the printed textile industry in England took place from the seventeenth to the nineteenth centuries, the technique of producing machinemade copies of the genuine Javanese batiks being introduced at the end of the nineteenth century. While the merchant converters in Manchester at first had the African wax prints produced in Holland, they later started English production in Lancashire (Butler 1958:12). The most famous of the English wax-print manufacturers was the Newton Banks Works of the Calico Printers' Association, Manchester, known today as the English Calico Ltd. A. Brunnschweiler (UK) Ltd.

is the contemporary trading name for the African division. L. Cooper[9] explained that in 1960 the Calico Printers' Association (CPA), which traded in printed cloth to West Africa, decided to acquire a direct line of wax prints for that market, and since Brunnschweiler was well established in the Madras trade to Africa (since 1874), the CPA bought the company and encouraged them to develop the wax-print trade further, just as they had done the Madras trade (Plate 3). Consequently these two specialities became the backbone of the Brunnschweiler trade with West Africa. Brunnschweiler was competing with the Dutch, and the French company C.F.A.O., which cooperated with the Japanese and made a serious attempt to acquire the wax-print market in Africa. After the Second World War the Japanese succeeded in taking the market in East Africa, while Brunnschweiler was concentrated on Zaire and the countries of West Africa. In 1974 English Calico was probably the only manufacturer of African "48" printed cotton textiles in Great Britain. This company has also joined with the government of Zaire and two other parties in the establishment of a print works at Kinshasa (Cooper, personal correspondence, 1974).

When some European governments, for example, France and Britain, issued decrees against import and printing of cotton goods in the seventeenth and eighteenth centuries, Switzerland did not have any such restrictions, and the printing textile industry flourished there. Many small print works were established, the most important areas being the cantons of Neuchâtel in the west and Glarus in the east (Robinson

Plate 3.   Woven Madras fabric with embroidery added. Madras is a woven cotton cloth originally from the area near Madras, India. It is often checked, or striped and has been produced continuously for about two hundred years. During this period it has pleased the tastes of the people of both West Africa and the West Indies (Brunnschweiler 1957:2)

[9]   L. Cooper is director of A. Brunnschweiler (UK) Ltd., Manchester, England.

1969b:120–121). In 1740 Johan Streiff of Glarus established the first plant for cloth printing, producing mainly wax or paste resists on an indigo-blue ground (Müller n.d.:11–12). By 1840 Glarus was renowned for its wide variety of printed cloths, and in 1860–1861 Egidius Trumpi at Glarus began to imitate the true wax effect by applying a reserve of colophony with wooden blocks and dyeing with indigo (M. L. Kartaschoff-Nabholz, personal communication with Joanne B. Eicher, 1973). Gradually the batik print works, as well as the formerly prosperous calico printers, closed down due to foreign competition, hindering tariff agreements, changing fashions, and the introduction of double printing. In 1971 Hohlenstein printing works in the town of Ennenda was the only factory producing wax-batik textiles for the African market. In the beginning Hohlenstein was operated by the Basel Trading Company (BTC), which was one of the first established trading companies on the coast of West Africa. In 1922–1924 the company attempted to obtain wax prints intended for West Africa from the United African Company (UAC), but they were unsuccessful and therefore decided to produce their own. The mill in Glarus–Ennenda was bought, the designs were ordered from UAC and sent to Glarus for reproduction, commencing the production of Swiss wax prints for West Africa. In 1960 BTC started to operate its own factories in Ghana and Nigeria, utilizing the Glarus system of textile printing, and in 1969 an additional factory was opened at Dakar in Senegal (Voirol, personal communication, 1971). The Hohlenstein company decided to close down its production of wax prints in the summer of 1973.

COMPARISON OF THE MANUFACTURERS' TECHNIQUES

The three manufacturers followed the same general procedure in production of wax-printed textiles for Africa, and the techniques followed at Brunnschweiler may serve as an example of how these were manufactured.

Brunnschweiler Production

Two major production lines of African prints exist: (1) wax prints, and (2) fancy prints (Cooper, personal communication, 1971). Wax prints are wax batiks which imitate the genuine Java batiks, but they are machine-printed rather than hand-painted. The fancy prints included green ground, alizarine, blotch print, and straightforward roller print, imitating the white spots and crackled lines distinctive to African wax prints. For many years the fancy prints formed a large part of the Brunnschweiler production, but as a result of the CPA takeover and growing Japanese competition in fancy prints the emphasis was changed to wax prints (Cooper, personal communication, 1971).

Brunnschweiler imported bulks of 117-yard-long pieces of *greige* cotton cloth from Taiwan, Korea, Japan, China, India, and Pakistan, which were sewn together in lengths of 12,000 yards for manufacturing of the printed cloth. The cotton was bleached, straightened, and printed with resins on both sides by engraved rollers, and as the fabric fell down in layers, the resin creased and the material acquired the "cracked" lines characteristic of Javanese batik. Sometimes it was sent through a wringer to produce the same effect. In this special process of waxing, both sides of the cloth were printed simultaneously, one side a little ahead of the other. Such a misfit was exploited for the purpose of adding a subtle effect to the cloth. Cooper pointed out that it was significant for good results that the temperature of the resin be exact. The next step involved passing the fabric through several indigo-dye baths, interrupted by oxidation between each bath. The cloth appeared green after the first dip, but turned more and more blue after each subsequent dip and airing. This was followed by a washing to remove nearly all the wax, but purposely leaving small spots called "lights". Application of further coloring was done by a continuous machine process, a treatment which had to be very exact for a satisfactory result and was regarded as a trade secret (Plate 4). Only occasionally did they use the hand-block technique (Plate 5). Throughout the printing every attempt was made to retain the effect and appearance produced by the old, established, hand-block method. No wash-and-wear finish was applied, because the African customer prefers design and eye appeal over convenience.

In 1971 Brunnschweiler presented 800 samples in their showroom, and offered a total range of 4,500 engraved designs, but had records of 20,000 different patterns on rollers, photographs, or cloth samples. The *chef d'atelier*, T. Jones, pointed out that a print was taken out of production if there were no sales during a four or five-year period; yet it was never considered dead, and was reintroduced when orders were received (Jones, personal interview, 1971). The company employed forty designers and produced about twenty-five new designs a week. Many of the traditional designs originated from the Scottish firm, Brown Flemming, which was taken over by F. W. Grafton in the 1920's. Between 1930 and 1960 several print producers were merged with Grafton's, and in 1961 Grafton and Brunnschweiler merged, both then being part of CPA. In 1930 Grafton rerecorded their designs embracing all collections. The Calico Printers' Association registered all designs printed by them and this procedure was continued for Brunnschweiler.

Plate 4. An illustration of how the depth and vividness of the same design can be improved by additional color application: (a) indigo and white only, (b) one color added, and (c) two colors added

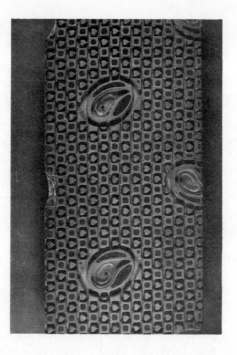

Plate 5.   One of the carved woodblocks still occasionally used for hand-printing

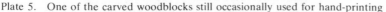

Texoprint Production

Krantz stated that Texoprint produced: (1) nonwax prints, and (2) wax prints (batiks) for the market in Africa. The nonwaxes were: (1) Javas–Dutch Java prints, alizarine-dyed and reserve-printed large repeats (Plate 2);(2) *khangas* — special prints with large repeats and a printed proverb, produced until recently for East Africa (Plate 6); and (3) imitation African waxes — cloth printed as direct roller prints, imitating the white spots and crackled lines distinctive of African wax prints.

Texoprint employed 1,500–2,000 people, including twenty-five designers, and was the only division of the Gamma Holding N.V. that employed designers; the others bought all their designs. The division held four thousand designs but only two thousand were in actual production in 1971. Two thousand designs were taken off production because no orders had been placed for them in the preceding two years. However, it was stated that any design could be brought into production at short notice, provided it was justified by demand. Approximately two hundred new designs were added annually (Krantz, personal communication, 1971).

Plate 6. A *khanga* print with proverb, produced by Texoprint

Differences in Technique

It appeared that there were certain distinct differences in the technique used by the three manufacturers. Much of the work was performed by hand in the Swiss production, while in England and the Netherlands the factories were largely mechanized. Furthermore, the Swiss employed a larger number of women in making the prints. Resin (wax) was imported, but the blending and standardization differed and was a trade secret. Since the Swiss used small amounts of resin, they were unable to blend. They all considered an exact temperature of the resin of the utmost importance. The English and the Dutch had extensive breaking of the resin; only a small amount of breaking took place on the Swiss cloth. The British and the Dutch purposely left spots of resin on the cloth until the terminal washing to produce spots called "lights", but the Swiss made no such attempts. Indigo-ground color was generally used in England and the Netherlands, while in Switzerland brown, or lately, brown–indigo was preferred. In Holland, brown, dark red, and lately dark orange, dull green, and combinations of indigo and orange, indigo and red, and indigo and brown, were also made. The Swiss apparently also differed in drawing the cloths on wheel frames during the dyeing process. Furthermore, the Swiss producers differed from the others in air-drying of the cloths in "hanging towers" at 40–45° F (apparently brown cloth cannot dry at high temperatures without detrimental effect). All manufacturers alternated dyeing and oxidation of the indigo cloth, repeated up to ten times. The Swiss claimed that the sand in the glacial water used for the washings aided in the removal of the resin. The Dutch stated that they used special soft water for washings which together with their special blend of resin produced clear edges and a bright appearance. Additional colors were added in England by special printing of the cloth on both sides, using engraved rollers. This was a procedure that demanded great exactness for satisfactory results and was a trade secret. Holland and Switzerland applied additional colors by hand-blocking which the English used in exceptional cases only. Typical for the Swiss was production of one-color prints (that is, one color in addition to the ground color) and relatively few two-color prints, but the others still produced two- or three-color prints. A wash-and-wear finish is now being used by the Dutch in a luxury article printed on a fine cambric cotton cloth, which has proved to be a success. No wash-and-wear finishes were used by the English or the Swiss manufacturers.

DESIGN OF AFRICAN WAX PRINTS

From the designer's viewpoint a good textile design is one that has a unified composition, serves the purpose intended for it, and represents the culture for which it is created. It may echo the past or anticipate the future but it must above all else reflect its actual origin (Birrell 1959:8). Artists and designers have been employed by the textile manufacturers to prepare imaginative forms and details in every known color, shade, and tone. The results have been a great variety of cotton goods which have been placed on the market through the years, few of which have been seen by the general public, as most people outside the textile industry are unaware of the great number of beautiful textiles available. This is especially true of the African wax prints.

African wax-printed textiles are carefully designed with exotic and beautiful motifs of unusual colors by designers steeped in the tastes and traditions of the Africans (Fraser 1948:103). The designers may be traditional or nontraditional: a wax-print design is declared traditional by manufacturers when in the course of time (after three or more years) it has been purchased regularly by the African market in varying quantities. Such a design is at one time or another named by some African consumer and is then marketed under that name. When the consumer buys the cloth it is kept throughout his life and often exhibited after death as commemoration of the life and status of the deceased. Therefore, the three criteria for designating a textile as a "traditional design" were: (1) that it was sold regularly over a course of years; (2) that it was given a name; and (3) that it was kept and valued. Some traditional designs dated back 85 years or more; the "Flying Duck" is such an example (Plate 1). Many others were dated before the First World War and between the wars; some were postwar designs. Apparently there are various degrees of traditional designs, that is, some are more traditional than others, and, of course, some are not traditional at all and therefore quickly drop out of production and use. Krantz suggested that perhaps the tradition could be kept alive by favorable construction of design and the very best use of color proportions. When wax prints are not significant enough to be named by the consumers, they are not kept, not considered traditional, and soon cease to be produced (personal communication, 1971).

The name of a design reflects either the consumer's conception of it or perhaps a personal experience or incident related to the purchase or wearing of the print. Therefore, a traditional design would indicate to the bystander certain known circumstances in which the person wearing the cloth was, is, or hopes to be (Krantz, personal communication, 1973). One writer stated that once the African public gives the design a name, sales will consistently continue to improve, even though the name may not appear to the non-African to have any connection with the design (Beauchamp 1957:209).

Cooper, Jones, Krantz, and Voirol all agree that it often took many years to produce a classic, and that there were no fixed rules or directions on how to produce an exceptional African design. The designer sometimes had certain expectations about a design but he would not know how well it was accepted until he, after some time, saw the sales record. The popularity of a design was the result of the totality of the African culture, language, geography and the environmental conditions of the people (personal communications, 1971).

The African wax-print designs were derived from the following inspirational sources.

INDIAN COTTONS.   Generally the Indian cottons provided a rich legacy for the designers, including the pattern book of the East India Company of the early nineteenth century (Robinson 1969b:114–116). According to Albert Müller, curator of the Glarus Museum, the Indian original patterns raise a fantastic world. The pattern books have page after page of naturalistic drawings and paintings in wild ecstasy suiting the tastes of the people in distant countries (Müller n.d.).

JAVANESE BATIKS.   Originally the designs and symbols of Java batik were derived from natural forms and evolved toward the abstract. Java batik was influenced by the myriad cultures and religions of Asia, and designs were based on historical and mythological events as well as local customs (*Writing of batik* 1968:6). The Dutch brought the Java batiks to Europe in the seventeenth century, and in the nineteenth century they started to make their own machine batik. Undoubtedly Java batiks served as inspirational sources for many years.

EUROPEAN PRINTS. Some of the European prints could be traced to other cultures and historic periods. According to Müller, the old pattern books at the Glarus canton museum at the Freuler palace in Näfels presented a vivid picture of nineteenth-century civilization; the colorful cheerfulness of the peasant ornamentation was preserved in the oldest cloths, which later on became the crucible of ornaments and symbols from the whole world, while batiks embodying amazing skill arose for destinations in Africa and elsewhere. Fabrics were saturated with timeless symbols and bits of history of civilization were handed down to us by the Glarus designers (Müller n.d.).

AFRICAN INDIGENOUS CLOTH. The designs of Manchester cloth, including the African wax prints, evolved from the indigenous hand textile industry of West Africa. The peoples of the west coast have a highly developed sense of design, color, and quality, and their cotton goods are an immensely important part of their indigenous culture (*West Africa* 1950:850).

TRADITIONAL AFRICAN OBJECTS AND SYMBOLS. Another important source of inspiration was the many traditional objects and symbols found in West Africa. For example, a favorite motif in Ghana was the stool used by rulers. Fertility was used as a motif for design in depicting a woman and two children's heads, suggesting twins, or in another instance a pod containing three beans which symbolize triplets (Beauchamp 1957:209).

CONTACTS WITH CONSUMERS, TRADERS, AND MARKET WOMEN IN AFRICA. Another source of inspiration was direct contact with consumers, the African traders, and especially the market women who at times came up with their own suggestions and requests. Designs from other companies were also used and altered.

HISTORICAL EVENTS, CURRENT EVENTS, POLITICAL FIGURES AND IDEAS. Generally nontraditional designs depicting political figures and events were of short duration, except when the individual died an extraordinary death, for example Lumumba and John F. Kennedy. In 1946 the Belgian Congo requested cloth with the allied victory design, which included the busts of President Dwight D. Eisenhower and Winston Churchill together with tanks and the dove of peace (Beauchamp 1957:209). However, the producers were generally reluctant to use politics in the making of designs. For example, Brunnschweiler refused to take sides in the Biafran conflict, when the two involved parties requested printed cloths with certain political and nationalistic sentiments and symbols.

RELIGION AND MYTHOLOGY.   Some designs can be traced to African mythology and a few prints have religious influence. There are many taboos in African cultures, and the producers take great care not to offend the African customer by violating such beliefs (Cooper, personal interview, 1971).

NATURAL FORMS.   Many designs were derived from nature; for example, from plants and their parts (roots, stems, leaves, flowers, and fruits) or from animals: mammals, birds, reptiles, amphibians, fish, insects, and other invertebrates. Celestial bodies, rocks, minerals, and diamonds are also inspirational sources.

GEOMETRICAL DESIGNS.   Since Mohammed forbade the making of the likenesses of living objects, great development of geometrical designs took place, especially in designs for areas with strong Muslim influence.

CLASSIFICATION OF AFRICAN WAX-PRINTED TEXTILES

To the knowledge of this writer, classification of African wax-printed textiles, necessary for the orderly arrangement and storage of collections, has never been seriously attempted. Classification systems have previously been worked out for other types of textiles, for example, Sir Peter Buck used motif as the basic criterion for grouping (Buck 1911:69–90). Buck was concerned with the evolutionary theory and attempted to determine the sequence of development of motifs. Phillips (1960) restated and improved on Buck's classification, emphasizing pattern analysis and description, and added another class of motifs. Emery (1966) developed an illustrated classification of fabrics according to structure. Harrell (1967) classified the Eicher collection of handcrafted Nigerian textiles according to region, fabric construction, design process, and the use for which the fabric was designed. Mead (1968) made a classification of the patterns of taaniko, a specialized ornamented cloth among the Maori of New Zealand, aiming at exhaustiveness and focusing attention on the dominant motif used. Patterns were graphed and photographed.

   It is proposed that an adequate classification system for wax-printed textiles intended for the African market should meet the following minimum criteria. The classifier should:

1.   State the classification clearly;
2.   Consider the dominant motif;
3.   Describe rather than interpret;
4.   Make the classification comprehensive and expansive;
5.   Make the classification simple and easy to use;

6. Facilitate grouping of samples for easy access; and
7. Number and catalog samples.

According to Johnston and Kaufman (1967:21), the motifs of printed African fabrics fall into three general categories, although more than one may be combined in a single fabric: first, there are those that tell a story; second, those that have symbolic significance or that serve as identification; and third, those that are simple ornamentations with a pattern. Such a general classification is not specific enough to make it practical for a large collection. Some other classification schemes which could be used follow.

TRADITIONAL OR NONTRADITIONAL DESIGNS. As previously mentioned, an African printed design is considered traditional when it is sold regularly, when it has received a name from the consumer, and when it is kept and cherished by the buyer. The criteria for nontraditional design therefore would be: lack of a name bestowed by the consumer, lack of sufficient admiration to make the print worth "treasuring", and lack of enough sales to keep the print on the market for several years. However, to divide the printed textiles into two groups only appears to be too simple. Furthermore, since it takes some years to determine if a design is traditional of not, it is impossible to predict whether new designs will be traditional.

SYMBOLIC MEANING. The symbolic meaning of a motif is often very obscure, because it involves time, cultural, and historical relationships which are not always clearly understood. Some designs selling today date back to originals prepared in the last century, and the meaning of the symbols has been lost. The temptation to attach meaning and even religious symbolism to the motifs of the decorative arts was always strong in the east, especially in Java, but the fact that such interpretations were often contradictory and inconsistent encouraged the assumption that invention of the forms sometimes preceded the meanings (Irwin and Murphy 1969:9). This is equally true for the African wax-printed textiles, as evidenced by the fact that the symbolic meaning and the naming of the print was often conceived in connection with the purchase of use of the fabric. Many designs apparently have no symbolic meaning, and others can only be ascertained by the specialist or the African consumer. Therefore, since the symbolic meaning is obscure and subject to interpretation, this particular classification method is less desirable, at least until further research has established the meaning of the symbolism.

INSPIRATIONAL SOURCES. Since the printed textiles were often inspired by other prints, traditional objects, and symbols; by direct contacts with the consumers, designers, and traders; by historical and current events, poli-

tical figures and concepts; by past masters in art; by religion and mythology; and by natural and geometric shapes, it would be possible to classify
the prints accordingly. Such a system would probably also involve
evolutionary developments, cultural, historical, and social relationships;
it would be an exhaustive task, requiring the work of a specialist. Furthermore, other inherent weaknesses are that the inspirational source of
many textiles is unknown and untraceable today, and such classification
would often involve a certain amount of interpretation by the classifier.

STYLE.   The concept of style, familiar to artists, anthropologists, and
archaeologists, is a rather difficult one, because style has different meanings to different people: it is subject to interpretation complicated by
one's value system, and somewhat limited by a person being conservative
(resisting change) or progressive (adopting innovations). Meyer Schapiro
(1953:287) defined style as "the constant form — and sometimes the
constant elements, qualities, and expression — in the art of an individual
or of a group." By this he meant that the work of an individual or a group
exhibits similarities of form, quality, and expression to a degree that an
investigator would have little difficulty in recognizing that the works
belong to that individual or group (Mead 1968:47). Classification according to style revealed in a design is certainly feasible, but has little practical
value for a collection used for general teaching purposes, although it may
be of value in art and costume history.

SHAPE.   The universe is composed of shapes of infinite variety, shapes
that have meaning for man, often in a symbolic sense. Giving them
connotations from his past experience, man learns to read shapes as he
reads handwriting (Bevlin 1970:37). Shapes can be divided into four
categories: (1) realistic shapes presenting a likeness of an object that is
easily recognizable; (2) abstract shapes derived from nature or familiar
objects simplified, distorted, or exaggerated to enhance their qualities;
(3) geometrical shapes, mathematical in character, often expressing the
manmade environment or exhibiting pure geometry; and (4) nonobjec-
tive shapes rarely resembling any recognizable object, nevertheless having a close relationship to nature, being biomorphic, since they are fluid
and express growth and flexibility. This method of classification by shape
of motif appears to be a useful instrument in grouping of textile designs,
but it presupposes considerable knowledge and understanding of design.
It would also necessitate subdivision since it is impractical to hold a large
textile collection in four categories.

COLOR.   Printed textiles could also be arranged in groups according to
the dominant color. Colors are impressive and important but for classification purposes not as significant as motifs. Therefore, such a grouping

would be of little value in arranging a printed textile collection, unless the collection was for the purpose of studying predominating colors.

COMBINATIONS.   Since none of the schemes listed are entirely satisfactory, perhaps a combination of two or more would be a valuable solution. That is, a textile collection could be arranged into major groups according to one of the preferred schemes, and it could possibly be further subdivided according to one or more of the other schemes. One limitation of this method would be that if two selected schemes had different purposes, it would not be practical. For example, classification according to shapes of the motifs would be at variance with classification according to color.

Considering the limitations of the described schemes, the writer suggests that a collection of African wax prints could be arranged for easy access in categories according to the subject matter inherent in the main motif. Religion, mythology, tradition, culture, history, current events, nature, science, technology, architecture, art artifacts, nonobjectives, musical instruments, personal objects, as well as all other aspects of daily life, could be drawn upon. A collection of early prints (1909–1939) for West Africa was studied and photographed at the Victoria and Albert Museum in London during the summer of 1971. Mrs. Morris of the museum's circulation department had made a tentative classification of these prints according to subject matter. Some of the interesting designs from the collection were classified as: (1) anatomical designs, (2) architectural designs, (3) occupational designs, (4) tie-dyed designs, and (5) umbrella designs.

A similar method was utilized in the classification of the Eicher and Nielsen collections, because it was easy to use, concentrated on the dominant motif, allowed for distinct classification into known subjects, could be cataloged and numbered, and suggested itself to further expansion.

At the courtesy of the three manufacturers their showrooms were visited and the designs of the African wax prints were studied and in some cases photographed. The collections obtained were classified and cataloged according to subject matter as listed in Table 2. For convenience the subjects covered in the present collections were arranged alphabetically. Additional letter combinations can be added when the collection expands into new subjects and subdivisions.

Table 2.   Key to classification system

Collection number: each sample was assigned a collection number composed of three parts:

1. *Producer*:
  I: Brunnschweiler
  II: Texoprint
  III: Hohlenstein

Table 2 — *continued*

2. *Category*: determined according to subject matter of dominant motif. Designated by uppercase letters, with subdivisions designated by lowercase letters

3. *Accession*: samples were assigned numbers in sequence of acquisition and appear as last numeral in the collection number, so an example of a complete number is I-A-sb-2

Category letters

Animals	A	Man	M
birds	A-b	eye	M-e
fish	A-f		
insects	A-i	Masks	Ma
mammals	A-m		
millipedes	A-ma	Nationalism	N
reptiles	A-r		
shells	A-s	Nonobjective	Na
snails	A-sa		
spiders	A-sb	Plants	P
wings	A-w		
Calendars	C	flowers	P-f
		fruits	P-fa
Combinations	Ca	seaweeds	P-s
Education	E	trees	P-t
		vines	P-v
Games	G		
		Umbrellas	U
Geometric designs	Ga		
Insignia	I		

DESCRIPTION OF SELECTED SAMPLES FROM THE AFRICAN WAX-PRINTED TEXTILE COLLECTION

Selected samples of African wax prints from the acquired collections were described and compared. To present a representative sampling of the collection, selection was based upon the following criteria: samples were selected (1) from each of the three manufacturers; (2) from various decades; (3) from a variety of motif categories; (4) from prints with available information, and (5) from representative types:
1. Traditional (and nontraditional);
2. Old and recent;
3. Old designs presented in new ways;
4. Combinations of several motifs;
5. Unusual motifs and striking colors;
6. Traceable inspirational sources;
7. Acceptable to or rejected by consumers;
8. Those known to have been named by consumers;
9. Designs with political influence.

Selected samples of wax-print designs are arranged in categories in Table 3. In describing each of the selected samples an attempt was made to present the following information:

1. Collection number and name of design (if known);

2. Reason for choice of sample, for example, traceable inspirational source, miscellaneous information;

3. Arrangement of design in one of four categories (Krantz, personal communication, 1973):

   a. "Centerpiece": a dominant motif in the center of field,

   b. "Four corners": two or four different motifs per repeat of 36 inches,

   c. "Patchwork": parts of various designs arranged systematically or scattered per square yard,

   d. "All-over": a square yard covered with similar motifs in the same position and dimensions;

4. Description of the repeat: the major section of the repeat is in this study designated as the *field*; the single or double panels surrounding the field or parallel to the selvage are named the *border*;

5. Size: size of repeat, motif or any parts of the design are presented in inches;

6. Color: the colors are listed and, as far as possible, based on the Calico Printers' Association's standard shades (Calico Printers' Association n.d.).

Table 3.   Selected samples of wax-print desings arranged in categories

Traditional designs
I-A-b-1	The Flying Duck (Plate 1)
I-Ca-20	The Banana
I-Na-19	The Shell
I-Na-22	The Good Husband
I-G-15	Dice Check

Old designs
I-Ga-8	The Target (pre-1920)
I-Ca-12	The Lamp (Plate 7)
I-Ca-11	The Staircase
I-Na-22	The Good Husband
II-Ca-80	Night and Day (Plate 8)

Recent designs
I-U-63	The Umbrella (Plate 9)
I-U-64	Umbrella stripe (1971)
I-E-25	The Alphabet (1970)
I-Ga-58	Tieplate (1970)
II-Ga-111	Name unknown (Plate 10)

Old designs presented in new ways
I-A-b-47	Migration
I-Ga-56	Eye Target

Table 3 — *continued*
I-Na-65   Damask
II-Ca-109   Back of Tortoise
III-Ca-114   Four Fields (Plate 11)

Combinations
I-Ca   The Batik
I-Ca-46   Diamond-Record-Shell
II-Ca-101   Broken Pots
III-Ca-113   Spinning Wheel (Plate 12)
III-Ca-114   Four Fields (Plate 11)
III-Ca-115   Linoleum

Designs with unusual motifs
  and colors
I-U-63   The Umbrella (Plate 9)
I-U-64   Umbrella stripe
II-Ca-78   Broken Pots
II-Na-107   Gecko Feet
III-A-r-113   Snake
III-A-i-113   Eye of Insect (Plate 13)

Traceable inspirational source
I-Ca-6   Java Lion (Java)
I-P-t-29   Tree of Life (Persia)
I-Na-65   Damask (Arabs)
I-Ca-36   The Arab Horseman (Arabs)
I-A-b-44   Bird in Maize (Plate 14)

Design named by consumers
II-Ga-69   A Red Eye Cannot Turn
                into Flames of Fire
II-P-t-77   Unity Is Strength/One Tree
                Alone Cannot Stand the
                Wind (Plate 15)
II-A-f-83   Women Are Fond of Fish
                (Plate 16)
II-M-e-86   The Eye/The Eye of God
II-Ga-92   African Mat/Show Your Love

Design well received by consumers
I-Ca-21   Yaw Donkor
I-M-45   Mask
III-A-b-118   Heron (Nigeria only)
III-Ca-124   Tarquajah (in Zaire)
III-Ga-128   Olympia (Plate 17)

Design rejected by consumers
III-Ca-124   Tarquajah (in Ghana)
III-A-b-118   Heron (all countries, except
                Nigeria)

Designs with political influence
I-N-62   Congo Independence
I-N-66   Uhuru (Plate 18)
I-N-67   4th Anniversaire
I-N-68   President Kennedy

Plate 7

Plate 8

Plate 9

Plate 10

Plate 7. "The Lamp" (I-Ca-12), a pre-1920 Brown Flemming design with a unique motif. Arrangement is centerpiece. The motif is a human hand with twelve dots in the palm, placed in the center of what appears to be an old lantern from which the rays of light emanate over a landscape of plants and standards. A row of hands is hanging as a cover over the motif, and a square of simulated script is placed between each lamp. Colors are traditional indigo, tange, and white

Plate 8. "Night and Day" (II-Ca-80), a popular old Brown Flemming design made by all three manufacturers. Arrangement is patchwork. The field is divided into two triangles, surrounded by an all-around border. The design is depicting night and day, illustrated by dark and light color backgrounds. The "day triangle" is covered with stylized flowers and flying birds. The "night triangle" is covered with a variety of symbols. Colors are indigo, brick-red and gourd-yellow

Plate 9. "The Umbrella" (I-U-63), a new and popular 1971 design. The umbrella is a significant status symbol in Ghana and to a lesser degree in some other African countries. It is an item of practical importance to all Africans living under the tropical sun and experiencing tropical rains. Arrangement is centerpiece. The motif is a large open umbrella and four smaller ones with tassels, flanked by a border of twenty small umbrellas. Colors are indigo, white, red and mustard

Plate 10. Name unknown (II-Ga-111), a new design produced in 1969 for the Ivory Coast and Nigeria. The arrangement is centerpiece. The pattern is a 45-inch-long indigo colored diamond shape with a twelve-inch center circle and "net" background. The circle appears in red, yellow, and pale blue consecutive rings. The diamond shape is viewed on a background of red, yellow, and pale blue stripes, radiating from the center and giving the illusion of rays streaming from the diamond shape. Colors are indigo, red, and yellow on white

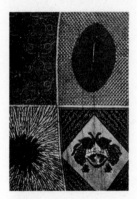

Plate 11

Plate 12

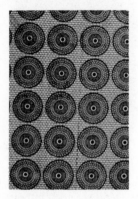

Plate 13

Plate 14

Plate 11. "Four Fields" (III-Ca-114), an example of how old favorites can be combined and used in new ways. Arrangement is four corners. The field is made up of four 23×17 inch rectangles, each with a different motif: (1) a centered star with rays of light; (2) two stylized peacocks enclosed in a diamond shape on a background of simulated script; (3) a stylized motif depicting an ostrich feather on "dice" background; and (4) stylized plant motifs. Colors are indigo, claret red, and buttercup yellow

Plate 12. "Spinning Wheel" (III-Ca-113). Arrangement is centerpiece. The spinning wheel is seen against a "scaly" background pattern and is surrounded by a ring of 32 wedges. A border with leaves runs parallel to the selvage. Colors are brown, light purple, light green, and light brown. A similar motif is named "Spider's Web" by Texoprint and Brunnschweiler

Plate 13. "Eye of Insect" (III-A-i-133), a one hundred percent Hohlenstein design produced only in the colors of the sample. All-over is the arrangement. The design is composed of four-inch-wide circles depicting the compound eye of an insect (*Omnitidia*), repeated on a light brown "honeycomb" background. Colors are brown and pink

Plate 14. "Bird in Maize" (I-A-b-44), a 1967 print with a definite Java influence. Arrangement is centerpiece. The motif is a large stylized bird with a smaller stylized bird to the right and a stylized flower to the left, enclosed in a parallelogram and flanked by triangles with tendril designs. The border is made of small rectangles with designs. Colors are indigo, tange and white

493

Plate 15

Plate 16

Plate 17

Plate 18

Plate 15. "Unity Is Strength" (II-P-t-77), a motif significant in being associated with the proverb: "One tree alone cannot stand the wind." The arrangement is centerpiece. The motif is composed of a single fallen tree in contrast to a group of standing trees. In the foreground are stylized flowers and close to the center is the inscription: "Dua Kur Gye Enum A Obu." The six-and-a-half-inch border is parallel to the selvage and contains leaves and flowers. Colors are indigo, rust and broken-gourd yellow

Plate 16. "Women Are Fond of Fish" (II-A-f-83), an example of a print named by the consumer. It is arranged as patchwork, and the motif is borrowed from the sea. The field is patterned with stylized seaweed and a school of fish, repeated on a background of undulating lines. Borders only at the selvage. One border is patterned with rows of "fish hooks", and the other border with "fishbones". The colors are indigo, brick red, and yellow

Plate 17. "Olympia" (III-Ga-128) illustrates acceptance of a new design. Arrangement is five olympic rings repeated on a "veined" background. It was designed in 1945 and millions of yards were sold the following seven years, not because the people of Ghana desired to honor the olympic games, but because the rings, to them, symbolized a very popular song at the time which in part read: "Don't be too unhappy because I am in prison and walk with my hands tied." The people of Ghana saw in the rings the chains that tied the prisoners' hands. It appeared to the writer that they chose to wear this particular cloth for similar reasons to those that caused many Americans to wear prisoner-of-war bracelets during the Vietnam conflict. The colors are brown and buttercup yellow

Plate 18. "Uhuru" (I-N-66), an example of a print which was used to commemorate an African political leader, and more than 50,000 yards were sold upon his death. Arrangement is centerpiece. A portrait of Lumumba is centered in a golden star, surrounded by a circle with the inscription: CONGO INDEPENDANCE 1960 MNC. Two portraits make up one repeat. Above and below the circles are Zaire flags and the inscription: UHURU, which means freedom. Colors are indigo, buttercup yellow, and white. This print is a typical example of extended use of "lights".

CONCLUSIONS

African wax-printed textiles provide an example of how cultural ideas are expressed and objectified in the designs. Great diversity in color and design reflect the varied acceptance of the many African countries. The search for the symbolic meaning of the wax-print designs is complicated by the fact that African consumers often perceive the motif differently from what was intended by the producers, and that the consumers often name the design according to certain circumstances in connection with the purchase or use of the cloth. Great changes take place in modern West Africa, but while the Africans are perfectly willing to innovate and modernize their society in many respects, it appears evident that the traditional wax-printed textiles will continue to be used and valued for a long time to come.

RECOMMENDATIONS

During this investigation the following possibilities for further research emerged and are suggested.

1. *African motivation for choice of design*: a study conducted in West Africa to interview consumers in an attempt to discover their motivation for preferences of certain designs.

2. *Naming of African wax prints*: a study among West African consumers to attempt to discover how they perceive various designs and reasons for consequent naming.

3. *Artistic expression of African wax prints*: a study of African wax prints from the point of view of elements and guidelines of design.

4. *Catalog of wax-prints*: a catalog of interesting African wax prints held in private and public collections.

5. *Comparative study of African- and European-produced wax prints.*

6. *Trade in African wax prints*: a comparison and analysis of the past 75 years of trade in wax-printed textiles to West Africa.

7. *Study of Java, Khanga, and Madras fabrics exported to Africa.*

8. *Japanese production of wax prints for Africa*: a study of Japanese wax-prints exported primarily to East Africa.

9. *Investigation of African nonwax prints*: an investigation of the socioeconomic importance of nonwax prints in various parts of Africa.

APPENDIX: THE USE OF PRINTED BATIKS BY AFRICANS

Justine M. Cordwell[10]

From the mid-nineteenth century when the first batik trade cloths were introduced into Africa, their acceptance and popularity were assured for three very basic reasons: first, cloth is an important medium for the visual communication of status and prestige in African society; second, the suppleness of the printed muslin allowed greater quantities of it to be worn without the weight of the indigenous weaving, hence it could be manipulated and tailored better to the human form, and its range of colors allowed greater individual aesthetic expression; and thirdly, its laundering properties were better than the indigenous, woven cloth, especially during periods of drought when available water for washing is at a premium. The mud of the rains and the dust of the dry season, plus the perspiration due to excessively high temperatures and humidity make washability an essential factor in the selection of a textile. Over the early years the trading companies soon informed the manufacturers of the acceptance or rejection of specific patterns and color combinations, and, as mentioned earlier, painstaking records of all this have been kept in the files of the textile firms. In spite of occasional mistakes in shipments, prints that were predominantly blue, for example, went to Nigeria, while those of orange and black went to the Gold Coast (now Ghana).

After the Second World War an increasing number of fabrics in patterns other than batik, such as stripes, checks, and ginghams, were added to the African markets, but the batiks remained the favorite cloth for the wrapped skirts. This particular use of the latter made it possible for the cloths with a political or commemorative motif to be used by the Africans to make quiet but effective commentary on the existing establishment. This was done by positioning the printed portrait of British or French rulers or their own political leaders in such a way that one could "innocently" and irreverently sit upon them. Some days such a print could be worn upside down "accidentally".

Many Africans are fond of traveling, but the portability of one's wardrobe poses a problem. Few travelers care to be parted from their luggage, so Africans have ingeniously adopted the large round tin containers in which European firms ship many items to the tropics, such as biscuits in wholesale lots. These containers, painted with European enamels, became a familiar sight in the fifties and sixties as Africans packed themselves onto converted lorries that became a form of omnibus with mahogany benches. The tin containers kept clothing dry or dust-free, and their size allowed the passenger to hold them in the lap. The size of them, however, prohibited the carrying of more than one extra outfit of the heavier indigenous cloth. On the other hand, up to three outfits of trade muslins could be packed in the same space.

The European muslin batiks became of great service to a person of high political status, for although such an individual would still select a well-made robe of indigenous cloth with much hand embroidery worked on it in order to display his wealth and his good taste and appropriateness to both rank and occasion, he could still afford a large wardrobe of damasks and batiks to show his wealth and taste further. Such a wealthy man might also be expected to give cloth to needy persons, and here economy could be practiced by use of batiks on muslin instead of the more costly handwoven cloths.

---

[10] This appendix was contributed at the request of the author.

The economy of the European muslin, coupled with the variety and richness of designs and color, were exactly the qualities that members of many West African societies needed to express materially certain values important to them. For example, not only is a Yoruba known for his or her taste, but is also judged by the taste of the company he or she keeps. These particular West Africans have a way of expeditiously handling this by the use of the social club to which a person belongs. Bascom (1952:497) describes this:

No man of high rank would be seen in the streets alone, while an ordinary individual invites the members of his club (egbe) to his house for food and drink at the time of a religious ceremony, funeral, wedding, or any other important event, so that he may have a large crowd dressed in fine clothes following him when he goes in the streets. This is one of the principal reasons for joining a club, and it is also related to the great interest of the Yoruba in children and large families. Both men's and women's clubs have their own distinctive clothing by which their members can be recognized, and one of the typical features of Yoruba religious ceremonies are the groups of about forty to sixty men or women, dressed alike, who are honoring one of their members as his or her guests.

European trading firms in West Africa became very aware of the business acumen of the women traders, and to those whose self-made wealth demonstrates this, the trading companies have extended a great amount of credit, in some instances up to the equivalent of $US40,000. These trading companies, in a perceptive and shrewd move, combine their knowledge of Yoruba tastes and culture patterns, such as those in the preceding paragraph, with their trust in the business sense of the women traders. A company would call in a wealthy woman trader and arrange to give her several bolts of new fabric that a textile firm was introducing to the African market. Enough cloth would be provided to make, say, blouses for every member of the woman's club, or enough for *lappas* [outer wrapped skirts] and perhaps another fabric for the head tie (*gele*). The company would also provide the money for a feast in the woman's compound and for drummers to precede a parade of the woman's club members wearing their outfits of the newly arrived fabrics. The seemingly casual course of the parade would be carefully planned through the quarter of the town and perhaps the marketplace in session that day so as to provide the maximum audience possible. Drawn by the drumming, the other women on the streets and the men as well would admire the cloths and, hopefully ask where they too could purchase such handsome and tasteful materials.

This type of advertising and use of textiles does not apply solely to the batiks, of course, for other cottons of European manufacture, such as gingham, plaids, and prints imitating eyelet embroidery (popular in the mid-sixties) are included as well. It is the combination of these other patterns with the batiks in African dress that makes any festival gathering of people in their best cloths a mixture of color and pattern reminiscent of paintings by Matisse.

REFERENCES

BASCOM, WILLIAM R.
   1952   Social status, wealth and individual differences among the Yoruba. *American Anthropologist* 53:490–505.
BEAUCHAMP, P. C.
   1957   "A gay garb for Ghana." *West Africa* 41:209.

BEVLIN, MARJORIE ELLIOT
1970   *Design through discovery.* New York: Holt, Rinehart and Winston.
BIRRELL, VERLA
1959   *The textile arts.* New York: Harper and Brothers.
BOAHEN, A. ADU
1971   "Kingdoms of West Africa," in *The horizon history of Africa.* Edited by Alvin M. Josephy, Jr. New York: American Heritage.
BRUNNSCHWEILER, A. O.
1957   "History of the Madras handkerchief trade." Unpublished notes, Manchester.
BUCK, SIR PETER (TE RANGIHIROA)
1911   On the Maori art of weaving cloaks, capes, and kilts. *New Zealand Dominion Museum Bulletin* 3:69–90.
BUTLER, RAY
1958   Sale of British cotton goods in West Africa. *The Times*, August 13, p. 12.
CALICO PRINTERS' ASSOCIATION
   n.d.   *Wax-prints; standard shades.* Manchester: F. W. Ashton.
DAVIDSON, BASIL
1966   *African kingdoms.* New York: Time-Life.
1971   "Kingdoms of West Africa," in *The horizon history of Africa.* Edited by Alvin M. Josephy, Jr. New York: American Heritage.
EICHER, JOANNE B.
1970   *African dress: a select and annotated bibliography of subsaharan countries.* East Lansing: Department of Human Environment and Design, African Studies Center, Michigan State University.
EMERY, IRENE
1966   *The primary structures of fabrics: an illustrated classification.* Washington, D.C.: Textile Museum.
FORDE, C. DARYLL, PHYLLIS M. KABERRY
1967   *West African kingdoms in the nineteenth century.* London: Oxford University Press.
FRASER, GRACE
1948   *Textiles by Britain.* London: George Allen and Unwin.
HARRELL, JANET
1967   "Classification and documentation of the Eicher collection of selected Nigerian textile fabrics." Unpublished Master's dissertation, Michigan State University, East Lansing.
IRWIN, J., V. MURPHY
1969   *Batik.* London: Victoria and Albert Museum.
JOHNSTON, MEDA PARKER, GLEN KAUFMAN
1967   *Design on fabrics.* New York: Reinhold.
JONES, G. I.
   n.d.   "Import trade of cloth into eastern Nigeria." Unpublished manuscript.
MEAD, SIDNEY M.
1968   *The art of taaniko weaving.* Wellington, New Zealand: A. H. A. W. Reed.
MÜLLER, ALBERT
   n.d.   *Der Zeugdruck im Museum des Landes Glarus im Nafels.* Glarus, Switzerland: Glarus Museum.
NEGRI, EVE DE
1966   Nigerian textile industry before independence. *Nigeria Magazine* 89:95–101.
PHILLIPS, W. J.
1960   *Maori rafter and taniko designs.* Wellington, New Zealand: Wingfield.

PLUMER, CHERYL
  1970   *African textiles: an outline of handcrafted sub-Saharan fabrics.* East Lansing: Department of Human Environment and Design, African Studies Center, Michigan State University.
ROBINSON, STUART
  1969a *A history of dyed textiles.* Cambridge Massachusetts: MIT Press.
  1969b *A history of printed textiles.* Cambridge, Massachusetts: MIT Press.
RODENBURG, G. H.
  1967   Dutch wax-block garments. *Textielhistorische Bijdragen* 39–50.
RYDER, A. F. C.
  1965   Dutch trade on the Nigerian coast during the seventeenth century. *Journal of the Historical Society of Nigeria* 3:195ff.
SCHAPIRO, MEYER
  1953   "Style," in: *Anthropology today.* Edited by A. L. Kroeber, 287–312. Chicago: University of Chicago Press.
SIEBER, ROY
  1972   *African textiles and decorative arts. New York:* Museum of Modern Art.
SKINNER, ELLIOTT P.
  1964   "West African economic systems," in *Economic transition in Africa.* Edited by Melville J. Herskovits and Mitchel Harwitz, 77–97. Evanston, Illinois: Northwestern University Press.
STEINMANN, ALFRED
  1958   *Batik: a survey of batik design.* Leigh-on-Sea, Essex: F. Lewis.
THORP, ELLEN
  1956   *Ladder of bones.* London: Jonathan Cape.
West Africa
  1950   Manchester's African trade. *West Africa* 1751:850–851.
WOLFSON, FREDA
  1958   *Pageant of Ghana.* London: Oxford University Press.
Writing of batik
  1968   *The writing of batik.* Wood-Ridge, New Jersey: Craftools.

Biographical Notes

ENYINNA CHUTA (1940–   ) received his M.A. in Economics and his Ph.D. in Agricultural Economics, both at Michigan State University, East Lansing. He has specialized in rural cooperatives and rural industries, and in small- and medium-scale industries. He has written pamphlets and occasional papers as well as working papers for the University. For the coming year, after publication of this volume, he will be in Geneva, Switzerland, in the Employment and Development Department of the Employment and Technology Branch of the International Labor Office.

HERBERT M. COLE (1935–   ) is Associate Professor of Art History at the University of California at Santa Barbara. He received his Ph.D. at Columbia University in 1968, working on Ibo art under the direction of Douglas Fraser. He is author of *African arts of transformation* and coauthor (with Doran Ross) of the catalogue *Arts of Ghana*. His book on Ibo Mbari houses is being published this year by Indiana University Press. He has made many trips to Africa, which is reflected in his numerous articles on art and personal adornment and in *African arts and leadership*, which he coedited with Douglas Fraser.

JUSTINE M. CORDWELL (1920–   ) received her Ph.D. in Anthropology from Northwestern University under the direction of Melville Herskovits. Her unpublished dissertation on Yoruba and Bini aesthetics is widely known and distributed on microfilm. She is editor of *The visual arts*. She has been a consultant in city planning and an urban ethnologist, as well as a lecturer in anthropology at Northwestern, Loyola, and Roosevelt Universities.

JOHN HENRY DREWAL (1943–   ) received his B.A. from Hamilton

College in 1964 and his Ph.D from Columbia University in 1973. He is presently Associate Professor of Art History at the Cleveland State University, Cleveland, Ohio. He has done fieldwork on art and culture in Ghana, Togo, Benin, and Nigeria, and on African art retention in Brazil, and has published several exhibition catalogues and numerous articles.

JOANNE B. EICHER (1930–   ) is Professor and Head of the Department of Textiles and Clothing at the University of Minnesota, St. Paul, Minnesota. She received her Ph.D. in a Sociology and Anthropology at Michigan State University, where she taught from 1969–1977. She has coauthored (with Mary Ellen Roach) two books on clothing, *Dress, adornment and the social order* and *The visible self: perspectives on dress*. She is the author of *African dress, an annotated bibliography* as well as a sociological study on high school girl's dress; she has supervised an outline of handcrafted, sub-Saharan textiles by Cheryl Plumer. A more recent book, published in Lagos, details Nigerian dress.

JANET BRODY ESSER (1930–   ) is currently Assistant Professor of Art History at San Diego State University. She received her B.F.A. in Studio Arts from the State University of Iowa, her B.S. in Art Education from Kent State University, her M.A. in Art History from California State University, Long Beach, and her Ph.D. in Art History from the University of California, Los Angeles. She previously taught at Occidental College, Los Angeles, Marymount College/Loyola University, California State University, Long Beach, and Kent State University. She is the author of numerous articles on Mexican art forms.

PAUL HOCKINGS (1935–   ) studied anthropology at the Universities of Sydney, Toronto, Chicago, Stanford, and California (Berkeley). He received his Ph.D. in Anthropology from the University of California (Berkeley). Now Associate Professor at the University of Illinois, Chicago Circle Campus, his broad interests range from Southeast Asian studies, through ethnography of Ireland and visual anthropology to the ethnology of Chicago's ethnic groups. He is author of *A bibliography for the Nilgiri Hills of Southern India, Ancient Hindu refugees: Badaga social history 1550–1975*, and *Sex and disease in a mountain community*. He is also editor of *Principles of visual anthropology*.

MARILYN HAMMERSLEY HOULBERG holds degrees from the University of Chicago in Art History and the University of London in Anthropology. She is currently teaching at the School of the Art Institute of Chicago. She has published on Yoruba art and religion in *African Arts*. Her special interests are Yoruba art and its symbolism, while her on-going research is on Yoruba twin cults, both in West Africa and in Afro-American cultures in the New World.

JOANN W. KEALI'INOHOMOKU (1930–   ) is currently teaching at Northern Arizona University, Flagstaff. She was previously Assistant Professor of Anthropology and Dance, World Campus Alfoat, Chapman College, Orange, California. Her interests are dance ethnology, theory and methodology, especially non-European, Hopi Indian pottery, and affective culture, especially Hopi Indian and Hawaiian. Her publications include "Folk dance," "Hopi and Polynesian dance: a study in cross-cultural comparisons," and "Dance and self-accompaniment."

AVIVA KLEIN (1936–   ) is Lecturer in Jewish Folklore Studies at the Hebrew University, Jerusalem, Israel. She has specialized in studies of immigration and acculturation, folk medicine, and material culture.

E. JEAN LANGDON (1944–   ) received her B.A. at Carleton College, Minnesota, her M.A. at the University of Washington, Seattle, and her Ph.D. at Tulane University, Louisiana. She is a cultural anthropologist interested in ethnomedicine, hallucinogens, and Latin American cultures. She is currently editing a volume on South American mythology and working on hallucinogenic art of South America.

EVAN MACLYN MAURER (1944–   ) received his M.A. in Art History from the University of Minnesota in 1969 and his Ph.D. in Art History from the University of Pennsylvania in 1974. Though an authority on both modern art and the late Renaissance in the Western world, he is Curator of Primitive Art at the Art Institute of Chicago. While his breadth of interests in this field are great, he has particular empathy for and interest in the language and composition of dress, particularly that of the North American Indian.

MARGARET THOMPSON MILLER. No biographical data available.

RUTH NIELSEN (1925–   ) received her M.A. at Michigan State University in 1974 in textiles and clothing under the direction of Joanne Eicher. Her thesis "The historical development of waxprinted textiles intended for West Africa and Zaire" is condensed in this volume. She is Director of the School of Home Economics in Skaodsborg, Denmark.

SIMON OTTENBERG (1923–   ) is Professor of Anthropology at the University of Washington, Seattle. He received his Ph.D. from Northwestern University under the direction of Melville Herskovits. As a result of his fieldwork in West Africa (where he is as this goes to press) he is author of two different volumes on the Afikpo Igbo culture, and coeditor (with Phoebe Ottenberg) of a well-known sourcebook on African societies. He received the Amaury Talbot Award for best book on Africa in 1976, *Masked rituals of Africa*.

ILA POKORNOWSKI (1928–   ) received both her B.S. and M.A. from Michigan State University in the field of textiles and clothing. She is an instructor in clothing in the Department of Family Resources and Human Environment at Michigan State University, where there is a close liaison between her department and that of the African Studies Program. Her on-going work is the updating of a bibliography on African dress with Joanne Eicher. She is also working on a history of apparel with Anna M. Creekmore.

LORETTA REINHARDT (1938–   ) received her B.F.A. degree in painting from the Maryland Institute before entering anthropology. She received her M.A. from Indiana University, with a study of Hopewellian art, and for her Ph.D. from Southern Illinois University. Her dissertation, *Mende carvers*, was based on her first fieldwork in art and aesthetics among the Mende of Sierra Leone, West Africa, in 1967–1968. A second period of fieldwork, on indigo dyeing in 1971, is reported in "Mrs. Kadiato Kamara: an expert dyer in Sierra Leone". Dr. Reinhardt has taught at Temple University, Philadelphia and, since 1971, at the University of Toronto. She has recently returned from a third period of fieldwork in Sierra Leone, 1977–1979, where she studied aesthetic values and process among the Mende of Sierra Leone, a study which emphasized audio-visual documentation.

MARY ELLEN ROACH (1921–   ) is Professor at the School of Family Resources and Consumer Sciences, University of Wisconsin, Madison. She received her Ph.D. in Sociology and Anthropology at Michigan State University. She collaborated with Joanne Eicher on two books on the sociology of dress and is the author of numerous articles and monographs on dress. She approaches the subject as a sociologist trained in anthropology.

RONALD A. SCHWARZ (1939–   ) received his B.A. in Philosophy from Colgate University, and his Ph.D. from Michigan State University. He has done post-doctoral studies at Tulane University, School of Public Health and Tropical Medicine. He is currently affiliated with the Department of Behavioral Sciences, The John Hopkins University, School of Hygiene and Public Health. He also works as a free-lance consultant on development projects in Latin American and Africa. He previously taught at Colgate University, Williams College, and Instituto

Norte Andino de Ciencias Sociales, Colombia. His research interests include social organization, social change, aesthetics and the medical system of the Guambiano Indians of Colombia, primary health care practitioners, midwives, and drug addiction in South America and the United States. He is coeditor (with David L. Browman) of two books: *Peasants, primitives, and proletariats* and *Spirits, shamans, and stars* and is currently working on a book on environmental health and development for the American Public Health Association.

A. G. TROFIMOVA. No biographical data available.

U. R. VON EHRENFELS (1901–   ) was educated at Prague and Vienna Universities. He lived in India and did field research there for over three decades. From 1949 he was Head of the Department of Anthropology at the University of Madras. In 1962 he joined the South Asia Institute of the University of Heidelberg. A specialist in matrilineal societies, he has written numerous articles, books (e.g. *Mother-right in India, Kadar of Chchin, Innere Entwicklungshilfe*) and contributed articles to such collected works as *Epistemology in anthropology* and *German scholars on India*.

MAUDE SOUTHWELL WAHLMAN (1942–   ) received her M.A. in Anthropology at Northwestern University, Evanston in 1969 and is currently working on her Ph.D. at Yale University under the direction of Robert Faris Thompson. She and her husband travelled throughout Africa gathering material for the Contemporary African Arts exhibit at the Field Museum, Chicago. She has also done fieldwork in Nigeria, Ghana, and Sierra Leone and in the American Southwest. She is author of two well-known exhibit catalogues, *Contemporary African Arts* and *Contemporary African Fabrics* and has written numerous articles on African art, pottery, fabrics, and clothing. She is currently working on her dissertation, "The optics of the Afro-American quilt".

BETTY WASS (1935–   ) received her M.A. and Ph.D. at Michigan State University under the direction of Joanne Eicher in the Department of Family Resources and Human Ecology in the field of textiles and clothing. She is Assistant Professor in the Department of Environment, Textiles and Design at the University of Wisconsin, Madison. She has done fieldwork in Sierra Leone, Nigeria, and Egypt, some of which is reported in *African Arts*. Her recent Egyptian work is on the applique work of the traditional Bedouin tentmakers.

Index of Names

Abercrombie, Thomas J., 59
Abraham, R. C., 192, 195n, 210n, 213, 214, 376, 380, 381, 392
Adamson, Joy, 92n
Addison, W., 253, 255, 256
Adedeji, J. A., 193
Adeleye, I. O., 192
Adepegba, -., 198, 224, 225
Ajisafe, A. K., 111
Akinsulure, A., 206n
Akinwole, A. O., 198, 199, 215
Alexander, Bryan, 143n
Alldridge, Thomas J., 232, 234, 237, 242, 244, 245, 248, 263
Amoda, Moyibi, 342
Andres, William, 16
Anthony, Susan B., 418
Aristova, T. F., 407, 410
Arkell, A. J., 106
Arroyo de Anda, Luis Aveleyra, 49, 53
Ashton, A. John, 16
Atwater, Mary, 426
Avdal, A., 410

Bakare, A., 203
Bankole, A., 199
Barnet, Hanna, 451
Bartels, M., 425n, 426, 426n, 429n
Bartlett, Edith, 327
Bascom, William R., 106, 107, 108, 109, 110, 113, 190, 368, 369, 372, 372n, 380n, 496
Battell, Andrew, 104
Beals, R., 24, 269, 271n
Beattie, John, 23
Beauchamp, P. C., 470, 482, 483
Beaumont, Peter, 50, 51

Beck, Horace C., 105, 106
Beier, H. Ulli, 193, 201n, 203, 204, 205
Belli Gowder, M. K., 150, 154, 155, 158, 169
Benbow, Jessie, 145, 152, 155
Benedict, Ruth, 24, 25, 27
Bevlin, Marjorie Elliott, 486
Beyioku, A. F., 200, 201, 203, 216
Bick, Mario, 26
Blair, Emma Helen, 328
Bliss, S. H., 25
Bloomer, Amelia, 418, 419
Boahen, A. Adu, 468
Bogatyrev, Peter G., 1, 32, 33
Bolland, M. A., 474
Boshier, Adrian, 51
Bouteiller, Marchelle, 54
Bowen, T. J., 210n
Brauer, Erich, 427
Braun-Ronsdorf, M., 436n
Breuil, Abbé, 51
Brody, Janet. See Esser
Brown, Jean, 87n, 100n
Buchlor, J., 29, 30
Buck, Sir Peter, 484
Bunzel, Ruth, 25, 27
Bush, George, 11, 331
Butler, Ray, 467, 472, 474
Butt-Thomson, F. W., 257

Campbell, Robert, 110
Carlyle, Thomas, 1, 28
Carmony, Donald F., 326
Carrasco, Pedro, 269
Carroll, Kevin, 381n, 385
Caton-Thomson, Gertrude, 105
Chuta, Enyinna, 3, 447–466, 499

Clapperton, Hugh, 109, 111
Clarke, J. D., 112
Clifford, Miles, 60
Cohn, J. C., 103
Cole, Herbert M., 2, 67, 87–102, 192, 499
Cooper, L., 475, 475n, 476, 477, 482, 484
Cordwell, Justine M., 2, 47–75, 112, 113, 114, 495, 499
Crawley, Ernest, 25
Crowfoot, Grace, 436n
Crowther, S., 195n, 204, 210n, 214n, 215, 216

Damien, Yvonne, 47n
Daniel, F., 112
Darbois, Dominique, 65
Dark, Philip, 231n, 233, 244
Davenport, Millia, 13, 16, 17
Davidson, Basil, 51, 105, 468, 469
Dawson, J. L. M., 249, 250
D'Azevedo, Warren, 235
Delano, Isaac, 334
DeNegri, E., 224, 469
Douglas, Mary, 31
Douglass, John M., 323
Dresser, Leland, 448, 461, 461n, 462
Drewal, Henry John, 2, 3, 189–229, 381, 499
Drewal, Margaret Thompson, 189n
Duchamp, Marcel, 272n
Dunlap, Knight, 25, 26
Durkheim, Emile, 233
DuToit, A. P., 114

Easmon, M. C. F., 243, 448n
Eberl-Elber, Ralph, 237
Eckholm, Gordon F., 49, 53
Efendiev, R. S., 405
Eicher, Joanne Bubolz, 2, 7–21, 28, 47, 48, 421, 467, 468n, 470n, 472n, 476, 500
Eisen, Gustavus, 105
Elgee, C. H., 110
Elisofon, Eliot, 402n
Ellis, A. B., 107
Ellis, Havelock, 26
Emeneau, Murray B., 143, 159, 169
Emory, Kenneth, 56, 57
Esser, Janet Brody, 2, 3, 267–294, 500
Etuobe, Alaiye, 210n
Evans-Pritchard, E. E., 27

Fadipe, N. A., 111, 201, 346
Fagg, William, 108, 109, 112, 113, 249
Familori, Funke, 362
Faris, James, 66, 67, 68
Faron, Louis, C., 31
Farrow, William, 107, 108
Field, Henry, 57, 58, 71
Film, Rebecca Beverly, 306

Flanagan, J. F., 426
Flemming, Ebenezer Brown, 470, 474
Flugel, John Carl, 25
Foray, Miriam, 463
Forbes, Robert J., 48, 49, 443n
Forde, C. Daryll, 107, 113, 469
Foster, George M., 270n
Fourneau, J., 105, 114
Francis, Walter, 145, 147
Franzero, Charles Marie, 11
Fraser, Grace, 481
Frazer, E., 206n
Frazer, James G., 25
Frobenius, Leo, 107, 112

Gardner, Robert, *Dead birds*, 66; *Gardens of war*, 66
Geijer, Agnes, 426, 436n
Gerbrands, S., 233, 244
Gerend, Alphonse, 327
Gillen, F. J., 25
Gluckman, Max, 391
Goffman, Erving, 26
Goitein, Sh. Dov., 427
Greenfield, Kent Roberts, 12
Grigg, Henry B., 147, 148, 150, 153
Guliev, G. A., 407, 409
Gwatkin, Nina, 353

Habara, Sh. Yosef, 427, 429n, 436n, 440
Hagen, Victor W. Von, 69
Hall,-., 248
Hambly, Wilfred D., 58, 111
Handy, E. S. Craighill, 57
Handy, Willowdean Chatterson, 57
Hardenburg, Walter E., 304
Harkness, Henry, 150, 155, 165, 168
Harley, George W., 232, 244
Harms, Ernst, 25
Harper, P., 201, 208, 213, 216n
Harrell, Janet, 484
Harris, W. T., 231, 245
Harrison, Michael, 418
Hays, Elinor, 419
Hearn, Lafcadio, 13
Heiden, Max, 426
Heider, Karl G., *Gardens of war*, 66
Helm, June, 28
Hernandez de Alba, Gregorio, 40
Hertz, Robert, 31
Hiler, Hilaire, 24, 25
Hiler, Meyer, 24, 25
Hill, L. Reinhardt, 235, 244
Hirn, Yrjo, 24, 25, 26, 27; *The origins of art*, 24
Hobley, C. W., 104
Hockings, Paul, 2, 47n, 143–174, 500
Hofstra, Sjoerd, 231, 232, 234

Hoijer, H., 24
Holm, Bill, 133
Hostetler, John A., 18
Houdek, Nancy, 448
Houlberg, Klindt, 349n, 350, 351, 352, 361, 362, 363, 388
Houlberg, Marilyn Hammersley, 3, 344, 349–397, 500
Hughes, Charles C., 31

Ibn Battuta, 104
Idowu, E. B., 193
Innes, Gordon, 234, 235, 236n, 239n, 241, 244, 245, 247, 249, 250, 254, 256
Irwin, J., 470, 485
Izmailova, A. A., 409, 410

Jackes, Mary, 231n
Jackson, W. H., 124, 125, 126, 130
Jagor, Andreas, F., 153
Jefferson, Louise, 62
Johnson, Gerald, 238
Johnson, Samuel, 108, 109, 111, 337, 368, 370, 383
Johnston, Meda Parker, 485
Johnston, Rhoda Omasunlola, 337
Jones, G. I., 184, 482
Jopling, Carol F., 28
Jordan, Alfred, 420, 421

Kaberry, Phyllis M., 469
Kafeh, Yosef, 427
Kamara, Kadiatu, 451, 452, 453, 454, 455, 456, 457, 458
Karakashly, K. T., 406, 407
Kariabettan, N., 145
Karl, William V., 145
Kartaschoff-Nabholz, M. L., 476
Kaufman, Glen, 485
Keali'nohomoku, Joann W., 2, 77–83, 501
Keely, Lawrence, 48n
Keimer, Louis, 57
Kil'chevskaia, Z. A., 406, 407
King, William Ross, 165
Kinietz, William Vernon, 314, 322
Klein, A., 3, 425–445, 501
Knapp, L., 425
Kosswig, Leonore, 425, 425n, 426, 429n, 431n, 435, 436n, 438n, 440
Kraditor, Aitken S., 419, 420
Krantz, C. H., 470, 470n, 474, 479, 482
Krapi-Askari, Eva, 110
Krauss, Samuel, 425, 430n
Krige, E. J., 104
Krige, J. D., 104
Kroeber, A. L., 32
Kurath, Gertrude Prokosch, 286n

La Baume, Wolfgang, 426, 443n
Lajoux, Jean-Dominique, 64
Lancet-Maller, A., 429n, 436n
Landa, Fray Diego de, 69, 70
Langdon, E. Jean, 3, 297–311, 501
Launois, John, 63
Lawal, B., 190, 204, 208, 208n, 213, 225
Lazar, Paul, 47n
Leach, Edmund R., 91, 367, 395
Lee, Thorold D., 425n, 440
Leechman, Douglas, 58
Lehmann-Filhes, M., 425, 426
Lehmann-Hautt, -., 426
Leuzinger, Elsy, 249
Lévi-Strauss, Claude, 31, 32, 40, 41, 389
Lewis, Oscar, 27
Lhote, Henri, 29
Lienhardt, Godfrey, 23
Lindblom, Carl, 448n
Lindfors, B., 189, 202
Little, Kenneth, 231, 232, 233, 234, 235, 236, 237, 238, 239, 242, 243, 244, 249, 250, 251, 253, 257, 257n, 258, 261, 263
Lloyd, P. C., 110, 111, 210n
London, Perry, 11, 331
Lucas, J. Olumide, 107
Lurie, Nancy Oestreich, 322

McCorkle, Thomas, 269
McCulloch, M., 234, 248, 253
McLuhan, T. C., 327
Macleane, Charles D., 170
Matteson, Esther, 33
Mauny, Raymond, 105
Maurer, Evan M., 2, 119–141, 501
Mauss, Marcel, 171, 172
Mead, Margaret, 57, 66
Mead, Sidney M., 484, 486
Mellor, W. F., 113
Melville, Herman, 56
Merchant, Whabiz D., 143n
Migeod, F. W. H., 237n, 251, 252, 256, 256n, 259
Miles, Arthur, 154
Miller, B. V., 410
Miller, Elizabeth Smith, 418, 419
Miller, Margaret Thompson, 3, 313–330, 501
Mörike, E.G.C., 160, 164
Morton-Williams, P., 193, 215, 383, 384
Moulero, T., 200, 201n, 203, 205, 206, 207, 208, 212, 215
Mountford, Charles P., 66
Müller, Albert, 476, 482, 483
Murphy, Robert F., 29, 40
Murphy, V., 470n, 485
Murray, K. C., 198, 201, 201n, 204n, 215, 217, 218

Nadel, S. F., 30
Natesa Sastri, S. M., 161, 164, 168
Needham, Rodney, 31
Newton, Herta, 452, 453, 454, 456, 458
Nielsen, Ruth, 3, 467–498, 501
Norris, Herbert, 17

Odugbesan, C., 204
Ogibenin, Boris L., 41
Ogundipe, Lasisi, 210n, 214, 215, 216
Ojo, G. J. Afolabi, 111, 112
O'Kelliher, Marjorie, 324, 325
Olabimtan, A., 190, 201n, 217
O'Meara, Walter, 325
Oni, M., 199
Orobiyi, A., 217
Osubi, S., 203, 205
Ottenberg, Simon, 2, 3, 177–187, 501
Overton, George, 323
Owomoyela, O., 189, 202

Pa Jobu, 245, 247, 249
Palau-Marti, M., 214n
Parsons, Elsie Clews, 27
Paxson, Barbara, 448
Paz, Octavio, 447
Phelps, Elizabeth Stuart, 418
Phillips, Ruth, 245, 247
Phillips, W. J., 484
Pinkley, Homer V., 305n
Plass, Margaret, 249
Plumer, Cheryl, 467
Pokornowski, Ila, 2, 103–117, 502
Poll, Solomon, 17, 18, 19
Powell, Father Peter J., 135
Prost, J. H., 80
Prucha, Francis Paul, 326
Putnam, John J., 402

Quiggin, A. Hingston, 114

Radcliffe-Brown, A. R., 12
Raffles, Sir Thomas Stamford, 470
Ranga, Nagayya G., 155
Rathjens, Carl, 426, 427, 427n, 436n
Redfield, Robert, 27
Reed, Charles, 47n
Reichel-Dolmatoff, Alicia, 27, 41
Reichel-Dolmatoff, Gerardo, 27, 41
Reinhardt, Loretta, 2, 3, 231–266, 448, 502
Rhiem, Hanna, 145, 153, 155, 165
Richardson, Jane, 32
Riet Lowe, Clarence van, 104, 105, 106
Ritter, Professor, 426
Ritzenthaler, Robert E., 328
Rivers, William H. R., 169, 170
Rivet, Paul, 33

Roach, Mary Ellen, 2, 3, 7–21, 28, 415–422, 502
Robinson, Scott, 300n
Robinson, Stuart, 426, 469, 470, 475, 482
Robley, Horatio Gordon, 56, 57
Rodenburg, G. H., 470, 474
Rosenblüth, Hadasa, 426, 427
Russell, Frances E., 417, 418, 419
Ryder, A. F. C., 105, 469

Sahagún, Fray Bernardino de, 69, 70
Samikannu, C. Paul, 154, 155
Sanborn, Herbert C., 25, 26
Santa Gertrudis, Fray Juan de, 303
Santos, D. M. dos, 193, 195n, 203n
Santos, J. E. dos, 193
Sapir, Jacob, 427
Saulner, Tony, 66
Sawyer, Harry A. E., 231, 245
Schapiro, Meyer, 486
Scharlau-Staudinger, Margarete, 425
Schiltz, Mark, 349n, 358, 382, 382n
Schoewe, Charles E., 326, 327
Schofield, J. F., 104, 105, 106, 114
Schuette, Marie, 425, 430n, 438n, 440, 440n, 443n
Schultz, Harald, 62
Schwarz, Ronald A., 2, 23–45, 47n, 502
Shaeffer, G., 429n
Shapiro, Harry, 48
Sherring, Matthew A., 165
Shor, Franc, 63
Shortt, John, 145, 147, 152
Sieber, Roy, 447, 467
Simnel, Georg, 26
Siskind, Janet, 302n
Skinner, Elliott P., 469
Sleen, W. F. N. van der, 106
Smith, Gerrit, 419, 422
Smith, Huron H., 327, 328, 329
Smith, John, 58
Smith, Robert, 106, 107, 109, 111
Smythe, Hugh H., 332, 343
Smythe, Mabel, 332, 343
Solarin, Sheila, 349n
Solarin, Tai, 349n
Spencer, Paul, 87n, 93n, 100n
Spencer, Walter B., 25
Sprague, Linda, 355n
Stacy, Miriam, 448, 448n
Stanton, Elizabeth Cady, 417, 418, 419, 421, 422
Steinen, Karl von den, 57
Steinmann, Alfred, 470n
Stone, James W. Van, 58
Stone, Lucy, 418, 419, 422
Sturtevant, William C., 28
Sutter, Frederic Koehler, 55

Tabib, Abraham, 427n
Taiwo, R., 195
Talbot, Amaury, 107, 110
Tallone, Peter, 87n
Tax, Sol, 47n
Thomas, Northcote W., 257n
Thomas, William I., 25
Thompson, Robert Faris, 107, 192, 193, 195, 201, 206, 214n, 216, 217, 374, 385, 386, 389
Thurston, Edgar, 145, 148, 152, 153, 161, 165, 167
Thwaites, R. G., 322
Tidhar, Amalia, 437n
Tignous, H. P. J. A., 145, 147, 152
Tilke, M., 407n
Torchinskaia, E. G., 406, 408
Trofimova, A. G., 3, 405–414
Tumiñá-Pillimué, Francisco, 40
Tunis, M. A., 448, 458
Turner, Victor, 31, 37, 351, 367, 395
Twala, Regina, G., 104

Underhill, Ruth Murray, 323, 326

Vandenburg, Mary M., 328
Vandenhoute, P. J., 232
Veblen, Thorstein, 417
Verger, R., 193, 201, 202, 204, 210n, 216
Verghese, Isaac, 145

Vettori, Aldo, 87n
Vicker, William, 308n
Vivekanandam Pillai, T. H., 147
Voght, Evan Z., 27
Voirol, E., 470, 470n, 476, 482
Von Ehrenfels, U. R., 3, 399–403, 503

Wahlman, James, 450, 457
Wahlman, Maude, 3, 447–466, 503
Walker, Anthony R., 169, 170
Wallis, C. Braithwaite, 245
Ward, Benjamin, 145, 147, 150
Wass, Betty M., 3, 112, 161, 331–348, 503
Weinberg, Martin S., 20
Weiner, Janet E., 268. *See also* Esser
Weiss, Gerald, 299
West, Robert Cooper, 268
Westcott, Joan, 385, 386, 388
Westermarck, Edward A., 26
Willett, Frank, 105, 108, 109, 110, 112, 113
Williams, D., 204n
Wilson, Monica, 30
Wolfe, Tom, 23, 42
Wright, Arthur R., 235, 244, 245

Yaiguaje, Estanislao, 304

Zohar, Mrs., 429n

Index of Subjects

Adornment. *See* Clothing and Adornment; Personal Adornment. *See also* Samburu of Kenya; Siona of Colombia; Yoruba beads

African beads: Frobenius' report on ancient glass bead making in Ife, 112; travellers' reports of bead trade and significance, 104, 105, 110, 111, 112; widespread use of, as a research topic, 104–105; Yoruba bead-wearing tradition, 107–108

African studies: acknowledgements to supportive institutions, 189n, 231n

African textile arts in the modern American market, 447

Alake of Abeokuta's state visit to London, 110

America, Central and South: cosmetic customs of, 69–70; shells as ancient trade item, 122. *See also* Siona of Colombia; Guambiano of Colombia

America, United States of: modern imports of kohl, 72; symbolism of personal adornment in, 7, 8, 10, 13–14; white-collar workers in, 14. *See also* North American Indian clothing; Potawatomi costume

American Institute of Indian Studies, 143n

Amulets, Samburu, 89, 97

Anthropological studies: of clothing and adornment, 23–24; of clothing and social change, 31–33; of environment, 31; of the Guambianos as a case study of clothing, 33–40; of material culture, 27–28, 29–31

Arabia. *See* Tablet weaving of Yemenite Jews

Archaeological evidence: of Alaskan tattooing, 58; of bead glass in early Nigeria, 104; of early mining of ores for cosmetic pigmentation, 49–51, 69; of first needles and textiles, 24; of Mayan skull deformation, 53; of New World cosmetic hematite, 69; of non-African cultures in Algeria, 51, 52; of pigmentation in Algerian rock paintings, 50–51, 64; of textile treasures at Birka, 426; of weaving from Viking tomb, 425

Azerbaidzhan clothing, traditional and modern: Baku as center of new Caucasian vogue, 411; Baku modern jewelry of high artistic value, 412; Caucasian folk costume as an ethnic standard, 405; decorative necklaces and filigree work, 412; female costume set, traditional, 406–408; footwear, old and new, 407, 408, 410; male costumes, warlike, 408–409; minority variations, Tat and Talysh, 409–410; modern disappearance of traditional clothes, 412; Muslim Kurdish foot bracelets and nose trinkets, 410; natural silk fabrics for general wear, 411, 412; post-Revolution elimination of the *yash-mak* and *rubend*, 410; recent postwar changes, 411–412

Badaga of South India: body ornaments, gold and silver, 148, 149; childhood rituals of clothing and adornment, 151–153; European influences on women's dress, 145–146, 147; female tattooing and scarring, 152–153; flow of clothing and jewelry at weddings, 155–157, 158; funeral clothing customs, 158–165; guru's gifts to a bride, 157, 158; a Hindu social remnant with distinctive costumes, 143,

Badaga of South India — *cont.*
144, 145; the Kaggusis *rudrakśa* bead,
154; Kota building of the catafalque, 165,
166; the *linga* phallic emblem, male,
153–154; male dress, basic, modern, 146,
147; *manji* cloth weaving, washing,
starching, 150–151; marriage rituals and
gifts, 154–158; relationships with other
tribes, 168–171; results of migration to
Nilgri plateau, 143, 144; rings, significance of, 149; umbrellas, 149–150, 170;
wearing and washing of clothes, 151;
women's dress, white, traditional, three-
part, 145, 146, 147
Batik: European, muslin, as symbol of
wealth and status, 495; Javanese, history
of, 469–470, 482. *See also* Wax-printed
textiles
Beads: as a "biography" of a Samburu
woman, 98–99, 100; Cambay factory,
106; colored, from ancient Ife, 112; colored, and Yoruba gods, 107–108; coral,
of regal importance, 109, 110, 111;
dating of Bantu ostrich egg, 105–106;
glass, imported, 98, 112, 323; glass,
imported for trade purposes, 104;
Guambiano, 37; historical, African, a
survey, 104–106; manufactured, stone
and glass, 112; nutshell, made by women,
111; and political status, 108, 110; royal,
sacred, trade, 104, 114; of the Samburu
of Kenya, 88, 89, 94, 95; significance of
manufacture and stringing, 105; Siona
necklaces, 305; stone, red, quartz, 112;
as a universal personal adornment,
103–104; as Yoruba woman's dowry,
111; Zulu, royal, 104
Bead decorations: of crowns and veils,
Yoruban, 192; embroidery for Yoruba
regalia, 113; of North American Indian
clothing, 121, 128, 129; Potawatomi,
315, 317, 318, 319, 323, 324
Benin, the Yoruba of. *See* Yoruba costuming
"Blue" Berbers, accidental dyeing of, 73
Body painting: in the Americas, 69;
Australian aboriginal, 25, 66; of Colombian Siona, 303; in Cro-Magnon burials,
49; Fuegian, 25; of the Maya, 69–70; of
the Nuba male, 67; Paleolithic Neanderthal, 24, 48; Pictish blue, 73; of the
Yoruba, 367, 372. *See also* Cosmetic art;
Dyes, cosmetic; Pigments, cosmetic
Bracelets: Badaga, 145; Samburu, 89
Britain: Beau Brummell, arbiter of fashion,
11; ceremonial investiture of Prince of
Wales, 15; the politics of beauty patches,
16

British textile trade with West Africa. *See*
Wax-printed textiles
Burial customs: Badaga, 158–165; bone
and body painting, 24, 25, 48–49; of the
Lingayat, 165; Zambian gold-decorated
skeletons, 105

Chetti, weaver tribe of Madras plains, trade
relationship with the Badaga, 170
Chicago: Edward Ayer Collection, 127,
128, 137, 141; Field Museum of Natural
History, 71n, 131, 138, 139, 447, 450;
Newberry Library, 124, 125, 126
Clothing: North American Indian, *see*
North American Indian clothing; pageantry and power, *see* Yoruba costuming
Clothing and adornment: as an anthropological study, 23, 24, 25; as an index of
status, 27; nudity and modesty, 26;
philosophical studies of, 29–31, 32–33,
40–41; as a primate disposition, 24; the
sexual attraction of, 26, 27; specific functions of, 28, 29; as a taboo subject, 23, 42.
See also Guambianos of Colombia; Siona
of Colombia
Clothing and colonialism: early contacts
between East and West, 399; European
dislike of native dress, 399–400;
examples of imposed acculturation,
401–403; examples of power abuse
through fashion, 402–403; socioeconomic influences of Western clothing, 401–402
Color and cosmetic art: blue of the
Requibat Berbers, 73; the dominance of
red, 64, 66, 69, 70, 71, 72; in Kenya and
Nuba society, 67; a key to human pleasure, 63; Nuba application and body oiling, 67–68; plant-dyes of Africa and the
East, 69–73; red of the Siona, 304–305;
the world of the Australian aborigine, 66.
See also Dyes, cosmetic; Pigments,
cosmetic
Color symbolism of North American
Indian tribes, 119
Colored beads: associated with the Yoruba
gods, 107–108; glass, made in ancient Ife,
112; royal blue of the Siona, 305
Coral, for royal adornment, 109, 110, 111
Cosmetic art: artistic creativity of New
Guinea society, 66; customs of women of
New Spain, (Mexico), 69; Dart's study of
South African pigmentation ores, 49–50;
early self-decoration, 48–49; and hair
bleaching, 71, 72; hair dyeing, 70–71,
367; kohl for eyes, 72; of Kenya and
Nuba, 66; the Mayan squint, 53n; mod-
ern, Euro-American, 61, 62; motivation,

sexual, ritual, medicinal, 52; Nuba techniques of application, 68; oil as a skin base, 52; permanent, deformative, 53, 61, 62; and protective sleeping racks, 68; scarification, permanent, of North and West Africa, illustrated, 58–59
Cosmetics, traditional, of Yoruba women, 367
Cosmetic transformation: make-up, 63; modern Western, 61–62
Costume: pageantry and power of, *see* Yoruba costuming; sexual differentiation and acculturation in, *see* Potawatomi costume; and the supernatural, *see* Mende secret societies
Cranbrook Institute of Science, 132
Cuba: Yoruban bead-wearing tradition in, 108
Culture: and aesthetics of African bead-wearing, 105; and clothing, *see* North American Indian clothing, cultural and spiritual significance of

Dance and costume, the implications of: Arabian belly-dancing, 78, 81–82; Arabian male dancing, 81, 82, 83; the Aztec head-dress, 80; the Japanese kimono, 77–78, 80, 81; Korean court style, 78, 82; long skirts, Burmese and Spanish, 79; masked dancers, 80; Pueblo padded calves, 79, 82; as reflections of history and culture, 80–83; the Samoan *tapa*, 79, 83; shoes as shapers of movement, 79
Dancing: at Badaga funerals, 163–164; in Mende secret society rites, 251, 252, 253, 254, 255, 263; of Uruapán hórtelanos, 288
Dyes, cosmetic: Amerind domesticated, animal and vegetable, 69; henna as a hair dye, 70–71; indigo, 71, 73, 367, 370, 448; indigo for Mende masks, 252; Mayan *achiotle*, 70; saffron paint, of Indian origin, 71; for Siona *cusmas*, 304
Dyes, mineral. *See* Pigments, cosmetic
Dyeing, Sierra Leone. *See* Resist-dyed textiles, Sierra Leone

Earrings: Azerbaidzhan, traditional, 408, 412; Badaga, 145, 152; Samburu, 96, 97
Edward Ayer photographic collection, 124, 125, 126, 127, 128, 130, 137, 141
Efe/Gelede. *See* Yoruba costuming
Egungun cult, Nigerian. *See* Masquerades, Yoruban; Yoruba costuming
Ethnic identification, African, by means of dress and personal adornment, 100–101
Ethnic importance of Caucasian folk-costume, 405. *See also* Azerbaidzhan clothing
Ethnographic data and analysis of hair behavior in Yoruba religious cults. *See* Hair behavior, Yoruban
Ethnohistory: the cultural functions of clothing, 144, 171; in Nigerian hair styles, 353; in post-independent Nigeria, 345
Exports of European textiles to Africa. *See* Wax-printed textiles

Face-painting: Algerian, 64; Caduevo, 41; Ivory Coast, 65; Samburu *balu*, 92; technique of red ocher application, 64, 65, 66; of Yoruba women, 367
Foundations and grants, Kress and Wenner-Gren, 349n

Gelede/Efe Gelede, Yoruban. *See* Masquerades; Yoruba costuming
Gifts, the ritual significance of: in Badaga cloth exchange, 171–172; in Badaga marriage ceremonies, 154–158; at Efe/Gelede performances, Nigeria, 191–192; at masked parades, Nigerian, 178, 180
Gold: Azerbaidzhan filigree, 412; significance of, in Badaga marriage gifts, 156
Guambiano of Colombia, a case study of clothing: the blue kilt, 35, 36; customs and social organization of, 34, 38; the distinctive hat, 35, 36, 37; a dualism in clothing, 37–38; egalitarian emphasis, 37; an isolate Spanish-Indian community, 33; the location and ecological zones of, 33–34; patterns of social and spatial unity, 38, 39, 40

Hair: Badaga styles, 152; dyeing, henna and indigo, 70–71, 370, 372; ornaments of Potawatomi women, 313, 316, 317; protecting the Nuba coiffure, 68; rituals of Badaga burials, 161, 162; of the Samburu *moran*, (warrior), 90, 91, 92; of the Siona, 305; styles, modern Nigerian, 344
Hair behavior in Yoruba religious cults: "born to die" children, 380–382; Eshu, the trickster god, 385–391; myths of Eshu, 388, 389, 390; priests of the Shango cult, 383–385; the sacred Dada children, 375–378; sexual role reversals in Balufon festival and Egungun masquerade, 391–392; Shango, the violent god, 383–385; social and symbolic aspects of Yoruba culture, 392–395; twin children, the ritual of, 378–380
Harvard University, the Oakes Ames Herbarium of Economic Plants, 305n

Hats: significance of Guambiano male-made hats, 34, 35, 36, 37, 38, 39, 40; symbolic, of the Fon of Benin, 28

Headgear: Azerbaidzhan, 407, 408, 409, 410; Badaga, South India, 145, 147; decline in status of the eagle feather, 321; Poro headdresses, Mende, 235, 239, 240, 254; Plains type bonnets, Potawatomi, 313, 314; Siona feather crowns, 305; status, male, of North American Indian tribes, 121; turbans, Badaga, 163, 164, 169; of Yoruba rituals, Nigeria, 192, 195

Heard Museum, Phoenix, Arizona: the Barry Goldwater Collection, 136

Henna (*Lawsonia alba; Lawsonia inermis*), widespread use of as hair dye, 70–71

Hopi Indians of Arizona: Kachina dancers, ritual, 132–133, 138

Hortelanos of Uruapán, Michoacán: the barrios, characteristics of, 269, 291; Barrio de la Magdalena fiesta, 271, 272–273; *cargos* and *cargueros*, 270, 271, 272, 290; disguises, individual and in character, 281, 282; *espantapájaros*, (guerilla) characters, 273, 282, 283, 290; fiestas and *cargos*, 269–270, 271; maringuillas, transvestite, 273, 278, 285, 286, 287, 291; masks, professional and participant, examples illustrated, 274–280, 282–285; masquerade of the gardeners, 267, 283–285, 291–293; mock abduction (*robo*) intra-barrio, 287–288; *negrito* dances of the meseta, 271, 271n; the parade, 290; peripheral nature of religious symbolism, 291–292; poles, symbolic, as comic props, 283–285, 288, 289; repertoire of characters, 273; ritual expression of community values, 291–292; sacred and profane origins of *hortelanos*, 282–283; similar meseta masquerades at Christmas, 291–292; Uruapán, the city, 268–269; young married men as masqueraders, 273–274

Igbo people of Afikpo, 177. *See also* Masked parade, Nigerian

Ivory, exclusive to warriors, Samburu, 89, 90

Japan: the kimono dance form, 77–78; sumptuary laws in, 13; tattooing as a fine art, 56

Kansas City Museum of History and Science, 140

Kenya National Museum, 87n

Kikuyu sacred beads for oath-taking, 104

Kohl, various ingredients and methods of making, 72

Korumba, tribal group among the Badaga, feared for sorcery, 169

Kota tribe of craftsmen within Badaga villages, 168–169, 171

Lagos, Nigeria, setting for study of changing forms of dress. *See* Yoruba dress

Lingayat, the: funeral customs, 160, 164, 165; worshippers of Shiva, 153. *See also* Badaga of South India

Liverpool City Museum: early dating of the woven Girdle of Rameses, 425

Logan Museum of Anthropology, Beloit, 129

Madras cloth trade in Africa, 475

"Manchester cloth", exported to Africa, 467, 467n, 470, 471

Manji cloth, Badaga, weaving, washing, and starching of, 150–151

Masks of Mende secret societies: black, wooden, 244, 245, 249, 253; "found", 262; leather, sacred, 235; life expectancy of, 263–264; Poro hoods, 239, 240; raffia and wood, 233; secular, cylindrical, 235, 241; society masks, ownership of, 246–247. *See also* Mende secret societies

Masked parade, Nigerian: aesthetic aspects of, 186; the *Aro* masked slave trader, 179–180; costumes and masks, 179; culturally historical, 184; a dry season festival, 183–184; a four-day festival of female visiting, 177–178; freedom and constraint, symbolic, 186; gunmen and praise singers, 178, 179; the Igbo people of Afikpo, 177; maskers as marriageable girls and married women, 180, 185; net-masked players, grouped, 179; new age set of young men, triennial, 178; the *njenji* walk-walk, 177, 178; paraders in modern and foreign dress, 180–181, 182; progression through Afikpo villages, 181, 183; psychological significance of, 185–186; role reversal and male status, 184–185; sociological implications, 183; village involvement, 183–184; wooden masks of madness, 179

Masking traditions of Mexican *hortelanos*: maringuilla, transvestite, 285–287, 291; masks constructed by professionals and participants, 274–280, 282; masks, impermanence of, 267; professionally made for *negritos* and *viejitos*, 271, 274, 279, 280; variety of mask material in Barrio de la Magdalena, 272–273. *See also* Hortelanos of Uruapán

Masquerades, Yoruban: Efe/Gelede, 192n,

197n, 197–200, 201–227; Egungun, 192n, 193–197. *See also* Yoruba costuming

Maya: cosmetic art, permanent, deformative, 53, 53n; tattooing, female, 70

Mende secret societies, West African: "Bundu devil", *normeh*, 245; dancing, sacred and secular, 261, 262, 263; devil masks, raffia and wood, 233; Falui, Nafalie, 239, 240, 261; Gɔbɔi, secular spirit, and attendants, 235–239, 240, 261; Guinea Coast masks, 232–233; Humci society, regulating sexual matters, 250, 251; Humci spirits and masks, 252–253; Jobai and Yavie, 241, 242; Kongoli and Jobuli, 259, 260, 261; Kpa-Mende, 253, 259; Mende view of the supernatural, 231; Muslim prayer boards, 236, 238; *ngafanga*, nonancestral cultic spirits, 232, 263; Njaye spirit, sacred, the Njokui, 249, 250; Njaye spirit, secular, Fakoi, 250, 251; nɔmɔli, definitions of, 231–232; Poro masks and costumes, 235; Poro society, male, initiatory, 233–234; Poro spirits, sacred and secular, 235–242; Paramount Chief Madame Mabadja of Bagbe, 243; Sande spirits, sacred, the *Sowie*, 244–247, 261, 262; Sande spirits, secular, the Gɔndi, 247–248, 262; Sande (Bundu), women's society, initiatory, 242–244, 257; Sande-Poro and other society interrelations, 256–258; Wunde dance described, 255; Wunde society for military training, 253. *See also* Masks of Mende secret societies

Mining of cosmetic ores: hematite, 49, 50; specculante, 49; Zambian pyrolusite, (manganese), 50, 51. *See also* Pigments, cosmetic

Moshe Dayan's eye-patch, politically symbolic, 15

National Endowment for the Humanities, (USA), 87n

Nigeria: national dress and political opposition, 15; myth and masquerade of Egungun and Efe/Gelede, 192. *See also* Lagos; Masked parade, Nigerian; *and* the Yoruba entries

North American Indian clothing: breechclouts, culturally symbolic, 122; color symbolism, tribal, 119; decorative accessories, 122, 124, 125, 126; and European materials and technology, 120–121, 124; headgear, skin and feathered, 121, 124; leggings, 122, 124, 126, 128; moccasins, plain and decorated, 122, 124; shirts, skin, decorated, 121, 140; social prestige of wearer and maker, 120; women's garments of social prestige, 122, 127, 129, 130, 131

North American Indian clothing, its cultural and spiritual significance: animal symbols of the Midé, 123; belief in spiritual power of the elements, 123; the Ghost Dance religion of Prairie and Plains tribes, 134, 140; group identification among Plain tribes, 134; the Midéwiwin medicine society of the Woodlands, 123; the phenomena of natural environment, 123, 129, 135; Plains and Prairie warrior clothing, 134–135; Pueblo fertility ceremonies and male secret societies, 132, 133; symbols and pictographs of war encounters, 135; totemic animals of group identification, 134; traditional costumes and masks, 132; tribal ceremonies of Northwest coast fishermen-hunters, 132, 133; social structure and heraldic system, NW coast, 133, 139; women's guilds for decoration of robes, 135, 141

North American Indian clothing, illustrative plates: Blackfoot warrior, Red Plume, 125; Cheyenne warrior, Plenty Horses, 128; Ghost Dance shirt, Arapaho, 140; Hamatsa ceremony costume, 138; heraldic garb, NW coast, 139; Hopi girls, 127; Hopi man and boy, 137; Kachina, Hopi dancer, 136; Midé bag, Winnebago, (Woodlands), 132; Navajo woman's dress, 130; Pawnee buffalo robe, 141; Pawnee chiefs, 126; Plains woman's dress, 129; Pomo woman's dress, 131; Woodlands-Prairie male, chiefs, 124

Northwestern University, Evanston, Illinois, Program of African Studies, 177n

Nose-rings, of Badaga widows, 160

Oba, paramount king of the Yoruba: coronation rites and regalia, 109–110; and political status of the town, 110; traditional style of crown, 113. *See also* Beads; Yoruba of Nigeria

Origins of art, The (Hirn), on self-decoration, 24, 25

Pageantry, and power. *See* Yoruba costuming

Periplus of the Erythrean Sea: evidence of early bead trade, East African, 104

Personal adornment: aesthetics of, 7–8; and Amish symbolism, 18–19; Beau Brummell's role, 11; ceremonial, traditional, 9,

Personal adornment — *cont.*
15; as expression of individuality, 8, 9, 10; functions of, 7; as index of social standing, 12–13; and political symbolism, 15–16; and radical unrest, 11; as a recreation, 19; and religious denomination, 17–18, 19; as a sexual symbol, 19–20; social definition of, 10–11; in social ritual, 18; symbols of economic status, 13–14; and women's liberation, 16. *See also* Beads; Clothing and adornment

Photographers: K. Houlberg, 350, 351; W. H. Jackson, 124, 125, 126, 130

Pigments, cosmetic: African pyrolusite, 50, 51; Aztec, black, 63; cinnabar, Indonesian, 64; cochineal beetle pastures, 69; Eskimo lignite, 58; green malachite, toxic, 52; ground camwood, 49; hematite of the Americas, 69; kohl, 61, 63; "male" and "female" ores, South African, 50; North African indigo, 59, 60, 73; red, universal use of, 64–66, 69; red ocher, preservative, 24, 48–49, 64–65; tattooing "inks", 55, 57, 59; toxic, arsenic and kohl, 61; vegetable dyes, 53. *See also* Dyes, cosmetic

Polynesia; Maori tattooing, Captain Cook's report on, 56; tattooing designs, significance of, 56–57

Ponchos, Guambiano, 36, 38, 39

Potawatomi costume: bandolier bags, beaded, 324; beaded garments and sashes, 318, 319, 320, 323, 324; beadwork, modern, Wabeno, 328; buckskin shirts, 315; buckskin dresses, 318; clothing artifacts grouped by bodily regions, 313; costume elements of sound and movement, 315; decorative body covering as new index of wealth, 322; effects of fur traders on, 322–323, 324–325; finger-woven sashes of French military origin, 326; headgear, male and female, 313, 314; Indian Service boarding schools and white man's clothing, 327; Pan-Indianism in dress encouraged by tourism, 328–329; protective clothing, the buffalo robe, 320; robes, hide and blanket, 315; silver gorgets, peace medals distributed by British, 327–328; status of hair styles and warrior feathers, 321; trade goods as personal adornment, 323; tourist trade and development of handicrafts, 328–329; United States policy of present giving, 326, 327; women's garments, traditional and modern, 315

Raffles, Sir Thomas Stamford, of Singapore, a study of Javanese batik, 469

Religion: and dress, Amish, Roman Catholic and Hasidic Jew, 17–18; Guambiano, male dominated, 39

Resist-dyed textiles of Sierra Leone: design and color quality, 449–450; design system and the dyer, 463–464; dyes, indigenous, preparations of, 458–460; dyes synthetic, imported, 458, 459; dyers, a family profession, 448, 449; economics of textile marketing, direct and co-operative, 460–461, 463, 465; export trade, 461–462; fabric types, 451, 456, 460, 461, 463; fashion and national identity, 462–463; finishing and pressing, 456–457; *gara*, indigo-dyed fabrics, 448, 462; indigo blue dye, 448, 451, 452, 458, 459; introduction of dyeing to Sierra Leone, 448; kola-nut brown dye, 452, 458, 459; Makeni, the center of dyeing, 448, 459; in the modern American market, 447; starch-resist patterns, 455–458; subsystems affecting the industry, 465; taxonomy of Sierra Leone textiles, 457; tie-dye cloud pattern technique, 451–452; tie-dye machine-sewn patterns, 453; tie-dye *siti* (sewn patterns), 451, 452, 453, 454; tie-eye *taka* (pleated), 451, 452–453, 454; wax-resist candeling, stamped and splattered, 454–455, 456, 457, 458

Saffron, cosmetic history of, 71

Samburu of Kenya, a study of living art: anklets and pendants, audible, 95; the beads of childhood, 88, 89; beads and the older woman, 99–100; bead significance, 98; cattle-rearing as major factor of life, 88; continuous wearing of ornamentation, 100; neck-beads, the girl's collection, 94, 95; earrings, 96, 97; ethnic "grammar" of tribal decoration, 101; face-painting, red ocher, 92; hair, significance of, to the *moran*, 90, 91; hair styles in detail, 91, 92, 93, 94; a Maasi-speaking tribe, 87; marks of pride, 90; marriage and the *moran*, 93, 93n; the married woman's bead collection, 95–96, 97; *moran* (warrior) status, 88, 93; *mparo* necklaces, 96, 97, 99; narcissism of the *moran*, 92; neck-beads, the girl's collection, 94, 95; personal ornamentation, male and female, 88; Samburu girl's self-decoration, 93, 94; sex and age grades expressed through ornamentation, 101

Scarification: Andaman, 12; of Badaga boys, 153; as means of tribal identification, 59, 60; keloidal scar tissue designs,

58, 59, 60, 95; Nuer, 27; permanent, cosmetic, of dark-skinned N. and W. African peoples, 58, 59; Samburu, 90, 95; social value of, 12; of the yellow-skinned Bini, 60; Yoruba, 190n

Secret societies. *See* Mende secret societies, West African

Shells, decorative, as trade item of ancient North America, 122

Sierra Leone textile industry. *See* Resist-dyed textiles, African

Siona of Colombia: class hierarchy, 302; clothing as social identity, 309–310; cosmology of the Siona stratified universe, 299, 300, 309; the *cusma* of Franciscan introduction, 300, 303–304; designs of hallucinogenic inspiration, 304, 305, 306; elaborate ornamentation, 304–305; fragrant herbs as adornment, 300, 303, 305; historical survey of the group, 298–299; jaguar teeth necklaces, 305; link with white "compadrazco" in Puerto Asis, 302–303, 310; low status of, Colombian, 302; modern decline in shaman power, 301–302; the modern Siona, 306, 307, 308, 310; necklaces, colored, 305; precontact nudity, adorned, 303; putting on the *cusma*, 309; rituals of hallucinogenic *yagé*, 298, 300, 301, 306; shaman leadership, 298, 300, 301, 305; spirits, beautifully adorned, 300; transformation of shaman into animal, 309; visionary motifs in face design, 305–306; Western clothing and social order, 310–311; Yagé people as intermediaries, 300, 301, 310

Sumptuary laws: among Japanese farmers, 13; of social classes in Nuremberg, 12

Suttee, symbolic, of the Badaga widow, 165

Tablet weaving of Yemenite Jews: antiquity of weaving, researches into, 425–427; the apparatus, or loom, 429–436; the beater, 434, 435; brocading, a definition, 443n; cards, 431; card weaving, the technique, 429n,; the comb, 430, 431; designs, 440, 441; finish and price of belt, 440, 441; gold and silver work, 426, 427, 436; heddles, 432–433, 439, 440; Iman's protection of from mass production, 428–429; modern interest in Yemenite traditional handicrafts, 426–427; San'a tablet weaving, a history of crises, 427–429; shuttles, 435; spindles, 434–435; the thread, type and color, 435–436; a *tizig*, Star of David design, 436–437, 440, 442; warp, 430, 432; weaving with metallic thread, 438,

439, 440; work method and description, 436–440

Tattooing: American Indian, 58; Badaga, 143, 145, 152–153; Burmese, 54; blue as a permanent color, 72; Cambodian, 55; designs, Islamic, symbolic, 57; Dyak, Borneo, 55; Eskimo technique and design, 58; facial, reasons for, 57–58; Islamic, Middle East and North Africa, 57, 60; Japanese, 54; of Mayan women, 70; Polynesian, 56; Samoan, 55; Thai, 54

Tattooing, *The illustrated man* (Steiger), 54

Textiles: African arts displayed in crafts exhibitions, 447; West African trade, 468. *See also* Resist-dyed textiles, Sierra Leone; Tablet weaving; Wax-printed textiles; Weaving

Tie-dye fabric techniques. *See* Resist-dyed textiles

Toda pastoral tribe: as embroiderers, 147, 169, 170; linked to Badaga by cloth exchange, 169–170

Tuareg of North Africa: blue veil identification, 27; Lhote's view of uses and psychology of the veil, 29

Umbrellas: of Badaga men, 147; Toda ceremonial, 170

University of California, Santa Barbara, 87n

Wax-printed textiles for export to Africa: African design requirements, 481, 482; African use of batik muslins, 495–496; Brown Flemming and Grafton designs, 477, 491; Brunnschweiler, history and production, 474–475; Brunnschweiler printing techniques, 476–477; categories of design from sample collections, 488–490; criteria for classification, 484–488; English Calico, Ltd., of Manchester, 474–475; English printing and overseas trade, 474–475, 477; European trade contacts, original, Eastern, 471; "Flying Duck" Manchester design, 472–473, 481; inspirational sources of design, Indian, Javanese, African, 482–484, 485; Madras trade, 475; "Manchester cloth" defined, 467n; "Manchester cloth" developed, 469; manufacturers' collections, 487–488; motifs, symbolic, 485, 486, 487, 494; named designs and motifs, illustrated, 491–493; Netherlands textile printing, to present, 473–474; Previnaire's print works, Haarlem, 473–474; sources for research study, 471–472; speciality prints for African markets, 467–468; Swiss

Wax-printed textiles — *cont.*
printing prosperity at Glarus, 475–476;
techniques, Swiss, British, Netherlands,
480–481; Texoprint nonwax and batik
prints, 479; textile trade in West Africa,
historical, 468–469, 470–471; Van
Vlissigen, survival of, 474; wax and
non-wax print, exported, 468; wealthy
women traders in textiles, 496; West
African batik, of Javanese introduction,
470
Weaving: of Badaga *manji* cloth, 150–151;
the Girdle of Rameses, 425, 440; historical survey of, 425–426; a tablet weaving
loom, Yemenite, 429–436. *See also*
Potawatomi costume
West African values expressed materially:
the wardrobe of damasks and batiks, 495;
the Yoruba social club, 496
Women, specific roles and status of: and
Azerbaidzhan *yashmak*, 407, 410;
among the Badaga, marriage and widowhood, 145, 154–158; and Badaga funeral
customs, 158–161, 163; and the batik
trade, 470, 496; domestic, Potawatomi,
321; and dyes, cosmetic, 71, 72, 73; and
gara dyeing, Sierra Leone, 464; guilds of,
North American Indian, 135; Guambiano, 34; in Mende secret society, the
Sande, 242–244; in modern Nigeria, 344;
and royal hairstyles, Yoruba, 375; Samburu bead-wearing, 93–98; and social
prestige in costume, 122; of the Uruapán
barrios, 287; the Yoruba bead dowry,
111
Women's dress, Western reforms in:
Amelia Bloomer's reformed costume,
418–419; American Dress Reform
Association, 417–418; role differences
and life patterns, 415–416; trousers, male
clothing, functional, 416–417; trousers as
women's wear, 421; unisex clothing and
display, 422; women's suffrage and work
opportunities, 420, 421, 422

Yoruba of Nigeria, the: the beaded, fringed
crown of royalty, 108–109, 113; beads as
dowry, 111; bead embroidery, a male
occupation, 113; colored beads associated with the gods, 107–108, 114; crowning of the Oba, 109; dress and dignity of
the Oba, 109–110, 113; the myth of
origin, 106, 108; slave master's ownership of beads, 111; variations in style of
crown, 113
Yoruba costuming, ritual: aesthetics of
clothing, 190; cloth equated with children, 189; the cloth myth and costume

display, 193, 193n; concept of covering
and concealment, 201; Efe/Gelede "borrowing" of cloth, 197–198; Efe/Gelede
ceremonies, 189–190, 192n; Efe nocturnal masquerade in detail, 201–217;
Egungun cult of ancestral males, 192n,
193; Egungun categories, funeral, magic,
spiritual, 194–196; Gelede dances, male
and female, 225–227; Gelede masquerade and costumes, 217–225; kinetic
qualities of cloth, 191; masks as ancestral
rite, 199–200; masqueraders of Egungun, 193–196; myths and origins of
Gelede concealment, 199–201; nakedness and insanity, 190; Oro Efe's costume
and performance, 210–217; Oro Efe,
masquerade singer, performance and
repertoire, 202–203, 207, 208–209; performers and costumers, 201; performance of the Great Mother, 204–207,
208; regional variations in Efe ensembles, 217; ritual adornment, the head as
focus, 192; ritual apparel and regalia,
191; veiling and masking, 192; Yorubaland sketch map, 193
Yoruba dress, a Lagos family studied: age-
role differences, 337–338; children and
indigenous dress, 345; conclusions drawn
from study, 347–348; conductors' suits,
modern, 344; constancy of urban family
pattern, 345–346; decline in wrappers
and shawls, 345; education and change in
dress, 332, 334, 338, 343, 344; female
indigenous dress with western additions,
339–342; increased nationalism and
indigenous dress, *1940–1959*, 338–342;
male dress in a patrilineal society, 337;
Nigerian independence and indigenous
dress, *1960–1974*, 342–345, 346, 347;
Nigerian hairstyles for women, 344;
organization of the study, 332; period of
study, *1900–1974*, 331; the professionally élite of Nigerian society, 332–333,
343, 347; tabulation of findings, 346;
traditional dress, 336; unit family as
source material, 333; Western dress
and education, *1900–1939*, 334–338;
woman's changing role, 344–345
Yoruba hairstyles: advertisements, illustrated, 350; Afro styles, American
inspired, 365–366; *agogo* for married
women, 368–369; barbers' shops and
signs, 363–365; braided olowo styles for
young girls, older women, 353, 354; children, ritual, 368, 375–380, 382; of court
messengers, various kingdoms, 370–373;
Egbe Hetayo hairdressers' union, 355;
Egungun masquerade styles, 371, 392,

393; Eko/bridge, Lagos style in detail, 352, 353; ethnic variations, 353; hairdressers, 350, 355; hairstyle signs, 355; indicative of social categories, 349; male-female relationship styles, 356–359; modern female styles, 351; modern male styles, 363–365; named styles, illustrated, 350, 351, 352, 353;*ọlọwọ* (hand-done style, 351, 352, 353, *olowu* (thread-wrapped) style, 351, 352, 353; political implications, 352, 355; and rites of passage, the life cycle, 367–370, 382; sculptural styles of modern status and wealth, 356–357; Second All-Africa

Games, the Olokun Head commemorative styles and bags, 360, 361, 362; thread-wrapped styles, 355; styles for royalty, 354, 374; shaven, long, tailed, for hunters, 374; transvestite, festival, 366, 392, 393

Yoruba religious cults. *See* Hair behavior; Yoruba costuming

Zaire. *See* Wax-printed textiles

Zambia, gold-decorated skeletons of Ingombe Ilede, 105

Zulu, beads as status symbols reserved for royalty, 104